HAESE & HARRIS PUBLICATIONS

Specialists in mat

Mathematics
for the international student

8 MYP 3

Pamela Vollmar
Michael Haese
Robert Haese
Sandra Haese
Mark Humphries

**for use with
IB Middle Years
Programme**

MATHEMATICS FOR THE INTERNATIONAL STUDENT 8 (MYP 3)

Pamela Vollmar   B.Sc.(Hons.), PGCE.
Michael Haese   B.Sc.(Hons.), Ph.D.
Robert Haese   B.Sc.
Sandra Haese   B.Sc.
Mark Humphries   B.Sc.(Hons.)

Haese & Harris Publications
3 Frank Collopy Court, Adelaide Airport, SA 5950, AUSTRALIA
Telephone: +61 8 8355 9444, Fax: + 61 8 8355 9471
Email: info@haeseandharris.com.au
Web: www.haeseandharris.com.au

National Library of Australia Card Number & ISBN 978-1-876543-35-8

© Haese & Harris Publications 2008

Published by Raksar Nominees Pty Ltd
3 Frank Collopy Court, Adelaide Airport, SA 5950, AUSTRALIA

| First Edition | 2008 |
| *Reprinted* | 2009 |

Cartoon artwork by John Martin. Artwork by Piotr Poturaj and David Purton.
Cover design by Piotr Poturaj.
Computer software by David Purton, Thomas Jansson and Troy Cruickshank.

Typeset in Australia by Susan Haese (Raksar Nominees). Typeset in Times Roman $10\frac{1}{2}/11\frac{1}{2}$

The textbook and its accompanying CD have been developed independently of the International Baccalaureate Organization (IBO). The textbook and CD are in no way connected with, or endorsed by, the IBO.

This book is copyright. Except as permitted by the Copyright Act (any fair dealing for the purposes of private study, research, criticism or review), no part of this publication may be reproduced, stored in a retrieval system, or transmitted in any form or by any means, electronic, mechanical, photocopying, recording or otherwise, without the prior permission of the publisher. Enquiries to be made to Haese & Harris Publications.

Copying for educational purposes: Where copies of part or the whole of the book are made under Part VB of the Copyright Act, the law requires that the educational institution or the body that administers it has given a remuneration notice to Copyright Agency Limited (CAL). For information, contact the Copyright Agency Limited.

Acknowledgements: The publishers acknowledge the cooperation of Oxford University Press, Australia, for the reproduction of material originally published in textbooks produced in association with Haese & Harris Publications.

While every attempt has been made to trace and acknowledge copyright, the authors and publishers apologise for any accidental infringement where copyright has proved untraceable. They would be pleased to come to a suitable agreement with the rightful owner.

Disclaimer: All the internet addresses (URL's) given in this book were valid at the time of printing. While the authors and publisher regret any inconvenience that changes of address may cause readers, no responsibility for any such changes can be accepted by either the authors or the publisher.

FOREWORD

This book may be used as a general textbook at about 8th Grade (or Year 8) level in classes where students are expected to complete a rigorous course in Mathematics. It is the third book in our Middle Years series 'Mathematics for the International Student'.

In terms of the IB Middle Years Programme (MYP), our series does not pretend to be a definitive course. In response to requests from teachers who use 'Mathematics for the International Student' at IB Diploma level, we have endeavoured to interpret their requirements, as expressed to us, for a series that would prepare students for the Mathematics courses at Diploma level. We have developed the series independently of the International Baccalaureate Organization (IBO) in consultation with experienced teachers of IB Mathematics. Neither the series nor this text is endorsed by the IBO.

In regard to this book, it is not our intention that each chapter be worked through in full. Time constraints will not allow for this. Teachers must select exercises carefully, according to the abilities and prior knowledge of their students, to make the most efficient use of time and give as thorough coverage of content as possible.

We understand the emphasis that the IB MYP places on the five Areas of Interaction and in response there are links on the CD to printable pages which offer ideas for projects and investigations to help busy teachers (see p. 5). Other features worth noting include 'Graphics Calculator Instructions' (p. 9) and 'Challenge Sets' on the CD (see p. 25). Chapter 25 is a collection of miscellaneous activities which we hope students will find interesting and challenging (see p. 495).

Frequent use of the interactive features on the CD should nurture a much deeper understanding and appreciation of mathematical concepts. The inclusion of our new **Self Tutor** software (see p. 4) is intended to help students who have been absent from classes or who experience difficulty understanding the material.

The book contains many problems to cater for a range of student abilities and interests, and efforts have been made to contextualise problems so that students can see the practical applications of the mathematics they are studying.

We welcome your feedback.   Email: info@haeseandharris.com.au
                                         Web: www.haeseandharris.com.au

PV, PMH, RCH, SHH, MH

Acknowledgements

The authors and publishers would like to thank all those teachers who have read proofs and offered advice and encouragement.

Among those who submitted courses of study for Middle Years Mathematics and who offered to read and comment on the proofs of the textbook are: Margie Karbassioun, Kerstin Mockrish, Todd Sharpe, Tamara Jannink, Yang Zhaohui, Cameron Hall, Brendan Watson, Daniel Fosbenner, Rob DeAbreu, Philip E. Hedemann, Alessandra Pecoraro, Jeanne-Mari Neefs, Ray Wiens, John Bush, Jane Forrest, Dr Andrzej Cichy, William Larson, Wendy Farden, Chris Wieland, Kenneth Capp, Sara Locke, Rae Deeley, Val Frost, Mal Coad, Pia Jeppesen, Wissam Malaeb, Eduardo Betti, Robb Kitcher, Catherine Krylova, Julie Tan, Rosheen Gray, Jan-Mark Seewald, Nicola Cardwell, Tony Halsey, Ros McCabe, Alison Ryan, Mark Bethune, Keith Black, Vivienne Verschuren, Mark Willis, Curtis Wood, Ufuk Genc, Fran O'Connor. Special thanks to Heather Farish. To anyone we may have missed, we offer our apologies.

The publishers wish to make it clear that acknowledging these individuals does not imply any endorsement of this book by any of them, and all responsibility for the content rests with the authors and publishers.

USING THE INTERACTIVE CD

The interactive CD is ideal for independent study.

Students can revisit concepts taught in class and undertake their own revision and practice. The CD also has the text of the book, allowing students to leave the textbook at school and keep the CD at home.

By clicking on the relevant icon, a range of new interactive features can be accessed:

- Self Tutor
- Areas of Interaction links to printable pages
- Printable Chapters
- Interactive Links – to spreadsheets, video clips, graphing and geometry software, computer demonstrations and simulations

INTERACTIVE LINK

SELF TUTOR is a new exciting feature of this book.

The *Self Tutor* icon on each worked example denotes an active link on the CD.

Simply 'click' on the *Self Tutor* (or anywhere in the example box) to access the worked example, with a teacher's voice explaining each step necessary to reach the answer.

Play any line as often as you like. See how the basic processes come alive using movement and colour on the screen.

Ideal for students who have missed lessons or need extra help.

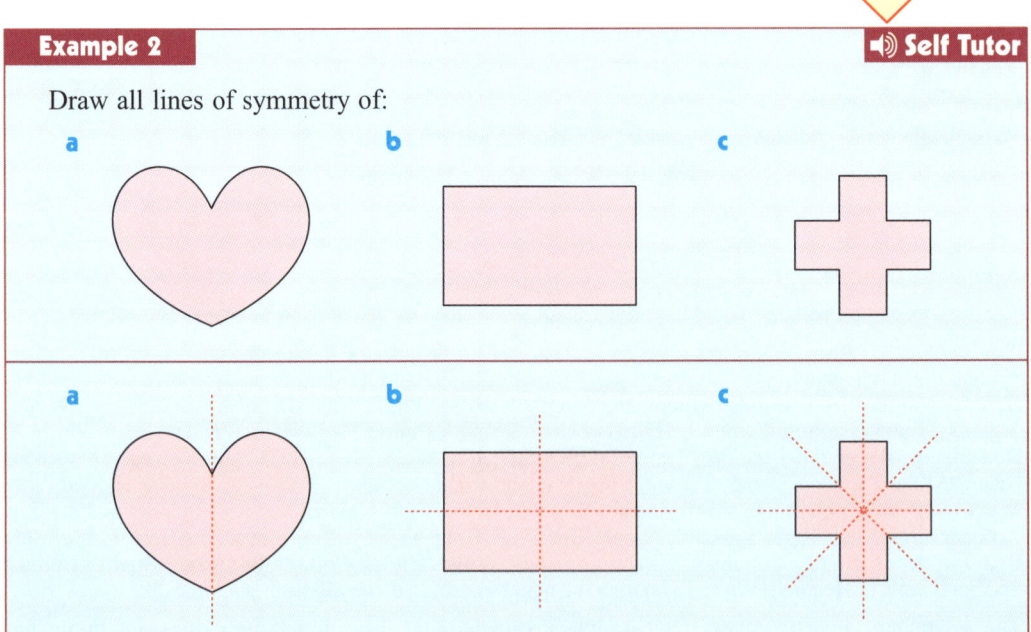

See **Chapter 16, Transformations, similarity and congruence**, p. 333

AREAS OF INTERACTION

The International Baccalaureate Middle Years Programme focuses teaching and learning through five Areas of Interaction:

- Approaches to learning
- Community and service
- Human ingenuity
- Environments
- Health and social education

The Areas of Interaction are intended as a focus for developing connections between different subject areas in the curriculum and to promote an understanding of the interrelatedness of different branches of knowledge and the coherence of knowledge as a whole.

Click on the heading to access a printable 'pop-up' version of the link.

In an effort to assist busy teachers, we offer the following printable pages of ideas for projects and investigations:

INFLATION RATES
Areas of interaction:
Approaches to learning, Community and service

LINKS click here

Links to printable pages of ideas for projects and investigations

Chapter 3: Percentage p. 97	**INFLATION RATES** Approaches to learning/Community and service
Chapter 7: The geometry of polygons p. 163	**AIRCRAFT NAVIGATION** Human ingenuity/ Approaches to learning
Chapter 8: Indices p. 187	**RUSSIAN PEASANT MULTIPLICATION** Human ingenuity/ Approaches to learning
Chapter 9: Radicals and Pythagoras p. 211	**CREATE YOUR OWN PYRAMIDS** Human ingenuity/ Approaches to learning
Chapter 10: Length and area p. 240	**HOW MUCH OXYGEN IS PRODUCED?** Environments/Health and social education
Chapter 12: Volume and capacity p. 274	**ICEBERGS** Environments/Approaches to learning
Chapter 13: Coordinate geometry p. 300	**HOW FAR IS IT FROM YOUR CHIN TO YOUR FINGERTIPS?** Approaches to learning
Chapter 16: Transformations, similarity and congruence p. 349	**THE MATHEMATICS OF AIR HOCKEY** Approaches to learning
Chapter 19: Quadratic equations p. 399	**HOW FAR WILL A CAR TRAVEL WHEN BRAKING?** Community and Service/Health and Social Education
Chapter 20: Quantitative statistics p. 417	**AT WHAT RATE SHOULD YOU BREATHE ?** Health and social education
Chapter 23: Trigonometry p. 468	**MEASURING INACCESSIBLE DISTANCES** Human ingenuity/ Approaches to learning

TABLE OF CONTENTS

GRAPHICS CALCULATOR INSTRUCTIONS — 9

- A Basic calculations — 10
- B Basic functions — 12
- C Secondary function and alpha keys — 15
- D Memory — 15
- E Lists — 18
- F Statistical graphs — 20
- G Working with functions — 21

CHALLENGE SETS — 25

1 NUMBER — 27

- A Natural numbers — 28
- B Divisibility tests — 30
- C Integers — 32
- D Order of operations — 34
- E Fractions and rational numbers — 37
- F Decimal numbers — 41
- G Ratio — 46
- H Prime numbers and index notation — 50
- Review set 1A — 53
- Review set 1B — 54

2 ALGEBRAIC OPERATIONS — 55

- A Algebraic notation — 56
- B The language of mathematics — 59
- C Changing words to symbols — 60
- D Generalising arithmetic — 63
- E Algebraic substitution — 64
- F Collecting like terms — 67
- G Product and quotient simplification — 69
- Review set 2A — 71
- Review set 2B — 71

3 PERCENTAGE — 73

- A Percentage — 74
- B The unitary method in percentage — 78
- C Finding a percentage of a quantity — 80
- D Percentage increase and decrease — 81
- E Percentage change using a multiplier — 85
- F Finding the original amount — 89
- G Simple interest — 90
- H Compound interest — 93
- Review set 3A — 97
- Review set 3B — 98

4 ALGEBRAIC EXPANSION — 99

- A The distributive law — 100
- B The expansion of $(a+b)(c+d)$ — 105
- C The expansion rules — 106
- D Expansion of radical expressions — 112
- Review set 4A — 115
- Review set 4B — 116

5 INTERPRETING AND DRAWING GRAPHS — 117

- A Interpreting graphs and charts — 118
- B Travel graphs — 123
- C Information from line graphs — 126
- D Using technology to graph data — 127
- Review set 5A — 129
- Review set 5B — 131

6 SOLVING EQUATIONS — 133

- A The solution of an equation — 134
- B Maintaining balance — 136
- C Isolating the unknown — 137
- D Formal solution of linear equations — 138
- E Equations with a repeated unknown — 141
- F Fractional equations — 143
- G Unknown in the denominator — 146
- Review set 6A — 148
- Review set 6B — 148

7 THE GEOMETRY OF POLYGONS — 149

- A Review of geometrical facts — 151
- B Triangles — 156
- C Isosceles triangles — 159
- D Quadrilaterals and other polygons — 162
- E Deductive geometry — 165
- F Special quadrilaterals — 167
- Review set 7A — 170
- Review set 7B — 171

8 INDICES — 173

- A Algebraic products and quotients in index notation — 174
- B Index laws — 176
- C Expansion laws — 178
- D Zero and negative indices — 180
- E Scientific notation (Standard form) — 183
- F Significant figures — 186
- Review set 8A — 188
- Review set 8B — 188

TABLE OF CONTENTS

9 RADICALS AND PYTHAGORAS   189
- A   Square roots   191
- B   Rules for square roots   192
- C   Solving equations of the form $x^2 = k$ 194
- D   The theorem of Pythagoras   196
- E   The converse of Pythagoras' theorem   202
- F   Pythagorean triples   203
- G   Problem solving using Pythagoras   205
- H   Three dimensional problems (Extension)   208
- I   Cube roots   209
- Review set 9A   211
- Review set 9B   212

10 LENGTH AND AREA   213
- A   Lengths and perimeters   214
- B   Circumference of a circle   218
- C   Area   223
- D   Areas of circles and ellipses   228
- E   Areas of composite figures   230
- F   Surface area   233
- G   Problem solving   238
- Review set 10A   240
- Review set 10B   241

11 ALGEBRA   243
- A   Converting into algebraic form   244
- B   Forming equations   246
- C   Problem solving using equations   248
- D   Finding an unknown from a formula   251
- E   Linear inequations   253
- F   Solving linear inequations   255
- Review set 11A   259
- Review set 11B   260

12 VOLUME AND CAPACITY   261
- A   Units of volume   262
- B   Volume formulae   263
- C   Capacity   268
- D   Problem solving   271
- Review set 12A   274
- Review set 12B   275

13 COORDINATE GEOMETRY   277
- A   Plotting points   279
- B   Linear relationships   281
- C   Plotting linear graphs   284
- D   The equation of a line   286
- E   Gradient or slope   287
- F   Graphing lines from equations   291
- G   Other line forms   294
- H   Finding equations from graphs   298
- I   Points on lines   299
- Review set 13A   301
- Review set 13B   302

14 SIMULTANEOUS EQUATIONS   303
- A   Trial and error solution   304
- B   Graphical solution   305
- C   Solution by substitution   306
- D   Solution by elimination   308
- E   Problem solving with simultaneous equations   311
- Review set 14A   314
- Review set 14B   314

15 ESTIMATING PROBABILITIES   315
- A   Probability by experiment   317
- B   Probabilities from tabled data   319
- C   Probabilities from two way tables   320
- D   Chance investigations   322
- Review set 15A   327
- Review set 15B   327

16 TRANSFORMATIONS, SIMILARITY AND CONGRUENCE   329
- A   Translations   330
- B   Reflections and line symmetry   331
- C   Rotations and rotational symmetry   334
- D   Enlargements and reductions   337
- E   Similar figures   338
- F   Similar triangles   340
- G   Areas and volumes of similar objects   341
- H   Congruence of triangles   346
- Review set 16A   350
- Review set 16B   351

17 ALGEBRAIC FACTORISATION   353
- A   Common factors   354
- B   Factorising with common factors   356
- C   Difference of two squares factorising   359
- D   Perfect square factorisation   361
- E   Factorising quadratic trinomials   363
- F   Miscellaneous factorisation   366
- Review set 17A   367
- Review set 17B   367

18 COMPARING CATEGORICAL DATA   369
- A   Categorical data   372
- B   Examining categorical data   376
- C   Comparing and reporting categorical data   380
- D   Data collection   382
- E   Misleading graphs   384
- Review set 18A   385
- Review set 18B   387

TABLE OF CONTENTS

19 QUADRATIC EQUATIONS — 389
- A   The Null Factor law — 390
- B   Equations of the form $ax^2 + bx = 0$ — 391
- C   Solving equations using the 'difference of squares' — 392
- D   Solving equations of the form $x^2 + bx + c = 0$ — 393
- E   Problem solving with quadratic equations — 394
- F   Simultaneous equations involving quadratic equations — 398
- Review set 19A — 399
- Review set 19B — 399

20 QUANTITATIVE STATISTICS — 401
- A   Quantitative data — 402
- B   Grouped discrete data — 406
- C   Measuring the centre — 409
- D   Comparing and reporting discrete data — 415
- Review set 20A — 417
- Review set 20B — 419

21 ALGEBRAIC FRACTIONS — 421
- A   Evaluating algebraic fractions — 422
- B   Simplifying algebraic fractions — 423
- C   Multiplying and dividing algebraic fractions — 425
- D   Adding and subtracting algebraic fractions — 427
- E   Simplifying more complicated fractions — 430
- Review set 21A — 435
- Review set 21B — 436

22 THEORETICAL PROBABILITY — 437
- A   Sample space — 438
- B   Theoretical probability — 439
- C   Using grids to find probabilities — 442
- D   Multiplying probabilities — 444
- E   Using tree diagrams — 445
- F   Expectation — 448
- G   Odds — 450
- Review set 22A — 451
- Review set 22B — 452

23 TRIGONOMETRY — 453
- A   Using scale diagrams in geometry — 454
- B   Trigonometry — 455
- C   The trigonometric ratios — 460
- D   Problem solving with trigonometry — 464
- Review set 23A — 468
- Review set 23B — 469

24 INTRODUCTION TO NETWORKS — 471
- A   Network diagrams — 472
- B   Constructing networks — 474
- C   Precedence networks — 477
- D   Counting pathways — 480
- Review set 24A — 482
- Review set 24B — 483

25 LOCUS — 485
- A   Everyday applications of loci — 486
- B   Experiments in locus — 488
- C   Locus in geometry — 491
- Review set 25 — 493

25 ACTIVITIES — 495
1. Triangular numbers — 496
2. Word maze — 496
3. Cops and robbers — 497
4. Translations on a chessboard — 497
5. Shortest distance — 498
6. Engaged couples — 499
7. Number chains — 500
8. Paper — 501
9. Jockeying for truth — 502

ANSWERS — 503

INDEX — 543

Graphics calculator instructions

Contents: A Basic calculations
B Basic functions
C Secondary function and alpha keys
D Memory
E Lists
F Statistical graphs
G Working with functions

In this course it is assumed that you have a **graphics calculator**. If you learn how to operate your calculator successfully, you should experience little difficulty with future arithmetic calculations.

There are many different brands (and types) of calculators. Different calculators do not have exactly the same keys. It is therefore important that you have an instruction booklet for your calculator, and use it whenever you need to.

However, to help get you started, we have included here some basic instructions for the **Texas Instruments TI-83** and the **Casio fx-9860G** calculators. Note that instructions given may need to be modified slightly for other models.

GETTING STARTED

Texas Instruments TI-83

The screen which appears when the calculator is turned on is the **home screen**. This is where most basic calculations are performed.

You can return to this screen from any menu by pressing [2nd] [MODE].

When you are on this screen you can type in an expression and evaluate it using the [ENTER] key.

Casio fx-9860g

Press [MENU] to access the Main Menu, and select **RUN·MAT**.

This is where most of the basic calculations are performed.

When you are on this screen you can type in an expression and evaluate it using the [EXE] key.

A   BASIC CALCULATIONS

Most modern calculators have the rules for **Order of Operations** built into them. This order is sometimes referred to as BEDMAS.

This section explains how to enter different types of numbers such as negative numbers and fractions, and how to perform calculations using grouping symbols (brackets), powers, and square roots. It also explains how to round off using your calculator.

NEGATIVE NUMBERS

To enter negative numbers we use the **sign change** key. On both the **TI-83** and **Casio** this looks like .

Simply press the sign change key and then type in the number.

For example, to enter −7, press [(−)] 7.

GRAPHICS CALCULATOR INSTRUCTIONS

FRACTIONS

On most scientific calculators and also the **Casio** graphics calculator there is a special key for entering fractions. No such key exists for the **TI-83**, so we use a different method.

Texas Instruments TI-83

To enter common fractions, we enter the fraction as a division.

For example, we enter $\frac{3}{4}$ by typing 3 ÷ 4. If the fraction is part of a larger calculation, it is generally wise to place this division in brackets, i.e.,   (3 ÷ 4) .

To enter mixed numbers, either convert the mixed number to an improper fraction and enter as a common fraction *or* enter the fraction as a sum.

For example, we can enter $2\frac{3}{4}$ as   (11 ÷ 4)   *or*   (2 + 3 ÷ 4) .

Casio fx-9860g

To enter fractions we use the **fraction** key a b/c .

For example, we enter $\frac{3}{4}$ by typing 3 a b/c 4 and $2\frac{3}{4}$ by typing 2 a b/c 3 a b/c 4. Press SHIFT a b/c ($a\frac{b}{c} \leftrightarrow \frac{d}{c}$) to convert between mixed numbers and improper fractions.

SIMPLIFYING FRACTIONS & RATIOS

Graphics calculators can *sometimes* be used to express fractions and ratios in simplest form.

Texas Instruments TI-83

To express the fraction $\frac{35}{56}$ in simplest form, press 35 ÷ 56 MATH 1 ENTER . The result is $\frac{5}{8}$.

To express the ratio $\frac{2}{3} : 1\frac{1}{4}$ in simplest form, press   (2 ÷ 3) ÷ (1 + 1 ÷ 4) MATH 1 ENTER .

The ratio is 8 : 15.

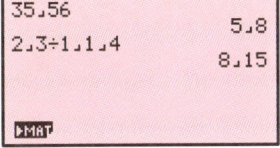

Casio fx-9860g

To express the fraction $\frac{35}{56}$ in simplest form, press 35 a b/c 56 EXE . The result is $\frac{5}{8}$.

To express the ratio $\frac{2}{3} : 1\frac{1}{4}$ in simplest form, press 2 a b/c 3 ÷ 1 a b/c 1 a b/c 4 EXE . The ratio is 8 : 15.

ENTERING TIMES

In questions involving time, it is often necessary to be able to express time in terms of hours, minutes and seconds.

Texas Instruments TI-83

To enter 2 hours 27 minutes, press 2 [2nd] [MATRX] (ANGLE)
1:^{o} 27 [2nd] [MATRX] 2:$'$.   This is equivalent to 2.45 hours.

To express 8.17 hours in terms of hours, minutes and seconds, press 8.17 [2nd] [MATRX] 4:▶DMS [ENTER].
This is equivalent to 8 hours, 10 minutes and 12 seconds.

Casio fx-9860g

To enter 2 hours 27 minutes, press 2 [OPTN] [F6] [F5] (ANGL) [F4] ($^{o\prime\prime\prime}$) 27 [F4] ($^{o\prime\prime\prime}$) [EXE].   This is equivalent to 2.45 hours.

To express 8.17 hours in terms of hours, minutes and seconds, press 8.17 [OPTN] [F6] [F5] (ANGL) [F6] [F3] (▶DMS) [EXE].
This is equivalent to 8 hours, 10 minutes and 12 seconds.

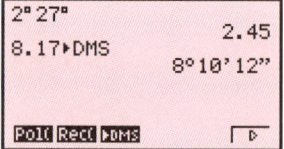

B BASIC FUNCTIONS

GROUPING SYMBOLS (BRACKETS)

Both the **TI-83** and **Casio** have bracket keys that look like [(] and [)].

Brackets are regularly used in mathematics to indicate an expression which needs to be evaluated before other operations are carried out.

For example, to enter $2 \times (4 + 1)$ we type 2 [×] [(] 4 [+] 1 [)].

We also use brackets to make sure the calculator understands the expression we are typing in.

For example, to enter $\frac{2}{4+1}$ we type 2 [÷] [(] 4 [+] 1 [)]. If we typed 2 [÷] 4 [+] 1 the calculator would think we meant $\frac{2}{4} + 1$.

In general, it is a good idea to place brackets around any complicated expressions which need to be evaluated separately.

POWER KEYS

Both the **TI-83** and **Casio** also have power keys that look like [^]. We type the base first, press the power key, then enter the index or exponent.

For example, to enter 25^3 we type 25 [^] 3.

Note that there are special keys which allow us to quickly evaluate squares.

Numbers can be squared on both **TI-83** and **Casio** using the special key [x^2].

For example, to enter 25^2 we type 25 [x^2].

SQUARE ROOTS

To enter square roots on either calculator we need to use a secondary function (see the **Secondary Function and Alpha Keys**).

Texas Instruments TI-83

The **TI-83** uses a secondary function key [2nd].

To enter $\sqrt{36}$ we press [2nd] [x^2] 36 [)].

The end bracket is used to tell the calculator we have finished entering terms under the square root sign.

Casio fx-9860g

The Casio uses a shift key [SHIFT] to get to its second functions.

To enter $\sqrt{36}$ we press [SHIFT] [x^2] 36.

If there is a more complicated expression under the square root sign you should enter it in brackets.

For example, to enter $\sqrt{18 \div 2}$ we press [SHIFT] [x^2] [(] 18 [÷] 2 [)].

ROUNDING OFF

You can use your calculator to round off answers to a fixed number of decimal places.

Texas Instruments TI-83

To round to 2 decimal places, press [MODE] then [▼] to scroll down to Float.

Use the [▶] button to move the cursor over the 2 and press [ENTER]. Press [2nd] [MODE] to return to the home screen.

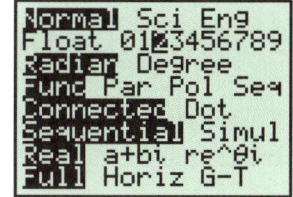

If you want to unfix the number of decimal places, press [MODE] [▼] [ENTER] to highlight Float.

Casio fx-9860g

To round to 2 decimal places, select **RUN·MAT** from the Main Menu, and press [SHIFT] [MENU] to enter the setup screen. Scroll down to Display, and press [F1] (**Fix**). Press 2 [EXE] to select the number of decimal places. Press [EXIT] to return to the home screen.

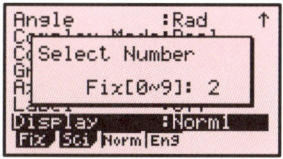

To unfix the number of decimal places, press [SHIFT] [MENU] to return to the setup screen, scroll down to Display, and press [F3] (**Norm**).

INVERSE TRIGONOMETRIC FUNCTIONS

To enter inverse trigonometric functions, you will need to use a secondary function (see the **Secondary Function and Alpha Keys**).

Texas Instruments TI-83

The inverse trigonometric functions $\sin^{-1}$, $\cos^{-1}$ and $\tan^{-1}$ are the secondary functions of $\boxed{\text{SIN}}$, $\boxed{\text{COS}}$ and $\boxed{\text{TAN}}$ respectively. They are accessed by using the secondary function key $\boxed{\text{2nd}}$.

For example, if $\cos x = \frac{3}{5}$, then $x = \cos^{-1}\left(\frac{3}{5}\right)$.

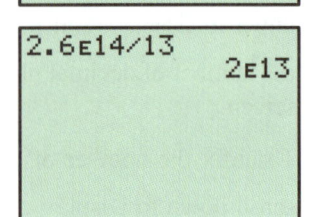

To calculate this, press $\boxed{\text{2nd}}$ $\boxed{\text{COS}}$ 3 $\boxed{\div}$ 5 $\boxed{)}$ $\boxed{\text{ENTER}}$.

Casio fx-9860g

The inverse trigonometric functions $\sin^{-1}$, $\cos^{-1}$ and $\tan^{-1}$ are the secondary functions of $\boxed{\sin}$, $\boxed{\cos}$ and $\boxed{\tan}$ respectively. They are accessed by using the secondary function key $\boxed{\text{SHIFT}}$.

For example, if $\cos x = \frac{3}{5}$, then $x = \cos^{-1}\left(\frac{3}{5}\right)$.

To calculate this, press $\boxed{\text{SHIFT}}$ $\boxed{\cos}$ $\boxed{(}$ 3 $\boxed{\div}$ 5 $\boxed{)}$ $\boxed{\text{EXE}}$.

SCIENTIFIC NOTATION

If a number is too large or too small to be displayed neatly on the screen, it will be expressed in scientific notation, that is, in the form $a \times 10^k$ where $1 \leqslant a \leqslant 10$ and k is an integer.

Texas Instruments TI-83

To evaluate 2300^3, press 2300 $\boxed{\wedge}$ 3 $\boxed{\text{ENTER}}$. The answer displayed is 1.2167E10, which means 1.2167×10^{10}.

To evaluate $\frac{3}{20\,000}$, press 3 $\boxed{\div}$ 20 000 $\boxed{\text{ENTER}}$. The answer displayed is 1.5E−4, which means 1.5×10^{-4}.

You can enter values in scientific notation using the EE function, which is accessed by pressing $\boxed{\text{2nd}}$ $\boxed{,}$.

For example, to evaluate $\frac{2.6 \times 10^{14}}{13}$, press 2.6 $\boxed{\text{2nd}}$ $\boxed{,}$ 14 $\boxed{\div}$ 13 $\boxed{\text{ENTER}}$. The answer is 2×10^{13}.

GRAPHICS CALCULATOR INSTRUCTIONS

Casio fx-9860g

To evaluate 2300^3, press 2300 [^] 3 [EXE]. The answer displayed is 1.2167E+10, which means 1.2167×10^{10}.

To evaluate $\frac{3}{20\,000}$, press 3 [÷] 20 000 [EXE]. The answer displayed is 1.5E−04, which means 1.5×10^{-4}.

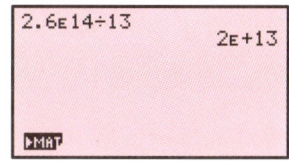

You can enter values in scientific notation using the [EXP] key. For example, to evaluate $\frac{2.6 \times 10^{14}}{13}$, press 2.6 [EXP] 14 [÷] 13 [EXE]. The answer is 2×10^{13}.

C SECONDARY FUNCTION AND ALPHA KEYS

Texas Instruments TI-83

The **secondary function** of each key is displayed in yellow above the key. It is accessed by pressing the [2nd] key, followed by the key corresponding to the desired secondary function. For example, to calculate $\sqrt{36}$, press [2nd] [x^2] 36 [)] [ENTER].

The **alpha function** of each key is displayed in green above the key. It is accessed by pressing the [ALPHA] key followed by the key corresponding to the desired letter. The main purpose of the alpha keys is to store values into memory which can be recalled later. Refer to the **Memory** section.

Casio fx-9860g

The **shift function** of each key is displayed in yellow above the key. It is accessed by pressing the [SHIFT] key followed by the key corresponding to the desired shift function.

For example, to calculate $\sqrt{36}$, press [SHIFT] [x^2] 36 [EXE].

The **alpha function** of each key is displayed in red above the key. It is accessed by pressing the [ALPHA] key followed by the key corresponding to the desired letter. The main purpose of the alpha keys is to store values which can be recalled later.

D MEMORY

Utilising the memory features of your calculator allows you to recall calculations you have performed previously. This not only saves time, but also enables you to maintain accuracy in your calculations.

SPECIFIC STORAGE TO MEMORY

Values can be stored into the variable letters A, B, ..., Z using either calculator. Storing a value in memory is useful if you need that value multiple times.

Texas Instruments TI-83

Suppose we wish to store the number 15.4829 for use in a number of calculations. Type in the number then press STO▶ ALPHA MATH (A) ENTER.

We can now add 10 to this value by pressing ALPHA MATH + 10 ENTER, or cube this value by pressing ALPHA MATH ^ 3 ENTER.

Casio fx-9860g

Suppose we wish to store the number 15.4829 for use in a number of calculations. Type in the number then press → ALPHA X,θ,T (A) EXE.

We can now add 10 to this value by pressing ALPHA X,θ,T + 10 EXE, or cube this value by pressing ALPHA X,θ,T ^ 3 EXE.

ANS VARIABLE

Texas Instruments TI-83

The variable **Ans** holds the most recent evaluated expression, and can be used in calculations by pressing 2nd (−).

For example, suppose you evaluate 3×4, and then wish to subtract this from 17. This can be done by pressing 17 − 2nd (−) ENTER.

If you start an expression with an operator such as +, −, etc, the previous answer **Ans** is automatically inserted ahead of the operator. For example, the previous answer can be halved simply by pressing ÷ 2 ENTER.

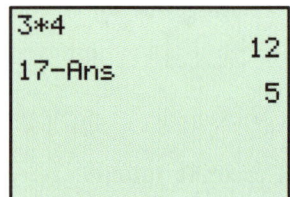

If you wish to view the answer in fractional form, press MATH 1 ENTER.

Casio fx-9860g

The variable **Ans** holds the most recent evaluated expression, and can be used in calculations by pressing SHIFT (−) . For example, suppose you evaluate 3×4, and then wish to subtract this from 17. This can be done by pressing 17 − SHIFT (−) EXE .

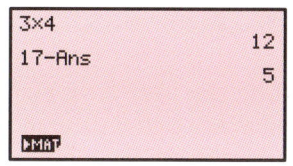

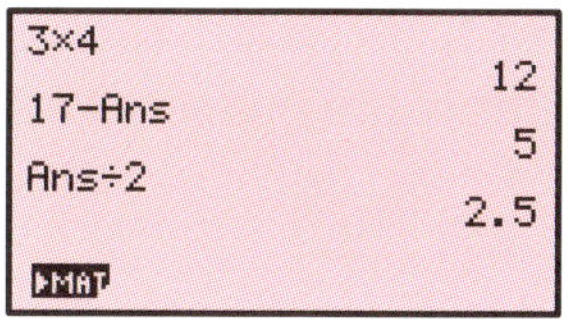

If you start an expression with an operator such as + , − , etc, the previous answer Ans is automatically inserted ahead of the operator. For example, the previous answer can be halved simply by pressing ÷ 2 EXE .

If you wish to view the answer in fractional form, press F↔D .

RECALLING PREVIOUS EXPRESSIONS

Texas Instruments TI-83

The **ENTRY** function recalls previously evaluated expressions, and is used by pressing 2nd ENTER .

This function is useful if you wish to repeat a calculation with a minor change, or if you have made an error in typing.

Suppose you have evaluated $100 + \sqrt{132}$. If you now want to evaluate $100 + \sqrt{142}$, instead of retyping the command, it can be recalled by pressing 2nd ENTER .

The change can then be made by moving the cursor over the 3 and changing it to a 4, then pressing ENTER .

If you have made an error in your original calculation, and intended to calculate $1500 + \sqrt{132}$, again you can recall the previous command by pressing 2nd ENTER .

Move the cursor to the first 0.

You can insert the digit 5, rather than overwriting the 0, by pressing 2nd DEL 5 ENTER .

Casio fx-9860g

Pressing the left cursor key allows you to edit the most recently evaluated expression, and is useful if you wish to repeat a calculation with a minor change, or if you have made an error in typing.

Suppose you have evaluated $100 + \sqrt{132}$.

If you now want to evaluate $100 + \sqrt{142}$, instead of retyping the command, it can be recalled by pressing the left cursor key.

Move the cursor between the 3 and the 2, then press DEL 4 to remove the 3 and change it to a 4. Press EXE to re-evaluate the expression.

E — LISTS

Lists are used for a number of purposes on the calculator. They enable us to enter sets of numbers, and we use them to generate number sequences using algebraic rules.

CREATING A LIST

Texas Instruments TI-83

Press STAT 1 to take you to the **list editor** screen.

To enter the data {2, 5, 1, 6, 0, 8} into **List1**, start by moving the cursor to the first entry of L_1. Press 2 ENTER 5 ENTER ...... and so on until all the data is entered.

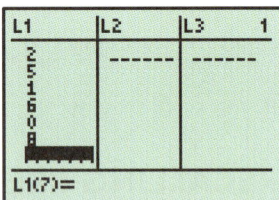

Casio fx-9860g

Selecting **STAT** from the Main Menu takes you to the **list editor** screen.

To enter the data {2, 5, 1, 6, 0, 8} into **List 1**, start by moving the cursor to the first entry of **List 1**. Press 2 EXE 5 EXE ...... and so on until all the data is entered.

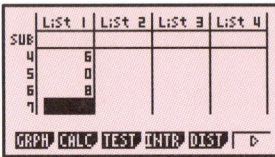

DELETING LIST DATA

Texas Instruments TI-83

Pressing STAT 1 takes you to the **list editor** screen.

Move the cursor to the heading of the list you want to delete then press CLEAR ENTER.

Casio fx-9860g

Selecting **STAT** from the Main Menu takes you to the **list editor** screen.

Move the cursor to anywhere on the list you wish to delete, then press F6 (▷) F4 (**DEL-A**) F1 (**Yes**).

REFERENCING LISTS

Texas Instruments TI-83

Lists can be referenced by using the secondary functions of the keypad numbers 1–6.

For example, suppose you want to add 2 to each element of **List1** and display the results in **List2**. To do this, move the cursor to the heading of L_2 and press 2nd 1 + 2 ENTER.

GRAPHICS CALCULATOR INSTRUCTIONS

Casio fx-9860g

Lists can be referenced using the List function, which is accessed by pressing SHIFT 1.

For example, if you want to add 2 to each element of **List 1** and display the results in **List 2**, move the cursor to the heading of **List 2** and press SHIFT 1 (**List**) 1 + 2 EXE.

Casio models without the List function can do this by pressing OPTN F1 (LIST) F1 (**List**) 1 + 2 EXE.

NUMBER SEQUENCES

Texas Instruments TI-83

You can create a sequence of numbers defined by a certain rule using the *seq* command.

This command is accessed by pressing 2nd STAT ▶ to enter the **OPS** section of the List menu, then selecting **5:seq**.

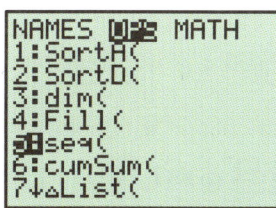

For example, to store the sequence of even numbers from 2 to 8 in **List3**, move the cursor to the heading of **L3**, then press 2nd STAT ▶ 5 to enter the *seq* command, followed by 2 X,T,θ,n , X,T,θ,n , 1 , 4) ENTER.

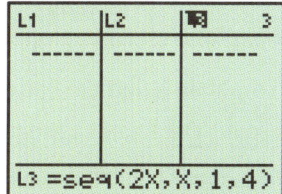

This evaluates $2x$ for every value of x from 1 to 4.

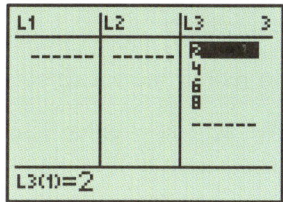

Casio fx-9860g

You can create a sequence of numbers defined by a certain rule using the *seq* command.

This command is accessed by pressing OPTN F1 (LIST) F5 (**Seq**).

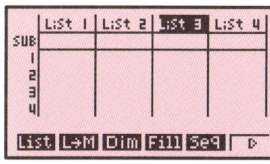

For example, to store the sequence of even numbers from 2 to 8 in **List 3**, move the cursor to the heading of **List 3**, then press OPTN F1 F5 to enter a sequence, followed by 2 X,θ,T , X,θ,T , 1 , 4 , 1) EXE.

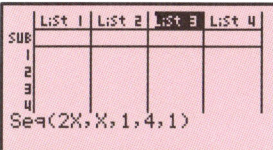

This evaluates $2x$ for every value of x from 1 to 4 with an increment of 1.

20   GRAPHICS CALCULATOR INSTRUCTIONS

F STATISTICAL GRAPHS

STATISTICS

Your graphics calculator is a useful tool for analysing data and creating statistical graphs.

In this section we will produce descriptive statistics and graphs for the data set   5 2 3 3 6 4 5 3 7 5 7 1 8 9 5.

Texas Instruments TI-83

Enter the data set into **List1** using the instructions on page **18**. To obtain descriptive statistics of the data set, press STAT ▶ **1:1-Var Stats** 2nd **1 (L1)** ENTER .

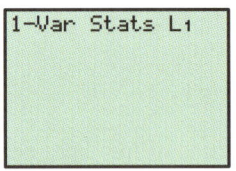
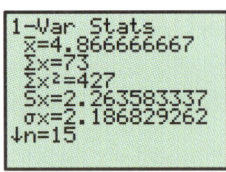

To obtain a boxplot of the data, press 2nd Y= (STAT PLOT) **1** and set up **Statplot1** as shown. Press ZOOM **9:ZoomStat** to graph the boxplot with an appropriate window.

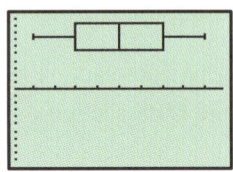

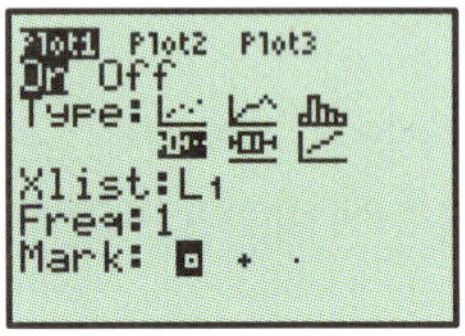

To obtain a vertical bar chart of the data, press 2nd Y= **1**, and change the type of graph to a vertical bar chart as shown. Press ZOOM **9:ZoomStat** to draw the bar chart. Press WINDOW and set the **Xscl** to 1, then GRAPH to redraw the bar chart.

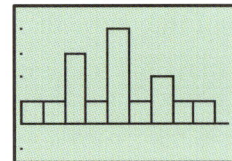

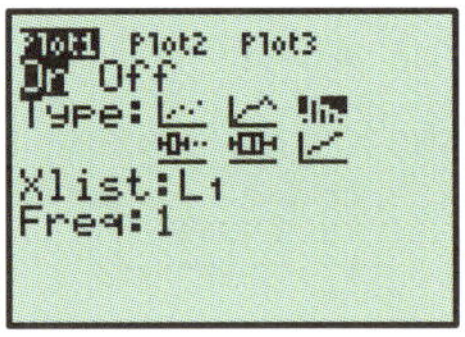

We will now enter a second set of data, and compare it to the first.

Enter the data set 9 6 2 3 5 5 7 5 6 7 6 3 4 4 5 8 4   into **List2**, press 2nd Y= **1**, and change the type of graph back to a boxplot as shown. Move the cursor to the top of the screen and select **Plot2**. Set up **Statplot2** in the same manner, except set the **XList** to **L2**. Press ZOOM **9:ZoomStat** to draw the side-by-side boxplots.

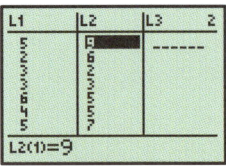

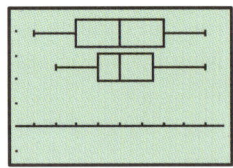

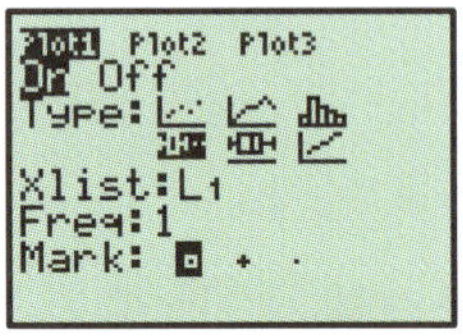

Casio fx-9860g

Enter the data into **List 1** using the instructions on page **18**. To obtain the descriptive statistics, press F6 (▷) until the **GRPH** icon is in the bottom left corner of the screen, then press F2 (**CALC**) F1 (**1VAR**).

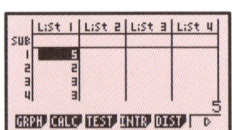
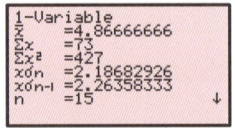

GRAPHICS CALCULATOR INSTRUCTIONS 21

To obtain a boxplot of the data, press [EXIT]
[EXIT] [F1] (GRPH) [F6] (SET), and set up
StatGraph 1 as shown. Press [EXIT] [F1]
(GPH1) to draw the boxplot.

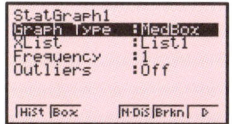 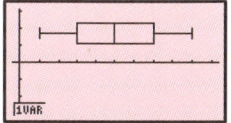

To obtain a vertical bar chart of the data, press
[EXIT] [F6] (SET) [F2] (GPH2), and set up
StatGraph 2 as shown. Press [EXIT] [F2]
(GPH2) to draw the bar chart (set Start to 0,
and Width to 1).

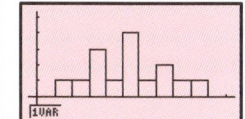

We will now enter a second set of data, and
compare it to the first.

Enter the data set   9 6 2 3 5 5 7 5 6 7 6 3 4
4 5 8 4   into **List 2**, then press [F6] (SET)
[F2] (GPH2) and set up **StatGraph 2** to draw a
boxplot of this data set as shown. Press [EXIT]
[F4] (SEL), and turn on both **StatGraph 1** and
StatGraph 2. Press [F6] (DRAW) to draw the side-by-side boxplots.

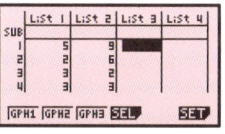 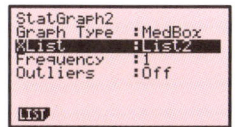
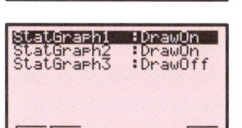 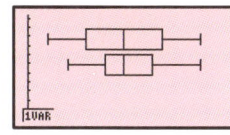

G WORKING WITH FUNCTIONS

GRAPHING FUNCTIONS

Texas Instruments TI-83

Pressing [Y=] selects the **Y=** editor, where you can store functions
to graph. Delete any unwanted functions by scrolling down to
the function and pressing [CLEAR].

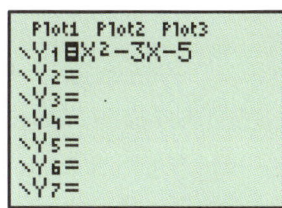

To graph the function $y = x^2 - 3x - 5$, move the cursor to
Y₁, and press [X,T,θ,n] [x²] [−] 3 [X,T,θ,n] [−] 5 [ENTER]. This
stores the function into **Y₁**. Press [GRAPH] to draw a graph of
the function.

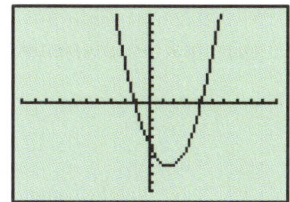

To view a table of values for the function, press [2nd] [GRAPH]
(TABLE). The starting point and interval of the table values can
be adjusted by pressing [2nd] [WINDOW] (TBLSET).

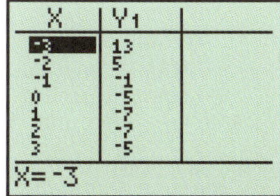

Casio fx-9860g

Selecting **GRAPH** from the Main Menu takes you to the Graph Function screen, where you can store functions to graph. Delete any unwanted functions by scrolling down to the function and pressing DEL F1 **(Yes)**.

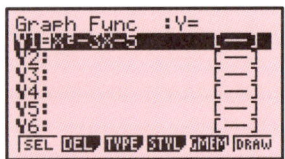

To graph the function $y = x^2 - 3x - 5$, move the cursor to **Y1** and press X,θ,T x^2 − 3 X,θ,T − 5 EXE . This stores the function into **Y1**. Press F6 **(DRAW)** to draw a graph of the function.

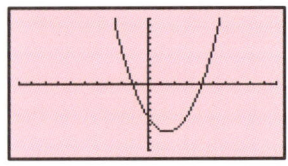

To view a table of values for the function, press MENU and select **TABLE**. The function is stored in **Y1**, but not selected. Press F1 **(SEL)** to select the function, and F6 **(TABL)** to view the table. You can adjust the table settings by pressing EXIT and then F5 **(SET)** from the Table Function screen.

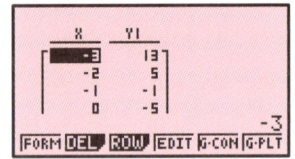

FINDING POINTS OF INTERSECTION

It is often useful to find the points of intersection of two graphs, for instance, when you are trying to solve simultaneous equations.

Texas Instruments TI-83

We can solve $y = 11 - 3x$ and $y = \dfrac{12 - x}{2}$ simultaneously by finding the point of intersection of these two lines. Press Y= , then store $11 - 3x$ into **Y1** and $\dfrac{12 - x}{2}$ into **Y2**. Press GRAPH to draw a graph of the functions.

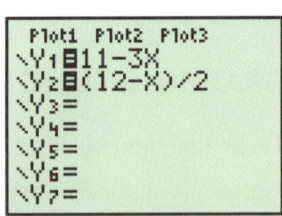

To find their point of intersection, press 2nd TRACE **(CALC) 5**, which selects **5:intersect**. Press ENTER twice to specify the functions **Y1** and **Y2** as the functions you want to find the intersection of, then use the arrow keys to move the cursor close to the point of intersection and press ENTER once more.

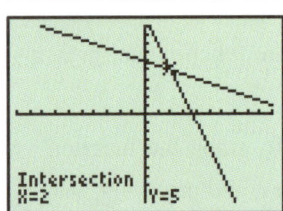

The solution $x = 2$, $y = 5$ is given.

Casio fx-9860g

We can solve $y = 11 - 3x$ and $y = \dfrac{12 - x}{2}$ simultaneously by finding the point of intersection of these two lines. Select **GRAPH** from the Main Menu, then store $11 - 3x$ into **Y1** and $\dfrac{12 - x}{2}$ into **Y2**. Press F6 **(DRAW)** to draw a graph of the functions.

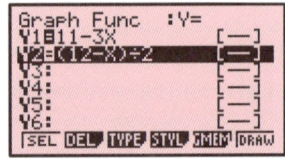

To find their point of intersection, press F5 (G-Solv) F5 (ISCT). The solution $x = 2$, $y = 5$ is given.

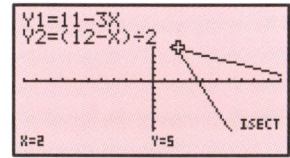

Note: If there is more than one point of intersection, the remaining points of intersection can be found by pressing ▶.

SOLVING $f(x) = 0$

In the special case when you wish to solve an equation of the form $f(x) = 0$, this can be done by graphing $y = f(x)$ and then finding when this graph cuts the x-axis.

Texas Instruments TI-83

To solve $x^3 - 3x^2 + x + 1 = 0$, press Y= and store $x^3 - 3x^2 + x + 1$ into Y1. Press GRAPH to draw the graph.

To find where this function first cuts the x-axis, press 2nd TRACE (CALC) 2, which selects **2:zero**. Move the cursor to the left of the first zero and press ENTER, then move the cursor to the right of the first zero and press ENTER. Finally, move the cursor close to the first zero and press ENTER once more. The solution $x \approx -0.414$ is given.

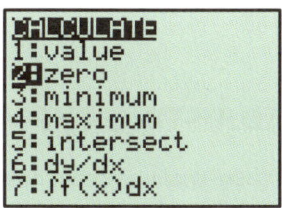

Repeat this process to find the remaining solutions $x = 1$ and $x \approx 2.41$.

Casio fx-9860g

To solve $x^3 - 3x^2 + x + 1 = 0$, select **GRAPH** from the Main Menu and store $x^3 - 3x^2 + x + 1$ into **Y1**. Press F6 (DRAW) to draw the graph.

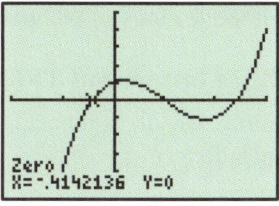

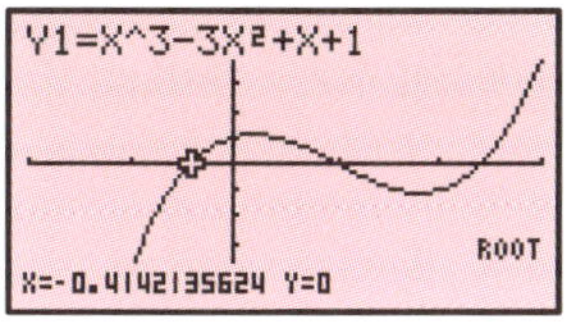

To find where this function cuts the x-axis, press F5 (G-Solv) F1 (ROOT). The first solution $x \approx -0.414$ is given.

Press ▶ to find the remaining solutions $x = 1$ and $x \approx 2.41$.

TURNING POINTS

Texas Instruments TI-83

To find the turning point (vertex) of $y = -x^2 + 2x + 3$, press Y= and store $-x^2 + 2x + 3$ into Y1. Press GRAPH to draw the graph.

From the graph, it is clear that the vertex is a maximum, so press 2nd TRACE (CALC) 4 to select **4:maximum**.

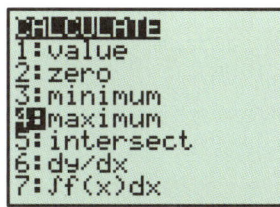

Move the cursor to the left of the vertex and press ENTER, then move the cursor to the right of the vertex and press ENTER. Finally, move the cursor close to the vertex and press ENTER once more. The vertex is (1, 4).

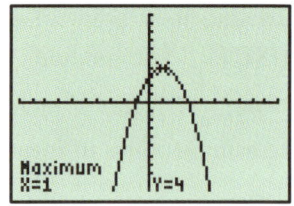

Casio fx-9860g

To find the turning point (vertex) of $y = -x^2 + 2x + 3$, select **GRAPH** from the Main Menu and store $-x^2 + 2x + 3$ into **Y1**. Press F6 **(DRAW)** to draw the graph.

From the graph, it is clear that the vertex is a maximum, so to find the vertex press F5 **(G-Solv)** F2 **(MAX)**.

The vertex is (1, 4).

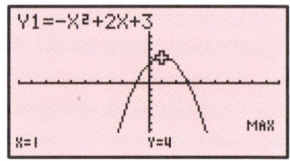

ADJUSTING THE VIEWING WINDOW

When graphing functions it is important that you are able to view all the important features of the graph. As a general rule it is best to start with a large viewing window to make sure all the features of the graph are visible. You can then make the window smaller if necessary.

Texas Instruments TI-83

Some useful commands for adjusting the viewing window include:

ZOOM **0:ZoomFit** :   This command scales the y-axis to fit the minimum and maximum values of the displayed graph within the current x-axis range.

ZOOM **6:ZStandard** :   This command returns the viewing window to the default setting of $-10 \leqslant x \leqslant 10$, $-10 \leqslant y \leqslant 10$.

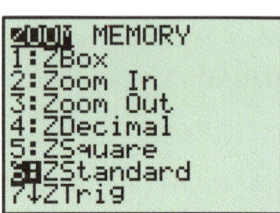

If neither of these commands are helpful, the viewing window can be adjusted manually by pressing WINDOW and setting the minimum and maximum values for the x and y axes.

Casio fx-9860g

The viewing window can be adjusted by pressing SHIFT F3 **(V-Window)**. You can manually set the minimum and maximum values of the x and y axes, or press F3 **(STD)** to obtain the standard viewing window $-10 \leqslant x \leqslant 10$, $-10 \leqslant y \leqslant 10$.

CHALLENGE SETS

Click on the icon to access printable Challenge Sets.

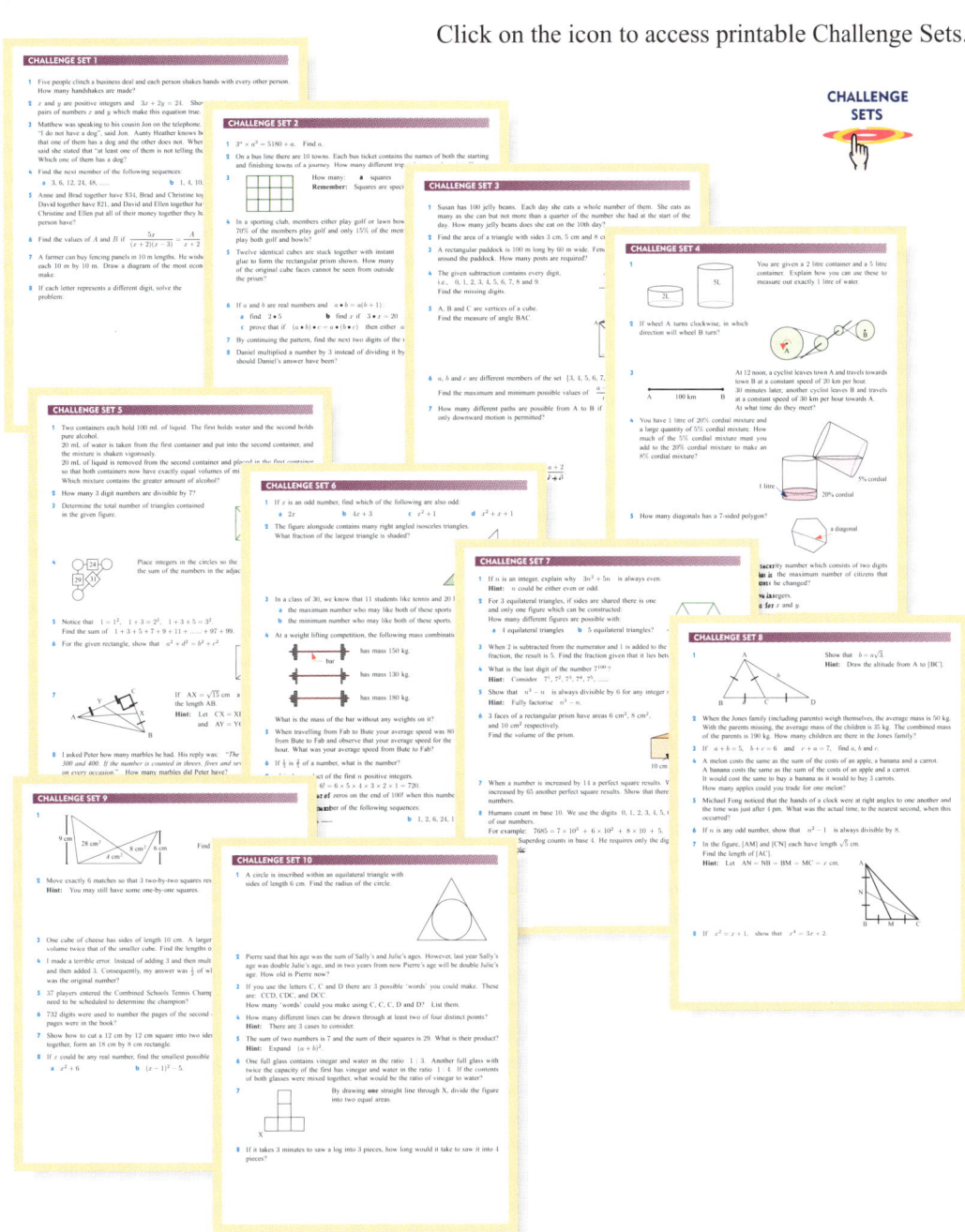

Chapter 1

Number

Contents:
- **A** Natural numbers
- **B** Divisibility tests
- **C** Integers
- **D** Order of operations
- **E** Fractions and rational numbers
- **F** Decimal numbers
- **G** Ratio
- **H** Prime numbers and index notation

Numbers have been part of human thinking since prehistoric times. Today, we live in numbered streets, have telephone numbers, registration numbers, bank account numbers, and tax file numbers. We use numbers to describe the value of things, to measure the universe and plot courses through time and space. We are "tagged" with a number when we are born and often after we die. Numbers are thus an essential part of our lives.

In this chapter we review integers, fractions, decimals, and ratio, and also investigate the notation called index form.

OPENING PROBLEM — "POCKET MONEY"

During a twelve week school term, Tim and his sister Becky agreed to do the dishes for their parents from Monday to Friday. Tim did them on Monday, Wednesday and Friday, leaving Becky to do them on Tuesday and Thursday. They negotiated with their parents to be paid 2 cents for the first week, 4 cents for the second week, 8 cents for the third week, and so on.

Consider the following questions:

1 What is the *ratio* of the work Tim does to the work Becky does?

2 What *fraction* of the work does Tim do?

3 How *much* will they be paid in weeks 4, 5 and 6?

4 What would *each* person be paid for the *final* week of term?

5 How much would *each* person be paid for doing the dishes during the term?

A   NATURAL NUMBERS

NATURAL NUMBERS

> The **natural numbers** are the counting numbers 1, 2, 3, 4, 5, 6, 7, 8, 9, ...

The set of natural numbers is endless. As there is no largest natural number, we say that the set is **infinite**.

FACTORS

> The **factors** of a natural number are all the natural numbers which divide exactly into it, leaving no remainder.

For example, the factors of 10 are: 1, 2, 5 and 10.

A number may have many factors. When a number is written as a **product** of factors, we say it is **factorised**.

For example, consider the number 20.

20 has factors 1, 2, 4, 5, 10, 20 and can be factorised into pairs as: 1×20, 2×10, or 4×5.
20 may also be factorised as the product of 3 factors, for example $20 = 2 \times 2 \times 5$.

The **highest common factor** or **HCF** of two or more natural numbers is the largest factor which is common to all of them.

Example 1 Self Tutor

Find the HCF of 24 and 40.

The factors of 24 are: $\{1, 2, 3, 4, 6, 8, 12, 24\}$

The factors of 40 are: $\{1, 2, 4, 5, 8, 10, 20, 40\}$

$\therefore$ the HCF of 24 and 40 is 8.

MULTIPLES

A **multiple** of any natural number is obtained by multiplying it by another natural number.

For example, the multiples of 3 are: 3, 6, 9, 12, 15, 18, ... These are obtained by multiplying 3 by each of the natural numbers in turn:
$3 \times 1 = 3$, $3 \times 2 = 6$, $3 \times 3 = 9$, $3 \times 4 = 12$, ...

Example 2 Self Tutor

a Find the largest multiple of 9 less than 500.
b Find the smallest multiple of 11 greater than 1000.

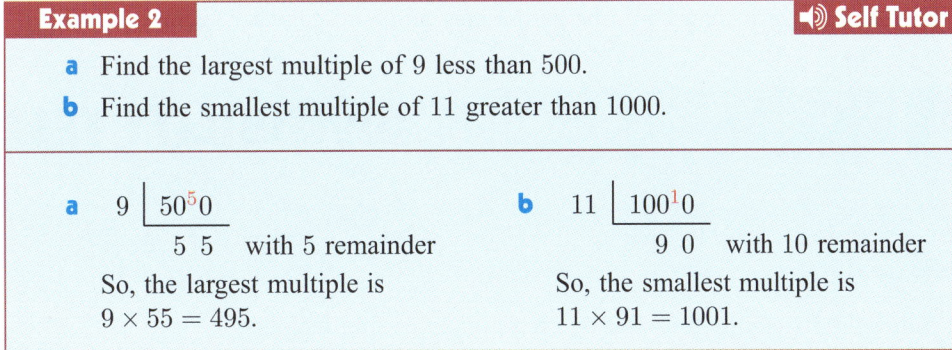

a $9 \overline{)50^50}$
  $5\ 5$ with 5 remainder
So, the largest multiple is
$9 \times 55 = 495$.

b $11 \overline{)100^10}$
  $9\ 0$ with 10 remainder
So, the smallest multiple is
$11 \times 91 = 1001$.

The **lowest common multiple** or **LCM** of two or more natural numbers is the smallest multiple which is common to all of them.

Example 3 Self Tutor

Find the LCM of 6 and 8.

The multiples of 6 are: $\{6, 12, 18, 24, 30, 36, 42, 48, 54, 60, ...\}$

The multiples of 8 are: $\{8, 16, 24, 32, 40, 48, 56, ...\}$

$\therefore$ the common multiples of 6 and 8 are: 24, 48, ...

$\therefore$ the LCM of 6 and 8 is 24.

EXERCISE 1A

1 List all the factors of:
   a 9
   b 12
   c 19
   d 60
   e 23
   f 48
   g 49
   h 84

2 List the first five multiples of:
   a 4
   b 7
   c 9
   d 15

3 Find the HCF of:
   a 6, 8
   b 12, 18
   c 24, 30
   d 72, 120
   e 6, 12, 15
   f 20, 24, 36
   g 12, 18, 27
   h 24, 72, 120

4 a Find the largest multiple of 7 which is less than 1000.
  b Find the smallest multiple of 13 which is greater than 1000.
  c Find the largest multiple of 17 which is less than 2000.
  d Find the smallest multiple of 15 which is greater than 10 000.

5 Find the LCM of:
   a 5, 8
   b 4, 6
   c 8, 10
   d 15, 18
   e 2, 3, 4
   f 3, 4, 5
   g 5, 9, 12
   h 12, 18, 27

6 Three bells chime at intervals of 4, 5 and 6 seconds respectively. If they all chime at the same instant, how long will it be before they all chime together again?

B DIVISIBILITY TESTS

One number is **divisible** by another if, when we divide, the answer is a *natural number*, or whole number.

The following divisibility tests can be used to help us find factors:

A natural number is **divisible by**:
2 if the **last digit is even** or **0**
3 if the **sum of the digits is divisible by 3**
4 if the **number formed by the last two digits is divisible by 4**
5 if the **last digit is 0 or 5**
6 if the **number is even and divisible by 3**.

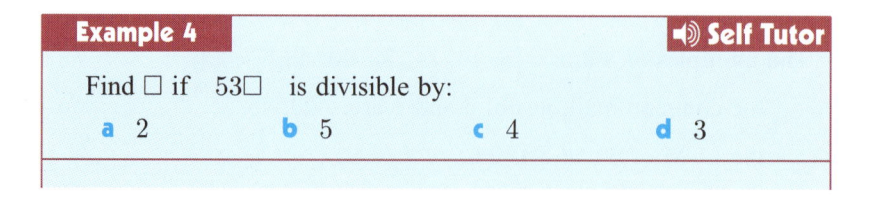

Example 4   ◄)) Self Tutor

Find ☐ if 53☐ is divisible by:
   a 2
   b 5
   c 4
   d 3

> **a** To be divisible by 2, □ must be even or 0.
>   ∴ □ = 0, 2, 4, 6 or 8
> **b** To be divisible by 5, □ must be 0 or 5.
>   ∴ □ = 0 or 5
> **c** To be divisible by 4, '3□' must be divisible by 4.
>   ∴ □ = 2 or 6   {as 32 and 36 are divisible by 4}
> **d** To be divisible by 3, 5 + 3 + □ must be divisible by 3.
>   ∴ 8 + □ must be divisible by 3.
>   ∴ □ = 1, 4 or 7   {as the number must be 9, 12 or 15}

EXERCISE 1B

1 Determine whether the following numbers are divisible by:

  i 2   **ii** 3   **iii** 4   **iv** 5   **v** 6

  a 1002   **b** 12 345   **c** 2816   **d** 123 210
  e 861   **f** 6039   **g** 91 839   **h** 123 456 789

2 Find □ if the following are divisible by 2:
  a 43□   **b** 592□   **c** 3□6   **d** □13

3 Find □ if the following are divisible by 3:
  a 31□   **b** 2□3   **c** □42   **d** 32□5

4 Find □ if the following are divisible by 4:
  a 42□   **b** 3□4   **c** 514□   **d** 68□0

5 Find □ if the following are divisible by 5:
  a 39□   **b** 896□   **c** 73□5   **d** 64□2

6 Find □ if the following are divisible by 6:
  a 42□   **b** 55□   **c** 6□8   **d** 41□2

Check your answers using your calculator!

7 Find the largest three digit number divisible by both 3 and 4.

8 Find the smallest whole number greater than 1 which leaves a remainder of 1 when divided by 3, 4 and 5.

9 How many three digit numbers are divisible by 7?

10 Find the digits X and Y if the number of form 'X7Y6' is divisible by 24.

11 | P | Q | R | S | is a four digit number. Find the number given the following clues:

  Clue 1: All digits are different.
  Clue 2: The product of digits R and S equals digit P.
  Clue 3: Digit Q is one more than P.
  Clue 4: The sum of all digits is 18.
  Clue 5: The four digit number is divisible by 11.

INTEGERS

The negative whole numbers, zero, and the natural numbers form the set of all **integers**.
......, $-5, -4, -3, -2, -1, 0, 1, 2, 3, 4, 5,$ ......

We can show these numbers on a number line. Zero is neither positive nor negative.

We can classify integers as follows:

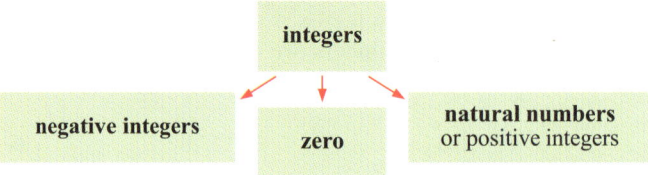

In previous courses we developed the following rules for the **addition** and **subtraction** of integers:

+ (positive) gives a (positive)
− (positive) gives a (negative)
+ (negative) gives a (negative)
− (negative) gives a (positive)

Example 5 — Self Tutor

Simplify:

a $4 + -9$	b $4 - -9$	c $-3 + -5$	d $-3 - -5$
a $4 + -9$ $= 4 - 9$ $= -5$	b $4 - -9$ $= 4 + 9$ $= 13$	c $-3 + -5$ $= -3 - 5$ $= -8$	d $-3 - -5$ $= -3 + 5$ $= 2$

The following rules were developed for **multiplication** with integers:

(positive) × (positive) gives a (positive)
(positive) × (negative) gives a (negative)
(negative) × (positive) gives a (negative)
(negative) × (negative) gives a (positive)

Example 6 — Self Tutor

Find the value of:

a 3×4	b 3×-4	c -3×4	d -3×-4
a $3 \times 4 = 12$	b $3 \times -4 = -12$	c $-3 \times 4 = -12$	d $-3 \times -4 = 12$

NUMBER (Chapter 1) 33

Example 7 🔊 Self Tutor

Simplify:
  a -4^2 **b** $(-4)^2$ **c** -2^3 **d** $(-2)^3$

a -4^2 **b** $(-4)^2$ **c** -2^3 **d** $(-2)^3$
    $= -4 \times 4$ $= -4 \times -4$ $= -2 \times 2 \times 2$ $= -2 \times -2 \times -2$
    $= -16$ $= 16$ $= -8$ $= -8$

The following rules were developed for **division** with integers:

    (positive) ÷ (positive) gives a (positive)
    (positive) ÷ (negative) gives a (negative)
    (negative) ÷ (positive) gives a (negative)
    (negative) ÷ (negative) gives a (positive)

Example 8 🔊 Self Tutor

Find the value of:
  a $14 \div 2$ **b** $14 \div -2$ **c** $-14 \div 2$ **d** $-14 \div -2$

a $14 \div 2$ **b** $14 \div -2$ **c** $-14 \div 2$ **d** $-14 \div -2$
    $= 7$ $= -7$ $= -7$ $= 7$

EXERCISE 1C

1 Find the value of:
  a $13 - 8$ **b** $13 + -8$ **c** $13 - -8$ **d** $-13 + 8$
  e $-13 - 8$ **f** $-13 - -8$ **g** $8 - 13$ **h** $13 + 8$
  i $16 + 25$ **j** $16 - 25$ **k** $16 + -25$ **l** $16 - -25$
  m $-16 + 25$ **n** $-16 + -25$ **o** $-16 - -25$ **p** $25 - 16$

2 Find the value of:
  a 6×7 **b** 6×-7 **c** -6×7 **d** -6×-7
  e 5×8 **f** 5×-8 **g** -5×8 **h** -5×-8

3 Find the value of:
  a -5^2 **b** $(-5)^2$ **c** $(-1)^3$ **d** -1^3
  e $3 \times -2 \times 5$ **f** $-3 \times 2 \times -5$ **g** $-3 \times -2 \times -5$ **h** $2 \times (-3)^2$
  i $-2 \times (-3)^2$ **j** -2^4 **k** $(-2)^4$ **l** $(-3)^2 \times (-2)^2$

4 Find the value of:
  a $15 \div 3$ **b** $15 \div -3$ **c** $-15 \div 3$ **d** $-15 \div -3$
  e $24 \div 8$ **f** $24 \div -8$ **g** $-24 \div 8$ **h** $-24 \div -8$
  i $\dfrac{4}{8}$ **j** $\dfrac{-4}{8}$ **k** $\dfrac{4}{-8}$ **l** $\dfrac{-4}{-8}$

34   NUMBER   (Chapter 1)

D   ORDER OF OPERATIONS

Some expressions contain more than one operation. To evaluate these correctly we use the following rules:

- Perform the operations within **brackets** first.
- Calculate any part involving **exponents**.
- Starting from the left, perform all **divisions** and **multiplications** as you come to them.
- Restart from the left, performing all **additions** and **subtractions** as you come to them.

The word **BEDMAS** may help you remember this order.

Grouping symbols or **brackets** are used to indicate a part of an expression which should be evaluated first.

- If an expression contains *one set* of brackets, evaluate that part first.
- If an expression contains *two or more sets* of brackets one inside the other, evaluate the *innermost* first.
- The division line of fractions also behaves as a grouping symbol. This means that the numerator and the denominator must be found separately before doing the division.

Example 9   ◆)) Self Tutor

Simplify: **a** $3 + 7 - 5$ **b** $6 \times 3 \div 2$

a $3 + 7 - 5$ {Work from left to right as only $+$ and $-$ are involved.}
$= 10 - 5$
$= 5$

b $6 \times 3 \div 2$ {Work from left to right as only $\times$ and $\div$ are involved.}
$= 18 \div 2$
$= 9$

Example 10   ◆)) Self Tutor

Simplify: **a** $23 - 10 \div 2$ **b** $3 \times 8 - 6 \times 5$

a $23 - 10 \div 2$ **b** $3 \times 8 - 6 \times 5$
$= 23 - 5$ {$\div$ before $-$} $= 24 - 30$ {$\times$ before $-$}
$= 18$ $= -6$

NUMBER (Chapter 1) 35

EXERCISE 1D.1

1 Simplify:
- **a** $5 + 8 - 3$
- **b** $5 - 8 + 3$
- **c** $5 - 8 - 3$
- **d** $2 \times 10 \div 5$
- **e** $10 \div 5 \times 2$
- **f** $5 \times 10 \div 2$

2 Simplify:
- **a** $4 + 7 \times 3$
- **b** $7 \times 2 + 8$
- **c** $13 - 3 \times 2$
- **d** $5 \times 4 - 20$
- **e** $33 - 3 \times 4$
- **f** $15 - 6 \times 0$
- **g** $2 \times 5 - 5$
- **h** $60 - 3 \times 4 \times 2$
- **i** $15 \div 3 + 2$
- **j** $8 \times 7 - 6 \times 3$
- **k** $5 + 2 + 3 \times 2$
- **l** $7 - 5 \times 3 + 2$
- **m** $28 - 8 \div 2$
- **n** $6 + 10 \div 2$
- **o** $23 - 3 \times 7$
- **p** $15 \div 5 + 8 \div 2$

Example 11 🔊 **Self Tutor**

Simplify: $3 + (11 - 7) \times 2$

$3 + (11 - 7) \times 2$
$= 3 + 4 \times 2$ {evaluate the brackets first}
$= 3 + 8$ {$\times$ before $+$}
$= 11$

3 Simplify:
- **a** $12 + (5 - 2)$
- **b** $(12 + 5) - 2$
- **c** $(8 \div 4) - 2$
- **d** $8 \div (4 - 2)$
- **e** $84 - (12 \div 6)$
- **f** $(84 - 12) \div 6$
- **g** $32 + (8 \div 2)$
- **h** $32 - (8 + 14) - 7$
- **i** $(32 - 8) + (14 - 7)$
- **j** $(16 \div 8) \div 2$
- **k** $16 \div (8 \div 2)$
- **l** $18 - (6 \times 3) - 4$
- **m** $24 \times 8 \div (4 - 2)$
- **n** $(16 + 4) - (8 \div 2)$
- **o** $2 \times (5 - 3) \div 4$

Example 12 🔊 **Self Tutor**

Simplify: $[12 + (9 \div 3)] - 11$

$[12 + (9 \div 3)] - 11$
$= [12 + 3] - 11$ {evaluate the inner brackets first}
$= 15 - 11$ {outer brackets next}
$= 4$

4 Simplify:
- **a** $8 - [(2 - 3) + 4 \times 3]$
- **b** $[16 - (9 + 3)] \times 2$
- **c** $13 - [(8 - 3) + 6]$
- **d** $[16 - (12 \div 4)] \times 3$
- **e** $200 \div [4 \times (6 \div 3)]$
- **f** $[(12 \times 3) \div (12 \div 3)] \times 2$

Example 13

Simplify: $\dfrac{12 + (5 - 7)}{18 \div (6 + 3)}$

$\dfrac{12 + (5 - 7)}{18 \div (6 + 3)} = \dfrac{12 + (-2)}{18 \div 9}$ {evaluate the brackets first}

$= \dfrac{10}{2}$ {simplifying numerator and denominator}

$= 5$

5 Simplify:

a $\dfrac{75}{5 \times 5}$ b $\dfrac{21}{16 - 9}$ c $\dfrac{18 \div 3}{14 - 11}$ d $\dfrac{7 + 9}{6 - 2}$

e $\dfrac{53 - 21}{9 - 5}$ f $\dfrac{3 \times 8 + 6}{6}$ g $\dfrac{57}{7 - (2 \times 3)}$ h $\dfrac{(3 + 8) - 5}{3 + (8 - 5)}$

6 Using $\times$, $\div$, $+$ or $-$ only, insert symbols between the following sets of numbers so that correct equations result. Remember that the operations must be evaluated in the correct order.

a 9   3   2 = 8   b 9   3   2 = 25   c 9   3   2 = 5

7 Insert grouping symbols where necessary to make the following true:

a $8 - 6 \times 3 = 6$ b $120 \div 4 \times 2 = 15$ c $120 \div 4 \times 2 = 60$
d $5 \times 7 - 3 - 1 = 15$ e $5 \times 7 - 3 - 1 = 33$ f $5 \times 7 - 3 - 1 = 19$
g $3 + 2 \times 8 - 4 = 36$ h $3 + 2 \times 8 - 4 = 11$ i $3 + 2 \times 8 - 4 = 15$

USING YOUR CALCULATOR TO PERFORM OPERATIONS

In this course it is assumed that you have a graphics calculator. A set of instructions for many common tasks can be found starting on page **9**.

In this section we consider evaluating expressions on your calculator. Your calculator already has the **order of operations** built into it. However, you may need to consult the sections about **negative numbers** and **grouping symbols** on pages **10** and **12**.

Example 14

Calculate: a $\dfrac{15}{3} + 2$ b $\dfrac{15}{3 + 2}$

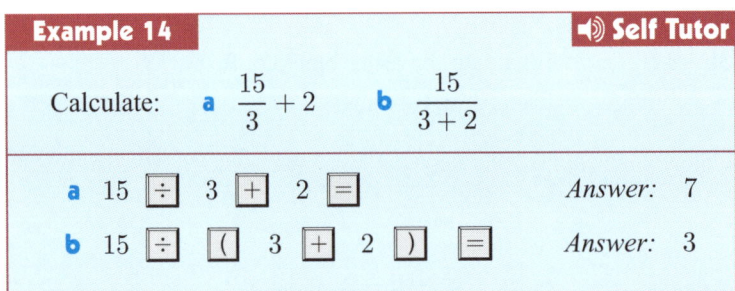

Try to remember BEDMAS!

NUMBER (Chapter 1) 37

> **Example 15** ◀ඛ **Self Tutor**
>
> Calculate: **a** $20 \div -4$ **b** $\dfrac{-8}{5-1}$
>
> **a** 20 ÷ (−) 4 =   Answer: −5
>
> **b** (−) 8 ÷ (5 − 1) =   Answer: −2

EXERCISE 1D.2

1 Evaluate each of the following using your calculator:

a $17 + 23 \times 15$
b $(17 + 23) \times 15$
c $128 \div 8 + 8$
d $128 \div (8 + 8)$
e 34×-8
f $-64 \div -16$
g $\dfrac{89 + -5}{-7 \times 3}$
h $-25 + 32 \div -4$
i $\dfrac{-15 - 5}{6 - (8 \div 4)}$
j $\dfrac{136 + 8}{4 \times 9}$
k $\dfrac{127 - 307}{2 \times 3 \times 5}$
l $\dfrac{28 - (8 \div 2)}{(5 + 1) \times 2}$

E FRACTIONS AND RATIONAL NUMBERS

> **Rational numbers** can be written as a **ratio** of two integers.
> They can be written in the form $\dfrac{a}{b}$ where a and b are integers and $b \neq 0$.

Rational numbers appear in many forms.

For example, $4, -2, 0, 10\%, -\tfrac{4}{7}, 1.3, 0.\overline{6}$ are all rational numbers.

They can be written in the form $\dfrac{a}{b}$ as: $\tfrac{4}{1}, \tfrac{-2}{1}, \tfrac{0}{1}, \tfrac{1}{10}, \tfrac{-4}{7}, \tfrac{13}{10}, \tfrac{2}{3}$.

> A **fraction** is an expression written in the form $\dfrac{a}{b}$ where $b \neq 0$.

The quantity a is called the **numerator** and the quantity b is called the **denominator**.

A **common fraction** consists of two integers separated by a bar symbol. For example,

$\dfrac{1}{4}$ ← numerator
← bar (which also means *divide*)
← denominator

The **reciprocal** of a fraction is obtained by swapping its numerator and denominator.
So, the reciprocal of $\dfrac{a}{b}$ is $\dfrac{b}{a}$.

TYPES OF FRACTIONS

$\frac{2}{3}$ is called a **proper fraction** as the numerator is less than the denominator.

$\frac{4}{3}$ is called an **improper fraction** as the numerator is greater than the denominator.

$2\frac{1}{2}$ is a **mixed number** as it is really $2 + \frac{1}{2}$.

$\frac{1}{3}$ and $\frac{2}{6}$ are **equivalent fractions** as both fractions represent equivalent portions.

ADDITION AND SUBTRACTION

To **add** (or **subtract**) two fractions we convert them to equivalent fractions with a common denominator. We then add (or subtract) the new numerators.

Example 16

Find: $\frac{2}{3} + \frac{3}{4}$

$\frac{2}{3} + \frac{3}{4}$ {LCD = 12}

$= \frac{2 \times 4}{3 \times 4} + \frac{3 \times 3}{4 \times 3}$ {to achieve a common denominator of 12}

$= \frac{8}{12} + \frac{9}{12}$

$= \frac{17}{12}$

$= 1\frac{5}{12}$

Example 17

Find: $2\frac{1}{2} - 1\frac{2}{5}$

$2\frac{1}{2} - 1\frac{2}{5}$

$= \frac{5}{2} - \frac{7}{5}$ {write as improper fractions}

$= \frac{5 \times 5}{2 \times 5} - \frac{7 \times 2}{5 \times 2}$ {to achieve a common denominator of 10}

$= \frac{25}{10} - \frac{14}{10}$

$= \frac{11}{10}$ or $1\frac{1}{10}$

EXERCISE 1E.1

1 Find:

    a $\frac{3}{14} + \frac{6}{14}$ **b** $\frac{7}{16} + \frac{2}{16}$ **c** $\frac{5}{8} + \frac{3}{4}$ **d** $\frac{2}{5} + \frac{1}{6}$

    e $\frac{2}{3} + 4$ **f** $1\frac{1}{2} + \frac{5}{8}$ **g** $1\frac{1}{2} + 2\frac{1}{6}$ **h** $2\frac{1}{3} + 3\frac{3}{4}$

2 Find:

    a $\frac{7}{9} - \frac{2}{9}$ **b** $\frac{3}{4} - \frac{5}{6}$ **c** $\frac{4}{7} - \frac{1}{2}$ **d** $1 - \frac{5}{8}$

    e $5 - 3\frac{1}{8}$ **f** $2\frac{4}{5} - 1\frac{1}{3}$ **g** $2\frac{1}{2} - 4\frac{1}{6}$ **h** $2\frac{1}{3} - 3\frac{3}{4}$

MULTIPLICATION

To **multiply** two fractions, we multiply the numerators together and multiply the denominators together. We cancel any common factors in the numerator and denominator before completing the multiplication.

In general, $\dfrac{a}{b} \times \dfrac{c}{d} = \dfrac{ac}{bd}$.

Example 18

Find: **a** $\dfrac{1}{2} \times \dfrac{2}{5}$ **b** $(2\tfrac{1}{3})^2$

a $\quad \dfrac{1}{2} \times \dfrac{2}{5}$
$= \dfrac{1}{2} \times \dfrac{2}{5}$
$= \dfrac{1}{5}$

b $\quad (2\tfrac{1}{3})^2$
$= 2\tfrac{1}{3} \times 2\tfrac{1}{3}$
$= \dfrac{7}{3} \times \dfrac{7}{3}$
$= \dfrac{49}{9}$ or $5\tfrac{4}{9}$

Remember to cancel any common factors before completing the multiplication.

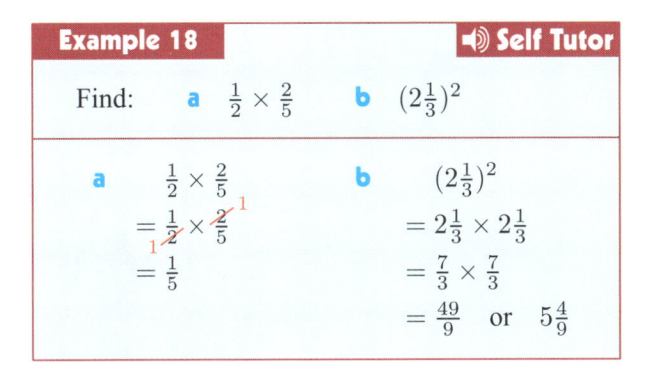

DIVISION

To **divide** by a fraction, we multiply by the reciprocal of that fraction.

$$\dfrac{a}{b} \div \dfrac{c}{d} = \dfrac{a}{b} \times \dfrac{d}{c}$$

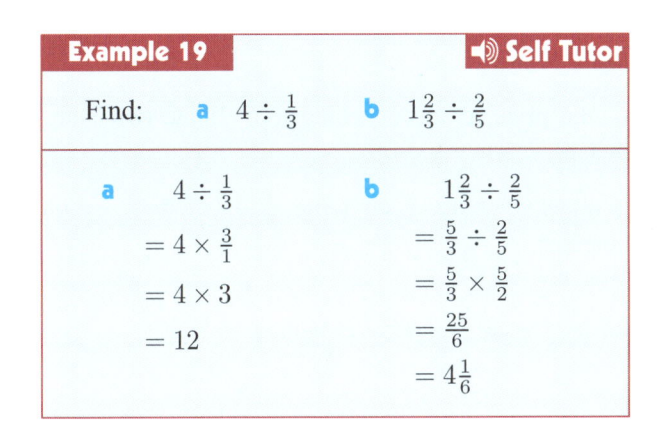

Example 19

Find: **a** $4 \div \tfrac{1}{3}$ **b** $1\tfrac{2}{3} \div \tfrac{2}{5}$

a $\quad 4 \div \tfrac{1}{3}$
$= 4 \times \tfrac{3}{1}$
$= 4 \times 3$
$= 12$

b $\quad 1\tfrac{2}{3} \div \tfrac{2}{5}$
$= \tfrac{5}{3} \div \tfrac{2}{5}$
$= \tfrac{5}{3} \times \tfrac{5}{2}$
$= \tfrac{25}{6}$
$= 4\tfrac{1}{6}$

The reciprocal of $\dfrac{c}{d}$ is $\dfrac{d}{c}$.

EXERCISE 1E.2

1 Calculate:

a $\tfrac{3}{4} \times \tfrac{5}{6}$ **b** $\tfrac{4}{7} \times \tfrac{1}{2}$ **c** $2 \times \tfrac{3}{4}$ **d** $\tfrac{2}{3} \times 4$

e $1\tfrac{1}{2} \times \tfrac{5}{8}$ **f** $1\tfrac{3}{8} \times \tfrac{4}{11}$ **g** $(2\tfrac{1}{3})^2$ **h** $(1\tfrac{1}{2})^3$

2 Evaluate:

a $\tfrac{3}{4} \div \tfrac{5}{6}$ **b** $\tfrac{3}{4} \div \tfrac{2}{3}$ **c** $\tfrac{7}{12} \div \tfrac{3}{4}$ **d** $\tfrac{2}{3} \div 4$

e $2 \div \tfrac{3}{4}$ **f** $1\tfrac{1}{2} \div \tfrac{5}{8}$ **g** $\tfrac{3}{4} \div 2\tfrac{1}{2}$ **h** $2\tfrac{1}{3} \div 3\tfrac{3}{4}$

3 Calculate:

  a $4\frac{3}{8} + 2\frac{2}{5}$
  b $(\frac{2}{3})^4$
  c $6 - 3 \times \frac{3}{4}$
  d $\frac{3}{4} \times 1\frac{1}{2} \div 2$
  e $\dfrac{6 \times 3 \times \frac{1}{2}}{\frac{3}{4}}$
  f $1 \div (\frac{1}{2} + \frac{3}{5})$
  g $1 \div \frac{1}{2} + \frac{3}{5}$
  h $\dfrac{4 - \frac{1}{2}}{3 \times \frac{2}{3}}$

PROBLEM SOLVING WITH FRACTIONS

Example 20 — Self Tutor

During a season, Joe hit $\frac{2}{5}$ of the home runs for his team.

How many home runs did he hit if there were 40 scored in total?

Joe hit $\frac{2}{5}$ of $40 = \frac{2}{5} \times 40$

$= \dfrac{2 \times \cancel{40}^{\,8}}{\cancel{5}_{\,1}}$

$= 16$ home runs.

Remember that 'of' means '×'.

EXERCISE 1E.3

1 Michael eats $\frac{1}{4}$ of a cheesecake and later eats $\frac{2}{5}$ of the cheesecake. What fraction remains?

2 The cost of a Ford is $\frac{2}{13}$ of the cost of a Rolls Royce. If the current price of a Rolls Royce is $211 250, what is the cost of a Ford?

3 The price of tracksuit pants is $\frac{4}{5}$ of the price of the matching top. If the two items together cost £36, find the price of each.

4 A family spends $\frac{1}{3}$ of its weekly budget on rent, $\frac{1}{4}$ on food, $\frac{1}{8}$ on clothes, $\frac{1}{12}$ on entertainment, and the remainder is banked.
How much is banked if the weekly income is €864.72?

5 Renee used $\frac{1}{3}$ of a length of pipe and later used $\frac{2}{3}$ of what remained.
What fraction of the pipe is left?

6 $\frac{9}{10}$ of the weight of a loaf of bread comes from the flour used in its baking.
$\frac{2}{9}$ of the weight of the flour is protein. What fraction of the weight of the loaf is protein?

7 A farmer has 364 ewes and each ewe has either one or two newborn lambs. If there are 468 lambs in total, what fraction of the ewes have twin lambs?

8 A tree is losing its leaves. Two thirds fall off in the first week, two thirds of those remaining fall off in the second week, and two thirds of those remaining fall off in the third week. Now there are 37 leaves. How many leaves did the tree have originally?

FRACTIONS ON A CALCULATOR

The instructions on page **11** discuss how to enter and evaluate fractions on a graphics calculator.

However, you must not forget how to manually perform operations with fractions.

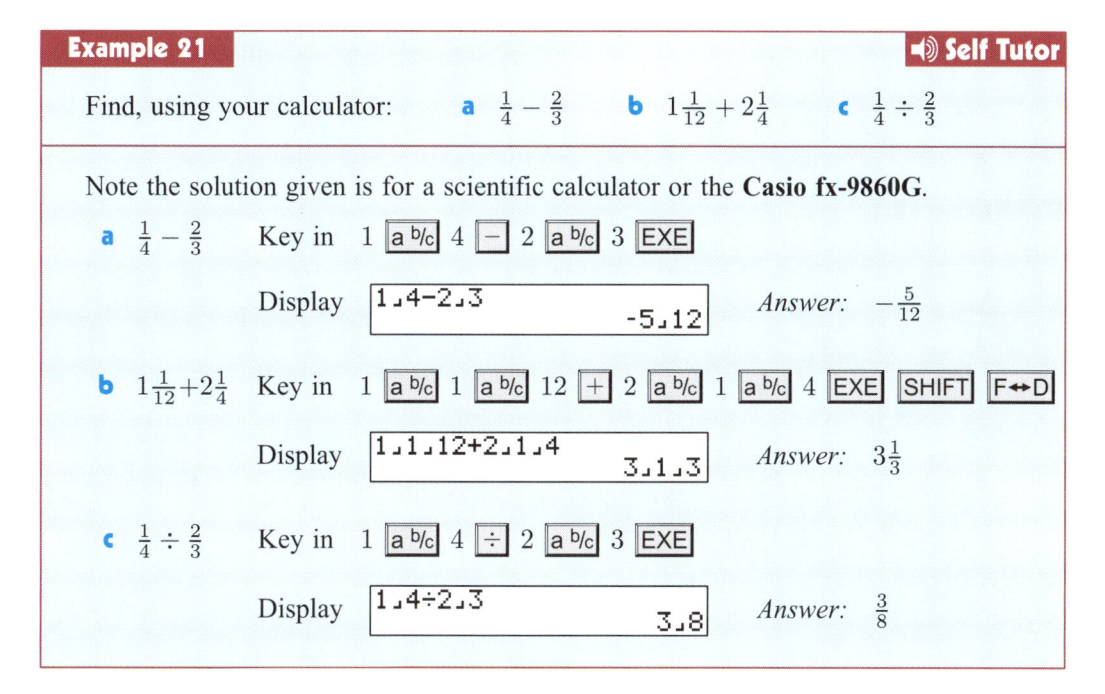

Example 21 — Self Tutor

Find, using your calculator: **a** $\frac{1}{4} - \frac{2}{3}$ **b** $1\frac{1}{12} + 2\frac{1}{4}$ **c** $\frac{1}{4} \div \frac{2}{3}$

Note the solution given is for a scientific calculator or the **Casio fx-9860G**.

a $\frac{1}{4} - \frac{2}{3}$ Key in   1 [a b/c] 4 [−] 2 [a b/c] 3 [EXE]

Display `1⌐4-2⌐3`
         `       -5⌐12`   Answer: $-\frac{5}{12}$

b $1\frac{1}{12} + 2\frac{1}{4}$ Key in   1 [a b/c] 1 [a b/c] 12 [+] 2 [a b/c] 1 [a b/c] 4 [EXE] [SHIFT] [F↔D]

Display `1⌐1⌐12+2⌐1⌐4`
         `       3⌐1⌐3`   Answer: $3\frac{1}{3}$

c $\frac{1}{4} \div \frac{2}{3}$ Key in   1 [a b/c] 4 [÷] 2 [a b/c] 3 [EXE]

Display `1⌐4÷2⌐3`
         `       3⌐8`   Answer: $\frac{3}{8}$

EXERCISE 1E.4

1 Find, using your calculator:

a $\frac{1}{3} + \frac{1}{4}$ **b** $\frac{1}{3} + \frac{5}{7}$ **c** $\frac{3}{8} - \frac{2}{7}$ **d** $\frac{1}{4} - \frac{1}{3}$

e $\frac{2}{9} \times \frac{3}{2}$ **f** $\frac{5}{7} \times \frac{2}{3}$ **g** $\frac{6}{7} \times \frac{1}{5}$ **h** $\frac{3}{5} \div \frac{2}{9}$

i $1\frac{1}{4} + 2\frac{1}{2} \times \frac{3}{4}$ **j** $1\frac{3}{7} \times 2\frac{1}{8} + 1\frac{1}{4}$ **k** $3\frac{1}{7} \div (2\frac{3}{4} \times \frac{4}{7})$

F DECIMAL NUMBERS

A **decimal number** is one which contains a decimal point. We can use decimal numbers to display fractions of whole numbers.

For example:
- 4.63 is a quick way of writing $4 + \frac{6}{10} + \frac{3}{100}$. This number can also be written as the **improper fraction** $\frac{463}{100}$ or as the **mixed number** $4\frac{63}{100}$.
- 14.062 is a quick way of writing $14 + \frac{6}{100} + \frac{2}{1000}$.

Expansions of decimals like those above are referred to as **expanded fractional form**.

Example 22

a Write 5.704 in expanded fractional form.
b Write $\quad 3 + \frac{2}{10} + \frac{4}{100} + \frac{1}{10\,000}\quad$ in decimal form.
c State the value of the digit 6 in $\quad 0.036\,24$.

---

a $5.704 = 5 + \frac{7}{10} + \frac{4}{1000}$ **b** $3 + \frac{2}{10} + \frac{4}{100} + \frac{1}{10\,000} = 3.2401$

c In $\;0.036\,24$, the 6 stands for $\frac{6}{1000}$.

EXERCISE 1F.1

1 Write the following in expanded fractional form:
  a 2.5 **b** 2.05 **c** 2.0501 **d** 4.0052 **e** 0.0106

2 Write the following in decimal form:
  a $3 + \frac{2}{10}$
  b $\frac{7}{10} + \frac{8}{100}$
  c $\frac{6}{10} + \frac{3}{1000}$
  d $\frac{7}{100} + \frac{9}{1000}$
  e $4 + \frac{1}{10\,000}$
  f $5 + \frac{3}{100} + \frac{2}{10\,000}$

3 State the value of the digit 6 in the following:
  a 7608 **b** 762 **c** 0.619 **d** 0.0762 **e** 0.000 164

4 Evaluate:
  a $10.76 + 8.3$
  b $16.21 + 13.84$
  c $16.21 - 13.84$
  d $2.5 - 0.6$
  e $12 - 7.254$
  f $0.26 + 3.09 + 0.985$
  g $0.0039 + 0.471$
  h $7.9 - 8.6$
  i $0.25 + 0.087 - 0.231$
  j $0.421 - 1$
  k $-0.258 + 3$
  l $-2.7 - 3.61$

Example 23

Evaluate:
a 24×0.8 **b** $3.6 \div 0.02$

---

a $\qquad 24 \times 8 = 192$
$\quad\therefore\quad 24 \times 0.8 = 19.2 \qquad \{\div 10 \text{ by shifting decimal 1 place left}\}$

b $\quad 3.6 \div 0.02$
$\quad = 3.60 \div 0.02 \qquad$ {shift both decimal points the same
$\quad = 360 \div 2 \qquad\qquad$ number of places to the right}
$\quad = 180$

5 Evaluate:
  a 13.7×100
  b $0.5 \div 100$
  c $15 \div 0.5$
  d 0.5×8
  e 0.5×0.08
  f 3000×0.6
  g 3.6×0.6
  h $1 \div 0.02$
  i $(0.3)^3$
  j $500 \times (0.2)^2$
  k $0.64 \div 160$
  l $0.0775 \div 2.5$

NUMBER   (Chapter 1)   43

Example 24	Self Tutor
Write 0.075 in simplest fraction form.	$0.075 = \frac{75}{1000}$ $= \frac{75 \div 25}{1000 \div 25}$ $= \frac{3}{40}$

6 Write in simplest fraction form:

   a 0.5   **b** 0.6   **c** 3.25   **d** 0.625   **e** 0.0375   **f** 0.0084

   g 2.75   **h** 9.1   **i** 3.125   **j** 0.076   **k** 0.0875   **l** 0.0005

Example 25	Self Tutor
Write the following in decimal form: **a** $\frac{7}{40}$ **b** $\frac{3}{7}$	

a $\frac{7}{40}$
     $= 7 \div 40$
     $= 0.175$
 	
 Calculator: 7 ÷ 40 =
	b $\frac{3}{7}$
	     $= 3 \div 7$
	     $= 0.\overline{428571}$
	
	 Calculator: 3 ÷ 7 =

When fractions are converted to decimals they either terminate or recur.

7 Write in decimal form:

   a $\frac{1}{2}$ **b** $\frac{3}{4}$ **c** $\frac{3}{5}$ **d** $\frac{17}{50}$ **e** $\frac{2}{3}$

   f $\frac{2}{9}$ **g** $\frac{9}{40}$ **h** $\frac{5}{6}$ **i** $\frac{7}{8}$ **j** $\frac{17}{80}$

   k $\frac{37}{125}$ **l** $\frac{5}{12}$ **m** $\frac{3}{20}$ **n** $\frac{4}{11}$ **o** $\frac{11}{25}$

   p $\frac{7}{9}$ **q** $\frac{7}{90}$ **r** $\frac{7}{99}$ **s** $\frac{7}{999}$ **t** $\frac{7}{9999}$

Example 26	Self Tutor
Jon bought four drinks for $1.30 each. How much change did he get from a $10 note?	

cost = $1.30 × 4
       = $5.20
	∴ change = $10 − $5.20
	               = $4.80

8 Solve the following problems:

a Benjamin fills his car with 50 litres of petrol. How much does it cost him if petrol is selling at 94.6 pence per litre?

b Potting mix sells at €3.80 per kg. How much would a 3.5 kg bag of potting mix cost?

c The sweet shop sells licorice at $9.40 per kg. How much would 250 g of licorice cost?

d The cost of electricity is 43.4 cents per kilowatt for each hour. What would:
  i 500 kilowatts of electricity cost for one hour
  ii it cost to burn a 60 watt globe for 10 hours?

e At a milk processing factory, cartons are filled from large refrigerated tanks that each hold 8400 litres. How many 600 mL cartons can be filled from one tank?

f A large mixer at a bakery holds 0.75 tonnes of dough. How many bread rolls, each of mass 150 g, can be made from the dough in the mixer?

g How many dozen bottles of wine can be filled from a 9000 litre fermentation tank if each bottle holds 750 mL?

h A trophy store wishes to make brass medallions, each of mass 17.5 g, from 140 kg of brass. How many medallions can be made?

ROUNDING DECIMAL NUMBERS

We often need to round numbers to a certain number of decimal places. This sometimes occurs when we measure quantities and when we calculate the price of a particular amount of an item.

RULES FOR ROUNDING

- **Rounding to the nearest whole number**
  Look at the *first* decimal place.
  If the digit is 5, 6, 7, 8 or 9,   round **up**.
  If the digit is 0, 1, 2, 3 or 4,   round **down**.

  5.6 — look at this, then round

- **Rounding to the nearest one decimal place**
  Look at the *second* decimal place.
  If the digit is 5, 6, 7, 8 or 9,   round **up**.
  If the digit is 0, 1, 2, 3 or 4,   round **down**.

  5.64 — look at this, then round

- **Rounding to the nearest two decimal places**
  Look at the *third* decimal place.
  If the digit is 5, 6, 7, 8 or 9,   round **up**.
  If the digit is 0, 1, 2, 3 or 4,   round **down**.

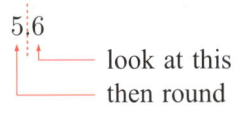

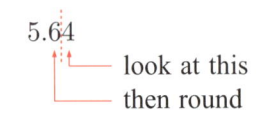

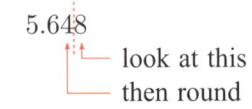

  5.648 — look at this, then round

Example 27

Round 39.748 to the nearest:

a whole number   **b** one decimal place   **c** two decimal places

a $39.748 \approx 40$ to the nearest whole number
b $39.748 \approx 39.7$ to one decimal place
c $39.748 \approx 39.75$ to two decimal places

Notice that: $0.5864 \approx 0.586$ (to 3 decimal places)
≈ 0.59 (to 2 decimal places)
≈ 0.6 (to 1 decimal place)

Example 28

Calculate, to 2 decimal places:

a $(2.8 + 3.7)(0.82 - 0.57)$ **b** $18.6 - \dfrac{12.2 - 4.3}{5.2}$

a (2.8 + 3.7) × (0.82 − 0.57) =
Screen: 1.625   Answer: 1.63

b 18.6 − (12.2 − 4.3) ÷ 5.2 =
Screen: 17.080 769 23   Answer: 17.08

EXERCISE 1F.2

1 Round to the nearest whole number:
  a 3.245   **b** 5.671   **c** 19.81   **d** 200.5

2 Round correct to 1 decimal place:
  a 3.12   **b** 10.41   **c** 4.85   **d** 3.96

3 Round correct to 2 decimal places:
  a 9.432   **b** 13.126   **c** 9.305   **d** 0.194

4 Find, giving your answers correct to 2 decimal places where necessary:
  a $(16.8 + 12.4) \times 17.1$ **b** $16.8 + 12.4 \times 17.1$ **c** $127 \div 9 - 5$
  d $127 \div (9 - 5)$ **e** $\dfrac{16.84}{7.9 + 11.2}$ **f** $37.4 - 16.1 \div (4.2 - 2.7)$
  g $\dfrac{27.4}{3.2} - \dfrac{18.6}{16.1}$ **h** $\dfrac{27.9 - 17.3}{8.6} + 4.7$ **i** $\dfrac{0.0768 + 7.1}{18.69 - 3.824}$

5 Seet Huang puts 25.42 litres of fuel in his motor bike. If the fuel costs 136.8 cents per litre, what price does Seet Huang need to pay?

G RATIO

A **ratio** is an ordered comparison of quantities of the same kind.

For example, if there are 13 boys and 17 girls in a class, the ratio of boys to girls is 13 to 17, written $13 : 17$.

If measurements are involved, we must use the **same units** for each quantity.

For example, suppose Andreas and Carol measure their heights. Carol records that Andreas is 1.76 m tall. Andreas records that Carol is 161 cm tall. The ratio of Andreas' height to Carol's height is not $1.76 : 161$ since these measurements have different units.

Rather, since 1.76 m = 176 cm, the ratio is $176 : 161$.

Example 29

Write as a ratio, without simplifying your answer:
- **a** Jack has $5 and Jill has 50 cents.
- **b** Mix 200 mL of cordial with 1 L of water.

a Jack : Jill = $5 : 50 cents   {write in the correct order}
                  = 500 cents : 50 cents   {write in the same units}
                  = 500 : 50   {express without units}

b cordial : water = 200 mL : 1 L   {write in the correct order}
                       = 200 mL : 1000 mL   {write in the same units}
                       = 200 : 1000   {express without units}

EXERCISE 1G.1

1 Write as a ratio, without simplifying your answer:
- **a** $10 is to $7
- **b** 2 L is to 5 L
- **c** 80 kg is to 50 kg
- **d** $2 is to 50 cents
- **e** 500 mL is to 2 L
- **f** 800 m is to 1.5 km

2 At my school there are 29 badminton players and 18 tabletennis players. Compare these quantities using a ratio.

3 The school cross-country race is 3.7 km long. The longest race at the athletics carnival is 800 m. Compare these distances using a ratio.

SIMPLIFYING RATIOS

Two ratios are **equal** if the quantities they compare are in the same proportions.

For example, if we have 9 oranges and 3 lemons, there are 3 oranges for every 1 lemon. So, the ratio $9:3$ equals the ratio $3:1$.

We can simplify a ratio by writing an equal ratio with integer components that are as small as possible.

To **simplify** a ratio we multiply or divide each part by the same non-zero number. This ensures we create an equal ratio.

Example 30 ◀ Self Tutor

Express the following ratios in simplest form:

   a $45:15$ **b** $2\frac{1}{2} : \frac{1}{2}$ **c** $0.4 : 1.4$

a $45 : 15$
$= 45 \div 15 : 15 \div 15$
$= 3 : 1$

b $2\frac{1}{2} : \frac{1}{2}$
$= \frac{5}{2} : \frac{1}{2}$
$= \frac{5}{2} \times 2 : \frac{1}{2} \times 2$
$= 5 : 1$

c $0.4 : 1.4$
$= 0.4 \times 10 : 1.4 \times 10$
$= 4 : 14$
$= 4 \div 2 : 14 \div 2$
$= 2 : 7$

EXERCISE 1G.2

1 Express as a ratio in simplest form:
   a $3 : 6$ **b** $\frac{3}{4} : \frac{1}{4}$ **c** $0.5 : 0.2$ **d** $18 : 24$
   e $2\frac{1}{2} : 1\frac{1}{2}$ **f** $1.5 : 0.3$ **g** 20 c to \$1.20   **h** 2 L to 500 mL

2 Use your calculator to find $1\frac{2}{3} \div 1\frac{1}{3}$. Simplify $1\frac{2}{3} : 1\frac{1}{3}$. What do you notice?

3 Simplify the ratios:
   a $\frac{1}{3} : \frac{1}{2}$ **b** $2\frac{1}{2} : 1\frac{1}{3}$ **c** $3\frac{1}{4} : \frac{2}{3}$ **d** $1\frac{2}{3} : 1\frac{3}{10}$

4 Express as a ratio in simplest form:
   a $0.5 : 0.3$ **b** $0.2 : 0.8$ **c** $0.6 : 1.5$ **d** $0.35 : 0.49$

EQUAL RATIOS

Ratios are **equal** if they can be expressed in the same simplest form.

48   NUMBER   (Chapter 1)

Example 31

Find $\square$ if: **a** $2:3 = 6:\square$ **b** $12:30 = \square:35$

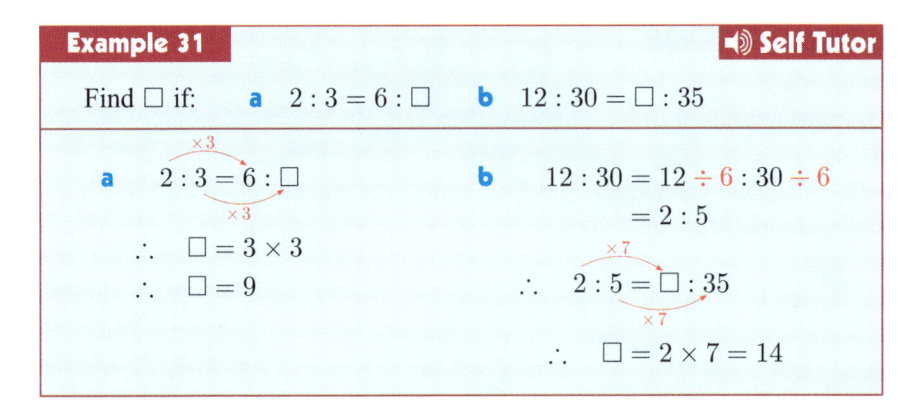

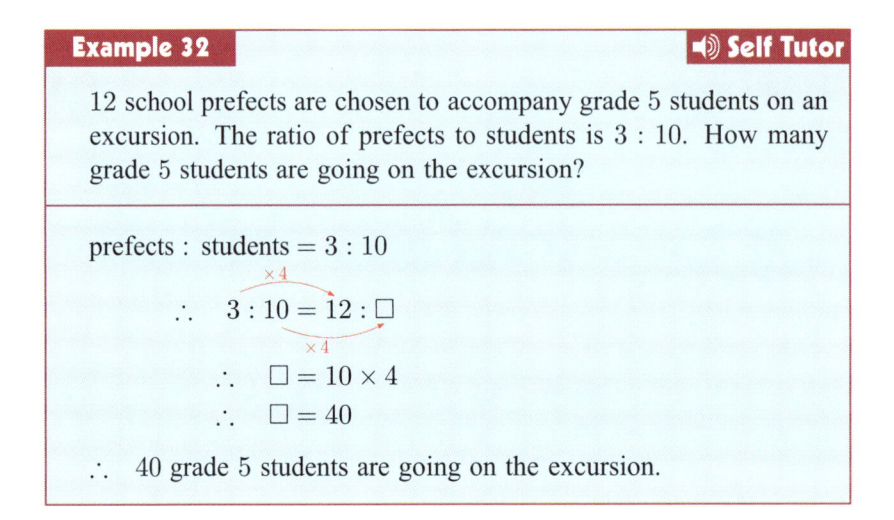

a $2:3 = 6:\square$ $\quad\quad$ (×3)

$\therefore\ \square = 3 \times 3$

$\therefore\ \square = 9$

b $12:30 = 12 \div 6 : 30 \div 6$

$\quad\quad = 2:5$

$\therefore\ 2:5 = \square:35$ (×7)

$\therefore\ \square = 2 \times 7 = 14$

Example 32

12 school prefects are chosen to accompany grade 5 students on an excursion. The ratio of prefects to students is $3:10$. How many grade 5 students are going on the excursion?

prefects : students $= 3:10$

$\therefore\ 3:10 = 12:\square$ (×4)

$\therefore\ \square = 10 \times 4$

$\therefore\ \square = 40$

$\therefore\ $ 40 grade 5 students are going on the excursion.

EXERCISE 1G.3

1 Find $\square$ if:
   a $2:5 = 8:\square$
   b $3:7 = \square:21$
   c $4:5 = 16:\square$
   d $2:6 = \square:27$
   e $12:9 = 16:\square$
   f $15:25 = 9:\square$

2 A hospital employs nurses and doctors in the ratio $7:2$. If there are 84 nurses, how many doctors are there?

3 A farmer has pigs and chickens in the ratio $3:8$. If she has 360 pigs, how many chickens does she have?

4 The price of a TV is reduced from $500 to $400. A DVD player costing $1250 is reduced in the same ratio as the TV. What does the DVD player sell for?

USING RATIOS TO DIVIDE QUANTITIES

Quantities can be divided in a particular ratio by considering the total **number of parts** the whole quantity is to be divided into.

NUMBER (Chapter 1)   49

Example 33   ◀)) Self Tutor

An inheritance of $60\,000$ is to be divided between Donny and Marie in the ratio $2:3$. How much does each receive?

There are $2 + 3 = 5$ parts in total.

$\therefore$ Donny gets $\frac{2}{5}$ of $\$60\,000$ and Marie gets $\frac{3}{5}$ of $\$60\,000$

$\quad = \frac{2}{5} \times 60\,000 \qquad\qquad\qquad = \frac{3}{5} \times 60\,000$

$\quad = \$24\,000 \qquad\qquad\qquad\quad\; = \$36\,000$

EXERCISE 1G.4

1 Divide: **a** $50 in the ratio $1:4$ **b** $35 in the ratio $3:4$

2 A fortune of £$800\,000$ is to be divided in the ratio $3:7$. What is the larger share?

3 The ratio of girls to boys in a tennis club is $4:5$. If there are 144 children in the club, how many are girls?

4 A glass contains alcohol and water in the ratio $1:4$. A second glass contains the same quantity of liquid, but this time the ratio of alcohol to water is $2:3$. Each glass is emptied into a third glass. What is the ratio of alcohol to water in the final mixture?

5 One full glass contains vinegar and water in the ratio $1:3$. Another glass with twice the capacity of the first has vinegar and water in the ratio $1:4$. If the contents of both glasses are mixed together, what is the ratio of vinegar to water?

INVESTIGATION 1   "POCKET-MONEY" SPREADSHEET

Consider again the **Opening Problem** on page 28. A spreadsheet can be used to analyse the problem and help calculate the answers.

What to do:

1 Open a new spreadsheet and enter the following headings and data:

	A	B	C	D	E
1		Days	Fraction of work	% of pay	1
2	Tim	3			
3	Becky	2			
4	Total				
5					

(week 1)

(2 cents for week 1) → $0.02

2 Complete your spreadsheet by entering the following formulae:

	A	B	C	D	E	F
1		Days	Fraction of work	% of pay	1	=E1+1
2	Tim	3	=B2/B4	=C2*100	=C2*E4	
3	Becky	2	=B3/B4	=C3*100	=C3*E4	
4	Total	=B2+B3			$0.02	=E4*2
5						

3 Fill the formulae in:

    a B4 **across** to column D   **b** E2 and E3 across to column F

    c F1, F2, F3 and F4 across to column P.

4 Use your spreadsheet to answer the questions posed on page **28**.

5 Investigate the split of the payments if:

    a the process continued for a further five weeks   **Hint:**   Fill across to column U.

    b Tim works 4 days to Becky's 1 day   **Hint:**   Enter 4 in B2 and 1 in B3.

    c the week 1 payment was 5 cents.   **Hint:**   Enter 0.05 in E4.

H   PRIME NUMBERS AND INDEX NOTATION

Rather than writing $2 \times 2 \times 2$, we can write such a product as 2^3. We call this **index notation**. We say that 2 is the **base** and that 3 is the **index** or **power**.

2^3 reads   "*two cubed*" or

           "*the third power of two*" or

           "*two to the power of three*".

2^3 index or power   base

If n is a positive integer, then a^n is the product of n factors of a.

$$a^n = \underbrace{a \times a \times a \times a \times a \times a \times \ldots \times a}_{n \text{ factors}}$$

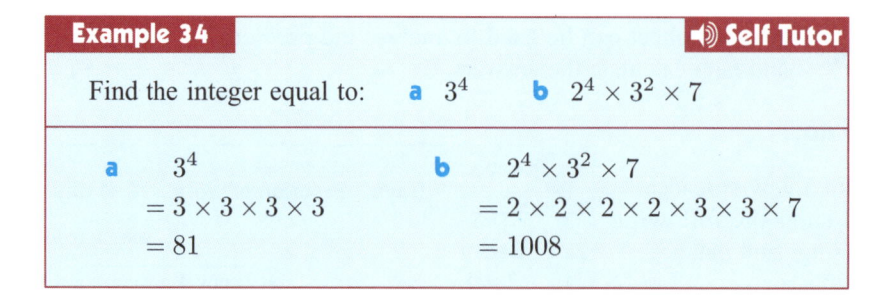

Example 34   🔊 Self Tutor

Find the integer equal to: **a** 3^4 **b** $2^4 \times 3^2 \times 7$

a 3^4
    $= 3 \times 3 \times 3 \times 3$
    $= 81$

b $2^4 \times 3^2 \times 7$
    $= 2 \times 2 \times 2 \times 2 \times 3 \times 3 \times 7$
    $= 1008$

You can evaluate powers on your calculator using a special key. Instructions for graphics calculators can be found on page **12**.

PRIMES AND COMPOSITES

A **prime number** is a natural number which has **exactly** two distinct factors, 1 and itself.

A **composite number** is a natural number which has more than two factors.

NUMBER (Chapter 1) 51

Notice that **one** (1) is neither prime nor composite.

17 is a **prime number** since it has only 2 factors, 1 and 17.

26 is a **composite number** since it has more than two factors. These are 1, 2, 13 and 26.

> Apart from order, every composite number can be written as a **product of prime factors** in **one and only one way**.

For example, $72 = 2 \times 2 \times 2 \times 3 \times 3$ or $72 = 2^3 \times 3^2$. We call this a **prime factorisation** and say the number is written in **prime factored form**.

One method for factorising a composite number in this way is to continue to divide the number by primes. Divide firstly by 2, and when 2 is exhausted divide by 3, and when 3 is exhausted divide by 5, and so on.

Example 35 ◀)) Self Tutor

a Write 32 as a power of a prime number.
b Write 264 as a product of prime factors in index form.

a $32 = 2 \times 2 \times 2 \times 2 \times 2$
   $= 2^5$

b
2	264
2	132
2	66
3	33
11	11
	1

$264 = 2 \times 2 \times 2 \times 3 \times 11$

∴ in index form,
$264 = 2^3 \times 3^1 \times 11^1$

EXERCISE 1H

1 Find the integer equal to:
  a 2^3
  b 2^4
  c 3^3
  d 3×5^2
  e $2^2 \times 3^2$
  f $2 \times 3^3 \times 5^2$
  g $2^2 \times 3 \times 7^2$
  h $2^4 \times 5^3 \times 11$

2 Find, using your calculator:
  a 5^4
  b 8^3
  c 12^5
  d $(-4)^9$
  e $(-7)^4$
  f $(-3)^3$
  g 2.8^6
  h 19^2

3 List the set of all primes less than 30.

4 Write the following as powers of a prime:
  a 8
  b 27
  c 64
  d 625
  e 343
  f 243
  g 1331
  h 529

5 Express the following as the product of prime factors in index form:
  a 56
  b 240
  c 504
  d 735
  e 297
  f 221
  g 360
  h 952

6 The **most abundant** number in a set of numbers is the number which has the highest power of 2 as a factor.

For example:
- the most abundant number of $\{1, 2, 3, 4, 5, 6, 7, 8, 9, 10\}$ is 8 as $8 = 2^3$.
- the most abundant number of $\{41, 42, 43, 44, 45, 46, 47, 48, 49, 50\}$ is 48 as $48 = 2^4 \times 3$.

Find the most abundant number of the set
$\{151, 152, 153, 154, 155, 156, 157, 158, 159, 160\}$.

7 Find, correct to 3 decimal places:

  a $(2.6 + 3.7)^4$ **b** $(8.6)^3 - (4.2)^3$ **c** $12.4 \times (10.7)^4$

  d $\left(\dfrac{3.2 + 1.92}{1.47}\right)^3$ **e** $\left(\dfrac{0.52}{0.09 \times 6.14}\right)^4$ **f** $\dfrac{648}{(3.62)^4}$

8 Find the last digit of 3^{100}.
Hint: Consider $3^1, 3^2, 3^3, 3^4, 3^5, 3^6, \ldots$ and look for a pattern.

9 Find the last digit of the number 7^{200}. **Hint:** Consider $7^1, 7^2, 7^3, 7^4, 7^5, \ldots$

10 The sum of two different odd numbers is 36. When their difference is factorised into primes, the sum of the primes is 10. Find the numbers.

11 $3^a \times a^3 = 518a$ or five thousand one hundred and eighty ...... Find a.

DISCUSSION

3^{3^3}

Which is correct?

3^{3^3}
$= (3^3)^3$
$= 27^3$
$= 19\,683$

or

3^{3^3}
$= 3^{(3)^3}$
$= 3^{27}$
$= 7\,625\,597\,484\,987$

INVESTIGATION 2   THE 3-DIGIT PROBLEM

What to do:

1 Choose any three different digits from 1 to 9. Write down the six possible two digit numbers that can be formed using these digits. For example, if we choose the digits 2, 7 and 8, we would write down: 27, 28, 72, 78, 82, 87 which add to 374. Find the **sum** of the six numbers and write their sum in prime factored form. Record your results in a table:

Digits chosen	Numbers	Sum of 6 numbers	Sum in prime factored form
2, 7, 8	27, 28, 72, 78, 82, 87	374	$2 \times 11 \times 17$
⋮	⋮	⋮	⋮

2 Choose another three digits and repeat the process outlined above.

3 Choose a further three digits and repeat.

4 Find the HCF of all the sums.

5 Prove that you will always obtain this HCF for all possible choices of 3 different digits.

   Hint: Any two digit number with digits a and b has the form $10a + b$.
   For example, $37 = 10 \times 3 + 7$.

INVESTIGATION 3   PRIME OR COMPOSITE?

Is 251 prime or composite?

A systematic approach to answering this question is to divide 251 by all the primes up to the square root of 251. We start with the smallest prime first.

For example, $\sqrt{251} \approx 15.84$. We divide 251 by the primes 2, 3, 5, 7, 11, 13 which are all less than 15.84. We discover that none of these primes divide exactly into 251, so 251 is a prime number.

What to do:

1 Use this method to determine which of the following numbers are prime:

   a 129   **b** 371   **c** 787   **d** 4321

2 Explain why we only need to check primes up to the square root of the number.

REVIEW SET 1A

1 **a** Evaluate $(-5) \times (-3)$.

   b Evaluate $18 \div (6 - 9)$.

   c Find □ if 69□ is divisible by 2.

   d Evaluate $\frac{3}{5} \times 1\frac{1}{3}$.

   e Write 400 mL is to 2 L as a ratio in simplest form.

   f Write 132 as a product of primes in index form.

   g Write $\frac{3}{8}$ as a decimal.

   h What natural number has the prime factorisation $2^3 \times 3^2 \times 5$?

2 Find the:

   a HCF and LCM of 24 and 36

   b largest multiple of 17 which is less than 1000.

3 Find $\frac{5}{12}$ of $48.60.

4 Use your calculator to find, correct to 2 decimal places:

    a $2.76 \times 5.7 - 2.9 \div 4$ **b** $2.3 \div 9.2$ **c** $\frac{1}{4} \div \frac{2}{3}$

5 **a** A butcher sells $\frac{2}{3}$ of his hamburger patties on Monday and $\frac{1}{2}$ of the remainder on Tuesday. What fraction of the patties remains unsold?

    b A lemon drink is mixed using one part lemon juice to seven parts water. If 250 mL of lemon juice is used, how much water should be added?

    c At a Falcons vs Crocs basketball match, the ratio of supporters is 5 : 3. If there are 4000 in the crowd, how many are Falcons supporters?

REVIEW SET 1B

1 **a** Evaluate 1.2×0.4.   **b** Evaluate $2\frac{3}{4} \times 1\frac{1}{3}$.

    c Find the value of $\dfrac{-8 \times -5}{-2}$.   **d** Evaluate $\frac{1}{2} + \frac{1}{3}$.

    e Write $\frac{7}{25}$ in decimal form.   **f** Evaluate $5 \times 3 - 4 \times 5$.

    g Write 2 m is to 40 cm as a ratio in simplest form.

    h Write 1188 as a product of primes in index form.

    i Find $\square$ if 27$\square$2 is divisible by 3.   **j** Evaluate $2^2 \times 3^3 \times 5^2$.

2 Find:

    a the HCF and LCM of 15 and 27

    b the smallest multiple of 13 which is greater than 2000.

3 Find, in minutes, $\frac{3}{8}$ of 2 hours and 16 minutes.

4 Use your calculator to find:

    a $3\frac{4}{5} - 1\frac{1}{9}$ **b** $4.65 - 7.87 \div 3.25$ correct to 3 decimal places.

5 **a** How many 2.4 m lengths of wire can be cut from a roll 156.4 m long? How much wire is wasted?

    b A profit of $85 000 is to be split amongst two business owners in the ratio 3 : 2. What is the smaller share?

    c A painter paints $\frac{1}{3}$ of a house on one day and $\frac{1}{4}$ of the house on the next day. What fraction of the house is yet to be painted?

Chapter 2

Algebraic operations

Contents:
- **A** Algebraic notation
- **B** The language of mathematics
- **C** Changing words to symbols
- **D** Generalising arithmetic
- **E** Algebraic substitution
- **F** Collecting like terms
- **G** Product and quotient simplification

Algebra is a powerful tool used in mathematics. It involves the use of letters or **pronumerals** to represent unknown values or **variables**.

We use algebra to construct mathematical **expressions** and **formulae** that describe problem solving situations.

For example, the area of any rectangle is found by multiplying its length by its width.

For a general rectangle, the length and width are unknown or variable. We let A represent the area of the rectangle, l represent its length, and w represent its width.

Using algebra, the area of the rectangle can be written as the formula

$$A = l \times w \quad \text{or} \quad A = lw.$$

Likewise, instead of writing "the perimeter of a rectangle is found by adding twice its length to twice its width", we write the formula $P = 2l + 2w$.

OPENING PROBLEM

A picture frame has height and width in the ratio $3:2$. It forms a border 5 cm wide around the painting.

Things to think about:

1 How can we use algebra to represent:
- **a** the height of the picture frame
- **b** the height of the painting
- **c** the width of the picture frame
- **d** the width of the painting
- **e** the area of the painting?

2 Find the area of the painting on display if the picture frame is 60 cm wide.

A ALGEBRAIC NOTATION

In algebra we use letters or pronumerals to represent variables.

We include the variables in expressions as though they were numbers.

However, we obey some rules which help make algebra easier.

In algebra we agree:

- to **leave out** the "$\times$" **signs** between any multiplied quantities provided that at least one of them is an unknown (letter)
- to write **numerals (numbers) first** in any product
- where products contain two or more letters, we write them in **alphabetical order**.

For example:
- $3b$ is used rather than $3 \times b$ or $b3$
- $3bc$ is used rather than $3cb$.

ALGEBRAIC OPERATIONS (Chapter 2)

Example 1

Write in product notation:

a $t \times 6s$ **b** $4 \times k + m \times 3$ **c** $3 \times (r + s)$

a $t \times 6s$
$= 6st$

b $4 \times k + m \times 3$
$= 4k + 3m$

c $3 \times (r + s)$
$= 3(r + s)$

WRITING SUMS AS PRODUCTS

Sums of identical terms can be easily written using **product notation**.

For example, $3 + 3 + 3 + 3 = 4 \times 3$ {4 lots of 3}
$\therefore \quad b + b + b + b = 4 \times b = 4b$ {4 lots of b}

and likewise $a + a + a = 3a$ and $y + y + y + y + y = 5y$.

Example 2

Simplify: **a** $r + r + r + s + s$ **b** $d + d - (a + a + a + a)$

a $r + r + r + s + s$
$= 3r + 2s$

b $d + d - (a + a + a + a)$
$= 2d - 4a$

INDEX NOTATION

When the same number is multiplied by itself two or more times we use **index notation** as a quick way of writing the product.

For example, $3 \times 3 \times 3 \times 3 = 3^4$, and $b \times b \times b \times b = b^4$.

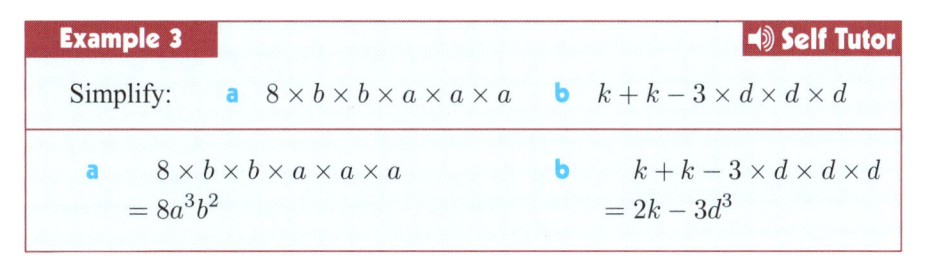

Example 3

Simplify: **a** $8 \times b \times b \times a \times a \times a$ **b** $k + k - 3 \times d \times d \times d$

a $8 \times b \times b \times a \times a \times a$
$= 8a^3b^2$

b $k + k - 3 \times d \times d \times d$
$= 2k - 3d^3$

SIMPLIFYING ALGEBRAIC PRODUCTS

$3 \times 2x$ and $a^2 \times 2ab$ are **algebraic products**.

Algebraic products can often be simplified using these steps:

- **Expand** out any brackets.
- Calculate the **coefficient** of the final product by multiplying all the numbers.
- **Simplify** the unknowns using index notation where appropriate. The unknowns should be written in alphabetical order.

EXERCISE 2A

1 Simplify using product notation:
   - **a** $3 \times m$
   - **b** $k \times 4$
   - **c** $n \times 7$
   - **d** $6 \times 2b$
   - **e** $7 \times 3a$
   - **f** $m \times 5d$
   - **g** $8m \times 3$
   - **h** $8m \times p$
   - **i** $p \times 7 \times q$
   - **j** $p \times q \times 2$
   - **k** $a \times b \times c$
   - **l** $p \times h \times d$

2 Simplify:
   - **a** $a \times b + n$
   - **b** $3 \times a + 2 \times b$
   - **c** $b \times a + m$
   - **d** $b \times a - c$
   - **e** $d - a \times c$
   - **f** $k - d \times 4$
   - **g** $c \times a + d \times b$
   - **h** $10 - a \times b \times 2$
   - **i** $8 \times (m + n)$
   - **j** $4 \times (d - 2)$
   - **k** $(b - d) \times 3$
   - **l** $a \times b \times (c + 1)$

3 Simplify using product notation:
   - **a** $t + t$
   - **b** $n + n + n$
   - **c** $p + p + q + q + q + 3$
   - **d** $d + d + d + e$
   - **e** $5 + y + y + x$
   - **f** $a + a + a + a + b + b$
   - **g** $a + a + 5 + a$
   - **h** $b - (a + a)$
   - **i** $b - a + a$
   - **j** $t + t + t + s + s$
   - **k** $5 + d + d + d$
   - **l** $2 + a + b + b + a$

4 Explain why:
   - **a** $3 - (a + a)$ is not the same as $3 - a + a$
   - **b** $m - (n + n + n)$ is not the same as $m - n + n + n$.

5 Write in expanded form:
   - **a** a^3
   - **b** b^4
   - **c** $3d^2$
   - **d** $4n^3$
   - **e** $10a^2b$
   - **f** $4ab^3$
   - **g** $(2a)^2$
   - **h** $2a^2$
   - **i** $a^2 + 2b^2$
   - **j** $a^3 - 3b^2$

6 Write in simplest form:
   - **a** $3 \times a \times a$
   - **b** $5 \times b \times b \times b$
   - **c** $2 \times a \times a \times 5$
   - **d** $8 \times a \times a \times b$
   - **e** $5 \times m \times n \times n \times n$
   - **f** $3 \times p \times 4 \times q \times q$
   - **g** $p \times p \times p \times q \times r \times r$
   - **h** $4 \times a \times 5 \times a$
   - **i** $3 \times d \times d \times 2 \times c$
   - **j** $a + a \times a$
   - **k** $a \times a \times a + a$
   - **l** $b \times b \times b - a \times a$
   - **m** $b \times b + 3 \times b$
   - **n** $c \times c \times c - 5 \times c$
   - **o** $3 \times a \times b \times b - 5 \times b \times c$
   - **p** $3 \times a \times a + a \times m$
   - **q** $4 \times x + 2 \times x \times x \times x$
   - **r** $4 \times (x + 2 + x) \times x$

In algebra we use shorthand notation to simplify the look of an expression.

B THE LANGUAGE OF MATHEMATICS

Some **key words** used in algebra are:

Word	Meaning	Example(s)
variable	an unknown value that is represented by a letter or symbol	$C = 2\pi r$ has variables C and r.
expression	an algebraic form consisting of numbers, variables and operation signs	$2x + y - 7$, $\dfrac{2a + b}{c}$
equation	an algebraic form which contains an $=$ sign	$3x + 8 = -1$, $\dfrac{x - 1}{2} = -4$
terms	algebraic forms which are separated by $+$ or $-$ signs, the signs being included	$3x - 2y + xy - 7$ has four terms. These are $3x$, $-2y$, xy and -7.
like terms	terms with exactly the same variable form	In $4x + 3y + xy - 3x$: • $4x$ and $-3x$ are like terms • $4x$ and $3y$ are unlike terms • xy and $3y$ are unlike terms.
constant term	a term which does not contain a variable	In $3x - y^2 + 7 + x^3$, 7 is a constant term.
coefficient	the number factor of an algebraic term	In $4x + 2xy - y^3$: • 4 is the coefficient of x • 2 is the coefficient of xy • -1 is the coefficient of y^3.

Example 4 ◆) Self Tutor

Consider $4y^2 - 6x + 2xy - 5 + x^2$.

a Is this an equation or an expression?
b How many terms does it contain?
c State the coefficient of: **i** x **ii** x^2.
d State the constant term.

a We have an expression, as there is no $=$ sign present.
b The expression contains five terms: $4y^2$, $-6x$, $2xy$, -5 and x^2.
c **i** The coefficient of x is -6.   **ii** The coefficient of x^2 is 1.
d The constant term is -5.

EXERCISE 2B

1 State the coefficient of x in the following:
- **a** $4x$
- **b** $-7x$
- **c** x
- **d** $-x$
- **e** $5 + 6x$
- **f** $xy - 3x$
- **g** $x^2 - 2x$
- **h** $2x^3 - \dfrac{1}{x} + x$

2 State the coefficient of y in the following:
- **a** $2y$
- **b** $-2y$
- **c** $11y$
- **d** $-3y$
- **e** $4x - y$
- **f** $3x - 7y + 1$
- **g** $y^3 + 3y$
- **h** $6y^2 - 13y + 8$

3 Consider $5x^2 + 6xy - y^2 + 3x - 4y + 6$:
- **a** Is this an equation or an expression?
- **b** How many terms does it contain?
- **c** State the coefficient of   **i** x^2 **ii** y^2 **iii** xy **iv** y.
- **d** What is the constant term?

4 How many terms are there in:
- **a** $3x + y - 7$
- **b** $x^2 - ab + c - 11$
- **c** $x^4 + x^2 + x - 6 + \dfrac{4}{x}$?

5 Which of the following are equations and which are expressions?
- **a** $a + b - 2c$
- **b** $3x^2 - 6x + 8$
- **c** $3x - y = 7$
- **d** $\dfrac{x}{2} = \dfrac{6}{x}$
- **e** $\dfrac{x}{2} - \dfrac{x-1}{3}$
- **f** $\dfrac{x}{2} - \dfrac{x-1}{3} = 8$

C   CHANGING WORDS TO SYMBOLS

In algebra we can convert sentences into **algebraic expressions** or **equations**.
For example,

<u>Twice a number</u>   <u>increased by 7</u>   is   <u>5 less than the number</u>

becomes $2x$ $+\ 7$ $=$ $x - 5$.

Many algebraic statements contain words such as sum, difference, product, and quotient.

© Jim Russell, General Features Pty Ltd.

Word	Meaning	Example
sum	The sum of two or more numbers is obtained by **adding** them.	$3+7$, $a+4$, $b+c+d$ are sums.
difference	The difference between two numbers is the larger one **minus** the smaller one.	$9-5$, $d-6$ (if $d > 6$) are differences.
product	The product of two or more numbers is obtained by **multiplying** them.	3×6, $3a$, xyz are products.
quotient	The quotient of two numbers is the first one mentioned **divided** by the second.	The quotient of x and y is $\dfrac{x}{y}$.
average	The **average** of a set of numbers is their sum divided by the number of numbers.	The average of a, b and c is $\dfrac{a+b+c}{3}$.

Example 5 ◀) Self Tutor

a State the sum of 4 and z.
b State the difference between x and y (if $y > x$).
c State the average of r, s and t.

a The sum of 4 and z is $4 + z$.
b The difference is $y - x$. {as y is larger than x}
c The average is $\dfrac{r+s+t}{3}$.

When writing products we leave out the multiplication signs between unknowns and write them in alphabetical order.

EXERCISE 2C

1 Write expressions for the sum of:
   a 7 and 3 **b** 4 and y **c** t and $2p$ **d** a, b and c

2 Write expressions for the product of:
   a 7 and 3 **b** 4 and y **c** t and $2p$ **d** a, b and c

3 Write expressions for the quotient of:
   a 7 and 3 **b** 4 and y **c** t and $2p$ **d** $a+b$ and c

4 Write expressions for the average of:
   a 7 and 3 **b** 4 and y **c** t and $2p$ **d** a, b and c

5 Write expressions for the difference between:
   a 7 and 3
   c 4 and y if $4 > y$
   b 4 and y if $4 < y$
   d $(a+b)$ and c if $(a+b) < c$

Example 6

Write down algebraic expressions for the sum of:

a a and b divided by 2 **b** a and b, all divided by 2

a $a + \dfrac{b}{2}$ **b** $\dfrac{a+b}{2}$

Example 7

Write down algebraic expressions for:

a the sum of b and a squared **b** the sum of b and a, all squared
c the sum of the squares of b and a

a $b + a^2$ **b** $(b+a)^2$ **c** $b^2 + a^2$

6 Write down algebraic expressions for the sum of:
  a b and c divided by 3
  b b and c, all divided by 3
  c 2 and x squared
  d 2 and x, all squared.

7 Write down algebraic expressions for:
  a one third of the sum of r and s
  b triple the sum of b and c
  c the sum of m and n cubed
  d the sum of m and n, all cubed.

8 Write down algebraic expressions for:
  a three times x, subtracted from b
  b the product of a and the square of b
  c the sum of a and five times b
  d 3 less than t
  e 4 more than a
  f the product of the square of x and 9
  g the square of the product of c and d
  h the sum of the squares of x and y
  i the sum of the squares of p, q and r
  j half the sum of c and d squared.

Example 8

Write, in sentence form, the meaning of:

a $b + 7$ **b** $2a + b$ **c** $2(a + b)$

a $b + 7$ is "the sum of b and 7" or "7 more than b".
b $2a + b$ is "the sum of twice a and b".
c $2(a + b)$ is "double the sum of a and b".

9 Write, in sentence form, the meaning of:
  a $a + 6$ **b** $7 + b$ **c** $c + d$ **d** $c + 3d$
  e $3(c + d)$ **f** bc **g** $(p + q)^2$ **h** $p^2 + q^2$

i $3x^2$ **j** $(3x)^2$ **k** $a + \dfrac{b}{5}$ **l** $\dfrac{a+b}{5}$

m $\dfrac{x}{y}$ **n** $\left(\dfrac{a}{b}\right)^2$ **o** $\dfrac{a^2}{b^2}$ **p** $\dfrac{a+b}{c}$

D   GENERALISING ARITHMETIC

To find algebraic expressions for many real world situations, we first think in terms of numbers or numerical cases. We then proceed to more general cases.

For example, suppose we are asked to find the total cost of x books which each cost €y. We could start by finding the total cost of 5 books which each cost €10.

In this case the total cost is $5 \times$ €$10 =$ €50.

We *multiplied* the two quantities, and so the total cost of x books at €y each is $x \times$ €$y =$ €xy.

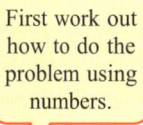

> First work out how to do the problem using numbers.

Example 9

Find:
  a the cost of m mandarins at 45 cents each
  b the change from £20 when buying n pens at £1.20 each.

a The cost of 3 mandarins at 45 cents each is 3×45 cents.
∴ the cost of m mandarins at 45 cents each is $m \times 45 = 45m$ cents.

b The change when buying 4 pens costing £1.20 each is $20 - (4 \times 1.20)$ pounds.
∴ the change when buying n pens costing £1.20 each is
$20 - (n \times 1.20)$ pounds $= 20 - 1.2n$ pounds.

EXERCISE 2D

1 Find the total cost (in yen) of buying:
  a 5 toys at ¥300 each   **b** a toys at ¥300 each   **c** a toys at ¥c each.

2 Find the total cost (in euros) of buying:
  a 8 pears at 50 cents each   **b** p pears at 50 cents each
  c p pears at y cents each.

3 Find the change from $100 when buying:
  a 3 boxes of chocolates at $11 each   **b** x boxes of chocolates at $11 each
  c x boxes of chocolates at $$y$ each.

64 ALGEBRAIC OPERATIONS (Chapter 2)

4 Zane is now 14 years old. How old was he x years ago?

5 Anne can paddle her canoe at 3 km per hour. How far can she paddle in t hours?

6 Katia is climbing the stairs to the top of a 35 m tower. Each step is 21 cm high. If Katia has climbed x steps:

  a how high has she climbed

  b how much further must she climb to the top?

7 Graham buys c chairs and t tables. Find the total cost if each chair costs £45 and each table costs £85.

8 Su Lin travelled a km in 3 hours and then b km in 2 hours. Find:

  a the total distance Su Lin travelled

  b the average speed for the whole trip.

> average speed = $\dfrac{\text{distance travelled}}{\text{time taken}}$

9 **a** A lorry driver travels at an average speed of 80 km per hour for 5 hours. How far has the driver travelled?

  b How far would the driver travel at an average speed of s km per hour for t hours?

E   ALGEBRAIC SUBSTITUTION

In **Exercise 2D** we found algebraic expressions for many real world situations. These expressions involve the variables present in the situation.

For example, suppose a triangle has base b units and height h units. Its area is given by the expression $\frac{1}{2}bh$.

If we are given the base and height of a triangle, we can evaluate the expression to find the area. We do this by substituting the given values of the variables into the equation.

For example, if the base of a triangle $b = 5$ cm and the height of the triangle $h = 2$ cm, then the area of the triangle is $\frac{1}{2} \times 5 \times 2 = 5$ cm^2.

> To **evaluate** a mathematical expression we find its value for particular numerical substitutions of the variables or unknowns.

If we substitute a negative value, we place it in brackets. This helps us to evaluate the signs in the expression correctly.

For example, consider the expression $5a + 3b$

If $a = -2$ and $b = 4$ then $5a + 3b = 5 \times (-2) + 3 \times 4$
$= -10 + 12$
$= 2$

> Notice how we place negative substitutions inside brackets.

Example 10

For $a = 2$, $b = -1$ and $c = 3$, evaluate:

a $3a - 2b$ **b** $c^2 + b$

a $\quad 3a - 2b$
$= 3 \times 2 - 2 \times (-1)$
$= 6 + 2$
$= 8$

b $\quad c^2 + b$
$= 3^2 + (-1)$
$= 9 - 1$
$= 8$

EXERCISE 2E

1 If $a = 1$, $b = 2$ and $c = 3$, find the value of:

- **a** $a + b$
- **b** $2a$
- **c** $a - c$
- **d** $b + 2c$
- **e** $5 - 2c$
- **f** bc
- **g** $ab - a$
- **h** $2b^2$
- **i** $2(a + b)$
- **j** $3(c - a)$
- **k** $(2a)^2$
- **l** $3c^2$

2 If $k = 4$, $l = -2$, $m = 3$, and $n = -1$, evaluate:

- **a** $2k + l$
- **b** $2m - 5$
- **c** $kl + n$
- **d** $2n^2$
- **e** $(2n)^2$
- **f** $l^2 - m$
- **g** k^3
- **h** $3l - 4n$
- **i** $k^2 - 2l$
- **j** $l(n + 2)$
- **k** $2(k + l)$
- **l** $2k + 3m$

3 If $p = 3$, $q = -2$, $r = -3$ and $s = 4$, evaluate:

- **a** p^2
- **b** $-p^2$
- **c** $r^2 s$
- **d** pqr
- **e** pq^2
- **f** $p^2 + q - 3$
- **g** $pr + 2s$
- **h** $p - q^2 + 2$
- **i** $q^2 + r$
- **j** $2(q + s)$
- **k** $p(r + s)$
- **l** $(p + q)(p - q)$

Example 11

If $p = 3$, $q = -2$ and $r = -4$, evaluate:

a $\dfrac{p - q}{r}$ **b** $\dfrac{q^2 + pr}{p + r}$

a $\quad \dfrac{p - q}{r}$
$= \dfrac{3 - (-2)}{(-4)}$
$= \dfrac{3 + 2}{-4}$
$= \dfrac{5}{-4}$
$= -\dfrac{5}{4}$

b $\quad \dfrac{q^2 + pr}{p + r}$
$= \dfrac{(-2)^2 + 3 \times (-4)}{3 + (-4)}$
$= \dfrac{4 - 12}{-1}$
$= \dfrac{-8}{-1}$
$= 8$

4 If $a = 2$, $b = -3$, $c = 4$, and $d = -1$, find the value of:

a $\dfrac{c}{a}$ **b** $\dfrac{b}{d}$ **c** $\dfrac{b+d}{c}$ **d** $\dfrac{a-d}{b}$

e $\dfrac{b+d}{b-d}$ **f** $\dfrac{b+2}{1-a}$ **g** $\dfrac{c}{2d}$ **h** $\dfrac{3a}{2b}$

i $\dfrac{a+c}{2b}$ **j** $\dfrac{-a}{b+d}$ **k** $\dfrac{a-b}{a-d}$ **l** $\dfrac{a+2c}{a-2c}$

5 For

p	q	r	s	t
-3	-2	2	4	-1

find the value of:

a $\dfrac{q}{r}$ **b** $\dfrac{q-r}{s}$ **c** $\dfrac{q+t}{2p}$ **d** $\dfrac{q+s}{r-t}$

e $\dfrac{2q}{-t}$ **f** $\dfrac{s-q}{q^2}$ **g** $\dfrac{2q}{q-s}$ **h** $\dfrac{r-t}{r-q}$

i $\dfrac{rs}{qt}$ **j** $\dfrac{q^2+t}{p^2}$ **k** $\dfrac{s+rt}{p}$ **l** $\dfrac{qst}{-pr}$

INVESTIGATION   "TO BE OR NOT TO BE" EQUAL

We can use substitution to give us a better understanding of whether two different looking algebraic expressions are equal or not.

We choose some values for the variables and substitute these values into both expressions. If the results are always equal no matter what values we choose for the variables, then the expressions are equal.

For example:

- $2(x+3)$ and $2x+6$ are **equal expressions** because no matter what value of x is substituted, the expressions are equal for this value of x.
- $2(x+3)$ and $2x+3$ cannot be equal, because when $x = 1$,

$$2(x+3) \quad\quad\quad \text{whereas} \quad\quad\quad 2x+3$$
$$= 2(1+3) \quad\quad\quad\quad\quad\quad\quad\quad = 2 \times 1 + 3$$
$$= 2 \times 4 \quad\quad\quad\quad\quad\quad\quad\quad\quad = 2 + 3$$
$$= 8 \quad\quad\quad\quad\quad\quad\quad\quad\quad\quad = 5$$

- One **counter example** is sufficient to show that two expressions are not equal.

What to do:

1 Copy and complete the following table of values:

a	b	$a + \dfrac{b}{4}$	$\dfrac{a+b}{4}$	$\dfrac{a}{4} + b$	$\dfrac{a}{4} + \dfrac{b}{4}$
8	4				
3	5				
6	-2				

ALGEBRAIC OPERATIONS (Chapter 2) 67

From the table, which of the four expressions are likely to be equal and which are definitely not equal?

2 Use a table like that in **1** or use a spreadsheet to test the following for equality:

  a $\frac{1}{2}x$ and $\frac{x}{2}$ using $x = 4, 6, -8$

  b $180 - (a + b)$ and $180 - a - b$ using $a = 20, b = 30$; and $a = 40, b = 75$

  c $(2x)^2$ and $2x^2$ using $x = 0, 1, 2, 3$

  d $(x + y)^2$ and $x^2 + y^2$ using $x = 1, y = 2$; and $x = 3, y = 5$

  e $(x - y)^2$ and $x^2 - 2xy + y^2$ using $x = 3, y = 1$; and $x = 4, y = -1$.

F COLLECTING LIKE TERMS

Like terms are algebraic terms which contain the same variables to the same indices.

For example:

- $2xy$ and $-2xy$ are **like terms**
- a^2 and $-3a$ are **unlike terms** because the indices of a are not the same.

Algebraic expressions can often be simplified by adding or subtracting like terms. This is sometimes called **collecting like terms**.

Consider $2a + 4a$ = $\underbrace{a + a}_{\text{"2 lots of }a\text{"}}$ + $\underbrace{a + a + a + a}_{\text{"4 lots of }a\text{"}}$.

In total we have 6 lots of a, and so $2a + 4a = 6a$.

Example 12

Simplify, where possible, by collecting like terms:

  a $3x + 2x$ **b** $7a - 3a$ **c** $-2x + 3 - x$
  d $3bc + bc$ **e** $2x - x^2$

  a $3x + 2x$
  $= 5x$

  b $7a - 3a$
  $= 4a$

  c $-2x + 3 - x$
  $= -3x + 3$
  {since $-2x$ and $-x$ are like terms}

  d $3bc + bc$
  $= 4bc$

  e $2x - x^2$ is in simplest form
  {since $2x$ and $-x^2$ are unlike terms}

EXERCISE 2F

1 Simplify, where possible, by collecting like terms:

   a $3 + x + 5$ **b** $8 + 7 + x$ **c** $p + 3 + 7$ **d** $12 + a + a$

   e $b + 3 + b$ **f** $b + b$ **g** $2x + x$ **h** $a + 3 + a + 7$

   i $x + 3x$ **j** $3x - 2x$ **k** $3x - x$ **l** $a^2 + a^2$

   m $7x + 3$ **n** $2x^2 + x^2$ **o** $17x - 7$ **p** $17x - x$

   q $3b^2 - b^2$ **r** $2ab + 3ab$ **s** $g + g + g$ **t** $9b - 7b - 2$

2 Simplify, where possible:

   a $11n - 11n$ **b** $11n - n$ **c** $11n - 11$

   d $3ab + ba$ **e** $xy + 2xy$ **f** $2p^2 - p^2$

   g $3a + 2 + a + 4$ **h** $2a + 3a + 4a$ **i** $b + 3 + 2b + 4$

   j $3xy + 4yx$ **k** $2a + b + 3a + b$ **l** $3a^2 + a + a^2 + 2a$

   m $3x + 2x - x$ **n** $n + 2n - 3n$ **o** $ab + b^2 + 2ab + b^2$

   p $3x + 7x - 10$ **q** $3x + 7x - 10x$ **r** $3x + 7x - x$

   s $r + r + 2r^2$ **t** $x^2 + x + 2$ **u** $3 + 6y - 1 + 2y$

3 Simplify, by collecting like terms:

   a $3x + 8x$ **b** $3x - 8x$ **c** $-3x + 8x$

   d $-3x - 8x$ **e** $5a + a$ **f** $5a - a$

   g $-5a + a$ **h** $-5a - a$ **i** $m^2 + 2m$

   j $-3d - 5d$ **k** $-3d + 5d$ **l** $3d - 5d$

   m $b + 2b - 3$ **n** $t - 3t - 2t$ **o** $-6g - g$

   p $4m - 7m + 1$ **q** $a + 2 - 3a$ **r** $-2b - -3b$

   s $3b - b$ **t** $3b - -b$ **u** $x - -2x$

Example 13   ◆) **Self Tutor**

Simplify, by collecting like terms:

   a $2 + 3a - 3 - 2a$ **b** $x^2 - 2x + 3x - 2x^2$

a $2 + 3a - 3 - 2a$
    $= 3a - 2a + 2 - 3$
    $= a - 1$
    {$3a$ and $-2a$ are like terms,
    2 and -3 are like terms.}

b $x^2 - 2x + 3x - 2x^2$
    $= x^2 - 2x^2 - 2x + 3x$
    $= -x^2 + x$
    {x^2 and $-2x^2$ are like terms,
    $-2x$ and $3x$ are like terms.}

---

4 Simplify, where possible:

   a $a + 2 - 2a - 5$ **b** $a - 2b + 3a + b$

   c $ab + 2 - 3ab - 4$ **d** $ab + 3ab - 4ab$

   e $3x - 4 + 4 - 4x$ **f** $2x^2 - 7 + x^2 - 3$

   g $-3n + 2 + n - 7$ **h** $3a + b - 2a - 7b$

ALGEBRAIC OPERATIONS (Chapter 2)

i $5bc - 8bc + 3$
j $3x^2 + x - x^2 - 2x$
k $-x^3 - x^2 + x^3 - 3x^2$
l $2x - y - -x - y$
m $xy + y - 2xy - 3y$
n $-2x - 4 - 3x - 6$

G PRODUCT AND QUOTIENT SIMPLIFICATION

In this section we will simplify products like $2x \times 3x^2$ and quotients or divisions like $4x^3 \div 2x$ or $\dfrac{4x^3}{2x}$.

PRODUCTS

The **product** of two factors is found by multiplying them together.

Example 14 ◄) **Self Tutor**

Simplify:

a $2x \times 5$ **b** $4x \times 3x^2$ **c** $6x^2 \times 5x^2$

a $2x \times 5$
$= 2 \times x \times 5$
$= 10x$

b $4x \times 3x^2$
$= 4 \times x \times 3 \times x \times x$
$= 12x^3$

c $6x^2 \times 5x^2$
$= 6 \times x \times x \times 5 \times x \times x$
$= 30x^4$

With practice, you should be able to do these **mentally**. The following procedure may help you:

Consider the factors $-2x$ and $3x^2$. Their product $-2x \times 3x^2$ can be simplified by following the steps below:

Step 1: Find the product of the **signs**.
Step 2: Find the product of the **numerals** or numbers.
Step 3: Find the product of the **variables** or letters.

For $-2x$, the sign is $-$, the numeral is **2**, and the variable is x.

So, $-2x \times 3x^2 = -6x^3$

$- \times + = -$
$2 \times 3 = 6$
$x \times x^2 = x^3$

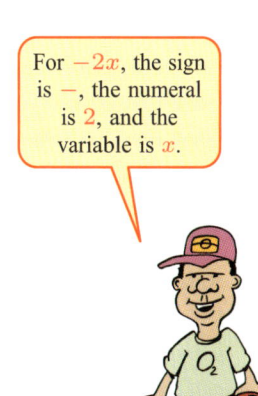

EXERCISE 2G.1

1 Write the following algebraic products in simplest form:

   a $x \times y$ **b** $x \times 3 \times y$ **c** $x \times y \times x$ **d** $a \times 2b$

   e $(-x)^2$ **f** $x^2 \times x$ **g** $(-x) \times 2x$ **h** $(-a) \times a^2$

2 Simplify the following:

   a $3a \times b$ **b** $3a \times b^2$ **c** $3ab \times 2b$ **d** $5ab \times 4ab$

   e $(4a)^2$ **f** $(3b)^2 \times b^2$ **g** $4y \times 2y^2$ **h** $5b^2 \times 2b$

   i $5b^2 \times b^2$ **j** $3b^2 \times 4b^3$ **k** $4x \times (-x)$ **l** $(-3x) \times x$

   m $2x \times (-3x)$ **n** $(-2x) \times (-4x)$ **o** $(-x^2) \times 2x$ **p** $3x^2 \times (-6x)$

   q $5 \times (-x^3)$ **r** $2x \times (-x)^3$ **s** $4d^2 \times (-d)$ **t** $(2x)^3$

3 **a** Find:

     i $x^2 \times x^2$ **ii** $x^3 \times x^2$ **iii** $x^4 \times x^3$ **iv** $x^3 \times x^6$

  b By considering your answers to **a**, simplify $x^m \times x^n$ where m and n are positive whole numbers.

QUOTIENTS

The **quotient** of two factors is found by dividing the first by the second. The result is an **algebraic fraction**.

When we divide algebraic expressions we can cancel common factors in exactly the same way as for numerical fractions.

Example 15   🔊 **Self Tutor**

Simplify: **a** $\dfrac{6x^3}{3x}$ **b** $\dfrac{4x^2}{12x^4}$

a $\dfrac{6x^3}{3x}$

$= \dfrac{\overset{2}{\cancel{6}} \times x \times x \times \cancel{x}^{\,1}}{{}_1\cancel{3} \times \cancel{x}_{\,1}}$

$= \dfrac{2x^2}{1}$

$= 2x^2$

b $\dfrac{4x^2}{12x^4}$

$= \dfrac{\overset{1}{\cancel{4}} \times \cancel{x} \times \cancel{x}^{\,1}}{{}_3\cancel{12} \times x \times x \times \cancel{x} \times \cancel{x}_{\,1}}$

$= \dfrac{1}{3x^2}$

EXERCISE 2G.2

1 Simplify the following:

   a $\dfrac{x^4}{x^2}$ **b** $\dfrac{x^4}{x}$ **c** $\dfrac{x^5}{x^2}$ **d** $\dfrac{x^5}{x^3}$

   e $\dfrac{3x^3}{x}$ **f** $\dfrac{5x^4}{x^2}$ **g** $\dfrac{10x^3}{2x}$ **h** $\dfrac{10x^4}{5x}$

i $\dfrac{4x^4}{2}$ **j** $\dfrac{4x^4}{2x}$ **k** $\dfrac{4x^4}{2x^2}$ **l** $\dfrac{2x^4}{4x^3}$

m $\dfrac{4x}{8x^2}$ **n** $\dfrac{4x}{8x^3}$ **o** $\dfrac{3x^2}{6x^3}$ **p** $\dfrac{3x^3}{9x^5}$

2 a Find:

  i $\dfrac{x^4}{x^2}$ **ii** $\dfrac{x^6}{x^3}$ **iii** $\dfrac{x^7}{x^2}$ **iv** $\dfrac{x^8}{x^5}$

b By considering your answers to **a**, find $\dfrac{x^m}{x^n}$ where m and n are positive whole numbers.

REVIEW SET 2A

1 Simplify:

  a $3 \times m \times n \times n$ **b** $(3x)^2 \times 2$ **c** $3 \times a \times b - 2 \times a \times a$

2 Consider the expression $7a + 12b - 4ab - 5a + 3ab - 4$.

  a How many terms are present? **b** State any like terms.
  c State the coefficient of b. **d** State the constant term.
  e If possible simplify the expression.

3 Find:

  a the number 6 more than y **b** the number p less than q
  c the change when p basketballs are bought for $\$q$ each from an amount of $\$r$.

4 If $x = 4$, $y = -3$, and $z = -2$, evaluate:

  a y^3 **b** $\dfrac{2xy}{z^2}$ **c** $(x - y)^2$

5 Simplify by collecting like terms:

  a $4p + 3p - 7$ **b** $3a + 7b - (-4b) - 2a$

6 Simplify:

  a $3m^2 \times 2m$ **b** $(3m^2)^2$ **c** $\dfrac{4a^3}{2a}$ **d** $\dfrac{6a^2}{9a^3}$

REVIEW SET 2B

1 Simplify:

  a $4 \times x \times 3 \times y \times y$ **b** $5x \times (2x)^2$ **c** $5 \times a \times a \times a - 5 \times a$

2 Consider the expression $5x + 7y - 8xy + 3 - 5y$.

  a How many terms are present? **b** State any like terms.
  c State the coefficient of xy. **d** State the constant term.
  e If possible, simplify the expression.

3 Find:

    a the number 4 less than x

    b the number q more than the square of p

    c the total cost in euros of buying p pens at q cents each, and r rulers at s cents each.

4 If $a = -3$, $b = 4$, and $c = -2$, find:

    a $-c^3$ **b** $\dfrac{3ab}{c^2}$ **c** $\dfrac{b-c}{2a}$

5 Simplify by collecting like terms:

    a $3q - 5q + 2$ **b** $3c + 5d - 8c - 2d$

6 Simplify:

    a $5x^2 \times 4x$ **b** $(-3x) \times (-2x^2)$ **c** $\dfrac{5x^4}{10x}$ **d** $\dfrac{12x^2}{18x^4}$

DAME KATHLEEN OLLERENSHAW
(1912 - ....)

Like many people **Kathleen Ollerenshaw** enjoyed attempting puzzles of various kinds. Her interest in mathematics was stimulated when she was ill as a child and started doing mathematical puzzles to fill in time. Kathleen was virtually deaf from the age of 8.

She was so fascinated by reading about some of the great mathematicians that she was determined to pursue mathematics as a career. Many people advised her against pursuing such a career because they saw no future in mathematics for a girl. Despite these opinions, Dame Ollerenshaw continued with her plan. She attended Somerville College at Oxford University and completed her degree.

After working as a statistician she returned to Oxford to teach during the war. Over a period of 10 years she produced a number of research papers and in fact was awarded her Doctor of Philosophy. Her main area of interest was in the study of the geometry of numbers. While continuing her interest in mathematics and education she became greatly involved in public duties and in 1971 became Dame Kathleen as a result of service to education. She served as a city councillor and was Lord Mayor of Manchester in 1975-76.

Chapter 3

Percentage

Contents:
- **A** Percentage
- **B** The unitary method in percentage
- **C** Finding a percentage of a quantity
- **D** Percentage increase and decrease
- **E** Percentage change using a multiplier
- **F** Finding the original amount
- **G** Simple interest
- **H** Compound interest

74   PERCENTAGE   (Chapter 3)

Percentages are commonly used every day around us. We may see headlines like:

- Imports now taxed at 10%.
- Earn 6.5% on your money.
- 65% of children are overweight.
- 40% off sale this week.
- Opera attendances down by 8%.

An understanding of percentages and how to operate with them is therefore vital.

OPENING PROBLEM

Roger's Racquets specialises in selling tennis racquets. The owner Roger purchases 120 racquets for $80 each. He applies a profit margin of 70% to the racquets, but finds he cannot sell any at that price. Consequently he has a 15% discount sale.

Consider the questions below:

a What was the price of each racquet before the sale?

b What was the price of each racquet after discounting?

c What was the percentage profit made on the cost price of each racquet?

d If 80% of the racquets were sold in the sale, how much profit was made?

e What is the overall percentage return on costs if the remaining racquets are given away?

A   PERCENTAGE

We use percentages to compare an amount with a whole which we call 100%.

> % reads "**per cent**" which is short for *per centum*.
> Loosely translated from Latin, per cent means *in every hundred*.

If an object is divided into one hundred parts then each part is called 1 per cent, written 1%.

Thus, $\frac{1}{100} = 1\%$ 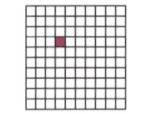   and $\frac{100}{100} = 100\%$

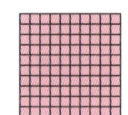

So, a percentage is like a fraction which has denominator 100.

In general: $\frac{x}{100} = x\%$

PERCENTAGE (Chapter 3)

CONVERTING FRACTIONS AND DECIMALS INTO PERCENTAGES

All fractions and decimals can be converted into percentages. We can do this either by:
- writing the fraction or decimal as a fraction with denominator 100, or
- multiplying by 100%, which is really just $\frac{100}{100}$ or 1.

Example 1

Convert each of the following to a percentage:

a $\frac{9}{20}$ b 3

a $\frac{9}{20}$
$= \frac{9 \times 5}{20 \times 5}$
$= \frac{45}{100}$
$= 45\%$

b 3
$= \frac{3 \times 100}{1 \times 100}$
$= \frac{300}{100}$
$= 300\%$

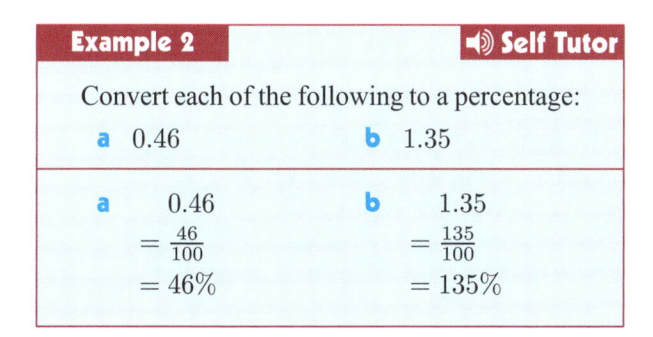

To convert to a percentage, we obtain a fraction with denominator 100.

Example 2

Convert each of the following to a percentage:

a 0.46 b 1.35

a 0.46
$= \frac{46}{100}$
$= 46\%$

b 1.35
$= \frac{135}{100}$
$= 135\%$

Remember that $\frac{x}{100} = x\%$

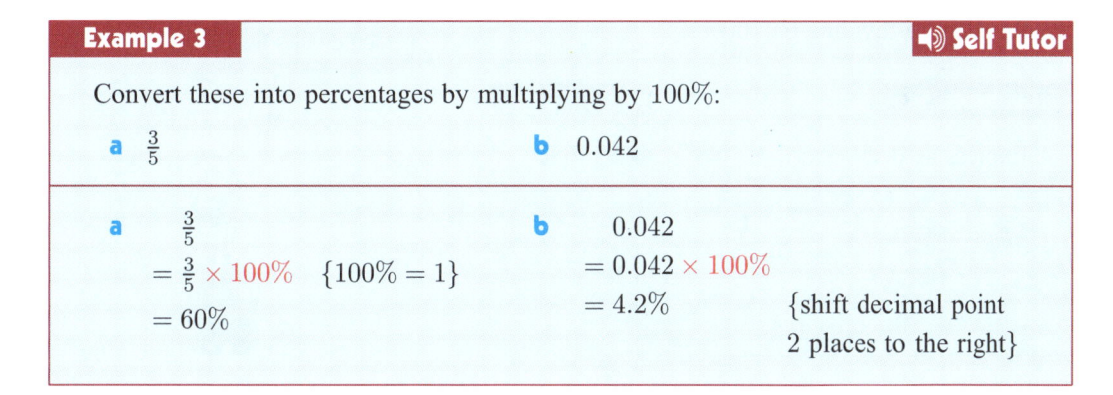

Example 3

Convert these into percentages by multiplying by 100%:

a $\frac{3}{5}$ b 0.042

a $\frac{3}{5}$
$= \frac{3}{5} \times 100\%$ {100% = 1}
$= 60\%$

b 0.042
$= 0.042 \times 100\%$
$= 4.2\%$ {shift decimal point 2 places to the right}

EXERCISE 3A.1

1 Write the following as fractions with denominator 100 and hence convert to a percentage:

a $\frac{7}{10}$ b $\frac{3}{4}$ c $\frac{7}{50}$ d $\frac{13}{25}$

e 1 f 4 g $\frac{11}{20}$ h $\frac{11}{40}$

2 Write each of the following as a percentage:
   a 0.06 **b** 0.1 **c** 0.92 **d** 0.75
   e 1.16 **f** 5.27 **g** 0.064 **h** 1.024

3 Convert the following into percentages by multiplying by 100%:
   a $\frac{2}{5}$ **b** 0.82 **c** 0.95 **d** 1.085
   e 5.16 **f** 1.012 **g** $3\frac{1}{4}$ **h** $\frac{17}{20}$
   i $\frac{4}{9}$ **j** $2\frac{5}{8}$ **k** $1\frac{2}{3}$ **l** $3\frac{3}{11}$

CONVERTING PERCENTAGES INTO FRACTIONS AND DECIMALS

A percentage may be converted into a fraction by first writing the percentage with a denominator of 100, then expressing it in its lowest terms.

Example 4

Express as fractions in lowest terms: **a** 115% **b** $12\frac{1}{2}$%

a $\quad 115\%$
$= \frac{115}{100}$
$= \frac{115 \div 5}{100 \div 5}$
$= \frac{23}{20}$

b $\quad 12\frac{1}{2}\%$
$= \frac{12.5}{100}$
$= \frac{125}{1000}$ {multiply both numerator and denominator by 10, then ÷ each by 125}
$= \frac{1}{8}$

Percentages may be converted into decimals by shifting the decimal point two places to the left. This is equivalent to dividing by 100%.

Shifting the decimal point 2 positions to the left divides by 100.

Example 5

Express as decimals: **a** 88% **b** 116%

a $\quad 88\%$
$= 088.\%$
$= 0.88$

b $\quad 116\%$
$= 116.\%$
$= 1.16$

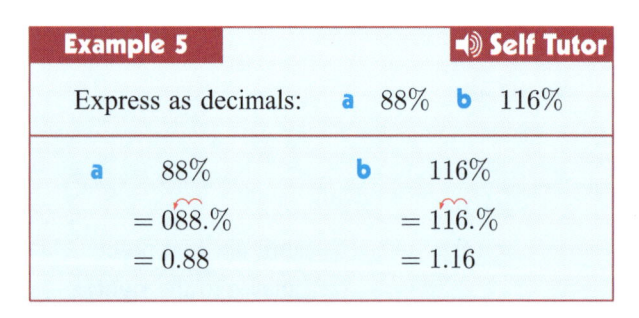

EXERCISE 3A.2

1 Express as fractions in lowest terms:
   a 85% **b** 42% **c** 105% **d** 15%
   e 48% **f** $7\frac{1}{2}$% **g** $6\frac{1}{4}$% **h** 132%
   i $16\frac{2}{3}$% **j** $33\frac{1}{3}$% **k** 160% **l** 0.25%

2 Express as decimals:
- **a** 92%
- **b** 106%
- **c** 112.4%
- **d** 88.2%
- **e** 7.5%
- **f** 1%
- **g** 256%
- **h** 0.05%
- **i** 1150%
- **j** 0.0037%
- **k** 342.8%
- **l** 63.7%

ONE QUANTITY AS A PERCENTAGE OF ANOTHER

We can *compare* quantities using percentages. To find one quantity as a percentage of another, we write the first as a **fraction** of the second, then multiply by 100%.

Example 6

Express as a percentage:
- **a** Mike ran 10 km out of 50 km
- **b** Rani spent 5 months of the last two years overseas.

a 10 km out of 50 km $= \frac{10}{50} \times 100\%$ {cancelling}

$= 20\%$

So, Mike ran 20% of 50 km.

b 5 months of the last two years

$= 5$ months of 24 months   {must have the *same* units}

$= \frac{5}{24} \times 100\%$ {Calculator: 5 ÷ 24 × 100 = }

$\approx 20.8\%$

So, Rani spent about 20.8% of the last 2 years overseas.

3 Express as a percentage:
- **a** 40 marks out of 50 marks
- **b** 21 marks out of 35 marks
- **c** 5 km out of 40 km
- **d** 500 m out of 1.5 km
- **e** 8 km out of 58 km
- **f** 130 kg out of 2.6 tonnes
- **g** 4 hours out of 1 day
- **h** 3 months out of 3 years

4 Anastasia was given €20 pocket money and Emma was given €24. Anastasia saved €7 while Emma saved €9. Who saved the greater percentage of their pocket money?

5 Matt spent $40 on jeans, $25 on a top and $65 on shoes. He received $20 change from $150. What percentage of his money did Matt spend on:
- **a** jeans
- **b** a top
- **c** shoes
- **d** all of his clothes?

6 Maya scored 32 out of 40 for a Maths test and 41 out of 55 for a Science test. For which test did she score a lower percentage?

INVESTIGATION 1 — SPORTING INJURIES

The graphs below show the number of players involved in eight different sports in England and the number of injuries suffered by players involved in those same eight sports.

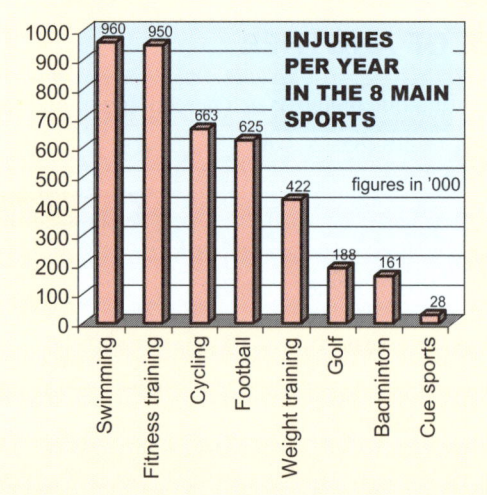

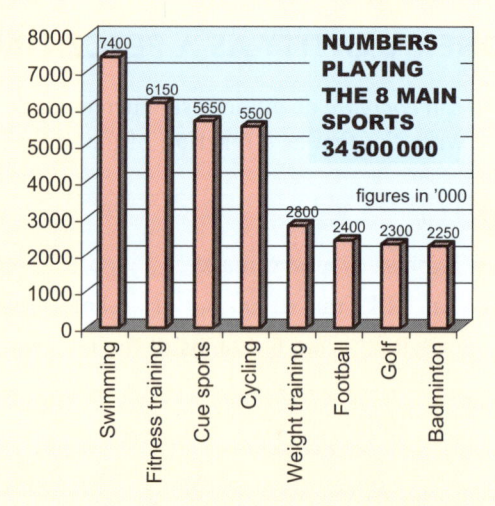

INJURIES PER YEAR IN THE 8 MAIN SPORTS (figures in '000)

- Swimming: 960
- Fitness training: 950
- Cycling: 663
- Football: 625
- Weight training: 422
- Golf: 188
- Badminton: 161
- Cue sports: 28

NUMBERS PLAYING THE 8 MAIN SPORTS 34 500 000 (figures in '000)

- Swimming: 7400
- Fitness training: 6150
- Cue sports: 5650
- Cycling: 5500
- Weight training: 2800
- Football: 2400
- Golf: 2300
- Badminton: 2250

What to do:

Investigate, using your calculator:

1. the total number of injuries per year in all 8 sports
2. injuries per year for each of the eight sports, expressed as a percentage of total injuries per year
3. the total number of people in England playing these 8 sports
4. the percentage of the total number of players playing each sport
5. the *injury rate* for each sport using

$$\text{Injury rate} = \frac{\text{number of injuries per year}}{\text{number playing that sport}} \times 100\%.$$

6. Use the injury rates to decide which sport appears to be the:
   a most dangerous **b** safest.

B THE UNITARY METHOD IN PERCENTAGE

Sometimes we know a certain percentage of the whole amount. For example,

Maddie knows that 16% of her wage is deducted for tax. Her payslip shows that $120 is taken out for tax. She wants to know her total income before tax.

The **unitary method** can be used to solve such problems.

Example 7

Find 100% of a sum of money if 16% is $120.

> 16% of the amount is $120
> ∴ 1% of the amount is $\dfrac{\$120}{16} = \$7.50$
> ∴ 100% of the amount is $\$7.50 \times 100$
> ∴ the amount is $750.

There is no need to actually calculate $\$\dfrac{120}{16}$. The final answer can be found in one step by multiplying $\$\dfrac{120}{16}$ by 100.

Example 8

Find 60% of a sum of money if 14% is $728.

> 14% is $728
> ∴ 1% is $\dfrac{\$728}{14} = \$52$
> ∴ 60% is $\$52 \times 60 = \$3120$.

Example 9

82% of fans at a basketball match support the Lakers. If there are 24 026 Lakers fans at the match, how many people attend the match?

> 82% is   24 026 fans
> ∴ 1% is $\dfrac{24\,026}{82} = 293$ fans
> ∴ 100% is $293 \times 100 = 29\,300$

So, 29 300 fans attend the match.

EXERCISE 3B

1 Find 100% if:
- **a** 20% is $360
- **b** 24% is 192 kg
- **c** 9% is 225 mL
- **d** 15% is 450 kg
- **e** 87% is $1044
- **f** 95% is 342 mL
- **g** 12% is 66 L
- **h** 35% is 252 kg
- **i** 47% is $585.

2 Find:
- **a** 30% if 7% is $126
- **b** 72% if 11% is 176 kg
- **c** 5% if 48% is $816
- **d** 15% if 90% is 1890 mL
- **e** 95% if 6% is 55 kg
- **f** 4% if 85% is $1000.

80   PERCENTAGE   (Chapter 3)

3 24% of the passengers on board a cruise ship are children. If there are 210 children aboard, determine the total number of passengers on board the ship.

4 80% of a plumbing contractor's income was from government contracts. If his income for the year from government contracts was $74 000, find his total annual income.

5 A country town has 1536 female residents. 48% of its population is female. Find the town's total population.

6 In the local high school 18% of the students play football and 32% play netball. If 126 students play football, how many students:

   a attend the school   **b** play netball?

C FINDING A PERCENTAGE OF A QUANTITY

To find a percentage of a quantity, convert the percentage to a fraction or a decimal and then **multiply**.

Example 10

Find: **a** 15% of 400 kg   **b** 4.5% of €210

a   15% of 400 kg
       $= 0.15 \times 400$ kg
       $= 60$ kg

b   4.5% of €210
       $= 0.045 \times 210$
       $=$ €9.45

Example 11

Sandra scored 86% in her exam out of 150. What mark did she score?

Sandra scored   86% of 150
              $= 0.86 \times 150$
              $= 129$ So, Sandra scored 129 marks.

Remember that 'of' means multiply!

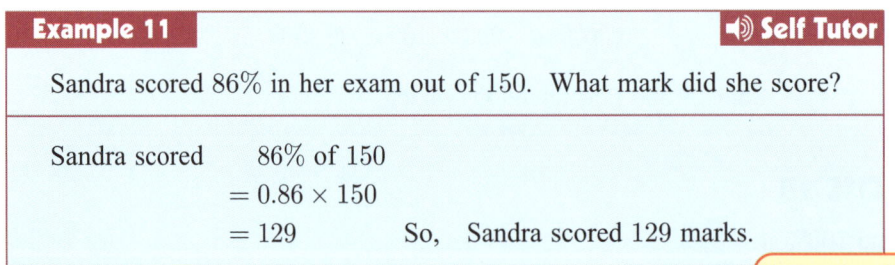

EXERCISE 3C

1 Find:

   a 30% of 90 kg   **b** 25% of €170
   c 4% of 50 L   **d** 75% of 40 km
   e 6.5% of $540   **f** 95% of 5 m
   g $47\frac{1}{2}$% of £1400   **h** $1\frac{1}{2}$% of $53 600

2 Solve the following problems:

a Su-la scored 45% in her test out of 80. What mark did she score?

b John scored 72% for an examination marked out of 150. How many marks did he actually score out of 150?

c A mixture of petrol and oil for a two-stroke lawn mower contains 85% petrol. How much oil is required for 18 litres of the fuel mixture?

d A real estate agent receives $4\frac{1}{2}$% commission on the sale of all property she handles. How much does she receive for a house she sells for £148 500?

e A share farmer receives 65% of the proceeds of the sale of a crop of wheat. If the wheat is sold for $62 400, how much does he receive?

f To insure goods to send them overseas it costs the exporter $2\frac{1}{2}$% of the value of the goods. If the goods are valued at €16 400, what will the insurance cost?

3 38.8% of Canada's population live in Ontario. The population of Ontario is 12.9 million.

a Use the unitary method to find the population of Canada.

b If 2.8% of Canadians live in Nova Scotia, how many actually live in Nova Scotia?

D PERCENTAGE INCREASE AND DECREASE

Every day we are faced with problems involving **money**. Many of these situations involve percentages. For example, we use percentages to describe profit, loss and discount.

Profit is an example of **percentage increase**. Loss and discount are examples of **percentage decrease**.

PROFIT AND LOSS

> **Profit or loss** is the difference between the **selling price** and the **cost price** of an item.
>
> Profit or loss = selling price − cost price.
>
> A **profit** occurs if the selling price is higher than the cost price.
>
> A **loss** occurs if the selling price is lower than the cost price.

Businesses make a profit by buying goods cheaply and then marking up or increasing the price when they sell them.

Example 12

A TV set is purchased for $450 and is marked up by 30%.

Find: **a** the profit   **b** the selling price.

a Profit = 30% of cost price
       = 30% of $450
       = $\frac{30}{100} \times \$450$
       = $135

b Selling price
       = cost price + profit
       = $450 + $135
       = $585

A profit is made when the selling price is greater than the cost price.

A retailer will often express their profit or loss as a **percentage of the cost price**.

For a profit we find the **percentage increase** in the price.

For a loss we find the **percentage decrease** in price.

Example 13

A bicycle costs $240 and is sold for $290.
Calculate the profit as a percentage of the cost price.

Profit = selling price − cost price
       = $290 − $240
       = $50

∴ profit as a *percentage* of cost price

= $\frac{\text{profit}}{\text{cost price}} \times 100\%$

= $\frac{50}{240} \times 100\%$

≈ 20.8%

We are really calculating the percentage increase in the price!

EXERCISE 3D.1

1 For the following items, find the: **i** profit or loss   **ii** selling price

   a a bicycle is purchased for $300 and marked up 80%

   b a ring is purchased for €650 and marked down 45%

   c a house is purchased for £137 000 and sold at a 15% profit

   d a car is purchased for ¥2 570 000 and sold at a 22% loss.

2 A bicycle costs $260 and is sold for $480. Calculate the profit as a percentage of the cost price.

3 A greengrocer buys fruit and vegetables from the market and sells them at a 25% mark up. On one particular morning, her fruit and vegetables cost her €500. If she sells all of her produce, find: **a** her profit   **b** her total income.

4 A 30 m roll of wire mesh was bought wholesale for £216. If it is sold for £8.50 per metre, find the profit and express it as a percentage of the wholesale or cost price.

Example 14   ◀» Self Tutor

Ali bought shares in Boral at $10.50 per share, but was forced to sell them at $9.30 each. Calculate:

  a her loss per share   **b** the loss per share as a percentage of the cost.

a   Loss
      = selling price − cost price
      = $9.30 − $10.50
      = −$1.20
    i.e., a $1.20 per share loss.

b   % loss
$$= \frac{\text{loss}}{\text{cost}} \times 100\%$$
$$= \frac{\$1.20}{\$10.50} \times 100\%$$
$$\approx 11.4\%$$

5 A used car firm pays $6000 for a car, but, because of financial difficulties, has to sell it immediately and receives only $4920 for the sale. Find the loss incurred by the used car firm and express this loss as a percentage of the cost price.

6 Ulrich and Jade purchased a new house for £320 000. Due to interest rate rises after 3 years they were unable to afford their mortgage repayments and had to sell the house for £285 000. Find:

  a the loss incurred   **b** the loss as a percentage of their total costs.

7 A hardware store has a closing down sale. They advertise an aluminium ladder at $256. If the wholesale or cost price of the ladder was $274, find the loss and express it as a percentage of the cost price.

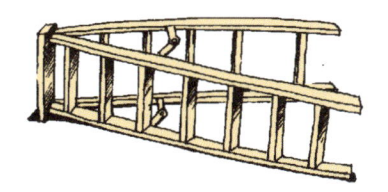

DISCOUNT

A **discount** is a **reduction** in the marked price of an item.

When retail stores advertise a **sale**, they offer a **percentage off** the **marked price** of most goods.

Discounts are often given to tradespeople as encouragement to buy goods at a particular store.

Example 15

A store offers a discount of 15% off the marked price of a shirt selling for $49.

Find the: **a** discount **b** sale price.

a Discount = 15% of $49
       = 0.15 × $49
       = $7.35

b Sale price = marked price − discount
       = $49 − $7.35
       = $41.65

EXERCISE 3D.2

1 Find the discount offered on the following items and hence find the sale price:
  a a pair of shoes marked at €70 and discounted 40%
  b a suit marked at £150 and discounted 25%
  c a cap marked at $24 and discounted $12\frac{1}{2}\%$.

2 A plumber buys supplies worth €220 but is given a 5% discount. What does she save with the discount?

3 A builder buys timber worth €4800 but is given a 12% discount. What does he pay for the timber?

4 A dressmaker buys material in bulk. It is marked at ¥13 200 but she is given a $7\frac{1}{2}\%$ discount. How much does she actually pay for the material?

Example 16

Kylie buys a pair of jeans marked at $90 but only pays $76.50. What percentage discount was she given?

We are really calculating the percentage decrease in the price.

Discount = $90 − $76.50 = $13.50

∴ % discount = $\dfrac{\text{discount}}{\text{marked price}} \times 100\%$

= $\dfrac{\$13.50}{\$90} \times 100\%$

= 15%

So, Kylie was given 15% discount.

5 Ronan purchases a CD marked at €28 but actually pays €23.80. What percentage discount was he given?

6 Nghia saw a car advertised for sale at $17 875, having been discounted from $27 500. Calculate the percentage discount.

7 A supermarket employee buys groceries worth ¥7600 but is only charged ¥7030. What employee discount did she receive?

E. PERCENTAGE CHANGE USING A MULTIPLIER

In the exercise on profit and loss, we dealt with **percentage change**. Another simple method for working with percentage change is to use a **multiplier**.

For example:

- If we *increase* an amount by 30%, we will have $100\% + 30\% = 130\%$ of the amount. So, to **increase** an amount by 30% we **multiply** by $\frac{130}{100}$ or 1.3. **1.3** is the **multiplier**.

- If we *decrease* an amount by 30%, we will have $100\% - 30\% = 70\%$ of the amount. So, to **decrease** an amount by 30% we **multiply** by $\frac{70}{100}$ or 0.7. **0.7** is the **multiplier**.

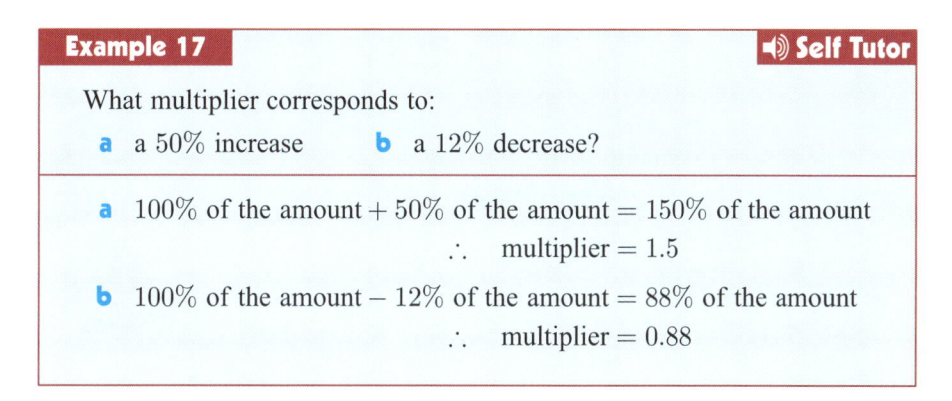

Example 17 — Self Tutor

What multiplier corresponds to:

a a 50% increase   b a 12% decrease?

a 100% of the amount + 50% of the amount = 150% of the amount
∴ multiplier = 1.5

b 100% of the amount − 12% of the amount = 88% of the amount
∴ multiplier = 0.88

Example 18 — Self Tutor

a Increase $300 by 20%.   b Decrease $300 by 20%.

a New amount
= 120% of $300
= 1.2 × $300
= $360

b New amount
= 80% of $300
= 0.8 × $300
= $240

EXERCISE 3E.1

1 What multiplier corresponds to a:

a 40% increase
b 6% increase
c 20% decrease
d 15% decrease
e 42% decrease
f 12% increase?

2 Perform the following calculations:

a Increase $120 by 15%.
b Increase 450 kg by 20%.
c Decrease £4800 by 24%.
d Decrease $720 by 8%.
e Increase 5000 hectares by 120%.
f Decrease 1600 tonnes by 12%.
g Decrease 12 500 m² by 1.46%.
h Increase €125 672 by 0.13%.

FINDING A PERCENTAGE CHANGE

The **multiplier method** can be used to find the percentage increase or decrease given the original and new amounts. We do this by expressing the new amount as a fraction of the original amount and then converting the result to a percentage.

$$\text{multiplier} = \frac{\text{new amount}}{\text{original amount}}$$

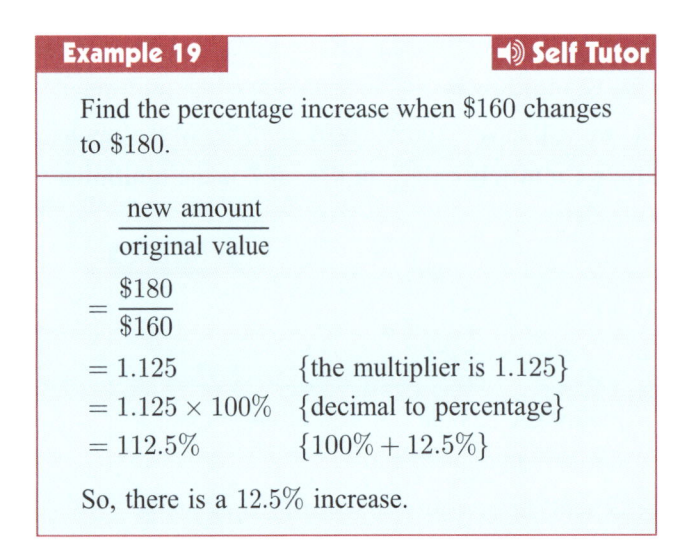

Example 19 — Self Tutor

Find the percentage increase when $160 changes to $180.

$\dfrac{\text{new amount}}{\text{original value}}$

$= \dfrac{\$180}{\$160}$

$= 1.125$ {the multiplier is 1.125}

$= 1.125 \times 100\%$ {decimal to percentage}

$= 112.5\%$ {100% + 12.5%}

So, there is a 12.5% increase.

Finding the fraction $\dfrac{\text{new amount}}{\text{original value}}$ can always be used to find percentage changes.

EXERCISE 3E.2

1 Find the percentage increase in the following, to 1 decimal place if necessary:

   a £80 changes to £96
   b €14 000 changes to €16 000
   c 32 hours changes to 37.5 hours
   d 180 cm changes to 185 cm
   e 42 kg changes to 49 kg
   f $156 000 changes to $164 000
   g 3.5 kg changes to 7 kg
   h 52.4 L changes to 61.7 L

2 My dairy herd produced a daily average of 467 L of milk last year. This year production has increased to 523 L. What is the percentage increase in milk production?

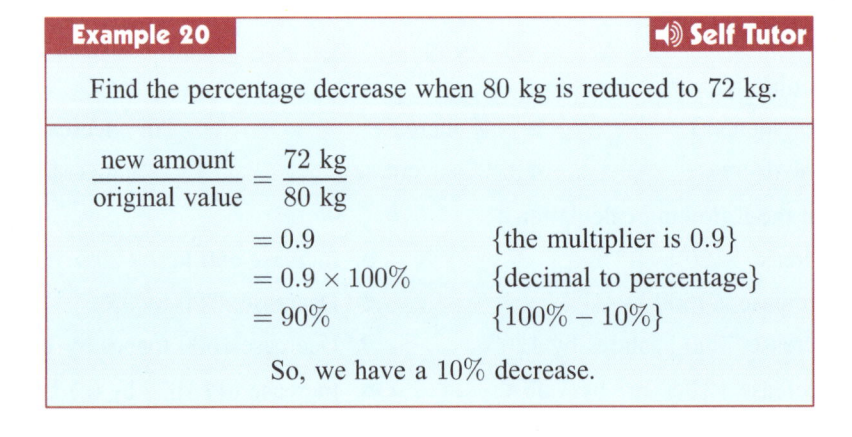

Example 20 — Self Tutor

Find the percentage decrease when 80 kg is reduced to 72 kg.

$\dfrac{\text{new amount}}{\text{original value}} = \dfrac{72 \text{ kg}}{80 \text{ kg}}$

$= 0.9$ {the multiplier is 0.9}

$= 0.9 \times 100\%$ {decimal to percentage}

$= 90\%$ {100% − 10%}

So, we have a 10% decrease.

3 Find the percentage decrease in the following:
   a $80 to $70
   b 95 kg to 90 kg
   c 60 hours to 40 hours
   d 8 km to 4 km
   e $155 to $140
   f €16 to €4

4 Increase $1000 by 10% and then decrease your answer by 10%. What do you notice?

5 My parents increased my pocket money by 10% and then three months later increased it by a further 10%. My father said this was an increase of 21%. Can you explain this?

APPLICATIONS OF THE MULTIPLIER

A simple application of the **multiplier** is in business problems where we are calculating the **selling price**. We are actually increasing or decreasing the **cost price** and so the **multiplier** can be used.

$$\text{Selling price} = \text{cost price} \times \text{multiplier}$$

Example 21

A warehouse owner buys a refrigerator for $750 and marks it up by 35%. At what price does the owner sell the refrigerator?

$100\% + 35\% = 135\%$

$\therefore$ multiplier $= 1.35$

selling price $=$ cost price $\times$ multiplier
$= \$750 \times 1.35$
$= \$1012.50$

The refrigerator is sold for $1012.50.

EXERCISE 3E.3

1 When a car priced at €14 200 is bought, a further 10% must be added for tax. What is the selling price of the car?

2 A leather coat costs a fashion store $150. They will sell it for a 70% profit. Find:
   a the selling price of the coat
   b the profit as a percentage of the selling price.

3 A real estate company buys a block of units for €326 000. They spend €22 000 on renovations and repairs. Three months later they are able to sell the units at a profit of 11% on their total investment. Find the total sale price for the block of units.

Example 22

Jody bought a block of land for $92 000, but was forced to sell it at a 12% loss. At what price did she sell the block of land?

selling price = cost price × multiplier
$$= \$92\,000 \times 0.88 \qquad \{100\% - 12\% = 88\% = 0.88\}$$
$$= \$80\,960$$

Jody sold her block for $80 960.

4 The car firm *A A Autos* paid $13 600 for a car, but were forced to sell it for a 15% loss. For what price did they sell the car?

5 A share trader buys WMC shares for $9.50 each. She will sell her shares if they lose 20% of their value. At what price will she sell her WMC shares?

6 A washing machine is priced at €440 but advertised for sale with a 30% discount. What will it cost to buy?

7 Answer the questions posed in the **Opening Problem** on page **74**.

8 Dan Brogen's Electrical buys a television set for $720. They add 30% to get the showroom price. At a sale the store offers a 15% discount. Find:
 a the customer's price   **b** the profit, as a percentage of the cost price.

9 My pocket money is €15 per week. When I turn 14 it will be increased by 200%. What will my pocket money be when I turn 14?

10 Find the percentage change in the area of a rectangle if all of its side lengths are:
 a increased by 20%   **b** decreased by 20%.

11 A machine costing $80 000 loses value or *depreciates* at 10% per year. Find its value after 2 years.

INVESTIGATION 2 DOUBLING AN INVESTMENT

Trevor invests in $1000 worth of shares. He expects the value of his investment to increase by 10% each year.

Trevor decides that he will sell the shares when they have *doubled in value*.

The purpose of this investigation is to find how long it takes for any investment to double in value at a particular rate. Doubling will usually occur **during** a year, but we are only interested in the whole number of years immediately **after** the doubling has occurred.

What to do:

1 Consider doubling the value of a $1000 investment which is increasing by 10% p.a. each year.

For an increase of 10%, we must multiply our investment amount by 110% = 1.1. So, our **multiplier** for each year is **1.1**.

New amount
= 1000×1.1
= 1100 at the end of the first year.

Copy and complete the given table:
How long will it take for the investment to double in value?

Number of years	Value
0	$1000
1	$1100
2	$1210
⋮	⋮

2 Would the answer be different if the initial value of $1000 was changed? Try some other initial values to see what happens.

3 Investigate what happens with other rates of increase, such as 4%, 6%, 8%, and 12%. You could use the **spreadsheet** which follows by clicking on the icon.
   Hint: For 4%, enter 0.04 in cell C1.

	A	B	C
1	Increase	V=$1000	0.1
2	Years	Value ($)	
3	0	1000	
4	=A3+1	=B3*(1+C$1)	
5	↓	↓	
6	fill down	fill down	

SPREADSHEET

4 Graph your results, with *investment rates* on the horizontal axis and *doubling time* on the vertical axis. Comment on your results.

F FINDING THE ORIGINAL AMOUNT

It is often useful to know what the original value of an item was before a percentage increase or decrease occurred.

For example, suppose an item is marked up by 30% and its new price is £156. How can we find its original price?

The following example illustrates a method for doing this.

Example 23   ◀)) Self Tutor

The price of a TV set is marked up by 25% for sale. Its selling price is $550.
For what price did the shopkeeper buy the TV set?

cost price × multiplier = selling price
∴ cost price × 1.25 = $550   {100% + 25% = 125% = 1.25}
∴ cost price = $\dfrac{\$550}{1.25}$ = $440

So, the television set cost the shopkeeper $440.

EXERCISE 3F

1. Find the original amount given that:
   a. after an increase of 25% the price was RM250
   b. after an increase of 35% the price was $243
   c. after a decrease of 10% the price was £81
   d. after a decrease of 17% the price was €37.35
   e. after a decrease of 37.5% the price was 115 pesos
   f. after a decrease of $22\frac{1}{2}$% the price was €9300

2. 'Blacks Furniture Mart' sells a lounge suite for $3280.50, making a profit of 35% on the cost price. How much did the business pay for the lounge suite?

3. A retailer sells a microwave oven for €640. This is a 25% profit on the cost price. How much did the retailer pay for the microwave oven?

4. An electrical firm sells a washing machine for $383.50, making a 30% profit on the wholesale or cost price. Find the wholesale price of the machine.

5. Jason sells a bicycle for $247 at a loss of 35%. What did Jason pay for the bicycle originally?

G SIMPLE INTEREST

When a person **borrows** money from a lending institution such as a bank or a finance company, the borrower must repay the loan in full, and also pay an additional **interest** payment. This is a charge for using the institution's money.

Similarly, when money is **invested** in a bank, the bank pays interest on any deposits.

SIMPLE INTEREST

> If the interest is calculated each year as a fixed percentage on the **original** amount of money borrowed or invested, then the interest is called **simple interest**.

For example, suppose $8000 is invested for 5 years at 10% per annum or per year simple interest.

$$\begin{aligned}\text{The simple interest paid for 1 year} &= 10\% \text{ of } \$8000 \\ &= 0.1 \times \$8000 \\ &= \$800\end{aligned}$$

$$\begin{aligned}\text{Thus, the simple interest for 2 years} &= 10\% \text{ of } \$8000 \times 2 \\ &= 0.1 \times \$8000 \times 2 \\ &= \$1600\end{aligned}$$

$$\vdots$$

$$\begin{aligned}\text{Thus, the simple interest for 5 years} &= 10\% \text{ of } \$8000 \times 5 \\ &= 0.1 \times \$8000 \times 5 \\ &= \$4000\end{aligned}$$

PERCENTAGE (Chapter 3) 91

These observations lead to the **simple interest formula**.

SIMPLE INTEREST FORMULA

If $C is borrowed or invested for n years at $r\%$ p.a. (per annum) simple interest, the **simple interest** I can be calculated using the formula:

$I = Crn$ where C is the **principal**,
                     r is the **flat rate of interest per annum**,
                     n is the **time** or **duration** of the loan in **years**.

Example 24   Self Tutor

Find the simple interest payable on an investment of $20 000 at 12% p.a. over a period of 4 years.

$C = 20\,000$ Now $I = Crn$
$r = 12 \div 100 = 0.12$ $\therefore \; I = 20\,000 \times 0.12 \times 4$
$n = 4$ $\therefore \; I = 9600$
                       $\therefore$ simple interest is $9600.

Example 25   Self Tutor

Calculate the simple interest payable on an investment of $15 000 at 8% p.a. over 9 months.

$C = 15\,000$ Now $I = Crn$
$r = 8 \div 100 = 0.08$ $\therefore \; I = 15\,000 \times 0.08 \times 0.75$
$n = \dfrac{9}{12} = 0.75$ $\therefore \; I = 900$
                      $\therefore$ simple interest is $900.

Remember to convert the time period to years.

In some areas of finance, sums of money may be invested over a period of **days**. However, the interest rate is still normally quoted per annum, so the time period n in the formula must be in **years**. So, the number of days *must be divided by* 365.

Example 26   Self Tutor

Determine the simple interest payable on an investment of $100 000 at 15% p.a. from April 28th to July 4th.

From April 28th there are 2 days left in April.

    $\therefore$ 2 days   left in April   ⟵ we exclude the first day (April 28)
         31 days   in May
         30 days   in June
         <u>4 days</u>   in July   ⟵ we include the last day (July 4)
         67 days

$C = 100\,000$ \qquad Now \quad $I = Crn$
$r = 15 \div 100 = 0.15$ \qquad $\therefore\ I = 100\,000 \times 0.15 \times 0.183\,562$
$n = \dfrac{67}{365} \approx 0.183\,562$ \qquad $\therefore\ I = 2753.42$

So, the interest payable is $2753.42.

EXERCISE 3G

1 Find the simple interest payable on an investment of:
   a $4000 at 8% p.a. for 5 years
   b £1500 at 11% p.a. for 3 years
   c €2500 at $10\tfrac{1}{2}$% p.a. for 2 years
   d $20 000 at $12\tfrac{1}{4}$% p.a. for 4 years.

2 Find the simple interest payable on an investment of:
   a $5000 at 7% p.a. over 6 months
   b €8000 at 9% over 3 months
   c ¥1 600 000 at $3\tfrac{1}{2}$% p.a. over 10 months
   d £11 500 at $5\tfrac{1}{4}$% p.a. over 18 months.

3 Stella Ho deposits €46 000 in a special investment account on March 17th. If the account pays $9\tfrac{1}{2}$% p.a. simple interest and she withdraws the money on June 30th, how much will her investment have earned during this time?

4 Tony Giacomin deposited $1600 on July 3rd in a special investment account which earns 13% p.a. simple interest. On August 17th he deposited another $5600 in the account. If he closed the account on November 12th by withdrawing the total balance, calculate how much his investment has earned over this period of time.

Example 27   ◀) Self Tutor

Calculate the total amount to be repaid if $5000 is borrowed for 3 years at 14% p.a. simple interest.

$C = 5000$ \qquad Now \quad $I = Crn$
$r = 14 \div 100 = 0.14$ \qquad $\therefore\ I = 5000 \times 0.14 \times 3$
$n = 3$ \qquad $\therefore\ I = 2100$

The total repayment = principal + interest
= $5000 + $2100
= $7100

5 If £2000 is borrowed under simple interest terms, how much must be repaid after:
   a 3 years at 5% p.a.
   b 8 months at 12% p.a.
   c 4 years at $8\tfrac{1}{2}$% p.a.?

6 Jamil borrows $5400 from the finance company to buy his first car. The rate of simple interest is 13% per annum and he borrows the money over a 5 year period. Find:
   a the amount Jamil must repay the finance company
   b his equal monthly repayments.   **Hint:** There are 60 months in 5 years.

7 An electric guitar with all attachments is advertised at €2400. If Klaus pays a deposit of €600, he then has to borrow the remainder or balance at 12% p.a. simple interest over 3 years. What are his monthly repayments?

H   COMPOUND INTEREST

When you deposit money in the bank, you are in effect, **lending** the money to the bank. The bank in turn uses your money to lend to other people. The bank will pay you interest to encourage your custom, and they charge interest to borrowers at a higher rate. This way the bank makes a profit.

If you leave the money in the bank for a period of time, the interest is automatically added to your account.

After the interest is added to your account, it will also earn interest in the next time period.

Consider the following example:

$1000 is placed in an account earning interest at a rate of 10% p.a. The interest is allowed to *compound* itself for three years. We say it is earning *10% p.a. compound interest*.

We can show this in a table:

Year	Amount at beginning of year	Compound Interest	Amount at end of year
1	$1000	10% of $1000 = $100	$1000 + $100 = $1100
2	$1100	10% of $1100 = $110	$1100 + $110 = $1210
3	$1210	10% of $1210 = $121	$1210 + $121 = $1331

After 3 years there is a total of $1331 in the account. We have earned $331 in compound interest.

If we construct a similar table for $1000 in an account earning 10% p.a. simple interest for 3 years, we can compare the values of the 2 different types of interest.

Year	Amount at beginning of year	Simple Interest	Amount at end of year
1	$1000	10% of $1000 = $100	$1000 + $100 = $1100
2	$1100	10% of $1000 = $100	$1100 + $100 = $1200
3	$1200	10% of $1000 = $100	$1200 + $100 = $1300

After 3 years there is a total of $1300 in the account, so we have earned $300 in simple interest.

Comparing the two,

Year	Compound Interest	Simple Interest
1	$100	$100
2	$110	$100
3	$121	$100

Notice that the *principal* on which the interest is calculated is *different* for the two forms of interest:

- For simple interest we always use the **initial amount** invested as the principal in each calculation.
- For compound interest we use the **amount** at the **end of the previous year** as the principal in each calculation.

For the *same rate of interest*, therefore, we will always earn *more interest* from compound interest accounts than from simple interest accounts over the same length of time.

Example 28

How much interest will I earn if I invest $10 000 for 3 years at:

a 15% p.a. simple interest   **b** 15% p.a. compound interest?

a We use the simple interest formula where $C = 10\,000$, $r = 0.15$, $n = 3$.

Now $I = Crn$

$\therefore \;\; I = 10\,000 \times 0.15 \times 3 = 4500$ Thus, the interest is $4500.

b

Year	Initial Amount	Interest	Final Amount
1	$10 000	15% of $10 000 = $1500.00	$11 500.00
2	$11 500	15% of $11 500 = $1725.00	$13 225.00
3	$13 225	15% of $13 225 = $1983.75	$15 208.75

Interest = final amount − initial amount
= $15 208.75 − $10 000
= $5208.75

EXERCISE 3H.1

1 Calculate:

    a the simple interest earned on €2000 at 5% p.a. for 3 years

    b using a table, the compound interest earned on €2000 at 5% p.a. for 3 years.

2 If £50 000 is invested at 9% p.a. compound interest, use a table to find:

    a the final amount after 2 years

    b how much interest was earned in the 2 year period.

3 Use a table to determine the interest earned for the following investments:

    a €4000 at 8% p.a. compound interest for 2 years

    b $12 000 at 6% p.a. compound interest for 3 years

    c £500 at 3% p.a. compound interest for 3 years.

PERCENTAGE (Chapter 3) 95

INVESTIGATION 3   COMPOUND INTEREST SPREADSHEET

A spreadsheet is an ideal way to investigate compound interest investments because it allows us to construct the table very rapidly.

Suppose $5000 is invested at 4% p.a. compound interest for 10 years.

What to do:

1 Open a new spreadsheet and enter the following:

	A	B	C	D
1	Investment	5000		
2	Interest rate	0.04		
3				
4	Year	Initial amount	Interest	Final amount
5	1	=B1	=B5*B$2	=B5+C5
6	=A5+1	=D5	=B6*B$2	=B6+C6

SPREADSHEET

2 Highlight the formulae in row 6. **Fill down** to row 14 for the 10th year of investment. **Format** all amounts in dollars.

3 Use your spreadsheet to answer the following questions:

    a What interest was paid in   **i** Year 1   **ii** Year 10?

    b How much is in the account after   **i** 5 years   **ii** 10 years?

4 Suppose $15 000 is invested at 6% p.a. compound interest for 10 years. Enter 15 000 in B1 and 0.06 in B2. For this investment, answer **a** and **b** in question **3** above.

5 How long would it take for $8000 invested at 5% p.a. compound interest to double in value?   **Hint:**   Enter 8000 in B1, 0.05 in B2, and **fill down** further.

6 What **compound interest rate** is needed for $12 000 to double in value after 6 years? **Hint:**   Enter 12 000 in B1 and repeatedly change the interest rate in B2.

THE COMPOUND INTEREST FORMULA

Suppose you invest €1000 in the bank for 3 years, earning 10% p.a. compound interest.

Since the interest rate is 10% p.a., your investment increases in value by 10% each year. Its new value is $100\% + 10\% = 110\%$ of the value at the start of the year, which corresponds to a *multiplier* of 1.1.

After one year your investment is worth	$\$1000 \times 1.1 = \$1100$
After two years it is worth	$\$1100 \times 1.1$
	$= \$1000 \times 1.1 \times 1.1$
	$= \$1000 \times (1.1)^2 = \$1210$
After three years it is worth	$\$1210 \times 1.1$
	$= \$1000 \times (1.1)^2 \times 1.1$
	$= \$1000 \times (1.1)^3 = \$1331$

This suggests that if the money was left in your account for n years, it would amount to $\$1000 \times (1.1)^n$.

We can write a formula for **Compound Growth**:

$$F_v = P_v(1+i)^n \quad \text{where}$$

- F_v is the **future value**
- P_v is the **present value** or original amount
- i is the **annual interest rate** as a decimal
- $(1+i)$ is the **multiplier**
- n is the **number of years of investment**

Notice that the formula for F_v above gives the total future value, which is the original amount plus interest.

To find the **interest only** we use:

$$\text{Compound interest} = F_v - P_v$$

Example 29

a What will $5000 invested at 8% p.a. compound interest amount to after 2 years?
b How much interest is earned?

a An interest rate of 8% indicates that $i = 0.08$.
For 2 years, $n = 2$ and so $F_v = P_v(1+i)^n$
$= \$5000 \times (1.08)^2$
$= \$5832$

b Interest earned $= \$5832 - \$5000 = \$832$.

EXERCISE 3H.2

1 a What will an investment of $3000 at 10% p.a. compound interest amount to after 3 years?
b What part of this is interest?

2 How much compound interest is earned by investing €20 000 for 4 years at 12% p.a.?

3 £5000 is invested for 2 years at 10% p.a. What will this investment amount to if the interest is calculated as:
a simple interest **b** compound interest?

4 a What will an investment of $30 000 at 10% p.a. compound interest amount to after 4 years?
b What part of this is interest?

5 How much compound interest is earned by investing €80 000 at 9% p.a. over a 3 year period?

6 £6000 is invested for 2 years at 15% p.a. What will this investment amount to if the interest is calculated as:
a simple interest **b** compound interest?

7 You have €8000 to invest for 3 years and there are 2 possible options you have been offered:

   Option 1: Invest at 9% p.a. simple interest.
   Option 2: Invest at 8% p.a. compound interest.

   a Calculate the amount accumulated at the end of the 3 years for both options and decide which option to take.

   b Would you change your decision if you were investing for 5 years?

8 What percentage increase will occur if I invest any amount over a 4 year period at 10% p.a. compound interest?   **Hint:** Let the principal be 1000 of your local currency.

9 An investment of $5000 at 7% interest compounded annually over x years will grow to $\$5000 \times (1.07)^x$. Enter the function $Y_1 = 5000 \times (1.07)\hat{\ }X$ into a **graphics calculator** and use the calculator to find:

   a the value of the investment after   **i** 5 years   **ii** 10 years   **iii** 20 years

   b how long it takes for the investment to increase to:

   i $10 000   **ii** $20 000   **iii** $40 000.

   Comment on your answers.

INFLATION RATES

Areas of interaction:
Approaches to learning, Community and service

INVESTIGATION 4   THE RATE OF INCREASE SPREADSHEET

Click on the icon to obtain a printable investigation on finding the annual average rate of increase in an investment.

REVIEW SET 3A

1 What multiplier corresponds to: **a** an 8% increase   **b** a 7% decrease?

2 Find the percentage change when €108 is increased to $144.

3 **a** Decrease $160 by 18% using a multiplier.
   b Increase 120 kg by 10% using a multiplier.

4 If 28% of a shipment of books weighs 560 kg, find the total weight of the shipment.

5 Jodie sold a dress for $224, making a loss of 30%. How much did the dress cost her?

6 Herb sold his house for £213 600 and made a 78% profit. How much did the house originally cost him?

7 See Kek inherited $33\frac{1}{3}\%$ of her uncle's estate of $420\,000$. However, she needs to pay 15% of her inheritance in tax.
   a What percentage did she actually inherit after the tax is paid?
   b How much did she actually inherit?

8 The local sports store buys sports shirts for $16 and adds a 40% mark up. In an end of season sale, a 25% discount is offered. Find the customer's price for a sports shirt.

9 Determine the simple interest on a loan of €7500 for 4 years at 8% p.a.

10 Determine the compound interest earned on £50 000 at 4% p.a. over a four year period.

11 A local manufacturing business has an increase of 6% in sales. Find the original weekly sales if the business now makes sales of $8533 per week.

REVIEW SET 3B

1 What multiplier corresponds to: **a** a $2\frac{1}{2}\%$ decrease   **b** a 7.3% increase?

2 Increase $240 by 24% using a multiplier.

3 A digital TV marked at $3000 is discounted by 12%. Find:
   a the discount given   **b** the selling price.

4 A television was bought for $560 and sold for $665. Find the profit as a percentage of the cost price.

5 The deposit of 40% for a concreting job costs £2400. How much will the remaining 60% cost?

6 Imran bought a cricket bat and then sold it for $250 at a profit of 25%. How much did the bat cost him?

7 Sergio exercised regularly to decrease his body weight by 14%. He now weighs 81.7 kg. How heavy was Sergio before he commenced the exercise program?

8 In the first year of business, Jennifer made a profit of €83 000. In the second year her profit increased to €98 000.
   a By what percentage did her profit increase?
   b What is her estimated profit for the next year assuming the same percentage increase as before?

9 **a** Determine the simple interest on a loan of $7800 for 3 years at 11% p.a.
   b Find the equal monthly repayments required to pay off the loan.

10 Determine the compound interest earned on $30 000 at 5% p.a. over a three year period.

11 Over a period of time, the value of a house increased by 15% to $455\,400$. Find the original value of the house.

Chapter 4

Algebraic expansion

Contents:
- **A** The distributive law
- **B** The expansion of $(a+b)(c+d)$
- **C** The expansion rules
- **D** Expansion of radical expressions

OPENING PROBLEM

Each week Jasmin earns €5 from her father for washing the family car and €7 from her grandfather for mowing the lawns.

If Jasmin does these tasks each week for an 11 week period, write a single expression for how much she earned over the period:

- from her father
- from her grandfather
- from them both.

A — THE DISTRIBUTIVE LAW

In the **Opening Problem**, Jasmin earned $11 \times €5$ from her father and $11 \times €7$ from her grandfather over the 11 week period.

Another way of looking at this is that Jasmin earned 11 lots of $€5 + €7$, which is $11 \times (5 + 7)$ euros.

Consequently, $11(5 + 7) = 11 \times 5 + 11 \times 7$.

Notice that the factor outside the brackets is multiplied by each term inside the brackets.

This process of removing the brackets in a product is known as **expansion**, and

$$a(b + c) = ab + ac$$ is called the **distributive law**.

Example 1

Expand and simplify:

a $5(x + 4)$ **b** $4(y - 3)$

a $5(x + 4)$
$= 5 \times x + 5 \times 4$
$= 5x + 20$

b $4(y - 3)$
$= 4(y + -3)$
$= 4 \times y + 4 \times (-3)$
$= 4y - 12$

Multiply each term inside the brackets by the quantity outside the brackets.

Example 2

Expand and simplify:

a $3(2a + 7)$ **b** $2(3x - 4)$

a $3(2a + 7)$
$= 3 \times 2a + 3 \times 7$
$= 6a + 21$

b $2(3x - 4)$
$= 2 \times 3x + 2 \times (-4)$
$= 6x - 8$

EXERCISE 4A

1 Expand and simplify:

- **a** $2(x+7)$
- **b** $3(x-2)$
- **c** $4(a+3)$
- **d** $5(a+c)$
- **e** $6(b-3)$
- **f** $7(m+4)$
- **g** $2(n-p)$
- **h** $4(p-q)$
- **i** $3(5+x)$
- **j** $5(y-x)$
- **k** $8(t-8)$
- **l** $4(7+m)$
- **m** $6(d+e)$
- **n** $2(x-11)$
- **o** $3(7+k)$
- **p** $5(p-q)$
- **q** $4(10-j)$
- **r** $7(y+n)$
- **s** $2(n-12)$
- **t** $8(11-d)$

2 Expand and simplify:

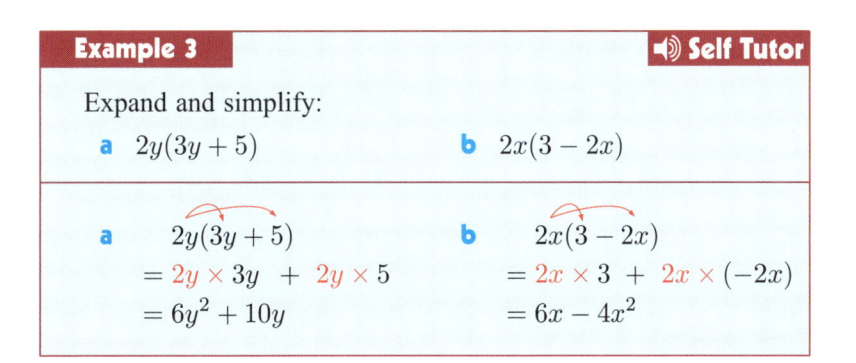

- **a** $9(2x+1)$
- **b** $3(1-3x)$
- **c** $5(2a+3)$
- **d** $11(1-2n)$
- **e** $6(3x+y)$
- **f** $5(x-2y)$
- **g** $4(3b+c)$
- **h** $2(a-2b)$
- **i** $7(a-5b)$
- **j** $12(2+3d)$
- **k** $8(3-4y)$
- **l** $6(5b+3a)$
- **m** $11(2x-y)$
- **n** $4(p+9q)$
- **o** $5(a-8b)$
- **p** $2(9+8x)$
- **q** $3(9x+y)$
- **r** $7(c-9d)$
- **s** $6(m+7n)$
- **t** $8(8a-c)$

Example 3 ◀) Self Tutor

Expand and simplify:

a $2y(3y+5)$ **b** $2x(3-2x)$

a $\quad 2y(3y+5)$
$= 2y \times 3y + 2y \times 5$
$= 6y^2 + 10y$

b $\quad 2x(3-2x)$
$= 2x \times 3 + 2x \times (-2x)$
$= 6x - 4x^2$

3 Expand and simplify:

- **a** $x(x+2)$
- **b** $x(5-x)$
- **c** $a(2a+4)$
- **d** $b(5-3b)$
- **e** $a(b+2c)$
- **f** $a(a^2+1)$
- **g** $a^2(2-a)$
- **h** $2x(3-4x)$
- **i** $3x(6-x)$
- **j** $5x(x-4)$
- **k** $4a(1-a)$
- **l** $7b(b+2)$
- **m** $(2x+3)x$
- **n** $(5-2x)x$
- **o** $ab(a+b)$
- **p** $a^2b(3-b)$
- **q** $mn(m-n)$
- **r** $ac(c-4a)$
- **s** $6p(4-7pq)$
- **t** $(3k+5l^2)k$
- **u** $(7a^2-5b)b$
- **v** $xy(x+9y)$
- **w** $(7-4x)xy$
- **x** $(3t-5s^2)t$

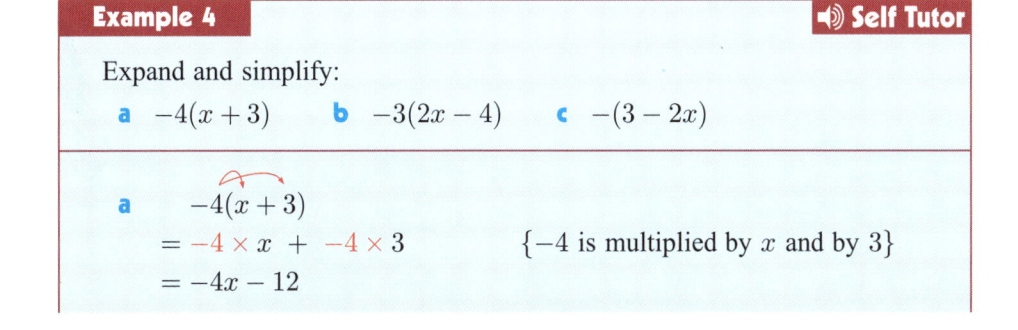

Example 4 ◀) Self Tutor

Expand and simplify:

a $-4(x+3)$ **b** $-3(2x-4)$ **c** $-(3-2x)$

a $\quad -4(x+3)$
$= -4 \times x + -4 \times 3 \qquad \{-4 \text{ is multiplied by } x \text{ and by } 3\}$
$= -4x - 12$

b $-3(2x-4)$
$= -3 \times 2x + -3 \times (-4)$ {-3 is multiplied by $2x$ and by -4}
$= -6x + 12$

c $-(3-2x)$
$= -1(3-2x)$ {-1 is multiplied by 3 and by $-2x$}
$= -1 \times 3 + -1 \times (-2x)$
$= -3 + 2x$

4 Expand and simplify:

a $-2(x+2)$	**b** $-3(x+4)$	**c** $-4(x-2)$	**d** $-5(5-x)$
e $-(a+2)$	**f** $-(x-3)$	**g** $-(5-x)$	**h** $-(2x+1)$
i $-3(4-x)$	**j** $-4(5x-2)$	**k** $-5(3-4c)$	**l** $-(x-2)$

Example 5

Expand and simplify:

a $-a(a+7)$ **b** $-4b(2b-3)$

a $-a(a+7)$
$= -a \times a + -a \times 7$
$= -a^2 - 7a$

b $-4b(2b-3)$
$= -4b \times 2b + -4b \times (-3)$
$= -8b^2 + 12b$

5 Expand and simplify:

a $-a(a+1)$	**b** $-b(b+4)$	**c** $-c(5-c)$	**d** $-x(2x+4)$
e $-2x(1-x)$	**f** $-3y(y+2)$	**g** $-4a(5-a)$	**h** $-6b(3-2b)$

Example 6

Expand and simplify:

a $3(x+5) + 2(4-x)$ **b** $5(3-x) - 2(x+1)$

a $3(x+5) + 2(4-x)$
$= 3 \times x + 3 \times 5 + 2 \times 4 + 2 \times (-x)$
$= 3x + 15 + 8 - 2x$
$= 3x - 2x + 15 + 8$
$= x + 23$

b $5(3-x) - 2(x+1)$
$= 5 \times 3 + 5 \times (-x) + -2 \times x + -2 \times 1$
$= 15 - 5x - 2x - 2$
$= 15 - 2 - 5x - 2x$
$= 13 - 7x$

In practice the second line of working is often left out.

6 Expand and simplify:

- **a** $3(x+2) + 2(x+3)$
- **b** $5(x+3) + 4(x+3)$
- **c** $4(x-2) + 5(x-4)$
- **d** $3(2x-7) + 2(1-x)$
- **e** $5(m+4) - 3(m-2)$
- **f** $5(m-3) - 2(m+1)$
- **g** $3(x-1) - 2(2x-4)$
- **h** $7(1-x) - (3x+2)$
- **i** $7(x+2) + 3(2-4x)$
- **j** $3(4-3x) - 2(2x+1)$
- **k** $-5(n-4) - 3(2n-5)$
- **l** $6(2y-1) + 4(2-y)$
- **m** $9(x+1) + 3(2x-3) - 15x$
- **n** $11(2t-1) - 3(5-3t) + 4$

Example 7   Self Tutor

Expand and simplify:

a $4 - 2(x+3)$ **b** $8 - 3(2y-1)$

a $4 - 2(x+3)$
$= 4 + -2(x+3)$
$= 4 + -2 \times x + -2 \times 3$
$= 4 - 2x - 6$
$= -2x - 2$

b $8 - 3(2y-1)$
$= 8 + -3(2y-1)$
$= 8 + -3 \times 2y + -3 \times (-1)$
$= 8 - 6y + 3$
$= 11 - 6y$

---

7 Expand and simplify:

- **a** $3x - (2x+1)$
- **b** $5 - 3(x+2)$
- **c** $7 - 6(2x-3)$
- **d** $11x - (2-x)$
- **e** $6 - 5(1-2x)$
- **f** $11 - (3-2x)$
- **g** $16 - 7(1-3x)$
- **h** $x + 6 - 3(4-x)$
- **i** $8x + 1 - 2(3-2x)$
- **j** $7 - (1-2x)$
- **k** $2x - (8-7x) + 3$
- **l** $8 - 5(11-3x)$

Example 8   Self Tutor

Expand and simplify:

a $a(a+2) + 2a(3a-2)$ **b** $y(3y-1) - 3y(2y-5)$

a $a(a+2) + 2a(3a-2)$
$= a \times a + a \times 2 + 2a \times 3a + 2a \times (-2)$
$= a^2 + 2a + 6a^2 - 4a$
$= 7a^2 - 2a$

b $y(3y-1) - 3y(2y-5)$
$= y \times 3y + y \times (-1) + -3y \times 2y + -3y \times (-5)$
$= 3y^2 - y - 6y^2 + 15y$
$= 14y - 3y^2$

8 Expand and simplify:

   a $x(x+1) + 2x(x-4)$ **b** $x(1-x) - x(2+x)$

   c $4(a+b) - 3(a-b)$ **d** $x^2(x+2) - 2x^2(1-x)$

   e $x(x^2 - 5) - 2x(1 - x^2)$ **f** $5(a+b-2) - 4(5-a+2b)$

Example 9 ◀)) Self Tutor

Expand and simplify:

   a $3(x^2 + 4x - 5)$ **b** $2a(a^2 - 3a + 1)$

a $3(x^2 + 4x - 5)$ **b** $2a(a^2 - 3a + 1)$
    $= 3 \times x^2 + 3 \times 4x + 3 \times (-5)$ $= 2a \times a^2 + 2a \times (-3a) + 2a \times 1$
    $= 3x^2 + 12x - 15$ $= 2a^3 - 6a^2 + 2a$

---

9 Expand and simplify:

   a $2(y^2 + 2y + 3)$ **b** $5(a^2 - 4a - 2)$ **c** $3(2x^2 + 3x - 1)$

   d $4(-3b^2 - 2b + 3)$ **e** $3y(y^2 - 2y + 7)$ **f** $2a(4a^2 + a - 1)$

   g $2x(-5x^2 - x + 4)$ **h** $-3b(2b^2 + 4b - 2)$ **i** $-2y(3y^2 - y + 5)$

INVESTIGATION   "THINK OF A NUMBER"

Algebra is a powerful tool in mathematical problem solving.
Algebra can help us to describe problems in general terms and often gives us an insight into *why* something works.

What to do:

1 Play the following 'think of a number' game with a partner:

   Think of a number.
   Double it.
   Subtract 4.
   Halve the result.
   Add 3.
   Subtract your original number.

Repeat the game choosing different numbers. You should find that the answer is always 1. Why is this so?

2 Algebra can provide an insight into why the answer to the game above is always 1. Let x represent the starting number.

Copy and complete the following argument by writing down each step in terms of x:

   Think of a number. x

   Double it.   gives $2x$

   Subtract 4.   gives $2x - 4$

   Halve the result.   gives $\frac{1}{2}(.... - ....)$ or .... $-$ ....

   Subtract your original number.   gives   .... $-$ .... $- x$ or ....

3 Try the following 'think of a number' game: Think of a number.
Treble it.
Add 9.
Divide the result by 3.
Subtract 3.

What is your answer? Repeat the game using different numbers.

4 For the game above, let x be the starting number. Use algebra to show how the game works.

5 Make up your own 'think of a number' game. Test it with algebra before you try it on others.

B THE EXPANSION OF $(a+b)(c+d)$

Products like $(a+b)(c+d)$ can be expanded by **repeated use** of the **distributive law**.

For example, $\quad (x+2)(x-1) \quad$ (1) $\qquad$ Compare: $\quad \square(x-1)$
$= (x+2)x + (x+2)(-1) \quad$ (2) $\qquad\qquad\qquad = \square \times x + \square \times (-1)$
$= x(x+2) - 1(x+2) \quad$ (3) $\qquad$ Notice that the distributive law for bracket
$= x^2 + 2x - x - 2 \quad$ (4) $\qquad$ expansion was used three times: once to
$= x^2 + x - 2 \qquad\qquad\qquad\qquad$ get line (2) and twice to get line (4).

Example 10

Expand and simplify by repeated use of the distributive law:

a $(x+5)(x+4)$ $\qquad\qquad$ **b** $(x-2)(2x-1)$

a $\quad (x+5)(x+4)$ $\qquad\qquad$ **b** $\quad (x-2)(2x-1)$
$= (x+5)x + (x+5)4 \qquad\qquad = (x-2)2x + (x-2)(-1)$
$= x(x+5) + 4(x+5) \qquad\qquad = 2x(x-2) - (x-2)$
$= x^2 + 5x + 4x + 20 \qquad\qquad = 2x^2 - 4x - x + 2$
$= x^2 + 9x + 20 \qquad\qquad\qquad = 2x^2 - 5x + 2$

Example 11

Expand using the distributive law repeatedly:

a $(x+5)^2$ $\qquad\qquad$ **b** $(x-5)^2$

a $\quad (x+5)^2$ $\qquad\qquad$ **b** $\quad (x-5)^2$
$= (x+5)(x+5) \qquad\qquad\quad = (x-5)(x-5)$
$= (x+5)x + (x+5)5 \qquad\quad = (x-5)x + (x-5)(-5)$
$= x(x+5) + 5(x+5) \qquad\quad = x(x-5) - 5(x-5)$
$= x^2 + 5x + 5x + 25 \qquad\quad = x^2 - 5x - 5x + 25$
$= x^2 + 10x + 25 \qquad\qquad\quad = x^2 - 10x + 25$

EXERCISE 4B

1 Expand and simplify by repeated use of the distributive law:
- **a** $(x+2)(x+3)$
- **b** $(a+4)(a+5)$
- **c** $(b+2)(b-5)$
- **d** $(a-3)(a-4)$
- **e** $(x+y)(a+b)$
- **f** $(a+b)(p+q)$
- **g** $(x+1)(2x+3)$
- **h** $(x-1)(2x+3)$
- **i** $(3x+4)(x-5)$
- **j** $(3x-4)(x+5)$
- **k** $(5x-7)(2x-1)$
- **l** $(x+1)(x^2+4)$

2 Expand by repeated use of the distributive law:
- **a** $(x+3)^2$
- **b** $(x-3)^2$
- **c** $(x+7)^2$
- **d** $(x-7)^2$
- **e** $(2x+5)^2$
- **f** $(2x-5)^2$
- **g** $(x+y)^2$
- **h** $(x-y)^2$
- **i** $(x-4)^2$
- **j** $(10+x)^2$
- **k** $(2-3x)^2$
- **l** $(1+4x)^2$

Example 12 ◀ Self Tutor

Use the distributive law to expand and simplify: $(x+2)(x^2+2x-3)$

$(x+2)(x^2+2x-3)$
$= (x+2)x^2 + (x+2)2x + (x+2)(-3)$
$= x^2(x+2) + 2x(x+2) - 3(x+2)$
$= x^3 + 2x^2 + 2x^2 + 4x - 3x - 6$
$= x^3 + 4x^2 + x - 6$

3 Use the distributive law to expand and simplify:
- **a** $(x+1)(x^2+x+3)$
- **b** $(x+2)(2x^2+x+5)$
- **c** $(x-2)(x^2-x-3)$
- **d** $(x^2+x+1)(x+4)$
- **e** $(x^2-x+2)(2x-3)$
- **f** $(2x^2+x-1)(3x+7)$
- **g** $(2x+7)(5-x+x^2)$
- **h** $(x+9)(x^2+7-2x)$

C THE EXPANSION RULES

The distributive law can also be seen by examining areas.

Consider the figure alongside.

The overall area is $a(b+c)$

So, $a(b+c)$ = area of rectangle (1) + area of rectangle (2)
$= ab + ac$

Now consider a rectangle with side lengths $(a+b)$ and $(c+d)$.

The overall area is $(a+b)(c+d)$.

But this area can also be obtained by adding the areas of the four smaller rectangles.

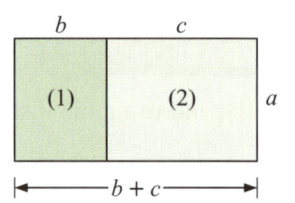

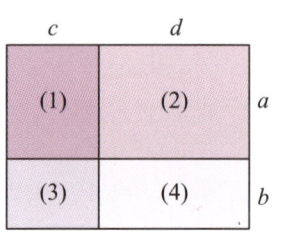

So, $(a+b)(c+d)$ = area of (1) + area of (2) + area of (3) + area of (4)
$$= ac + ad + bc + bd$$

Hence $$(a+b)(c+d) = ac + ad + bc + bd$$

This expansion rule is sometimes called the **FOIL** rule as:

$$(a+b)(c+d) = \underset{\text{Firsts}}{ac} + \underset{\text{Outers}}{ad} + \underset{\text{Inners}}{bc} + \underset{\text{Lasts}}{bd}$$

with inners $b \cdot c$ and outers $a \cdot d$.

Example 13 ◀)) Self Tutor

Expand and simplify: **a** $(x+3)(x+7)$ **b** $(x-2)(x+4)$

a $(x+3)(x+7)$
$= x \times x + x \times 7 + 3 \times x + 3 \times 7$
$= x^2 + 7x + 3x + 21$
$= x^2 + 10x + 21$

b $(x-2)(x+4)$
$= x \times x + x \times 4 - 2 \times x - 2 \times 4$
$= x^2 + 4x - 2x - 8$
$= x^2 + 2x - 8$

The second line is often done mentally and not written down.

Example 14 ◀)) Self Tutor

Expand and simplify:

a $(x+7)^2$ **b** $(3x-2)^2$

a $(x+7)^2$
$= (x+7)(x+7)$
$= x^2 + 7x + 7x + 49$
$= x^2 + 14x + 49$

b $(3x-2)^2$
$= (3x-2)(3x-2)$
$= 9x^2 - 6x - 6x + 4$
$= 9x^2 - 12x + 4$

The middle two terms are identical.

Example 15 ◀)) Self Tutor

Expand and simplify using $(a+b)(c+d) = ac + ad + bc + bd$:

a $(x+3)(x-3)$ **b** $(2x-5)(2x+5)$

a $(x+3)(x-3)$
$= x^2 - 3x + 3x - 9$
$= x^2 - 9$

b $(2x-5)(2x+5)$
$= 4x^2 + 10x - 10x - 25$
$= 4x^2 - 25$

The middle two terms add to zero!

108   ALGEBRAIC EXPANSION   (Chapter 4)

EXERCISE 4C.1

1 Use the rule $(a+b)(c+d) = ac+ad+bc+bd$ to expand, and then simplify if possible:

- **a** $(p+q)(m+n)$
- **b** $(x+y)(r+s)$
- **c** $(x+4)(x+7)$
- **d** $(x+3)(x+1)$
- **e** $(y+3)(y+2)$
- **f** $(a+3)(a+7)$
- **g** $(x+2)(x-2)$
- **h** $(x-4)(x+2)$
- **i** $(x+7)(x-3)$
- **j** $(x-9)(x+2)$
- **k** $(x-4)(x+3)$
- **l** $(x+6)(x-2)$
- **m** $(x-4)(x-3)$
- **n** $(x-5)(x-8)$
- **o** $(x-11)(x-4)$
- **p** $(2x+3)(x-1)$
- **q** $(x-4)(3x+2)$
- **r** $(2x+3)(2x-4)$

2 Expand and simplify using the rule $(a+b)(c+d) = ac+ad+bc+bd$:

- **a** $(x+1)^2$
- **b** $(x+4)^2$
- **c** $(x-2)^2$
- **d** $(x-5)^2$
- **e** $(3+y)^2$
- **f** $(3-y)^2$
- **g** $(2x+1)^2$
- **h** $(2x-1)^2$
- **i** $(1+4a)^2$
- **j** $(1-4a)^2$
- **k** $(a+b)^2$
- **l** $(a-b)^2$
- **m** $(3x+2)^2$
- **n** $(4x-3)^2$
- **o** $(9x-5)^2$
- **p** $(7x+2)^2$

3 Expand and simplify using the rule $(a+b)(c+d) = ac+ad+bc+bd$:

- **a** $(x+2)(x-2)$
- **b** $(y-5)(y+5)$
- **c** $(a+7)(a-7)$
- **d** $(b-4)(b+4)$
- **e** $(3+x)(3-x)$
- **f** $(6-y)(6+y)$
- **g** $(1+a)(1-a)$
- **h** $(8-b)(8+b)$
- **i** $(2x+1)(2x-1)$
- **j** $(3a-2)(3a+2)$
- **k** $(3+5b)(3-5b)$
- **l** $(5-4y)(5+4y)$

4 Write down your observations from question **3**.

PERFECT SQUARES

Perfect squares have form $(a+b)^2$, and because we see them often in algebraic expressions we use a rule for writing down their expansions:

$$(a+b)^2 = a^2 + 2ab + b^2$$

This rule is easily established by repeated use of the distributive law.

$(a+b)^2 = a^2 + 2ab + b^2$ can be demonstrated using areas.

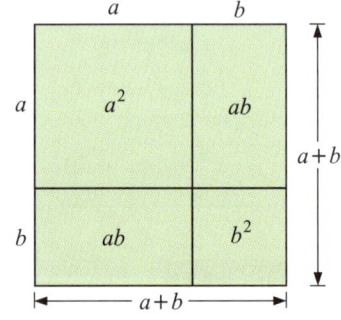

The following is a useful way of remembering the perfect square rules:

$$(a+b)^2 \;=\; a^2 \;+\; 2ab \;+\; b^2$$

1st term   2nd term   square of first term   twice product of 2 terms   square of 2nd term

Example 16

Expand and simplify: **a** $(x+6)^2$ **b** $(2x+5)^2$

a $(x+6)^2$
$= x^2 + 2 \times x \times 6 + 6^2$
$= x^2 + 12x + 36$

b $(2x+5)^2$
$= (2x)^2 + 2 \times 2x \times 5 + 5^2$
$= 4x^2 + 20x + 25$

Example 17

Expand and simplify: **a** $(5-x)^2$ **b** $(3x-7)^2$

a $(5-x)^2$
$= (5 + -x)^2$
$= 5^2 + 2 \times 5 \times (-x) + (-x)^2$
$= 25 - 10x + x^2$

b $(3x-7)^2$
$= (3x + -7)^2$
$= (3x)^2 + 2 \times 3x \times (-7) + (-7)^2$
$= 9x^2 - 42x + 49$

EXERCISE 4C.2

1 Expand and simplify using the rule $(a+b)^2 = a^2 + 2ab + b^2$:

  a $(c+d)^2$ **b** $(r+s)^2$ **c** $(m+n)^2$ **d** $(a+3)^2$
  e $(x+5)^2$ **f** $(x+11)^2$ **g** $(2x+1)^2$ **h** $(3x+2)^2$
  i $(4x+3)^2$ **j** $(5+3x)^2$ **k** $(7x+1)^2$ **l** $(2x+y)^2$
  m $(6+x)^2$ **n** $(3+5x)^2$ **o** $(x^2+1)^2$ **p** $(x^2+x)^2$

2 Expand and simplify using the rule $(a+b)^2 = a^2 + 2ab + b^2$:

  a $(x-y)^2$ **b** $(r-s)^2$ **c** $(d-c)^2$ **d** $(d-3)^2$
  e $(4-a)^2$ **f** $(7-x)^2$ **g** $(3x-1)^2$ **h** $(5-d)^2$
  i $(2x-5)^2$ **j** $(3-4a)^2$ **k** $(3a-2b)^2$ **l** $(x^2-2)^2$
  m $(6-x)^2$ **n** $(3-5x)^2$ **o** $(x^2-x)^2$ **p** $(x-2x^2)^2$

DIFFERENCE OF TWO SQUARES

An expression of the form $(a+b)(a-b)$ is called a **difference of two squares**.

Expanding this expression using the FOIL rule, $(a+b)(a-b) = a^2 + a(-b) + ba - b^2$
$= a^2 - ab + ab - b^2$
$= a^2 - b^2$

Thus $(a+b)(a-b) = a^2 - b^2$.

Example 18

Expand and simplify using the rule $(a+b)(a-b) = a^2 - b^2$:

a $(x+3)(x-3)$ **b** $(2x-5)(2x+5)$

a $\quad (x+3)(x-3)$
$= (x)^2 - (3)^2$
$= x^2 - 9$

b $\quad (2x-5)(2x+5)$
$= (2x)^2 - (5)^2$
$= 4x^2 - 25$

EXERCISE 4C.3

1 Expand and simplify using the rule $(a+b)(a-b) = a^2 - b^2$:

a $(y+4)(y-4)$ **b** $(b+1)(b-1)$ **c** $(x-9)(x+9)$
d $(a-8)(a+8)$ **e** $(5-b)(5+b)$ **f** $(2-x)(2+x)$
g $(10+a)(10-a)$ **h** $(7+y)(7-y)$ **i** $(3x-2)(3x+2)$
j $(4x+3)(4x-3)$ **k** $(1-2y)(1+2y)$ **l** $(5-3a)(5+3a)$

MISCELLANEOUS EXPANSION

Example 19

Expand and simplify using expansion rules:

a $(2x-3)(x+5)$ **b** $(x+9)^2$ **c** $(3x-7)(3x+7)$

a $\quad (2x-3)(x+5)$
$= 2x^2 + 10x - 3x - 15$ {FOIL}
$= 2x^2 + 7x - 15$

b $\quad (x+9)^2$
$= x^2 + 2 \times x \times 9 + 9^2$ {perfect square}
$= x^2 + 18x + 81$

c $\quad (3x-7)(3x+7)$
$= (3x)^2 - (7)^2$ {difference of two squares}
$= 9x^2 - 49$

EXERCISE 4C.4

1 Expand and simplify using expansion rules:

a $(x+4)(x-2)$ **b** $(x-3)(x+2)$ **c** $(x+3)^2$
d $(1-x)(2-x)$ **e** $(4-x)(x-2)$ **f** $(x-7)^2$
g $(x+6)(x-6)$ **h** $(x+10)^2$ **i** $(2x+7)(2x-7)$
j $(x-5)(2x+3)$ **k** $(2x+11)^2$ **l** $(x+a)(x-a)$
m $(3x+2)(x-5)$ **n** $(2x-9)^2$ **o** $(3x+5)(3x-5)$
p $(3x+4)(2-x)$ **q** $(5-x)^2$ **r** $(3+2x)(5x-1)$

2 **a** Show that $(n + \frac{1}{2})^2 = n^2 + n + \frac{1}{4}$ using the perfect square expansion rule.

  b Hence, find the value of $(2\frac{1}{2})^2$. **Hint:** Let $n = 2$.

  c Find: **i** $(3\frac{1}{2})^2$ **ii** $(10\frac{1}{2})^2$ **iii** $(20\frac{1}{2})^2$

EXTENSION

Great care must be taken to avoid errors in more complicated algebraic simplification. It is often wise to put in all steps of the simplification so that not too much is performed mentally.

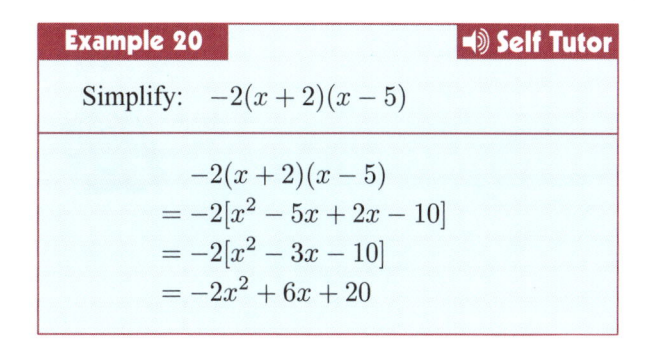

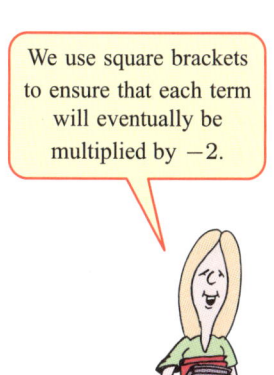

Example 20

Simplify: $-2(x + 2)(x - 5)$

$-2(x + 2)(x - 5)$
$= -2[x^2 - 5x + 2x - 10]$
$= -2[x^2 - 3x - 10]$
$= -2x^2 + 6x + 20$

We use square brackets to ensure that each term will eventually be multiplied by -2.

EXERCISE 4C.5

1 Expand and simplify:

  a $2(x + 1)(x + 4)$ **b** $3(x + 4)(x + 5)$ **c** $4(x - 1)(x - 5)$
  d $2(2 - x)(3 - x)$ **e** $-5(x + 2)(x + 7)$ **f** $-3(x + 2)(x - 3)$
  g $-4(2 - x)(1 - x)$ **h** $-(3 - x)(x + 2)$ **i** $-(5 - x)(2 + x)$
  j $-7(x - 3)(x + 3)$ **k** $-2(5 + x)(5 - x)$ **l** $-3(x - 4)^2$

Example 21

Expand and simplify: **a** $4(x - 5)^2$ **b** $5 - 2(x + 3)^2$

a $4(x - 5)^2$
$= 4[(x)^2 + 2 \times x \times (-5) + (-5)^2]$ {expand the perfect square}
$= 4(x^2 - 10x + 25)$ {simplify}
$= 4x^2 - 40x + 100$ {multiply through by 4}

b $5 - 2(x + 3)^2$
$= 5 - 2[(x)^2 + 2 \times x \times 3 + (3)^2]$ {expand the perfect square}
$= 5 - 2(x^2 + 6x + 9)$ {simplify}
$= 5 - 2x^2 - 12x - 18$ {multiply through by -2}
$= -2x^2 - 12x - 13$ {collect like terms}

2 Expand and simplify:

a $2(x+3)^2$
b $3(2-x)^2$
c $5(a+b)^2$
d $-4(x+1)^2$
e $-(x+2)^2$
f $2(2x+1)^2$
g $4+2(x-2)^2$
h $1-3(x+2)^2$
i $8-2(4-x)^2$

Example 22 — Self Tutor

Expand and simplify: $(2x-1)(x+2) - (x-2)^2$

$(2x-1)(x+2) - (x-2)^2$
$= [2x^2 + 4x - x - 2] - [x^2 + 2 \times x \times (-2) + (-2)^2]$
$= [2x^2 + 3x - 2] - [x^2 - 4x + 4]$
$= 2x^2 + 3x - 2 - x^2 + 4x - 4$
$= x^2 + 7x - 6$

*The use of brackets is **essential**.*

3 Expand and simplify:

a $(x+2)^2 + 3(x+1)$
b $(x+3)^2 - 8(2-x)$
c $(x-1)^2 + 2(x+1)^2$
d $4 + 3(x+1)(x+4)$
e $(x+2)(x-2) - (x-1)^2$
f $(x+1)^2 + 3(x-1)^2$
g $3(x+1)^2 + 2(x-2)^2$
h $3(2-x)^2 - 5(x+1)^2$
i $2(x+3)(x+5) - 3(x-1)^2$
j $2(x-1)^2 + 3(4-x)$
k $2(x-4)^2 - 5(1+2x)^2$
l $3(x+1)^2 - 2(x-2)^2$

D. EXPANSION OF RADICAL EXPRESSIONS

We have seen previously that a **radical** is a number expressed using the radical sign $\sqrt{}$.

In particular, the **square root** of a number a is the number which, when multiplied by itself, gives a. So, $\sqrt{a} \times \sqrt{a} = a$.

OPERATIONS WITH RADICALS

Example 23 — Self Tutor

Simplify: a $\sqrt{11} \times \sqrt{11}$ b $(\sqrt{13})^2$

a $\sqrt{11} \times \sqrt{11}$
$= 11$

b $(\sqrt{13})^2$
$= \sqrt{13} \times \sqrt{13}$
$= 13$

Example 24

Simplify: a $4\sqrt{3} \times \sqrt{3}$ b $(2\sqrt{5})^2$

a $4\sqrt{3} \times \sqrt{3}$
$= 4 \times \sqrt{3} \times \sqrt{3}$
$= 4 \times 3$
$= 12$

b $(2\sqrt{5})^2$
$= 2\sqrt{5} \times 2\sqrt{5}$
$= 2 \times 2 \times \sqrt{5} \times \sqrt{5}$
$= 4 \times 5$
$= 20$

Radicals in simplest form can be 'collected' in the same way as 'like' algebraic terms. For example, since $2x + 3x = 5x$,
$2\sqrt{2} + 3\sqrt{2} = 5\sqrt{2}$.

Compare **a** with $4a + 2a = 6a$.

Example 25

Simplify: a $4\sqrt{3} + 2\sqrt{3}$ b $3 + \sqrt{2} + 4 - 5\sqrt{2}$

a $4\sqrt{3} + 2\sqrt{3}$
$= 6\sqrt{3}$

b $3 + \sqrt{2} + 4 - 5\sqrt{2}$
$= 7 - 4\sqrt{2}$

EXERCISE 4D

1 Simplify:

a $\sqrt{7} \times \sqrt{7}$ b $\sqrt{5} \times \sqrt{5}$ c $\sqrt{21} \times \sqrt{21}$ d $\sqrt{19} \times \sqrt{19}$
e $\sqrt{8} \times \sqrt{8}$ f $(\sqrt{17})^2$ g $(\sqrt{35})^2$ h $(\sqrt{24})^2$

2 Simplify:

a $3\sqrt{5} \times \sqrt{5}$ b $2\sqrt{7} \times \sqrt{7}$ c $\sqrt{2} \times 4\sqrt{2}$ d $\sqrt{3} \times 7\sqrt{3}$
e $(3\sqrt{2})^2$ f $(4\sqrt{5})^2$ g $(2\sqrt{3})^2$ h $(5\sqrt{2})^2$
i $2\sqrt{3} \times 5\sqrt{3}$ j $3\sqrt{5} \times 2\sqrt{5}$ k $3\sqrt{2} \times 4\sqrt{2}$ l $(\sqrt{2})^4$

3 Simplify:

a $5\sqrt{2} + 4\sqrt{2}$ b $7\sqrt{3} - 5\sqrt{3}$ c $6\sqrt{7} + 7\sqrt{7}$
d $3\sqrt{3} - \sqrt{3}$ e $4\sqrt{2} + \sqrt{2}$ f $\sqrt{2} + \sqrt{3} + \sqrt{2}$
g $\sqrt{3} - 2\sqrt{3}$ h $3\sqrt{2} + 2\sqrt{2} - \sqrt{2}$ i $\sqrt{2} + 2\sqrt{3} + 2\sqrt{2} - \sqrt{3}$
j $3\sqrt{3} + 4\sqrt{3} - 8\sqrt{3}$ k $\sqrt{7} + 5\sqrt{7} - 2\sqrt{7}$ l $4\sqrt{5} - 2\sqrt{5} + 3\sqrt{5}$

Example 26

Expand and simplify:

a $\sqrt{2}(\sqrt{2}+3)$ **b** $3\sqrt{3}(6-2\sqrt{3})$

a $\sqrt{2}(\sqrt{2}+3)$
$= \sqrt{2} \times \sqrt{2} + \sqrt{2} \times 3$
$= 2 + 3\sqrt{2}$

b $3\sqrt{3}(6-2\sqrt{3})$
$= 3\sqrt{3} \times 6 + 3\sqrt{3} \times (-2\sqrt{3})$
$= 18\sqrt{3} - 6 \times 3$
$= 18\sqrt{3} - 18$

The number outside the brackets is multiplied by each number inside the brackets.

4 Expand and simplify:

a $\sqrt{2}(3-\sqrt{2})$ **b** $\sqrt{3}(\sqrt{3}+1)$ **c** $\sqrt{3}(1-\sqrt{3})$
d $\sqrt{7}(7-\sqrt{7})$ **e** $\sqrt{5}(2-\sqrt{5})$ **f** $\sqrt{11}(2\sqrt{11}-1)$
g $\sqrt{6}(1-2\sqrt{6})$ **h** $2\sqrt{2}(2+\sqrt{2})$ **i** $3\sqrt{2}(\sqrt{2}-1)$
j $2\sqrt{2}(3-\sqrt{2})$ **k** $2\sqrt{5}(3-\sqrt{5})$ **l** $3\sqrt{3}(\sqrt{3}+5)$

Example 27

Expand and simplify:

a $-\sqrt{2}(\sqrt{2}+3)$ **b** $-\sqrt{3}(4-\sqrt{3})$

a $-\sqrt{2}(\sqrt{2}+3)$
$= -\sqrt{2} \times \sqrt{2} + -\sqrt{2} \times 3$
$= -2 - 3\sqrt{2}$

b $-\sqrt{3}(4-\sqrt{3})$
$= -\sqrt{3} \times 4 + -\sqrt{3} \times (-\sqrt{3})$
$= -4\sqrt{3} + 3$

Be careful with the negative signs!

5 Expand and simplify:

a $-\sqrt{2}(3-\sqrt{2})$ **b** $-\sqrt{2}(4-\sqrt{2})$ **c** $-\sqrt{3}(1+\sqrt{3})$
d $-\sqrt{3}(\sqrt{3}+2)$ **e** $-\sqrt{5}(2+\sqrt{5})$ **f** $-(\sqrt{2}+3)$
g $-\sqrt{5}(\sqrt{5}-4)$ **h** $-(3-\sqrt{7})$ **i** $-\sqrt{11}(2-\sqrt{11})$
j $-2\sqrt{2}(1-\sqrt{2})$ **k** $-3\sqrt{3}(5-\sqrt{3})$ **l** $-7\sqrt{2}(\sqrt{2}+3)$

Example 28

Expand and simplify: $(3-\sqrt{2})(2+3\sqrt{2})$

$(3-\sqrt{2})(2+3\sqrt{2})$
$= 3 \times 2 + 3 \times 3\sqrt{2} - \sqrt{2} \times 2 - \sqrt{2} \times 3\sqrt{2}$
$= 6 + 9\sqrt{2} - 2\sqrt{2} - 6$
$= 7\sqrt{2}$

*Remember to use the **FOIL** rule.*

6 Expand and simplify:

a $(1+\sqrt{2})(2+\sqrt{2})$
b $(2+\sqrt{3})(3+\sqrt{3})$
c $(\sqrt{3}+2)(\sqrt{3}-1)$
d $(4-\sqrt{2})(3+\sqrt{2})$
e $(1+\sqrt{3})(1-\sqrt{3})$
f $(5+\sqrt{7})(2-\sqrt{7})$
g $(\sqrt{5}+2)(\sqrt{5}-3)$
h $(6-\sqrt{3})(2+\sqrt{3})$
i $(4-\sqrt{2})(3-\sqrt{2})$
j $(4-3\sqrt{3})(2-\sqrt{3})$
k $(-1+2\sqrt{2})(2-\sqrt{2})$
l $(2\sqrt{2}+3)(2\sqrt{2}+5)$

Example 29

Expand and simplify the following perfect squares:

a $(\sqrt{3}+2)^2$
b $(\sqrt{5}-3)^2$

a $(\sqrt{3}+2)^2$
$= (\sqrt{3})^2 + 2 \times \sqrt{3} \times 2 + 2^2$
$= 3 + 4\sqrt{3} + 4$
$= 7 + 4\sqrt{3}$

b $(\sqrt{5}-3)^2$
$= (\sqrt{5})^2 + 2 \times \sqrt{5} \times (-3) + (-3)^2$
$= 5 - 6\sqrt{5} + 9$
$= 14 - 6\sqrt{5}$

7 Expand and simplify the following perfect squares:

a $(1+\sqrt{2})^2$
b $(2-\sqrt{3})^2$
c $(\sqrt{3}+2)^2$
d $(1+\sqrt{5})^2$
e $(5-\sqrt{2})^2$
f $(4-\sqrt{6})^2$
g $(5\sqrt{2}-1)^2$
h $(3-2\sqrt{2})^2$
i $(1+3\sqrt{2})^2$
j $(4\sqrt{3}+5)^2$
k $(3-\sqrt{7})^2$
l $(2\sqrt{11}+3)^2$

8 Use the difference of two squares expansion rule $(a+b)(a-b) = a^2 - b^2$ to expand and simplify:

a $(4+\sqrt{3})(4-\sqrt{3})$
b $(5-\sqrt{2})(5+\sqrt{2})$
c $(6-\sqrt{5})(6+\sqrt{5})$
d $(3-\sqrt{7})(3+\sqrt{7})$
e $(1-\sqrt{3})(1+\sqrt{3})$
f $(2+\sqrt{5})(2-\sqrt{5})$
g $(3\sqrt{2}-1)(3\sqrt{2}+1)$
h $(4\sqrt{3}+5)(4\sqrt{3}-5)$
i $(2\sqrt{5}-5)(2\sqrt{5}+5)$

REVIEW SET 4A

1 Expand the following expressions:

a $2(x+11)$
b $2x(7-2x)$
c $-4(3-2x)$

2 Expand and simplify:

a $2(1-3x) + 5(2x-1)$
b $3x(x+1) - 2x(2x-7)$

3 Expand and simplify:

a $(x^2+3)(x+8)$
b $(x-4)^2$
c $(7-2x)^2$

4 Expand and simplify:

a $-x(x^2+2x-3)$
b $(x+2)(x^2-3x+1)$

5 Expand and simplify:

a $3\sqrt{2} - 5\sqrt{2}$
b $2\sqrt{3}(\sqrt{3} + \frac{1}{2}\sqrt{2})$
c $-\sqrt{5}(3\sqrt{5} - 2)$

6 Expand and simplify:

   a $(2-\sqrt{3})^2$ **b** $(2\sqrt{2}+3)(\sqrt{2}-1)$ **c** $(3-\sqrt{2})(3+\sqrt{2})$

7 Expand and simplify: $(3x+1)(x-2) - (x+2)^2$

REVIEW SET 4B

1 Expand and simplify:

   a $3(x-8)$ **b** $-2(6-3x)$ **c** $2x^2(x^2-x+1)$

2 Expand and simplify:

   a $3x(1-x) + x(2x+1)$ **b** $2(2x-3) - 5(x+2)$

3 Expand and simplify:

   a $(x+6)^2$ **b** $(2x-5)^2$ **c** $(3x+7)(3x-7)$

4 Expand and simplify:

   a $-3x(1-5x-2x^2)$ **b** $(2x-3)(x^2-x+4)$

5 Expand and simplify:

   a $3\sqrt{3} + 4\sqrt{3}$ **b** $4\sqrt{5}(1-\sqrt{5})$ **c** $-\sqrt{7}(7-\sqrt{7})$

6 Expand and simplify:

   a $(3+\sqrt{3})^2$ **b** $(3\sqrt{2}+1)(2-\sqrt{2})$

   c $(3\sqrt{2}+\sqrt{3})(3\sqrt{2}-\sqrt{3})$

7 Expand and simplify: $(2x-1)^2 - (x+2)^2$

Chapter 5

Interpreting and drawing graphs

Contents:
- **A** Interpreting graphs and charts
- **B** Travel graphs
- **C** Information from line graphs
- **D** Using technology to graph data

A INTERPRETING GRAPHS AND CHARTS

Newspapers and magazines contain graphs, charts and tables which display information. It is important to interpret the information correctly. We often use **percentages** in our analysis.

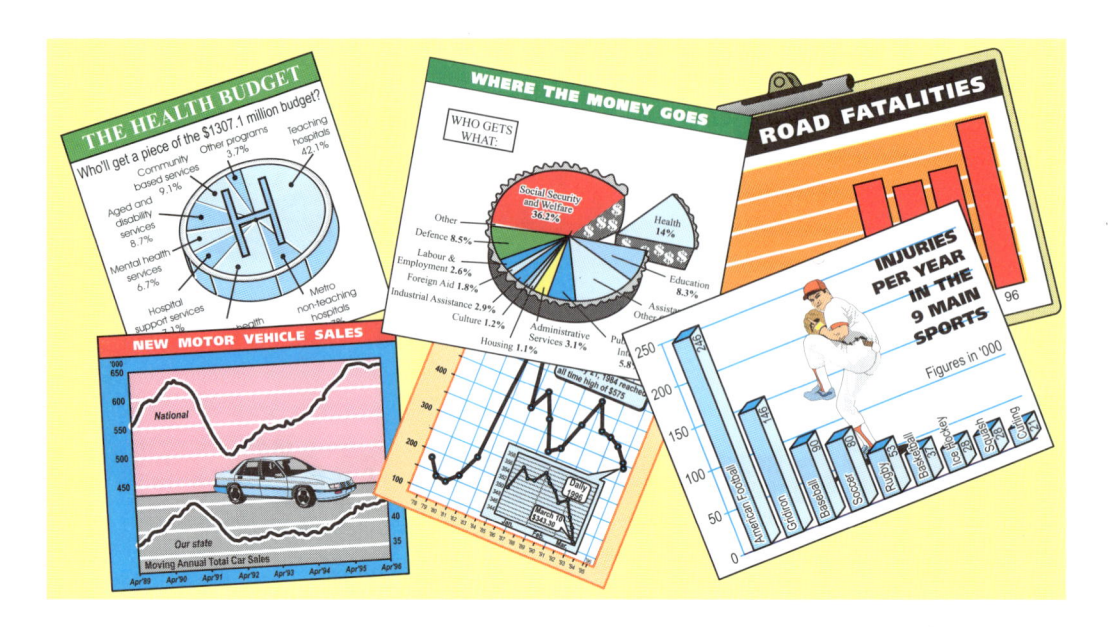

Example 1

The bar graph shows the number of different items sold in an electrical goods store in a given month.

a How many DVD players were sold for the month?

b How many more computers were sold than television sets?

c What percentage of the items sold were cooling fans?

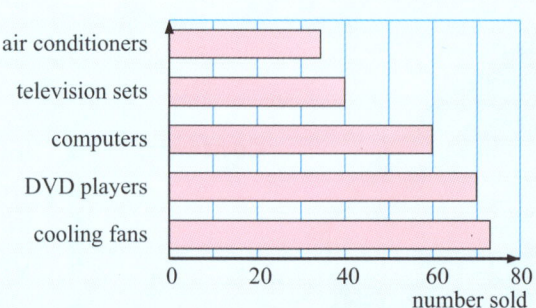

a 70 DVD players were sold.

b 60 computers were sold. 40 television sets were sold.
∴ 20 more computers than television sets were sold.

c 34 air conditioners, 40 television sets, 60 computers, 70 DVD players and 73 cooling fans were sold.
So, the total is $34 + 40 + 60 + 70 + 73 = 277$
∴ cooling fans as a percentage of total items sold $= \dfrac{73}{277} \times 100\% \approx 26.4\%$

EXERCISE 5A

1 The graph shows attendances at various Friday night events at an Arts festival.

  a Which event was most popular?

  b How many more people attended the Drama than attended Modern Dance?

  c What percentage of people attended the Jazz?

2

  a What information is contained in the graph alongside?

  b How many Daily News papers were sold in:

    i March 2006   **ii** March 2007?

  c During which 6 month period did net sales increase the most?

  d What was the increase in sales from:

    i September 2004 to September 2005

    ii September 2005 to September 2006?

  e Find the September 2005 sales as a percentage of the September 2007 sales.

3 **a** Estimate the median house price in 2008 in:

    i London   **ii** Liverpool

  b How much higher is the median house price in Edinburgh than in Glasgow?

  c What percentage is the median Birmingham price of the median Liverpool price, in the year 2008?

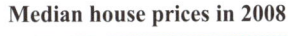

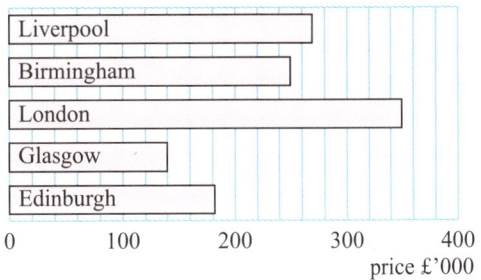

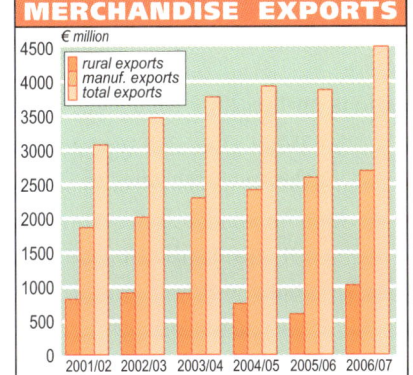

4 According to the graph:

  a **i** What was the total value of exports in 2006/07?

    ii What percentage of the total exports in 2006/07 were rural exports?

  b In which years was the value of manufacturing exports more than triple the value of rural exports?

  c In which year was the value of rural exports at its lowest? Can you suggest a possible reason for this?

Example 2

Use the pie chart alongside to answer the following questions regarding the health budget.

a How much money was allocated to the health care budget?

b What percentage of Australian budget was spent on mental health services?

c Which service received the most money?

d How much money was spent on:
   i hospital support services
   ii other programs?

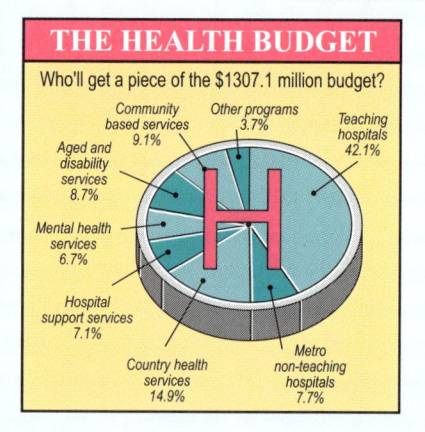

THE HEALTH BUDGET
Who'll get a piece of the $1307.1 million budget?
- Community based services 9.1%
- Other programs 3.7%
- Teaching hospitals 42.1%
- Aged and disability services 8.7%
- Mental health services 6.7%
- Hospital support services 7.1%
- Country health services 14.9%
- Metro non-teaching hospitals 7.7%

---

a $1307.1 million was allocated to the health care budget.

b 6.7% of the budget was allocated to mental health services.

c Teaching hospitals received the most money, with 42.1% of the budget.

d
   i 7.1% of $1307.1 million
   $= \frac{7.1}{100} \times \$1307.1$ million
   $\approx \$92.80$ million

   ii 3.7% of $1307.1 million
   $= \frac{3.7}{100} \times \$1307.1$ million
   $\approx \$48.36$ million

---

5 Use the pie chart below to answer the following questions on Australia's immigrants.

a Which region supplied most of the immigrants?

b What percentage of Australian immigrants arrived from:
   i New Zealand
   ii South Africa?

c If the total number of immigrants was 31 600:
   i how many arrived from the Philippines
   ii how many arrived from Europe?

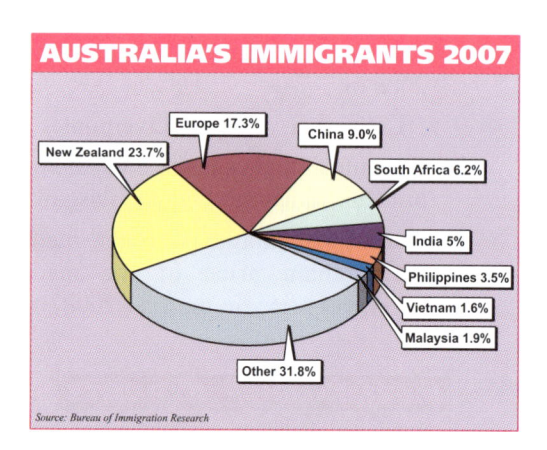

AUSTRALIA'S IMMIGRANTS 2007
- Europe 17.3%
- New Zealand 23.7%
- China 9.0%
- South Africa 6.2%
- India 5%
- Philippines 3.5%
- Vietnam 1.6%
- Malaysia 1.9%
- Other 31.8%

Source: Bureau of Immigration Research

6 Use this pie chart to answer the following questions on the 2007 road toll.

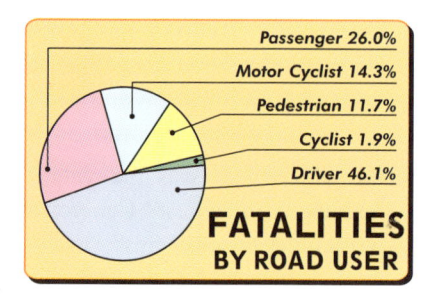

FATALITIES BY ROAD USER
- Passenger 26.0%
- Motor Cyclist 14.3%
- Pedestrian 11.7%
- Cyclist 1.9%
- Driver 46.1%

a What road user type accounted for the most fatalities in 2007?

b The road toll for 2007 was 154. Of those killed on the road, how many were:
   i passengers
   ii motor cyclists
   iii pedestrians?

7 The graph alongside displays the results of a national phone-in of children aged six to sixteen as to what they do at home between 3 pm and 6 pm.

   a Use the graph to determine the percentage of children who:

   i watch TV, videos, play with computers or listen to music

   ii spend time with friends, siblings or pets.

   b If 240 children were surveyed:

   i how many do schoolwork

   ii how many more spend time on the phone rather than do chores?

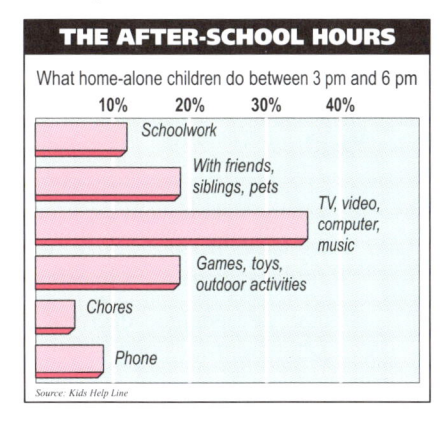

Example 3

The column graph shows the number of women diagnosed with breast cancer from 1999 to 2007. Use the graph to determine:

a the number of women diagnosed in 2007

b how many more women were diagnosed in 2004 then in 2002

c the percentage increase in cases diagnosed from 2001 to 2006.

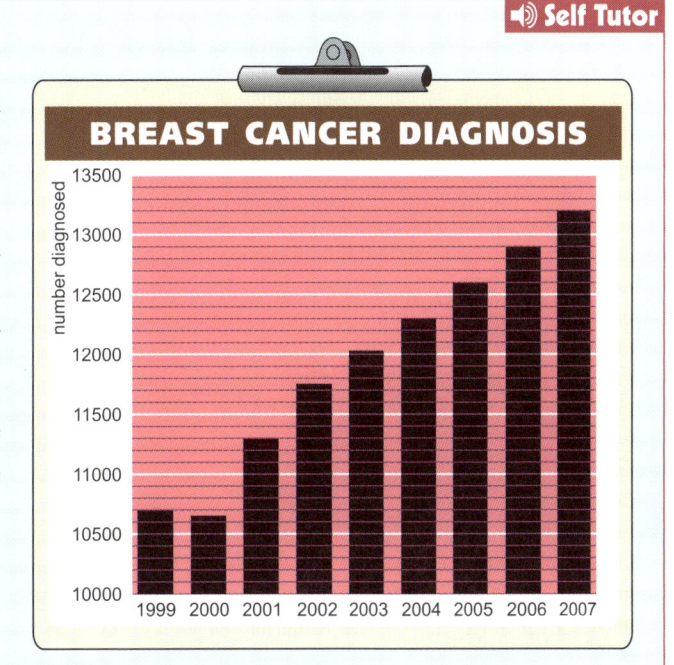

---

a The number of women diagnosed in 2007 was 13 200.

b The number diagnosed in 2004 was 12 300.
The number diagnosed in 2002 was 11 750.
∴ 12 300 − 11 750 = 550 more cases were diagnosed in 2004.

c The number of cases in 2001 was 11 300.
The number of cases in 2006 was 12 900.
∴ the increase = 12 900 − 11 300 = 1600
∴ percentage increase $\frac{1600}{11\,300} \times 100\% \approx 14.2\%$

Note: The concept of a **multiplier** could also be used in **c**.

> Percentage change = $\frac{\text{change}}{\text{original}} \times 100\%$

8 The graph alongside indicates the number of speeding offences over a 10 year period. Determine:

  a the decrease in the number of offences from 2003 to 2007

  b the percentage decrease in offences from 2003 to 2007

  c which year showed the greatest increase in offences from the previous year

  d the percentage decrease in offences from 2002 to 2007.

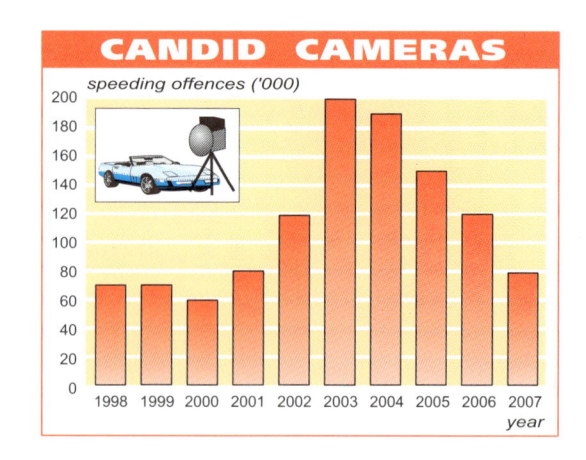

9 This line graph shows the variation in the value a gram of gold over a number of years. Determine:

  a the year during which the greatest increase in value occurred

  b the value in July
    i 2004
    ii 2006

  c the percentage increase from the start of 2004 to the end of 2005

  d the percentage decrease from April 2006 to October 2006.

10 The table alongside compares the consumption of a range of foods in India for 1988 and 2007.

  a For which foods has the consumption increased from 1988 to 2007?

  b From the table, what is the change in the consumption of wheat over this time period?

  c Calculate the percentage decrease over this time period in the consumption of:
    i rice   **ii** pulses.

  d Calculate the percentage increase in the consumption of edible oils over this time period.

  e Do your calculations in **c** and **d** agree with the % change given in the table?

Food items	1988	2007	%Change
Consumption/Capita (kg/30 days)			
Rice	5.65	4.85	−14.2
Wheat	4.57	4.03	−11.7
Cereals	11.05	9.44	−14.5
Pulses	1.06	0.86	−18.8
Dairy	4.52	5.25	16.2
Edible Oils	0.56	0.69	23.6
Meat/Fish/Eggs	2.01	2.49	23.8
Veg/Fruit	11.46	13.44	17.3
Sugar/Spices	1.63	1.46	−10.4

11 Sally is going to New Zealand for a holiday. She has a road map which shows this chart. Sally notices that the chart is made up of two triangles.

The bottom left triangle shows the distances between towns. For example, the distance between Auckland and Wellington is 666 km.

	Auckland	Hamilton	Palmerston North	Rotorua	Taupo	Wellington
Auckland		2:20	9:20	4:10	4:40	11:30
Hamilton	131		7:00	1:50	2:20	9:10
Palmerston North	453	412		6:05	4:40	2:35
Rotorua	239	108	341		1:25	8:15
Taupo	280	149	263	78		6:50
Wellington	666	535	145	464	386	

The top right triangle shows the times taken to drive safely between towns. For example, it takes 11 hours 30 minutes to drive between Auckland and Wellington.

a i How far is it between Auckland and Hamilton?
   ii How long would it take to drive this distance?

b i How long would it take to drive between Hamilton and Rotorua?
   ii How far apart are these two towns?

c i What is the shortest distance between towns given on the chart?
   ii What are the names of the towns?

d i Name the two towns with the same travelling times from Taupo and give their distances from Taupo.
   ii Name the two towns with the same travelling times from Hamilton and give their distances from Hamilton.
   iii Discuss why you do not always take the same time to travel the same distance on different roads.

B   TRAVEL GRAPHS

Suppose car A travels 120 kilometres in 1.5 hours.

Car A has average speed $= \dfrac{\text{distance}}{\text{time}}$

$= \frac{120}{1.5} = 80$ km per hour.

Now suppose car B travels 120 km in 1 hour.

Car B has average speed $= \dfrac{\text{distance}}{\text{time}}$

$= \frac{120}{1} = 120$ km per hour.

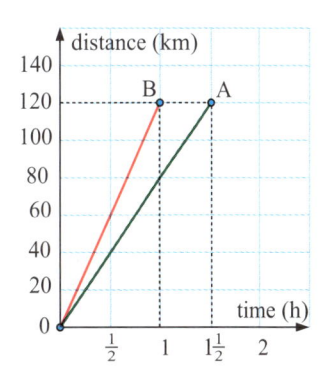

Car B is travelling much faster than Car A. We can observe this fact is noticeable on the graph alongside. The line for Car B is much steeper than that for car A.

Example 4

Consider the illustrated distance-time graph. Use it to describe a possible journey from home undertaken by a sales representative travelling in the country.

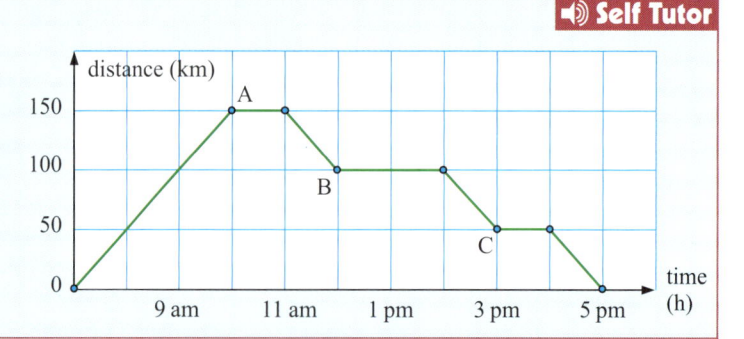

The sales representative leaves home at 7 am and travels 150 km to town A in 3 hours, where he spends an hour with customers.

He then travels 50 km back towards home to town B, where he arrives at 12 noon.

He spends an hour with customers and then has an hour for lunch.

At 2 pm he travels another 50 km back towards home and arrives at town C at 3 pm.

He spends an hour there with customers.

At 4 pm he travels 50 km back to his home, arriving there at 5 pm.

EXERCISE 5B

1 Thomas drives for 15 minutes to the supermarket, which is 15 km away. He shops for 30 minutes and then drives home, taking 15 minutes. Draw a *distance-time graph* of his journey.

2 The *distance-time graph* shown describes the journey of a family travelling from their home in Bangalore to Goa for a holiday. The distance is 560 km.

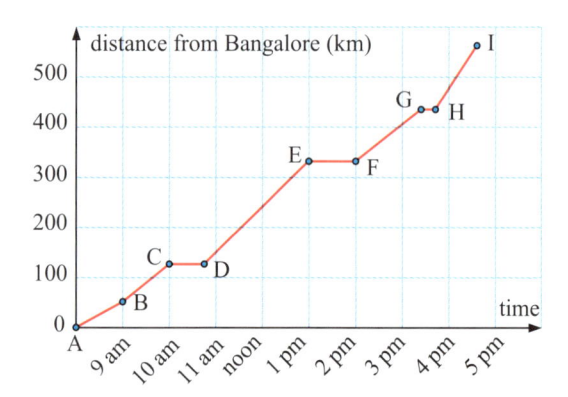

  a Describe their trip.

  b Explain where the following comments are made in the journey. You may need to organise them in the correct order first.

  i "We will have lunch now."
  ii "This is the fastest section."
  iii "At last we have arrived."
  iv "We are only stopping for petrol."
  v "This is the slowest section."
  vi "This is the longest section."

3 The annual *Hare versus Tortoise* 1 km race took place at the end of spring (so the tortoise was fully awake after his winter hibernation). The tortoise plodded on at a steady 50 metres per minute while the hare raced at an amazing 400 metres per minute. Unfortunately the hare could only do this for 30 seconds at a time, then required a rest for 5 minutes before his next run.

  a Who won this year?

b Construct graphs of the distances travelled by both the hare and the tortoise with time on the horizontal axis and distance travelled on the vertical axis. Hence justify your answer to **a** above.

c Last year the hare only had to rest for 3 minutes after each run. Who won last year?

d Construct a distance-time graph to justify your answer to **c**.

4 There are three routes from Summerville to Ingleside. Match the route descriptions to the appropriate *distance-time graphs*:

Route A: A two-lane highway direct with speed limit of 110 km per hour.
A thirty minute wait at bridge-works.

Route B: A winding mountain road with steep gradients and curves requiring travel at a constant slower speed.

Route C: A two-lane highway with speed limit of 110 km per hour and then a winding detour to avoid bridge-works.

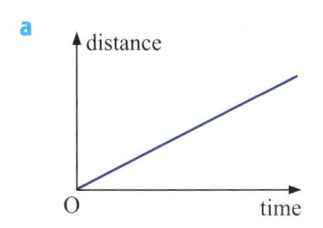

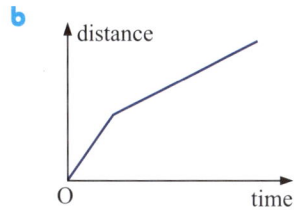

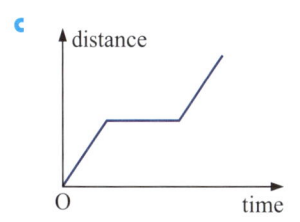

Example 5 — Self Tutor

The graph alongside indicates the distance a homing pigeon travelled from its point of release until it reached its home.

Use the graph to determine:

a the total length of the flight
b the time taken for the pigeon to reach home
c the time taken to fly the first 200 km
d the time taken to fly from the 240 km mark to the 400 km mark
e the average speed for the first 4 hours
f the average speed for the whole flight.

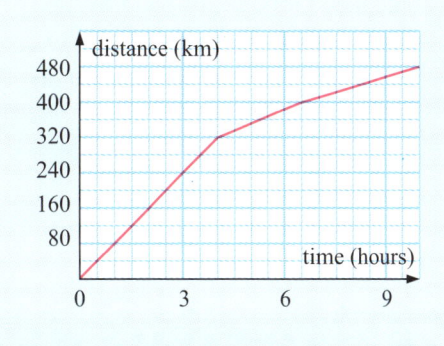

a Length of flight is 480 km.
b Time to reach home is 10 hours.
c Time for first 200 km is $2\frac{1}{2}$ hours.
d It takes 3 hours to fly 240 km. It takes $6\frac{1}{2}$ hours to fly 400 km.
∴ it takes $3\frac{1}{2}$ hours to fly from 240 km to 400 km.
e In the first 4 hours it flies 320 km
∴ average speed = $\frac{320}{4}$ = 80 km per hour.
f It travels a distance of 480 km in 10 hours
∴ average speed = $\frac{480}{10}$ = 48 km per hour.

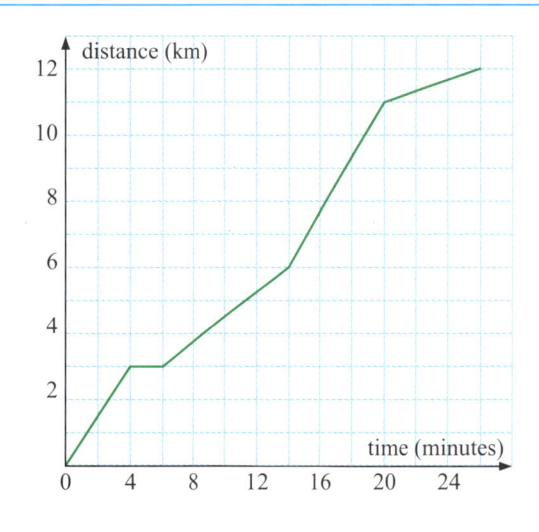

5 The graph alongside indicates the distance a cyclist must travel to work. Use the graph to determine:

- **a** the distance to work
- **b** the time taken to get to work
- **c** the distance travelled after
  - **i** 10 minutes
  - **ii** 17 minutes
- **d** the time taken to travel
  - **i** 6 km
  - **ii** 10 km
- **e** the average speed for the whole distance.

6 Two rally cars were involved in a handicap time trial. The distance-time graph indicates how far each has travelled.

Use the graph to determine:

- **a** the handicap advantage given to car Y
- **b** the distance travelled by each car
- **c** how far both cars had travelled when car X caught car Y
- **d** how long it took each car to travel 300 km
- **e** how much faster X completed the time trial than Y
- **f** the average speed of each car.

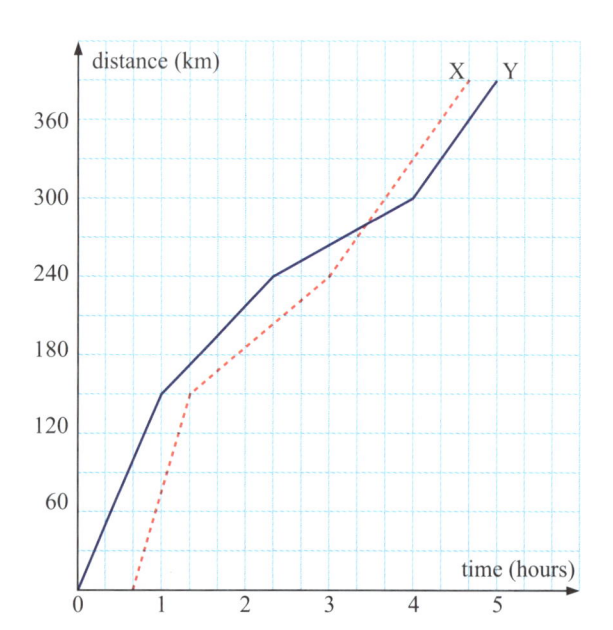

C   INFORMATION FROM LINE GRAPHS

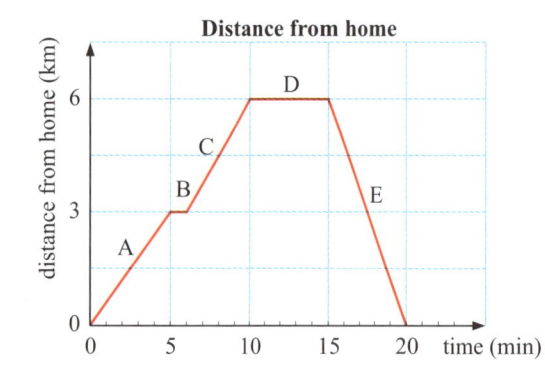

The graph shows Max's distance from his home when he drove to the hardware store to buy some paint.

A shows that he started out slowly.

B shows where he had to stop at traffic lights. His distance remains the same.

C shows that he continued towards the store faster than he was travelling earlier.

D shows the time when he was stopped at the store while he collected the paint. His distance remains the same.

E shows that he returned home at quite a fast speed.

When the graph is steeper, Max is travelling more distance in a particular time. He is thus travelling faster.

EXERCISE 5C

1 Match the graph to the story.

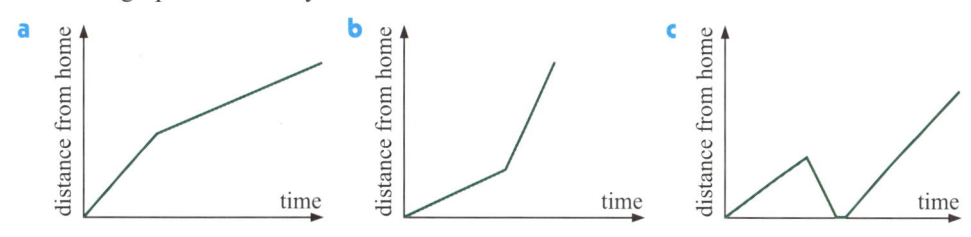

a, **b**, **c** (graphs of distance from home vs time)

A I am walking steadily to school. After a while I meet a friend and we walk together. We walk slower than when I was by myself.

B I am part-way to school when I remember that I have left my homework at home. I run back home to get it then run to school.

C I start to walk to school then I accept a ride with a friend.

2 Match the graph to the story.

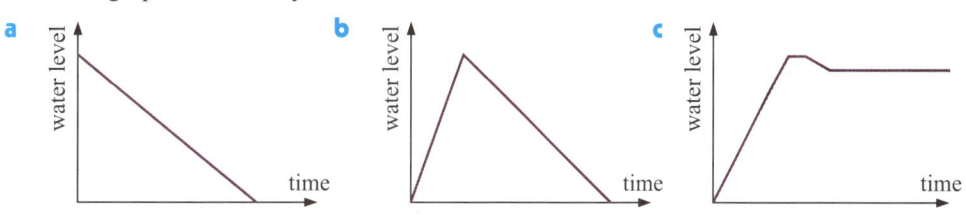

a, **b**, **c** (graphs of water level vs time)

A I fill a bucket with water. After a few minutes my dog drinks some of the water. I decide to leave the water in the bucket in case he wants a drink later.

B I quickly fill a bucket with water but the bucket is split and the water runs out.

C I start with a full bucket of water and pour the water slowly over my seedlings until the bucket is empty.

D USING TECHNOLOGY TO GRAPH DATA

Many special computer programs are used to help us organise and graph data.

Click on the icon to run the statistical graphing software.
Change the data in the table and see the effect on the graph.

STATISTICS PACKAGE

- Notice that the graph's heading and the labels on the axes can be changed.
- The type of graph can be changed by clicking on the icon to give the type that you want.

Experiment with the package and use it whenever possible.

INVESTIGATION — SPREADSHEETS FOR GRAPHING DATA

The colours of cars in a supermarket carpark are recorded below. Suppose you want to draw a frequency column graph of this data.

Colour	white	red	blue	green	other
Frequency	38	27	19	18	11

The following steps using a computer spreadsheet enable you to do this quickly and easily.

Step 1: Start a new spreadsheet, type in the table, and then highlight the area as shown.

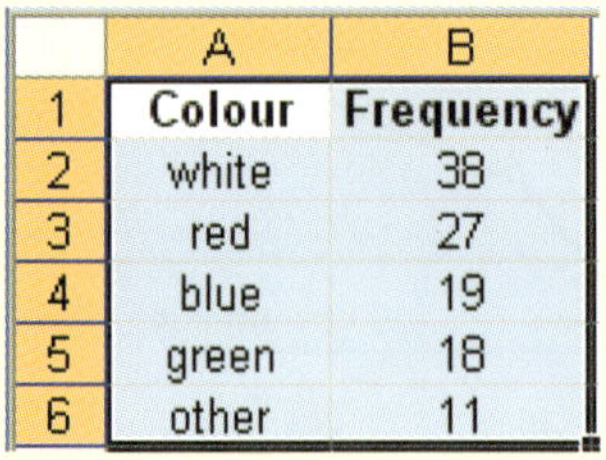

Step 2: Click on [Chart Wizard] from the menu bar.

Step 3: Choose Standard Types, Chart type: Column.

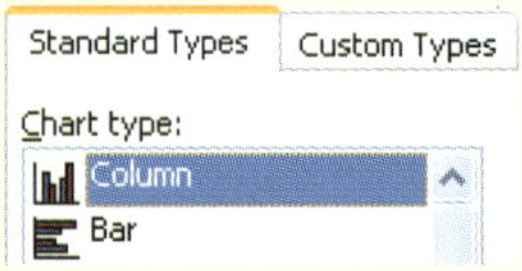

This is probably already highlighted. Click Finish.

You should get: [frequency column graph]

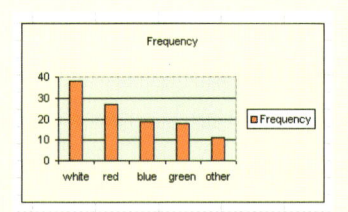

This demonstration takes you through all the steps. DEMO

Now suppose the colours of cars in the neighbouring car park were also recorded. The results are summarised in the table alongside.

Colour	white	red	blue	green	other
Frequency 1	38	27	19	18	11
Frequency 2	15	18	21	9	3

Step 4: Into the C column type the *Frequency 2* data and highlight the three columns as shown.

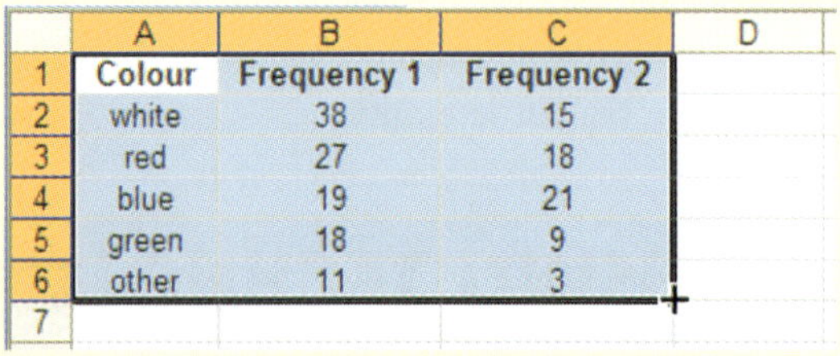

Step 5: Click on [Chart Wizard] then Standard Types, Chart type: Column.

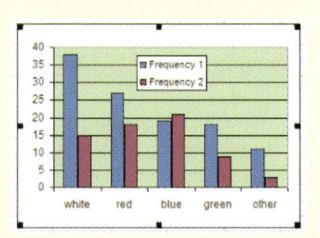

Step 6: Choose Chart sub-type, then Finish.

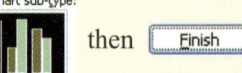

Step 7: Experiment with other types of graphs and data.

What to do:

1 Gather statistics of your own or use data from questions in the previous exercise. Use the spreadsheet to draw an appropriate statistical graph of the data.

2 Find out how to adjust labels, scales, legends, and other features of the graph.

EXERCISE 5D

1 The given data is to be displayed on a pie chart.

   a Find the sector angles to the nearest degree for each category.

   b Use technology to draw the pie chart for this data.

Favourite colour	Frequency
Green	38
Blue	34
Red	29
Purple	21
Other	34

2 In a pie chart on *leisure activities* the sector angle for *roller-blading* is 34° and this represents 136 students.

   a The sector angle for *cycling* is 47°. How many students cycle for leisure?

   b If 38 students *collect stamps or coins*, what sector angle would represent them?

   c How many students were used in the sample?

3 After leaving school, four graduates compare their weekly incomes at 5 year intervals. Their incomes are shown in the table alongside.

	After 5 years	After 10 years
Kaylene	685	2408
Harry	728	1345
Wei	820	2235
Matthew	1056	1582

   a Draw side-by-side column graphs to represent the data.

   b Draw back-to-back bar graphs to represent the data.

   c Find the percentage increase for each person for the data given.

   d Two of the four gained university qualifications. Which ones are they likely to be?

REVIEW SET 5A

1 The pie chart alongside illustrates the percentage of capital works expenditure spent in different areas. The total expenditure was $240 million.

   a Determine the amount of money spent on:

   i education   ii law and order.

   b How much more was spent on education than law and order?

   c If the total expenditure was increased to $300 million, calculate:

   i the percentage increase in expenditure

   ii the increase in expenditure for health.

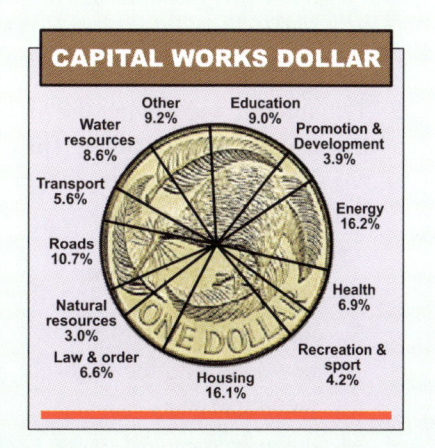

CAPITAL WORKS DOLLAR

Other 9.2%
Education 9.0%
Water resources 8.6%
Promotion & Development 3.9%
Transport 5.6%
Energy 16.2%
Roads 10.7%
Health 6.9%
Natural resources 3.0%
Law & order 6.6%
Recreation & sport 4.2%
Housing 16.1%

2  The graph alongside shows the representatives of a local council according to gender and age.

WHO'S ON COUNCIL
(Bar graph showing males and females by age group)
- 18-24: Males 7, Females 2
- 25-34: Males 20, Females 13
- 35-44: Males 62, Females 26
- 45-54: Males 147, Females 58
- 55-64: Males 204, Females 72
- 65+: Males 107, Females 27

Source: State Electoral Office

a Determine the total number of representatives.
b Determine the percentage of representatives who are female.
c Determine the percentage of representatives who are 45 years of age or older.
d Which age group shows the greatest difference between numbers of males and numbers of females?
e What percentage of representatives in the 65+ age group are female?

3 This graph shows what the average Australian owns in assets. It includes the value of houses, cars, superannuation, investments and savings.

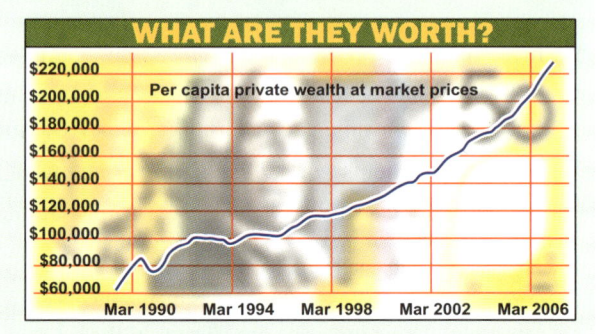

WHAT ARE THEY WORTH?
Per capita private wealth at market prices
(Line graph from Mar 1990 to Mar 2006, values from $60,000 to $220,000)

a Estimate the assets of the average Australian in:
  i March 1990
  ii March 2006
b Calculate the percentage increase in wealth between March 1990 and March 2006.
c Which 4-year period shows the greatest increase in wealth? Explain your answer.

4 a Briefly describe the information presented in the graph.
b At what time was the UV radiation index extreme?
c What was the UV index at 3 pm?
d Between what times was the UV index considered very high or extreme?

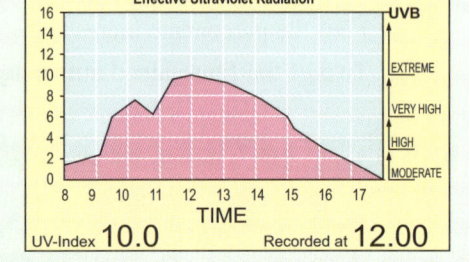

Effective Ultraviolet Radiation
(Graph showing UV index from time 8 to 17, with levels: MODERATE, HIGH, VERY HIGH, EXTREME, UVB)
UV-Index 10.0   Recorded at 12.00

5 Two aircraft were flying the air route from A to B but in opposite directions. Their distances from A are shown on the graph alongside. Use the graph to determine:

a the distance from A to B
b in which direction the flight was completed more rapidly, and by how much
c how long into the flight the planes were when they crossed
d the average speed of the flight in each direction.

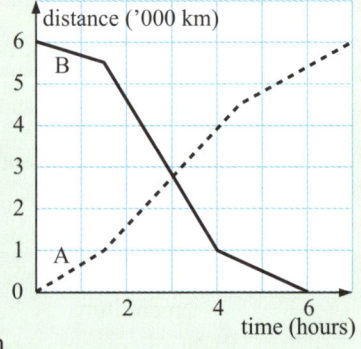

(Graph: distance ('000 km) vs time (hours), showing curves A and B)

REVIEW SET 5B

1 A small business classified its expenditure into five areas. The pie chart shows the percentage of expenditure in each area.

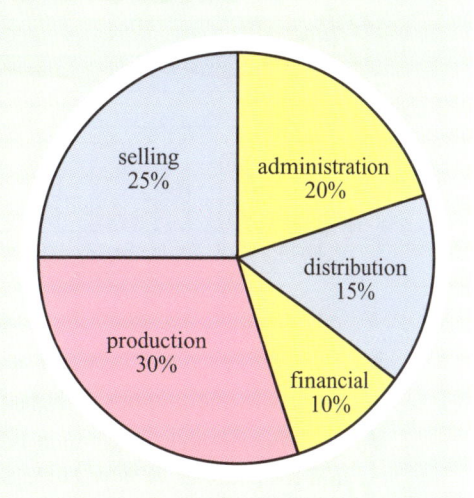

   a Which area accounted for the largest proportion of expenditure?

   b If the total expenditure was €2.5 million, determine:

      i the cost of administration

      ii by how much the expenditure on production exceeded that on selling.

   c The company decided to reduce expenditure from €2.5 million to €2 million. Calculate the percentage decrease in spending.

Pie chart: selling 25%, administration 20%, distribution 15%, financial 10%, production 30%.

2

SPEEDING FINES

Year	Total detections	Total revenue
2004	268,964	£33,881,402
2005	293,351	£35,163,339
2006	272,907	£34,630,818
2007	168,556	£23,676,638

   a What information is shown in the table?

   b Which year showed the greatest number of detections?

   c What was the highest total revenue?

   d Comment on the data for the year 2007.

3

   a What information is contained in the pie chart shown?

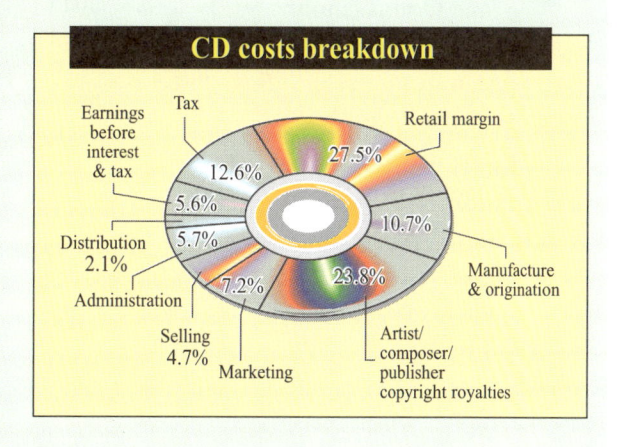

   b What factor accounts for most of the cost of a compact disc?

   c What factor accounts for the least?

   d What percentage of the cost of a CD goes to artist, composer, publisher, and copyright royalties?

CD costs breakdown: Tax 12.6%, Earnings before interest & tax 5.6%, Distribution 2.1%, Administration 5.7%, Selling 4.7%, Marketing 7.2%, Artist/composer/publisher copyright royalties 23.8%, Manufacture & origination 10.7%, Retail margin 27.5%.

   e If you pay $29.95 for a CD in a music shop, how much goes towards:

      i marketing   **ii** manufacture and origination   **iii** tax?

   f Add up all the percentages given in the pie chart. Explain your answer.

4

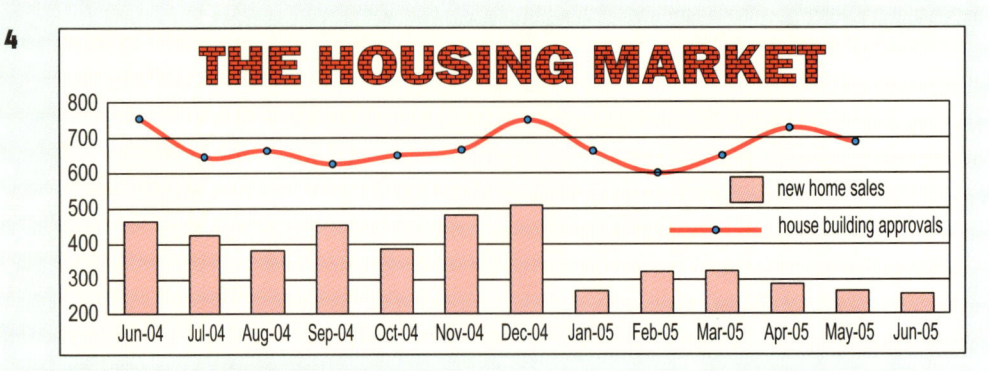

Graph: THE HOUSING MARKET — bar chart of new home sales and line graph of house building approvals from Jun-04 to Jun-05.

    a Which month recorded the greatest number of new home sales?

    b Find the difference between new home sales in June '04 and January '05.

    c What was the number of house building approvals in October '04?

    d Find the greatest difference between the number of house building approvals and the number of new home sales in the period June '04 to February '05.

    e Comment on the sales figures in the two periods June '04 to December '04, and January '05 to June '05.

5 The graph alongside describes the journeys of families between Naples and Turin.

Use the graph to determine:

    a the distance from Naples to Turin

    b how much quicker the Gallelli family completed the trip than the Ortuso family

    c the average speed for each family over the first three hours

    d the average speed for each family over the whole trip.

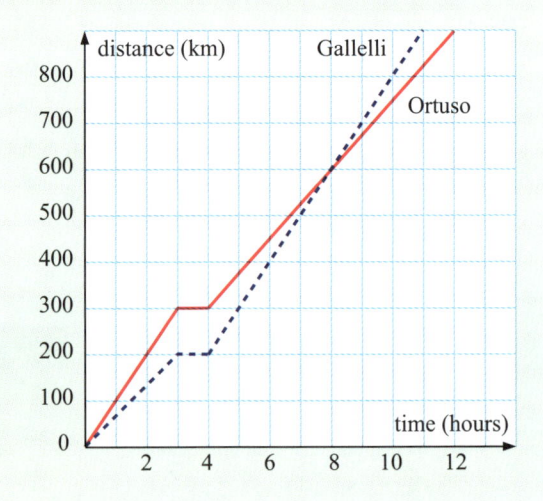

Chapter 6
Solving equations

Contents:
- **A** The solution of an equation
- **B** Maintaining balance
- **C** Isolating the unknown
- **D** Formal solution of linear equations
- **E** Equations with repeated unknowns
- **F** Fractional equations
- **G** Unknown in the denominator

Many mathematical situations can be described using an **equation**. This is a formal statement that one expression is equal to another. The expressions are connected by the **equals sign** $=$.

An **algebraic equation** is an equation which involves at least one variable.

For example, $3x + 5 = 8$ is an algebraic equation.

We read the symbol $=$ as 'equals' or 'is equal to'.

By following a formal procedure, we can **solve** the equation to find the value of the variable which makes it true. In this case we see that x must be 1, since $3 + 5 = 8$.

LINEAR EQUATIONS

A **linear equation** contains at least a variable which can only be raised to the power 1.

For example, $3x + 5 = 8$, $\frac{1}{2}x - 3 = 2$ and $\frac{1+x}{3} = x$ are linear equations

whereas $x^2 - 3x + 2 = 0$, $\frac{1}{x} = \sqrt{x}$, and $x^3 = 8$ are not linear equations.

SIDES OF AN EQUATION

The **left hand side** (LHS) of an equation is on the left of the $=$ sign.

The **right hand side** (RHS) of an equation is on the right of the $=$ sign.

For example, $\underbrace{3x + 5}_{\text{LHS}} = \underbrace{8}_{\text{RHS}}$

OPENING PROBLEM

If possible, solve the following equations:

a $2x - 3 = 5$ **b** $x^2 - x = 0$ **c** $x - 1 = x$

Do equations always have a solution?

If there is a solution, is there always only one possible solution?

A THE SOLUTION OF AN EQUATION

The **solution** of a linear equation is the value of the variable which makes the equation true. In other words, it makes the **left hand side** (LHS) equal to the **right hand side** (RHS).

In the example $3x + 5 = 8$ above, the only value of the variable x which makes the equation true is $x = 1$.

$$\begin{aligned}
\text{When } x = 1, \quad \text{LHS} &= 3x + 5 \\
&= 3 \times 1 + 5 \\
&= 3 + 5 \\
&= 8 \\
&= \text{RHS} \quad \therefore \text{ LHS} = \text{RHS}
\end{aligned}$$

Simple linear equations involving one unknown may often be solved either by inspection or by trial and error.

Example 1 — Self Tutor

The solution of the equation $3x - 7 = -4$ is one of the following integers $\{-1, 1, 3\}$. Find the solution by trial and error.

We *substitute* each possible solution into the LHS until it equals -4.

$$\begin{array}{lll}
\text{When } x = -1, & \text{when } x = 1, & \text{when } x = 3, \\
3x - 7 & 3x - 7 & 3x - 7 \\
= 3 \times (-1) - 7 & = 3 \times 1 - 7 & = 3 \times 3 - 7 \\
= -3 - 7 & = 3 - 7 & = 9 - 7 \\
= -10 & = -4 & = 2
\end{array}$$

$\therefore$ the solution is $x = 1$.

EXERCISE 6A

1 The solution of each of the following equations is one of the given possibilities. Find the solution by trial and error.

  a $2x - 9 = 5$ $\{3, 5, 7\}$
  b $3 - a = -1$ $\{2, 4, 6\}$
  c $\dfrac{x+6}{2} = 1$ $\{-4, -2, 0\}$
  d $\dfrac{6}{1+y} = 3$ $\{1, 2, 3\}$

2 Which of the following equations are:
  A true for *exactly one* value of x
  B true for *two* values of x
  C true for *all* values of x
  D *never* true
  E true for *all* values of x except 0?

  a $x + 3 = 5$
  b $x^2 = 0$
  c $\dfrac{1}{x} = 0$
  d $2x = 11$
  e $x^2 = 9$
  f $x - x = 0$
  g $x - 1 = x$
  h $2 + 5x = 12$
  i $x - x^2 = 0$
  j $3x \times 2x = 6x^2$
  k $\dfrac{1}{x} \times x = 1$
  l $2 - \dfrac{1}{x} = 3$

B — MAINTAINING BALANCE

For any equation the LHS must always equal the RHS. We can therefore think of an equation as a set of scales that must always be in **balance**.

The balance of an equation is maintained provided we perform the same operation on **both sides** of the equals sign.

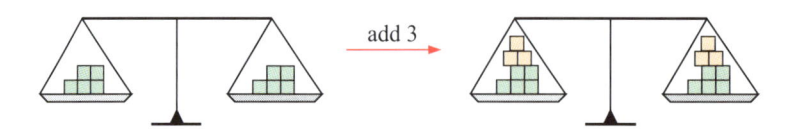

Any mathematical operation we perform on one side of an equation we must also perform on the other side.

Example 2

What equation results when:

a adding 5 to both sides of $2x - 5 = 7$
b subtracting 3 from both sides of $5x + 3 = 18$?

a $\qquad 2x - 5 = 7$
$\therefore \quad 2x - 5 + 5 = 7 + 5$
$\therefore \qquad 2x = 12$

b $\qquad 5x + 3 = 18$
$\therefore \quad 5x + 3 - 3 = 18 - 3$
$\therefore \qquad 5x = 15$

Example 3

What equation results when:

a both sides of $\dfrac{3x - 2}{4} = -1$ are multiplied by 4
b both sides of $5x = -15$ are divided by 5?

a $\qquad \dfrac{3x - 2}{4} = -1$
$\therefore \quad 4 \times \dfrac{3x - 2}{4} = 4 \times -1$
$\therefore \quad 3x - 2 = -4$

b $\qquad 5x = -15$
$\therefore \quad \dfrac{5x}{5} = \dfrac{-15}{5}$
$\therefore \qquad x = -3$

EXERCISE 6B

1 What equation results from *adding*:

    a 6 to both sides of $x - 6 = 4$
    b 7 to both sides of $x - 7 = 6$
    c 11 to both sides of $2x - 11 = 3$
    d 13 to both sides of $3x - 13 = -2$?

2 What equation results from *subtracting*:

    a 2 from both sides of $x + 2 = 3$ **b** 4 from both sides of $x + 4 = -2$

    c 5 from both sides of $2x + 5 = 0$ **d** 9 from both sides of $3x + 9 = -1$?

3 What equation results from *multiplying* both sides of:

    a $x = -3$ by 3   **b** $3x = 1$ by 5   **c** $\frac{x}{2} = 4$ by 2

    d $\frac{x}{4} = -1$ by 4   **e** $\frac{x}{-3} = -2$ by -3 **f** $\frac{x}{-10} = 4$ by -10?

4 What equation results from *dividing* both sides of:

    a $3x = 12$ by 3   **b** $-5x = 30$ by -5

    c $2x + 8 = 0$ by 2   **d** $3x - 9 = 24$ by 3

    e $4(x + 2) = -12$ by 4   **f** $-6(x - 1) = -24$ by -6?

C   ISOLATING THE UNKNOWN

In order to solve an equation, we need to isolate the variable or unknown on one side of the equation. Before we can do this, however, we need to understand how the expression containing the unknown is built up.

For example, consider the expression $3x + 5$. It can be **built up** as follows.

Start with x, multiply by 3 to give $3x$, then add 5 to give $3x + 5$.

Remember that the rule of BEDMAS must be applied. We need to build up an expression in brackets first. A fraction bar acts like a bracket and implies division.

Example 4   ◀) Self Tutor

Show how to 'build up' the expression $\frac{x + 2}{3} - 1$.

We start with x.	x
We then add 2.	$x + 2$
We divide the result by 3.	$\frac{x + 2}{3}$
We then subtract 1.	$\frac{x + 2}{3} - 1$

We **isolate the unknown** on one side of the equation by **reversing** the building up process. To do this we use **inverse operations**. Addition and subtraction are inverse operations; so are multiplication and division.

So, consider the expression $\frac{x + 2}{3} - 1$ in **Example 4**.

To 'build up' the expression we performed the operations: $+2$, $\div 3$, -1.

138   SOLVING EQUATIONS   (Chapter 6)

So, to isolate x in $\dfrac{x+2}{3} - 1$ we perform the inverses of these operations in the reverse order, i.e., $+1$, $\times 3$, -2.

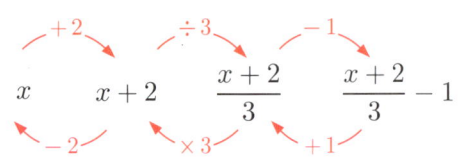

$x \xrightarrow{+2} x+2 \xrightarrow{\div 3} \dfrac{x+2}{3} \xrightarrow{-1} \dfrac{x+2}{3} - 1$

(reverse: -2, $\times 3$, $+1$)

$+$ and $-$ are inverse operations, and $\times$ and $\div$ are inverse operations.

This means that $\dfrac{x+2}{3} - 1$ becomes $\dfrac{x+2}{3}$ {adding 1}

then $\dfrac{x+2}{3}$ becomes $x+2$ { $\times$ by 3}

then $x+2$ becomes x {taking 2}.

EXERCISE 6C

1 Show how to 'build up' the expression:

a $5x + 2$
b $-x + 7$
c $5(x+6)$
d $8(x-3)$
e $\dfrac{x+2}{3}$
f $\dfrac{x-4}{5}$
g $\dfrac{x}{7} + 2$
h $\dfrac{x}{3} - 4$
i $\dfrac{-2x+1}{3}$
j $\dfrac{3x-4}{2}$
k $\dfrac{x+6}{3} + 5$
l $\dfrac{2x-1}{4} - 11$

2 Explain how to isolate x in the following:

a $x + 5$
b $x - 7$
c $2x$
d $\dfrac{x}{5}$
e $3x$
f $\dfrac{x}{4}$
g $x - 6$
h $-x + 11$
i $2x + 1$
j $3x - 2$
k $5x + 7$
l $1 - 2x$
m $2 - 4x$
n $17 - 3x$
o $\dfrac{x}{3} + 2$
p $\dfrac{x}{4} - 2$
q $\dfrac{3x-1}{2}$
r $\dfrac{2x+5}{3}$
s $\dfrac{x+1}{3} - 2$
t $\dfrac{x+3}{2} + 5$
u $\tfrac{2}{3}x + 1$
v $6 - \tfrac{3}{4}x$
w $\tfrac{1}{2}(6x - 5)$
x $\tfrac{1}{3}(4x + 1)$

D FORMAL SOLUTION OF LINEAR EQUATIONS

When we use the $=$ sign between two algebraic expressions we have an equation which is in **balance**. Whatever we do to one side of the equation, we must do the same to the other side to **maintain the balance**.

SOLVING EQUATIONS (Chapter 6) 139

Compare the balance of weights:

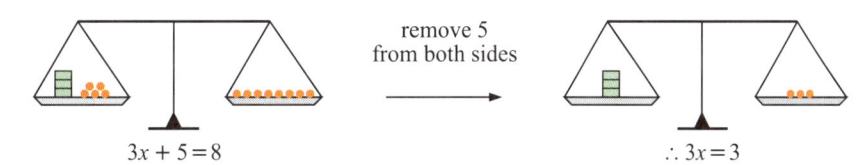

$3x + 5 = 8$ → remove 5 from both sides → $\therefore 3x = 3$

As we perform the inverse operations necessary to **isolate the unknown**, we must perform the same operations on the other side to maintain the balance.

Consider how the expression has been built up and then isolate the unknown by using **inverse operations** in **reverse order**.

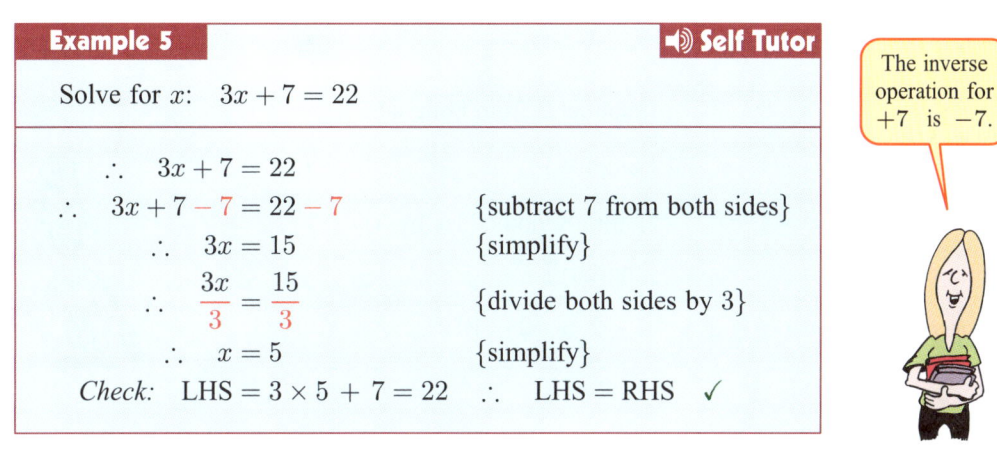

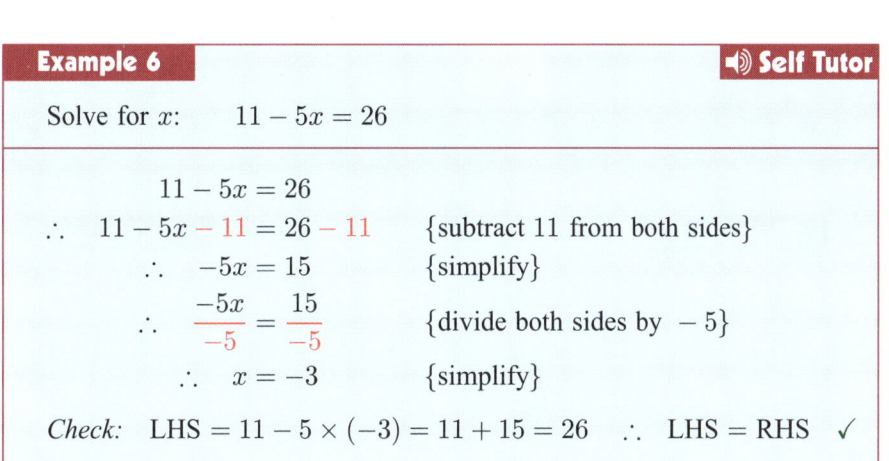

Example 5 ◀) Self Tutor

Solve for x: $3x + 7 = 22$

$\therefore \quad 3x + 7 = 22$
$\therefore \quad 3x + 7 - 7 = 22 - 7$ {subtract 7 from both sides}
$\therefore \quad 3x = 15$ {simplify}
$\therefore \quad \dfrac{3x}{3} = \dfrac{15}{3}$ {divide both sides by 3}
$\therefore \quad x = 5$ {simplify}

Check: LHS $= 3 \times 5 + 7 = 22$ $\therefore$ LHS = RHS ✓

The inverse operation for $+7$ is -7.

Example 6 ◀) Self Tutor

Solve for x: $11 - 5x = 26$

$11 - 5x = 26$
$\therefore \quad 11 - 5x - 11 = 26 - 11$ {subtract 11 from both sides}
$\therefore \quad -5x = 15$ {simplify}
$\therefore \quad \dfrac{-5x}{-5} = \dfrac{15}{-5}$ {divide both sides by -5}
$\therefore \quad x = -3$ {simplify}

Check: LHS $= 11 - 5 \times (-3) = 11 + 15 = 26$ $\therefore$ LHS = RHS ✓

EXERCISE 6D

1 Solve for x:

a $x + 3 = 0$
b $3x = -9$
c $3x + 6 = 0$
d $3x - 4 = -6$
e $5x + 8 = 18$
f $4x - 9 = 1$
g $8x - 7 = 9$
h $3x + 6 = -7$
i $6 + 7x = -1$
j $9 = 3x + 7$
k $6x - 7 = -1$
l $-1 = 2x + 6$

2 Solve for x:

   a $6 - x = -5$ **b** $-4x = 15$ **c** $3 - 2x = 7$

   d $5 - 4x = -7$ **e** $3 - 7x = -2$ **f** $17 - 2x = -1$

   g $11 = 3 - 2x$ **h** $15 - 2x = -1$ **i** $8 = 3 - 2x$

   j $6 = -1 - 7x$ **k** $-15 = 3 - 6x$ **l** $11 = -4 - 3x$

Example 7   *Self Tutor*

Solve for x: $\dfrac{x}{3} + 2 = -2$

$\dfrac{x}{3} + 2 = -2$

$\therefore \; \dfrac{x}{3} + 2 - 2 = -2 - 2$ {subtract 2 from both sides}

$\therefore \; \dfrac{x}{3} = -4$ {simplify}

$\therefore \; \dfrac{x}{3} \times 3 = -4 \times 3$ {multiply both sides by 3}

$\therefore \; x = -12$ {simplify}

Check: LHS $= -\dfrac{12}{3} + 2 = -4 + 2 = -2 =$ RHS. ✓

Remember that $\dfrac{x}{3}$ is really $x \div 3$ and the inverse operation of $\div 3$ is $\times 3$.

---

3 Solve for x:

   a $\dfrac{x}{2} = 5$ **b** $\dfrac{2x}{3} = -4$ **c** $\dfrac{x}{4} + 1 = -3$

   d $\dfrac{x}{3} - 2 = 1$ **e** $\dfrac{x-1}{2} = 1$ **f** $\dfrac{x+5}{3} = -1$

Example 8   *Self Tutor*

Solve for x: $\dfrac{4x+3}{5} = -2$

$\dfrac{4x+3}{5} = -2$

$\therefore \; 5 \times \dfrac{(4x+3)}{5} = -2 \times 5$ {multiply both sides by 5}

$\therefore \; 4x + 3 = -10$ {simplify}

$\therefore \; 4x + 3 - 3 = -10 - 3$ {subtract 3 from both sides}

$\therefore \; 4x = -13$ {simplify}

$\therefore \; \dfrac{4x}{4} = -\dfrac{13}{4}$ {divide both sides by 4}

$\therefore \; x = -3\tfrac{1}{4}$ {simplify}

4 Solve for x:

a $\dfrac{2x+7}{5} = 0$ **b** $\frac{1}{2}(1-3x) = -1$ **c** $\dfrac{1+4x}{7} = 3$

d $\dfrac{3x-1}{2} = 4$ **e** $\frac{1}{5}(4-3x) = -1$ **f** $\frac{1}{4}(1+2x) = -2$

INVESTIGATION 1 — SOLVING EQUATIONS BY SPREADSHEET

Consider the equation $5x + 2 = 2x + 14$.
To **solve** the equation, we need to find the value of x that makes the LHS equal to the RHS.
This can be done by trial and error using a spreadsheet.

What to do:

1 Open a new spreadsheet and enter the following:

	A	B	C
1	x	5x+2	2x+14
2	-3	=A2*5+2	=A2*2+14
3	=A2+1		
4			
5			
6		fill down	

2 **Fill** the formulae in A3, B2 and C2 **down** to Row 10.

3 Your spreadsheet should look like this:
If we examine Row 3, we find that when $x = -2$, $5x+2 = -8$ but $2x+14 = 10$.
So, $x = -2$ is *not a solution*, since the LHS $\neq$ RHS.
Use your spreadsheet to find the solution to $5x + 2 = 2x + 14$.

	A	B	C
1	x	5x+2	2x+14
2	-3	-13	8
3	-2	-8	10
4	-1	-3	12
5	0	2	14
6	1	7	16

4 Change your spreadsheet to find the solution to the equation $7x - 1 = 3x - 5$.

5 Change your spreadsheet to try to solve the equation $4x + 3 = x - 2$.

6 Why does the spreadsheet method fail to provide the solution of the equation in **5**? Can you adjust the spreadsheet so it will provide the solution? Do you think a spreadsheet will be a practical method of solution for more complicated equations?

E — EQUATIONS WITH A REPEATED UNKNOWN

Equations in which the unknown appears more than once need to be solved systematically.
We use the following procedure:

Step 1: If necessary **expand** any **brackets** and **collect like terms**.
Step 2: If necessary, remove the unknown from one side. Aim to be left with a **positive unknown** on one side.
Step 3: Use inverse operations to **isolate the unknown** and maintain balance.
Step 4: **Check** that your solution satisfies the equation, i.e., LHS = RHS.

Example 9

Solve for x: $5(x+1) - 2x = -7$

$5(x+1) - 2x = -7$
$\therefore \quad 5x + 5 - 2x = -7$ 　　{expand brackets}
$\therefore \quad 3x + 5 = -7$ 　　{collect like terms}
$\therefore \quad 3x + 5 - 5 = -7 - 5$ 　　{subtract 5 from both sides}
$\therefore \quad 3x = -12$ 　　{simplify}
$\therefore \quad \dfrac{3x}{3} = \dfrac{-12}{3}$ 　　{divide both sides by 3}
$\therefore \quad x = -4$ 　　{simplify}

EXERCISE 6E

1 Solve for x:
- **a** $4(x-1) - 2x = 2$
- **b** $2(x-3) + 3x = 9$
- **c** $5(x+2) - 2x = 4$
- **d** $3(2x+3) - 4x = -3$
- **e** $6(3x+2) - 5x = -1$
- **f** $-4(2x-1) + 5x = -12$

2 Solve for x:
- **a** $3(x+1) + 4(x+2) = -3$
- **b** $5(x+3) - 2(x-1) = 2$
- **c** $4(x-2) - (x+1) = 6$
- **d** $5(3+2x) + 2(x+1) = -7$
- **e** $3(2x+1) - 4(x+2) = 9$
- **f** $3(5x-2) - 2(3x-4) = 2$

Example 10

Solve for x: $5x + 2 = 3x - 5$

$5x + 2 = 3x - 5$
$\therefore \quad 5x + 2 - 3x = 3x - 5 - 3x$ 　　{subtract $3x$ from both sides}
$\therefore \quad 2x + 2 = -5$ 　　{simplify}
$\therefore \quad 2x + 2 - 2 = -5 - 2$ 　　{subtract 2 from both sides}
$\therefore \quad 2x = -7$ 　　{simplify}
$\therefore \quad \dfrac{2x}{2} = \dfrac{-7}{2}$ 　　{divide both sides by 2}
$\therefore \quad x = -3\tfrac{1}{2}$ 　　{simplify}

3 Solve for x:
- **a** $3x + 2 = x + 10$
- **b** $7x + 2 = 4x - 8$
- **c** $8x + 3 = 4x + 4$
- **d** $3x - 1 = 6x - 4$
- **e** $4x - 2 = 8x + 10$
- **f** $5 + 2x = 18 + 4x$

SOLVING EQUATIONS   (Chapter 6)   143

Example 11

Solve for x: $15 - 2x = 11 + x$

$15 - 2x = 11 + x$
$\therefore\ 15 - 2x + 2x = 11 + x + 2x$ {add $2x$ to both sides}
$\therefore\ 15 = 11 + 3x$ {simplify}
$\therefore\ 15 - 11 = 11 + 3x - 11$ {subtract 11 from both sides}
$\therefore\ 4 = 3x$ {simplify}
$\therefore\ \dfrac{4}{3} = \dfrac{3x}{3}$ {divide both sides by 3}
$\therefore\ x = 1\tfrac{1}{3}$ {simplify}

4 Solve for x:
- **a** $3x + 5 = 1 - x$
- **b** $6 + 2x = 15 - x$
- **c** $6 + x = 13 - 2x$
- **d** $9 - 2x = 12 - 7x$
- **e** $4 - 3x = 8 - x$
- **f** $9 - 3x = x + 2$

5 Solve for x:
- **a** $3(x + 1) - x = 15$
- **b** $5(x + 2) - 2x = 11$
- **c** $6(1 - 2x) = -4 - 7x$
- **d** $2(x + 4) + 8(x - 2) = 12$
- **e** $4(3x + 1) + 18 = x$
- **f** $7x - 2(x + 1) = 13$
- **g** $14x - 5(2x + 5) = 7$
- **h** $19 - (3 - x) = 5x$
- **i** $2x - 4(4 - 3x) = x + 10$
- **j** $2(x + 4) = 7 - (3 + x)$
- **k** $2(x - 6) + 7x = 3(3x - 4)$
- **l** $5(2x - 4) = 4x - 2(1 - 3x)$

F   FRACTIONAL EQUATIONS

More complicated fractional equations can be solved by:

- writing all fractions with the same **lowest common denominator (LCD)**, and then
- **equating numerators**.

To solve equations involving fractions, we make the denominators the same so that we can equate the numerators.

Example 12

Solve for x: $\dfrac{x}{3} = \dfrac{2}{5}$

$$\frac{x}{3} = \frac{2}{5} \qquad \text{has LCD of 15}$$

$$\therefore \quad \frac{x \times 5}{3 \times 5} = \frac{2 \times 3}{5 \times 3} \qquad \text{\{to achieve a common denominator\}}$$

$$\therefore \quad 5x = 6 \qquad \text{\{equating numerators\}}$$

$$\therefore \quad x = 1\tfrac{1}{5} \qquad \text{\{divide both sides by 5\}}$$

Example 13 ◀) Self Tutor

Solve for x: $\quad \dfrac{2x+3}{4} = \dfrac{x-2}{3}$

$$\frac{2x+3}{4} = \frac{x-2}{3} \qquad \text{has LCD of 12}$$

$$\therefore \quad \frac{3 \times (2x+3)}{3 \times 4} = \frac{4 \times (x-2)}{4 \times 3} \qquad \text{\{to achieve a common denominator\}}$$

$$\therefore \quad 3(2x+3) = 4(x-2) \qquad \text{\{equating numerators\}}$$

$$\therefore \quad 6x+9 = 4x-8 \qquad \text{\{expanding brackets\}}$$

$$\therefore \quad 6x+9-4x = 4x-8-4x \qquad \text{\{subtracting } 4x \text{ from both sides\}}$$

$$\therefore \quad 2x+9 = -8 \qquad \text{\{simplifying\}}$$

$$\therefore \quad 2x+9-9 = -8-9 \qquad \text{\{subtracting 9 from both sides\}}$$

$$\therefore \quad 2x = -17 \qquad \text{\{simplifying\}}$$

$$\therefore \quad \frac{2x}{2} = \frac{-17}{2} \qquad \text{\{dividing both sides by 2\}}$$

$$\therefore \quad x = -8\tfrac{1}{2}$$

EXERCISE 6F

1 Solve for x:

  a $\dfrac{x}{4} = \dfrac{5}{2}$ **b** $\dfrac{2}{3} = \dfrac{x}{5}$ **c** $\dfrac{6x}{4} = \dfrac{3}{2}$ **d** $\dfrac{1}{4} = \dfrac{x}{3}$

  e $\dfrac{3x}{4} = \dfrac{3}{2}$ **f** $\dfrac{1}{5} = \dfrac{5x}{3}$ **g** $\dfrac{3}{5} = \dfrac{x}{2}$ **h** $\dfrac{4x}{5} = \dfrac{1}{2}$

2 Solve for x:

  a $\dfrac{3x+1}{4} = \dfrac{5}{2}$ **b** $\dfrac{x+4}{3} = \dfrac{x}{2}$ **c** $\dfrac{2x+3}{5} = \dfrac{2x}{3}$

  d $\dfrac{x+1}{3} = \dfrac{2x+5}{4}$ **e** $\dfrac{4-x}{2} = \dfrac{x+1}{3}$ **f** $\dfrac{5x+2}{4} = \dfrac{2x-1}{3}$

  g $\dfrac{3-2x}{2} = x+4$ **h** $\dfrac{x+2}{3} = \dfrac{5-x}{4}$ **i** $\dfrac{3x+8}{3} = x-5$

SOLVING EQUATIONS (Chapter 6) 145

Example 14

Solve for x: $\quad \dfrac{x}{2} + \dfrac{2x}{3} = -4$

$\dfrac{x}{2} + \dfrac{2x}{3} = \dfrac{-4}{1}$ $\qquad$ has LCD of 6

$\therefore \quad \dfrac{x \times 3}{2 \times 3} + \dfrac{2x \times 2}{3 \times 2} = \dfrac{-4 \times 6}{1 \times 6}$ $\qquad$ {to achieve a common denominator}

$\therefore \quad 3x + 4x = -24$ $\qquad$ {equating numerators}

$\therefore \quad 7x = -24$ $\qquad$ {simplifying LHS}

$\therefore \quad x = -\dfrac{24}{7}$ $\qquad$ {dividing by 7}

$\therefore \quad x = -3\dfrac{3}{7}$

3 Solve for x:

a $\dfrac{x}{2} + \dfrac{x}{5} = 2$ $\qquad$ **b** $\dfrac{x}{2} - \dfrac{2x}{3} = \dfrac{5}{6}$ $\qquad$ **c** $\dfrac{3x}{2} - \dfrac{x}{8} = 11$

d $\dfrac{3x}{4} + \dfrac{2x}{3} = -\dfrac{1}{2}$ $\qquad$ **e** $\dfrac{5x}{2} - \dfrac{x}{6} = \dfrac{3}{8}$ $\qquad$ **f** $\dfrac{x}{7} - \dfrac{3x}{2} = 4$

Example 15

Solve for x: $\quad \dfrac{x+1}{3} + \dfrac{2x+3}{2} = 4$

$\dfrac{x+1}{3} + \dfrac{2x+3}{2} = \dfrac{4}{1}$ $\qquad$ has LCD of 6

$\therefore \quad \dfrac{2 \times (x+1)}{2 \times 3} + \dfrac{3 \times (2x+3)}{3 \times 2} = \dfrac{6 \times 4}{6 \times 1}$ $\qquad$ {to achieve a common denominator}

$\therefore \quad 2(x+1) + 3(2x+3) = 24$ $\qquad$ {equating numerators}

$\therefore \quad 2x + 2 + 6x + 9 = 24$ $\qquad$ {expanding brackets}

$\therefore \quad 8x + 11 = 24$ $\qquad$ {collecting like terms}

$\therefore \quad 8x = 13$ $\qquad$ {subtracting 11 from both sides}

$\therefore \quad x = \dfrac{13}{8}$ $\qquad$ {dividing both sides by 8}

$\therefore \quad x = 1\dfrac{5}{8}$

4 Solve for x:

a $\dfrac{x}{3} + \dfrac{2x+1}{6} = 0$ $\qquad$ **b** $\dfrac{2x+3}{5} + \dfrac{x-1}{2} = \dfrac{3}{4}$

c $\dfrac{2x-3}{5} + \dfrac{x+4}{2} = -2$ $\qquad$ **d** $\dfrac{x-2}{3} + \dfrac{2x+1}{12} = 2$

e $\dfrac{4x-3}{5} + \dfrac{x+2}{3} = -\dfrac{1}{4}$ $\qquad$ **f** $\dfrac{x-4}{3} + \dfrac{2x-3}{8} = \dfrac{5}{6}$

146 SOLVING EQUATIONS (Chapter 6)

Example 16

Solve for x: $\dfrac{2x+1}{3} - \dfrac{x-2}{2} = 5$

$\dfrac{(2x+1)}{3} - \dfrac{(x-2)}{2} = \dfrac{5}{1}$ has LCD of 6

$\therefore \dfrac{2 \times (2x+1)}{2 \times 3} - \dfrac{3 \times (x-2)}{3 \times 2} = \dfrac{6 \times 5}{6 \times 1}$ {to achieve a common denominator}

$\therefore 2(2x+1) - 3(x-2) = 30$ {equating numerators}

$\therefore 4x + 2 - 3x + 6 = 30$ {expanding brackets}

$\therefore x + 8 = 30$ {collecting like terms}

$\therefore x = 22$

Notice the use of brackets in the original fractions.

5 Solve for x:

   a $\dfrac{x+1}{2} - \dfrac{2x}{5} = 4$

   b $\dfrac{3x-2}{3} - \dfrac{x-1}{2} = \dfrac{1}{2}$

   c $\dfrac{4x}{5} - \dfrac{x-2}{2} = -3$

   d $\dfrac{2x-1}{4} - \dfrac{x+2}{3} = -\dfrac{1}{3}$

   e $\dfrac{4x+1}{2} - \dfrac{2x-3}{6} = 1$

   f $\dfrac{x-5}{6} - \dfrac{x+1}{4} = -2$

G UNKNOWN IN THE DENOMINATOR

If the unknown appears as part of the denominator, we still solve by writing the equations with the same lowest common denominator (LCD), and then **equating numerators**.

Example 17

Solve for x: $\dfrac{3x+1}{x-1} = -2$

$\dfrac{3x+1}{x-1} = \dfrac{-2}{1}$ has LCD of $x-1$

$\therefore \dfrac{3x+1}{x-1} = \dfrac{-2 \times (x-1)}{1 \times (x-1)}$ {to achieve a common denominator}

$\therefore 3x + 1 = -2(x-1)$ {equating numerators}

$\therefore 3x + 1 = -2x + 2$ {expanding brackets}

$\therefore 3x + 1 + 2x = -2x + 2 + 2x$ {adding $2x$ to both sides}

$\therefore 5x + 1 = 2$ {simplifying both sides}

$\therefore 5x + 1 - 1 = 2 - 1$ {subtracting 1 from both sides}

$\therefore 5x = 1$

$\therefore x = \tfrac{1}{5}$ {dividing both sides by 5}

EXERCISE 6G

1 Solve for x:

a $\dfrac{2}{x} = \dfrac{1}{5}$ b $\dfrac{8}{x} = \dfrac{2}{3}$ c $\dfrac{4}{7} = \dfrac{2}{x}$ d $\dfrac{3}{5} = \dfrac{1}{x}$

e $\dfrac{1}{3x} = \dfrac{3}{4}$ f $\dfrac{4}{3x} = 2$ g $\dfrac{7}{2x} = -4$ h $-5 = \dfrac{3}{7x}$

2 Solve for x:

a $\dfrac{2x+1}{4x} = -3$ b $\dfrac{3x+5}{x+4} = 2$ c $\dfrac{6x+1}{x-3} = 2$

d $\dfrac{-9}{2x+1} = 3$ e $\dfrac{3x-1}{x+4} = 3$ f $\dfrac{4x+1}{x+5} = -3$

INVESTIGATION 2   RECURRING DECIMALS

Consider the recurring decimal 0.555...... which we can also write as $0.\overline{5}$. What fraction gives this decimal?

We can use an equation to find a fraction equal to 0.555......

What to do:

1 Let $x = 0.555.....$ and call this equation (1).

2 Multiply both sides of (1) by 10. Call the result equation (2).

3 Subtract (1) from (2).

4 Solve the resulting equation. What fraction is equal to 0.555...?

You should have written down the following solution:

$$\begin{aligned}
\text{Let } \quad & x = 0.555...... \quad (1) \\
\therefore \quad & 10 \times x = 10 \times 0.555...... \\
\therefore \quad & 10x = 5.555...... \quad (2) \\
& -x = 0.555...... \\
\hline
& 9x = 5 \quad \{(2) - (1)\} \\
\therefore \quad & x = \tfrac{5}{9}
\end{aligned}$$

So, $0.555...... = \tfrac{5}{9}$

5 Follow similar steps to convert the following recurring decimals to fractions:

   a 0.777....   b 0.888....   c 0.333....   d 0.444....

6 Convert the following recurring decimals to fractions:

   a 1.262626....   b 1.0202....   c 1.0909....   d 2.0909....

Hint: Multiply both sides of equation (1) by 100.

7 Convert the following recurring decimals to fractions:

   a 0.5333....   b 1.7333....   c 0.9444....   d 2.0555....

REVIEW SET 6A

1. The solution of the equation $3x + 8 = 29$ is one of the integers $\{-7, 9, 7\}$. Find the solution.

2. Is the equation $5 - 2x = 7$ true for:
   A all values of x
   B exactly one value of x?

3. Explain how the expression $\dfrac{2x+1}{3}$ is 'built up' from x.

4. Explain how to isolate x in $5x - 7$.

5. Explain how to isolate x in $2(x - 3)$.

6. Solve for x:
   a $5 + 2x = -11$
   b $\dfrac{3 - 2x}{7} = -6$
   c $3 - 2x = 3x + 8$

7. Solve for x:
   a $\dfrac{x}{5} = \dfrac{3}{4}$
   b $\dfrac{2x+1}{3} = \dfrac{x}{2}$

8. Solve for x:
   a $\dfrac{1}{2x} = 5$
   b $\dfrac{x+1}{1-2x} = -1$
   c $\dfrac{x-1}{2} - \dfrac{2-x}{3} = 8$

REVIEW SET 6B

1. The solution of the equation $2x - 5 = -11$ is one of the integers $\{3, -3, 8\}$. Find the solution.

2. Is the equation $2x + 3x = 6x - x$:
   A true for all values of x
   B never true?

3. Show how the expression $4(x - 3)$ is 'built up' from x.

4. Show how the expression $\dfrac{x}{5} + 3$ is 'built up' from x.

5. Explain how to isolate x in $\dfrac{2x+3}{4}$.

6. Solve for x:
   a $12x + 4 = 28$
   b $\dfrac{2x}{3} + 1 = -2$
   c $3(2x - 1) + 5 = 2(x + 7)$

7. Solve for x:
   a $\dfrac{x}{2} = \dfrac{5}{4}$
   b $\dfrac{1-3x}{6} = \dfrac{x-2}{3}$

8. Solve for x:
   a $\dfrac{7}{3x} = \dfrac{3}{2}$
   b $\dfrac{3-2x}{x+4} = -6$
   c $\dfrac{2x+1}{3} - \dfrac{1-x}{6} = -2$

Chapter 7

The geometry of polygons

Contents:
- **A** Review of geometrical facts
- **B** Triangles
- **C** Isosceles triangles
- **D** Quadrilaterals and other polygons
- **E** Deductive geometry
- **F** Special quadrilaterals

THEOREMS

Discoveries in geometry may be made by drawing accurate figures and then making precise measurements of sizes of angles and lengths of sides.

For example, if we draw a series of triangles of various sizes and shapes and on each occasion measure the interior angles we may discover an important fact about all triangles.

Consider these:

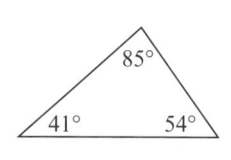

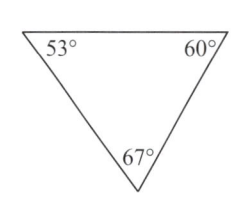

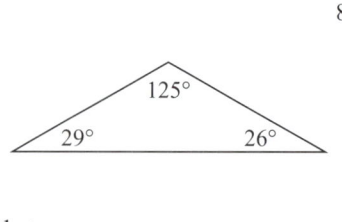

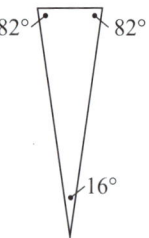

From an investigation like this, we may propose that:

"The sum of the interior angles of any triangle is 180°."

However, this geometrical proposition requires logical proof before it can be accepted as true.

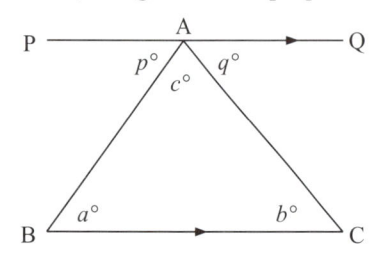

One such proof uses the diagram shown.
[PQ] is drawn parallel to [BC].

$$p + c + q = 180 \quad \text{\{angles on a line\}}$$
But $p = a$ and $q = b$
$$\therefore \quad a + c + b = 180 \quad \text{\{alternate angles\}}$$

So, the angles of a triangle add to 180°.

"The sum of the interior angles of any triangle is 180°" is a very useful result and is called a theorem.

A **theorem** is an important result which can be called upon when solving other problems or proving other theorems.

OPENING PROBLEM

Luciano makes aluminium window frames to be placed in new houses. They are supposed to be rectangular, but because aluminium is very light and flexible, they are sometimes pushed out of shape in transport.

Things to think about: 
- If a rectangular frame is 'out of square', what is its shape?
- Explain how a measuring tape can be used to check that all corners are right angles.
- How could Luciano help keep the rectangular frames in shape during transport?
- The frames often show identical shapes such as triangles. What special name is used to indicate identical shapes?

A REVIEW OF GEOMETRICAL FACTS

DEFINING ANGLES

Revolution	Straight Angle	Right Angle
One complete turn. One revolution = 360°.	$\frac{1}{2}$ turn. 1 straight angle = 180°.	$\frac{1}{4}$ turn. 1 right angle = 90°.
Acute Angle	**Obtuse Angle**	**Reflex Angle**
Less than a $\frac{1}{4}$ turn. An acute angle has size between 0° and 90°.	Between $\frac{1}{4}$ turn and $\frac{1}{2}$ turn. An obtuse angle has size between 90° and 180°.	Between $\frac{1}{2}$ turn and 1 turn. A reflex angle has size between 180° and 360°.

ANGLE PAIRS

- Two angles which have sizes which add to 90° are called **complementary angles**.
- Two angles which have sizes which add to 180° are called **supplementary angles**.
- Two angles which have the same vertex and share a common arm are called **adjacent angles**.
  $P\hat{A}Q$ and $Q\hat{A}R$ are adjacent angles.
- For intersecting lines, angles which are directly opposite each other are called **vertically opposite angles**.

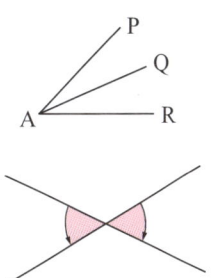

TRIANGLE CLASSIFICATION

By sides:

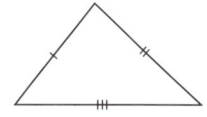

Scalene triangle
no equal sides

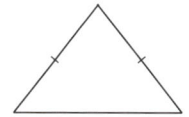

Isosceles triangle
two equal sides

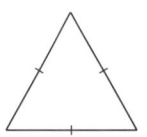

Equilateral triangle
three equal sides

By angles:

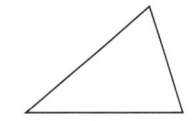

Acute angled triangle	Obtuse angled triangle	Right angled triangle
all acute angles	one obtuse angle	one right angle

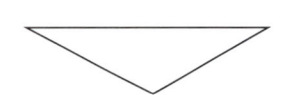

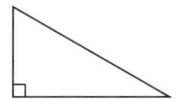

LINE TERMINOLOGY

- **Line (AB)** is the endless straight line passing through the points A and B.

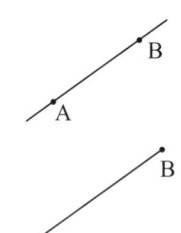

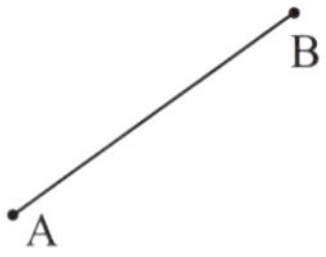

- **Line segment [AB]** is the part of the straight line connecting A to B.

- **Concurrent lines** are three or more lines all passing through a common point.

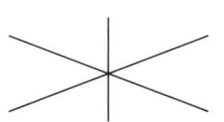

- **Collinear points** are points which lie in a straight line.

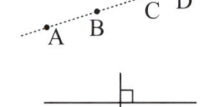

- **Perpendicular lines** intersect at right angles.

- **Parallel lines** are lines which never intersect. Arrow heads indicate parallelism.

- A **transversal** is a line which crosses over two other lines.

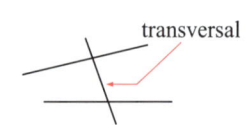

GEOMETRIC THEOREMS

Title	Theorem	Figure
Angles at a point	The sum of the sizes of the angles at a point is 360°.	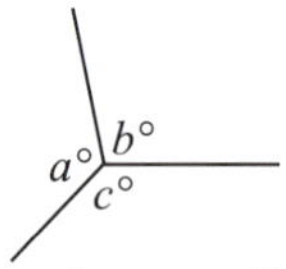 $a + b + c = 360$
Adjacent angles on a straight line.	The sum of the sizes of the angles on a line is 180°. The angles are supplementary.	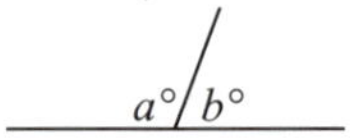 $a + b = 180$

Title	Theorem	Figure
Adjacent angles in a right angle	The sum of the sizes of the angles in a right angle is 90°. The angles are complementary.	$a + b = 90$
Vertically opposite angles	Vertically opposite angles are equal in size.	$a = b$
Corresponding angles	When two *parallel* lines are cut by a third line, then angles in corresponding positions are equal in size.	$a = b$
Alternate angles	When two *parallel* lines are cut by a third line, then angles in alternate positions are equal in size.	$a = b$
Co-interior angles (also called allied angles)	When two *parallel* lines are cut by a third line, co-interior angles are supplementary.	$a + b = 180$
Angles of a triangle	The sum of the interior angles of a triangle is 180°. **GEOMETRY PACKAGE**	$a + b + c = 180$
Exterior angle of a triangle	The size of the exterior angle of a triangle is equal to the sum of the interior opposite angles. **GEOMETRY PACKAGE**	$c = a + b$
Angles of a quadrilateral	The sum of the interior angles of a quadrilateral is 360°. **GEOMETRY PACKAGE**	$a + b + c + d = 360$

EXERCISE 7A

1. State whether the following are true (T) or false (F):
   a. An angle measuring 89° is an acute angle.
   b. An angle measuring 91° is an obtuse angle.
   c. The size of an angle depends on the lengths of its arms.
   d. When a vertical line crosses a horizontal line the angle formed is a straight angle.
   e. $\frac{3}{4}$ of a straight angle is an acute angle.
   f. A right angle is neither an acute angle nor an obtuse angle.

2. [XY] is a fixed line segment and [OP] can rotate about O between [OX] and [OY]. 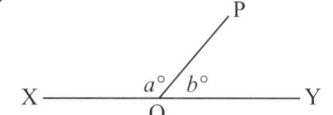
   a. If $a = 135$, find b.
   b. If $b = 67$, find a.
   c. What is a if b is 27?
   d. If a is 0, what is b?
   e. If $a = 89$, find b.
   f. If $a = b$, what is the value of each?

3. Find the complement of:
   a. 36°
   b. 71°
   c. $a°$
   d. $(90 - x)°$

4. Find the supplement of:
   a. 79°
   b. 113°
   c. $n°$
   d. $(180 - m)°$
   e. $(90 + a)°$

5. Find the values of the variables, giving brief reasons:

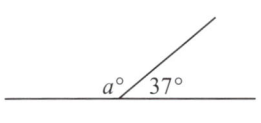

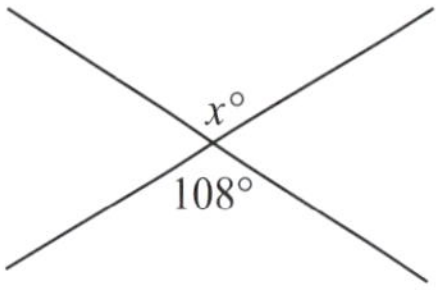

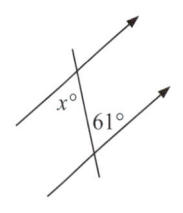

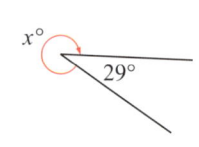

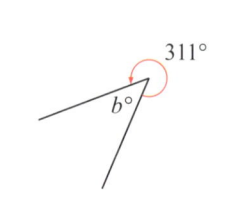

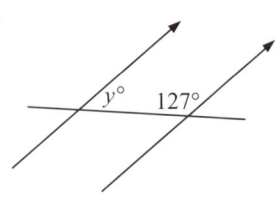

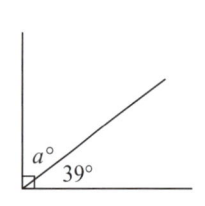

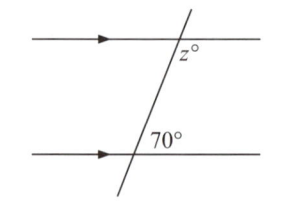

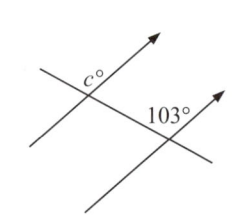

THE GEOMETRY OF POLYGONS   (Chapter 7)   155

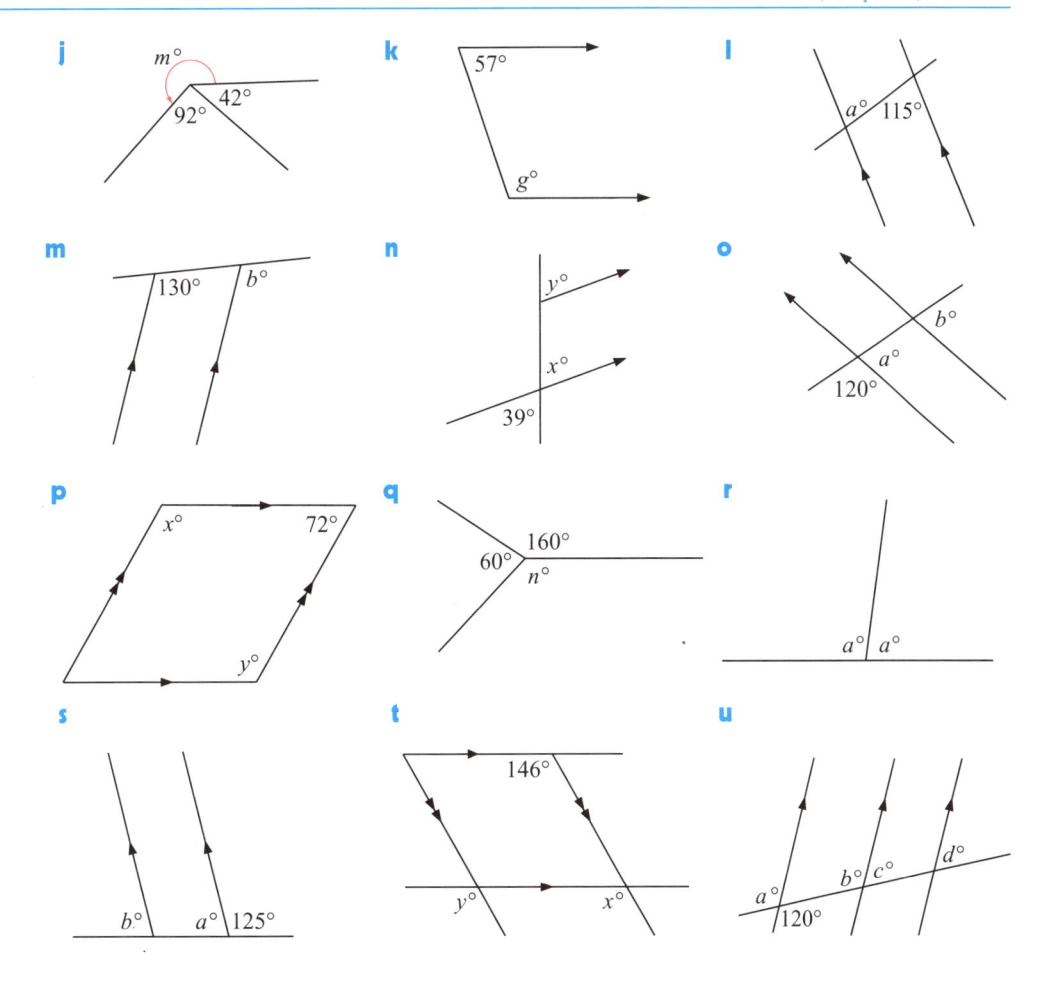

j, **k**, **l**, **m**, **n**, **o**, **p**, **q**, **r**, **s**, **t**, **u**

Example 1

Find, giving brief reasons, the value of the unknown in:

a, **b**

a
$$90 + a + 40 = 180 \quad \text{\{angles on a line\}}$$
$$\therefore \quad a + 130 = 180$$
$$\therefore \quad a = 50$$

b
$$2x - 100 = x \quad \text{\{equal corresponding angles\}}$$
$$\therefore \quad 2x - 100 - x = x - x \quad \text{\{subtracting } x \text{ from both sides\}}$$
$$\therefore \quad x - 100 = 0 \quad \text{\{simplifying\}}$$
$$\therefore \quad x = 100$$

156 THE GEOMETRY OF POLYGONS (Chapter 7)

6 Find, giving brief reasons, the value of the unknown in:

a 140°, $d°$

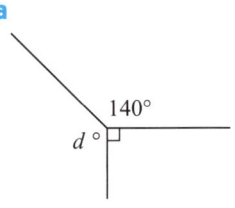

b $2g°$, $3g°$

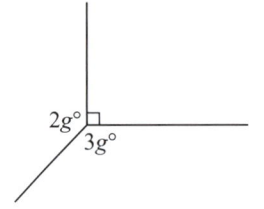

c $e°$, $e°$, $e°$

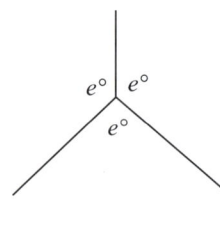

d $h°$, $2h°$

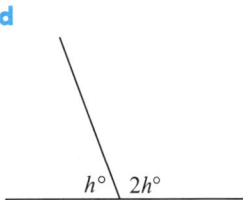

e $3n°$, $2n°$

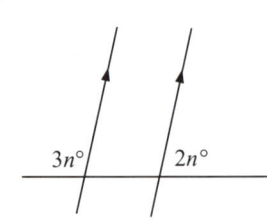

f $(x+30)°$, $x°$

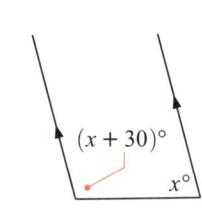

g $(x+30)°$, $(2x+15)°$

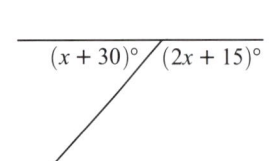

h $15x°$, $(2x+5)°$

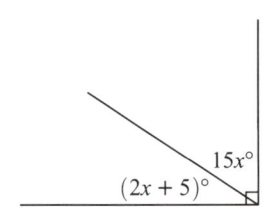

i $3x°$, $(3x+30)°$, $67°$, $(x-31)°$

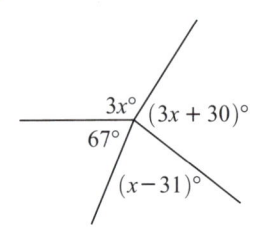

7 State whether [KL] is parallel to [MN], giving a brief reason for your answer. These diagrams are sketches only and have not been drawn to scale.

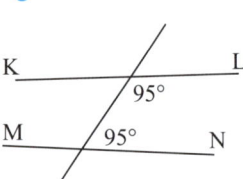

a 95°, 95°

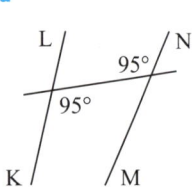

b 95°, 95°

c 95°, 95°

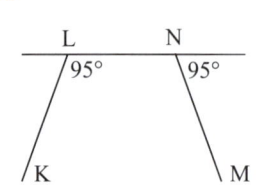

B TRIANGLES

A **triangle** is a polygon which has three sides.
All triangles have the following properties:

- The sum of the interior angles of a triangle is $180°$.
- Any exterior angle is equal to the sum of the interior opposite angles.
- The longest side is opposite the largest angle.
- The triangle is the only **rigid** polygon.

RESEARCH

Research the use of triangles in the construction of bridges. Explain what is meant by the statement "*the triangle is the only rigid polygon*" and how this helps the bridge structure.

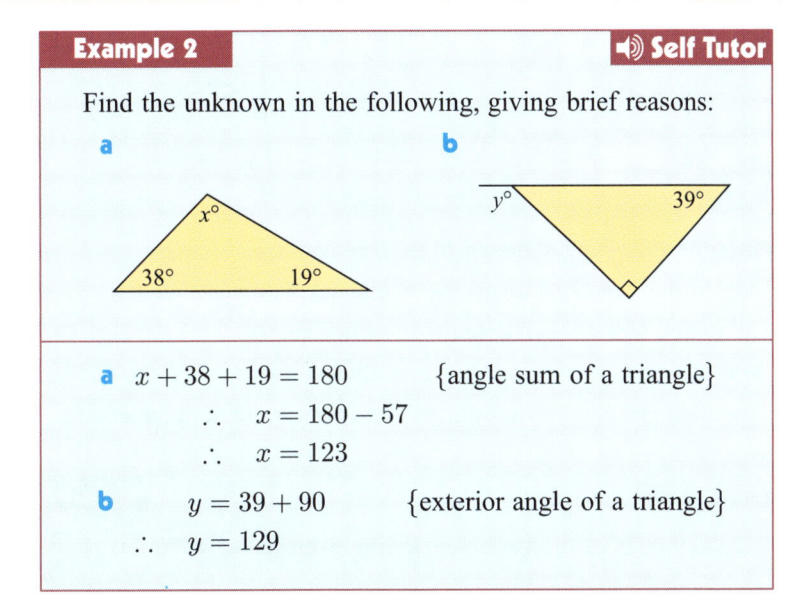

Example 2

Find the unknown in the following, giving brief reasons:

a Triangle with angles $x°$, $38°$, $19°$.

b Right triangle with angles $y°$, $39°$, and $90°$.

a $x + 38 + 19 = 180$ {angle sum of a triangle}
∴ $x = 180 - 57$
∴ $x = 123$

b $y = 39 + 90$ {exterior angle of a triangle}
∴ $y = 129$

EXERCISE 7B

1 Find the unknown in the following, giving brief reasons:

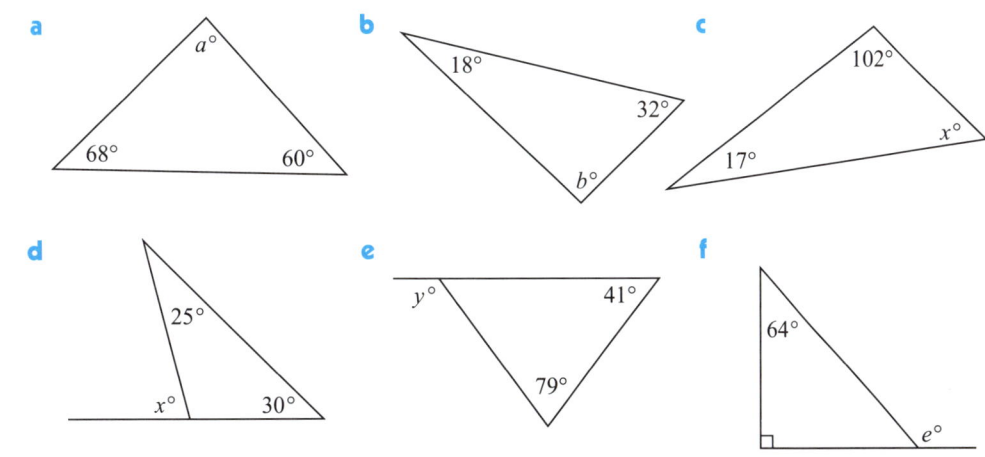

a Triangle with angles $a°$, $68°$, $60°$.

b Triangle with angles $18°$, $32°$, $b°$.

c Triangle with angles $102°$, $17°$, $x°$.

d Triangle with interior angles $25°$, $30°$, and exterior angle $x°$.

e Triangle with angles $y°$, $79°$, $41°$.

f Right triangle with angles $64°$, $90°$, and exterior angle $e°$.

2 The following triangles are *not* drawn to scale. State the longest side of each triangle.

a Triangle with B = 102°, A = 58°, C

b Triangle with B = 80°, A = 10°, C = 90°

c Triangle with A, B = 28°, C = 28°

d Triangle with B = 27°, C = 16°, A

e Triangle with C = 21°, A = 100°, B

f Triangle with B, C = 19°, A = 81°

g Triangle with C = 82°, A, B = 12°

h Triangle with A = 12°, B = 75°, C

i Triangle with C, A = 90°, B

> The longest side is opposite the largest angle.

3 State whether the following statements are *true* or *false*:
  a The sum of the angles of a triangle is equal to two right angles.
  b A right angled triangle can contain an obtuse angle.
  c The sum of two angles of a triangle is always greater than the third angle.
  d The two smaller angles of a right angled triangle are supplementary.

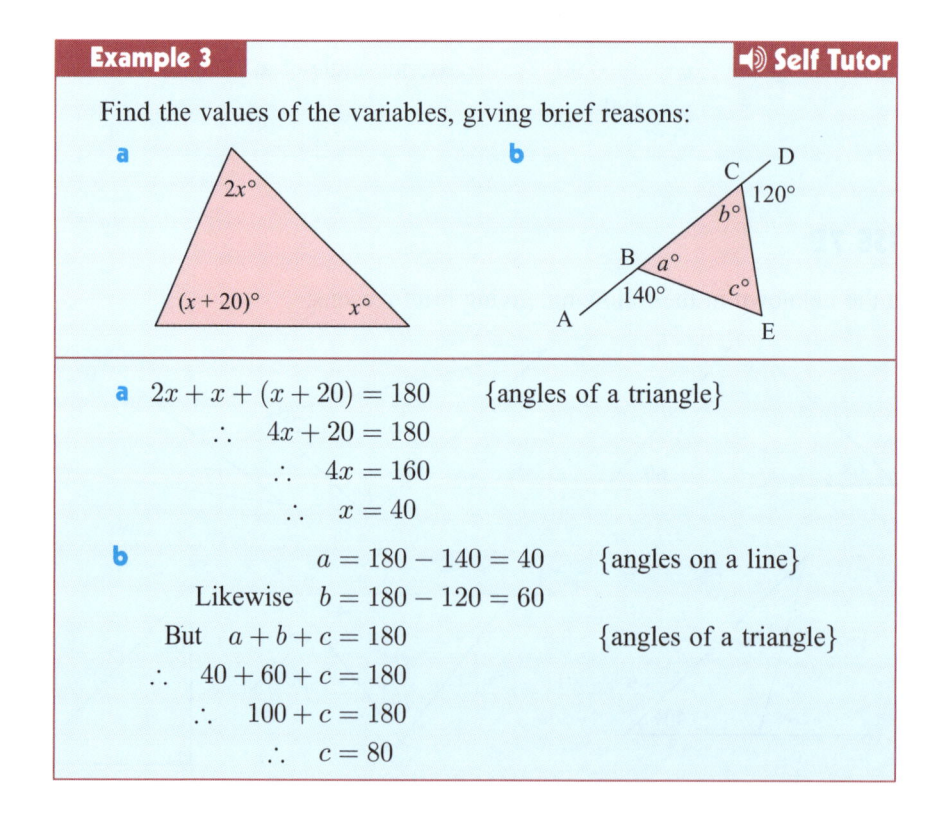

Example 3 🔊 **Self Tutor**

Find the values of the variables, giving brief reasons:

a Triangle with angles $2x°$, $(x+20)°$, $x°$

b Figure with $a°$ at B (with 140° on line A-B extended), $b°$ at C (with 120° at D on line extended), $c°$ at E

a $2x + x + (x + 20) = 180$ {angles of a triangle}
  $\therefore \quad 4x + 20 = 180$
  $\therefore \quad 4x = 160$
  $\therefore \quad x = 40$

b $\qquad a = 180 - 140 = 40$ {angles on a line}
  Likewise $b = 180 - 120 = 60$
  But $a + b + c = 180$ {angles of a triangle}
  $\therefore \quad 40 + 60 + c = 180$
  $\therefore \quad 100 + c = 180$
  $\therefore \quad c = 80$

THE GEOMETRY OF POLYGONS (Chapter 7) 159

4 Find the values of the variables, giving brief reasons:

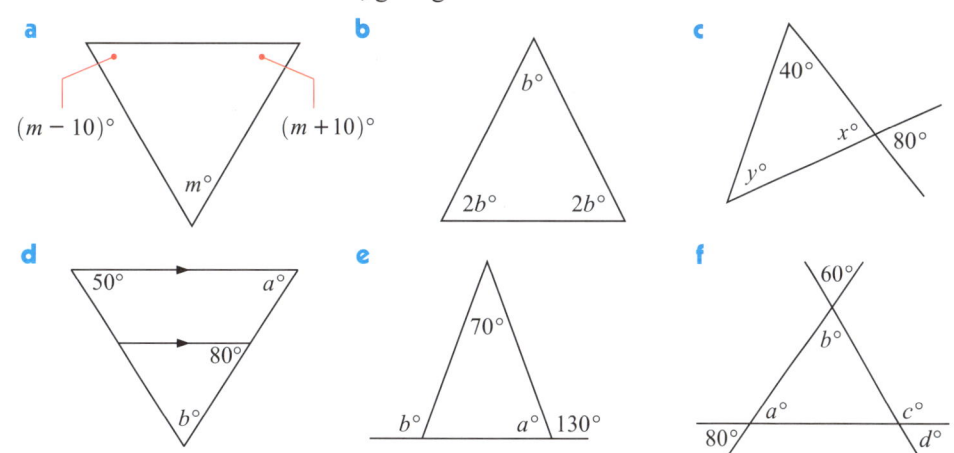

a $(m-10)°$, $(m+10)°$, $m°$

b $b°$, $2b°$, $2b°$

c $40°$, $x°$, $80°$, $y°$

d $50°$, $a°$, $80°$, $b°$

e $70°$, $b°$, $a°$, $130°$

f $60°$, $b°$, $a°$, $80°$, $c°$, $d°$

5 The three angles of a scalene triangle are $x°$, $(x+6)°$ and $(2x-10)°$. What are the sizes of these angles?

C   ISOSCELES TRIANGLES

An **isosceles triangle** is a triangle in which two sides are equal in length.

The angles opposite the two equal sides are called the **base angles**.

The vertex where the two equal sides meet is called the **apex**.

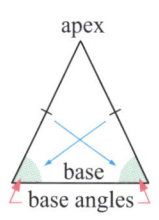

THE ISOSCELES TRIANGLE THEOREM

In any isosceles triangle:
- the base angles are equal
- the line joining the apex to the midpoint of the base bisects the vertical angle and meets the base at right angles.

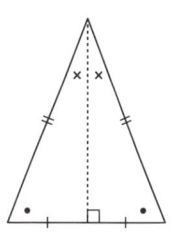

CONVERSES

With many theorems there are converses which we can use in problem solving.

Converse 1: If a triangle has two equal angles then it is isosceles.

Converse 2: The angle bisector of the apex of an isosceles triangle bisects the base at right angles.

Converse 3: The perpendicular bisector of the base of an isosceles triangle passes through its apex.

DISCUSSION

What does the word *converse* mean?

Can you find any other converses to the isosceles triangle theorem?

Example 4

Find x, giving brief reasons:

a

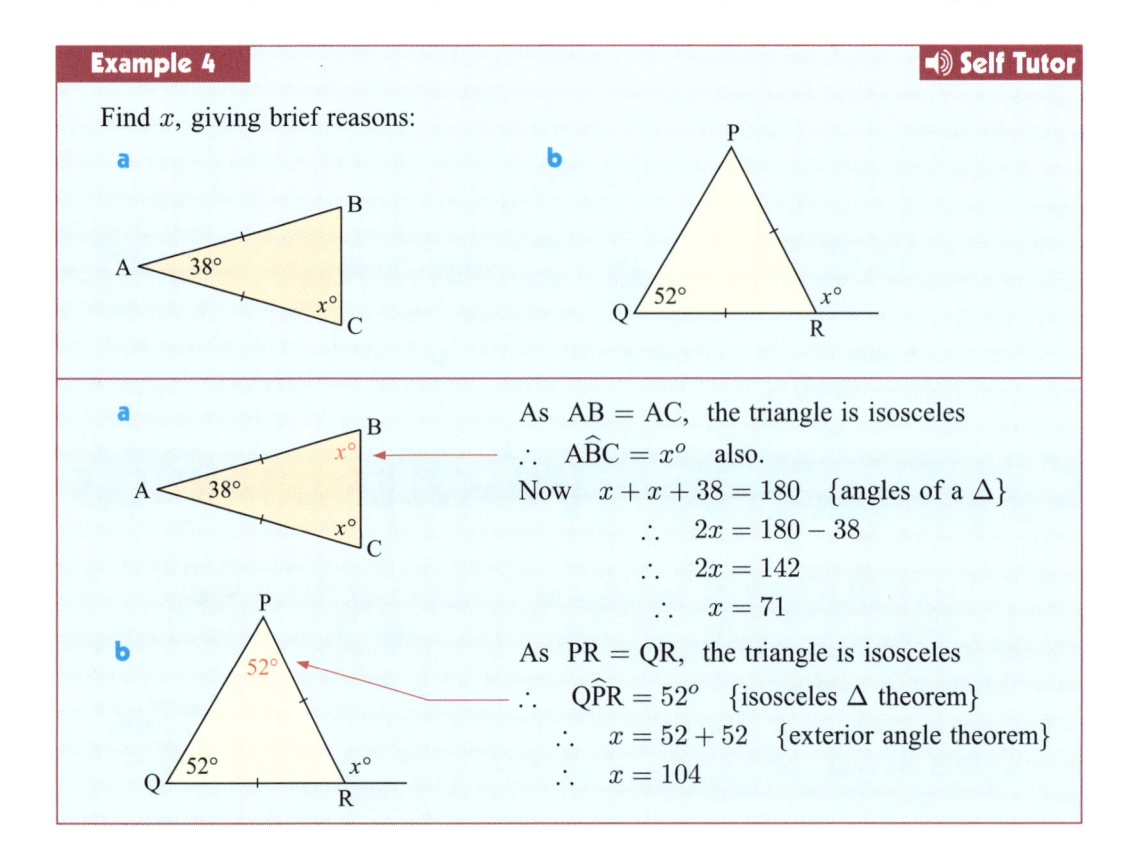

b

a As $AB = AC$, the triangle is isosceles
∴ $A\widehat{B}C = x°$ also.
Now $x + x + 38 = 180$ {angles of a $\triangle$}
∴ $2x = 180 - 38$
∴ $2x = 142$
∴ $x = 71$

b As $PR = QR$, the triangle is isosceles
∴ $Q\widehat{P}R = 52°$ {isosceles $\triangle$ theorem}
∴ $x = 52 + 52$ {exterior angle theorem}
∴ $x = 104$

EXERCISE 7C

1 Find x, giving reasons:

a

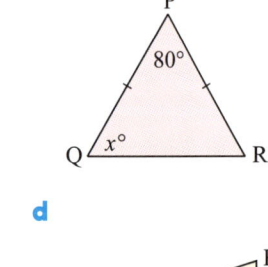

b

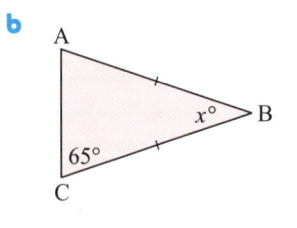

c

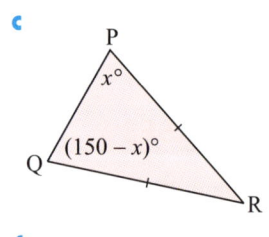

d

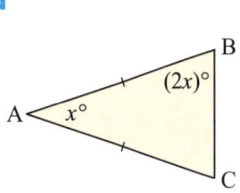

e

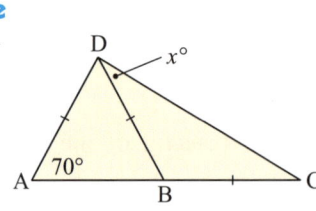

f

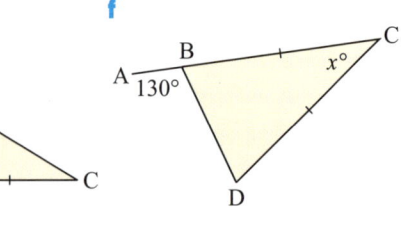

2 Find x, giving brief reasons:

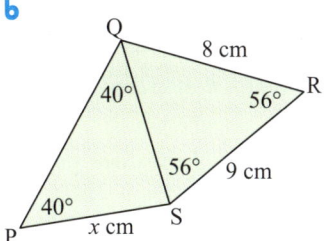

a Triangle ABC with angle B = 70°, angle C = 70°, AB = x cm, AC = 12 cm.

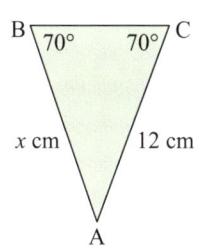

b Quadrilateral PQRS with angle QPS = 40°, angle PQR split into 40° and (angle at Q near R), angle at S = 56°, QR = 8 cm, RS = 9 cm, PS = x cm, and angle PSR shown as 56°.

c Triangle XZY with marks showing XZ = XY, ZM = MY, and angle at M = $x°$.

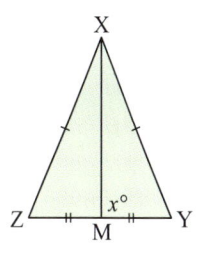

3 The following triangles are not drawn to scale. Classify them as equilateral, isosceles or scalene. The information marked on them is correct.

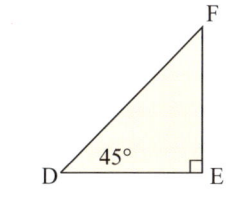

a Triangle ABC with angle A = 60° and AB = AC (tick marks).

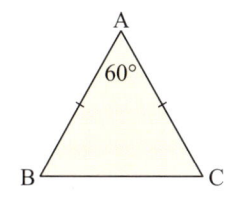

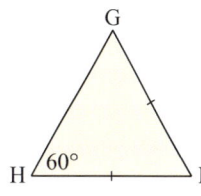

b Triangle DEF with angle D = 45° and right angle at E.

c Triangle GHI with angle I = 60° and HI marked with tick marks on H side and I side.

d Triangle JKL with angle J = 70°, angle K = 40°.

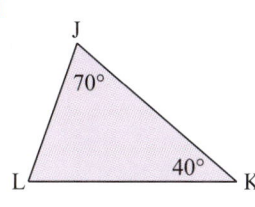

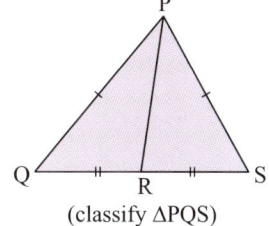

e Triangle PQS with R on QS; QR = RS (tick marks), PR drawn, PQ = PS (tick marks). (classify $\triangle PQS$)

f Triangle WXY with Z on WY; WZ = ZY (tick marks), XZ perpendicular to WY. (classify $\triangle WXY$)

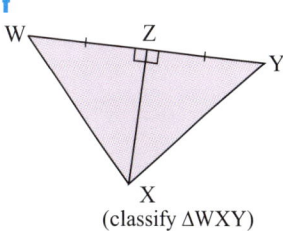

4 The figure alongside has not been drawn to scale:

a Find x.

b What can be deduced about the triangle?

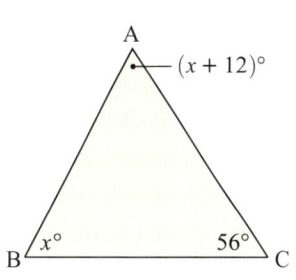

Triangle ABC with angle at A = $(x+12)°$, angle B = $x°$, angle C = 56°.

5

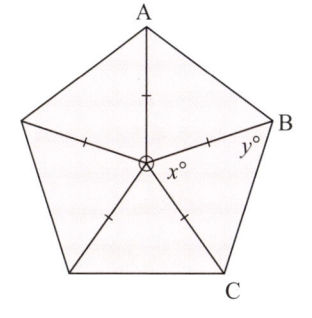

Because of its symmetry, a regular pentagon can be made up of five isosceles triangles.

a Find the size of x, the angle at the centre of the pentagon.

b Hence, find y.

c Hence, find the measure of one interior angle such as $A\hat{B}C$.

6 Repeat question **5** but use an octagon.

D QUADRILATERALS AND OTHER POLYGONS

A **quadrilateral** is a four-sided polygon.
The sum of the interior angles of a quadrilateral is 360°.

Suppose a quadrilateral is drawn on a piece of paper.
If the four angles are torn off and reassembled at a point, we notice that the angle sum must be 360°.

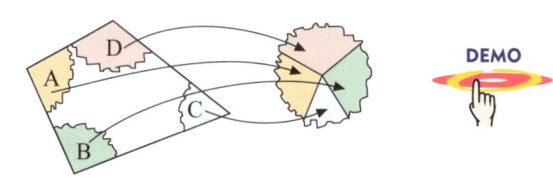

A **polygon** is a closed plane figure which has straight lines for sides.
The sum of the interior angles of an n-sided polygon is $s = (n-2) \times 180°$

For example, if $n = 6$ we split the hexagon into $6 - 2 = 4$ triangles, each having an angle sum of 180°.

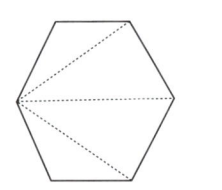

A **regular polygon** has all sides equal in length and all angles equal in size.

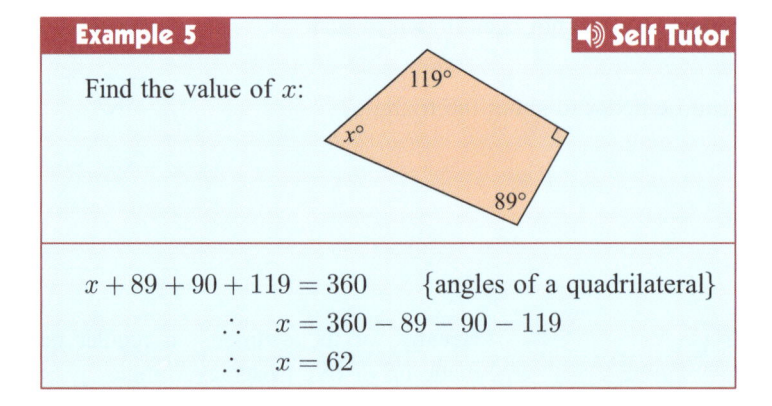

Example 5

Find the value of x:

$x + 89 + 90 + 119 = 360$ {angles of a quadrilateral}
$\therefore x = 360 - 89 - 90 - 119$
$\therefore x = 62$

EXERCISE 7D.1

1 Copy and complete:

a A quadrilateral can be split into .... triangles and so the sum of its interior angles is .... $\times 180° = ...°$.

b A pentagon can be split into .... triangles and so the sum of its interior angles is .... $\times 180° = ...°$.

c A 9-gon can be split into .... triangles and so the sum of its interior angles is .... $\times 180° = ...°$.

2 Find the value of x:

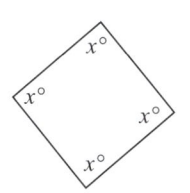

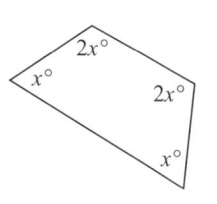

a (quadrilateral with angles 113°, 70°, $x°$, and a right angle)

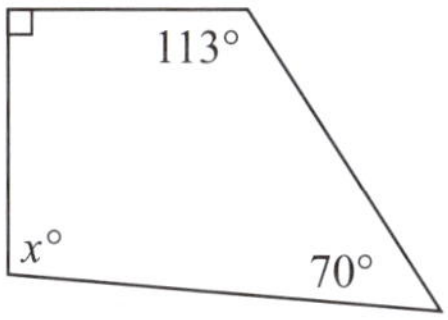

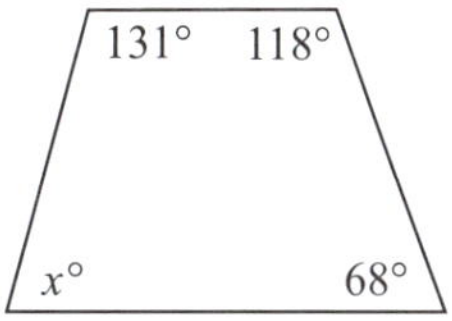

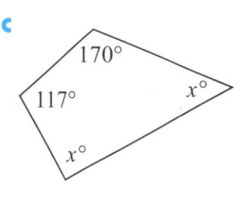

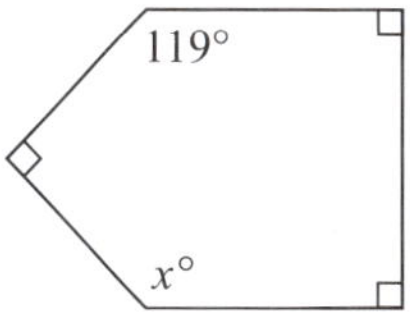

b (quadrilateral with angles 131°, 118°, 68°, $x°$)

c (quadrilateral with angles 170°, 117°, $x°$, $x°$)

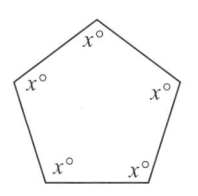

d (quadrilateral with four angles all $x°$)

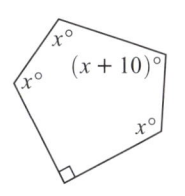

e (quadrilateral with angles $2x°$, $2x°$, $x°$, $x°$)

f (pentagon with angles 119°, $x°$, and three right angles)

g (pentagon with five angles all $x°$)

h (pentagon with angles $x°$, $x°$, $(x+10)°$, $x°$, and a right angle)

i (hexagon with six angles all $x°$)

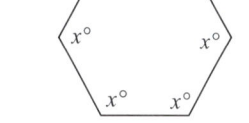

3 The sum of the angles of a polygon is $1980°$. How many angles has the polygon?

4 Juan claims to have found a polygon which has angles with a sum of $2500°$. Comment on Juan's finding.

5 Copy and complete the following table for regular polygons:

Regular polygon	Number of sides	Number of angles	Size of each angle
equilateral triangle			
square			
pentagon			
hexagon			
octagon			
decagon			

6 Copy and complete:
  - the sum of the angles of an n-sided polygon is ......
  - the size of each angle of a regular n-sided polygon is ......

7 Find the number of sides of a regular polygon which has angles of $150°$.

8 Is there a regular polygon which has angles of $158°$?

164   THE GEOMETRY OF POLYGONS   (Chapter 7)

INVESTIGATION 1 — EXTERIOR ANGLES OF POLYGONS

What to do:

Step 1: Draw any triangle and measure one exterior angle from each vertex. These are a, b and c in the figure alongside. Find the sum of these angles.

Repeat this procedure with two other triangles of your choice. What conclusion can you make?

Step 2: Draw any quadrilateral and measure one exterior angle from each vertex. Find the sum of the exterior angles. What conclusion can you make?

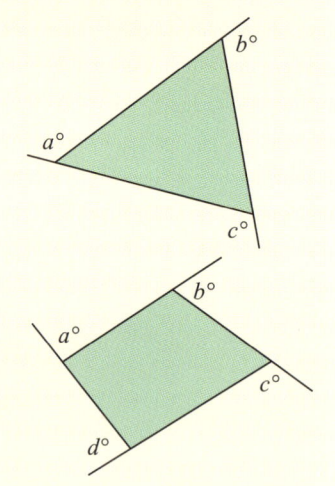

Step 3: From your results for triangles and quadrilaterals, suggest a value for the sum of the exterior angles of any polygon. Check your value by drawing any pentagon and hexagon, measuring each of the exterior angles, and calculating their sum.

In the previous investigation you should have discovered that:

"the sum of the exterior angles of any polygon is $360°$".

GEOMETRY PACKAGE

FLEA PROOF

Fred flea stood at A, facing towards his girlfriend Freda at X. He decided to march around the triangle ABC. He turned through $X\hat{A}B$, marched along [AB], turned through $Y\hat{B}C$, marched along [BC], turned through $Z\hat{C}A$ and marched along [CA].

On reaching A he saw Freda for the second time and proclaimed: "I have turned through one complete turn, so the sum of the exterior angles of a triangle must be $360°$."

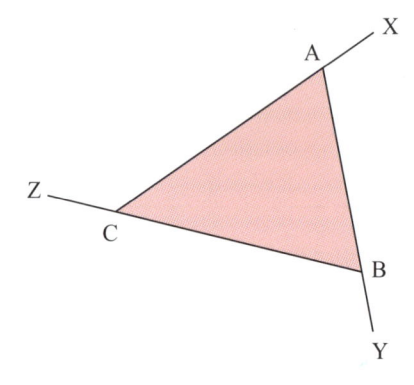

EXERCISE 7D.2

1 Find x in:

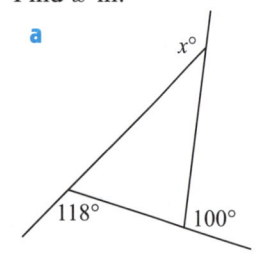

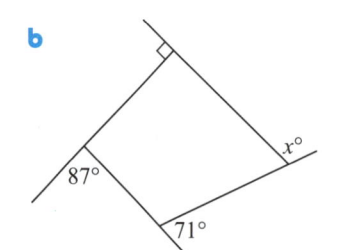

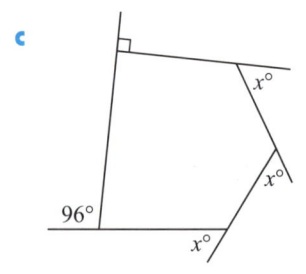

a $x°$, $118°$, $100°$

b $87°$, $71°$, $x°$

c $96°$, $x°$, $x°$, $x°$

2 Copy and complete:

Regular polygon	Sum of exterior angles	Size of each exterior angle	Size of each interior angle
equilateral triangle	$360°$	$360° \div 3 = 120°$	$180° - 120° = 60°$
square			
pentagon			
hexagon			
octagon			

Check that your answers agree with the angle size found in question **5** of **Exercise 7D.1**.

E DEDUCTIVE GEOMETRY

Fatima found many diagrams like these on Abdul's desk:

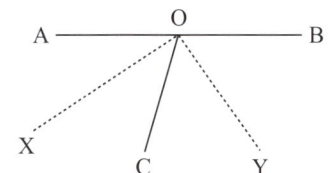

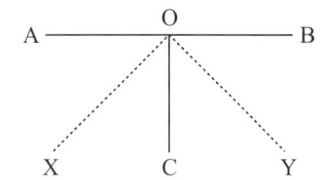

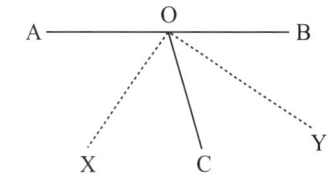

When Fatima asked Abdul what he was doing, he said that he suspected that no matter where [OC] was drawn from line segment [AB], the angle bisectors [OX] and [OY] were at right angles. Fatima wrote down the following argument to prove Abdul's discovery was true.

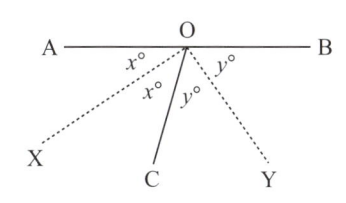

Let [OX] divide $A\hat{O}C$ into two equal angles of $x°$, and [OY] divide $B\hat{O}C$ into two equal angles of $y°$.

Now $2x + 2y = 180$ {angles on a line}
$\therefore \quad x + y = 90$ {dividing each term by 2}
$\therefore \quad X\hat{O}Y = 90°$

Fatima's proof is an example of **deductive geometry**. She has used some **theorems** or special results of geometry to prove Abdul's suspicion true.

EXERCISE 7E

1 ABC is an isosceles triangle in which AB = AC. [BA] is extended to D and [AE] is drawn parallel to [BC].

It is suspected that [AE] bisects $C\hat{A}D$. If we let $A\hat{B}C = x°$, find in terms of x:

   a $A\hat{C}B$ **b** $C\hat{A}E$ **c** $D\hat{A}E$

State your conclusion.

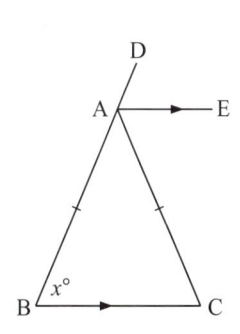

2 **a** Draw three large diagrams of a semi-circle with centre O and diameter [AB], but with P on the semi-circle in different positions.

b Measure $A\hat{P}B$ with a protractor in each case.

c What do you suspect about $A\hat{P}B$?

d Use the geometry package to take a closer look at the problem.

e Copy and complete the following argument:
We first join [OP]. We have created two .... triangles as AO = ... and OB = ...
If $O\hat{A}P = x°$ and $O\hat{B}P = y°$ then $O\hat{P}A$ = ... and $O\hat{P}B$ = ... {isosceles triangle theorem}
So, in triangle APB, $A\hat{P}B$ = ...
But $x + (..........) + y = 180$ {angles of a $\triangle$}
$\therefore$ $2x + ... = 180$ and so $x + ... = 90$
So, $A\hat{P}B$ is always a ....

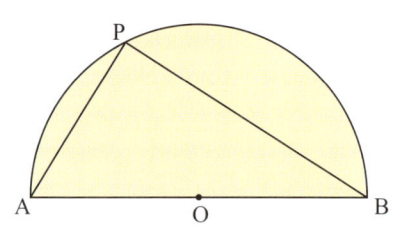

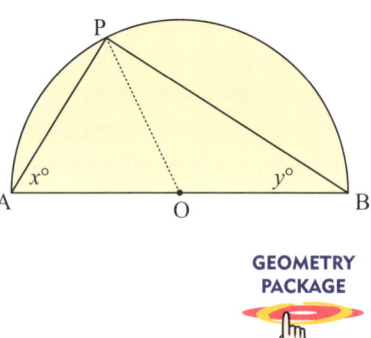

GEOMETRY PACKAGE

3 **a** Draw three large diagrams like the one given but vary the size of $A\hat{O}B$.

b In each case measure the sizes of $A\hat{O}B$ and $A\hat{C}B$.

c What connection do you suspect between the sizes of these angles?

d Use the geometry package to take a closer look at this problem.

e Copy and complete the following argument:
We first join [CO] and extend it to X. We have created two .... triangles as OA = ... = ...
If we let $O\hat{A}C = a°$ and $O\hat{B}C = b°$ then $O\hat{C}A$ = ... and $O\hat{C}B$ = ... {isosceles triangle theorem}
$\therefore$ $A\hat{C}B$ = ...
Now $A\hat{O}X$ = ... {exterior angle of a $\triangle$}
Likewise $B\hat{O}X$ = ...
$\therefore$ $A\hat{O}B$ = ...
So, $A\hat{O}B$ is always twice ....

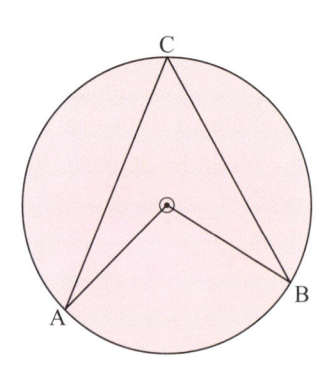

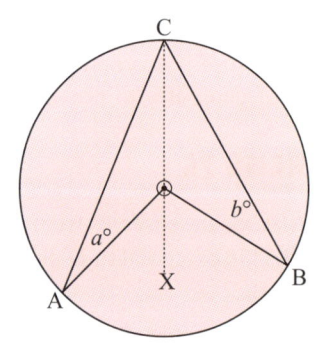

GEOMETRY PACKAGE

THE GEOMETRY OF POLYGONS   (Chapter 7)   167

4

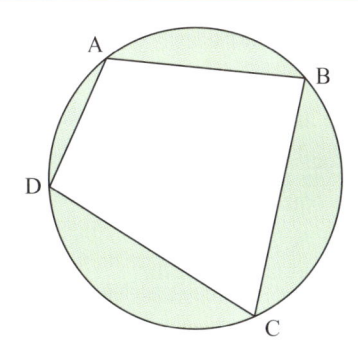

a Draw three diagrams like the one given but at least twice the size.

b Measure the size of each angle of the quadrilateral with a protractor.

c We know that the four angles add up to 360°. What do you suspect about the opposite angles?

d Use the geometry package to take a closer look at the situation.

GEOMETRY PACKAGE

e Copy and complete the following argument:
We locate the circle's centre and call it O.
We join [OA], [OB], [OC] and [OD].
We have created four .... triangles as
OA = ... = ... = ...
If $O\hat{A}D = a°$, $O\hat{B}A = b°$,
$O\hat{C}B = c°$ and $O\hat{D}C = d°$ then
$O\hat{D}A = ...$, $O\hat{A}B = ...$,
$O\hat{B}C = ...$ and $O\hat{C}D = ...$
{isosceles triangle theorem}
Now $D\hat{A}B + D\hat{C}B = ...$
But the sum of the four original angles is
$(a + b) + (.......) + (.......) + (.......) = 2a + ...$
$\therefore \quad 2a + ... = 360$
$\therefore \quad a + ... = 180$
So opposite angles of the quadrilateral add to ....°

5 ABC is an isosceles triangle with AB = AC. It seems that every time I draw a perpendicular from some point E on [BC] to meet the extension of [CA] at D, the triangle DAX seems to be isosceles.
Can you help me prove my suspicion?

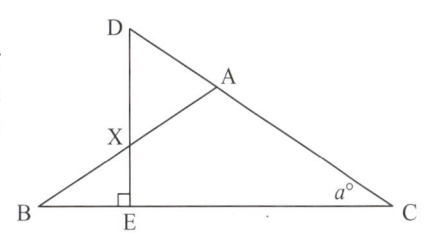

F   SPECIAL QUADRILATERALS

There are six special quadrilaterals. They are:

1 A **parallelogram** is a quadrilateral which has opposites sides parallel.

Properties:
- opposite sides are equal in length
- opposite angles are equal in size
- diagonals bisect each other.

GEOMETRY PACKAGE

2 A **rectangle** is a parallelogram with four equal angles of 90°.

Properties:
- opposite sides are parallel and equal
- diagonals bisect each other
- diagonals are equal in length.

3 A **rhombus** is a quadrilateral in which all sides are equal in length.

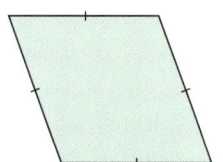

Properties:
- opposite sides are parallel
- opposite angles are equal in size
- diagonals bisect each other at right angles
- diagonals bisect the angles at each vertex.

4 A **square** is a rhombus with four equal angles of 90°.

Properties:
- opposite sides are parallel
- all sides are equal in length
- diagonals bisect each other at right angles
- diagonals bisect the angles at each vertex
- diagonals are equal in length.

5 A **trapezium** is a quadrilateral which has a pair of parallel opposite sides.

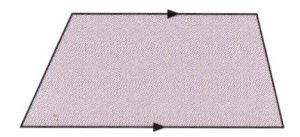

6 A **kite** is a quadrilateral which has two pairs of adjacent sides equal in length.

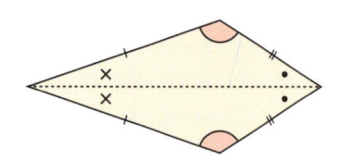

Properties:
- one diagonal is an axis of symmetry
- one pair of opposite angles are equal
- diagonals cut each other at right angles
- **one** diagonal bisects **one** pair of angles at the vertices.

DISCUSSION

Which of the following are true? Give reasons for your answers.
- A rectangle is a quadrilateral.
- A rectangle is a square.
- A square is a rhombus.
- A rhombus is a parallelogram.
- A quadrilateral is a rectangle.
- A square is a rectangle.
- A rhombus is a square.
- A parallelogram is a rhombus.

If you are unsure, look at the basic definition of each shape.

THE GEOMETRY OF POLYGONS (Chapter 7) 169

INVESTIGATION 2 — THE PROPERTIES OF A RHOMBUS

What to do:

1 Copy the figure alongside.
   △ADC is isosceles. Mark its base angles as a^o.
   △DCB is isosceles. Mark its base angles as b^o.
   △CBA is isosceles. Mark its base angles as c^o.
   △BAD is isosceles. Mark its base angles as d^o.

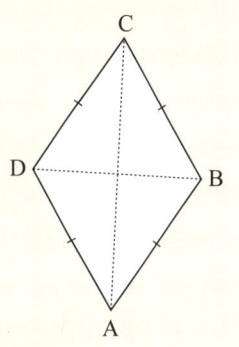

2 Find the sizes of the angles of the rhombus at A, B, C and D. What property of a rhombus have you just established?

3 Add all the angles of the rhombus and equate to $360°$.
   Now simplify your equation.
   Add the angles: $\hat{A} + \hat{D}$ and then $\hat{A} + \hat{B}$.
   What property of the rhombus has just been proven?

4 Following on from **3**, explain why we can now say that $a = c$ and $b = d$.
   What property of a rhombus has now been proven?

5 Prove that "the diagonals of a rhombus are at right angles" using the simplified equation from **3** and the result of **4**.

The properties of other special quadrilaterals can be established using deductive geometry.

Example 6 — Self Tutor

Draw three diagrams to show all the properties of a parallelogram.

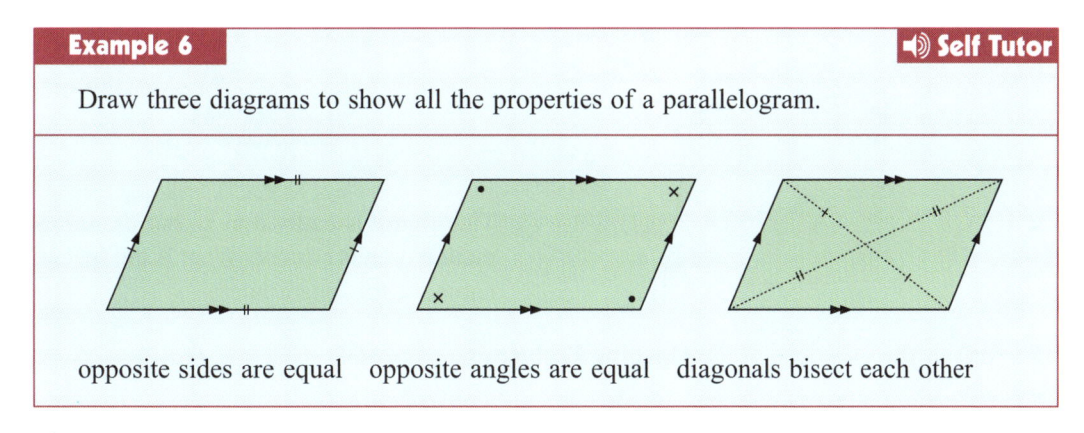

opposite sides are equal   opposite angles are equal   diagonals bisect each other

Example 7 — Self Tutor

Find x, giving a brief reason for your answer:

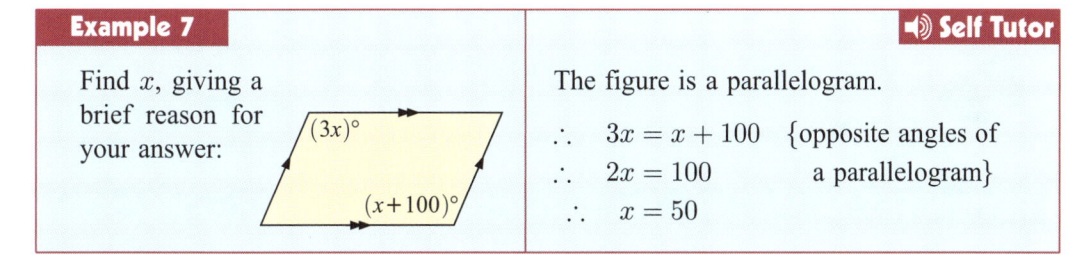

$(3x)°$
$(x + 100)°$

The figure is a parallelogram.

∴ $3x = x + 100$ {opposite angles of
∴ $2x = 100$ a parallelogram}
∴ $x = 50$

EXERCISE 7F

1 Draw four diagrams which show the four properties of:
   a a rhombus   **b** a kite.

THE GEOMETRY OF POLYGONS (Chapter 7)

2 Find the values of the variables in:

a. $(x+80)°$, $3x°$

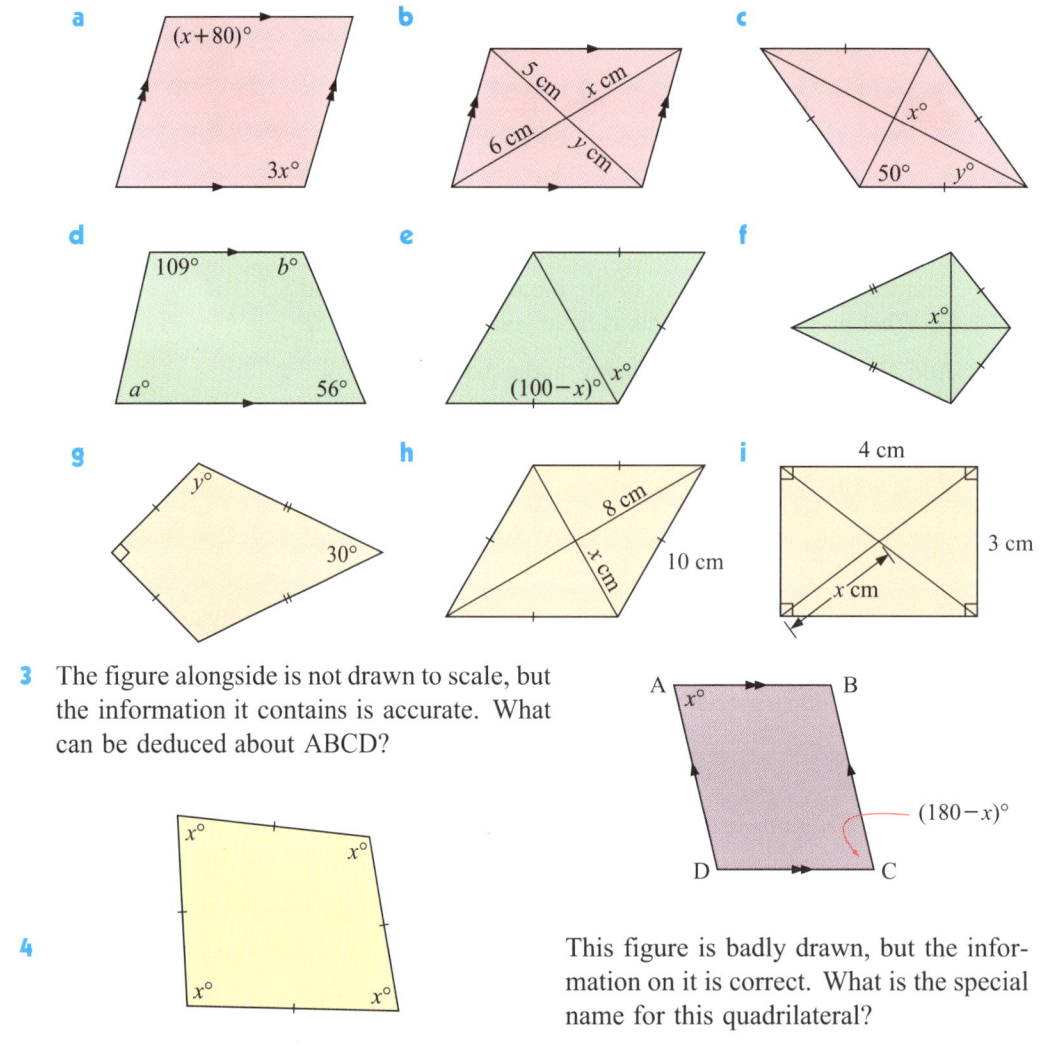

b. 5 cm, 6 cm, x cm, y cm

c. $x°$, $50°$, $y°$

d. $109°$, $b°$, $a°$, $56°$

e. $(100-x)°$, $x°$

f. $x°$

g. $y°$, $30°$

h. 8 cm, 10 cm, x cm

i. 4 cm, 3 cm, x cm

3 The figure alongside is not drawn to scale, but the information it contains is accurate. What can be deduced about ABCD?

A $x°$ — B, D — C $(180-x)°$

4 This figure is badly drawn, but the information on it is correct. What is the special name for this quadrilateral?

($x°$, $x°$, $x°$, $x°$)

5 Answer the questions in the **Opening Problem** on page **150**.

INVESTIGATION 3 — THE MIDPOINTS ON A QUADRILATERAL

Click on the icon to obtain a printable investigation.

REVIEW SET 7A

1 Find the values of the variables, giving brief reasons for your answers:

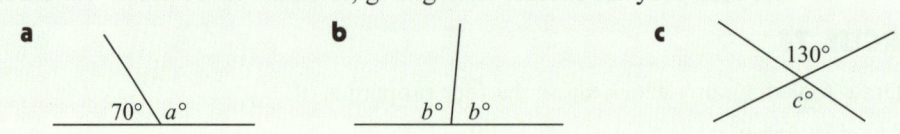

a. $70°$, $a°$

b. $b°$ | $b°$

c. $130°$, $c°$

d, **e**, 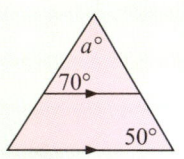 **f** (figures with angles: d shows parallel lines with 70°, a°, b°; e shows triangle with a°, 70°, 50° and parallel marks; f shows triangle with 75°, 65°, b°, c°, a°)

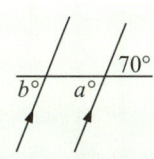

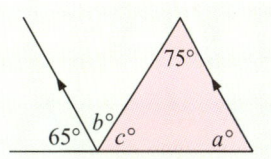

2 Find the value of the variable in each figure, giving a brief reason for your answer:

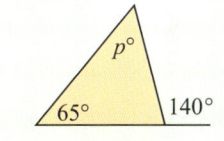

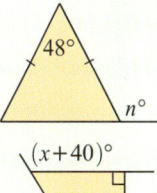

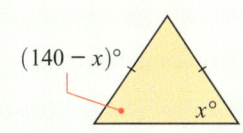

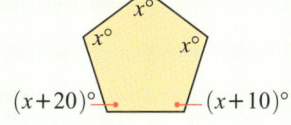

a triangle with angles $x°$, $x°$, $x°$

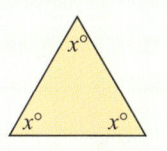

b triangle with $p°$, $65°$, $140°$ (exterior)

c triangle with $48°$ and $n°$

d triangle with $(140-x)°$ and $x°$ (with equal side marks)

e pentagon with angles $x°$, $x°$, $x°$, $(x+20)°$, $(x+10)°$

f quadrilateral with $(x+40)°$, $(x+50)°$, $x°$ and a right angle

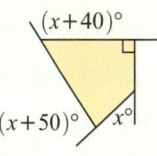

3 State whether the following are true or false:

a The sum of the lengths of two sides of a triangle is always greater than the length of the third side.

b A square is a parallelogram.

c The sum of the interior angles of an n-sided polygon is $n \times 180°$.

d A rhombus is a regular polygon.

4 Classify each triangle, in as much detail as possible:

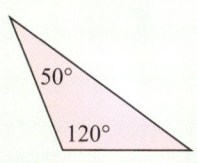

a triangle with $70°$, $40°$

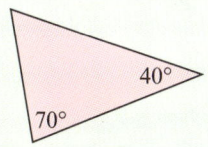

b triangle with $50°$, $120°$

c triangle with $2x°$, $x°$, $x°$

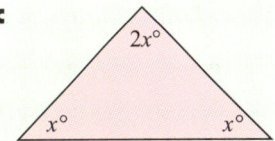

5 Classify each quadrilateral given below. The diagrams are not drawn to scale but the information on them is correct.

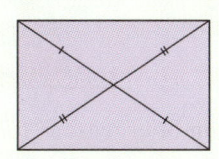

a kite-shaped figure with right angle and equal side marks

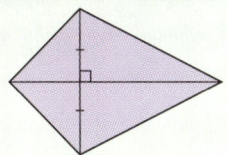

b rectangle-shaped figure with equal diagonal marks

c quadrilateral with two equal angles marked

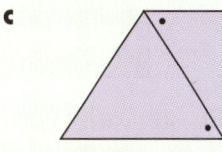

6 Show that in parallelogram ABCD alongside, x and y are supplementary, i.e., $x + y = 180$.

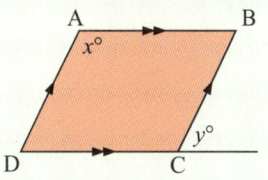

(Parallelogram ABCD with $x°$ at A and $y°$ at C)

REVIEW SET 7B

1 Find the values of the variables, giving brief reasons for your answers:

a angles $50°$, $b°$, $170°$

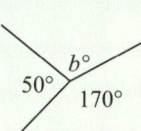

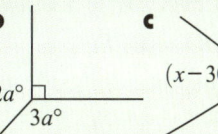

b angles $2a°$, $3a°$ with right angle

c angles $(x-30)°$, $(100-x)°$ at intersecting lines

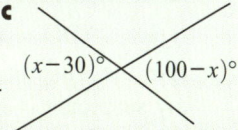

d (parallelogram with 70° and x°) **e** (rhombus with 120°, y°, x°) **f** (rectangle with diagonals, 40°, y°, x°)

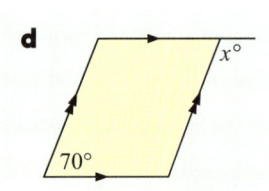

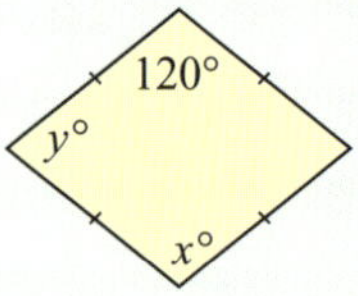

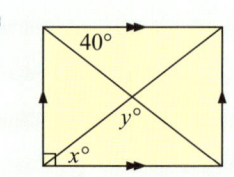

2 Find the values of the variables, giving brief reasons for your answers:

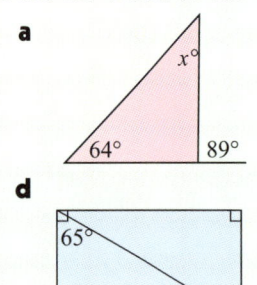

a (triangle with x°, 64°, 89°) **b** (triangle with 50°, y°, x° and parallel marks) **c** (trapezium with 3y°, 2x°, y°, x°)

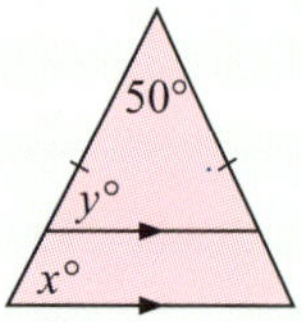

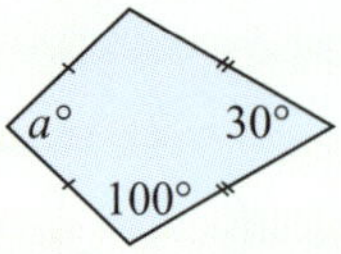

d (rectangle with diagonal, 65°, x°) **e** (kite with a°, 30°, 100°) **f** (triangle with x cm, 10 cm, 12 cm)

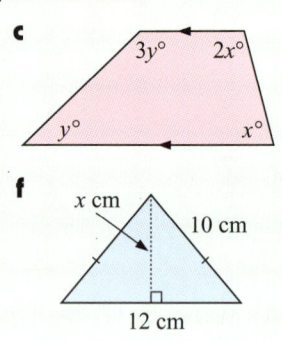

3 Classify each triangle, in as much detail as possible:

a (triangle with 36°, 54°) **b** (triangle with 60° and equal marks) **c** (triangle in circle with 100°, centre C)

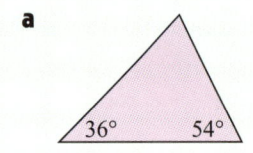

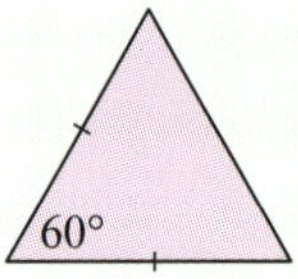

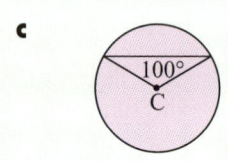

4 Find the value of the variable in each figure, giving brief reasons for your answers:

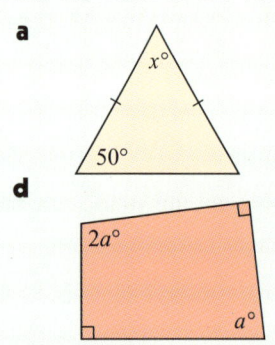

a (isosceles triangle with x°, 50°) **b** (right triangle with 40°, x°) **c** (isosceles triangle with 65°, x°)

d (quadrilateral with 2a°, a°, right angle) **e** (quadrilateral with 2x°, x°, 116°, 94°) **f** (figure with 29°, 29°, 50°, 50°, 8 cm, x cm)

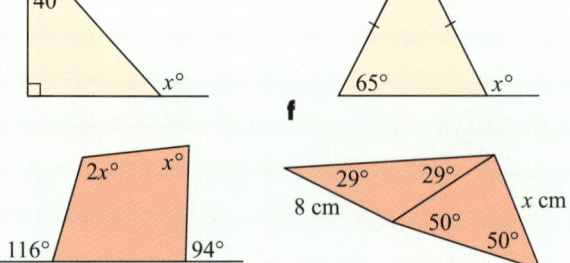

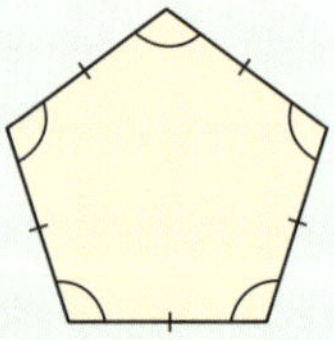

5 Classify each figure, giving brief reasons for your answers:

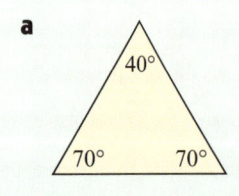

a (triangle with 40°, 70°, 70°) **b** (pentagon with equal sides and angles) **c** (parallelogram)

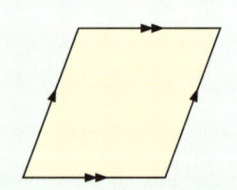

6 ABCD is a trapezium in which [AB] is parallel to [DC] and AD = BC. It seems that every time I draw such a figure, $A\hat{D}C = B\hat{C}D$.
Use the diagram alongside to prove my suspicion is always true.

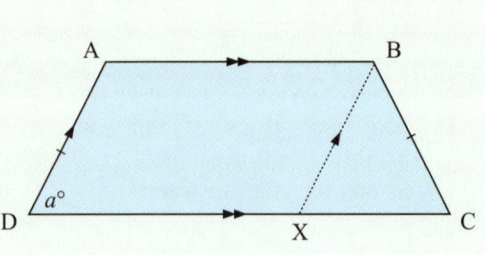

(Diagram: trapezium ABCD with A, B on top, D, C on bottom, X on DC, dashed line BX, angle a° at D)

Chapter 8

Indices

Contents:
- **A** Algebraic products and quotients in index notation
- **B** Index laws
- **C** Expansion laws
- **D** Zero and negative indices
- **E** Scientific notation (Standard form)
- **F** Significant figures

174 INDICES (Chapter 8)

OPENING PROBLEM

Hilbert wanted to find the number of atoms in one kilogram of pure gold. He was surprised to find that some scientists actually define what a kilogram means in terms of gold. They do this because gold is a perfectly stable element. Hilbert found that under such a definition, a kilogram equals 3 057 443 616 231 138 188 734 962 atoms of gold.

Things to think about:

- How can we best approximate this number?
- How can we write this number to make it easier to use?
- Can such a form be used to write very small numbers?

Some other large numbers include:

- The number of grains of sand in a large beach is about 100 000 000 000 000.
- The weight of sea water throughout the world is about 150 000 000 000 000 000 000 kg.
- Each drop of water contains about 2 000 000 000 000 000 000 000 molecules.

A — ALGEBRAIC PRODUCTS AND QUOTIENTS IN INDEX NOTATION

We have seen that:

If n is a positive integer, then a^n is the product of n factors of a.

$$a^n = \underbrace{a \times a \times a \times a \times a \times a \times \ldots \times a}_{n \text{ factors}}$$

Example 1

Simplify: **a** $m^3 \times m^2$ **b** $p^5 \times p$

a $m^3 \times m^2$
$= (m \times m \times m) \times (m \times m)$
$= m^5$

b $p^5 \times p$
$= (p \times p \times p \times p \times p) \times p$
$= p^6$

p^5 is the product of five ps.

EXERCISE 8A

1 Simplify:

a	$a \times a$	**b**	$b^2 \times b$	**c**	$c \times c^3$	**d**	$n^2 \times n^2$
e	$m \times m^2$	**f**	$s \times s^4$	**g**	$e^3 \times e^3$	**h**	$k^3 \times k^2$
i	$p^2 \times p^4$	**j**	$p^2 \times p$	**k**	$k^6 \times k^3$	**l**	$m^3 \times m$
m	$k^6 \times k$	**n**	$n \times n^4 \times n$	**o**	$e^4 \times e^3 \times e$	**p**	$n \times n \times n^2$

Example 2 🔊 Self Tutor

Simplify: **a** $(x^2)^2$ **b** $(5b^3)^2$

a $(x^2)^2$
$= x^2 \times x^2$
$= x \times x \times x \times x$
$= x^4$

b $(5b^3)^2$
$= 5b^3 \times 5b^3$
$= 5 \times b \times b \times b \times 5 \times b \times b \times b$
$= 25b^6$

---

2 Simplify:

a	$(a^2)^2$	**b**	$(s^3)^2$	**c**	$(g^2)^3$	**d**	$(ac)^2$
e	$(m^4)^2$	**f**	$(3ab)^2$	**g**	$(2a^2)^2$	**h**	$(5b^2)^2$
i	$(3ab^2)^2$	**j**	$(7m^2n)^2$	**k**	$(8a^2c)^2$	**l**	$(3x^2y)^3$
m	$(-a)^2$	**n**	$(-2a)^2$	**o**	$(-3b)^3$	**p**	$-2a \times (-5a)^2$

Example 3 🔊 Self Tutor

Simplify these quotients: **a** $\dfrac{x^5}{x}$ **b** $\dfrac{a^6}{a^3}$

a $\dfrac{x^5}{x}$
$= \dfrac{x \times x \times x \times x \times x \times \cancel{x}^{\;1}}{\cancel{x}^{\;1}}$
$= x^4$

b $\dfrac{a^6}{a^3}$
$= \dfrac{a \times a \times a \times \cancel{a} \times \cancel{a} \times \cancel{a}^{\;1}}{\cancel{a} \times \cancel{a} \times \cancel{a}^{\;1}}$
$= a^3$

---

3 Simplify:

a	$\dfrac{a^2}{a}$	**b**	$\dfrac{m^3}{m}$	**c**	$\dfrac{t^2}{t^2}$	**d**	$\dfrac{y^4}{y^2}$
e	$\dfrac{k^5}{k^2}$	**f**	$\dfrac{p^5}{p^3}$	**g**	$\dfrac{2n^6}{n^2}$	**h**	$\dfrac{6r^5}{3r^4}$
i	$\dfrac{12g^7}{3g^4}$	**j**	$\dfrac{8d^8}{12d^3}$	**k**	$\dfrac{10e^7}{2e^2}$	**l**	$\dfrac{5h^9}{15h^4}$

B   INDEX LAWS

INVESTIGATION 1 — DISCOVERING INDEX LAWS

Look for any patterns as you complete the following:

1 Copy and complete:

    a $2^2 \times 2^3 = (2 \times 2) \times (2 \times 2 \times 2) = 2^5$

    b $3^3 \times 3^1 = \boxed{} = \boxed{}$

    c $a^3 \times a^4 = \boxed{} = \boxed{}$

From the above examples, $a^m \times a^n = \boxed{}$.

2 Copy and complete:

    a $\dfrac{2^5}{2^3} = \dfrac{2 \times 2 \times 2 \times 2 \times 2}{2 \times 2 \times 2} = 2^2$ **b** $\dfrac{3^4}{3^1} = \boxed{} = \boxed{}$

    c $\dfrac{a^5}{a^2} = \boxed{} = \boxed{}$ **d** $\dfrac{x^7}{x^4} = \boxed{} = \boxed{}$

From the above examples, $\dfrac{a^m}{a^n} = \boxed{}$.

3 Copy and complete:

    a $(2^3)^2 = 2^3 \times 2^3 = (2 \times 2 \times 2) \times (2 \times 2 \times 2) = \boxed{}$

    b $(3^2)^4 = \boxed{} = \boxed{} = \boxed{}$

From the above examples, $(a^m)^n = \boxed{}$.

From **Investigation 1** you should have found these **index laws** for **positive indices**:

If m and n are positive integers, then:

- $a^m \times a^n = a^{m+n}$ To **multiply** numbers with the **same base**, keep the base and **add** the indices.
- $\dfrac{a^m}{a^n} = a^{m-n}, \ a \neq 0$ To **divide** numbers with the **same base**, keep the base and **subtract** the indices.
- $(a^m)^n = a^{m \times n}$ When **raising** a **power** to a **power**, keep the base and **multiply** the indices.

Example 4 — Self Tutor

Simplify using the laws of indices:

    a $2^3 \times 2^2$ **b** $x^4 \times x^5$

a $2^3 \times 2^2$
$= 2^{3+2}$
$= 2^5$
$= 32$

b $x^4 \times x^5$
$= x^{4+5}$
$= x^9$

When multiplying, keep the base and add the indices.

INDICES (Chapter 8) 177

EXERCISE 8B

1 Simplify using the index laws:

    a $2^2 \times 2^4$ **b** $3^2 \times 3^2$ **c** $5^3 \times 5^4$ **d** $7^2 \times 7^3$

    e $a^2 \times a^3$ **f** $n^4 \times n$ **g** $x^5 \times x^6$ **h** $b^2 \times b^5$

Example 5 — Self Tutor

When dividing, keep the base and subtract the indices.

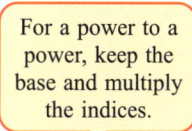

Simplify using the index laws:

    a $\dfrac{3^5}{3^3}$ **b** $\dfrac{p^7}{p^3}$

a $\dfrac{3^5}{3^3}$
$= 3^{5-3}$
$= 3^2$
$= 9$

b $\dfrac{p^7}{p^3}$
$= p^{7-3}$
$= p^4$

2 Simplify using the index laws:

    a $\dfrac{2^5}{2^2}$ **b** $\dfrac{3^4}{3^3}$ **c** $\dfrac{5^6}{5^4}$ **d** $\dfrac{10^7}{10^4}$

    e $\dfrac{x^7}{x^2}$ **f** $\dfrac{y^8}{y^2}$ **g** $a^6 \div a^5$ **h** $b^9 \div b^4$

For a power to a power, keep the base and multiply the indices.

Example 6 — Self Tutor

Simplify using the index laws:

    a $(2^3)^2$ **b** $(x^4)^5$

a $(2^3)^2$
$= 2^{3 \times 2}$
$= 2^6$
$= 64$

b $(x^4)^5$
$= x^{4 \times 5}$
$= x^{20}$

3 Simplify using the index laws:

    a $(2^2)^3$ **b** $(10^4)^2$ **c** $(3^3)^4$ **d** $(2^3)^5$

    e $(x^3)^4$ **f** $(x^5)^2$ **g** $(a^4)^5$ **h** $(b^3)^7$

4 Simplify using the index laws:

    a $a^3 \times a^2$ **b** $b^7 \div b^2$ **c** $c^4 \times c^3$ **d** $d^4 \times d$

    e $(a^4)^3$ **f** $b^8 \div b^5$ **g** $(b^2)^5$ **h** $a^3 \times a^n$

    i $b^4 \div b^3$ **j** $m^4 \times m^2 \times m^3$ **k** $(a^2)^3 \times a$ **l** $(g^3)^3 \times g^2$

178   INDICES   (Chapter 8)

Example 7 ◀)) Self Tutor

Simplify using the index laws:

a $2b^2 \times 3a^2b^3$
b $\dfrac{6x^4y^3}{3x^2y}$

a $2b^2 \times 3a^2b^3$
$= 2 \times 3 \times a^2 \times b^2 \times b^3$
$= 6 \times a^2 \times b^{2+3}$
$= 6a^2b^5$

b $\dfrac{6x^4y^3}{3x^2y}$
$= \dfrac{6}{3} \times x^{4-2} \times y^{3-1}$
$= 2x^2y^2$

5 Simplify using the index laws:

a $\dfrac{a^3}{a}$
b $4b^2 \times 2b^3$
c $10hk^3 \times 4h^4$
d $\dfrac{14a^7}{2a^2}$

e $\dfrac{12a^2b^3}{3ab}$
f $\dfrac{m^5n^4}{m^2n^3}$
g $\dfrac{m^{21}}{(m^2)^8}$
h $\dfrac{p^2 \times p^7}{(p^3)^2}$

C EXPANSION LAWS

INVESTIGATION 2   DISCOVERING EXPANSION LAWS

Look for any patterns as you complete the following:

1 Copy and complete the following:

a $(ab)^4 = ab \times ab \times ab \times ab = a \times a \times a \times a \times b \times b \times b \times b = \boxed{}$

b $(ab)^3 = \boxed{} = \boxed{} = \boxed{}$

c $(2a)^5 = \boxed{} = \boxed{} = \boxed{}$

In general, $(ab)^n = \boxed{}$.

2 Copy and complete:

a $\left(\dfrac{a}{b}\right)^3 = \dfrac{a}{b} \times \dfrac{a}{b} \times \dfrac{a}{b} = \dfrac{a \times a \times a}{b \times b \times b} = \boxed{}$

b $\left(\dfrac{a}{b}\right)^4 = \boxed{} = \boxed{} = \boxed{}$

In general, $\left(\dfrac{a}{b}\right)^n = \boxed{}$ for $b \neq 0$.

From **Investigation 2** you should have found these **expansion laws** for **positive indices**:

If n is a positive integer, then:
- $(ab)^n = a^n b^n$
- $\left(\dfrac{a}{b}\right)^n = \dfrac{a^n}{b^n}$ provided $b \neq 0$.

Example 8

Remove the brackets and simplify:

a $(ab)^5$ b $(2xy)^3$

a $(ab)^5$
$= a^5 b^5$

b $(2xy)^3$
$= 2^3 \times x^3 \times y^3$
$= 8x^3 y^3$

Raise each factor to the given power.

EXERCISE 8C

1 Remove the brackets of the following and simplify:

a $(ab)^4$ b $(xy)^3$ c $(ac)^4$ d $(xyz)^3$
e $(2x)^5$ f $(3a)^4$ g $(2m)^3$ h $(5ab)^3$

Example 9

Remove the brackets and simplify:

a $\left(\dfrac{m}{n}\right)^4$ b $\left(\dfrac{2}{b}\right)^3$

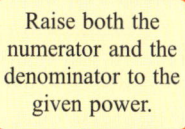

a $\left(\dfrac{m}{n}\right)^4$
$= \dfrac{m^4}{n^4}$

b $\left(\dfrac{2}{b}\right)^3 = \dfrac{2^3}{b^3}$
$= \dfrac{8}{b^3}$

Raise both the numerator and the denominator to the given power.

2 Remove the brackets of the following and simplify:

a $\left(\dfrac{x}{y}\right)^2$ b $\left(\dfrac{a}{b}\right)^3$ c $\left(\dfrac{p}{q}\right)^4$ d $\left(\dfrac{c}{d}\right)^5$
e $\left(\dfrac{3}{x}\right)^2$ f $\left(\dfrac{y}{5}\right)^3$ g $\left(\dfrac{2}{a}\right)^4$ h $\left(\dfrac{b}{2}\right)^5$

Example 10

Express the following in simplest form, without brackets:

a $(3a^2)^2$ b $(4a^2 b)^3$

a $(3a^2)^2$
$= 3^2 \times (a^2)^2$
$= 9a^4$

b $(4a^2 b)^3$
$= 4^3 \times (a^2)^3 \times b^3$
$= 64 a^6 b^3$

3 Express the following in simplest form, without brackets:

a $(2a^3)^2$ b $(5n^2)^2$ c $(3x^2)^2$ d $(3a^3)^2$

e $(xy^2)^2$ f $(x^2y)^3$ g $(2a)^2 \times 3a$ h $(3a^2b)^2$

i $(3ab^2)^3$ j $(7a^3c)^2$ k $(2a^2b)^4$ l $(3ab^3)^3$

Example 11   ◀)) **Self Tutor**

Express the following in simplest form, without brackets:

a $\left(\dfrac{xy}{3}\right)^2$ b $\left(\dfrac{2b}{3a^3}\right)^4$

a $\left(\dfrac{xy}{3}\right)^2$
$= \dfrac{x^2 \times y^2}{3^2}$
$= \dfrac{x^2 y^2}{9}$

b $\left(\dfrac{2b}{3a^3}\right)^4$
$= \dfrac{2^4 b^4}{3^4 (a^3)^4}$
$= \dfrac{16 b^4}{81 a^{12}}$

---

4 Express the following in simplest form, without brackets:

a $\left(\dfrac{ab}{2}\right)^2$ b $\left(\dfrac{3}{bc}\right)^2$ c $\left(\dfrac{2m}{n}\right)^3$ d $\left(\dfrac{m^2}{4}\right)^2$

e $\left(\dfrac{2a^2}{b}\right)^2$ f $\left(\dfrac{c^2}{2d}\right)^3$ g $\left(\dfrac{4a^2}{3b}\right)^2$ h $\left(\dfrac{2a}{3b^3}\right)^4$

D   ZERO AND NEGATIVE INDICES

From our original definition $a^n = \underbrace{a \times a \times a \times \ldots \times a}_{n \text{ times}},$ a^0 has no meaning.

However, consider the pattern:

$2^3 = 8$
$2^2 = 4$
$2^1 = 2$

If we continue the pattern, we get: $2^0 = 1$

$2^{-1} = \tfrac{1}{2} = \dfrac{1}{2^1}$

$2^{-2} = \tfrac{1}{4} = \dfrac{1}{2^2}$

> Each time the power of 2 decreases by 1, the result is halved.

In other bases such as 3 or 5, the same pattern will occur. We therefore define the following laws for zero and negative indices:

ZERO INDEX LAW

$$a^0 = 1 \quad \text{for all} \quad a \neq 0.$$

NEGATIVE INDEX LAW

If a is any non-zero number and n is an integer, then $a^{-n} = \dfrac{1}{a^n}$

This means that a^n and a^{-n} are **reciprocals** of one another.

In particular notice that $a^{-1} = \dfrac{1}{a}$.

Example 12

Simplify: **a** 7^0 **b** x^0 **c** $\dfrac{y^4}{y^4}$ **d** $2 + 5^0$

a 7^0
$= 1$

b x^0
$= 1$

c $\dfrac{y^4}{y^4}$
$= y^{4-4}$
$= y^0$
$= 1$

d $2 + 5^0$
$= 2 + 1$
$= 3$

Example 13

Simplify:
a 3^{-1} **b** 5^{-2} **c** 10^{-4}

a 3^{-1}
$= \dfrac{1}{3^1}$
$= \dfrac{1}{3}$

b 5^{-2}
$= \dfrac{1}{5^2}$
$= \dfrac{1}{25}$

c 10^{-4}
$= \dfrac{1}{10^4}$
$= \dfrac{1}{10\,000}$

*The negative index indicates the **reciprocal**.*

EXERCISE 8D

1 Simplify:

a 3^0 **b** 6^0 **c** 10^0 **d** 8^0
e y^0 **f** a^0 **g** $2x^0$ **h** $(2x)^0$
i $\dfrac{x^3}{x^3}$ **j** $\dfrac{b^5}{b^5}$ **k** $3 + 2^0$ **l** $5 - 7^0$

2 Simplify, giving answers in simplest rational form:

a 4^{-1} **b** 2^{-1} **c** 6^{-1} **d** 8^{-1} **e** 2^{-2}
f 3^{-2} **g** 7^{-2} **h** 9^{-2} **i** 3^{-3} **j** 10^{-5}

Example 14

Simplify, giving answers in simplest rational form:

a $\left(\frac{2}{3}\right)^{-1}$ **b** $\left(\frac{3}{5}\right)^{-2}$ **c** $8^0 - 8^{-1}$

a $\left(\frac{2}{3}\right)^{-1}$
$= \left(\frac{3}{2}\right)^1$
$= \frac{3}{2}$

b $\left(\frac{3}{5}\right)^{-2}$
$= \left(\frac{5}{3}\right)^2$
$= \frac{5^2}{3^2}$
$= \frac{25}{9}$

c $8^0 - 8^{-1}$
$= 1 - \frac{1}{8}$
$= \frac{7}{8}$

3 Simplify, giving answers in simplest rational form:

a $\left(\frac{1}{2}\right)^{-1}$ **b** $\left(\frac{1}{4}\right)^{-1}$ **c** $\left(\frac{4}{5}\right)^{-1}$ **d** $\left(\frac{5}{3}\right)^{-1}$ **e** $\left(\frac{1}{9}\right)^{-1}$

f $2^0 + 2^{-1}$ **g** $\left(\frac{2}{3}\right)^{-2}$ **h** $\left(1\frac{3}{4}\right)^{-2}$ **i** $\left(\frac{3}{4}\right)^{-3}$ **j** $3^0 + 3^1 - 3^{-1}$

Example 15

Write the following without brackets or negative indices:

a $8ab^{-1}$ **b** $8(ab)^{-1}$

a $8ab^{-1}$
$= \frac{8a}{1} \times \frac{1}{b}$
$= \frac{8a}{b}$

b $8(ab)^{-1}$
$= 8 \times \frac{1}{ab}$
$= \frac{8}{ab}$

4 Write the following without brackets or negative indices:

a $2a^{-1}$ **b** $(2a)^{-1}$ **c** $4b^{-1}$ **d** $(4b)^{-1}$
e $3b^{-2}$ **f** $(3b)^{-2}$ **g** $(5c)^{-2}$ **h** $5c^{-2}$
i xy^{-1} **j** $(xy)^{-1}$ **k** xy^{-2} **l** $(xy)^{-2}$
m $2ab^{-1}$ **n** $(2ab)^{-1}$ **o** $2(ab)^{-1}$ **p** $(3n^{-2})^{-1}$

5 Write as powers of 10:

a 1000 **b** 1 000 000 **c** 0.001 **d** 0.000 000 01

6 Write as powers of 2, 3 or 5:

a 8 **b** $\frac{1}{8}$ **c** 9 **d** $\frac{1}{9}$
e 125 **f** $\frac{1}{125}$ **g** 32 **h** $\frac{1}{32}$
i 81 **j** $\frac{1}{81}$ **k** $\frac{1}{25}$ **l** 1

INDICES (Chapter 8)   183

E   SCIENTIFIC NOTATION (STANDARD FORM)

Observe the pattern:

$10\,000 = 10^4$
$1000 = 10^3$
$100 = 10^2$
$10 = 10^1$
$1 = 10^0$
$\frac{1}{10} = 10^{-1}$
$\frac{1}{100} = 10^{-2}$
$\frac{1}{1000} = 10^{-3}$

As we divide by 10, the **exponent** or **power** of 10 decreases by one.

We can use this pattern to simplify the writing of very large and very small numbers.

For example,

$$300\,000 = 3 \times 100\,000 = 3 \times 10^5$$

and

$$0.0002 = \frac{2}{10\,000} = \frac{2}{1} \times \frac{1}{10\,000} = 2 \times 10^{-4}$$

SCIENTIFIC NOTATION

Scientific notation or **standard form** involves writing any given number as *a number between* 1 *inclusive and* 10, multiplied by a *power of* 10, i.e., $a \times 10^k$ where $1 \leqslant a < 10$ and k is an integer.

Example 16   ◀) Self Tutor

Write in scientific notation: **a** 37 600   **b** 0.000 86

a $37\,600 = 3.76 \times 10\,000$
$= 3.76 \times 10^4$ {shift decimal point 4 places to the left and × 10 000}

b $0.000\,86 = 8.6 \div 10^4$
$= 8.6 \times 10^{-4}$ {shift decimal point 4 places to the right and ÷ 10 000}

Notice that:
- If the original number is > 10, the power of 10 is **positive** (+).
- If the original number is < 1, the power of 10 is **negative** (−).
- If the original number is between 1 and 10, we write the number as it is and multiply it by 10^0, which is really just 1.

EXERCISE 8E.1

1 Write the following as powers of 10:
   a 100
   b 1000
   c 10
   d 100 000
   e 0.1
   f 0.01
   g 0.0001
   h 100 000 000

2 Express the following in scientific notation:
   a 259
   b 259 000
   c 2.59
   d 0.259
   e 0.000 259
   f 40.7
   g 4070
   h 0.0407
   i 407 000
   j 407 000 000
   k 0.000 040 7

3 Express the following in scientific notation:
   a The distance from the earth to the sun is 149 500 000 000 m.
   b Bacteria are single cell organisms, some of which have a diameter of 0.0003 mm.
   c A speck of dust is smaller than 0.001 mm.
   d The probability that your six numbers will be selected for Lotto on Monday night is 0.000 000 141 62.
   e The central temperature of the sun is 15 million degrees Celsius.
   f A single red blood cell lives for about four months and during this time it will circulate around the body 300 000 times.

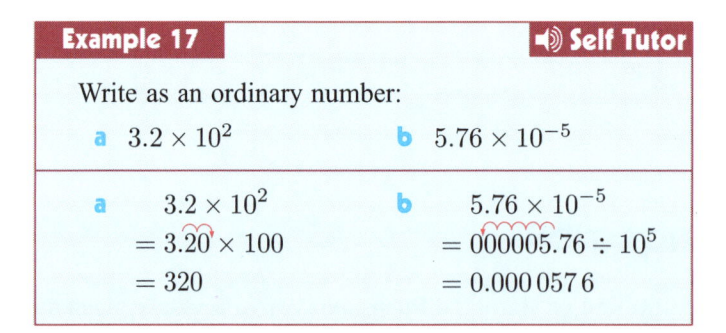

Example 17

Write as an ordinary number:
a 3.2×10^2
b 5.76×10^{-5}

a 3.2×10^2
  $= 3.20 \times 100$
  $= 320$

b 5.76×10^{-5}
  $= 000005.76 \div 10^5$
  $= 0.000\,057\,6$

4 Write as an ordinary decimal number:
   a 4×10^3
   b 5×10^2
   c 2.1×10^3
   d 7.8×10^4
   e 3.8×10^5
   f 8.6×10^1
   g 4.33×10^7
   h 6×10^7

5 Write as an ordinary decimal number:
   a 4×10^{-3}
   b 5×10^{-2}
   c 2.1×10^{-3}
   d 7.8×10^{-4}
   e 3.8×10^{-5}
   f 8.6×10^{-1}
   g 4.33×10^{-7}
   h 6×10^{-7}

6 Express the following quantities as ordinary decimal numbers:
   a The wavelength of light is 9×10^{-7} m.
   b The estimated world population for the year 2000 was 6.130×10^9.
   c The diameter of our galaxy, the Milky Way, is 1×10^5 light years.
   d The smallest viruses are 1×10^{-5} mm in size.
   e The mass of a bee's wing is 10^{-7} kg.

INDICES (Chapter 8) 185

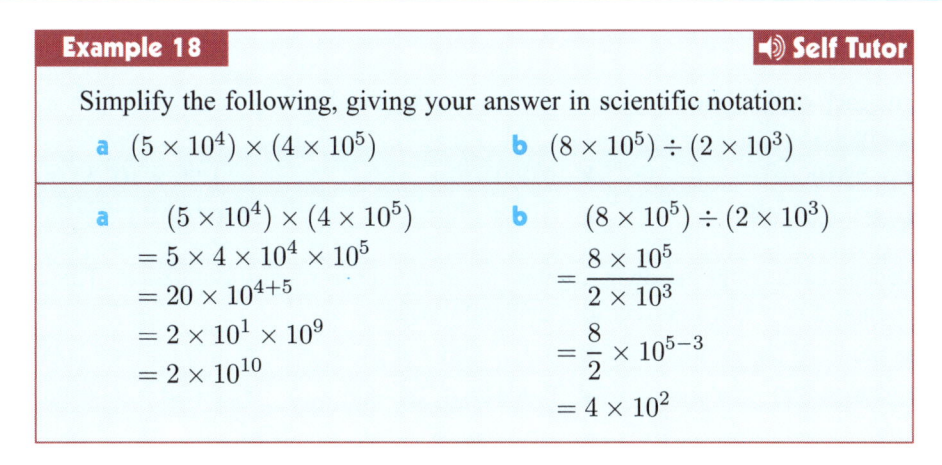

> **Example 18** ◀)) **Self Tutor**
>
> Simplify the following, giving your answer in scientific notation:
> a $(5 \times 10^4) \times (4 \times 10^5)$
> b $(8 \times 10^5) \div (2 \times 10^3)$
>
> a $(5 \times 10^4) \times (4 \times 10^5)$
> $= 5 \times 4 \times 10^4 \times 10^5$
> $= 20 \times 10^{4+5}$
> $= 2 \times 10^1 \times 10^9$
> $= 2 \times 10^{10}$
>
> b $(8 \times 10^5) \div (2 \times 10^3)$
> $= \dfrac{8 \times 10^5}{2 \times 10^3}$
> $= \dfrac{8}{2} \times 10^{5-3}$
> $= 4 \times 10^2$

7 Simplify the following, giving your answer in scientific notation:

a $(3 \times 10^3) \times (2 \times 10^2)$
b $(5 \times 10^2) \times (7 \times 10^5)$
c $(5 \times 10^4) \times (6 \times 10^3)$
d $(3 \times 10^3)^2$
e $(5 \times 10^4)^2$
f $(8 \times 10^{-2})^2$
g $(8 \times 10^4) \div (4 \times 10^2)$
h $(8 \times 10^5) \div (2 \times 10^3)$

SCIENTIFIC NOTATION ON A CALCULATOR

Scientific calculators can display very large and very small numbers using **scientific notation**.

If you perform the operation $2\,300\,000 \times 400\,000$ on your calculator, it will display 9.2^{11} or $9.2E11$ or something similar. This actually represents 9.2×10^{11}.

Likewise, if you perform $0.0024 \div 10\,000\,000$ your calculator will display 2.4^{-10} or $2.4E-10$ or something similar. This actually represents 2.4×10^{-10}.

Numbers which are already represented in scientific notation can be entered into the calculator using the EXP or EE key.

For example, 4.022×10^4 can be entered as: 4.022 EXP 4 or 4.022 EE 4 and will appear as 4.022^{04} or $4.022E4$ on the display.

Likewise, 5.446×10^{-11} can be entered as 5.446 EXP 11 +/− or 5.446 EE (−) 11 and will appear as 5.446^{-11} or $5.446E-11$.

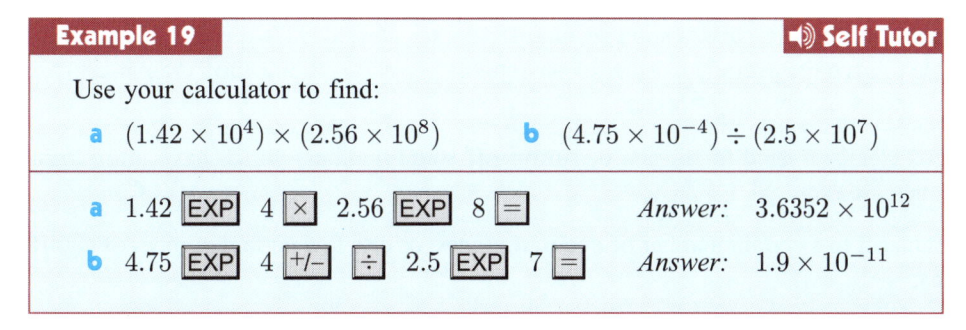

> **Example 19** ◀)) **Self Tutor**
>
> Use your calculator to find:
> a $(1.42 \times 10^4) \times (2.56 \times 10^8)$
> b $(4.75 \times 10^{-4}) \div (2.5 \times 10^7)$
>
> a 1.42 EXP 4 × 2.56 EXP 8 =   Answer: 3.6352×10^{12}
> b 4.75 EXP 4 +/− ÷ 2.5 EXP 7 =   Answer: 1.9×10^{-11}

EXERCISE 8E.2

1 Write each of the following as it would appear on the display of a calculator in scientific notation:

    a 1 220 000   **b** 0.000 046 4   **c** 1.26×10^{-4}

    d 2.464×10^{10} **e** 21 400 000   **f** 0.000 007 31

2 Calculate each of the following, giving your answer in scientific notation. The decimal part should be written correct to 2 decimal places.

    a $0.06 \times 0.002 \div 4000$ **b** $426 \times 760 \times 42\,000$ **c** $627\,000 \times 74\,000$

    d $320 \times 600 \times 51\,400$ **e** $0.004\,28 \div 120\,000$ **f** $0.026 \times 0.00\,42 \times 0.08$

3 Find, in scientific notation with decimal part correct to 2 places:

    a $(3.42 \times 10^5) \times (4.8 \times 10^4)$ **b** $(6.42 \times 10^{-2})^2$ **c** $\dfrac{3.16 \times 10^{-10}}{6 \times 10^7}$

    d $(9.8 \times 10^{-4}) \div (7.2 \times 10^{-6})$ **e** $\dfrac{1}{3.8 \times 10^5}$ **f** $(1.2 \times 10^3)^3$

4 If a missile travels at 5400 km per hour, how far will it travel in:

    a 1 day   **b** 1 week   **c** 2 years?

Give your answers in scientific notation with decimal part correct to 2 places. Assume that 1 year $\approx$ 365.25 days.

5 Light travels at a speed of 3×10^8 metres per second. How far will light travel in:

    a 1 minute   **b** 1 day   **c** 1 year?

Give your answers in scientific notation with decimal part correct to 2 places. Assume that 1 year $\approx$ 365.25 days.

F SIGNIFICANT FIGURES

There are many occasions when it is sensible to give an **approximate answer** to an arithmetic calculation.

For example, if we want to know how many people attended a football match, a figure of 32 000 would be acceptable even though the exact number was 31 964.

Likewise, if a traffic survey showed that 1852 cars carried 4376 people, it would not be sensible to give the average number of passengers per car as 2.362 850 972. An approximate answer of 2.4 is more appropriate.

There is clearly a need to shorten or **round off** some numbers which have more figures in them than are required.

We round off to a certain number of **decimal places**, or else to a certain number of **significant figures**.

THE PROCEDURE FOR ROUNDING OFF TO SIGNIFICANT FIGURES

To round off to n significant figures, look at the $(n+1)$th digit from the left:
- if it is 0, 1, 2, 3 or 4, do not change the nth figure,
- if it is 5, 6, 7, 8 or 9, increase the nth figure by 1.

Delete all figures after the nth figure, replacing by 0's if necessary.

Converting to **scientific notation** provides us with a safe method of rounding off.

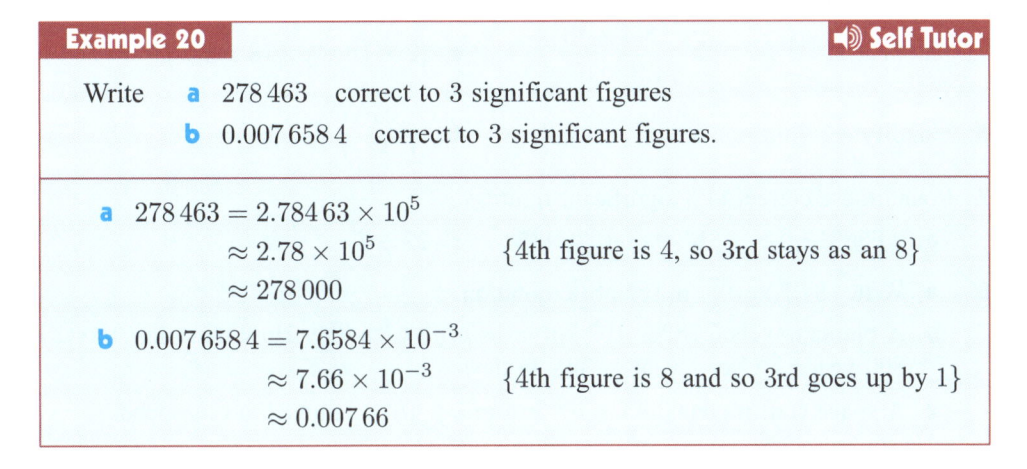

Example 20

Write **a** 278 463 correct to 3 significant figures
       b 0.007 658 4 correct to 3 significant figures.

a $278\,463 = 2.784\,63 \times 10^5$
       $\approx 2.78 \times 10^5$ {4th figure is 4, so 3rd stays as an 8}
       $\approx 278\,000$

b $0.007\,658\,4 = 7.6584 \times 10^{-3}$
       $\approx 7.66 \times 10^{-3}$ {4th figure is 8 and so 3rd goes up by 1}
       $\approx 0.007\,66$

EXERCISE 8F

1 Write correct to 2 significant figures:

   a 567   **b** 16 342   **c** 70.7   **d** 3.001   **e** 0.716
   f 49.6   **g** 3.046   **h** 1760   **i** 0.040 9   **j** 45 600

2 Write correct to 3 significant figures:

   a 43 620   **b** 10 076   **c** $0.\overline{6}$
   d 0.036 821   **e** 0.318 6   **f** 0.719 6
   g $0.\overline{63}$ **h** 0.063 71   **i** 18.997
   j 256 800

> A bar over a digit indicates a recurring decimal.
> $0.\overline{6} = 0.666\,666\,....$
> $0.\overline{63} = 0.636\,363\,......$

3 Write correct to 4 significant figures:

   a 28.039 2   **b** 0.005 362   **c** 23 683.9   **d** 42 366 709
   e 0.038 792   **f** 0.006 377 9   **g** 0.000 899 95   **h** 43.076 321

4 Consider the **Opening Problem** on page **174**. Write the number of atoms in a kilogram of gold in standard form with decimal part correct to 3 significant figures.

RUSSIAN PEASANT MULTIPLICATION

LINKS
click here

Areas of interaction:
Human ingenuity, Approaches to learning

REVIEW SET 8A

1. Simplify using index laws: **a** $x^8 \times x^3$ **b** $(a^4)^3$ **c** $\dfrac{b^8}{b^3}$

2. Express as powers of 3: **a** $3^2 \times 3^3 \times 3$ **b** $3^{11} \div 3^7$

3. Write in scientific notation: **a** 3762 **b** $0.000\,104\,3$ **c** 8.62

4. Simplify: **a** $6^0 + 6^1 + 6^2$ **b** $2^{-1} + (\tfrac{1}{3})^{-1}$ **c** $(\tfrac{5}{8})^{-2}$

5. Simplify, giving your answer in scientific notation:

    a $(4 \times 10^4)^3$ **b** $\dfrac{8.4 \times 10^4}{1.2 \times 10^{-3}}$ **c** $(2 \times 10^{-4}) \times (8 \times 10^7)$

6. Simplify: **a** $2x^3 \times 4x^{10}$ **b** $\left(\dfrac{2a^2}{b^2}\right)^3$

7. Round these correct to 3 significant figures:

    a 2.65831 **b** $0.000\,620\,435$ **c** $22 \div 7$

8. **a** Write 34.7×10^7 in scientific notation.

   b A planet travels 5.782×10^8 km in its orbit each day. How far will it travel in 800 years? Use 1 year ≈ 365.25 days.

   c A space craft travels 3.45×10^8 km in 5×10^{-3} hours. Find its speed.

REVIEW SET 8B

1. Simplify the following: **a** $a^{12} \div a^3$ **b** $(2x^3)^5$ **c** $6c^3 \times 7c^5$

2. Write as powers of 7: **a** 1 **b** $7^2 \times 7^3$

3. Write in scientific notation: **a** $0.003\,15$ **b** $413\,200$ **c** 0.8904

4. Simplify: **a** $(\tfrac{3}{2})^{-2}$ **b** $3^0 - 3^{-1}$ **c** $-(-1)^{10}$

5. Simplify, giving your answers in scientific notation:

    a $(8 \times 10^{-3})^2$ **b** $\dfrac{4.5 \times 10^4}{9 \times 10^{-2}}$ **c** $(4 \times 10^{-3}) \times (9 \times 10^7)$

6. Simplify:

    a $4d^{13} \times 5d^{18}$ **b** $\left(\dfrac{4x}{y^3}\right)^2$

7. Round these correct to 3 significant figures:

    a 58.049991 **b** $0.008\,255$ **c** $31 \div 11$

8. **a** Write 32×10^{-7} in scientific notation.

   b On average a bank receives €4.578×10^7 per week. How much will it receive in 20 years? Use 1 year ≈ 365.25 days.

   c A sub-atomic particle travels a distance of 5×10^5 cm in 8×10^{-6} sec. Find its speed.

Chapter 9

Radicals and Pythagoras

Contents:
- A Square roots
- B Rules for square roots
- C Solving equations of the form $x^2 = k$
- D The theorem of Pythagoras
- E The converse of Pythagoras' Theorem
- F Pythagorean triples
- G Problem solving using Pythagoras
- H Three dimensional problems (Extension)
- I Cube roots

HISTORICAL NOTE

For many centuries people have used right angled corners to construct buildings and to divide land into rectangular fields. They have done this quite accurately by relatively simple means.

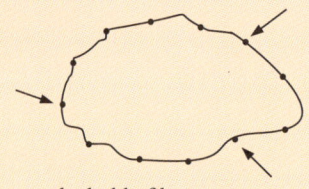

Over 3000 years ago the Egyptians knew that a triangle with sides in the ratio 3 : 4 : 5 was a right angled triangle. They used a loop of rope with 12 knots equally spaced along it to make corners in their building construction.

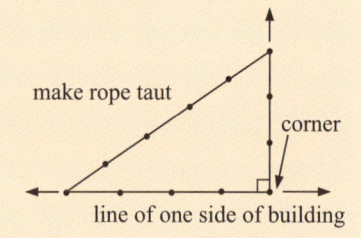

Around 500 BC, the Greek mathematician Pythagoras found a rule which connects the lengths of the sides of any right angled triangle. It is thought that he discovered the rule while studying tessellations of tiles on bathroom floors. Such patterns, like the one illustrated, were common on the walls and floors of bathrooms in ancient Greece.

The discovery of **Pythagoras' Theorem** led to the discovery of a different type of number which does not have a terminating or recurring decimal value, but which does have a distinct place on the number line. These numbers are called **surds** and are **irrational numbers**.

OPENING PROBLEM

A building is on fire and the fire department are called. They need to evacuate people from the third floor and second floor windows with the extension ladder attached to the back of the truck. The base of the ladder is 2 m above the ground. The fully extended ladder is 25 m in length.

Consider the following questions:

a If the fire truck parks so the base of the ladder is 7 m from the building, will it reach the third floor window which is 26 m above the ground?

b The second floor window is 22 m above the ground. By how much should the ladder be retracted so that it will just reach the second floor window?

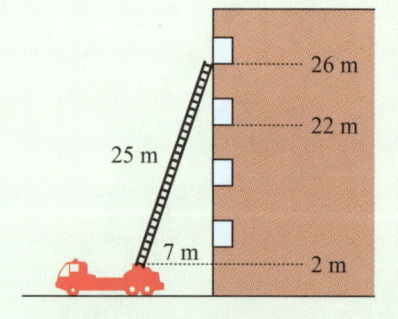

c If the ladder gets stuck in the fully extended position, how much further should the fire truck move *away* from the building to just reach the second floor window?

A SQUARE ROOTS

We have seen previously that 5×5 can be written as 5^2, which we read as "five squared". We know that $5^2 = 25$.

We say the *square root* of 25 is 5 and write $\sqrt{25} = 5$.

> $\sqrt{}$ is called the **radical** or **square root sign**. It reads "the square root of".

Finding the **square root** of a number is the opposite of **squaring** a number.

To find the square root of 9, we need to find a positive number which when multiplied by itself equals 9.

As $3 \times 3 = 9$, the number is 3. So, $\sqrt{9} = 3$.

> - $\sqrt{a}$ has meaning for $a \geqslant 0$, and is meaningless if $a < 0$.
> - $\sqrt{a}$ is always either positive or zero, so $\sqrt{a} \geqslant 0$.

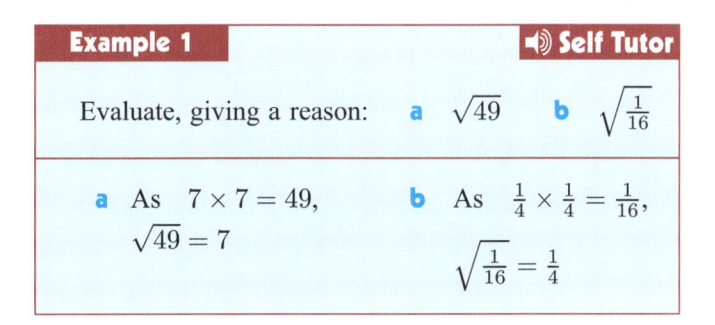

Example 1 ◀) Self Tutor

Evaluate, giving a reason: **a** $\sqrt{49}$ **b** $\sqrt{\frac{1}{16}}$

a As $7 \times 7 = 49$, $\sqrt{49} = 7$

b As $\frac{1}{4} \times \frac{1}{4} = \frac{1}{16}$, $\sqrt{\frac{1}{16}} = \frac{1}{4}$

IRRATIONAL NUMBERS

Finding the square roots of **square numbers** such as 1, 4, 9, 25, 36, and 49 is relatively easy. Other square roots such as $\sqrt{6}$ are more difficult to find.

What number multiplied by itself gives 6? We can use a calculator to find $\sqrt{6}$ by pressing $\sqrt{}$ 6 $=$. We get the answer $2.449\,489\,743$, which is an approximation to the actual value of $\sqrt{6}$.

$\sqrt{6}$ is an example of an **irrational number**, as it cannot be written as a *fraction* of any two integers.

> Any number written with the radical sign $\sqrt{}$ is called a **radical**.
> An irrational radical is called a **surd**.

Example 2

Between which two consecutive integers does $\sqrt{11}$ lie?

$\sqrt{9} = 3$ and $\sqrt{16} = 4$ and $9 < 11 < 16$
$\therefore \quad \sqrt{9} < \sqrt{11} < \sqrt{16}$
$\therefore \quad 3 < \sqrt{11} < 4$

$\therefore \quad \sqrt{11}$ lies between 3 and 4.

$\sqrt{11}$ lies between $\sqrt{9}$ and $\sqrt{16}$.

Example 3

Use your calculator to find $\sqrt{19}$ correct to 2 decimal places.

Calculator: $\sqrt{}$ 19 $=$ Display: 4.358898944

$\therefore \quad \sqrt{19} \approx 4.36$

EXERCISE 9A

1 Evaluate, giving a reason:
   - a $\sqrt{16}$
   - b $\sqrt{36}$
   - c $\sqrt{64}$
   - d $\sqrt{144}$
   - e $\sqrt{81}$
   - f $\sqrt{121}$
   - g $\sqrt{4}$
   - h $\sqrt{1}$
   - i $\sqrt{0}$
   - j $\sqrt{\frac{1}{9}}$
   - k $\sqrt{\frac{1}{49}}$
   - l $\sqrt{\frac{25}{64}}$

2 Between which two consecutive integers do the following square roots lie?
   - a $\sqrt{3}$
   - b $\sqrt{5}$
   - c $\sqrt{15}$
   - d $\sqrt{29}$
   - e $\sqrt{69}$
   - f $\sqrt{105}$
   - g $\sqrt{41}$
   - h $\sqrt{57}$

3 Use your calculator to find, correct to 2 decimal places:
   - a $\sqrt{8}$
   - b $\sqrt{15}$
   - c $\sqrt{24}$
   - d $\sqrt{67}$
   - e $\sqrt{83}$
   - f $\sqrt{111}$
   - g $\sqrt{140}$
   - h $\sqrt{200}$
   - i $\sqrt{3.14}$
   - j $\sqrt{0.04}$
   - k $\sqrt{\frac{3}{4}}$
   - l $\sqrt{7.29}$

B RULES FOR SQUARE ROOTS

$\sqrt{2}$ has the property that $(\sqrt{2})^2 = \sqrt{2}\sqrt{2} = 2$.

In fact, $(\sqrt{a})^2 = \sqrt{a}\sqrt{a} = a$ for all positive numbers a.

In the following investigation we discover other properties of square roots or radicals.

RADICALS AND PYTHAGORAS (Chapter 9)

INVESTIGATION 1 — PROPERTIES OF RADICALS

Notice that
$$(\sqrt{2}\sqrt{3})^2 = \sqrt{2}\sqrt{3} \times \sqrt{2}\sqrt{3}$$
$$= \sqrt{2}\sqrt{2}\sqrt{3}\sqrt{3}$$
$$= 2 \times 3$$
$$= 6$$
$$= (\sqrt{6})^2 \quad \text{and so} \quad \sqrt{2}\sqrt{3} = \sqrt{6}$$

What to do:

1 Use the technique above to show that:

   a $\sqrt{2}\sqrt{7} = \sqrt{14}$ **b** $\sqrt{3}\sqrt{5} = \sqrt{15}$ **c** $\sqrt{3}\sqrt{7} = \sqrt{21}$

2 Since $\sqrt{2}\sqrt{3} = \sqrt{6}$, $\dfrac{\sqrt{6}}{\sqrt{2}} = \sqrt{3}$ and $\dfrac{\sqrt{6}}{\sqrt{3}} = \sqrt{2}$. Use the results from **1** to find:

   a $\dfrac{\sqrt{14}}{\sqrt{2}}$ **b** $\dfrac{\sqrt{14}}{\sqrt{7}}$ **c** $\dfrac{\sqrt{15}}{\sqrt{3}}$ **d** $\dfrac{\sqrt{15}}{\sqrt{15}}$ **e** $\dfrac{\sqrt{21}}{\sqrt{3}}$ **f** $\dfrac{\sqrt{21}}{\sqrt{7}}$

Give reasons for your answers.

3 What do you suggest that $\sqrt{a}\sqrt{b}$ and $\dfrac{\sqrt{a}}{\sqrt{b}}$ simplify to?

From the investigation above you should have discovered that:

> for positive numbers a and b, $\sqrt{ab} = \sqrt{a}\sqrt{b}$ and $\sqrt{\dfrac{a}{b}} = \dfrac{\sqrt{a}}{\sqrt{b}}$.

Example 4   ◀) Self Tutor

Simplify: **a** $\sqrt{3}\sqrt{5}$ **b** $\dfrac{\sqrt{18}}{\sqrt{3}}$ **c** $(2\sqrt{3})^2$

a $\sqrt{3}\sqrt{5}$
$= \sqrt{3 \times 5}$
$= \sqrt{15}$

b $\dfrac{\sqrt{18}}{\sqrt{3}}$
$= \sqrt{\dfrac{18}{3}}$
$= \sqrt{6}$

c $(2\sqrt{3})^2$
$= 2\sqrt{3} \times 2\sqrt{3}$
$= 4 \times 3$
$= 12$

RADICALS IN SIMPLEST FORM

Some radicals can be rewritten in a form so the number under the square root sign is smaller than the original.

For example, $\sqrt{12} = \sqrt{4 \times 3} = \sqrt{4}\sqrt{3} = 2\sqrt{3}$.

> If a radical is written so the number under the square root sign is as small as possible, we say it is in **simplest radical form**.

To write a radical in simplest form, look for the highest perfect square factor under the radical sign.

> **Example 5** ◆) Self Tutor
>
> Write in simplest form: a $\sqrt{20}$ b $\sqrt{98}$
>
> a $\sqrt{20}$
> $= \sqrt{4 \times 5}$
> $= \sqrt{4}\sqrt{5}$
> $= 2\sqrt{5}$
>
> b $\sqrt{98}$
> $= \sqrt{49 \times 2}$
> $= \sqrt{49}\sqrt{2}$
> $= 7\sqrt{2}$

EXERCISE 9B

1 Simplify:

a $(\sqrt{3})^2$ b $(\sqrt{7})^2$ c $(\sqrt{13})^2$ d $(\sqrt{24})^2$

e $\dfrac{\sqrt{14}}{\sqrt{7}}$ f $\dfrac{\sqrt{24}}{\sqrt{6}}$ g $\dfrac{\sqrt{18}}{\sqrt{2}}$ h $\dfrac{\sqrt{39}}{\sqrt{13}}$

i $(2\sqrt{2})^2$ j $(3\sqrt{5})^2$ k $(7\sqrt{2})^2$ l $(2\sqrt{7})^2$

2 Write in simplest form:

a $\sqrt{8}$ b $\sqrt{24}$ c $\sqrt{28}$ d $\sqrt{52}$

e $\sqrt{18}$ f $\sqrt{32}$ g $\sqrt{27}$ h $\sqrt{48}$

i $\sqrt{72}$ j $\sqrt{50}$ k $\sqrt{125}$ l $\sqrt{63}$

m $\sqrt{80}$ n $\sqrt{200}$ o $\sqrt{75}$ p $\sqrt{112}$

Look for the highest perfect square factor under the radical sign.

C SOLVING EQUATIONS OF THE FORM $x^2 = k$

In the previous section we dealt with surds like $\sqrt{7}$.

Notice that $\sqrt{7} \times \sqrt{7} = 7$ and $-\sqrt{7} \times -\sqrt{7} = 7$ {as negative × negative = positive}.

So, if we were asked to solve the equation $x^2 = 7$, it is clear that x could equal $\sqrt{7}$ or $-\sqrt{7}$. The squares of both of these numbers are 7.

We write the solutions as $x = \pm\sqrt{7}$. This reads "plus or minus the square root of 7".

If $x^2 = k$ where $k > 0$, then $x = \pm\sqrt{k}$.

$\sqrt{k}$ exists only when $k \geqslant 0$. If $k < 0$ then there are **no solutions** to the equation $x^2 = k$.

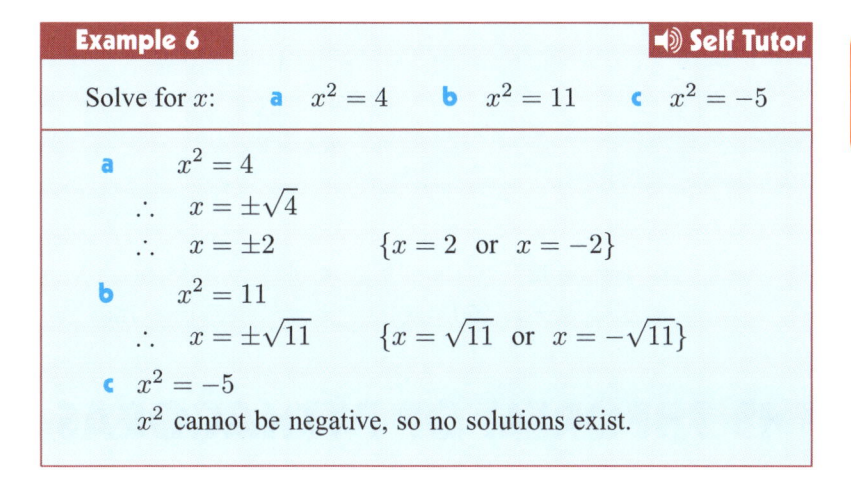

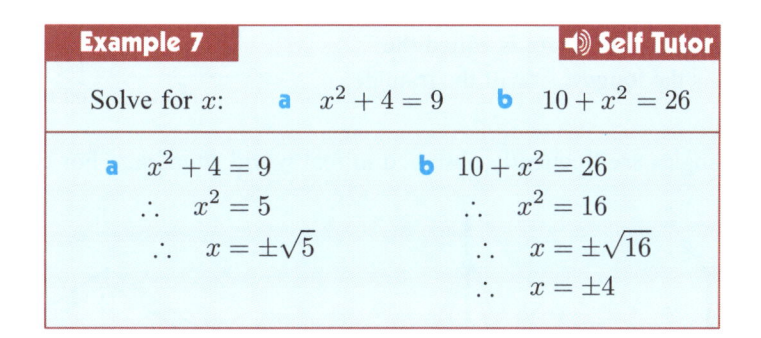

Example 6 ◀ Self Tutor

Solve for x: **a** $x^2 = 4$ **b** $x^2 = 11$ **c** $x^2 = -5$

a $x^2 = 4$
$\therefore\ x = \pm\sqrt{4}$
$\therefore\ x = \pm 2$ $\{x = 2$ or $x = -2\}$

b $x^2 = 11$
$\therefore\ x = \pm\sqrt{11}$ $\{x = \sqrt{11}$ or $x = -\sqrt{11}\}$

c $x^2 = -5$
x^2 cannot be negative, so no solutions exist.

*If $x^2 = k$ where k is greater than zero then there are **two** solutions.*

Example 7 ◀ Self Tutor

Solve for x: **a** $x^2 + 4 = 9$ **b** $10 + x^2 = 26$

a $x^2 + 4 = 9$
$\therefore\ x^2 = 5$
$\therefore\ x = \pm\sqrt{5}$

b $10 + x^2 = 26$
$\therefore\ x^2 = 16$
$\therefore\ x = \pm\sqrt{16}$
$\therefore\ x = \pm 4$

EXERCISE 9C

1 Solve for x:

  a $x^2 = 9$ **b** $x^2 = 36$ **c** $x^2 = 0$ **d** $x^2 = 100$

  e $x^2 = 13$ **f** $x^2 = 29$ **g** $x^2 = 32$ **h** $x^2 = 49$

  i $x^2 = -4$ **j** $x^2 = -3$ **k** $x^2 = 18$ **l** $x^2 = -26$

2 Solve for x:

  a $x^2 + 7 = 11$ **b** $x^2 + 9 = 25$ **c** $x^2 + 3 = 39$

  d $5 + x^2 = 30$ **e** $1 + x^2 = 5$ **f** $4 + x^2 = 12$

  g $x^2 + 16 = 34$ **h** $x^2 + 17 = 29$ **i** $10 + x^2 = 50$

Example 8

Solve for x: **a** $2x^2 = 24$ **b** $x^2 + (2x)^2 = 20$

a $2x^2 = 24$
$\therefore x^2 = 12$
$\therefore x = \pm\sqrt{12}$
$\therefore x = \pm\sqrt{4 \times 3}$
$\therefore x = \pm 2\sqrt{3}$

b $x^2 + (2x)^2 = 20$
$\therefore x^2 + 4x^2 = 20$
$\therefore 5x^2 = 20$
$\therefore x^2 = 4$
$\therefore x = \pm\sqrt{4}$
$\therefore x = \pm 2$

3 Solve for x:

a $3x^2 = 27$
b $2x^2 = 32$
c $4x^2 = 100$
d $x^2 + x^2 = 48$
e $x^2 + 2x^2 = 150$
f $x^2 + (2x)^2 = 160$

D THE THEOREM OF PYTHAGORAS

A **right angled triangle** is a triangle which has a right angle as one of its angles.

The side **opposite** the right angle is called the **hypotenuse** and is the **longest** side of the triangle.

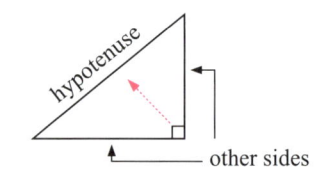

Right angled triangles are frequently observed in real world situations. For example:

ladder leaning against a wall

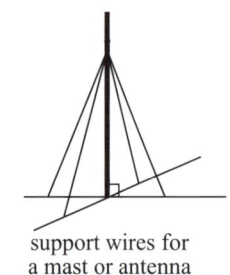

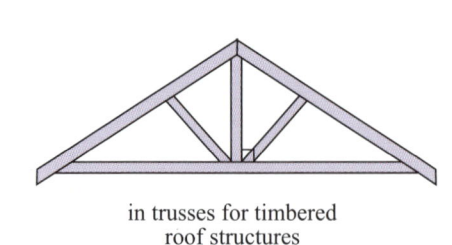

support wires for a mast or antenna

in trusses for timbered roof structures

INVESTIGATION 2   DISCOVERING THE THEOREM OF PYTHAGORAS

What to do:

1 Draw a horizontal line of length 4 cm. At right angles, draw a vertical line of length 3 cm as shown:

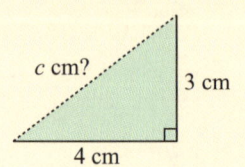

2 Complete a right angled triangle by drawing in the hypotenuse. If the shorter sides have lengths a cm and b cm, then $a = 3$ and $b = 4$. Let the hypotenuse have length c cm. Measure the hypotenuse and find c.

3 Copy and complete the table:

a	b	c	a^2	b^2	c^2	a^2+b^2
3	4		9			

4 Repeat the procedure above for three more right angled triangles. The sides of length a and b are specified in the table alongside:

a	b	c	a^2	b^2	c^2	a^2+b^2
6	8					
5	12					
4	7					

5 Complete the table in **4**. State any conclusions you draw from information in this table.

6 Construct two more right angled triangles with lengths a and b of your choosing. Does your conclusion hold for these triangles?

7 Click on the icon and further explore the lengths of sides of right angled triangles of any shape.   **PYTHAGORAS SIMULATION**

8 Discuss how a builder could use this discovery to measure right angles in a building.

THE THEOREM OF PYTHAGORAS

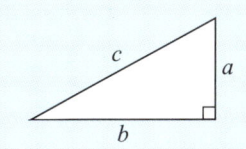

In a right angled triangle with hypotenuse of length c and other sides of length a and b,

$$c^2 = a^2 + b^2.$$

In geometric form, **Pythagoras' Theorem** states:

In any right angled triangle, the area of the square on the hypotenuse is equal to the sum of the areas of the squares on the other two sides.

WORKSHEET Look back at the tile pattern on page **190**. Can you see this figure in the pattern?

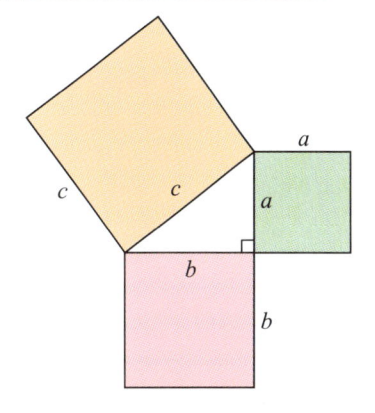

INVESTIGATION 3   PRESIDENT GARFIELD'S DIAGRAM

Presidents of the United States are remembered for many different things. Prior to being President, James Garfield used the diagram alongside to prove Pythagoras' Theorem. When he stumbled on this proof he was so pleased he gave cigars out to his many friends.

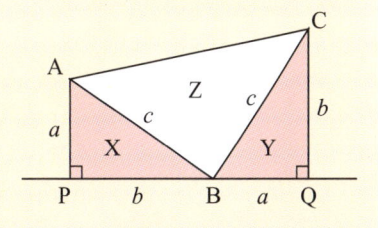

What to do:

1. Two identical right angled triangles, ABP and CQB, are placed on line (PBQ). What can you deduce about $A\hat{B}C$? Give all reasons.

2. Find the area of each triangle X, Y and Z.
   Hence, express   area X + area Y + area Z   in simplest form.

3. The combined regions X, Y and Z form a trapezium. Find:
   a the average of the parallel sides
   b the distance between the parallel sides
   c the area of the trapezium in terms of a and b using the area of a trapezium formula.

4. Use the results of **2** and **3c** to find a relationship between a, b and c.

DISCUSSION — PYTHAGORAS' THEOREM

How did Pythagoras prove the theorem he discovered? Algebra was probably not used as there is no evidence it was invented until well after his lifetime.

Try the CD link for a possible answer.

PYTHAGORAS' PROOF

FINDING SIDES OF TRIANGLES USING PYTHAGORAS' THEOREM

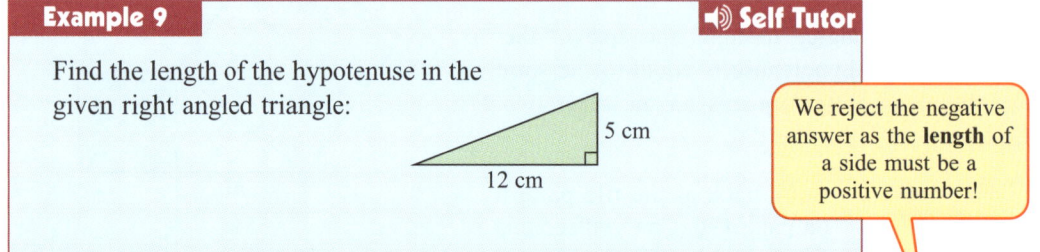

Example 9 — Self Tutor

Find the length of the hypotenuse in the given right angled triangle:

5 cm
12 cm

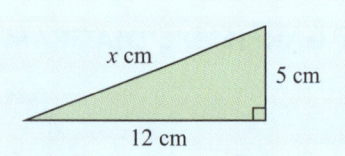

We reject the negative answer as the **length** of a side must be a positive number!

Let the hypotenuse have length x cm.

$\therefore \ x^2 = 12^2 + 5^2$ {Pythagoras}
$\therefore \ x^2 = 144 + 25$
$\therefore \ x^2 = 169$
$\therefore \ x = \pm\sqrt{169}$
$\therefore \ x = 13$ {as $x > 0$}

The hypotenuse has length 13 cm.

RADICALS AND PYTHAGORAS (Chapter 9) 199

EXERCISE 9D

1 Find the length of the hypotenuse in each of the following right angled triangles. Leave your answers in simplest radical form.

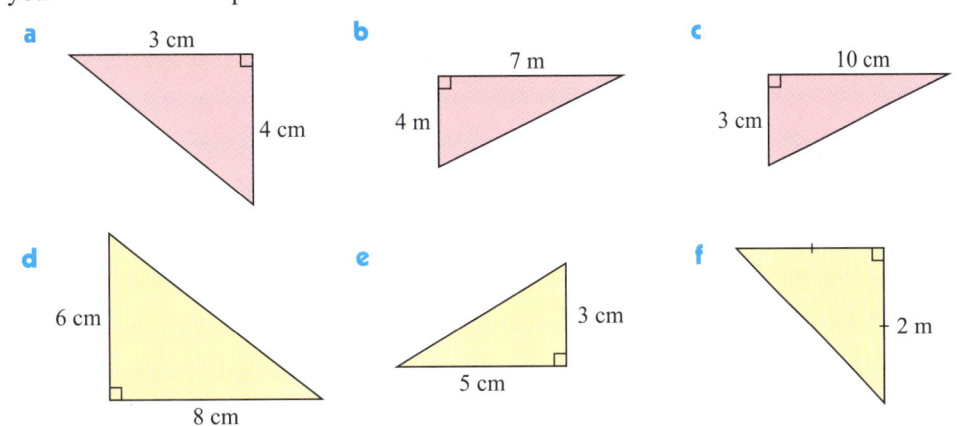

a 3 cm, 4 cm

b 7 m, 4 m

c 10 cm, 3 cm

d 6 cm, 8 cm

e 3 cm, 5 cm

f 2 m (isosceles)

Example 10 ◀)) Self Tutor

A right angled triangle has hypotenuse of length 6 cm and one other side of length 3 cm. Determine the length of the third side to the nearest millimetre.

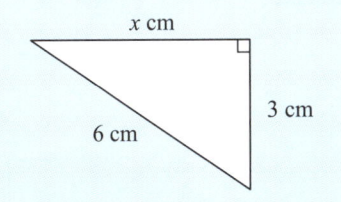

Let the third side have length x cm.

$\therefore \quad x^2 + 3^2 = 6^2$ {Pythagoras}
$\therefore \quad x^2 + 9 = 36$
$\therefore \quad x^2 = 27$
$\therefore \quad x = \pm\sqrt{27}$ (or $\pm 3\sqrt{3}$)
$\therefore \quad x = \sqrt{27}$ {as $x > 0$}

Thus the third side has length ≈ 5.2 cm.

---

2 Find the lengths of the unknown sides of the following right angled triangles. Leave your answers in simplest radical form.

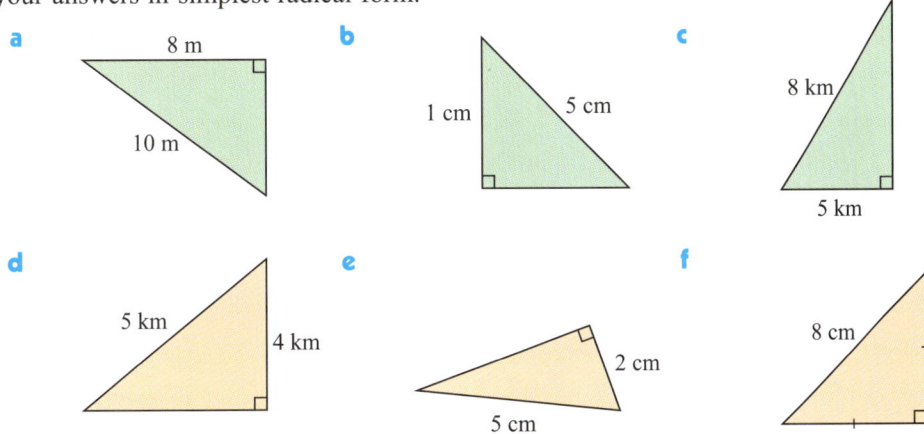

a 8 m, 10 m

b 1 cm, 5 cm

c 8 km, 5 km

d 5 km, 4 km

e 2 cm, 5 cm

f 8 cm (isosceles)

Example 11

Find the value of y in the following triangles:

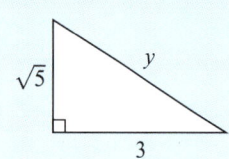

a (triangle with legs 3 and $\sqrt{5}$, hypotenuse y)

b (triangle with leg 2, hypotenuse $\sqrt{13}$, other leg y)

Make sure you identify the hypotenuse.

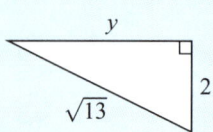

a $y^2 = 3^2 + (\sqrt{5})^2$ {Pythagoras}
∴ $y^2 = 9 + 5$
∴ $y^2 = 14$
∴ $y = \pm\sqrt{14}$
∴ $y = \sqrt{14}$ {as y is positive}

b $y^2 + 2^2 = (\sqrt{13})^2$
∴ $y^2 + 4 = 13$
∴ $y^2 = 9$
∴ $y = \pm\sqrt{9}$
∴ $y = 3$ {as y is positive}

3 Find the value of y in the following triangles:

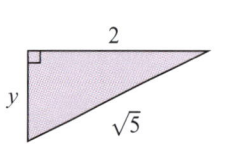

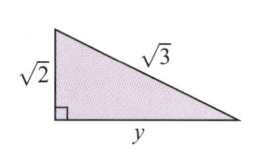

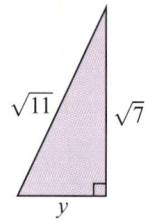

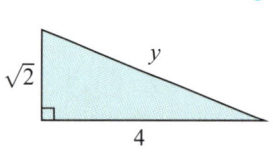

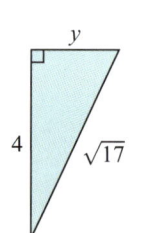

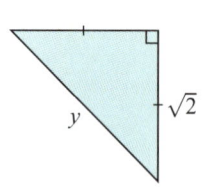

a (legs 2 and y, hypotenuse $\sqrt{5}$)

b ($\sqrt{2}$, $\sqrt{3}$, y)

c ($\sqrt{11}$, $\sqrt{7}$, y)

d ($\sqrt{2}$, 4, y)

e (4, $\sqrt{17}$, y)

f ($\sqrt{2}$, y — isosceles right triangle)

Example 12

Find the unknown lengths:

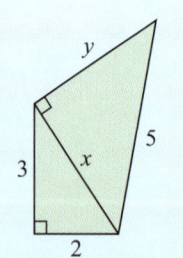

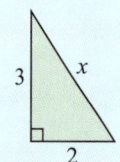

(triangle with sides 3, x, 2, and y, 5)

$x^2 = 3^2 + 2^2$ {Pythagoras}
∴ $x^2 = 9 + 4$
∴ $x^2 = 13$
∴ $x = \sqrt{13}$ {as x is positive}

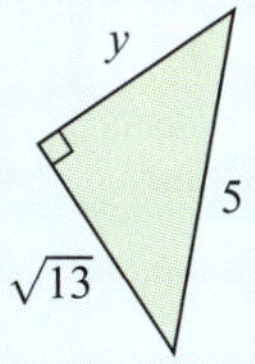

RADICALS AND PYTHAGORAS (Chapter 9) 201

$$y^2 + (\sqrt{13})^2 = 5^2 \quad \{\text{Pythagoras}\}$$
$$\therefore \quad y^2 + 13 = 25$$
$$\therefore \quad y^2 = 12$$
$$\therefore \quad y = \sqrt{12} \quad \{\text{as } y \text{ is positive}\}$$
$$\therefore \quad y = 2\sqrt{3}$$

4 Find the unknown lengths:

a, b, 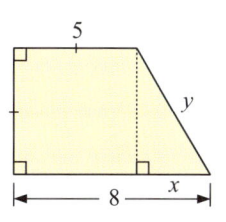 c, 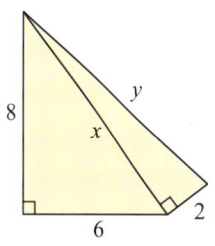 d, 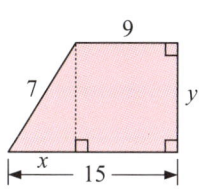 e, 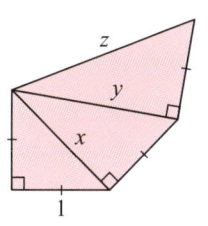 f, 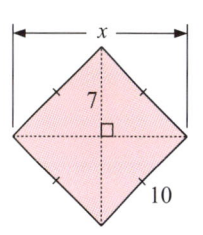 g, 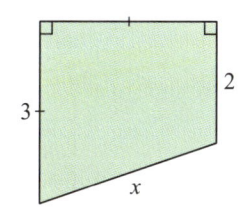 h, 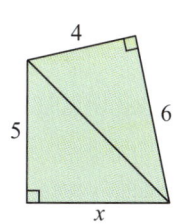 i

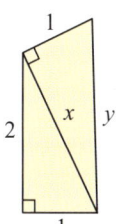

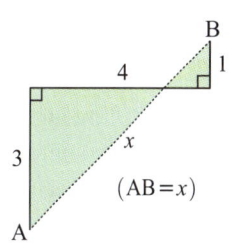

INVESTIGATION 4   LOCATING RADICALS ON A NUMBER LINE

What to do:

1. On a number line mark the position 3.

2. At 3 construct a right angle and draw a side of length 2 units.

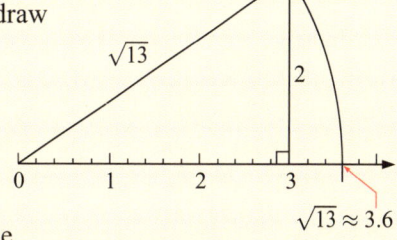

3. Complete the triangle. By Pythagoras' Theorem, the length of the hypotenuse is $\sqrt{13}$ units.

   $\sqrt{13} \approx 3.6$

4. With compass point at O, and radius equal to the length of the hypotenuse, draw an arc to cut the number line at $\sqrt{13}$. Estimate the value of $\sqrt{13}$ as accurately as you can.

5. Repeat the above procedure for: **a** $\sqrt{5}$ **b** $\sqrt{17}$ **c** $\sqrt{29}$ **d** $\sqrt{45}$

E THE CONVERSE OF PYTHAGORAS' THEOREM

If we are given the lengths of three sides of a triangle, the **converse** of **Pythagoras' Theorem** gives us a simple **test** to determine whether the triangle is right angled.

THE CONVERSE THEOREM

If a triangle has sides of length a, b and c units where $a^2 + b^2 = c^2$, then the triangle is right angled.

PYTHAGORAS SIMULATION

Example 13 ◀)) Self Tutor

Is the triangle with sides 8 cm, 9 cm and 12 cm right angled?

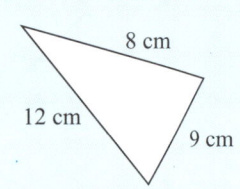

The two shorter sides have lengths 8 cm and 9 cm.

Now $8^2 + 9^2 = 64 + 81 = 145$

whereas $12^2 = 144$

$\therefore \ 8^2 + 9^2 \neq 12^2$

$\therefore$ the triangle is not right angled.

The **hypotenuse** would be the **longest** side!

EXERCISE 9E

1 The following figures are not drawn to scale. Which of the triangles are right angled?

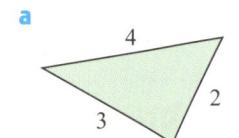

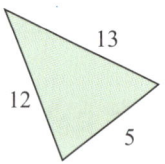

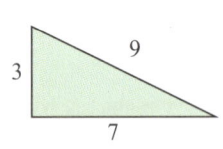

a 4, 2, 3

b 13, 12, 5

c 3, 9, 7

d 12, 7, 14

e 3, 7, 5

f 17, 8, 15

The right angle must be **opposite** the hypotenuse or longest side.

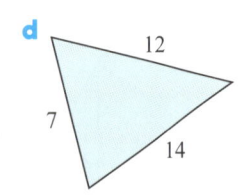

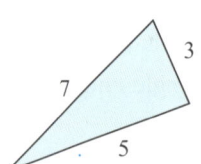

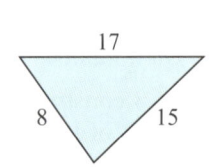

2 The following figures are not drawn to scale. Which of the triangles are right angled? If it exists, indicate which angle is the right angle.

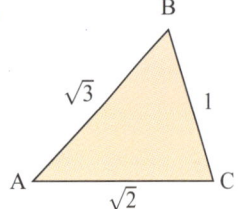

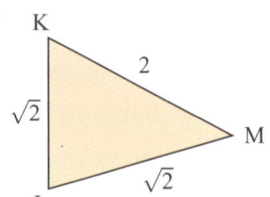

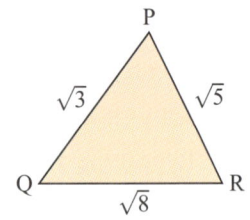

a Triangle ABC with AB = $\sqrt{3}$, BC = 1, AC = $\sqrt{2}$

b Triangle KLM with KL = $\sqrt{2}$, KM = 2, LM = $\sqrt{2}$

c Triangle PQR with PQ = $\sqrt{3}$, PR = $\sqrt{5}$, QR = $\sqrt{8}$

RADICALS AND PYTHAGORAS (Chapter 9) 203

d Triangle ABC with A to C = $2\sqrt{3}$ cm, A to B = 3 cm, C to B = $\sqrt{7}$ cm.

e Triangle PQR with P to Q = $\sqrt{5}$ m, P to R = $2\sqrt{2}$ m, Q to R = $2\sqrt{3}$ m.

f Triangle XYZ with X to Z = $3\sqrt{3}$ m, Z to Y = $4\sqrt{3}$ m, X to Y = $5\sqrt{3}$ m.

F PYTHAGOREAN TRIPLES

The simplest right angled triangle with sides of integer length is the **3-4-5 triangle**. The numbers 3, 4 and 5 satisfy the rule $3^2 + 4^2 = 5^2$.

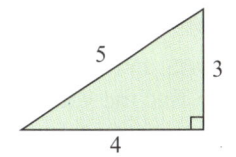

The set of numbers {3, 4, 5} is called a **Pythagorean triple** since it obeys the rule $a^2 + b^2 = c^2$ where a, b and c are **integers**.

Some other examples are: {5, 12, 13}, {7, 24, 25}, {8, 15, 17}.

We have seen that the ancient Egyptians used the 3-4-5 triangle when building. However, long before this, the **Babylonians** discovered a way of finding Pythagorean triples. A long list of them is given on the **Plimpton 322**, a clay tablet dating from almost 2000 years BC.

Example 14   ◀)) Self Tutor

Which of the following sets of numbers form Pythagorean triples?

a {3, 7, 9}   **b** {14, 48, 50}   **c** {7.5, 10, 12.5}

Let 'c' be the largest number!

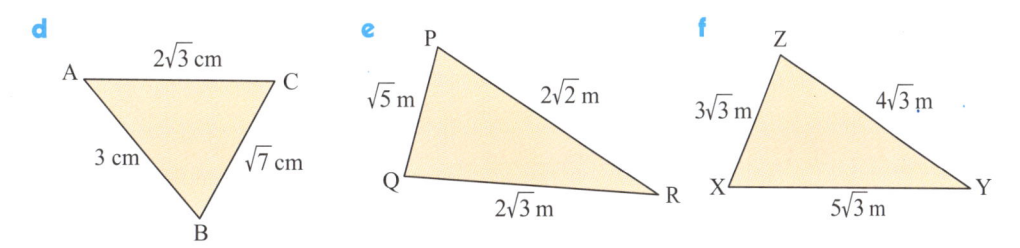

a $3^2 + 7^2 = 9 + 49 = 58$ and $9^2 = 81$
∴ {3, 7, 9} is not a Pythagorean triple.

b $14^2 + 48^2 = 196 + 2304 = 2500$ and $50^2 = 2500$
∴ $14^2 + 48^2 = 50^2$
∴ {14, 48, 50} is a Pythagorean triple.

c {7.5, 10, 12.5} is not a Pythagorean triple as these numbers are not all integers.

You will see in the following exercise how Pythagorean triples can be generated using **multiples**.

EXERCISE 9F

1 Determine, giving reasons, which of the following are Pythagorean triples:

  a {10, 24, 26}   **b** {4.5, 6, 7.5}   **c** {17, 19, 25}
  d {12, 16, 20}   **e** {11, 60, 61}   **f** {23, 36, 45}

2 **a** Show that $\{3, 4, 5\}$ is a Pythagorean triple.
    b Is $\{6, 8, 10\}$ a Pythagorean triple?
    c Write $6 : 8 : 10$ as a ratio in simplest form.
    d Is $\{9, 12, 15\}$ a Pythagorean triple?
    e Write $9 : 12 : 15$ as a ratio in simplest form.
    f Using your observations above, find x if $\{18, 24, x\}$ is a Pythagorean triple.

3 If $k > 0$ and a, b and c are the sides of a right angled triangle as shown, show that any triangle with sides ka, kb and kc must also be right angled.

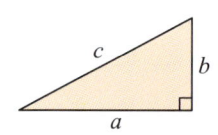

Example 15   ◀)) Self Tutor

Use *multiples* and the right angled triangle opposite to find the values of the unknowns in the following triangles:

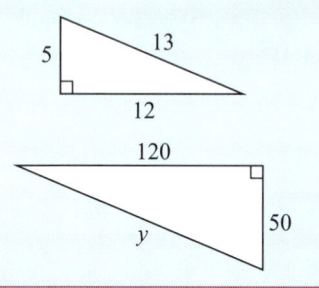

a

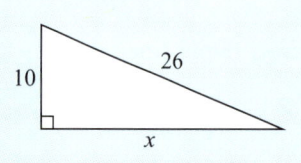

b

a $5 : 12 : 13 = 10 : x : 26$ (×2)

     $\therefore \quad x = 12 \times 2$

     $\therefore \quad x = 24$

b $5 : 12 : 13 = 50 : 120 : y$ (×10)

     $\therefore \quad y = 13 \times 10$

     $\therefore \quad y = 130$

4 Use *multiples* and the right angled triangle opposite to find the values of the unknowns in the following triangles:

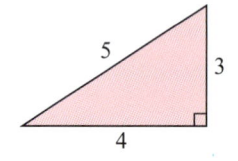

a 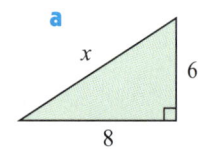   **b** 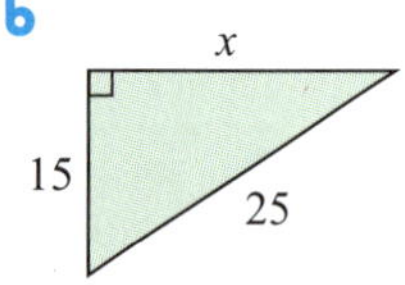   **c**   **d**

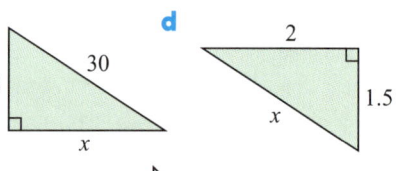

5 Use *multiples* and the right angled triangle opposite to find the values of the unknowns in the following triangles:

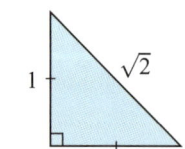

a 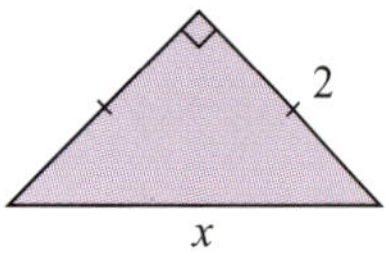   **b** 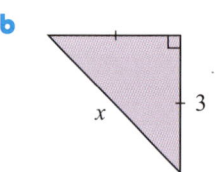   **c** 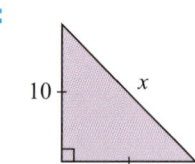   **d**

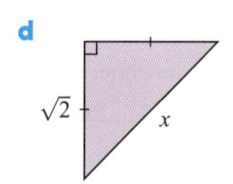

RADICALS AND PYTHAGORAS (Chapter 9) 205

> **Example 16** ◀)) **Self Tutor**
>
> Find k if $\{10, k, 26\}$ is a Pythagorean triple.
>
> Now, $10^2 + k^2 = 26^2$
> $\therefore k^2 = 26^2 - 10^2 = 576$
> $\therefore k = \pm\sqrt{576} = \pm 24$
>
> But $k > 0$, so $k = 24$.

6 Find k given that the following are Pythagorean triples:

   a $\{9, k, 15\}$ **b** $\{8, 15, k\}$ **c** $\{k, 24, 26\}$ **d** $\{11, k, 61\}$

G   PROBLEM SOLVING USING PYTHAGORAS

Right angled triangles occur in many practical problems. In these situations we can apply Pythagoras' Theorem to help find unknown side lengths.

The problem solving approach involves the following steps:

> *Step 1:* Draw a neat, clear diagram of the situation.
> *Step 2:* Mark known lengths and right angles on the diagram.
> *Step 3:* Use a symbol such as x to represent the unknown length.
> *Step 4:* Write down Pythagoras' Theorem for the given information.
> *Step 5:* Solve the equation.
> *Step 6:* Where necessary, write your answer in sentence form.

The following special geometrical figures contain right angled triangles:

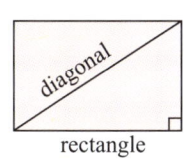

In a **rectangle**, right angles exist between adjacent sides.

Construct a **diagonal** to form a right angled triangle.

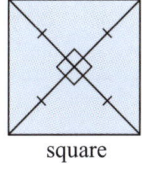

In a **square** and a **rhombus**, the diagonals bisect each other at right angles.

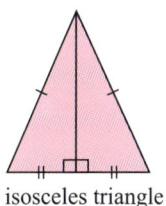

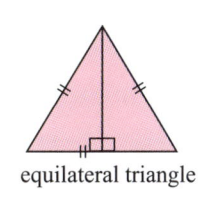

In an **isosceles triangle** and an **equilateral triangle**, the altitude bisects the base at right angles.

Example 17

Determine, to the nearest centimetre, the length of the diagonal support of a rectangular gate 3 m by 5 m.

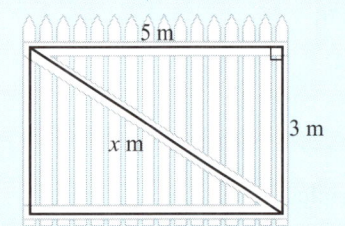

Let the diagonal support have length x m.

Now $x^2 = 3^2 + 5^2$ {Pythagoras}

$\therefore \quad x^2 = 9 + 25$

$\therefore \quad x^2 = 34$

$\therefore \quad x = \sqrt{34}$ {as x is positive}

$\therefore$ the support is $\sqrt{34} \approx 5.83$ m long.

EXERCISE 9G

1 Consider the diagonal of a 6 cm by 9 cm rectangle. Find the diagonal's length:
   a in radical form   **b** to the nearest mm.

2 Find the length of the diagonal of a square with sides of length 4.2 cm. Give your answer in radical form and also as a decimal to the nearest mm.

3 What is the longest length of iron rod which can be placed flat across the diagonal of the 3 m by 2 m floor of a garden shed?

4 A rhombus has diagonals of length 4 cm and 6 cm. Find its perimeter.

5 Three roads [AB], [BC] and [CA] form a right angled triangle. AC is 7 km and BC is 4 km. Qi rides his bicycle from A to B to C. What extra distance does he travel compared with going directly from A to C?

6 A baseball 'diamond' is a square whose sides are 27 m long. Find, to the nearest $\frac{1}{10}$ metre, the distance from the home plate to second base.

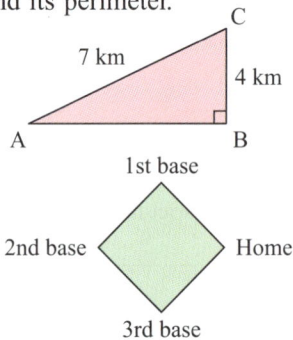

Example 18

An 8 m long ladder has its feet placed 3 m out from a vertical wall. How far up the wall will the ladder reach (to the nearest cm)?

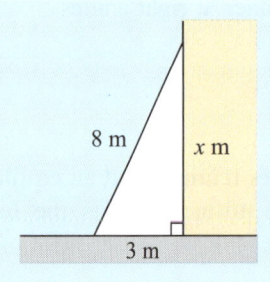

Let x m be the height up the wall.

$\therefore \quad x^2 + 3^2 = 8^2$ {Pythagoras}

$\therefore \quad x^2 + 9 = 64$

$\therefore \quad x^2 = 55$

$\therefore \quad x = \sqrt{55}$ {as x is positive}

$\therefore$ the ladder reaches $\sqrt{55} \approx 7.42$ m up the wall.

7 A 6 m ladder rests against a vertical wall at a point 4.9 m above the ground. Find the distance of the feet of the ladder from the base of the wall (to the nearest cm).

8 Answer the questions posed in the **Opening Problem** on page **190**.

9 A cyclist rides 8 km due west and then 10 km due north. How far is she from her starting point?

10 A runner is 22 km east and 15 km south of his starting point.

   a How far is he in a direct line from his starting point?

   b How long would it take him to return to his starting point in a direct line if he can run at 10 km per hour?

11 Two ships B and C leave a port A at the same time. B travels due west at a constant speed of 16 km per hour. C travels due south at a constant speed of 18 km per hour.

   a How far have B and C each travelled after two hours?

   b Find the distance between them after 2 hours.

12 A giant radio mast is held to the ground by 8 wires, 4 of which are illustrated. The other wires are fixed in the same positions on the other sides of the mast. If the wires have to be replaced, what length of wire must be purchased?

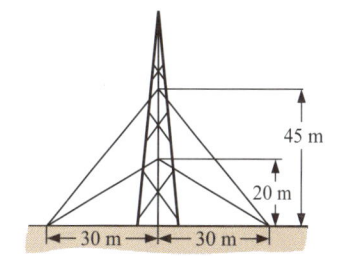

Example 19   ◀) Self Tutor

An equilateral triangle has sides of length 8 cm. Find its height to the nearest mm.

We draw an altitude which *bisects* the base.

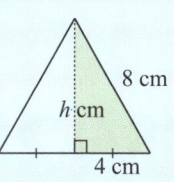

$h^2 + 4^2 = 8^2$ {Pythagoras}

$\therefore h^2 + 16 = 64$

$\therefore h^2 = 48$

$\therefore h = \sqrt{48}$ {as h is positive}

$\therefore$ the height of the triangle ≈ 6.9 cm

13 Find the height of an equilateral triangle with sides of length 6 cm.

14 An isosceles triangle has equal sides measuring 5 cm and a base which is 6 cm long.

   a Find the length of the altitude of the triangle from the apex to the base.

   b Hence, find the area of the triangle.

15 A cone has slant height 17 cm and base radius 8 cm.

   a Determine the height of the cone.

   b Find the volume of the cone using the formula $V_{cone} = \frac{1}{3}\pi r^2 h$.

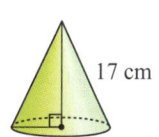

Example 20

A square has diagonals of length 10 cm. Find the length of a side to the nearest mm.

Let the sides have length x cm.

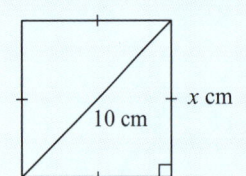

$\therefore \quad x^2 + x^2 = 10^2$ {Pythagoras}
$\therefore \quad 2x^2 = 100$
$\therefore \quad x^2 = 50$
$\therefore \quad x = \sqrt{50}$ {as x is positive}
$\therefore$ the lengths are $\sqrt{50} \approx 7.1$ cm.

16 A square has diagonals of length 12 cm. Find its perimeter.

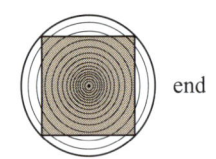

17 A log is 40 cm in diameter. Find the dimensions of the largest square section beam which can be cut from the log.

18 The longer side of a rectangle is four times the length of the shorter side. If the diagonal is 17 cm long, find the dimensions of the rectangle.

19 An equilateral triangle has an altitude of length 10 cm. Find the length of a side.

20 An equilateral triangle has sides of length 10 cm. Find its area.

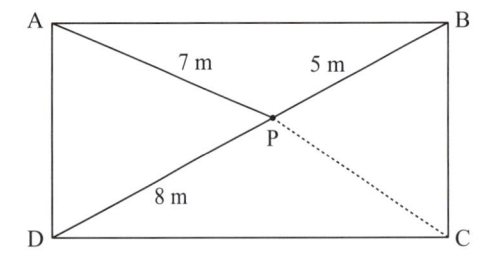

21 ABCD is a rectangular garden plot. P is a garden water tap. Find the distance from the tap to corner C.

(Diagram: rectangle ABCD with diagonals meeting at P; AP = 7 m, PB = 5 m, DP = 8 m)

H   THREE DIMENSIONAL PROBLEMS (EXTENSION)

Pythagoras' Theorem is often used *twice* to solve problems involving three dimensions. We look for right angled triangles for which two sides have known length.

Example 21

A room has floor dimensions 5 m by 4 m. The height of the room is 3 m. Find the distance from a corner point on the floor to the opposite corner point on the ceiling.

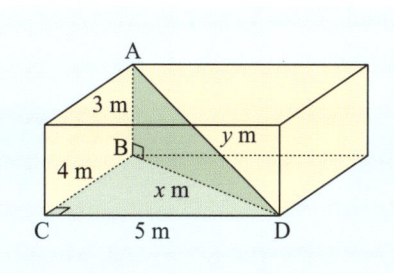

The required distance is AD. We join [BD].

In $\triangle$BCD, $x^2 = 4^2 + 5^2$ {Pythagoras}
In $\triangle$ABD, $y^2 = x^2 + 3^2$
$\therefore\ y^2 = (4^2 + 5^2) + 3^2$
$\therefore\ y^2 = 16 + 25 + 9$
$\therefore\ y^2 = 50$
$\therefore\ y = \sqrt{50}$ {as y is positive}

$\therefore$ the required distance is $\sqrt{50} \approx 7.07$ m

EXERCISE 9H

1 A cube has sides of length 1 cm.
Find the length of a diagonal of the cube.

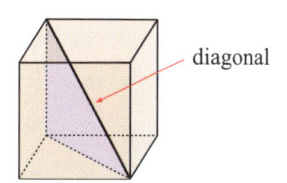

2 A room is 4 m by 3 m and has a height of 3 m. Find the distance from a corner point on the floor to the opposite corner of the ceiling.

3 A rectangular box has internal dimensions 5 cm by 3 cm by 1 cm.
Find the length of the longest matchstick that can be placed within the box.

4 ABCDE is a square-based pyramid. The apex of the pyramid E is directly above M, the point of intersection of [AC] and [BD]. If all edges of the pyramid have the same length of 10 cm, find the height of the pyramid to the nearest mm.

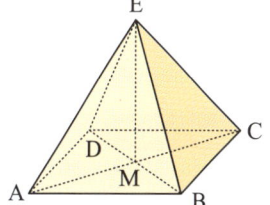

I   CUBE ROOTS

We have seen previously that $2 \times 2 \times 2$ can be written as 2^3, which we read as '2 cubed'. We know that $2^3 = 8$.

We say that the *cube root* of 8 is 2, and write $\sqrt[3]{8} = 2$.

$\sqrt[3]{\ }$ is called the **cube root sign**. It reads "the cube root of".

Finding the cube root of a number is the opposite of cubing the number or writing the number to the power 3.

To find the cube root of 27, we need to find the number which when multiplied by itself three times, gives 27.

As $3 \times 3 \times 3 = 27$, the number is 3. So $\sqrt[3]{27} = 3$.

We can also find the cube root of a negative number.

As $-3 \times -3 \times -3 = -27$, $\sqrt[3]{-27} = -3$.

Finding the cube roots of cubes such as 1, 8, 27, 64, and 125 is easy, but other cube roots such as $\sqrt[3]{20}$ are more difficult to find and we use a calculator.

Example 22

Evaluate, giving a reason: a $\sqrt[3]{216}$ b $\sqrt[3]{-64}$

a As $6 \times 6 \times 6 = 216$,
$\sqrt[3]{216} = 6$.

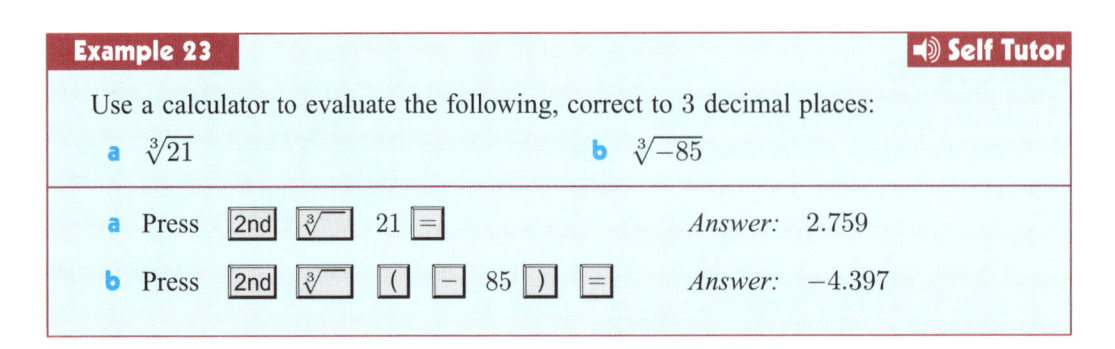

b As $-4 \times -4 \times -4 = -64$,
$\sqrt[3]{-64} = -4$.

Example 23

Use a calculator to evaluate the following, correct to 3 decimal places:
   a $\sqrt[3]{21}$ b $\sqrt[3]{-85}$

a Press [2nd] [$\sqrt[3]{\ }$] 21 [=]   Answer: 2.759

b Press [2nd] [$\sqrt[3]{\ }$] [(] [−] 85 [)] [=]   Answer: −4.397

We can use cube roots to solve equations of the form $x^3 = k$.

If $x^3 = k$, then $x = \sqrt[3]{k}$.

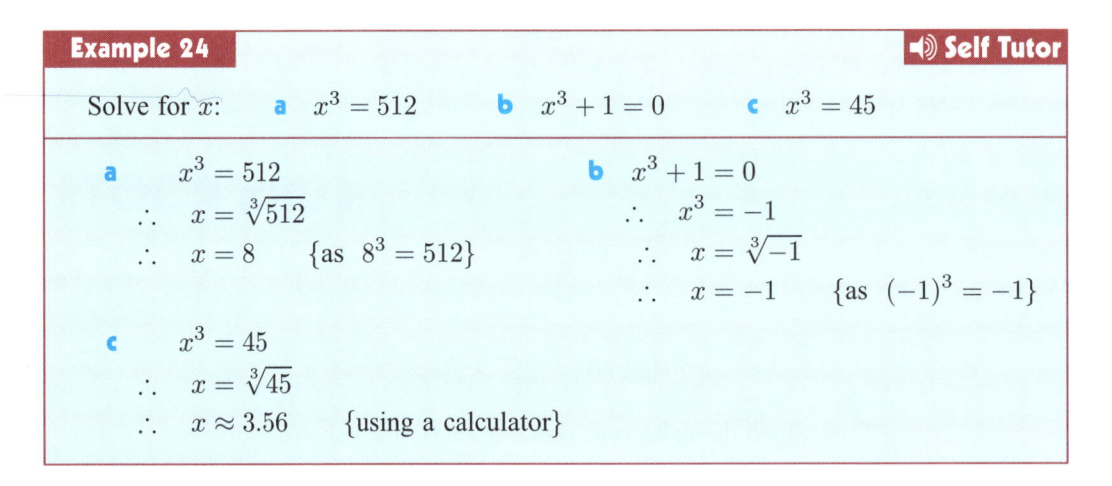

Example 24

Solve for x: a $x^3 = 512$ b $x^3 + 1 = 0$ c $x^3 = 45$

a $x^3 = 512$
$\therefore x = \sqrt[3]{512}$
$\therefore x = 8$ {as $8^3 = 512$}

b $x^3 + 1 = 0$
$\therefore x^3 = -1$
$\therefore x = \sqrt[3]{-1}$
$\therefore x = -1$ {as $(-1)^3 = -1$}

c $x^3 = 45$
$\therefore x = \sqrt[3]{45}$
$\therefore x \approx 3.56$ {using a calculator}

EXERCISE 9I

1 Evaluate:

a $\sqrt[3]{1}$ b $\sqrt[3]{-1}$ c $\sqrt[3]{-8}$ d $\sqrt[3]{64}$ e $\sqrt[3]{-216}$

f $\sqrt[3]{125}$ g $\sqrt[3]{-125}$ h $\sqrt[3]{1000}$ i $\sqrt[3]{-1000}$ j $\sqrt[3]{343}$

2 Use your calculator to find, correct to 2 decimal places:

a $\sqrt[3]{4}$ b $\sqrt[3]{20}$ c $\sqrt[3]{-100}$ d $\sqrt[3]{250}$ e $\sqrt[3]{-2000}$

3 Solve for x:

   a $x^3 = 8$ **b** $x^3 + 125 = 0$ **c** $x^3 - 64 = 0$ **d** $x^3 = 0$

   e $x^3 = -27$ **f** $x^3 + 1 = 0$ **g** $x^3 = 1\,000\,000$ **h** $x^3 = -729$

4 Use a calculator to solve for x:

   a $x^3 = 70$ **b** $x^3 = 256$ **c** $x^3 + 49 = 0$ **d** $x^3 - 900 = 0$

5 A cube has volume 300 cm^3. What is the length of one edge?

CREATE YOUR OWN PYRAMIDS

LINKS click here

Areas of interaction:
Human ingenuity, Approaches to learning

REVIEW SET 9A

1 Solve for x: **a** $x^2 = -14$ **b** $x^2 = 23$ **c** $3 + x^2 = 11$

2 Simplify: **a** $(\sqrt{11})^2$ **b** $(2\sqrt{3})^2$ **c** $\dfrac{\sqrt{50}}{\sqrt{2}}$ **d** $\sqrt[3]{-27}$

3 Write in simplest radical form: **a** $\sqrt{18}$ **b** $\sqrt{288}$

4 Find the perimeter of a rectangle which has an 8 cm diagonal and one side of length 5 cm.

5 An isosceles triangle has height 12 cm and equal sides of length 13 cm. Find the length of the base.

6 Find the exact value of x in the following:

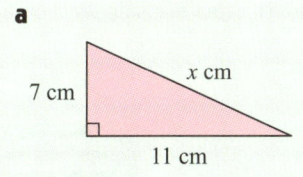

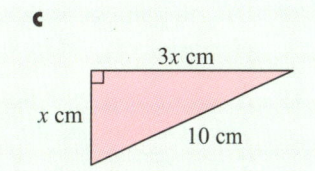

   a right triangle with legs 7 cm and 11 cm, hypotenuse x cm

   b right triangle with legs 4 cm and x cm, hypotenuse 8 cm

   c right triangle with legs x cm and 10 cm, hypotenuse $3x$ cm

7 The following triangles are not drawn to scale. Explain, with reasons, whether either triangle is right angled.

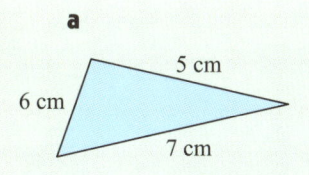

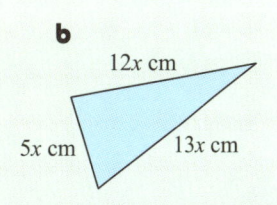

   a triangle with sides 6 cm, 5 cm, 7 cm

   b triangle with sides $12x$ cm, $5x$ cm, $13x$ cm

8 A ladder of length 6 m leans against a vertical wall. If the top of the ladder reaches 5 m up the wall, find the distance of the feet of the ladder from the wall. Give your answer to the nearest centimetre.

9 A rhombus has sides of length 10 cm. One of its diagonals is twice as long as the other. Find the length of the shorter diagonal to the nearest mm.

REVIEW SET 9B

1 Solve for x: **a** $x^2 = 49$ **b** $2x^2 = 26$ **c** $x^2 + 5 = 17$

2 Simplify: **a** $\left(\frac{1}{\sqrt{3}}\right)^2$ **b** $\left(\frac{1}{2}\sqrt{8}\right)^2$ **c** $\frac{\sqrt{48}}{\sqrt{3}}$

3 Write $\sqrt{50}$ in simplest form.

4 Solve for x: $x^3 + 125 = 0$

5 Find the exact value of x in the following:

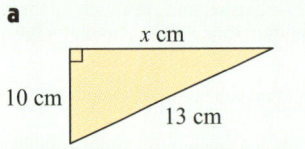

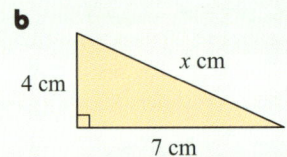

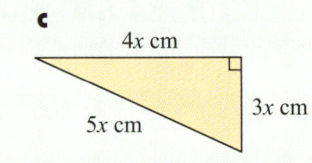

a right triangle with legs 10 cm and x cm, hypotenuse 13 cm.

b right triangle with legs 4 cm and 7 cm, hypotenuse x cm.

c right triangle with legs $4x$ cm and $3x$ cm, hypotenuse $5x$ cm.

6 The following triangles are not drawn to scale. Explain, with reasons, whether either triangle is right angled.

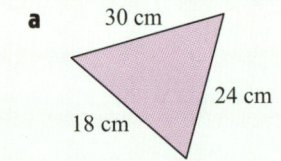

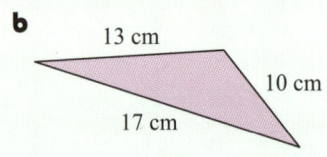

a triangle with sides 30 cm, 24 cm, 18 cm.

b triangle with sides 13 cm, 10 cm, 17 cm.

7 A cone has slant height 8 cm and base diameter 6 cm. Find the height of the cone.

8 Jason travels from A for 5 km due north and then 7 km due west to B. He then travels back directly from B to A. Find the total length of Jason's journey.

9 Find the length of the longest steel rod which could fit into a cardboard carton of dimensions 1.2 m by 0.8 m by 0.6 m.

10 A 4.5 m long pipe rests against a 2 m high tank. One end of the pipe is on the ground 3 m from the base of the tank. How much of the pipe overhangs the tank?

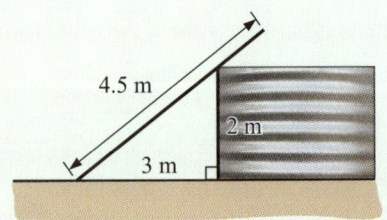

Chapter 10

Length and area

Contents:
- **A** Lengths and perimeters
- **B** Circumference of a circle
- **C** Area
- **D** Areas of circles and ellipses
- **E** Areas of composite figures
- **F** Surface area
- **G** Problem solving

LENGTH AND AREA   (Chapter 10)

Many people such as builders, engineers, architects, landscapers and surveyors rely on accurate measurement of **lengths** and **areas** to carry out their jobs.

OPENING PROBLEM

Sandy agrees to build a children's sandpit for the local kindergarten. Its sides and base will be made of wood, and it will be 5 m long, 3 m wide and 30 cm high.

Consider the following questions:

1 What *length* of 30 cm wide board is needed to make the border or *perimeter* of the sandpit?

2 What *area* of wood is needed to make the base of the sandpit?

3 What is the total *surface area* of wood needed to build the sandpit?

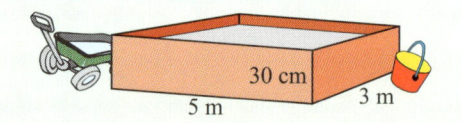

A   LENGTHS AND PERIMETERS

A **length** is a measure of the distance between two points.

The **metre** (m) is the base unit for length in the metric system.

When the metric system was being developed in 18th century France, the metre was defined as one ten-millionth of the distance from the North Pole to the equator through Paris.

Since 1983, the metre has been defined as the distance light travels in a vacuum in $\frac{1}{299\,792\,458}$ of a second.

From the metre, other units of length have been devised to handle smaller or larger distances. Millimetres (mm), centimetres (cm) and kilometres (km) are commonly used.

1 kilometre (km) = 1000 metres (m)	is $2\frac{1}{2}$ times around an athletics track.
1 metre (m) = 100 cm (cm)	is about an adult's stride length.
1 centimetre (cm) = 10 millimetres (mm)	is about the width of a fingernail.

The ability to **estimate** lengths and use appropriate units to describe them are important skills.

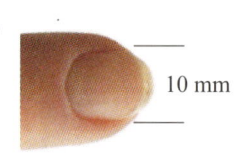

CONVERTING UNITS

To convert units of length, a conversion diagram can be used.

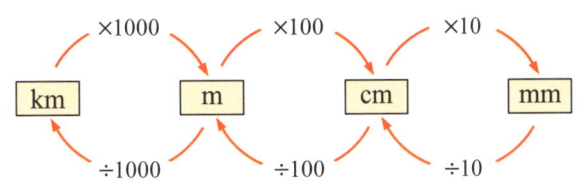

```
       ×1000        ×100         ×10
       ↙   ↘        ↙   ↘        ↙   ↘
    [ km ]      [ m ]       [ cm ]      [ mm ]
       ↖   ↗        ↖   ↗        ↖   ↗
       ÷1000        ÷100         ÷10
```

When converting from larger units to smaller units, we **multiply** by the conversion factor.

When converting from smaller units to larger units, we **divide** by the conversion factor.

Example 1 ◀)) Self Tutor

Convert:
a 200 cm to m   **b** 25 km to m

a 200 cm
   $= 200 \div 100$ m
   $= 2$ m

b 25 km
   $= 25 \times 1000$ m
   $= 25\,000$ m

EXERCISE 10A.1

1 What unit would you use to measure:
   a the distance between two towns
   b the length of a basketball court
   c the length of a plane
   d the diameter of a drink can
   e the length of a tooth pick
   f the width of a coin?

2 Choose the correct answer.
   a The width of a road would be:
      A 5 cm   **B** 5 m   **C** 50 m   **D** 500 mm
   b The length of a bee would be:
      A 14 km   **B** 140 cm **C** 14 mm   **D** 1400 m
   c The distance from New York to Seattle would be:
      A 39 000 m **B** 390 cm **C** 39 mm   **D** 3900 km

3 Estimate the following lengths, in the units given, then check your estimates by measuring:
   a the length of your pen (mm)
   b the width of your exercise book (mm)
   c the height of your desk (cm)
   d the length of the whiteboard (cm)
   e the height of your teacher (m)
   f the length of a soccer oval (m).

4 Convert:
   a 15 km to m
   b 240 mm to cm
   c 32 m to cm
   d 4.5 m to mm
   e 4320 m to km
   f 384 cm to km

5 A giant squid was caught and stretched from tentacle to tentacle. It measured 9625 mm. Find its length in:

    a centimetres   **b** metres.

6 A submarine dived to a depth of 635 600 cm. What is this depth in:

    a metres   **b** kilometres?

PERIMETER

The **perimeter** of a closed figure is the total length around its **boundary**.

The following perimeter formulae are for commonly occurring shapes:

PERIMETER FORMULAE

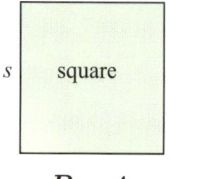

square: $P = 4s$

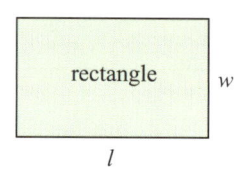

rectangle: $P = 2(l + w)$

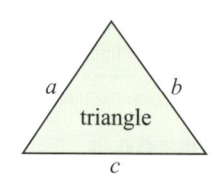

triangle: $P = a + b + c$

Example 2

Find the perimeter of:

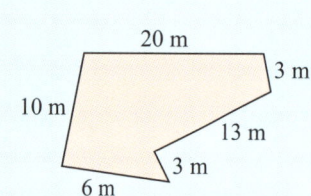

a (shape with sides 20 m, 3 m, 13 m, 3 m, 6 m, 10 m)

b right triangle with legs 6 cm and 8 cm

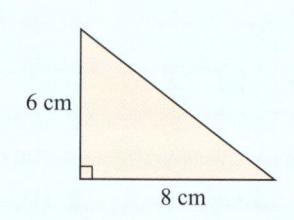

a Perimeter
$= 10 + 20 + 3 + 13 + 3 + 6$ m
$= 55$ m

b 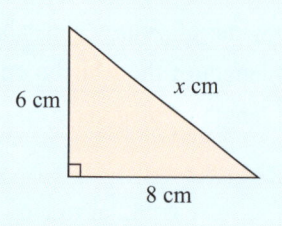
$x^2 = 6^2 + 8^2$ {Pythagoras}
$\therefore \ x^2 = 36 + 64$
$\therefore \ x^2 = 100$
$\therefore \ x = \sqrt{100} = 10$ {as $x > 0$}
$\therefore$ perimeter $= 6 + 8 + 10$ cm
$= 24$ cm

EXERCISE 10A.2

1 Find the perimeter of the following:

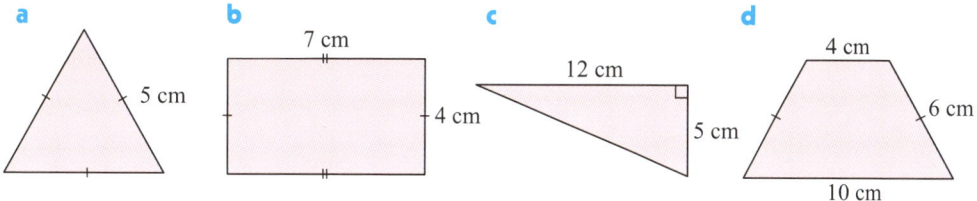

a Triangle with sides 5 cm (equilateral markings)

b Rectangle 7 cm by 4 cm

c Right triangle with 12 cm and 5 cm

d Trapezium with top 4 cm, sides 6 cm, base 10 cm

2 A farmer decides to fence a 400 m by 350 m field with a 4-strand wire fence. Find:
   a the perimeter of the field
   b the total length of wire required
   c the total cost of wire required if a single strand of wire costs 12.4 cents per metre.

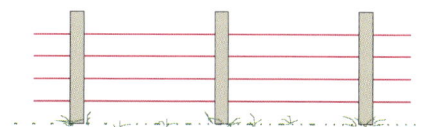

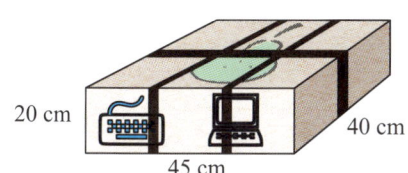

3 Boxes containing computers are fastened with three pieces of tape, as shown.
Each piece of tape is overlapped 5 cm at the join.
Calculate the total length of tape required for 20 boxes.

Box dimensions: 20 cm × 45 cm × 40 cm

4 Kim decides to get fit by running laps of a nearby shopping complex. Its dimensions are shown in the diagram alongside.
How many laps does he have to run if he wants to run 13 km in total?

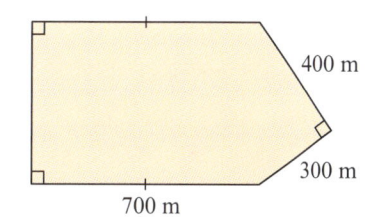

Shape dimensions: 400 m, 300 m, 700 m

Example 3

Find the perimeter P of:

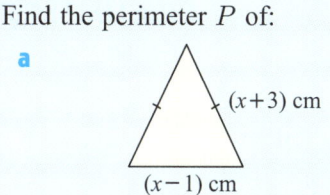

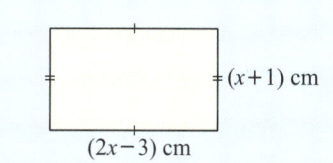

a Triangle with equal sides $(x+3)$ cm and base $(x-1)$ cm

b Rectangle with sides $(x+1)$ cm and $(2x-3)$ cm

a $P =$ two lots of $(x+3)$ + one lot of $(x-1)$
$P = 2(x+3) + (x-1)$
$P = 2x + 6 + x - 1$
$\therefore \ P = 3x + 5$ cm

b $P =$ two lots of $(x+1)$ + two lots of $(2x-3)$
$P = 2(x+1) + 2(2x-3)$
$P = 2x + 2 + 4x - 6$
$\therefore \ P = 6x - 4$ cm

5 Find the perimeter P of the following given all sides are measured in cm:

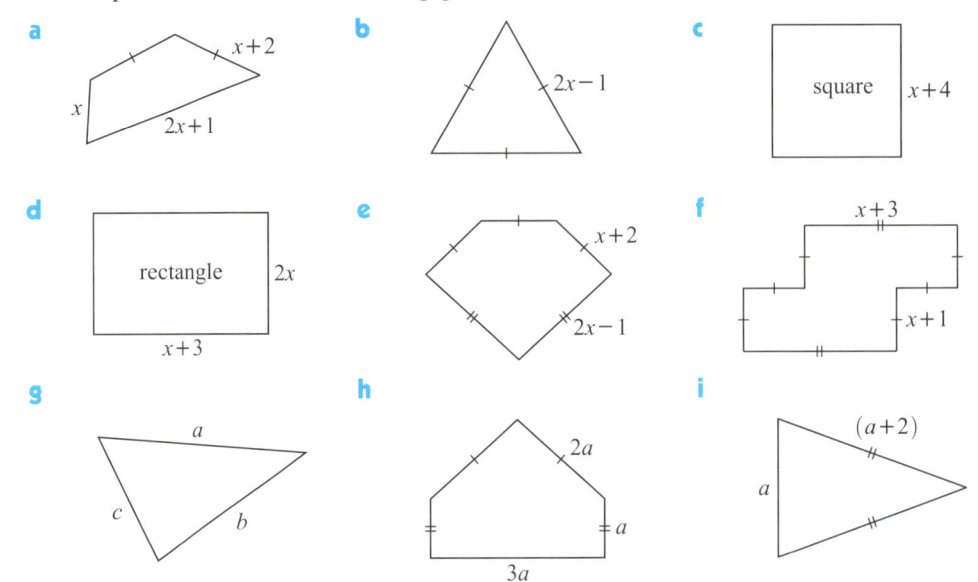

a (quadrilateral with sides x, $2x+1$, $x+2$, and one unmarked side equal to $x+2$)

b (equilateral triangle with side $2x-1$)

c square with side $x+4$

d rectangle with sides $x+3$ and $2x$

e (kite/rhombus-like shape with two sides $x+2$ and two sides $2x-1$)

f (step-shaped figure with $x+3$ and $x+1$ marked)

g triangle with sides a, b, c

h (pentagon with top sides $2a$ and $2a$, bottom $3a$, and two sides a)

i (isosceles triangle with two equal sides $(a+2)$ and base a)

B CIRCUMFERENCE OF A CIRCLE

The **diameter** of a circle is the distance across the circle measured through its centre.

The **circumference** of a circle is the perimeter or length around its boundary.

The following investigation should enable you to find the relationship between the circumference and diameter of any circle.

INVESTIGATION 1   CIRCUMFERENCE

You will need:

some cylinders such as soft drink cans, a toilet roll, and a piece of pipe, two set squares, a ruler and a pencil.

What to do:

Step 1: Measure the diameter d of one object using the two set squares as shown. The distance between the two marks is the diameter of your object.

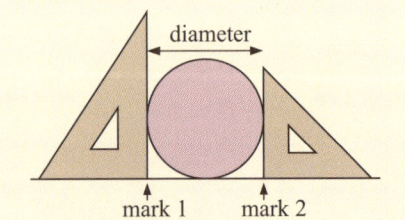

Step 2: Mark a point on the circumference of your object and then roll it along a flat surface for one complete revolution as shown. The distance between the two marks is the circumference or distance around the perimeter of your object.

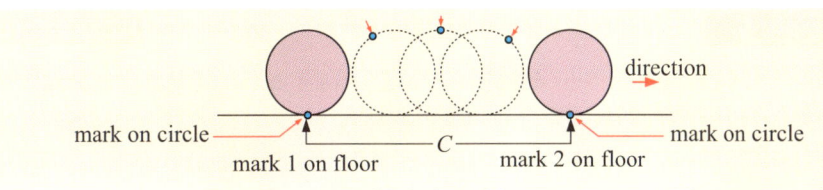

Step 3: Copy the table below and fill it in with measurements from your objects.

Circular object	Circumference	Diameter	$\dfrac{Circumference}{Diameter}$
⋮	⋮	⋮	⋮

Step 4: Compare your results with those of other students. What do you notice?

It has been known for thousands of years that whenever the circumference of a circle is divided by its diameter the answer is always the same. You should have found this in the investigation above, allowing for slight inaccuracies in measurements.

The actual value for $\dfrac{\text{circumference}}{\text{diameter}}$ for any circle lies between 3.14 and 3.15.

The exact value is symbolised by the Greek letter π known as 'pi'.

For any circle, $\dfrac{\text{circumference}}{\text{diameter}} = \pi$

and so circumference $= \pi \times$ diameter   or $C = \pi \times d$.

Since the diameter of the circle is twice the length of its radius, we can also write

circumference $= \pi \times 2 \times$ radius   or $C = 2 \times \pi \times r$.

$C = \pi d$ where d is the **diameter** of the circle and C is its **circumference**.

$C = 2\pi r$ where r is the **radius** of the circle.

The exact value for π cannot be written down because it is a decimal number which neither terminates (stops) nor recurs. It cannot even be expressed as a fraction. The value of π correct to 36 decimal places is
$\pi \approx 3.141\,592\,653\,589\,793\,238\,462\,643\,383\,279\,502\,884$.

In practice we use $\pi \approx 3.14$ which is correct to 3 significant figures, or else use the $\boxed{\pi}$ key on our calculator.

When using a calculator, we round off the **final answer** only.

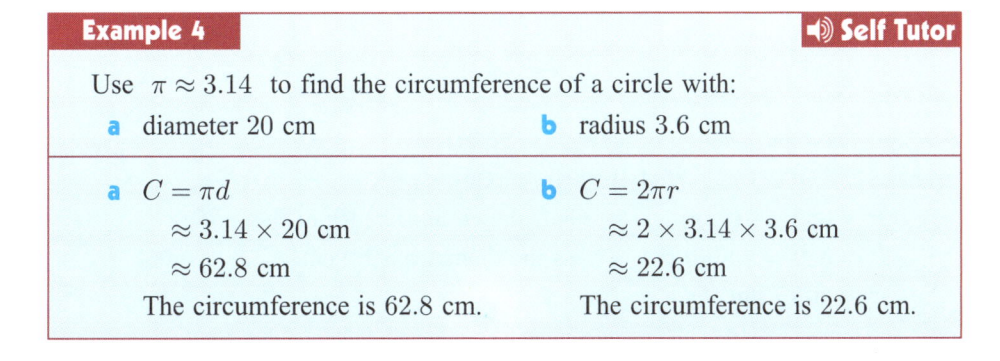

Example 4

Use $\pi \approx 3.14$ to find the circumference of a circle with:

a diameter 20 cm   **b** radius 3.6 cm

a $C = \pi d$
$\approx 3.14 \times 20$ cm
≈ 62.8 cm
The circumference is 62.8 cm.

b $C = 2\pi r$
$\approx 2 \times 3.14 \times 3.6$ cm
≈ 22.6 cm
The circumference is 22.6 cm.

Example 5

Using your calculator, find the circumference of a circle of radius 2.5 m. Give your answer correct to 2 decimal places.

$C = 2\pi r$
$= 2 \times \pi \times 2.5$ m
≈ 15.71 m   *Calculator:* 2 × 2nd F π × 2.5 =

So, the circumference is 15.71 m (approx).

EXERCISE 10B

1 Use $\pi \approx 3.14$ to find the circumference of:

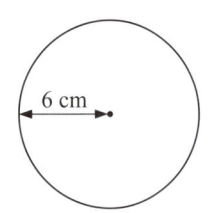

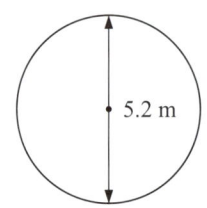

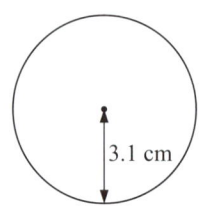

a 6 cm   **b** 5.2 m   **c** 3.1 cm

2 Using your calculator, find correct to 2 decimal places the circumference of a circle with:

a radius 4 cm   **b** diameter 18 m   **c** radius 7.2 km.

3 A cylindrical water tower has a base diameter of 7 m. Find the circumference of the base.

4 A circular flower bed has a radius of 2.5 m. Find the perimeter of the flower bed.

5 A bicycle wheel has radius 40 cm.
  a Find the circumference of the wheel.
  b How many kilometres would be travelled if the wheel rotates 10 000 times?
  c How many times does the wheel rotate if the bicycle is ridden 10 km?

Example 6

Find the perimeter of the door, giving your answer correct to 1 decimal place.

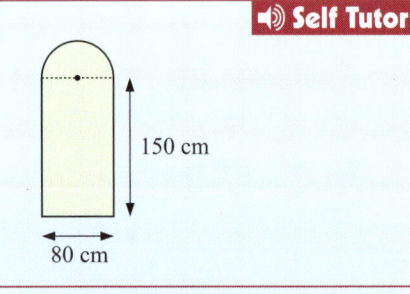

(150 cm, 80 cm)

Perimeter = 150 + 150 + 80 + the semi-circle
∴ $P = 380 + \frac{1}{2}(2\pi r)$ {half the circumference of the circle}
∴ $P = 380 + \pi \times 40$ cm   {as the diameter is 80 cm}
∴ $P \approx 505.7$ cm

LENGTH AND AREA (Chapter 10) 221

6 Find the perimeter, correct to 2 decimal places, of:

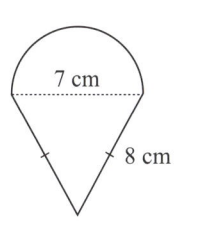

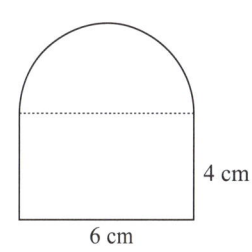

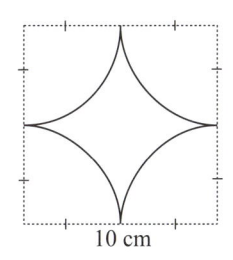

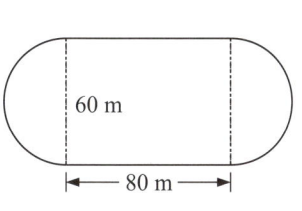

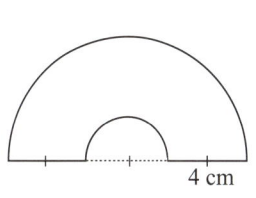

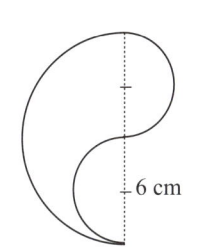

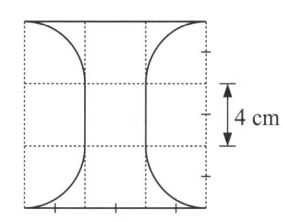

a (semicircle, 10 cm)

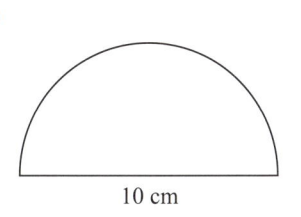

b (ice-cream cone shape, 7 cm across top, 8 cm slant sides)

c (rectangle with semicircular top, 6 cm wide, 4 cm tall sides)

d (square 10 cm with four inward circular arcs)

e (stadium/discorectangle, 60 m height, 80 m between centres)

f (semicircular annulus, inner radius 4 cm)

g (yin-yang style shape, 6 cm)

h (square with four inward semicircles, 4 cm)

i (three small semicircles atop one larger semicircle, 18 cm)

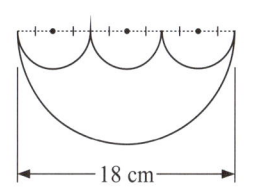

7 The minute hand of a clock is 8 cm long. How far does the tip travel between 2.00 pm and 2.45 pm?

8 Which is the shorter path from A to B: around the 2 smaller semi-circles or around the large semi-circle?

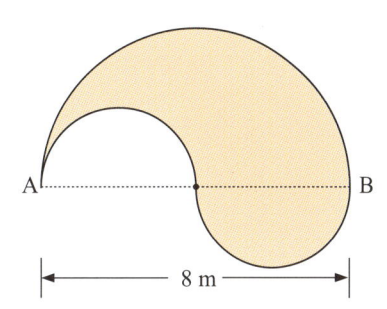

(Diagram: large semicircle from A to B with 8 m diameter, and two smaller semicircles)

Example 7

Find, correct to 2 decimal places, the radius of a circular pond which has a circumference of 30.5 m.

Using $C = 2\pi r$

$\therefore 30.5 = 2\pi r$

$\therefore \dfrac{30.5}{2\pi} = r$

$\therefore r \approx 4.85$ {Calculator: 30.5 ÷ (2 × 2nd F π) = }

So, the radius is about 4.85 m.

9 A machine makes circular paper plates which have circumference 50 cm. Find the diameter of a plate correct to the nearest mm.

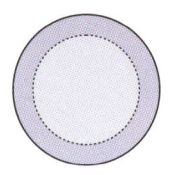

10 A bicycle wheel has diameter 0.6 m.
  a Find the circumference of the wheel to the nearest mm.
  b Through how many revolutions must the wheel turn during a 100 km trip?

11 A satellite has a circular orbit 800 km above the earth's equator. The radius of the earth is 6400 km and the satellite must complete exactly 14 orbits in one day.
  a Find the circumference of the satellite's orbit to the nearest km.
  b At what speed is the satellite moving?

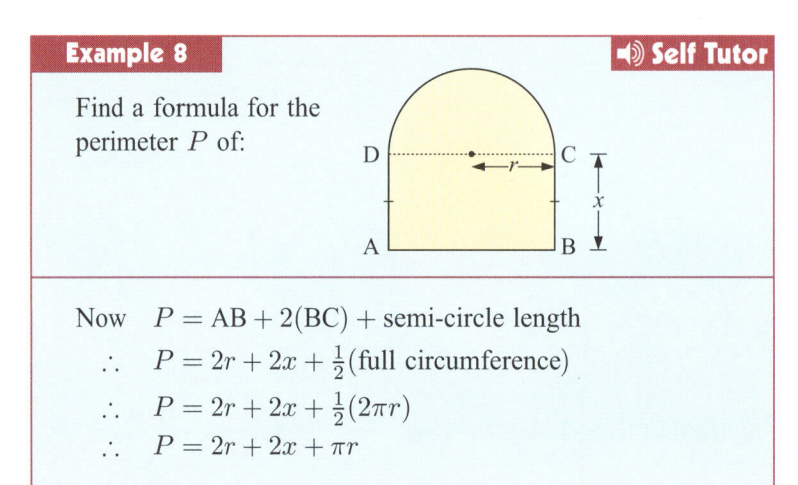

Example 8 — Self Tutor

Find a formula for the perimeter P of:

Now $P = AB + 2(BC) + $ semi-circle length
∴ $P = 2r + 2x + \frac{1}{2}($full circumference$)$
∴ $P = 2r + 2x + \frac{1}{2}(2\pi r)$
∴ $P = 2r + 2x + \pi r$

12 Find a formula for the perimeter P of:

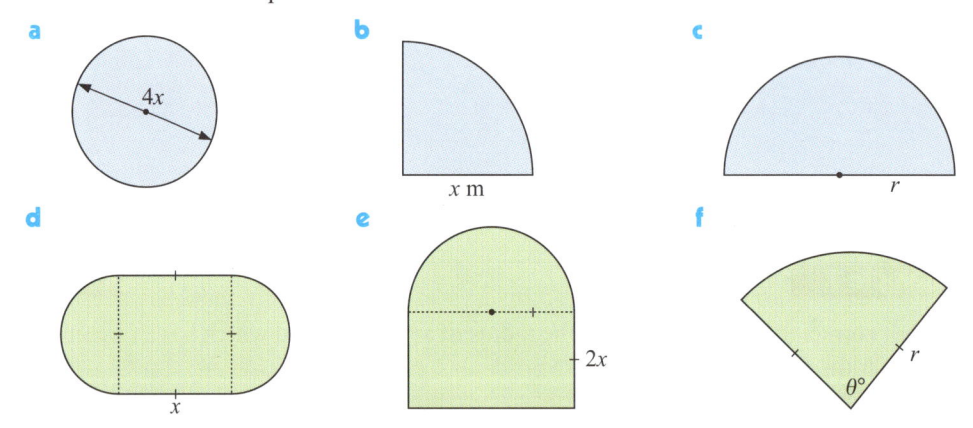

a (circle, diameter $4x$)

b (quarter circle, radius x m)

c (semicircle, radius r)

d (stadium shape, width x)

e (rectangle with semicircle on top, width $2x$)

f (sector, radius r, angle $\theta°$)

HISTORICAL NOTE — THE HISTORY OF PI

2000 BC Babylonians used $\pi \approx 3\frac{1}{8}$.

1000 BC Use of $\pi \approx 3$ in the **Bible** (1 Kings 7:23).

250 BC Archimedes found π to lie between $3\frac{10}{71}$ and $3\frac{1}{7}$.

1579	**Viete** calculated π to 9 decimal places.	
1665	**Sir Isaac Newton** calculated π to 16 decimal places.	
1706	The **Greek** letter π or 'pi' was first used.	
1949	The **ENIAC** computer took 70 hours to calculate π to over 2000 decimal places.	
1984	A computer in **Japan** was used to calculate π to 16 million decimal places!	

ACTIVITY 1   TRUNDLE WHEEL

A trundle wheel is an instrument used for measuring distances.
It consists of a wheel on a handle and a device which counts the number of revolutions of the wheel.

What to do:

1 Obtain a trundle wheel of circumference 1 metre. Find the radius of the wheel using the formula $C = 2\pi r$.

2 Use your trundle wheel to make measurements around your school, such as the distance around the oval, the length of a school building, the length of a tennis court, the perimeter of a tennis court, or the length of the fence around the school.

3 Find the error in your measurement of a kilometre if your trundle wheel has a radius which is too small by: **a** 1 cm   **b** 1 mm.

C   AREA

Around your school, you can see many surfaces such as walls, ceilings, paths and ovals. All of these surfaces are enclosed within boundaries that help to define the surface.

> **Area** is the amount of *surface* inside a two-dimensional shape.

We use areas in many aspects of life. For example, when buying land or a house we describe its size by its area.

Descriptions on cans of paint and bottles of weed killer refer to the **area** they can cover.

> The **area** of the surface of a closed figure is measured in terms of the number of square units it encloses.

The units of measurement of area are:

- square millimetres (mm^2)
- square centimetres (cm^2)
- square metres (m^2)
- hectares (ha)
- square kilometres (km^2).

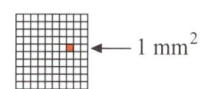

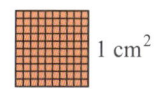

CONVERTING AREA UNITS

The square alongside has an area of 1 cm².

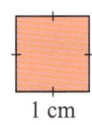

However, we could also give the lengths on the square in mm.

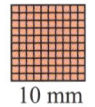

Thus, the area is also 10 mm × 10 mm = 100 mm²

So, to convert cm² into mm², we need to multiply by $10^2 = 100$.

The relationships between the units of area are shown below:

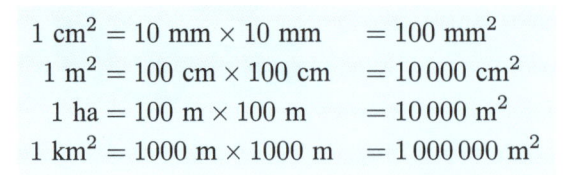

It is easier to convert the units of length before the area is calculated!

$$1 \text{ cm}^2 = 10 \text{ mm} \times 10 \text{ mm} \quad = 100 \text{ mm}^2$$
$$1 \text{ m}^2 = 100 \text{ cm} \times 100 \text{ cm} \quad = 10\,000 \text{ cm}^2$$
$$1 \text{ ha} = 100 \text{ m} \times 100 \text{ m} \quad = 10\,000 \text{ m}^2$$
$$1 \text{ km}^2 = 1000 \text{ m} \times 1000 \text{ m} \quad = 1\,000\,000 \text{ m}^2$$

To convert units of length, we can use a conversion diagram:

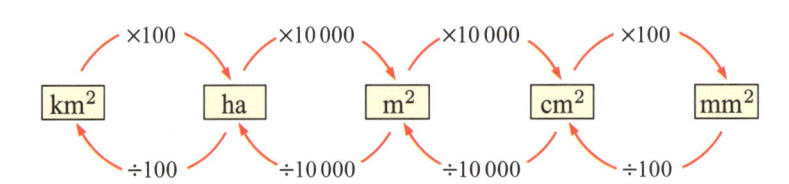

km² —×100→ ha —×10000→ m² —×10000→ cm² —×100→ mm²

km² ←÷100— ha ←÷10000— m² ←÷10000— cm² ←÷100— mm²

When converting from larger units to smaller units, we **multiply** by the conversion factor.

When converting from smaller units to larger units, we **divide** by the conversion factor.

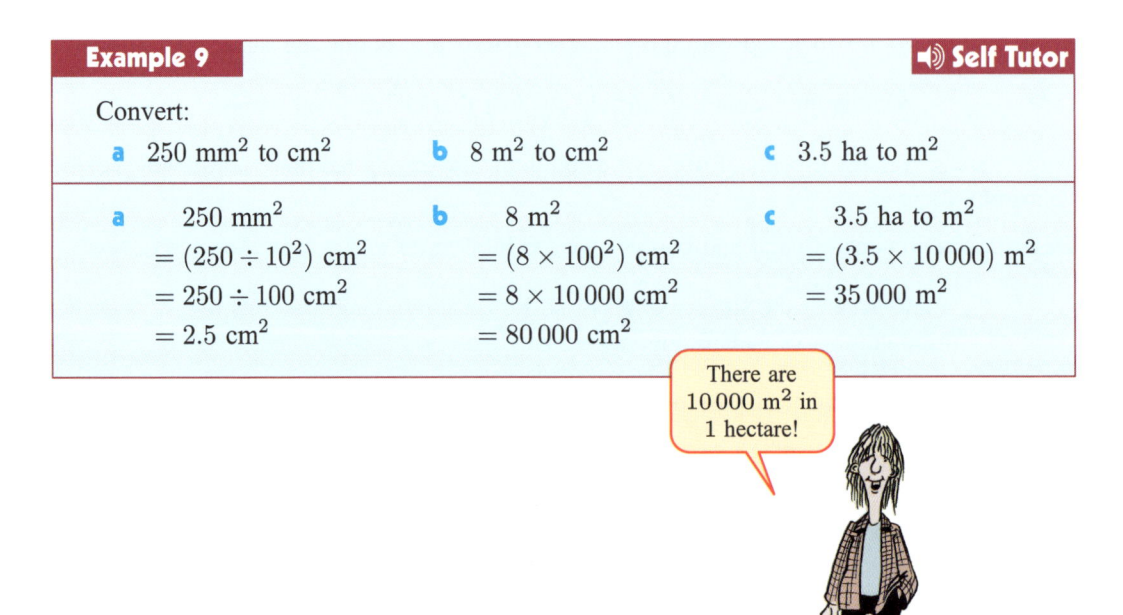

Example 9

Convert:
  a 250 mm² to cm²   **b** 8 m² to cm²   **c** 3.5 ha to m²

a   250 mm²
= $(250 \div 10^2)$ cm²
= $250 \div 100$ cm²
= 2.5 cm²

b   8 m²
= (8×100^2) cm²
= $8 \times 10\,000$ cm²
= 80\,000 cm²

c   3.5 ha to m²
= $(3.5 \times 10\,000)$ m²
= 35\,000 m²

There are 10\,000 m² in 1 hectare!

EXERCISE 10C.1

1 What units of area would be most suitable to measure the following areas:

   a the floor space in a classroom   **b** a horse's hoof

   c a fingernail   **d** barley grown on a farm

   e a soccer pitch   **f** Liechtenstein?

2 Convert:

   a 235 m^2 to cm^2 **b** 36.5 ha to m^2 **c** 3280 mm^2 to cm^2

   d 3 654 200 cm^2 to m^2 **e** 782 000 m^2 to ha   **f** 8.8 cm^2 to mm^2

   g 5 km^2 to ha   **h** 3000 ha to km^2 **i** 50 km^2 to m^2

AREA FORMULAE

The following area formulae have been used previously:

RECTANGLES

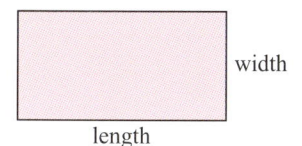

Area = length × width

TRIANGLES

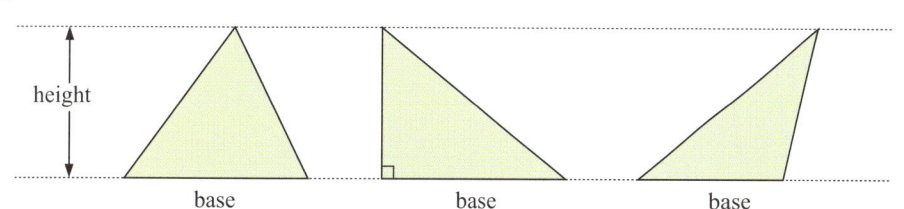

Area = $\frac{1}{2}$ (base × height)

PARALLELOGRAMS

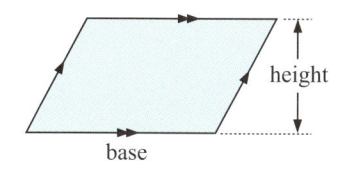

Area = base × height

TRAPEZIA

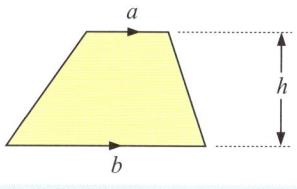

Area = [The average of the lengths of the two parallel sides] × [the distance between the parallel sides]

or   Area = $\left(\dfrac{a+b}{2}\right) \times h$

Example 10

Find the area of:

a

5 m
12 m

b

5 cm
10 cm

c

11 m
4 m
16 m

a Area
= $\frac{1}{2}$ base × height
= $\frac{1}{2}$ × 12 × 5
= 30 m^2

b Area
= base × height
= 10 × 5
= 50 cm^2

c Area
= $\left(\dfrac{a+b}{2}\right) \times h$
= $\left(\dfrac{11+16}{2}\right) \times 4$
= 54 m^2

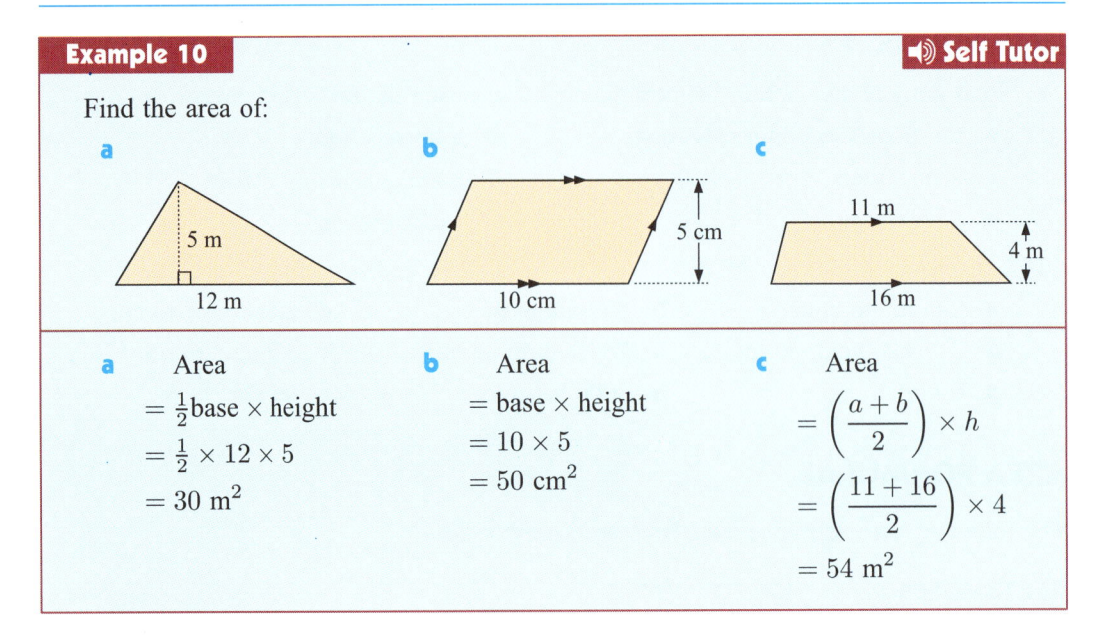

EXERCISE 10C.2

1 Find the area of the shaded region:

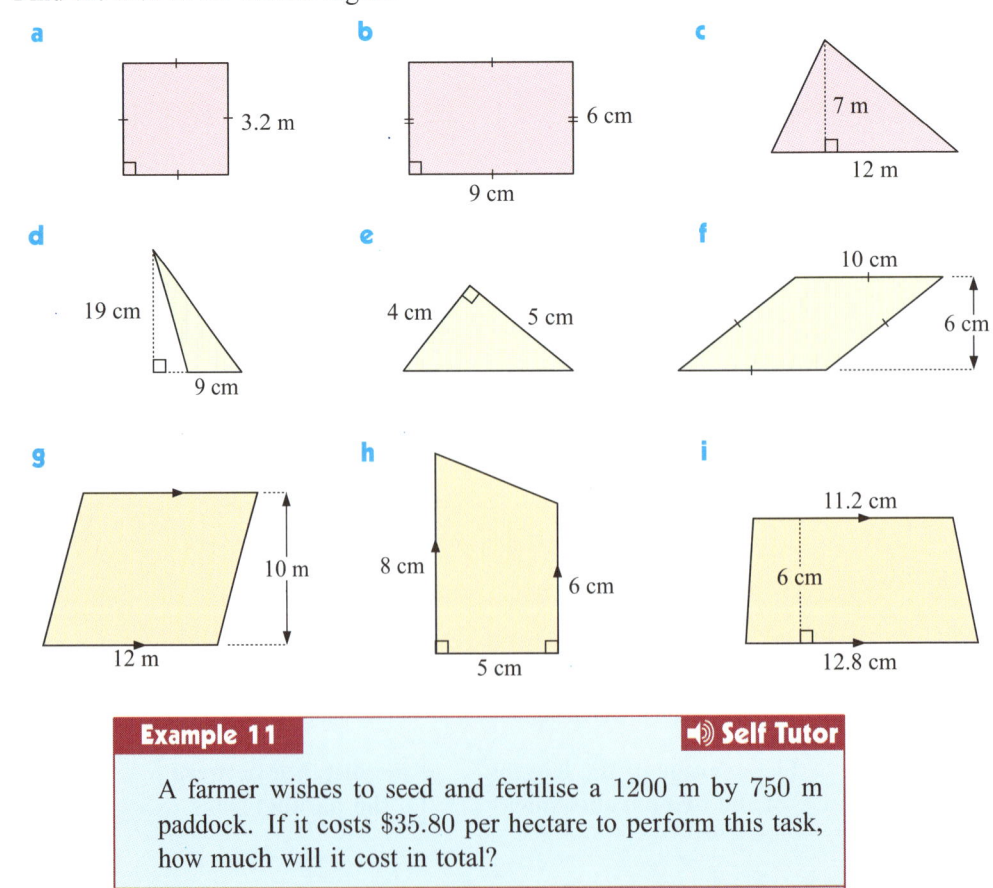

a 3.2 m

b 6 cm, 9 cm

c 7 m, 12 m

d 19 cm, 9 cm

e 4 cm, 5 cm

f 10 cm, 6 cm

g 10 m, 12 m

h 8 cm, 6 cm, 5 cm

i 11.2 cm, 6 cm, 12.8 cm

Example 11

A farmer wishes to seed and fertilise a 1200 m by 750 m paddock. If it costs $35.80 per hectare to perform this task, how much will it cost in total?

$$\text{Area of paddock} = \text{length} \times \text{width}$$
$$= 1200 \times 750 \text{ m}^2$$
$$= \frac{1200 \times 750}{10\,000} \text{ ha}$$
$$= 90 \text{ ha}$$
$$\therefore \text{ total cost} = 90 \times \$35.80$$
$$= \$3222.00$$

2 A school yard has dimensions 320 metres by 156 metres. It is completely surrounded by a wall that is 1.6 metres high. Both sides of the wall and the gates are to be painted. Find the total area to be painted.

3 Anya's farm measures 800 metres by 1.2 km. If 36 hectares are sown with wheat, find the percentage of her farm that is sown with wheat.

4 A square paving brick has an area of 225 cm². If each brick fits tightly in place, how many bricks are needed to pave a path 1.2 m by 12 m?

5 Find the area A of the following shaded regions if all measurements are in cm:

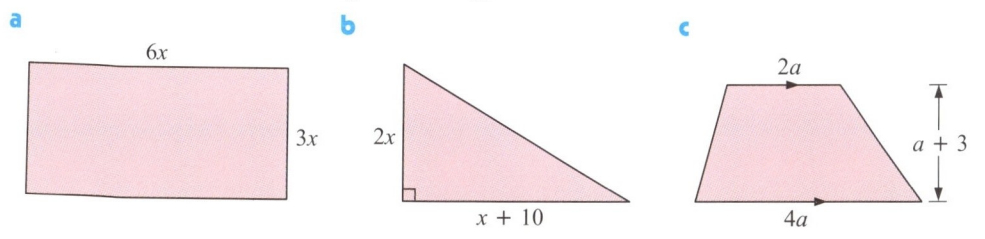

a rectangle with sides $6x$ and $3x$

b right triangle with base $x+10$ and height $2x$

c trapezium with parallel sides $2a$ (top) and $4a$ (bottom), height $a+3$

INVESTIGATION 2 — THE SHADEHOUSE

You wish to build a shadehouse against an existing brick wall. The structure is to be made from square section metal and is to be covered with dark green shadecloth. The tubing costs $3.95 per metre and the shadecloth comes in 3 m wide strips which cost $6.50 per metre.

Dimensions: existing wall 4.5 m, height 2.4 m, depth 3 m, with roll-up door. Joiners: 'corner', 'T', '4-way'.

What to do:

1 Find the total length of tubing required and hence its cost.

2 Find the length of cloth required and hence its cost.

3 Find the total cost of all joiners if corner joiners cost $5.00 each, T joiners cost $3.50 each, and 4-way joiners cost $6.50 each.

4 The floor of the shadehouse is to be covered with clay-brick pavers which can be purchased for $29.50 per square metre. Find the area of the floor and hence the total cost of the pavers required.

5 Find the total cost of making the shadehouse.

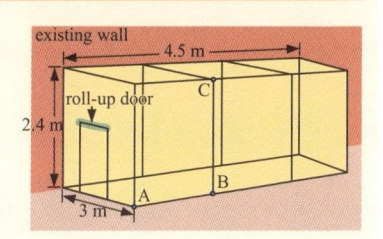

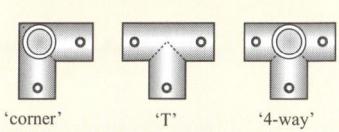

ACTIVITY 2 — THE AREA OF A CIRCLE

You will need: A pair of scissors, a pencil, glue, and a highlighter.

What to do:

1. Click on the icon and print the giant protractor. Measure its radius.

2. Highlight the circumference of the circular protractor.

3. Carefully cut out sectors of $10°$ then neatly paste the sectors side by side on a horizontal line drawn across the page as shown.

4. What familiar shape is similar to the shape you have made with the sectors?

5. What would happen to the shape which you have created if each sector had an angle of $1°$?

6. Calculate the area of the shape you have made. This is an estimate of the area of the protractor.

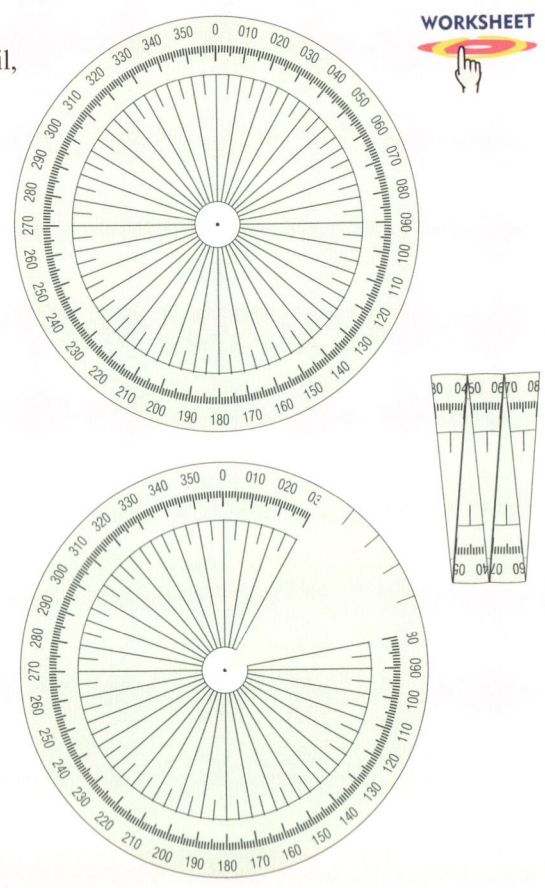

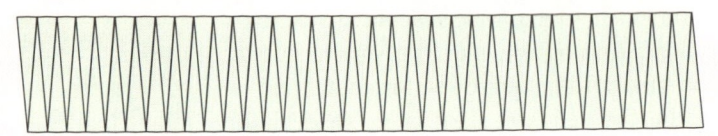

7. Divide the area you have found by the square of the radius. What do you suspect?

D AREAS OF CIRCLES AND ELLIPSES

Consider cutting a circle of radius r into 16 equal sectors and arranging them as shown:

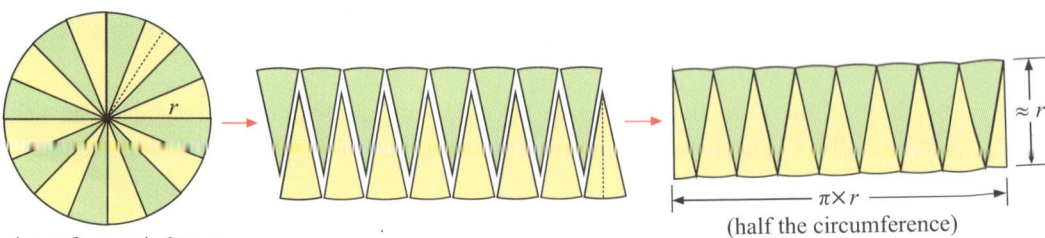

circumference is $2 \times \pi \times r$

$\pi \times r$ (half the circumference)

$\approx r$

The figure obtained closely resembles a rectangle. The height of the rectangle is the radius of the circle.

The top "edge" is the sum of all the arc lengths of the green sectors. This is half the circumference of the circle, which is

$$\tfrac{1}{2} \times 2 \times \pi \times r = \pi \times r.$$

The bottom "edge" is made up from the arcs of the yellow sectors in a similar way.

If the original circle is cut into 1000 equal sectors and arranged in the same way as before, the resulting figure is indistinguishable from a rectangle.

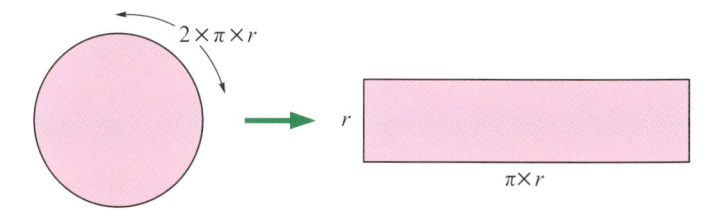

So, the area of the circle $\quad A = $ length $\times$ width $\;$ of the rectangle
$$\therefore \quad A = \pi \times r \times r$$
$$\therefore \quad A = \pi r^2$$

The area of a circle of radius r is given by $\;$ **Area $= \pi r^2$**.

Example 12

Find the area of the circle, giving your answer correct to 1 decimal place.

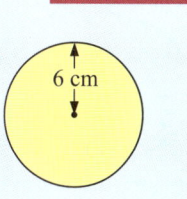

6 cm

$$A = \pi r^2$$
$$\therefore \quad A = \pi \times 6^2 \quad \text{\{the radius is 6 cm\}}$$
$$\therefore \quad A \approx 113.1 \text{ cm}^2$$

So, the area is approximately 113.1 cm².

ELLIPSES

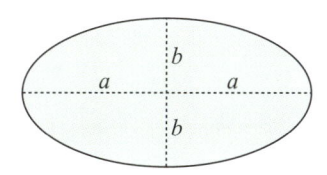

The area of an ellipse with **semi-axes** a and b is given by

Area $A = \pi ab$

Notice that when $a = b$, the ellipse becomes a circle with radius a, and area is πa^2.

LENGTH AND AREA (Chapter 10)

EXERCISE 10D

1 Find the area of the following figures, correct to 2 decimal places:

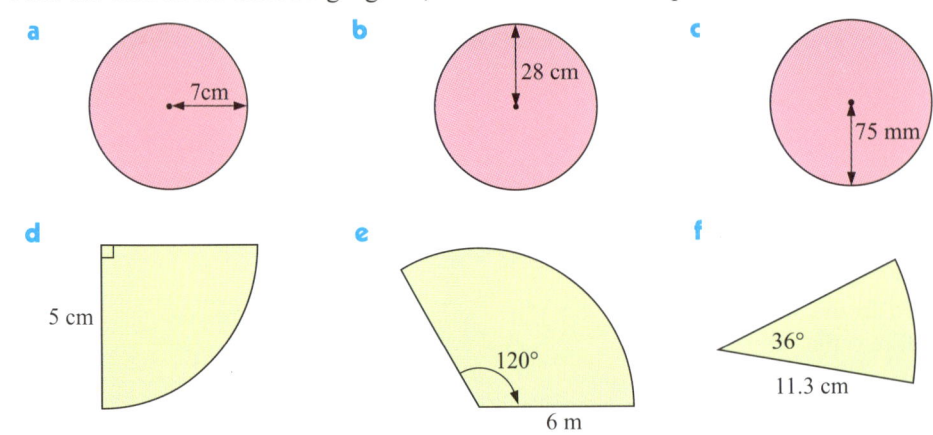

a circle, 7 cm radius

b circle, 28 cm diameter

c circle, 75 mm radius

d quarter circle, 5 cm

e sector, 120°, 6 m

f sector, 36°, 11.3 cm

2 For a circle of diameter 2.6 cm find, correct to 2 decimal places:

   a its perimeter   **b** its area.

3 A sprinkler sprays water in a circle with radius 3.4 m. Calculate the area of lawn it waters.

4 A goat is tethered to a post by a 5.4 m long rope. What area can the goat graze?

5 Find the area of the following:

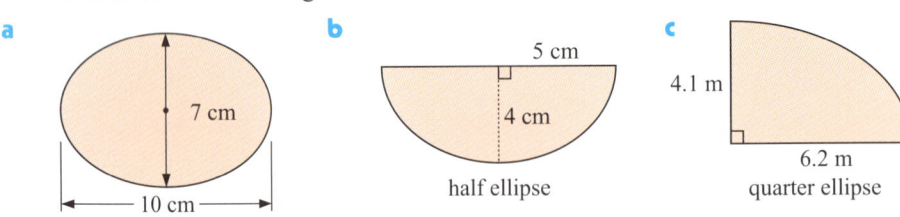

a ellipse, 7 cm, 10 cm

b half ellipse, 5 cm, 4 cm

c quarter ellipse, 4.1 m, 6.2 m

E   AREAS OF COMPOSITE FIGURES

Composite figures are figures made up from two or more basic shapes.

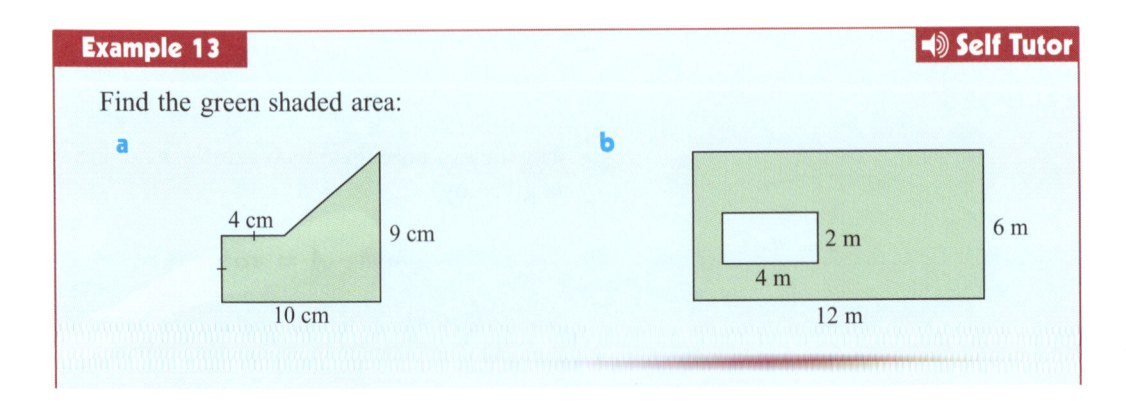

Example 13

Find the green shaded area:

a 4 cm, 9 cm, 10 cm

b 6 m, 2 m, 4 m, 12 m

a We divide the figure into a rectangle and a triangle as shown.

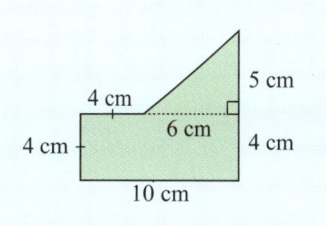

Area = area of rectangle + area of triangle
$= 10 \times 4 + \frac{1}{2} \times 6 \times 5$
$= 40 + 15$
$= 55$ cm^2

b Area = area large rectangle − area small rectangle
$= 12 \times 6 - 4 \times 2$ m^2
$= 64$ m^2

EXERCISE 10E

1 Find the area shaded:

a 5 m, 12 m, 8 m

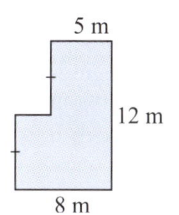

b 4 m, 6 m, 7 m, 10 m

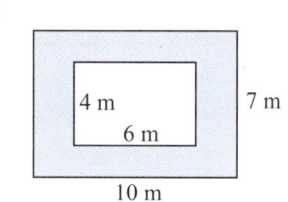

c 4 cm, 8 cm, 7 cm

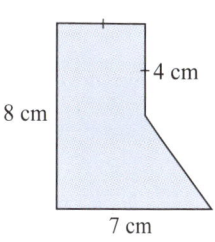

d 16 m, 3 m, 8 m

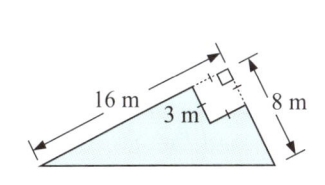

e 8 cm, 9 cm, 4 cm, 4 cm

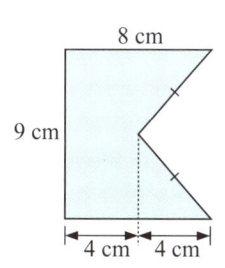

f 2 cm, 12 cm

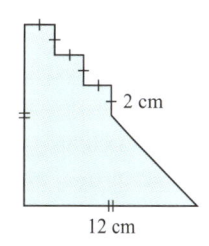

Example 14

Find, correct to 1 decimal place, the pink shaded area:

a 40 cm, 60 cm

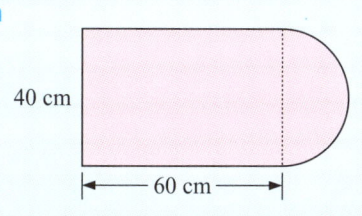

b 5 cm, 2 cm

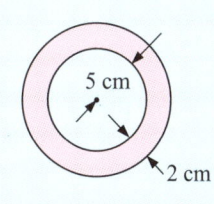

a Area = area of rectangle + area of semi-circle
$= 40 \times 60 + \frac{1}{2} \times (\pi \times 20^2)$ {area of circle $= \pi r^2$}
≈ 3028.3 cm^2

b Area = area large circle − area small circle
$= \pi \times 7^2 - \pi \times 5^2$
≈ 75.4 cm^2

2 Find the areas of the shaded regions, giving your answers correct to 2 decimal places:

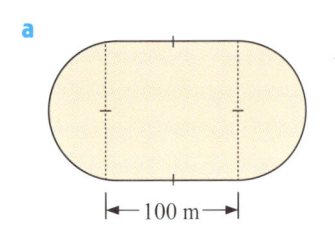

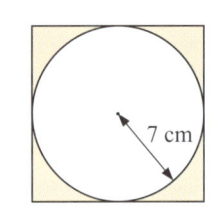

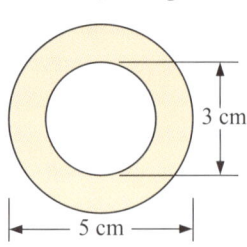

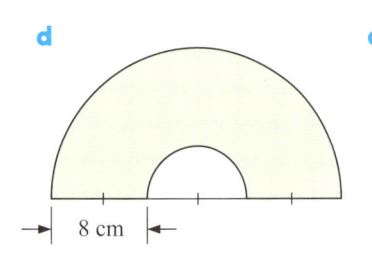

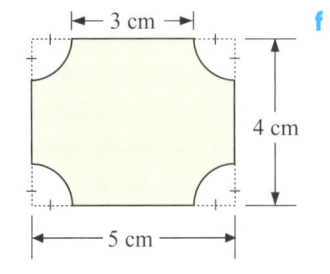

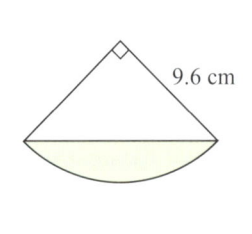

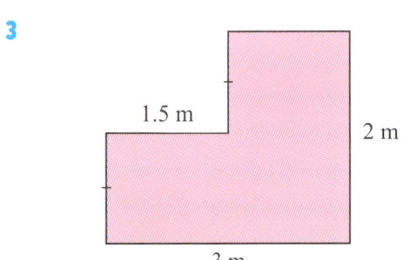

a. [shape: rectangle with semicircles on each end, width 100 m]

b. [circle of diameter 7 cm inscribed in a square]

c. [annulus with outer diameter 5 cm and inner radius ... width 3 cm shown]

d. [semicircular annulus with inner diameter 8 cm]

e. [square 5 cm by 4 cm with quarter-circles of radius 3 cm removed from each corner]

f. [quarter circle of radius 9.6 cm]

3

[L-shaped figure with dimensions 1.5 m, 2 m, 3 m]

A wall to be tiled has dimensions as illustrated. If tiles 10 cm by 20 cm are used, how many tiles are needed?

4 A circular garden of radius 2.5 m is planted within a rectangular back yard measuring 12 m by 7 m. Draw a diagram of the yard and find the area of the back yard which is not garden.

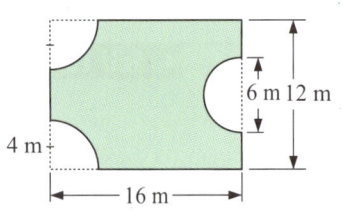

5 [diagram: rectangle 16 m by 12 m with quarter-circles of radius 4 m removed from two corners on the left and a half-circle of radius 6 m removed from the right side]

A gardener plans a lawn with three garden beds. Two of the beds are quarter-circles in shape, while the third is a half circle. Use the diagram to calculate the area of lawn.

6 A 2 m wide path is placed around a circular pond of diameter 4 m. Find the area of the path.

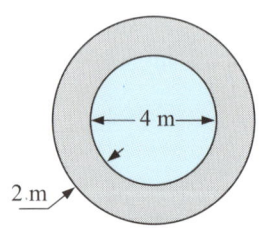

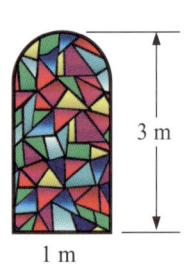

[diagram: circular pond diameter 4 m with 2 m wide path around it]

7 [stained glass window: rectangle 1 m wide and 3 m tall topped with a semicircle]

The illustration shows the dimensions of a stained glass window. Find the area of the window.

8 A rectangle is 12 cm by 8 cm. If the length of the rectangle is increased by 2 cm, by how much must the width be changed so that the area remains the same?

9 Find the area A of the following shaded regions if all measurements are in cm:

a

b

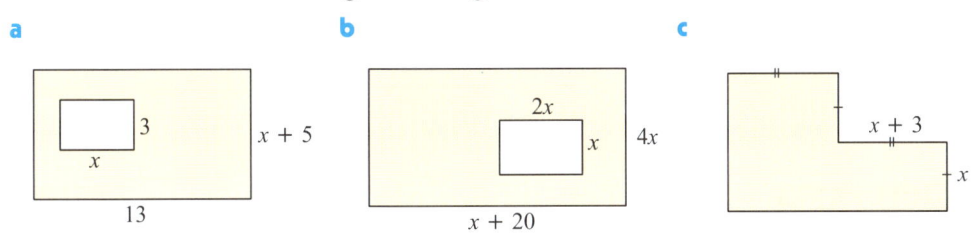

c

F   SURFACE AREA

SOLIDS WITH PLANE FACES

The **surface area** of a three-dimensional figure with plane faces is the sum of the areas of the faces.

The surface area of a solid will equal the area of the **net** which forms it. It is thus often helpful to draw the **net** first.

Software that demonstrates **nets** can be found at http://www.peda.com/poly/

Example 15   ◀◗ Self Tutor

Find the total surface area of the rectangular box:

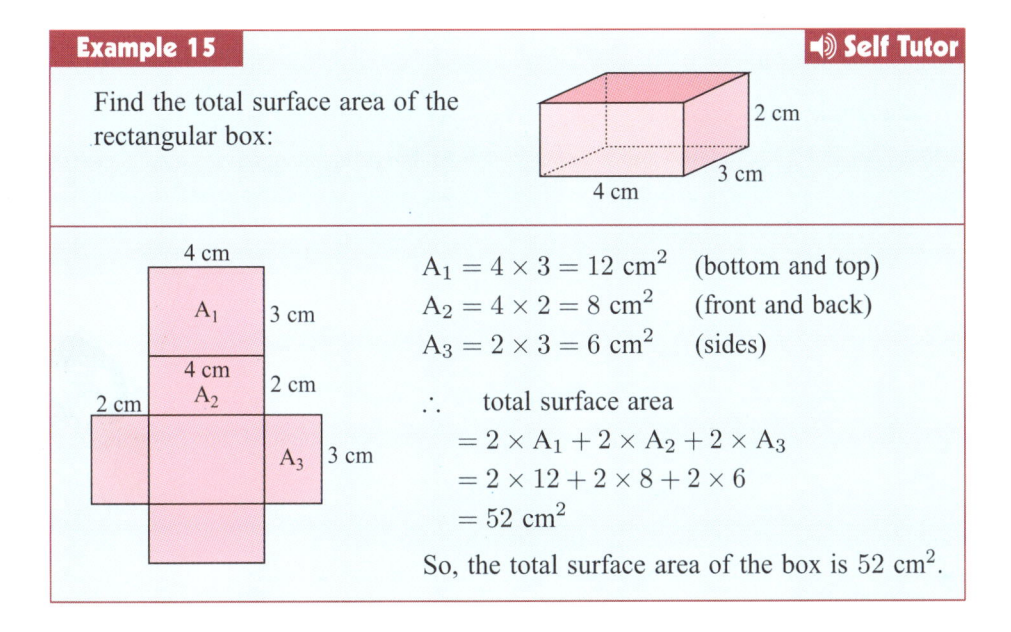

$A_1 = 4 \times 3 = 12$ cm^2 (bottom and top)
$A_2 = 4 \times 2 = 8$ cm^2 (front and back)
$A_3 = 2 \times 3 = 6$ cm^2 (sides)

$\therefore$ total surface area
$= 2 \times A_1 + 2 \times A_2 + 2 \times A_3$
$= 2 \times 12 + 2 \times 8 + 2 \times 6$
$= 52$ cm^2

So, the total surface area of the box is 52 cm^2.

EXERCISE 10F.1

1 Find the surface area of a cube with sides:

   a 5 mm   **b** 4.2 cm   **c** 8.5 cm

2 Find the surface area of the following rectangular prisms:

a 10 cm, 12 cm, 8 cm

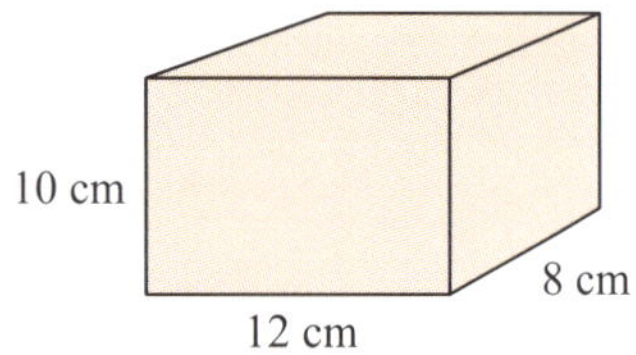

b 45 mm, 15 mm, 60 mm

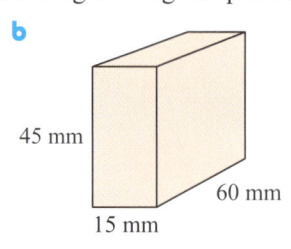

c 2 m, 20 m

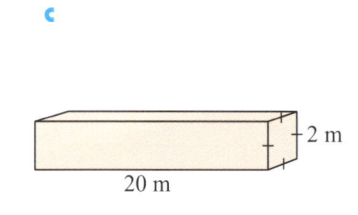

Example 16

What is the total surface area of this wedge?

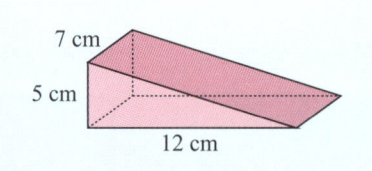

7 cm, 5 cm, 12 cm

We draw a net of the solid:

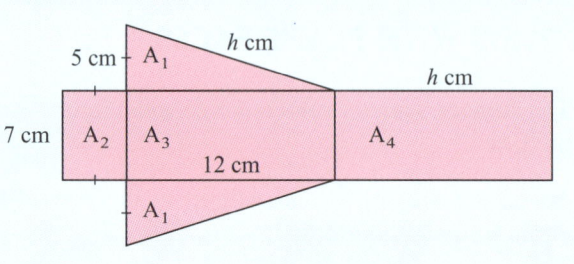

We next find h using Pythagoras:
$$h^2 = 12^2 + 5^2$$
$$h^2 = 169$$
$$\therefore \quad h = \sqrt{169} = 13 \quad \{\text{as } h > 0\}$$

Now, $A_1 = \frac{1}{2}bh$ $A_2 = 7 \times 5$ $A_3 = 12 \times 7$ $A_4 = 13 \times 7$
       $= \frac{1}{2} \times 12 \times 5$ $= 35 \text{ cm}^2$ $= 84 \text{ cm}^2$ $= 91 \text{ cm}^2$
       $= 30 \text{ cm}^2$

$\therefore$ total surface area $= 2 \times A_1 + A_2 + A_3 + A_4$
                            $= 2 \times 30 + 35 + 84 + 91$
                            $= 270 \text{ cm}^2$

Sometimes we need Pythagoras' Theorem to find a missing dimension.

---

3 Find the surface area of the following triangular prisms:

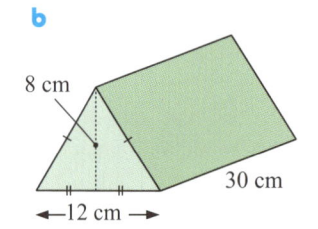

a 3 cm, 5 cm, 8 cm

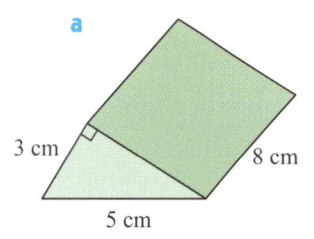

b 8 cm, 12 cm, 30 cm

c 5 m, 12 m, 15 m

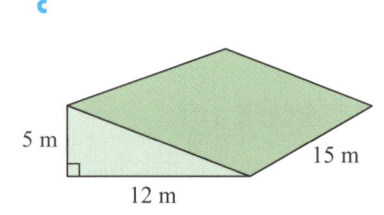

4 Find the surface areas of the following prisms:

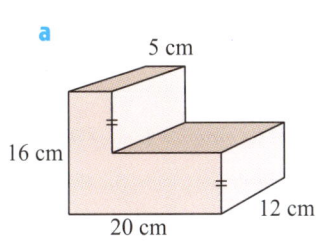

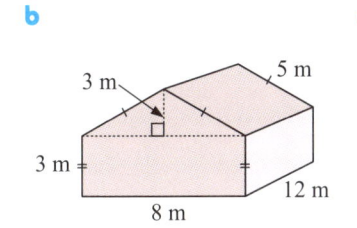

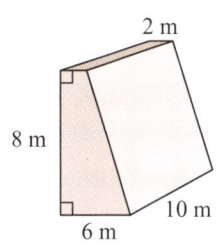

a (dimensions: 5 cm, 16 cm, 20 cm, 12 cm)

b (dimensions: 3 m, 5 m, 3 m, 8 m, 12 m)

c (dimensions: 2 m, 8 m, 10 m, 6 m)

Example 17   ◀) Self Tutor

Find the cost of erecting a 6 m by 4 m rectangular garden shed that is 2 m high if the metal sheeting costs $15 per square metre.

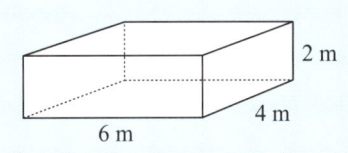

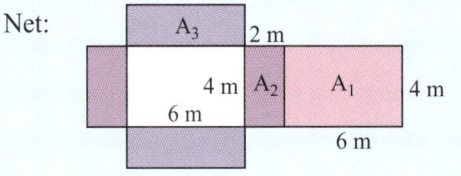

The shed: (6 m by 4 m by 2 m)

Net: (showing A_1, A_2, A_3)

$A_1 = 6 \times 4$ $A_2 = 4 \times 2$ $A_3 = 6 \times 2$
$ = 24 \text{ m}^2$ $ = 8 \text{ m}^2$ $ = 12 \text{ m}^2$

$\therefore$ total surface area $= A_1 + 2 \times A_2 + 2 \times A_3$
$\phantom{\therefore \text{ total surface area }} = 24 + 2 \times 8 + 2 \times 12$
$\phantom{\therefore \text{ total surface area }} = 64 \text{ m}^2$

$\therefore$ cost $= 64 \times \$15$
$\phantom{\therefore \text{ cost }} = \$960$

---

5 A cellar has dimensions 4 m by 3 m by 2.4 m high. Find the cost of painting the inside of the cellar (walls and ceiling) if 1 litre of paint costs €13.20 and each litre covers 5 square metres.

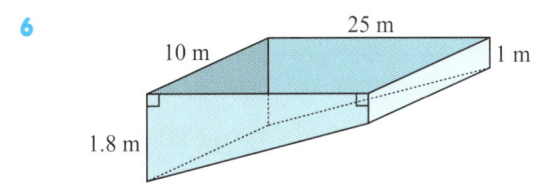

6 (swimming pool: 25 m, 10 m, 1 m, 1.8 m)

The walls and floor of the swimming pool shown are to be tiled. Determine the total area of tiles required.

7 A tent with the dimensions shown is made from canvas. Find the total cost of the canvas if it costs £12.80 per square metre. Add 3% extra area to allow for seams. (The floor of the tent is also canvas.)

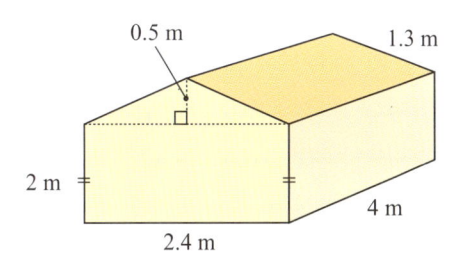

(tent dimensions: 0.5 m, 1.3 m, 2 m, 2.4 m, 4 m)

SOLIDS WITH CURVED SURFACES

We will consider the outer surface area of two types of objects with curved surfaces. These are **cylinders** and **spheres**.

CYLINDERS

Consider the cylinder shown alongside. If the cylinder is cut, opened out and flattened onto a plane, it takes the shape of a rectangle.

You can verify this by peeling the label off a cylindrical can.

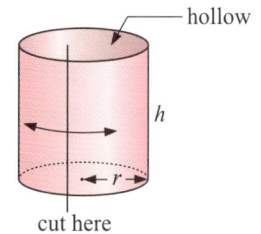

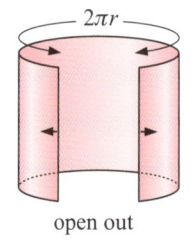

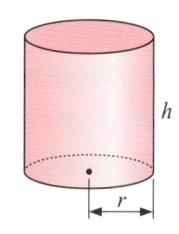

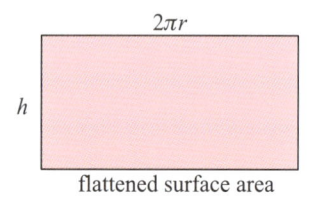

The length of the rectangle is the same as the circumference of the cylinder.

So, for a hollow cylinder, the outer surface area A = area of rectangle
$\therefore\ A = \text{length} \times \text{width}$
$\therefore\ A = 2\pi r \times h$
$\therefore\ A = 2\pi rh$

Object	Figure	Outer surface area
Hollow cylinder		$A = 2\pi rh$ (no ends)
Hollow can		$A = 2\pi rh + \pi r^2$ (one end)
Solid cylinder		$A = 2\pi rh + 2\pi r^2$ (two ends)

LENGTH AND AREA (Chapter 10) 237

Example 18 — Self Tutor

Find the surface area of the solid cylinder:

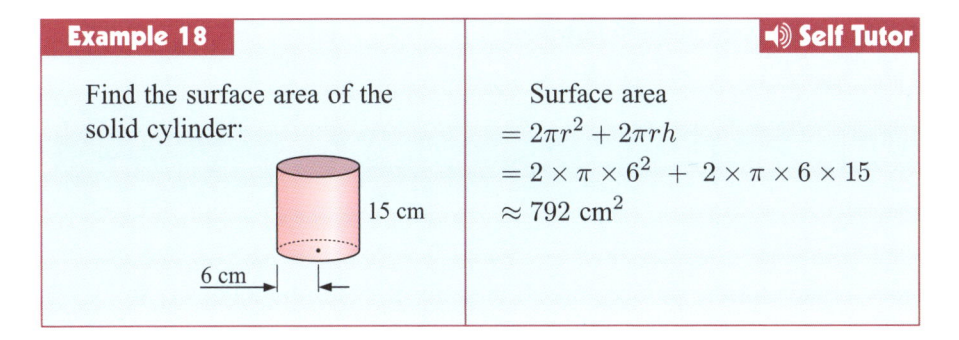

15 cm, 6 cm

Surface area
$= 2\pi r^2 + 2\pi rh$
$= 2 \times \pi \times 6^2 + 2 \times \pi \times 6 \times 15$
≈ 792 cm^2

SPHERES

The surface area of a sphere is related to the square of its radius. In particular we can use the formula:

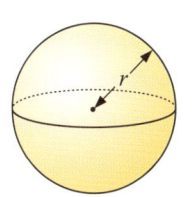

Surface area of a sphere $= 4\pi r^2$

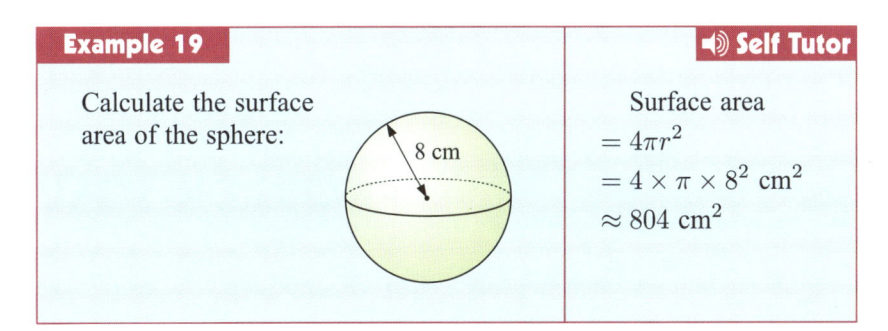

The mathematics required to prove this formula is beyond the scope of this course.

Example 19 — Self Tutor

Calculate the surface area of the sphere:

8 cm

Surface area
$= 4\pi r^2$
$= 4 \times \pi \times 8^2$ cm^2
≈ 804 cm^2

EXERCISE 10F.2

1 Find the outer surface area of the following:

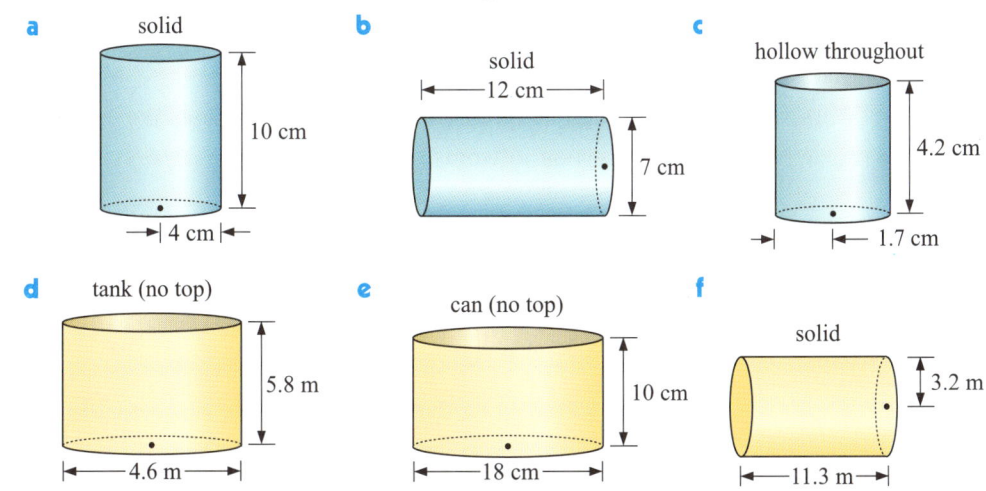

a solid — 10 cm height, 4 cm diameter

b solid — 12 cm, 7 cm

c hollow throughout — 4.2 cm, 1.7 cm

d tank (no top) — 5.8 m, 4.6 m

e can (no top) — 10 cm, 18 cm

f solid — 3.2 m, 11.3 m

2 Find the surface area of the following:

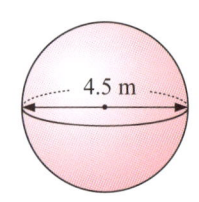

a sphere, 30 cm (radius)

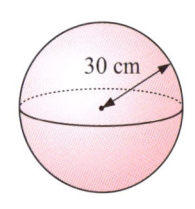

b sphere, 4.5 m (diameter)

c hemisphere, 9 cm

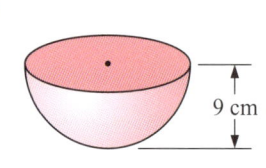

3 Find a formula for the surface area A, in terms of x, for the following solids:

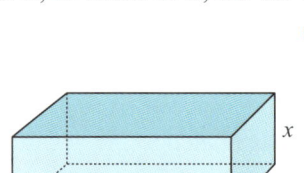

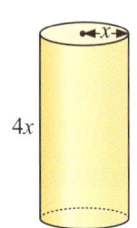

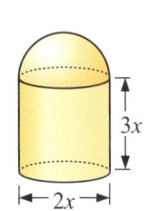

a cube with side $5x$

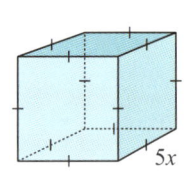

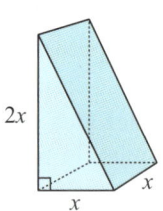

b rectangular prism, $3x \times x \times x$

c triangular prism, $2x \times x \times x$

d cylinder, radius x, height $4x$

e cylinder with hemisphere on top, diameter $2x$, cylinder height $3x$

f triangular prism, $3x \times 4x \times 6x$ with x

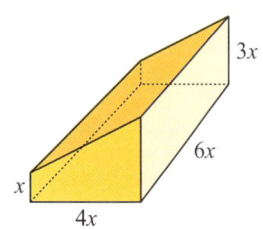

G   PROBLEM SOLVING

To solve the problems in this section you will need to select and apply the appropriate formulae from any of the previous sections.

There are simple **steps** to follow when **solving problems**:

- Read the question carefully.
- Draw a diagram with the information clearly marked on it.
- Label the unknowns.
- Choose the correct formula or formulae.
- Work step by step through the problem, making sure the units are correct.
- Answer the original question in words.

EXERCISE 10G

1 Ian needs to cut 12 circles of pastry from a 30 cm by 40 cm sheet. What percentage of the pastry remains?

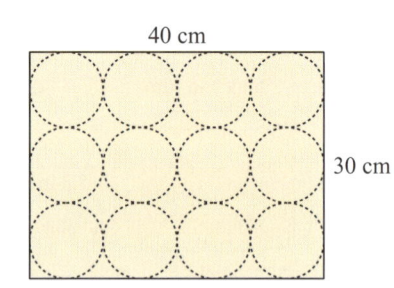

2 Using the formula for the surface area of a sphere, find:

  a the surface area of a soccer ball of diameter 20 cm

  b the cost of painting the outer hemispherical dome of the new Opera House given the diameter of the dome is 40 m and the painter's quote is €3.45 per square metre.

3 A garden shed 6 m by 3 m is surrounded by a paved path which is 1.2 m wide. Find the area of the path.

4 An indoor bike track has two 'straights' and two semi-circular ends as shown alongside. Lines are to be marked on the track to divide it into 4 lanes. Each lane will have width 1 m. Find the total length of lines to be marked.

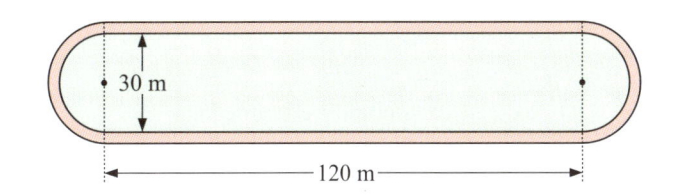

30 m

120 m

5 An 8 cm by 10 cm rectangle has the same perimeter as an isosceles triangle with base 10 cm and equal sides 13 cm. Which figure has the greater area and by how much?

Example 20   ◀)) Self Tutor

A circle has the same area as a square with sides 10 cm. Find its radius.

10 cm

10 cm

Area of circle $= \pi r^2$

Area of square $= 10 \text{ cm} \times 10 \text{ cm} = 100 \text{ cm}^2$

So, $\pi r^2 = 100$

$\therefore r^2 = \dfrac{100}{\pi}$ {$\div$ both sides by π}

$\therefore r = \sqrt{\dfrac{100}{\pi}} \approx 5.642$

So, the radius is about 5.64 cm

6 A circular arena has an area of 2000 m². Find its radius.

7 A circle has the same area as a square with sides 20 cm. Find its radius.

8 A cylindrical can has base radius 8 cm and total surface area 1000 cm². Find its height.

Example 21   ◀)) Self Tutor

Jane is painting cylindrical tin cans of height 12 cm and diameter 8 cm. She paints the top, bottom and sides of each.

If she has enough paint to cover an area of 5 square metres, how many cans is she able to paint?

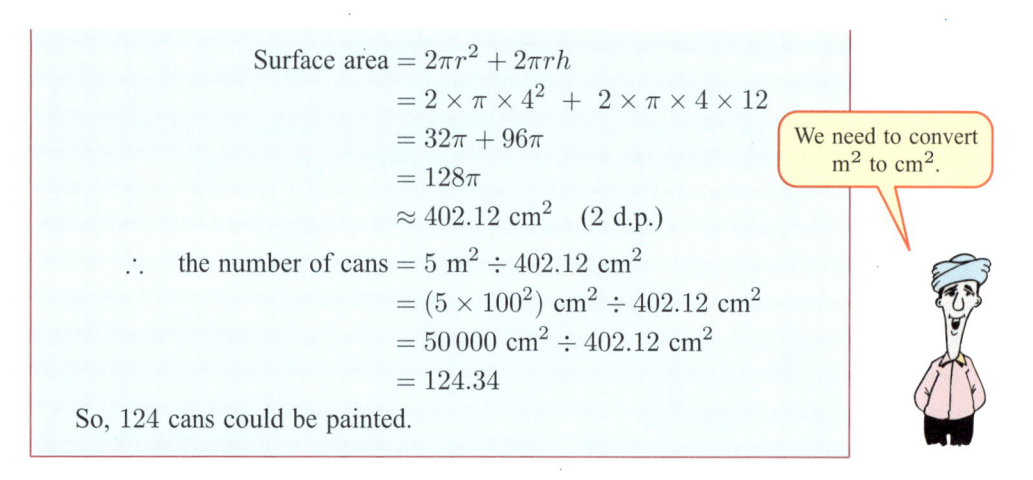

$$\begin{aligned}
\text{Surface area} &= 2\pi r^2 + 2\pi rh \\
&= 2 \times \pi \times 4^2 + 2 \times \pi \times 4 \times 12 \\
&= 32\pi + 96\pi \\
&= 128\pi \\
&\approx 402.12 \text{ cm}^2 \quad \text{(2 d.p.)}
\end{aligned}$$

$$\begin{aligned}
\therefore \text{ the number of cans} &= 5 \text{ m}^2 \div 402.12 \text{ cm}^2 \\
&= (5 \times 100^2) \text{ cm}^2 \div 402.12 \text{ cm}^2 \\
&= 50\,000 \text{ cm}^2 \div 402.12 \text{ cm}^2 \\
&= 124.34
\end{aligned}$$

So, 124 cans could be painted.

We need to convert m^2 to cm^2.

9 Determine how much paint is required to paint the outside of a cylindrical tank 12 m long with diameter 10 m if each litre of paint covers 15 square metres.

10 How many spherical balls of diameter 15 cm can be covered by 40 square metres of material?

11 Which has the greater surface area: a solid cylinder of height 16 cm and radius 8 cm, or a sphere of radius 10 cm?

12 We use a sphere to model earth, even though our planet is not a *perfect* sphere. Earth has a radius of approximately 6400 km. Find the approximate surface area of earth.

LINKS
click here

HOW MUCH OXYGEN IS PRODUCED?
Areas of interaction:
Environments, Health and social education

REVIEW SET 10A

1 Convert:

    a 95 mm to cm   **b** 4.8 km to m   **c** 3.15 ha to m^2

    d 55 000 cm^2 to m^2 **e** 3.4 m^2 to cm^2 **f** 18 500 m^2 to ha

2 Find the perimeter of:

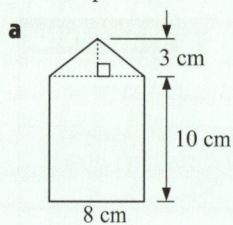

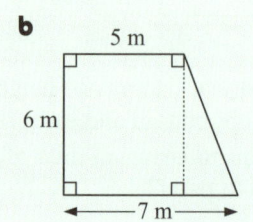

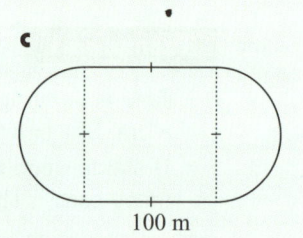

    a 3 cm, 10 cm, 8 cm

    b 5 m, 6 m, 7 m

    c 100 m

3 Find the pink shaded area of:

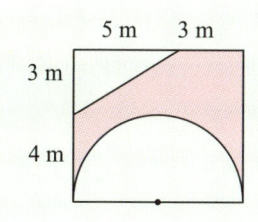

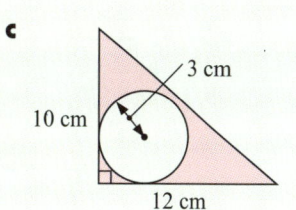

a (trapezium: parallel sides 8 cm and 12 cm, height 5 cm)

b (5 m, 3 m, 3 m, 4 m with semicircle removed)

c (right triangle 10 cm and 12 cm with inscribed circle radius 3 cm)

4 Find the surface area of:

a (rectangular prism: 5 cm by 4 cm by 2 cm)

b (cylinder: diameter 8 cm, height 15 cm)

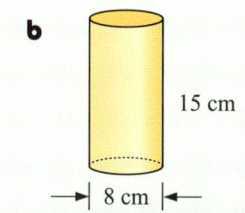

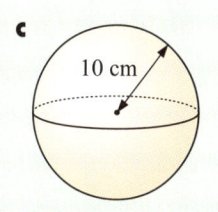

c (sphere: radius 10 cm)

5 A netball court 12 m by 24 m is surrounded by a grassed area 4 m wide. Find:

   a the area of grass

   b the cost of laying the grass as "instant lawn" at a cost of $6.40 per square metre.

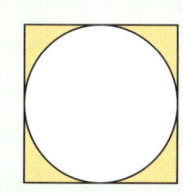

6 The outer square in the shape alongside has an area of 64 cm². Find the area of the yellow shaded region.

7 Find the perimeter P and the area A, in terms of x:

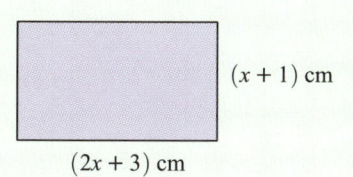

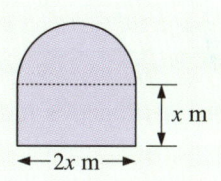

a (rectangle: $(2x+3)$ cm by $(x+1)$ cm)

b (shape: rectangle $2x$ m by x m topped with semicircle)

REVIEW SET 10B

1 Convert:

   a 6890 m to km   **b** 29.4 cm to mm   **c** 8800 m² to ha

   d 7.6 ha to m²   **e** 85 cm² to mm²   **f** 340 mm² to cm²

2 Find the perimeter of:

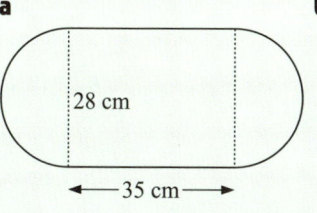

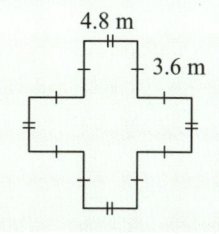

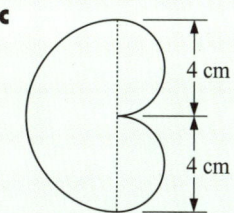

a (stadium shape: 28 cm, 35 cm)

b (cross shape: 4.8 m, 3.6 m)

c (shape with two semicircular cut-outs: 4 cm, 4 cm)

3 Find the yellow shaded area:

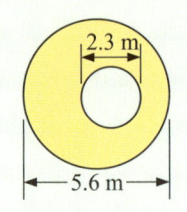

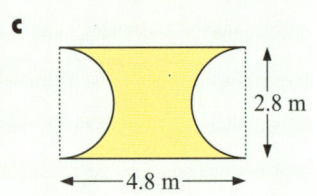

a 2.7 m, 3 m, 4 m, 5.2 m

b 2.3 m, 5.6 m

c 2.8 m, 4.8 m

4 Find the surface area of:

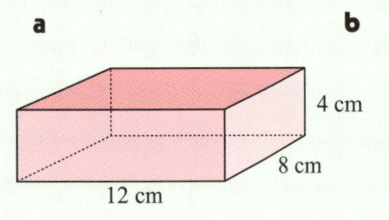

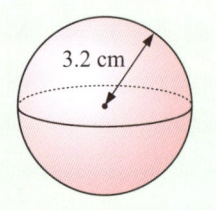

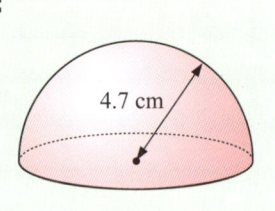

a 12 cm, 8 cm, 4 cm

b 3.2 cm

c 4.7 cm

5 Find the perimeter P and the area A of:

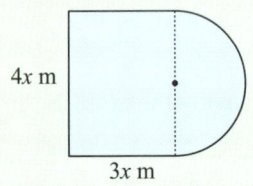

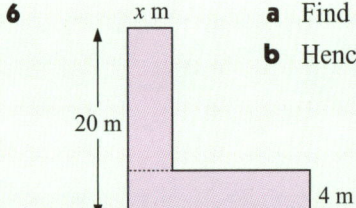

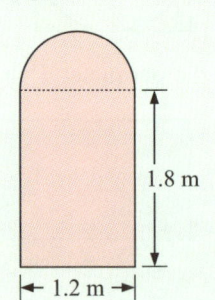

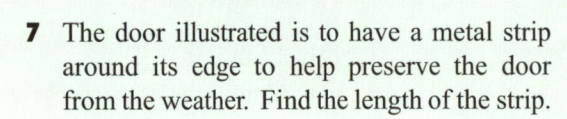

4x m, 3x m

6 x m, 20 m, 20 m, 4 m

a Find x if the area of the shape is 140 m².

b Hence, find the perimeter of the figure.

7 The door illustrated is to have a metal strip around its edge to help preserve the door from the weather. Find the length of the strip.

1.8 m, 1.2 m

8 If a sphere has a surface area of 1000 cm², find its radius correct to the nearest millimetre.

Chapter 11

Algebra

Contents:
- **A** Converting into algebraic form
- **B** Forming equations
- **C** Problem solving using equations
- **D** Finding an unknown from a formula
- **E** Linear inequations
- **F** Solving linear inequations

OPENING PROBLEM

A water tank is 2.3 m high, and is filled with water to a height of 1.1 m.

After some rain, the water level rises by x m.

Things to think about:

1. Can you write an **expression** for the new height of the water in terms of x?
2. Suppose the tank is now at full capacity. Can you write an **equation** involving x?
3. Suppose the tank is still not full. Can you write an **inequation** involving x?

Most real life problems do not start off written in mathematical language. We need to read sentences of words and convert them into mathematical form. We use the language of **algebra** to write **expressions**, **equations** or **inequations** that describe the problem.

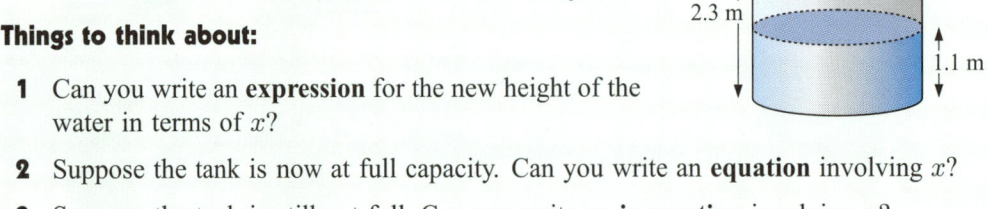

A CONVERTING INTO ALGEBRAIC FORM

Example 1   ◀)) Self Tutor

Convert into algebraic form:

a 18 more than a number
b 7 less than a number
c double a number
d double the sum of a number and 7

a 18 more than a number is   the number plus 18   i.e., $x + 18$
b 7 less than a number is   the number minus 7   i.e., $x - 7$
c double a number is   the number multiplied by 2   i.e., $2 \times x$ or $2x$
d The sum of a number and 7 is $x + 7$, so double this sum is $2 \times (x + 7)$ i.e., $2(x + 7)$

double ↗ ↑ sum of the number and 7

Note: Any letter, for example, y, could have been used here.

EXERCISE 11A

1 Translate the following into algebraic expressions:

a x is increased by 5
b 7 more than x
c 9 less than a
d x is decreased by 2
e the sum of d and 8
f x is divided by 4
g the product of 2 and b
h double x and add 11
i 5 more than 3 times s

2 Translate the following into algebraic expressions:

a 3 less than a number
b double a certain number
c 4 more than a certain number
d one half of a number
e 10 minus a number
f one third of a number
g 3 less than double a number
h 7 more than treble a number

ALGEBRA (Chapter 11)   245

3 Copy and complete:
   a Two numbers have sum 8. If one of them is x, then the other is ......
   b Two numbers are in the ratio 1 : 3. If the larger one is x then the smaller one is ......
   c Two numbers in the ratio 2 : 5 can be represented by $2x$ and ......
   d There are 30 members in a debating club. If x are boys then there are ...... girls.
   e If the smaller of two consecutive integers is x, then the larger is ......
   f Three consecutive integers in ascending order are x, ..., and ......
   g Two consecutive odd integers in ascending order are x and ......
   h Three consecutive integers in descending order are x, ..., and ......
   i If the middle integer of three consecutive integers is x, then the other two are ...... and ......
   j Two numbers differ by 7. If the smaller one is x then the other is ......

4 Express each of the following quantities as an algebraic expression in terms of the given variable:
   a The sum of two numbers is 7. One of the numbers is a. What is the other number?
   b The smaller of two consecutive integers is b. What is the larger integer?
   c c is the largest of three consecutive integers. What are the other two integers?
   d The smaller of two consecutive even integers is d. What is the larger one?
   e The middle of three consecutive odd integers is p. What are the other two integers?
   f There are n lollies in a jar. t of them are lemon flavoured. How many are *not* lemon flavoured?

Example 2   ◀)) **Self Tutor**

Translate into an algebraic expression:
   a the sum of three consecutive odd numbers, where the smallest is n
   b the total value of x 43 cent stamps and $(7 - x)$ 75 cent stamps.

---

a If n is the smallest number then the others are $n + 2$ and $n + 4$
   $\therefore$ the sum is $n + (n + 2) + (n + 4)$.
b The x stamps each costing 43 cents have total value $43x$ cents.
   The $(7 - x)$ stamps each costing 75 cents have total value $75(7 - x)$ cents.
   $\therefore$ the total value $= 43x + 75(7 - x)$ cents.

---

5 Translate into an algebraic expression:
   a the sum of two consecutive whole numbers
   b the product of two consecutive even numbers
   c the total value of x 20 pence coins and $(x - 2)$ 50 pence coins
   d the total power output of x 60 watt globes and $(x + 5)$ 80 watt globes.

B   FORMING EQUATIONS

Algebraic equations are mathematical sentences which indicate that two expressions have the same value. They always contain the "=" sign.

The following **steps** help us to convert a worded problem into an algebraic equation.

Step 1: Decide what the unknown quantity is and choose a variable such as x to represent it.

Step 2: Look for the operation(s) involved in the problem. For example,

Step 3: Form the equation with an "=" sign. These phrases all indicate equality: "the answer is", "will be", "the result is", "is equal to", or simply "is".

Statement	Translation
decreased by	subtract
more than	add
double	multiply by 2
halve	divide by 2

Example 3

Translate into an equation:
a   "When a number is added to 6 the result is 15."
b   "Twice a certain number is 7 more than the number."

a   *In words*   *Indicates*
    "a number"   We let x be the number
    "a number is added to 6" $6 + x$
    "the result is" $6 + x =$
                            So, $6 + x = 15$

b   *In words*   *Indicates*
    "a certain number"   Let x be the number
    "twice a certain number" $2x$
    "7 more than the number" $x + 7$
    "is"   So, $2x = x + 7$

In the following exercise, you do not have to set out your answers like those given in the example.

With practice you will be able to combine the steps, but you should note:

- the mathematical sentence you form must be an accurate translation of the information
- for these types of problems, you must have only one variable in your equation.

EXERCISE 11B

1   Translate into linear equations but *do not solve*:
    a   When a number is increased by 5, the answer is 7.
    b   When a number is decreased by 3, the result is -1.
    c   When a number is increased by 5 and the resulting number is doubled, the answer is 33.

d A number is doubled and 3 is added. The result is 7.
e Twice a number is 5 less than the number.
f Four times a number is equal to 35 minus the number.

Example 4 ◀) Self Tutor

Translate into an equation: "The sum of 2 consecutive even integers is 34."

Let the smaller even integer be x.

∴ the next even integer is $x + 2$.

So, $x + (x + 2) = 34$ is the equation.

2 Translate into equations, but *do not solve*:
   a The sum of two consecutive integers is 21.
   b The sum of 3 consecutive integers is 162.
   c The sum of two consecutive even integers is 78.
   d The sum of 3 consecutive odd integers is 123.

Example 5 ◀) Self Tutor

Apples cost 13 cents each and oranges cost 11 cents each.

If I buy 5 more apples than oranges and the total cost of the apples and oranges is $2.33, write a linear equation involving the total cost.

Type of fruit	Number of pieces of fruit	Cost per piece of fruit	Total cost
oranges	x	11 cents	$11x$ cents
apples	$x + 5$	13 cents	$13(x+5)$ cents
			233 cents

From the table we know the total cost, and so $11x + 13(x + 5) = 233$.

3 Form an equation for the following:
   a Bananas cost 12 cents each and dragonfruit cost 23 cents each. If I buy 3 more bananas than dragonfruit, the total cost will be $2.81.
   Hint: Let the variable n represent the number of dragonfruit.
   b Paul buys identical hammers for $8 each and identical mallets for $6 each. Altogether 11 of these tools are purchased and their total cost is $80.
   Hint: Let the number of hammers be h.
   c Jessica has a collection of old 2-cent and 5-cent stamps with a total value of $1.23. She has 2 more 2-cent stamps than 5-cent stamps.
   Hint: Let the variable f represent the number of 5-cent stamps.

Example 6

At present Ronaldo is three years younger than Paquita. In 5 years' time Ronaldo's age will be four fifths of Paquita's age. Write a linear equation to find Paquita's age.

Let Paquita's age be x years.

	Age Now	Age in 5 years' time
Paquita	x years	$(x+5)$ years
Ronaldo	$(x-3)$ years	$(x-3+5) = (x+2)$ years

From the table and the written information we know $\quad x + 2 = \frac{4}{5}$ of $(x + 5)$

so, $\quad x + 2 = \frac{4}{5}(x+5)$.

4 Form an equation for the following:

a A man is 3 times as old as his son. In 11 years' time he will be twice as old as his son will be.
Hint: Let the variable s represent the son's age in years now.

b At present a woman is twice as old as her daughter. Twenty one years ago she was 3 times older than her daughter.
Hint: Let the daughter's current age be x years.

c Wei is 10 years older than Bic. In 3 years' time Wei will be 3 times as old as Bic.
Hint: Let Bic's current age be x years.

C PROBLEM SOLVING USING EQUATIONS

PROBLEM SOLVING METHOD

- Identify the unknown quantity and allocate a variable to it.
- Decide which operations are involved.
- Translate the problem into an equation and check that your translation is correct.
- Solve the equation by isolating the variable.
- Check that your solution does satisfy the original problem.
- Write your answer in sentence form.

Example 7

The sum of 3 consecutive even integers is 132. Find the smallest integer.

Let x be the smallest even integer
$\therefore$ the next is $x + 2$ and the largest is $x + 4$.

So, $x + (x + 2) + (x + 4) = 132$ {their sum is 132}
$\therefore \quad 3x + 6 = 132$ {simplifying}
$\therefore \quad 3x + 6 - 6 = 132 - 6$ {subtract 6 from both sides}
$\therefore \quad 3x = 126$
$\therefore \quad \dfrac{3x}{3} = \dfrac{126}{3}$
$\therefore \quad x = 42$

So, the smallest integer is 42.

EXERCISE 11C

1 If two consecutive integers have a sum of 127, find the numbers.

2 When a number is doubled and then increased by 7, the answer is 19. Find the number.

3 If three consecutive integers add to 27, find the smallest of them.

Example 8   ◆) Self Tutor

If twice a number is subtracted from 11, the result is 4 more than the number. What is the number?

Let x be the number.
The LHS algebraic expression is $11 - 2x$.
The RHS algebraic expression is $x + 4$.

$\therefore \quad 11 - 2x = x + 4$ {the equation}
$\therefore \quad 11 - 2x + 2x = x + 4 + 2x$ {add $2x$ to both sides}
$\therefore \quad 11 = 3x + 4$
$\therefore \quad 11 - 4 = 3x + 4 - 4$ {subtract 4 from both sides}
$\therefore \quad 7 = 3x$
$\therefore \quad \dfrac{7}{3} = \dfrac{3x}{3}$ {divide both sides by 3}
$\therefore \quad x = 2\tfrac{1}{3}$

So, the number is $2\tfrac{1}{3}$.

4 When a number is subtracted from 11, the result is 6 more than the number. Find the number.

5 When a number is decreased by 3 and the result is doubled, the answer is equal to the original number. Find the number.

6 When one half of a number is added to one third of a number, the answer is 30. Find the number.

Example 9

Canned peaches come in two sizes. Small cans cost $2 each and large cans cost $3 each. If 15 cans of peaches are bought for a total of $38, how many small cans were purchased?

Size	Cost per can	Number bought	Value
small	$2	x	$\$2x$
large	$3	$15-x$	$\$3(15-x)$
		15	$38

So, $2x + 3(15-x) = 38$
$\therefore\ 2x + 45 - 3x = 38$ {expanding brackets}
$\therefore\ 45 - x = 38$ {simplifying}
$\therefore\ 45 - x - 45 = 38 - 45$ {subtract 45 from both sides}
$\therefore\ -x = -7$
$\therefore\ x = 7$

So, 7 small cans were bought.

7 I have 25 coins in my pocket all of which are 5 penny or 20 penny coins. If their total value is £2.90, how many 5 penny coins do I have?

8 Onions cost 25 cents each whereas peppers cost 35 cents each. If I buy 5 more onions than peppers and the total bill is €5.45, how many onions did I buy?

9 Our club shirts are available in two sizes: small shirts cost $27 each and large shirts cost $31 each. Last week a total of 14 shirts were sold with total cost $398. How many of each shirt size were bought?

Example 10

Matt is 5 years older than Kerry. In 7 years' time Kerry's age will be three quarters of Matt's age. How old is Kerry now?

Person	Age now (years)	Age in 7 years
Matt	$x+5$	$x+5+7$
Kerry	x	$x+7$

So $x + 7 = \frac{3}{4}(x+12)$
$\therefore\ 4(x+7) = 4 \times \frac{3}{4}(x+12)$ {multiply both sides by 4}
$\therefore\ 4(x+7) = 3(x+12)$
$\therefore\ 4x + 28 = 3x + 36$ {simplifying}
$\therefore\ 4x + 28 - 3x = 3x + 36 - 3x$ {subtract $3x$ from both sides}
$\therefore\ x + 28 = 36$
$\therefore\ x = 8$ {subtract 28 from both sides}

$\therefore$ Kerry is 8 years old now.

10 The sum of two numbers is 12. When one number is subtracted from three times the other, the result is 5. Find the numbers.

11 Two numbers differ by 3. Twice the smaller number is added to the larger number and the result is 14. Find the numbers.

12 3 consecutive even integers are such that the sum of the smaller two equals six more than the largest one. Find the integers.

13 A man is currently 4 times as old as his son. In 4 years from now he will be three times as old as his son will be then. How old is his son now?

14 At present Phil is 8 years older than Bob. If Phil was one year younger, his age would be double Bob's present age. How old is Bob?

15 In 5 years' time Pam will be twice as old as Sam was two years ago. Pam is 8 years older than Sam. How old is Sam?

D FINDING AN UNKNOWN FROM A FORMULA

A **formula** is an equation which connects two or more variables.

If we wish to find the value of one of the variables in a formula and we know the value(s) of the remaining variables, we **substitute** into the formula and **solve** the resulting equation.

Example 11

$A = \frac{1}{2}bh$ is the formula for finding the area, A, of a triangle given its base b and height h. Find the height of a triangle of base 12 cm and area 60 cm^2.

$b = 12$ and $A = 60$ $\therefore$ $60 = \frac{1}{2} \times 12 \times h$

$\therefore$ $60 = 6h$

$\therefore$ $\frac{60}{6} = h$ {dividing both sides by 6}

$\therefore$ $h = 10$

So, the height is 10 cm.

EXERCISE 11D

1 The area of a parallelogram with base b and height h is given by the formula $A = bh$. Find:

   a the base when the area is 48 cm^2 and the height is 6 cm

   b the height when the area is 7.5 m^2 and the base is 3 m.

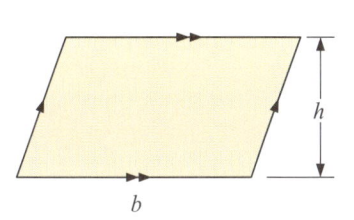

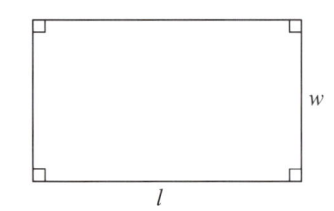

2 A rectangle with length l and width w has perimeter $P = 2l + 2w$. Find:

a the length of a rectangle with perimeter 26 m and width 3 m

b the width of a rectangle with length 5 cm and perimeter 31 cm.

3 If a block of wood of length l cm is cut into n planks of equal thickness, the thickness of each plank is given by $t = \dfrac{l}{n}$ cm.

a Find the length of wood required to make 20 planks of thickness 4 cm.

b Find the number of planks of thickness 5 cm which can be cut from a block of wood of length 60 cm.

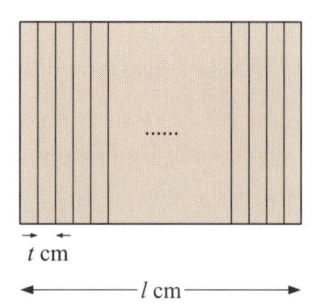

4 A ball is thrown directly upwards at a speed of u metres per second. Its velocity v metres per second after t seconds is calculated using the formula $v = u - gt$ where g is the gravitational constant of 9.8 metres per second per second. Find:

a the speed u at which the ball was thrown upwards if it has a velocity of 10.4 metres per second after 2 seconds

b the time taken for a ball thrown upwards at 25 metres per second to reach a velocity of 0.5 metres per second.

5 The surface area of a closed rectangular box is given by the formula $A = 2(lw + dl + dw)$ where l is its length, w is its width and d is its depth. Find:

a the length of a box with width 5 cm, depth 3 cm, and surface area 62 cm^2

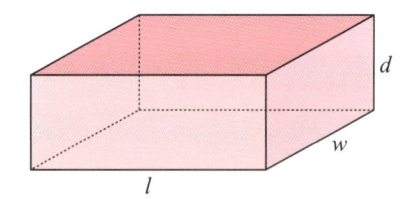

b the depth of a box with surface area 188 cm^2, length 6 cm, and width 4 cm.

Example 12 ◀) Self Tutor

When a stone is dropped from a stationary position, the distance travelled downwards is given by $s = \tfrac{1}{2}gt^2$ m, where g is the gravitational constant of 9.8 m per second per second and t is the time in seconds. Find:

a the depth of a well given that a stone takes 1.3 seconds to hit the bottom

b the time taken for a stone to reach the bottom of a 1000 m high vertical cliff.

a $\quad s = \tfrac{1}{2}gt^2 \quad$ where $\quad g = 9.8 \quad$ and $\quad t = 1.3$

$\therefore \quad s = \tfrac{1}{2} \times (9.8) \times (1.3)^2 \qquad$ {substituting}

$\therefore \quad s = 8.281 \qquad\qquad\qquad\qquad$ {calculator}

So, the well is 8.281 m deep.

b $s = \frac{1}{2}gt^2$ where $g = 9.8$ and $s = 1000$

∴ $1000 = \frac{1}{2} \times 9.8 \times t^2$ {substituting}

∴ $1000 = 4.9 \times t^2$

∴ $\frac{1000}{4.9} = t^2$ {dividing both sides by 4.9}

∴ $t = \pm\sqrt{\frac{1000}{4.9}}$ {if $x^2 = k$ then $x = \pm\sqrt{k}$}

∴ $t \approx 14.2857$ {as $t > 0$}

The stone would take ≈ 14.3 seconds to reach the bottom.

6 The volume of a cylinder is given by the formula $V = \pi r^2 h$ where r is the base radius and h is the height. Find:

a the height of a cylinder of radius 5 cm and volume 500 cm^3

b the radius of the base of a cylinder of volume 300 cm^3 and height 10 cm.

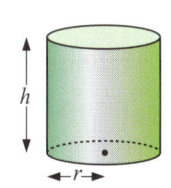

E   LINEAR INEQUATIONS

For safety reasons, many rides at theme parks have height restrictions. For example: "You must be at least 120 cm tall to go on this ride."

We could write this as   height $\geqslant 120$ or $H \geqslant 120$.

This means that if a person has height $H = 120$, 120.5, 125, or 140 then he or she can go on the ride.

All of these values **satisfy** the **inequality** $H \geqslant 120$.

All solutions to $H \geqslant 120$ can be represented on a **number line**:

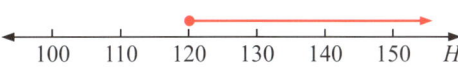

An **algebraic inequation** is a mathematical sentence which compares the values of two expressions using one of the signs $>$, $<$, $\geqslant$, $\leqslant$.

For example, $5x - 2 > 7$ is a *linear inequation* which indicates that the value of the expression $5x - 2$ is greater than 7.

INEQUATION SIGNS

Symbol	Meaning	Examples
$>$	is greater than	$5 > 3$, $x > 7$, $2\frac{1}{2} > x$
$<$	is less than	$3 < 5$, $7 < x$, $x < 2\frac{1}{2}$
$\geqslant$	is greater than or equal to	$5 \geqslant 4$, $b \geqslant 20$, $\frac{4}{5} \geqslant y$
$\leqslant$	is less than or equal to	$4 \leqslant 5$, $20 \leqslant b$, $y \leqslant \frac{4}{5}$

Notice in the examples above that if we interchange the LHS and RHS, the **inequation sign** is **reversed**. However, it is customary to write the variable on the **LHS** of the inequation.

Example 13 ◆) Self Tutor

Rewrite the following inequation with the variable on the LHS:

a $8 < x$ **b** $1.5 \geqslant y$

a $8 < x$ is written as $x > 8$ **b** $1.5 \geqslant y$ is written as $y \leqslant 1.5$

Note the reversal of the inequation sign!

EXERCISE 11E

1 Write a mathematical sentence for:

a the speed limit S is 40 km per hour   **b** the minimum age A is 18
c a is greater than 3   **d** b is less than or equal to -3
e d is less than 5   **f** -20 is greater than or equal to x
g 4 is less than y **h** z is greater than or equal to 0.

2 Rewrite the following inequations with the variable on the LHS:

a $2 < x$ **b** $5 > b$ **c** $2\frac{1}{2} \leqslant c$ **d** $-7 \geqslant d$ **e** $-19 > a$ **f** $-3 < p$

NUMBER LINES

A linear inequation is true for many values of the variable, whereas a linear equation usually only has one solution.

For example,
$x = 2$ indicates that the only possible value which satisfies the equation is 2
$x > 2$ indicates that any number greater than 2 will satisfy the inequation, and so there are infinitely many solutions.

There are usually infinitely many solutions to an inequation since we can have decimal numbers and fractions too. For example, for the inequation $x > 2$ the value of the unknown could be $2.1, 3, 5\frac{1}{2}, 109$ or any other value that fits the condition $x > 2$.

One way of showing $x > 2$ is to use a **number line**.

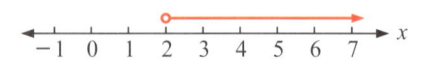

The arrow indicates that all values of x beyond 2 **satisfy** the inequation and the open circle shows that 2 is excluded.

To use a number line to indicate solutions to inequations we use the following convention:

- The value of the unknown is represented by a ray → or ← written above the number line.
- If the sign is $>$ or $<$, the ray has an open circle ○→ or ←○ .
  This indicates that the value at the ○ is **not included** in the solution.
- If the sign is $\geqslant$ or $\leqslant$, the ray has a closed circle ●→ or ←● .
  This indicates that the value at the ● is **included** in the solution.

ALGEBRA (Chapter 11) 255

Example 14

Draw number lines to show the following inequations:

a $a > 1$ **b** $a < -1$ **c** $a \geqslant 1$ **d** $a \leqslant -1$

a $a > 1$

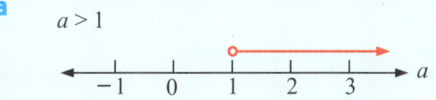

b $a < -1$

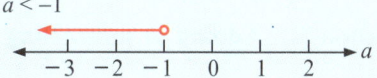

c $a \geqslant 1$

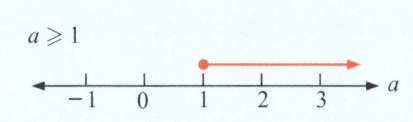

d $a \leqslant -1$

3 Draw separate number lines to show the following inequations:

a $x > 2$ **b** $a > -3$ **c** $b \leqslant 2$ **d** $m \geqslant -1$
e $3 < x$ **f** $2 > a$ **g** $-2 \geqslant b$ **h** $-2 \leqslant m$

4 Given that $a > 2$, decide if the following statements are true or false. Draw a number line to help you if necessary.

a 3.9 is a possible value for a
b -5.3 is a possible value for a
c 2 is a possible value for a
d 10 is *not* a possible value for a
e -100.8 is *not* a possible value for a
f 0 is a possible value for a.

F   SOLVING LINEAR INEQUATIONS

When we have a mathematical equation or inequation, we have a symbol between two expressions. We often refer to these expressions as the **left hand side (LHS)** and the **right hand side (RHS)**.

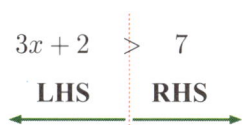

$$3x + 2 \quad > \quad 7$$
$$\text{LHS} \qquad \text{RHS}$$

An inequation is like an **unbalanced** set of scales.

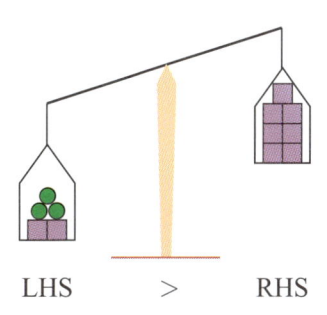

To solve linear inequations we treat the situation in a similar way to ordinary linear equations. We need to maintain the **imbalance** while carrying out the *same operation* on *both sides of the inequation sign*.

However, there is one consideration we must check first. Does performing an operation on both sides of an inequation sign always maintain the inequation? The following investigation should help answer this question.

LHS $>$ RHS

INVESTIGATION — OPERATIONS WITH INEQUATIONS

As you fill in the tables and answer the questions, remember that $a > b$ if a is to the right of b on the number line.

WORKSHEET

What to do:

Section 1: Adding or subtracting a positive or negative number

1 Copy and complete the following table where T means *true* and F means *false*:

True Inequation	Operation	Working	Simplify	T or F
$5 > 1$	add 3 to both sides	$5 + 3 > 1 + 3$	$8 > 4$	T
$11 > 7$	add 6 to both sides			
$8 > -3$	add 4 to both sides			
$-7 < -4$	add 5 to both sides			
$-6 < 5$	add 11 to both sides			
$8 > 6$	subtract 2 from both sides			
$9 > 7$	subtract 4 from both sides			
$2 > -1$	subtract 2 from both sides			
$-7 < -5$	subtract 5 from both sides			

2 Does *adding* a number to both sides of an inequation keep the inequation true, or does it make it false?

3 Does *subtracting* a number from both sides of an inequation keep the inequation true, or does it make it false?

4 Copy and complete: "Adding to, or subtracting from, both sides of an inequation ....."

Section 2: Multiplying or dividing by a positive or negative number

1 Copy and complete the following table:

True Inequation	Operation	Working	Simplify	T or F
$5 > 2$	multiply by 3	$5 \times 3 > 2 \times 3$	$15 > 6$	T
$-3 < -2$	multiply by 4			
$4 > 3$	multiply by (-3)			
$-2 > -5$	multiply by (-4)			
$7 > 3$	multiply by 2			
$-4 < -2$	multiply by 3			
$2 > -6$	multiply by (-2)			
$-5 < -3$	multiply by (-4)			
$6 > 3$	divide by 3			
$-6 > -8$	divide by 2			
$6 > 3$	divide by (-3)	$\frac{6}{-3} > \frac{3}{-3}$	$-2 > -1$	F
$-6 > -8$	divide by (-2)			
$7 < 14$	divide by 7			
$-10 < -5$	divide by 5			
$7 < 14$	divide by (-7)			

2 Does multiplying or dividing both sides of an inequation by a positive number keep the inequation true, or does it make it false?

3 Does multiplying or dividing both sides of an inequation by a negative number keep the inequation true, or does it make it false?

4 Write a sentence which describes your discovery about the effect on an inequation when:

    a multiplying or dividing by a positive number

    b multiplying or dividing by a negative number.

From the investigation you should have discovered the following facts about operations on inequations:

- Adding or subtracting a positive or negative number keeps the inequation **true**.
- Multiplying or dividing by a positive number keeps the inequation **true**.
- Multiplying or dividing by a negative number makes the inequation **false**.

This means that we may solve linear inequations in the same way as if they are ordinary linear equations, carrying out the same operations on both sides of the inequation sign, **except**, when we **multiply** (or **divide**) by a **negative number** we need to reverse the inequation sign.

SUMMARY OF RULES

- If we **swap** the LHS and RHS, we **reverse** the inequation sign.
- If we **add to** or **subtract from** both sides of an inequation, the sign is maintained.
- If we **multiply** or **divide** both sides by:
  - a **positive** number we **keep** the same inequation sign
  - a **negative** number we **reverse** the inequation sign.

The reverse of $>$ is $<$, and the reverse of $\geqslant$ is $\leqslant$. Remember to reverse the sign when dividing by a negative number!

So, for example, to solve $\;-3x > 18$

we need to divide both sides by -3.

$$\therefore \quad \frac{-3x}{-3} < \frac{18}{-3} \quad \{\text{reverse inequation sign}\}$$

$$\therefore \quad x < -6$$

Example 15   ◀)) Self Tutor

Solve the following inequations and plot the solutions on separate number lines:

  a $a - 4 > 5$ **b** $3b \leqslant 9$ **c** $4 - 2x > 0$

a $a - 4 > 5$

    $\therefore \quad a - 4 + 4 > 5 + 4$

    $\therefore \quad a > 9$

Check: If $a = 10$

then $10 - 4 = 6$

and $6 > 5$ is true. ✓

b $3b \leqslant 9$

$\therefore \dfrac{3b}{3} \leqslant \dfrac{9}{3}$

$\therefore b \leqslant 3$

Check: If $b = 2$
then $3 \times 2 = 6$
and $6 \leqslant 9$ is true. ✓

c $4 - 2x > 0$

$\therefore 4 - 4 - 2x > 0 - 4$

$\therefore -2x > -4$

$\therefore \dfrac{-2x}{-2} < \dfrac{-4}{-2}$ {reversing the sign}

$\therefore x < 2$

Check: If $x = 0$
then $4 - 2 \times 0 = 4$
and $4 > 0$ is true. ✓

EXERCISE 11F

1 Solve the following inequations and show their solutions on separate number lines:

a $a + 4 > 6$
b $3b \leqslant -9$
c $\dfrac{c}{3} < 2$
d $s - 4 < 2$
e $-4b > 16$
f $5 + t > 0$
g $-\dfrac{m}{5} \geqslant 12$
h $3x + 12 \geqslant -3$
i $5 - 3b \leqslant 7$
j $3a - 2 \geqslant 8$
k $4a + 9 < 1$
l $7 - 2b < -3$
m $16 + 7s > 2$
n $2a - 4 \leqslant 0$
o $12 - 5b > -3$
p $3b - 1 \geqslant 0$
q $5n + 7 < -3$
r $11 - 4b \leqslant 4$

Example 16   ◀)) Self Tutor

Solve the inequation $\dfrac{x}{4} - 2 \geqslant 3$ and show its solution on a number line.

$\dfrac{x}{4} - 2 \geqslant 3$

$\therefore \dfrac{x}{4} - 2 + 2 \geqslant 3 + 2$ {add 2 to both sides}

$\therefore \dfrac{x}{4} \geqslant 5$

$\therefore \dfrac{x}{4} \times 4 \geqslant 5 \times 4$ {multiply both sides by 4}

$\therefore x \geqslant 20$

Check: If $x = 32$ then
$\dfrac{32}{4} - 2 = 8 - 2 = 6$ and $6 \geqslant 3$ is true. ✓

2 Solve the following inequations and show their solutions on separate number lines:

a $\dfrac{x}{3} + 1 > 4$
b $\dfrac{b}{5} - 2 \leqslant -3$
c $\dfrac{c}{4} + 4 \geqslant 8$
d $\dfrac{2x}{3} - 2 < 4$
e $\dfrac{3x}{2} + 5 \geqslant -2$
f $1 - \dfrac{3x}{2} < 4$
g $2 - \dfrac{x}{4} \geqslant -3$
h $3 - \dfrac{2x}{5} < 2$
i $5 - \dfrac{3x}{4} > -2$

3 Solve the following inequations and show their solutions on separate number lines:

　a $\dfrac{a-3}{2} < 6$　　**b** $\dfrac{b+5}{4} \geqslant 1$　　**c** $\dfrac{4c+3}{5} \leqslant -1$

　d $\dfrac{4-a}{2} > 5$　　**e** $\dfrac{5-3x}{2} \leqslant -6$　　**f** $\dfrac{3-2x}{3} \geqslant -1$

4 Solve the following inequations by first expanding the brackets:

　a $3(c+1) > 8$　　**b** $5(1+3a) \leqslant -4$　　**c** $3(1-2a) \geqslant -5$

　d $2(2a+1) - 3 \leqslant -5$　　**e** $2(3-4a) + 3 < 7$　　**f** $4(2a+5) - 12 > 9$

5 Solve the following inequations by first interchanging the LHS and RHS:

　a $5 > 4 + x$　　**b** $2 \leqslant 6c + 14$　　**c** $-4 > 2b$

　d $7 \leqslant \dfrac{a}{3}$　　**e** $3 < \dfrac{d-2}{4}$　　**f** $6 \geqslant 3(p+2) - 11$

6 Solve for x and show the solution on a number line:

　a $5x - 3 > 3x + 1$　　**b** $2x + 1 \geqslant 4x + 7$　　**c** $8x + 6 < 3x + 1$

　d $2x + 7 > 7x + 3$　　**e** $6x + 2 \leqslant 3x - 7$　　**f** $x - 11 \leqslant 6x - 1$

REVIEW SET 11A

1 Translate into algebraic expressions:

　a the sum of a number and 5　　**b** 10 less than a number

　c 1 more than double a number

2 **a** The difference between two numbers is 7. If the smaller number is x, write an expression for the other number.

　b Write an expression for the number which is 3 less than the square of x.

　c If x is an even number, write an expression for the next larger even number.

3 Write an expression for the total value of x 50 cent coins and $(x+2)$ 10 cent coins.

4 Translate into linear equations but *do not solve*:

　a When a number is decreased by 5 and the result is doubled, the answer is 64.

　b The sum of three consecutive integers is 12.

5 When 4 times a certain number is increased by 3, the result is 21 more than the number. Find the number by solving an equation.

6 If I have 30 coins consisting of 5 penny and 20 penny coins. If the total value is £4.05, how many 5 penny coins do I have?

7 The velocity (v metres per second) of a ball falling from a stationary position is given by $v^2 = 2gs$ where s is the distance fallen in metres and $g = 9.8$ metres per second per second. Find:

　a the velocity of the ball after falling 40 m

　b the distance fallen when the velocity reaches 50 metres per second.

8 Write the following in symbolic form:

   a x is greater than 7   **b** -11 is less than or equal to x

9 Draw separate number lines to illustrate: **a** $x \geqslant 5$ **b** $3 > x$

10 Solve the following inequations:

   a $3 - 2x \geqslant -4$ **b** $\dfrac{2x+3}{2} < -3$ **c** $3(x+2) - 1 \leqslant 1 - 4x$

REVIEW SET 11B

1 Translate into algebraic expressions:

   a x is decreased by 5   **b** 6 more than a number

   c half of the sum of a number and 1.

2 **a** The sum of two numbers is 12 and one of them is x. Write an expression for the other number.

   b Write an expression for the number which is "3 less than five times x".

   c If there are x girls in a class of 25 students, write an expression for the number of boys in the class.

3 Write an expression for the total value of x €10 notes and twice that number of €20 notes.

4 Translate into linear equations, but *do not solve*:

   a Three times a number is equal to 48 minus the number.

   b The sum of two consecutive odd integers is 16.

5 Seven more than a certain number is nine less than twice the number. Find the number.

6 Sean has 19 coins in his pocket. The coins are all either worth 5 cents, 10 cents or 20 cents. He has twice as many 5 cent coins as 10 cent coins, and the total value of all coins is $2.20. How many 10 cent coins does Sean have in his pocket?

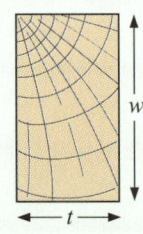

7 The strength S of a wooden beam is given by $S = 200w^2 t$ units where w cm is its width and t cm is its thickness. Find:

   a the strength of a beam of width 20 cm and thickness 4 cm

   b the width of a 3 cm thick beam of strength 60 000 units.

8 Draw separate number lines to illustrate:

   a $a \geqslant -2$ **b** $b < -1$ **c** $c > 0$

9 Solve the following inequations:

   a $3 - 2x \geqslant 0$ **b** $\dfrac{x}{5} - 3 < -1$ **c** $6(2x+1) \geqslant 6 - 13x$

10 Sue is three times as old as Michelle. 10 years ago she was seven times as old as Michelle was. How old is Sue now?

Chapter 12

Volume and capacity

Contents:
- **A** Units of volume
- **B** Volume formulae
- **C** Capacity
- **D** Problem solving

VOLUME AND CAPACITY (Chapter 12)

OPENING PROBLEM

Consider the cylindrical glasses A and B.

Pedro says that both glasses hold the same amount, since glass A is twice as wide as glass B but only half as high.

Glass A: 6 cm high, 8 cm wide.
Glass B: 12 cm high, 4 cm wide.

Things to think about:

1. Do you agree with Pedro's reasoning?
2. If not, which glass do you think holds more?

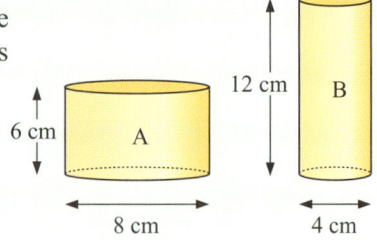

A UNITS OF VOLUME

The **volume** of a solid is the amount of space it occupies.

We measure volume in **cubic units**.

For example, we could use:
- cubic millimetres (mm^3)
- cubic centimetres (cm^3)
- cubic metres (m^3)

We can see from the diagrams following that one cubic centimetre occupies the *same* space as one thousand cubic millimetres.

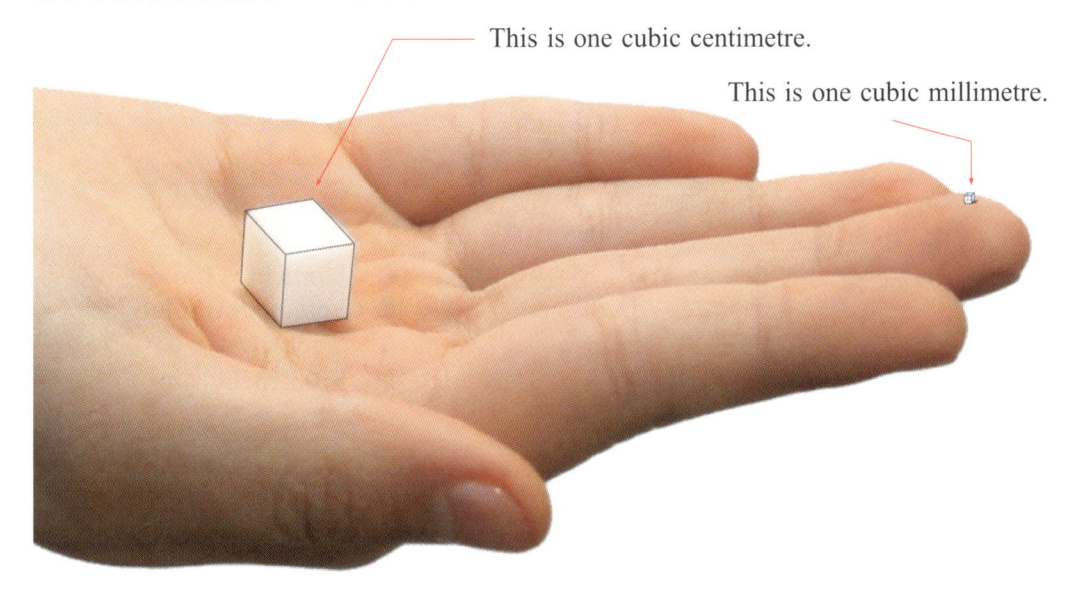

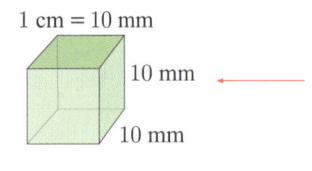

This is one cubic centimetre.

This is one cubic millimetre.

1 cm = 10 mm, 10 mm, 10 mm

This is one thousand cubic millimetres.
10 mm × 10 mm × 10 mm = 1000 mm^3

Likewise, 1 m^3 = 100 cm × 100 cm × 100 cm
= 1 000 000 cm^3

VOLUME CONVERSIONS

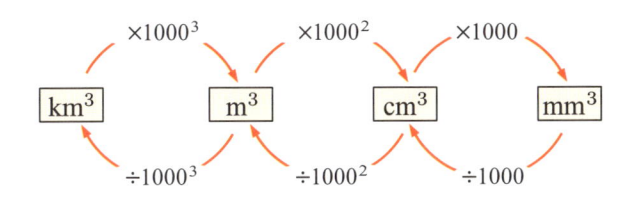

$$km^3 \xrightarrow{\times 1000^3} m^3 \xrightarrow{\times 1000^2} cm^3 \xrightarrow{\times 1000} mm^3$$

$$km^3 \xleftarrow{\div 1000^3} m^3 \xleftarrow{\div 1000^2} cm^3 \xleftarrow{\div 1000} mm^3$$

Remember, it is easier to convert the units of length before *the volume is calculated.*

Example 1 — Self Tutor

Convert:
a 23 cm³ to mm³
b 24 000 cm³ to m³

a 23 cm³
　　= (23 × 10³) mm³
　　= 23 000 mm³

b 24 000 cm³
　　= (24 000 ÷ 100³) m³
　　= (24 000 ÷ 1 000 000) m³
　　= 0.024 m³

EXERCISE 12A

1 What units of volume would be most suitable to measure the space occupied by:
　a a bucket of sand　**b** a grand piano　**c** a pencil
　d a mountain　**e** a paper clip　**f** a ship
　g a spoon　**h** a motor car　**i** a dressmaker's pin?

2 Convert:
　a 2400 mm³ to cm³　**b** 6.8 m³ to cm³　**c** 8.3 mm³ to cm³
　d 7 480 000 cm³ to m³　**e** 348 cm³ to mm³　**f** 2 × 10⁹ m³ to km³
　g 7.2 km³ to m³　**h** 38 100 mm³ to cm³　**i** 3500 cm³ to mm³

B VOLUME FORMULAE

RECTANGULAR PRISM (BOX)

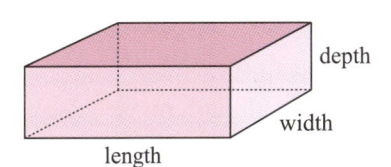

Volume = length × width × depth

SOLIDS OF UNIFORM CROSS-SECTION

Notice in the triangular prism alongside, that vertical slices parallel to the front triangular face will all be the same size and shape as that face. We say that solids like this are solids of *uniform cross-section*. The cross-section in this case is a triangle.

Another example is the hexagonal prism shown opposite.

For any solid of uniform cross-section:

Volume = area of cross-section × length

In particular, for a **cylinder**, the cross-section is a circle, and so:

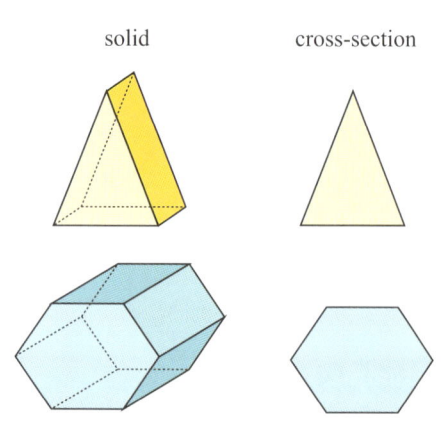

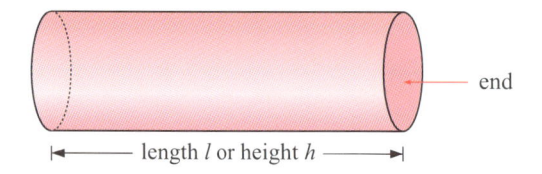

Volume = area of circle × length
$= \pi r^2 \times l$

$$V = \pi r^2 l \quad \text{or} \quad V = \pi r^2 h$$

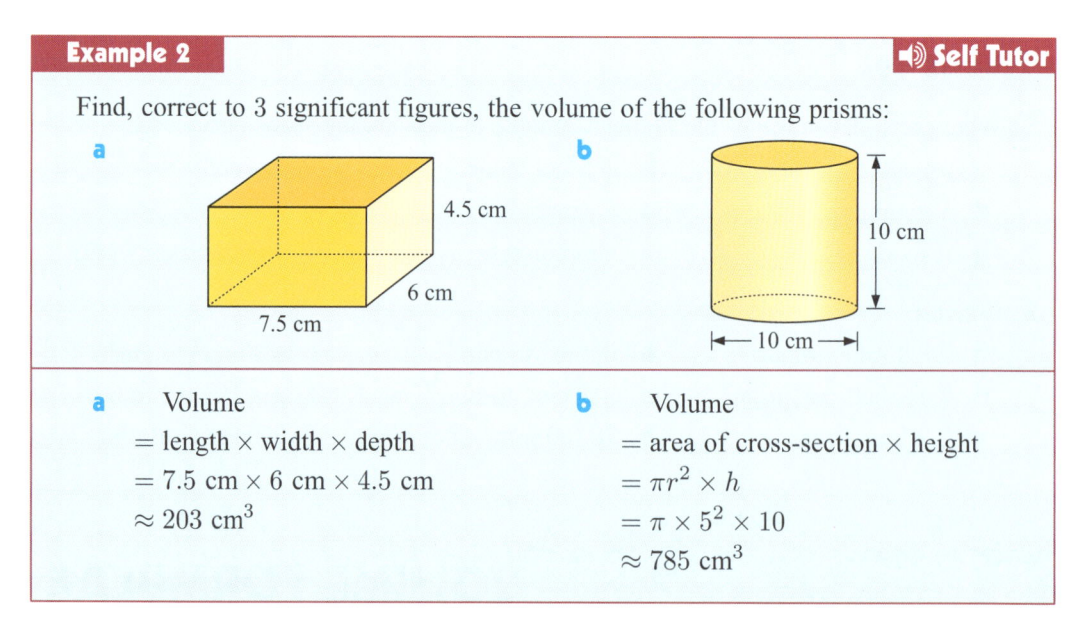

Example 2

Find, correct to 3 significant figures, the volume of the following prisms:

a (rectangular prism: 7.5 cm × 6 cm × 4.5 cm)

b (cylinder: diameter 10 cm, height 10 cm)

a Volume
= length × width × depth
= 7.5 cm × 6 cm × 4.5 cm
≈ 203 cm³

b Volume
= area of cross-section × height
= $\pi r^2 \times h$
= $\pi \times 5^2 \times 10$
≈ 785 cm³

TAPERED SOLIDS (PYRAMIDS AND CONES)

INVESTIGATION 1 — VOLUMES OF TAPERED SOLIDS

To find a formula for the volume of tapered solids, we will compare the volumes of tapered solids with those of solids with uniform cross-sections that have the same base and the same height.

We will compare:

- a cone and a cylinder

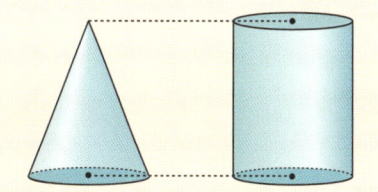

- a square-based pyramid and a square-based prism.

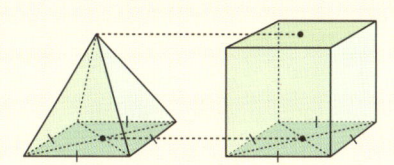

What to do:

1. Click on the icon to obtain a printable sheet containing nets for the solids described above.

2. Print the nets onto card, cut them out, and construct each of the solids. Use sticky tape to hold the models together.

3. Fill the model of the cone with sand completely, then pour the contents into the cylinder.

4. Repeat **3** until the cylinder is full. How many times do you need to fill up the cone in order to fill the cylinder?

5. Write an expression for the volume of the cone in terms of the volume of the cylinder.

6. Repeat steps **3-5** for the square-based pyramid and square-based prism.

7. Given that the volume of a solid with uniform cross-section is
$V = $ area of base $\times$ height, find a formula for the volume of a tapered solid.

Tapered solids have a flat base and come to a point called the **apex**. They **do not** have identical cross-sections. The cross-sections always have the same shape, but not the same size.

For example:

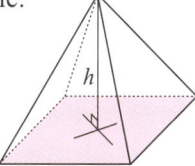

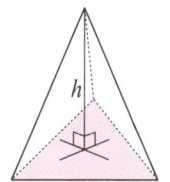

square-based pyramid   triangular-based pyramid   cone

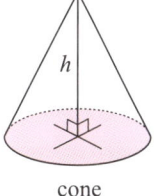

The perpendicular cross-section of a cone is always a circle, but its radius varies depending on how high up the cone we are.

For any tapered solid:

Volume = $\frac{1}{3}$ (area of base $\times$ height)

Example 3

Find the volumes of these solids:

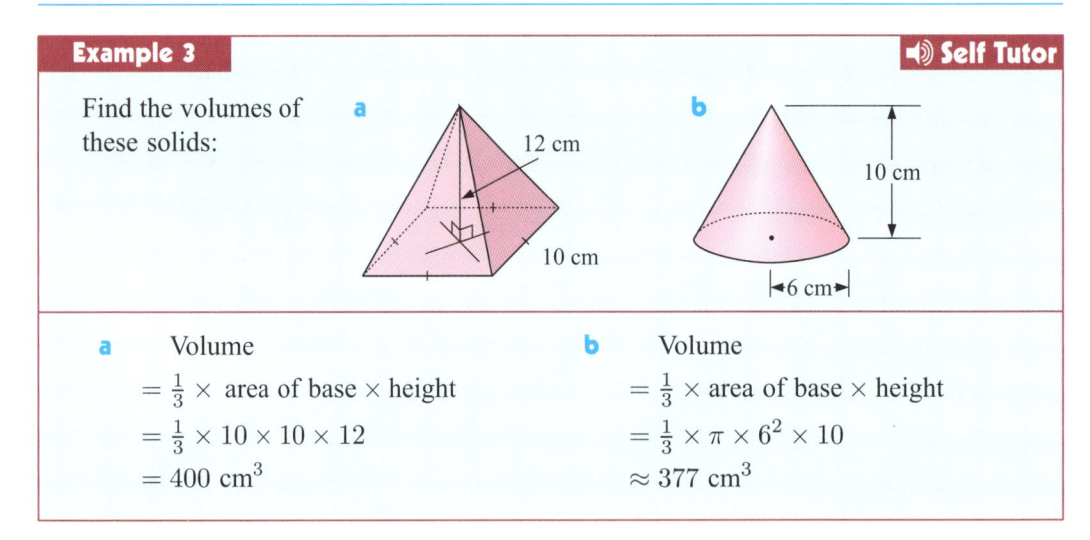

a (square pyramid, slant 12 cm, base 10 cm)

b (cone, height 10 cm, radius 6 cm)

a Volume
$= \frac{1}{3} \times$ area of base $\times$ height
$= \frac{1}{3} \times 10 \times 10 \times 12$
$= 400$ cm^3

b Volume
$= \frac{1}{3} \times$ area of base $\times$ height
$= \frac{1}{3} \times \pi \times 6^2 \times 10$
≈ 377 cm^3

SPHERES

The Greek philosopher **Archimedes** was born in Syracuse in 287 BC. Amongst many other important discoveries, he found that the volume of a sphere is equal to two thirds of the volume of the smallest cylinder which encloses it.

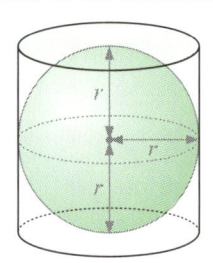

Volume of cylinder $= \pi r^2 \times h$
$= \pi r^2 \times 2r$
$= 2\pi r^3$

$\therefore$ volume of sphere $= \frac{2}{3} \times$ volume of cylinder
$= \frac{2}{3} \times 2\pi r^3$
$= \frac{4}{3} \pi r^3$

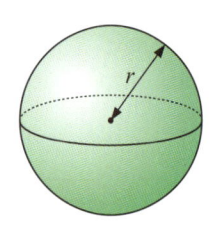

Archimedes' tomb was marked by a sphere inscribed in a cylinder!

Thus, $V = \frac{4}{3}\pi r^3$

Change the units to centimetres before calculating the volume.

Example 4

Find the volume of the sphere in cubic centimetres, to the nearest whole number:

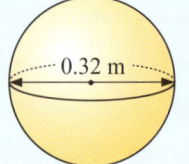

(sphere, diameter 0.32 m)

First, convert 0.32 m to cm.

0.32 m $= 32$ cm

$\therefore$ the radius $= 16$ cm

$V = \frac{4}{3}\pi r^3$

$\therefore V = \frac{4}{3}\pi \times 16^3$

$\therefore V \approx 17\,157$ cm^3

VOLUME AND CAPACITY (Chapter 12)

EXERCISE 12B

1 Find the volume of the following:

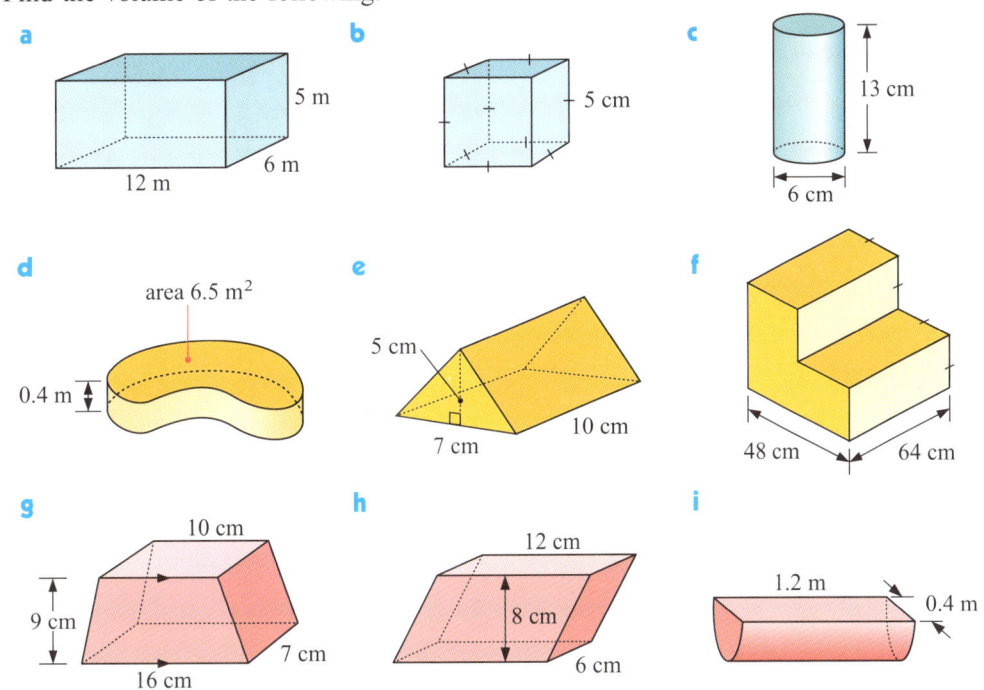

a 12 m × 6 m × 5 m rectangular prism

b cube with side 5 cm

c cylinder, diameter 6 cm, height 13 cm

d prism with cross-sectional area 6.5 m², height 0.4 m

e triangular prism, 5 cm, 7 cm, 10 cm

f L-shaped solid, 48 cm × 64 cm

g trapezoidal prism, 10 cm, 16 cm, 7 cm, 9 cm

h oblique prism, 12 cm, 6 cm, 8 cm

i 1.2 m × 0.4 m prism

2 Find the volume of the following:

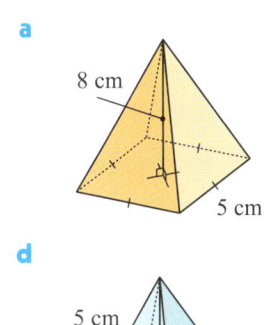

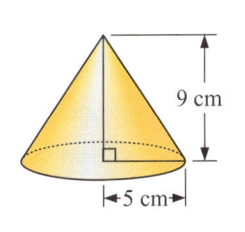

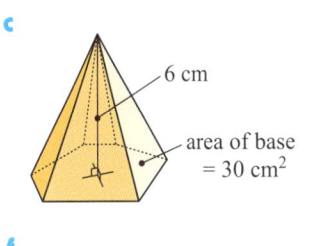

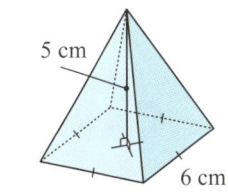

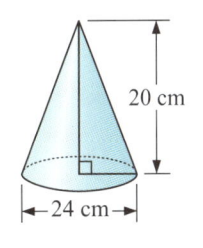

a square-based pyramid, slant 8 cm, base 5 cm

b cone, height 9 cm, radius 5 cm

c pyramid, height 6 cm, area of base = 30 cm²

d square-based pyramid, 5 cm, 6 cm

e cone, height 20 cm, diameter 24 cm

f pyramid, slant 14 cm, base 8 cm × 4 cm

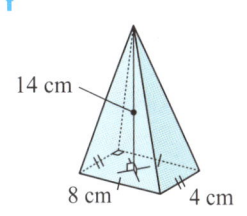

3 Find the volume of the following:

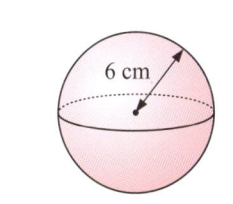

a sphere, radius 6 cm

b sphere, diameter 10.2 m

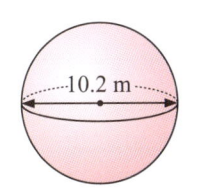

c hemisphere, radius 3 m

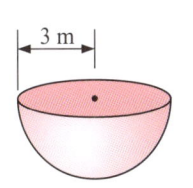

4 Find in terms of x, the volumes of these solids:

a. sphere, radius x m

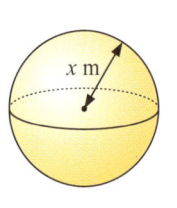

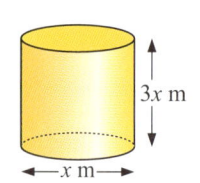

b. cylinder, diameter x m, height $3x$ m

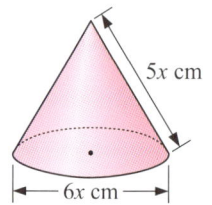

c. pyramid, height $4x$ cm, area of base $= 8x^2$ cm²

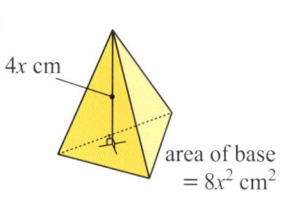

d. cone, height $7x$ cm, base diameter $6x$ cm

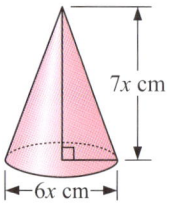

e. cone, slant height $5x$ cm, base diameter $6x$ cm

f. step solid with dimensions $2x$ cm and $3x$ cm

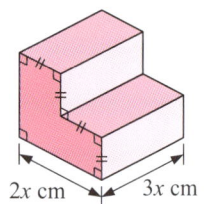

5 A triangular-based pyramid is shown alongside. Find its volume.

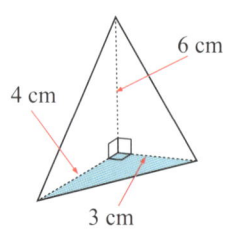

(dimensions: 6 cm, 4 cm, 3 cm)

6 Find the volume of the following figure:

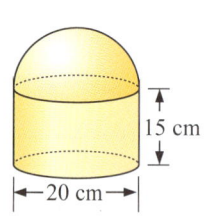

(cylinder of height 15 cm and diameter 20 cm with hemisphere on top)

7 A large rivet is illustrated. Find its volume.

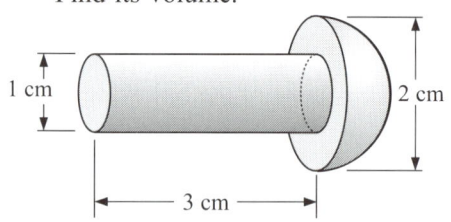

(cylinder of diameter 1 cm and length 3 cm with head of diameter 2 cm)

8 A cylindrical roller has diameter 1 m and width 1 m. The cylinder is solid metal which weighs 8 grams per cm³. Find the weight of the roller in kg.

C CAPACITY

The **capacity** of a container is the amount of material (solid or fluid) that it can contain.

The units for capacity are:

- millilitres (mL)
- litres (L)
- kilolitres (kL)
- megalitres (ML).

$$1 \text{ L} = 1000 \text{ mL}$$
$$1 \text{ kL} = 1000 \text{ L} = 1\,000\,000 \text{ mL}$$
$$1 \text{ ML} = 1000 \text{ kL} = 1\,000\,000 \text{ L}$$

Some items you are familiar with are:

Item	Estimate of Capacity
Medicine glass	25 mL
Cup	250 mL
Milk carton	1 L
Petrol tank	65 L
Hot water system	170 L
50 m swimming pool	1500 kL
Dam	10 ML
Reservoir	1000 ML

CAPACITY CONVERSIONS

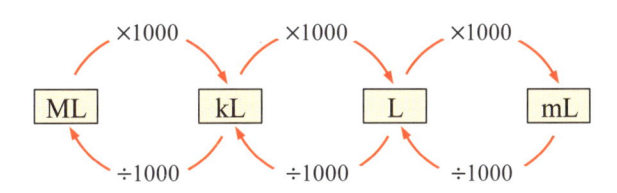

ML →×1000→ kL →×1000→ L →×1000→ mL
ML ←÷1000← kL ←÷1000← L ←÷1000← mL

Example 5

Convert:
a 4500 mL to L
b 6.4 kL to L

a   4500 mL
  = (4500 ÷ 1000) L
  = 4.5 L

b   6.4 kL
  = (6.4 × 1000) L
  = 6400 L

EXERCISE 12C.1

1 Which units of capacity would be most suitable to measure the capacity of:
 a a drink can   b a bath tub   c a syringe   d a rainwater tank
 e a lake   f a bucket   g a spa   h a rubbish dumpster?

2 Convert:
 a 3480 mL to L   b 4.85 ML to kL   c 72.5 L to kL
 d 8600 kL to ML   e 7.8 kL to L   f 15.3 L to mL
 g 545 mL to L   h 48 L to kL   i 372 100 kL to ML
 j 65 000 mL to L   k 0.82 kL to L   l 0.2 kL to mL

VOLUME AND CAPACITY

There is a close relationship between the units of **capacity** and **volume**.

1 mL of fluid will fill a cube 1 cm × 1 cm × 1 cm,

> so   1 mL is equivalent to 1 cm^3
> or   1 mL ≡ 1 cm^3.

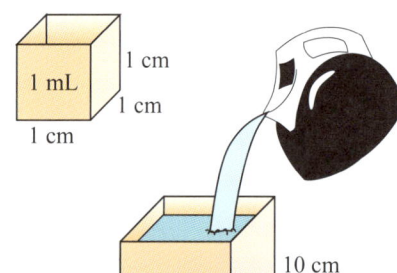

1 L of fluid will fill a cube 10 cm × 10 cm × 10 cm,

> so   1 L is equivalent to 1000 cm^3
> or   1 L ≡ 1000 cm^3.

1 kL of fluid will fill a cube 1 m × 1 m × 1 m,

> so   1 kL is equivalent to 1 m^3
> or   1 kL ≡ 1 m^3.

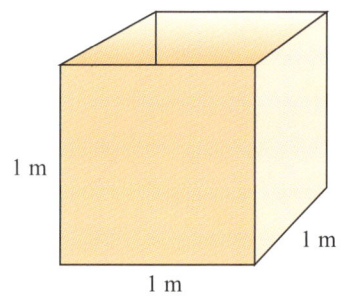

You could pour 1000 L into this cube!

Example 6   ◆) Self Tutor

Convert:
  a 4500 cm^3 to L   **b** 13.4 L to cm^3

  a 4500 cm^3 = (4500 ÷ 1000) L   **b** 13.4 L = (13.4 × 1000) cm^3
                     = 4.5 L   = 13 400 cm^3

Example 7   ◆) Self Tutor

Find the capacity in kilolitres of a cylindrical rainwater tank of height 3 m and diameter 4 m.

The volume occupied by the tank when full
     = area of base × height
     = $\pi \times 2^2 \times 3$
     = 12π m^3
∴ capacity = 12π kL   {as 1 kL ≡ 1 m^3}
            ≈ 37.7 kL

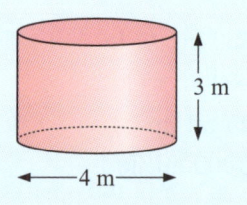

EXERCISE 12C.2

1 Convert:
- **a** 250 mL to cm^3
- **b** 9 L to cm^3
- **c** 3.9 mL to m^3
- **d** 750 cm^3 to mL
- **e** 4100 cm^3 to L
- **f** 18.5 m^3 to kL

2 A hemispherical bowl has internal diameter 30 cm. How many litres of water could it contain?

3 A conical tank has diameter 4 m and height 5 m. How many kL of water could it contain?

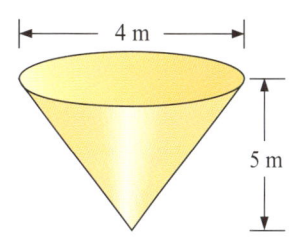

4 Mrs Foster has made $3\frac{1}{2}$ L of marmalade. She ladles it into cylindrical jars 12 cm high with 7 cm internal diameter. How many jars can she completely fill?

5 A conical pile of spice has radius 20 cm and height 50 cm. Find:
- **a** the volume of spice in the pile
- **b** the total capacity required to store the spice
- **c** the number of rectangular boxes 3 cm by 5 cm by 2 cm which could be completely filled from the pile.

6 Find the number of kilolitres of water required to fill a swimming pool with the dimensions shown:

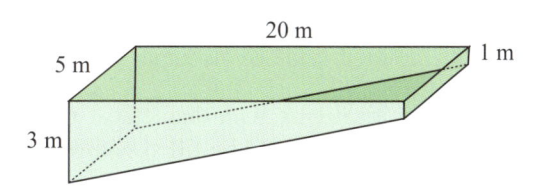

D   PROBLEM SOLVING

In this section you will need to select and apply the appropriate formula from any of the previous sections to solve problems.

> There are simple **steps** to follow when **solving problems**:
> - Read the question carefully.
> - Draw a diagram with the information clearly marked on it.
> - Label the unknowns.
> - Choose the correct formula or formulae.
> - Work step by step through the problem, making sure the units are correct.
> - Answer the original question in words.

Example 8

Sand from a quarry pours out from a giant hose and forms a conical heap on the ground. The heap has a base diameter of 25 m and a height of 8.9 m.

a Find the volume of sand in the heap to the nearest m^3.

b Find the total mass (to the nearest 10 tonne) of the sand given that 1 m^3 of it weighs 2.35 tonnes.

The diameter is 25 m, so $r = 12.5$.
The height is 8.9 m, so $h = 8.9$.

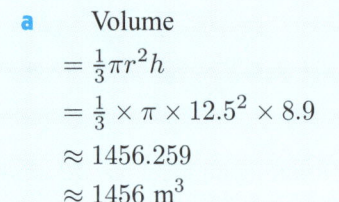

a Volume
$= \frac{1}{3}\pi r^2 h$
$= \frac{1}{3} \times \pi \times 12.5^2 \times 8.9$
≈ 1456.259
≈ 1456 m^3

b Total mass
= number of m^3 × weight per m^3
$\approx 1456.259 \times 2.35$
≈ 3422.209
≈ 3420 tonne

*In **b** we use the unrounded volume from **a**.*

EXERCISE 12D

1 Sugar runs out from a hole in the bottom of a shipping container and forms a conical heap on the floor. The heap is 2.6 m in diameter and 0.83 m high. Find:

a the volume of the heap of sugar

b the total mass of sugar given that 1 m^3 weighs 961 kg

c the total value of the sugar given that 1 kg is worth £0.80 retail price.

2 A cylindrical tank with diameter 3 m contains wine to a depth of 2.3 m. How many 750 mL bottles could be filled with wine from the tank?

3 A rectangular swimming pool 15 m by 6 m will be surrounded by a concrete path 2 m wide. Find:

a the area of the path

b the cost of concreting to a depth of 10 cm if the concrete costs $165 per cubic metre.

4 How many spherical fishing sinkers with diameter 1 cm could be made by melting a rectangular block of lead 20 cm by 5 cm by 6 cm and casting the molten product?

5 3 litres of water is poured into a rectangular box container which has a 20 cm by 20 cm square base. To what height does the water rise?

6 For the three illustrated solids find and compare the ratios of surface area : volume.

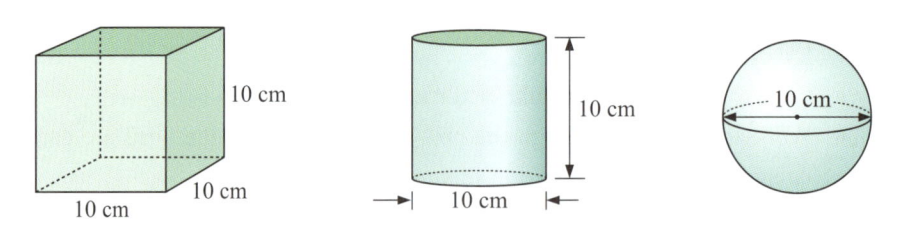

Example 9

Concrete pipes have an internal diameter of 90 cm and an external diameter of 1 m. The concrete weighs 1.25 tonnes per cubic metre. If each pipe is 3 m long and has a uniform cross-section, find its weight to the nearest kg.

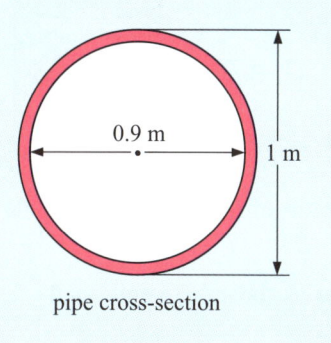

pipe cross-section

Area of end = area of large circle − area of small circle
$= \pi \times (0.5)^2 - \pi \times (0.45)^2$
$\approx 0.14923 \text{ m}^2$

Volume = area of end × length
∴ $V \approx 0.14923 \times 3 \text{ m}^3$
∴ $V \approx 0.44768 \text{ m}^3$
∴ weight $\approx 0.44768 \times 1250$ kg
≈ 559.596 kg
≈ 560 kg {nearest kg}

∴ the weight is approximately 560 kg.

Keep the accuracy of answers on your calculator as you work through the problem.

7 Concrete pipes have the dimensions shown:
  a Find the area of one end of the pipe.
  b Hence, find the volume of one pipe.
  c If concrete costs $135 per cubic metre, find the cost of the concrete needed to make one pipe.
  d If the concrete weighs 2.43 grams per cm^3, find the weight of one pipe in kilograms.

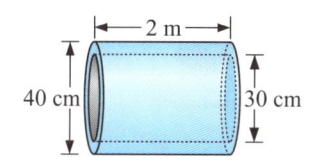

8 Fred Cooper has been asked to convene the toffee apple stall at the local school fair. To estimate the amount of toffee required for 1500 apples, he assumes that each apple is a sphere of diameter 6 cm and will be entirely coated with toffee to a thickness of 2 mm. What is the total volume of toffee required?

Example 10

A sphere has a volume of 200 cm^3. Find its radius.

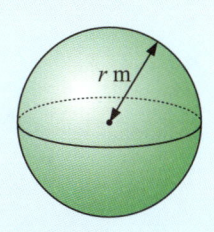

Volume of sphere $= \frac{4}{3}\pi r^3$
∴ $\frac{4}{3}\pi r^3 = 200$
∴ $\frac{3}{4} \times \frac{4}{3}\pi r^3 = \frac{3}{4} \times 200$ {× both sides by $\frac{3}{4}$}
∴ $\pi r^3 = 150$
∴ $r^3 = \frac{150}{\pi} \approx 47.746.....$
∴ $r = \sqrt[3]{47.746.....} \approx 3.628$

∴ the radius is approximately 3.63 cm.

9 A spherical ball has a volume of 500 cm^3. Find its radius.

10 A cylindrical paint can has base radius 10 cm and volume 1500 cm^3. Find its height.

11 Sand is deposited on a flat surface in a conical heap. How high is the heap if:

a its diameter equals its height and its volume is 1 m^3

b its diameter is twice its height and its volume is 5 m^3?

12 A sphere fits exactly into a cylinder. What fraction of the cylinder is air? **Hint:** Let the radius of the sphere be 1 unit.

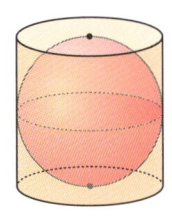

13 A sphere and a cube have the same volume. Find the ratio of the length of the side of the cube to the radius of the sphere.

14 A sphere has radius r. A cone has the same base radius as the sphere and height h. If they have the same volume, find the ratio of $h : r$.

PROJECT — SURFACE AREA AND VOLUME COMPARISON

Click on the icon to access this project.

ICEBERGS

Areas of interaction:
Environments, Approaches to learning

REVIEW SET 12A

1 Convert:

a 95 mm to cm
b 4.8 km to m
c 18 500 m^2 to ha
d 55 000 cm^2 to m^2
e 2.5 m^3 to cm^3
f 2500 cm^3 to L

2 Find the volume of:

a cylinder, 20 cm high, 5 cm radius

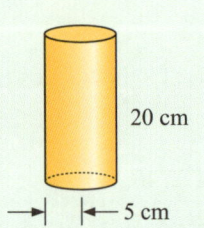

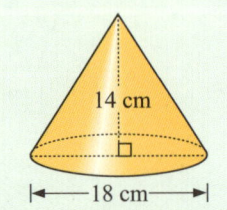

b cone, 14 cm high, 18 cm base

c sphere, 60 cm radius

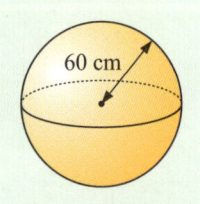

3 How many metal doorstops 15 cm by 10 cm by 5 cm can be cast from a spherical ball of metal of diameter 400 mm?

4 How long would it take to fill a petrol tank 24 cm by 40 cm by 60 cm if it can be filled at a rate of 16 litres per minute?

5 A cylindrical water tank of height 4 m is used to fill containers with dimensions 20 cm × 30 cm × 50 cm. If the tank can fill exactly 200 of these containers, find its base radius.

6 A basketball fits exactly into a cube which has sides equal in length to the diameter of the basketball. What percentage of the cube's volume does the basketball occupy?
Hint: Let the ball have radius r cm.

7 A semi-circular tunnel with dimensions shown is made of concrete.
  a What is the cross-sectional area of the tunnel? 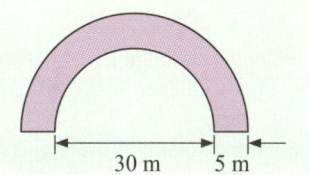
  b If the tunnel is 200 m long, find the cost of the concrete at $120 per cubic metre.

30 m   5 m

8 A cone has the same base radius as the radius of a sphere. If the volumes of the cone and the sphere are equal, by what factor is the height of the cone larger than its base radius?

REVIEW SET 12B

1 Convert:
  a 6890 m to km
  b 29.4 cm to mm
  c 7400 mL to L
  d 7.6 ha to m^2
  e 85 cm^2 to mm^2
  f 3.2 cm^3 to mm^3

2 Find the volume of:

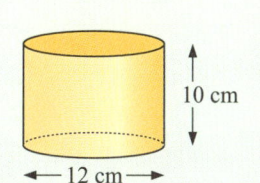

  a 3.2 cm × 2.8 cm × 1.6 cm
  b cylinder, diameter 12 cm, height 10 cm
  c cone, height 8 m, base radius 3 m

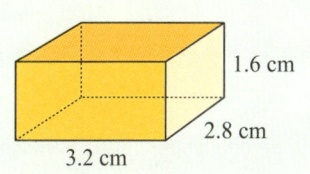

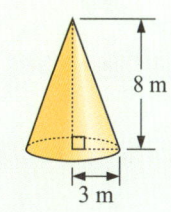

3 A rectangular garden plot 8 m by 3 m is surrounded by a concrete path which is 1.2 m wide. Find:
  a the area of the path
  b the volume of concrete required if it is to be 8 cm deep
  c the cost of the path if the concrete costs £75 per cubic metre.

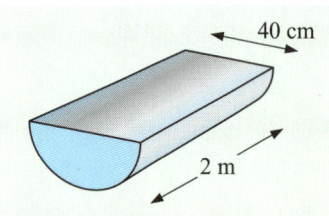

4 A horse's drinking trough has the dimensions shown. How long will it take to fill the trough if water flows into it at 12 litres per minute?

40 cm
2 m

5 A petrol can is a rectangular prism with base measurements 15 cm by 30 cm. If the can has capacity 18 litres, find its height.

6 A concrete driveway is to be 28 m long, 3 m wide, and have an average depth of 12 cm.
How much will it cost to lay the driveway if the contractor charges €160 per cubic metre of concrete?

7 A 50 m long swimming pool is completely filled with water. Find:
   a the area of the trapezium side
   b the capacity of the pool in kL.

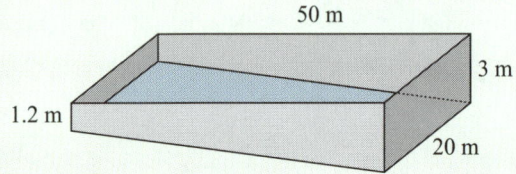

50 m
3 m
1.2 m
20 m

8 If a sphere has a surface area of 1000 cm², find to 1 decimal place:
   a its radius   **b** its volume.

Chapter 13

Coordinate geometry

Contents:
- **A** Plotting points
- **B** Linear relationships
- **C** Plotting linear graphs
- **D** The equation of a line
- **E** Gradient or slope
- **F** Graphing lines from equations
- **G** Other line forms
- **H** Finding equations from graphs
- **I** Points on lines

HISTORICAL NOTE

Sir Isaac Newton is recognised by many as one of the great mathematicians of all time. His achievements are remarkable considering mathematics, physics and astronomy were enjoyable pastimes after his main interests of chemistry, theology and alchemy.

Despite his obvious abilities, there is a story from Newton's childhood which indicates that even the greatest thinkers can find silly solutions for simple problems. He was asked to go out and cut a hole in the bottom of the barn door for the cats to go in and out. He decided to cut two holes: one for the cat and a smaller one for the kittens.

After completing school, Newton was initially made to work on a farm, but when his uncle discovered his enthusiasm for mathematics it was decided that he should attend Cambridge University.

Newton's contribution to the field of coordinate geometry included the introduction of negative values for coordinates. In his *Method of Fluxions*, Newton suggested eight new types of coordinate systems, one of which we know today as **polar coordinates**.

However, **René Descartes** is credited with developing the x-y coordinate system for locating points that we know as the **number plane** or **Cartesian plane**.

THE CARTESIAN PLANE

One way to specify the exact position of a point on the **two-dimensional number plane** is to use an **ordered pair** of numbers in the form (x, y).

We start with a point of reference O called the **origin**. Through it we draw two fixed lines, which are perpendicular to each other. They are a horizontal line called the x-**axis** and a vertical line called the y-**axis**.

The x-**axis** is an ordinary number line with positive numbers to the right of O and negative numbers to the left of O. Similarly, on the y-**axis** we have positives above O and negative numbers below O.

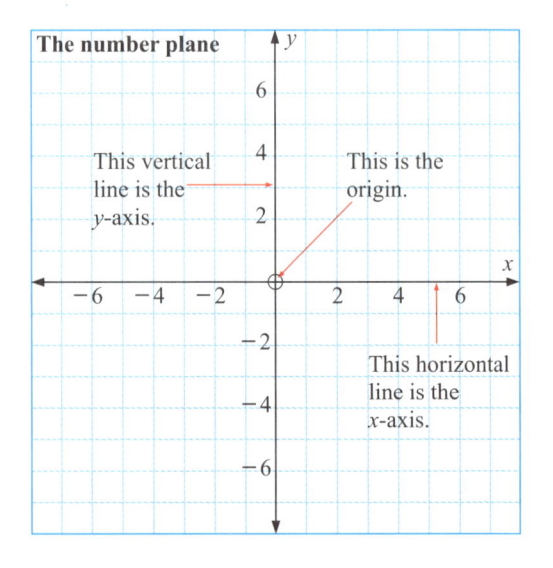

A PLOTTING POINTS

To help us identify particular points we often refer to them using a capital letter. For example, consider the points A(1, 3), B(4, −3) and C(−4, −2).

To plot the point A(1, 3):

- start at the origin O
- move right along the x-axis 1 unit
- then move upwards 3 units.

We say that 1 is the **x-coordinate** of A
and 3 is the **y-coordinate** of A.

To plot the point B(4, −3):

- start at the origin O
- move right along the x-axis 4 units
- then move downwards 3 units.

To plot the point C(−4, −2):

- start at the origin O
- move left along the x-axis 4 units
- then move downwards 2 units.

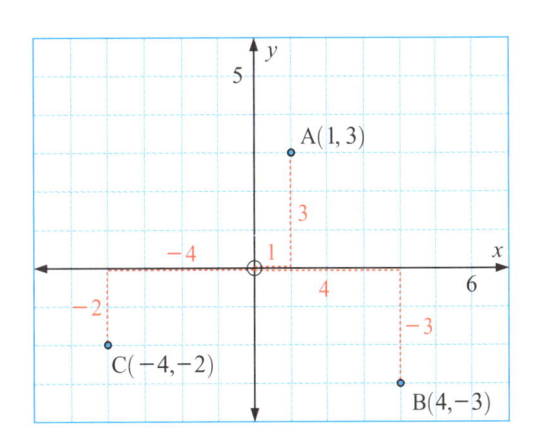

The x-coordinate is always given first. It indicates the movement away from the origin in the horizontal direction.

QUADRANTS

The x and y-axes divide the Cartesian plane into four regions referred to as **quadrants**. These quadrants are numbered in an **anti-clockwise direction** as shown alongside.

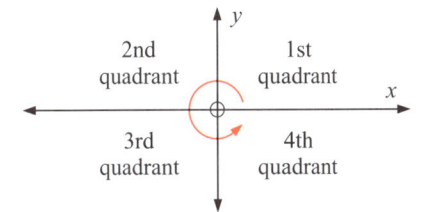

DISCUSSION — LOCATING PLACES

How can we locate the position of:

- a town or city in some country like Argentina
- a street in Auckland, New Zealand
- a point on an A4 sheet of paper?

Example 1

Plot the points A(3, 5), B(−1, 4), C(0, −3), D(−3, −2) and E(4, −2) on the same set of axes.

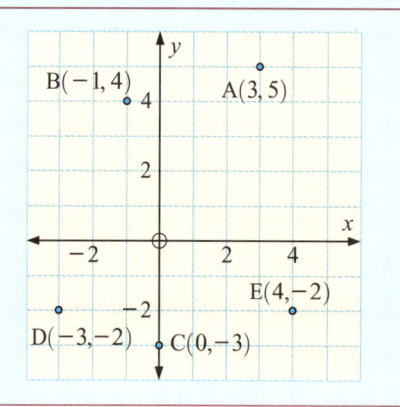

Start at O and move horizontally, then vertically.
→ is positive
← is negative
↑ is positive
↓ is negative.

EXERCISE 13A

1 State the coordinates of the points P, Q, R, S and T:

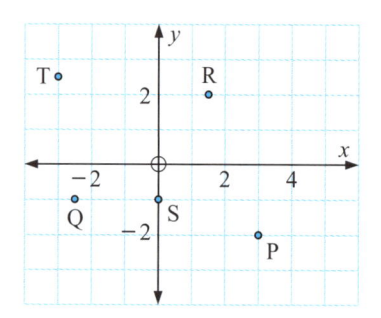

2 On the same set of axes plot the following points:
- **a** A(3, 4)
- **b** B(4, 3)
- **c** C(2, 6)
- **d** D(−3, 2)
- **e** E(5, −3)
- **f** F(−2, −4)
- **g** G(0, 5)
- **h** H(−3, 0)

3 State the quadrant in which each of the points in question **2** lies.

Example 2

On a Cartesian plane, show all the points with positive x-coordinate and negative y-coordinate.

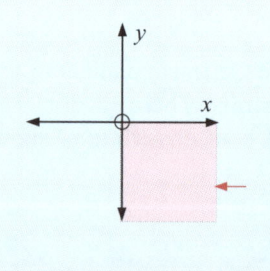

This shaded region contains all points where x is positive and y is negative. The points on the axes are not included.

4 On different sets of axes show all points with:
- **a** x-coordinate equal to 0
- **b** y-coordinate equal to 0
- **c** x-coordinate equal to 3
- **d** y-coordinate equal to −2
- **e** positive x-coordinate
- **f** negative y-coordinate
- **g** negative x and y-coordinates
- **h** negative x and positive y-coordinates

5 On separate axes plot the following sets of points:

   a $\{(0, 0), (1, 2), (2, 4), (3, 6), (4, 8)\}$ **b** $\{(0, 5), (1, 4), (2, 3), (3, 2), (4, 1)\}$

     i Are the points collinear?
     ii Do any of the following rules fit the set of points?

   A $y = x + 1$ **B** $y = x + 5$ **C** $y = 5 - x$
   D $y = 2x - 1$ **E** $y = 2x$

B   LINEAR RELATIONSHIPS

Consider the pattern:

    1st   2nd   3rd

We can construct a table of values which connects the diagram number n to the number of dots P.

n	1	2	3	4
P	3	5	7	9

We see that to go from one diagram to the next we need to add *two more* dots.

The **equation** which connects n and P in this case is $P = 2n + 1$.

This equation is easily checked by substituting $n = 1, 2, 3, 4, \ldots\ldots$ to find P.

For example, if $n = 3$ then $P = 2 \times 3 + 1 = 6 + 1 = 7$ ✓

Since the number of dots P *depends* on the diagram number n, we say that n is the **independent variable** and P is the **dependent variable**.

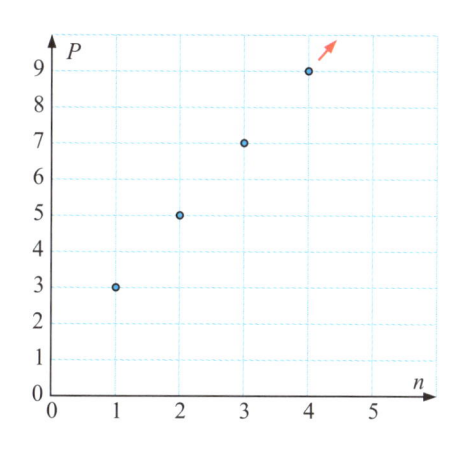

Note:

- This is an example of a **linear** relationship because the points form a straight line. We say the points are **collinear**.
- If $n = -1$, $P = 2(-1) + 1$
  $ = -1$

  But $(-1, -1)$ is meaningless here because we can't have a -1th diagram.

- If $n = 2\frac{1}{2}$, $P = 2(2\frac{1}{2}) + 1$
  $\phantom{If n = 2\tfrac{1}{2}, P} = 6$

  which is meaningless because we can't have a $2\frac{1}{2}$th diagram.

  For this reason we do not connect the points by a straight line.

The independent variable is placed on the horizontal axis.

Example 3

Each time when Max has only 10 litres of fuel left in his car's petrol tank, he fills it at at the petrol station. Petrol runs into the tank at 15 litres per minute. The petrol tank can only hold 70 litres.

a Identify the independent and dependent variables.
b Make a table of values for the number of litres L of petrol in the tank after time t minutes and plot the graph of L against t.
c Is the relationship between L and t linear?
d Is it sensible to join the points graphed with a straight line?
e For every time increase of 1 minute, what is the change in L?
f In filling the tank: **i** what amount is fixed **ii** what amount is variable?
g Find the number of litres of petrol in the tank after $1\frac{1}{2}$ minutes.

a The *number of litres of petrol* in the tank depends on the *time* it has been filling.
∴ time is the independent variable and the *number of litres of petrol* is the dependent variable.

b Each 1 minute the tank is filling adds another 15 litres of petrol.

t (min)	0	1	2	3	4
L (litres)	10	25	40	55	70

c The points lie in a straight line so the relationship is linear.

d Yes, as we could add petrol for $2\frac{1}{2}$ minutes, say, or put 56 litres of petrol in the tank.

e an increase of 15 litres

f **i** The fixed amount is 10 litres.
   ii The variable amount is 15 litres per minute.

g After $1\frac{1}{2}$ minutes there are $32\frac{1}{2}$ litres of petrol in the tank.

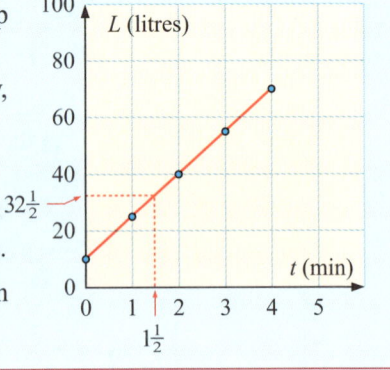

EXERCISE 13B

1 Each week a travel agent receives a basic salary of €200. In addition the agent is paid €30 for each ticket sold to Europe.

a What are the independent and dependent variables?
b Construct a table and draw a graph of income I against tickets sold t where $t = 0$, 1, 2, 3, ..., 10.
c Is the relationship linear?
d Is it sensible to join the points with a straight line?
e For each ticket sold, what will be the increase in income?
f **i** What is the fixed income? **ii** What is the variable income?

2 One litre cartons of 'Long-life' milk can be bought for 85 pence each.

  a Copy and complete the table:

Number of cartons n	0	1	2	3	4	5	6	7	8
Cost in pounds £C									

  b Plot the graph of C against n.
  c Identify the independent and dependent variables.
  d Is the relationship between C and n linear?
  e Is it sensible to join the points graphed with a straight line?
  f For each extra carton of milk bought, what is the change in C?
  g Find the cost of 4 cartons of milk.
  h How many cartons of milk could be bought for £5.95?

3 Jason has a large container for water. It already contains 4 litres when he starts to fill it using a 1.5 litre jug.

  a Make a table of values for the volume of water (V litres) in the container after Jason has emptied n full jugs of water ($n = 0, 1, 2, ..., 8$) into it.
  b What are the independent and dependent variables?
  c Plot the graph of V against n.
  d Is the relationship between V and n linear?
  e Is it sensible to join the points graphed with a straight line?
  f For each full jug of water added, what is the change in V?
  g What volume of water is in the container after Jason has emptied 5 full jugs into it?
  h How many full jugs must be emptied into the container to give a volume of 14.5 litres in the container?

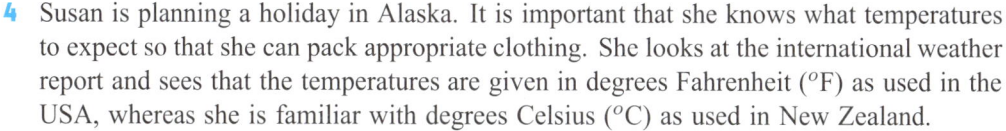

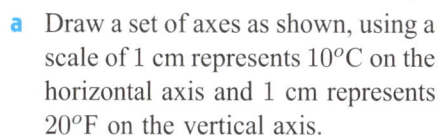

4 Susan is planning a holiday in Alaska. It is important that she knows what temperatures to expect so that she can pack appropriate clothing. She looks at the international weather report and sees that the temperatures are given in degrees Fahrenheit (°F) as used in the USA, whereas she is familiar with degrees Celsius (°C) as used in New Zealand.

  a Draw a set of axes as shown, using a scale of 1 cm represents 10°C on the horizontal axis and 1 cm represents 20°F on the vertical axis.
  b Identify the independent and dependent variables.
  c There is a linear relationship between °F and °C. The boiling point of water is 100°C or 212°F. The freezing point of water is 0°C or 32°F.

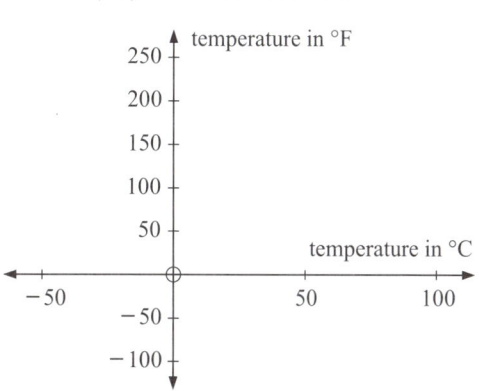

  Mark these points on your graph and join them with a straight line.

d Find the point where the number of degrees Celsius equals the same number of degrees Fahrenheit. What is the temperature?

e Susan sees that the maximum temperatures were:

    i 46°F on Monday   **ii** 36°F on Tuesday.

Convert these temperatures to °C.

f Use your graph to complete the following chart:

Temperature °F				20	10	0
Temperature °C	10	20	30	40		

C   PLOTTING LINEAR GRAPHS

Consider the equation $y = \frac{1}{2}x - 1$ which describes the relationship between two variables x and y.

For any given value of x, we can use the equation to find the value of y. These values form the coordinates (x, y) of a point on the graph of the equation.

The value of y depends on the value of x, so the independent variable is x and the dependent variable is y.

When $x = -2$, $y = \frac{1}{2}(-2) - 1$ When $x = 2$, $y = \frac{1}{2}(2) - 1$
$= -1 - 1$ $= 1 - 1$
$= -2$ $= 0$

From calculations like these we construct a **table of values**:

x	-3	-2	-1	0	1	2	3
y	$-2\frac{1}{2}$	-2	$-1\frac{1}{2}$	-1	$-\frac{1}{2}$	0	$\frac{1}{2}$

So, the points $(-3, -2\frac{1}{2})$, $(-2, -2)$, $(-1, -1\frac{1}{2})$, $(0, -1)$, ... all satisfy $y = \frac{1}{2}x - 1$ and lie on its graph.

Notice also that if $x = 1.8$ then $y = \frac{1}{2}(1.8) - 1$
$= 0.9 - 1$
$= -0.1$

$\therefore$ $(1.8, -0.1)$ also satisfy $y = \frac{1}{2}x - 1$.

In fact there are infinitely many points which satisfy $y = \frac{1}{2}x - 1$.

These points make up a **continuous** straight line which continues indefinitely in both directions. We indicate this using arrowheads.

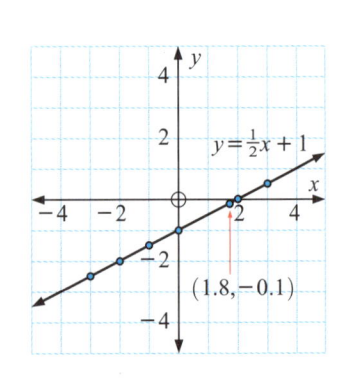

Example 4

Consider the equation $y = x - 2$.

a What are the independent and dependent variables?
b Construct a table of values using $x = -3, -2, -1, 0, 1, 2$ and 3.
c Draw the graph of $y = x - 2$.

a x is the independent variable.
y is the dependent variable.

b

x	-3	-2	-1	0	1	2	3
y	-5	-4	-3	-2	-1	0	1

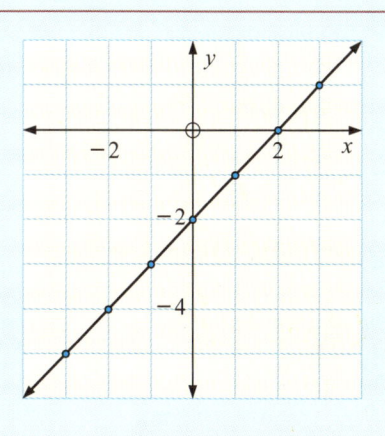

c

EXERCISE 13C

1 For the following equations:

  i State the independent and dependent variables.
  ii Construct a table of values using $x = -3, -2, -1, 0, 1, 2, 3$.
  iii Plot the graph.

  a $y = x$ **b** $y = 2x$ **c** $y = \frac{1}{2}x$ **d** $y = -2x$
  e $y = 2x + 3$ **f** $y = -2x + 3$ **g** $y = \frac{1}{4}x + 1$ **h** $y = -\frac{1}{4}x + 1$

2 Arrange the graphs of $y = x$, $y = 2x$ and $y = \frac{1}{2}x$ in order of steepness. What part of the equation do you suspect controls the degree of steepness of a line?

3 Compare the graphs of $y = 2x$ and $y = -2x$. What part of the equation do you suspect controls whether the graph slopes forwards or backwards?

4 Compare the graphs of $y = 2x$, $y = 2x + 3$ and $y = \frac{1}{4}x + 1$. What part of the equation do you suspect controls where the graph cuts the y-axis?

DISCUSSION

How many points lie on the line with equation $y = 2x + 3$?

Are there gaps between the points on the line?

Does the line have finite length?

D — THE EQUATION OF A LINE

Consider the line with equation $y = 2x$.

For all points on the line, the y-coordinate is always double the x-coordinate.

For example, the points:
$(-2, -4)$, $(-1, -2)$, $(0, 0)$, $(1, 2)$, $(2, 4)$ and $(3, 6)$ all lie on the line.

The graph of $y = 2x$ including these points is shown plotted alongside.

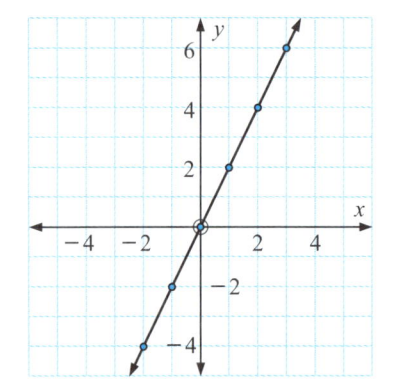

EQUATION OF A LINE

The **equation of a line** is an equation which connects the x and y-coordinates of **all** points on the line.

Example 5 — Self Tutor

State in words the meaning of the equation $y = 3x + 7$.

$y = 3x + 7$ connects the x and y values for every point on the line where the y-coordinate is three times the x-coordinate, plus 7.

Example 6 — Self Tutor

By inspection only, find the equations of the straight lines passing through the following points:

a
x	1	2	3	4	5
y	-3	-6	-9	-12	-15

b
x	1	2	3	4	5
y	5	4	3	2	1

a Each y-value is -3 times its corresponding x-value, so $y = -3x$.
b The sum of each x and y-value is always 6, so $x + y = 6$.

EXERCISE 13D

1 State in words the meaning of the equation:
  a $y = x + 3$ b $y = 5x$ c $y = 2x - 6$ d $x + y = 5$

2 By inspection only, find the equations of the straight lines passing through the following points:

a
x	1	2	3	4	5
y	4	8	12	16	20

b
x	2	3	4	5	6
y	4	5	6	7	8

c

x	0	1	2	3
y	0	-2	-4	-6

d

x	0	1	2	3
y	3	2	1	0

e

x	1	2	3	4	5
y	3	5	7	9	11

f

x	1	2	3	4	5
y	1	3	5	7	9

E GRADIENT OR SLOPE

Consider the two diagrams below. As we go from left to right along each line, the line from A to B travels **up**, but the line from C to D travels **down**. We say that [AB] has an upwards **gradient** whereas [CD] has a downwards gradient.

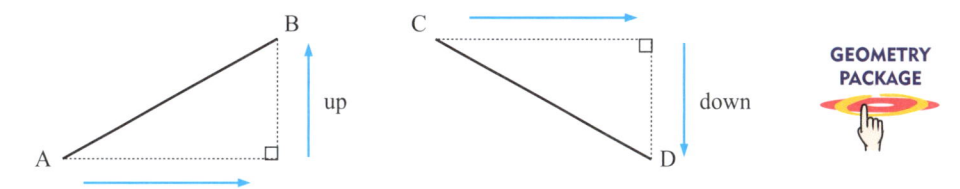

We use **gradient** or **slope** as a measure of a line's steepness. Horizontal lines are said to have **zero gradient**. Upwards sloping lines have positive gradients, whereas downwards sloping lines have negative gradients.

Gradient is the comparison of the vertical step to the horizontal step.

$$\text{gradient} = \frac{\text{vertical step}}{\text{horizontal step}}$$

When calculating the gradient of a line, it is a good idea to first move horizontally in the positive direction.

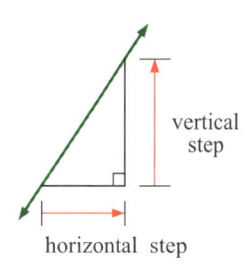

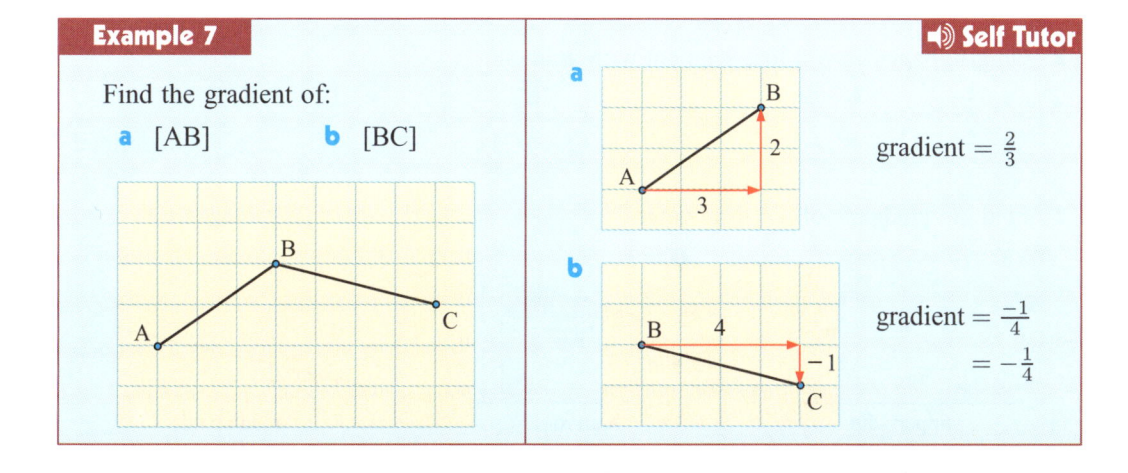

Example 7   ◀)) Self Tutor

Find the gradient of:

a [AB]   **b** [BC]

a gradient $= \frac{2}{3}$

b gradient $= \frac{-1}{4}$
$= -\frac{1}{4}$

288　COORDINATE GEOMETRY　(Chapter 13)

We see examples of gradient every day:

gradient of road = $\frac{1}{6}$

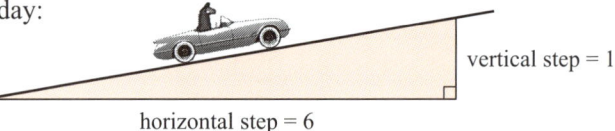

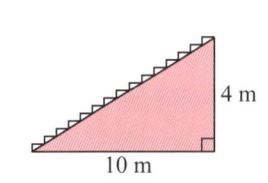

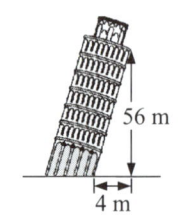

vertical step = 1
horizontal step = 6

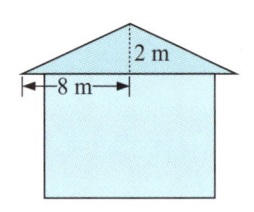

gradient of roof = $\frac{2}{8}$
= $\frac{1}{4}$

gradient of stairs = $\frac{4}{10}$
= $\frac{2}{5}$

gradient of tower = $\frac{56}{4}$
= 14

For a **horizontal line** the vertical step is 0. This gives 0 as the numerator, so the **gradient of a horizontal line is 0**.

For a **vertical line**, the horizontal step is 0. So the denominator is 0 and the **gradient of the vertical line is undefined**.

EXERCISE 13E.1

1 State the gradients of the lines labelled:

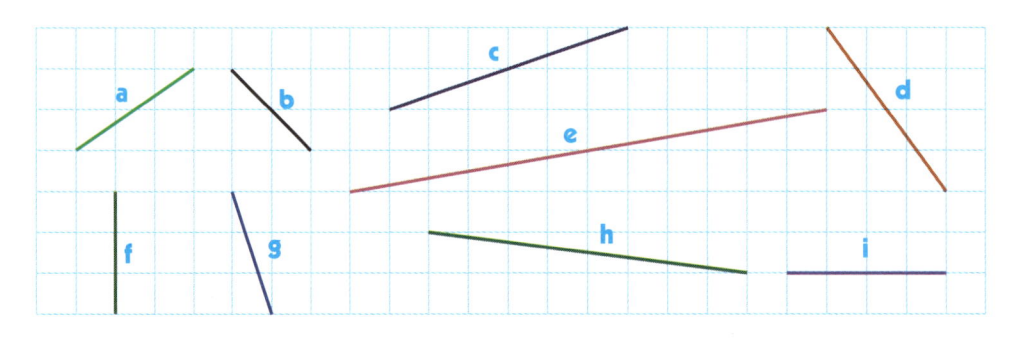

2 On grid paper draw a line segment with gradient:

　a $\frac{1}{2}$　　**b** $\frac{2}{3}$　　**c** $-\frac{1}{4}$　　**d** $2 = \frac{2}{1}$　　**e** 1　　**f** -3

　g $\frac{4}{3}$　　**h** $-\frac{5}{2}$　　**i** 0　　**j** $1\frac{1}{5}$　　**k** 10　　**l** undefined

3 Find the gradients of the following:

　a slippery-dip　　**b** barn roof　　**c** road up hill

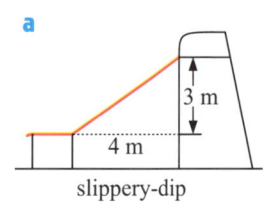

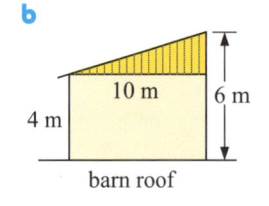

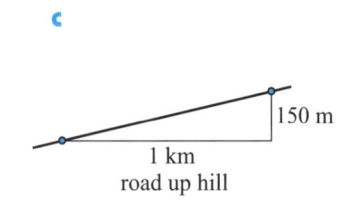

COORDINATE GEOMETRY (Chapter 13)

4 **a** Determine the gradient of:
  i [OA]   **ii** [OB]   **iii** [OC]
  iv [OD]   **v** [OE]   **vi** [OF]
  vii [OG]   **viii** [OH] **ix** [OI]

b Using the results of **a**, copy and complete the following statements:
  i The gradient of a horizontal line is ......
  ii The gradient of a vertical line is ......
  iii As line segments become steeper, their gradients ......

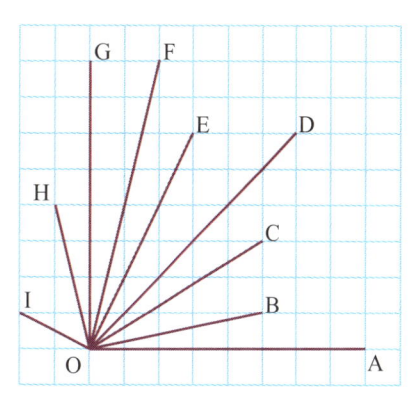

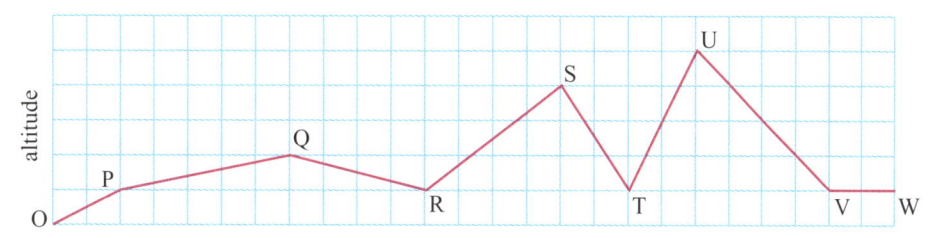

5 Imagine that you are walking across the countryside from O to W, i.e., from left to right.

a Indicate when you are going uphill.
b Indicate when you are going downhill.
c Where is the steepest positive gradient?
d Where is the steepest negative gradient?
e Where is the gradient 0?
f Where is the gradient positive and least?

6 By plotting the points on graph paper, find the gradients of the lines joining the following pairs of points:

  a O(0, 0) and A(2, 6)
  b O(0, 0) and B(−4, 2)
  c G(0, −1) and H(2, 5)
  d K(1, 1) and L(−2, −2)
  e M(3, 1) and N(−1, 3)
  f P(−2, 4) and Q(2, 0)

INVESTIGATION 1   THE GRADIENT OF A LINE

What to do:

1 Copy and complete:

Line segment	x-step	y-step	$\dfrac{y\text{-step}}{x\text{-step}}$
[BC]	2	1	$\frac{1}{2}$
[DE]			
[AC]			
[BE]			
[AE]			
[FG]			

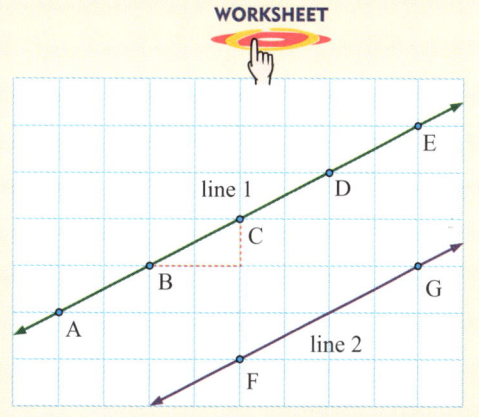

2 Copy and complete:

    a Lines [AB] and [CD] are ......

    b Lines [PQ] and [RS] are ......

    c gradient of [AB] = ...
       gradient of [PQ] = ...
       gradient of [CD] = ...
       gradient of [RS] = ...

    d gradient of [AB] × gradient of [CD] = ...
       gradient of [PQ] × gradient of [RS] = ...

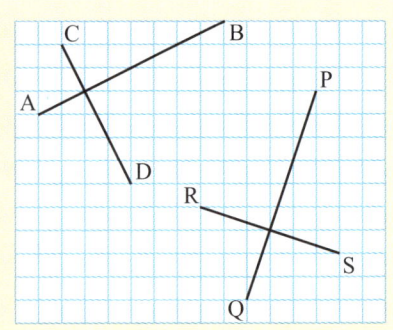

3 Copy and complete:

- The gradient of a straight line is ......
- Parallel lines have ......
- Perpendicular lines have gradients whose product is ......

THE GRADIENT FORMULA

Although we can find gradients easily using steps on a diagram, it is often quicker to use a formula.

For points $A(x_1, y_1)$ and $B(x_2, y_2)$, the vertical step is $y_2 - y_1$ and the horizontal step is $x_2 - x_1$.

$\therefore$ the gradient is $\dfrac{y_2 - y_1}{x_2 - x_1}$.

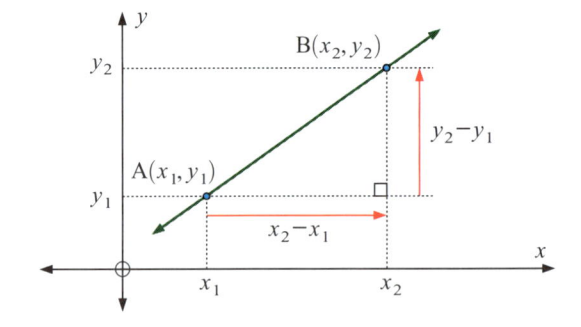

So,   the **gradient** of the line through (x_1, y_1) and (x_2, y_2) is $\dfrac{y_2 - y_1}{x_2 - x_1}$.

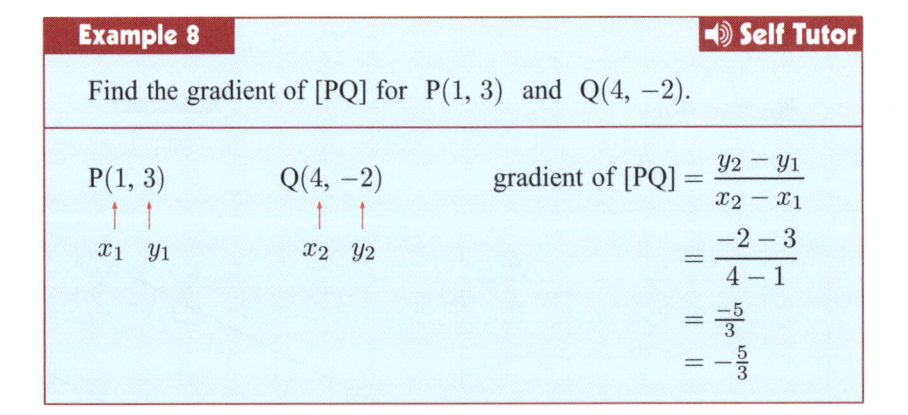

Example 8   ◀) Self Tutor

Find the gradient of [PQ] for P(1, 3) and Q(4, −2).

$P(1, 3)$ $Q(4, -2)$ gradient of $[PQ] = \dfrac{y_2 - y_1}{x_2 - x_1}$
   x_1 y_1 x_2 y_2
                                                   $= \dfrac{-2 - 3}{4 - 1}$

                                                   $= \dfrac{-5}{3}$

                                                   $= -\dfrac{5}{3}$

The advantage of finding the gradient by using a formula is that we do not have to plot the points on a graph.

COORDINATE GEOMETRY (Chapter 13)

EXERCISE 13E.2

1 For the following graphs, find the gradients by:
  i considering horizontal and vertical steps
  ii using the gradient formula.

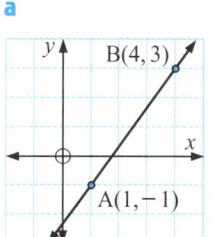

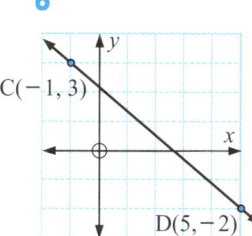

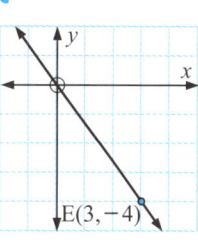

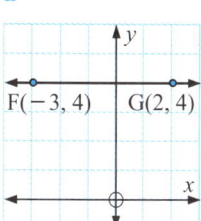

  a B(4, 3), A(1, −1)
  b C(−1, 3), D(5, −2)
  c E(3, −4)
  d F(−3, 4), G(2, 4)

2 Use the gradient formula to find the gradients of the lines joining the following pairs of points:

  a O(0, 0) and A(2, 6)
  b O(0, 0) and B(−4, 2)
  c O(0, 0) and C(2, −12)
  d O(0, 0) and D(1, −5)
  e E(1, 0) and F(1, 5)
  f G(0, −1) and H(2, −1)
  g I(1, 1) and J(3, 3)
  h K(1, 1) and L(−2, −2)
  i M(3, 1) and N(−1, 3)
  j P(−2, 4) and Q(2, 0)

3 Which method do you think is easier to use to find the gradient of the line joining R(−50, 460) and S(115, 55)? Explain your answer.

4 Suppose a straight line makes an angle $\theta°$ with the positive x-axis. Copy and complete:

  a The gradient of any horizontal line is ......
  b The gradient of any vertical line is ......
  c
    i If $\theta = 0°$, the gradient is ......
    ii If $\theta = 45°$, the gradient is ......
    iii If $\theta = 90°$, the gradient is ......
    iv If θ is acute, the gradient is ......
    v If θ is obtuse, the gradient is ......

F GRAPHING LINES FROM EQUATIONS

INVESTIGATION 2   GRAPHS OF THE FORM $y = mx + c$

The use of a **graphics calculator** or suitable **graphing package** is recommended for this investigation.

GRAPHING PACKAGE

What to do:

1 On the same set of axes, graph the family of lines of the form $y = mx$:

  a where $m = 1, 2, 3, \frac{1}{2}, \frac{1}{3}$
  b where $m = -1, -2, -3, -\frac{1}{2}, -\frac{1}{3}$

2 Find the gradients of the lines in **1**.

3 Describe the effect of m in the equation $y = mx$.

4 On the same set of axes, graph the family of lines of the form $y = 2x + c$ where $c = 0, 2, 4, -1, -3$.

5 Describe the effect of c in the equation $y = 2x + c$.

The point where a straight line meets the x-axis is called its **x-intercept**.

The point where a straight line meets the y-axis is called its **y-intercept**.

From **Investigation 2** you should have discovered that:

$y = mx + c$ is the equation of a straight line with gradient m and y-intercept c.

Example 9 ◀⃝ Self Tutor

Give the gradient and y-intercept of the line with equation:

a $y = 3x - 2$ **b** $y = 7 - 2x$ **c** $y = 0$

a $y = 3x - 2$ has $m = 3$ and $c = -2$
∴ gradient is 3 and y-intercept is -2

b $y = 7 - 2x$
or $y = -2x + 7$ has $m = -2$ and $c = 7$
∴ gradient is -2 and y-intercept is 7

c $y = 0$
or $y = 0x + 0$ has $m = 0$ and $c = 0$
∴ gradient is 0 and y-intercept is 0

EXERCISE 13F.1

1 Write down the equation of a line with:
  a gradient 2 and y-intercept 11
  b gradient 4 and y-intercept -6
  c gradient -3 and y-intercept $\frac{1}{2}$
  d gradient -1 and y-intercept 4
  e gradient 0 and y-intercept 7
  f gradient $\frac{2}{3}$ and y-intercept 6.

2 Give the **i** gradient **ii** y-intercept of the line with equation:
  a $y = 4x + 8$
  b $y = -3x + 2$
  c $y = 6 - x$
  d $y = -2x + 3$
  e $y = -2$
  f $y = 11 - 3x$
  g $y = \frac{1}{2}x - 5$
  h $y = 3 - \frac{3}{2}x$
  i $y = \frac{2}{5}x + \frac{4}{5}$
  j $y = \dfrac{x + 1}{2}$
  k $y = \dfrac{2x - 10}{5}$
  l $y = \dfrac{11 - 3x}{2}$

GRAPHING $y = mx + c$

To draw the graph of $y = mx + c$ we could do one of the following:
- construct a table of values using at least 3 points and then graph the points
- use the y-intercept and gradient
- use the x and y-intercepts.

GRAPHING USING y-INTERCEPT AND GRADIENT

To draw the graph of $y = mx + c$ using the y-intercept and gradient:
- find m and c
- locate the y-intercept and plot this point
- from the gradient, use the x and y-steps to locate another point
- join these two points and extend the line in either direction.

Example 10

Use the y-intercept and gradient of $y = \frac{2}{3}x + 1$ to graph the line.

For $y = \frac{2}{3}x + 1$, $m = \frac{2}{3}$ and $c = 1$

$\therefore$ the y-intercept is 1

and the gradient is $\dfrac{2 \leftarrow y\text{-step}}{3 \leftarrow x\text{-step}}$

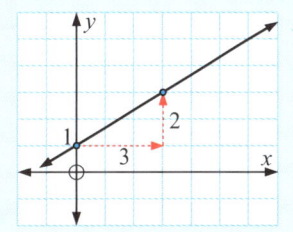

Example 11

Use the y-intercept and gradient of $y = -2x - 3$ to graph the line.

For $y = -2x - 3$, $m = -2$ and $c = -3$

$\therefore$ the y-intercept is -3

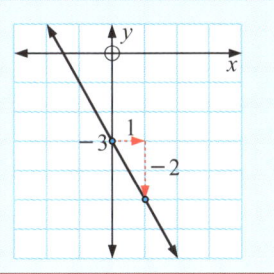

and $m = \dfrac{-2 \leftarrow y\text{-step}}{1 \leftarrow x\text{-step}}$

Always let the x-step be positive.

EXERCISE 13F.2

1 For each of the following:
   i find the gradient and y-intercept   **ii** sketch the graph.

   a $y = x + 3$
   b $y = -x + 4$
   c $y = 2x + 2$
   d $y = \frac{1}{2}x - 1$
   e $y = 3x$
   f $y = -\frac{1}{2}x$
   g $y = -2x + 1$
   h $y = 3 - \frac{1}{3}x$
   i $y = 3$

GRAPHING USING THE AXES INTERCEPTS

The y-intercept gives us one point to plot.

The x-intercept can be found by letting $y = 0$ in the equation of the line and then solving for x.

Any points on the x-axis have a y-coordinate of zero.

Example 12

Use axes intercepts to graph the line with equation $y = 2x - 5$.

The y-intercept is -5.

When $y = 0$, $2x - 5 = 0$
$\therefore \ 2x = 5$
$\therefore \ x = \frac{5}{2}$

So, the x-intercept is $2\frac{1}{2}$.

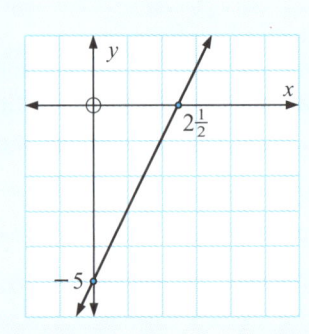

EXERCISE 13F.3

1 Use axes intercepts to graph the line with equation:

  a $y = x + 4$ **b** $y = -x + 3$ **c** $y = 2x + 4$

  d $y = -2x + 5$ **e** $y = \frac{1}{2}x - 2$ **f** $y = 3 - \frac{1}{2}x$

  g $y = \frac{1}{3}x + 1$ **h** $y = 2 - \frac{x}{3}$ **i** $y = \frac{x+2}{3}$

2 Can lines of the form $y = mx$ be graphed using intercepts only? How could you graph these lines?

G   OTHER LINE FORMS

HORIZONTAL AND VERTICAL LINES

Lines parallel to the x-axis and lines parallel to the y-axis are special cases which we need to treat with care.

INVESTIGATION 3   HORIZONTAL AND VERTICAL LINES

What to do:

1 Using graph paper, plot the following sets of points on the Cartesian plane. Rule a line through each set of points.

  a $(5, 2)$, $(5, 4)$, $(5, -2)$, $(5, -4)$, $(5, 0)$

b $(-1, 2)$, $(-1, 4)$, $(-1, -2)$, $(-1, -4)$, $(-1, 0)$
   c $(0, 2)$, $(0, 4)$, $(0, -2)$, $(0, -4)$, $(0, 0)$
   d $(-1, 3)$, $(2, 3)$, $(0, 3)$, $(4, 3)$, $(-3, 3)$
   e $(0, -4)$, $(1, -4)$, $(4, -4)$, $(-2, -4)$, $(3, -4)$
   f $(1, 0)$, $(0, 0)$, $(5, 0)$, $(-1, 0)$, $(-2, 0)$

2 Can you state the gradient of each line? If so, what is it?

3 Can you state the y-intercept of each line? If so, what is it?

4 How are these lines different from other lines previously studied?

5 Can you state the equation of the line?

VERTICAL LINES

The graph alongside shows the vertical lines $x = -1$ and $x = 3$.

For all points on a vertical line, regardless of the value of the y-coordinate, the value of the x-coordinate is the same.

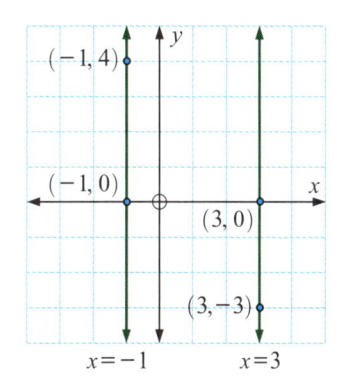

All **vertical** lines have equations of the form $x = a$.

The gradient of a vertical line is **undefined**.

HORIZONTAL LINES

The graph alongside shows the horizontal lines $y = -2$ and $y = 1$.

For all points on a horizontal line, regardless of the value of the x-coordinate, the value of the y-coordinate is the same.

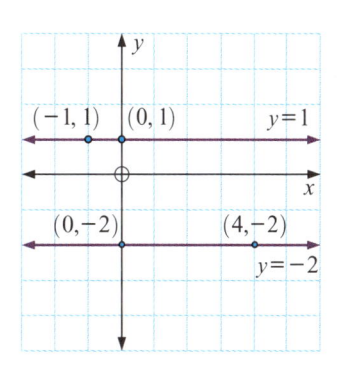

All **horizontal** lines have equations of the form $y = c$.

The gradient of a horizontal line is **zero**.

EXERCISE 13G.1

1 Identify as either a vertical or horizontal line and hence plot the graphs of:
   a $y = 3$
   b $x = 4$
   c $y = -2$
   d $x = -6$

2 Identify as either a vertical or horizontal line:
   a a line with zero gradient
   b a line with undefined gradient.

3 Find the equation of:
   a the x-axis
   b the y-axis
   c a line parallel to the x-axis and two units above it
   d a line parallel to the y-axis and 3 units to the left of it.

THE GENERAL FORM

Equations of the form $Ax + By = C$ where A, B and C are constants are also **linear**. This form is called the **general form** of the equation of a line.

For example, $2x - 3y = -6$ is the equation of a straight line in general form. In this case $A = 2$, $B = -3$ and $C = -6$.

We can rearrange equations given in general form into the $y = mx + c$ form and hence find their gradient.

Example 13   ◀)) Self Tutor

Make y the subject of the equation and hence find the gradient of:
   a $x - y = 4$
   b $2x + 3y = -6$

> A line in the form $y = mx + c$ has gradient m.

a
$x - y = 4$
$\therefore x - y - x = 4 - x$ {subtracting x from both sides}
$\therefore -y = 4 - x$ {simplifying}
$\therefore \dfrac{-y}{-1} = \dfrac{4}{-1} - \dfrac{x}{-1}$ {dividing each term by -1}
$\therefore y = -4 + x$ {simplifying}
$\therefore y = x - 4$ and so the gradient is 1.

b
$2x + 3y = -6$
$\therefore 2x + 3y - 2x = -6 - 2x$ {subtracting $2x$ from both sides}
$\therefore 3y = -6 - 2x$ {simplifying}
$\therefore \dfrac{3y}{3} = \dfrac{-6}{3} - \dfrac{2x}{3}$ {dividing both sides by 3}
$\therefore y = -2 - \tfrac{2}{3}x$
$\therefore y = -\tfrac{2}{3}x - 2$ and so the gradient is $-\tfrac{2}{3}$.

DISCUSSION

We can graph equations given in general form by converting them into the $y = mx + c$ form and then using the gradient and y-intercept.
Is there a better or quicker method of graphing equations in the general form?

EXERCISE 13G.2

1 Find the gradient of the line with equation:

    a $y = 2x - 3$ **b** $y = -3x + 4$ **c** $y = \dfrac{2x}{3} + 5$

    d $y = \dfrac{3x + 1}{4}$ **e** $y = 5 - 2x$ **f** $y = \frac{3}{5} - x$

2 Make y the subject of the equation and hence find the gradient of:

    a $x + y = 5$ **b** $2x + y = 4$ **c** $y - 3x = 5$

    d $2x - 3y = 6$ **e** $2y + x - 6 = 0$ **f** $6 - 2y + 5x = 0$

    g $3x + 7y = -21$ **h** $2x - 5y = 10$ **i** $5x + 3y = 30$

3 Match each equation to one of the graphs by using y-intercepts and gradients:

    a $y = x + 1$ **b** $y = 1 - x$

    c $2y = 3x + 4$ **d** $x + y = 5$

    e $2x + 5y = 10$ **f** $4 - 2x = 4y$

    g $x - y = 3$ **h** $\frac{1}{2}y = \frac{1}{2}x - 1$

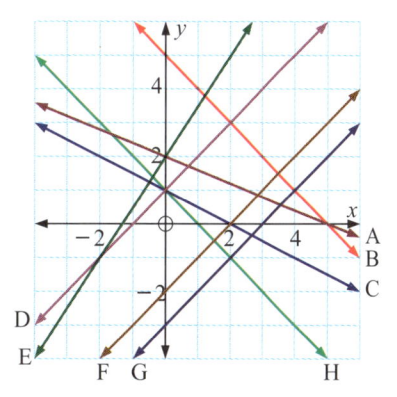

Example 14   Self Tutor

Use axes intercepts to draw the graph of the line $2x - 3y = -6$.

The line cuts the y-axis when $x = 0$

$\therefore \quad -3y = -6$

$\therefore \quad \dfrac{-3y}{-3} = \dfrac{-6}{-3}$

$\therefore \quad y = 2$

The line cuts the x-axis when $y = 0$

$\therefore \quad 2x = -6$

$\therefore \quad \dfrac{2x}{2} = \dfrac{-6}{2}$

$\therefore \quad x = -3$

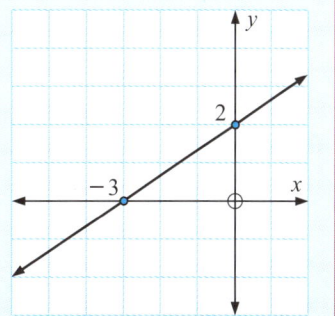

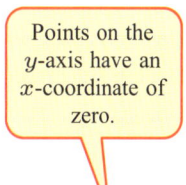

Points on the y-axis have an x-coordinate of zero.

4 Use axes intercepts to draw the graph of:

   a $x + y = 6$ **b** $2x + y = 4$ **c** $3x - y = 5$

   d $2x + 3y = 6$ **e** $3x - 4y = 12$ **f** $x + 3y = -6$

   g $2x - 5y = 10$ **h** $2x + 7y = 14$ **i** $3x - 4y = 8$

H FINDING EQUATIONS FROM GRAPHS

To determine the equation of a line we need to know its gradient and at least one other point on it.

If we are given two points on a graph then we can find its gradient m by using $m = \dfrac{y_2 - y_1}{x_2 - x_1}$.

So, if we know the y-intercept and one other point then we can find the **equation** connecting x and y.

Example 15

For the graph alongside, determine:

a the gradient of the line

b the y-intercept

c the equation of the line.

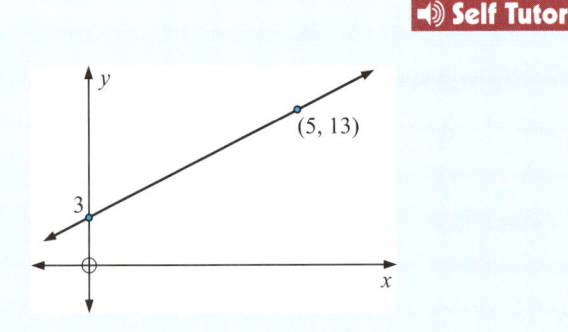

a $(0, 3)$ and $(5, 13)$ lie on the line

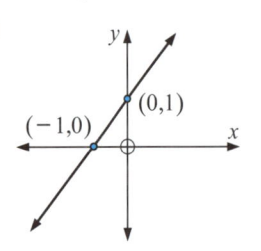

$\therefore$ the gradient $m = \dfrac{13 - 3}{5 - 0}$

$= \dfrac{10}{5}$

$= 2$

b The y-intercept is 3.

c The equation of the line is $y = 2x + 3$.

EXERCISE 13H

1 For each of the following lines, find:

   i the gradient   **ii** the y-intercept   **iii** the equation of the line.

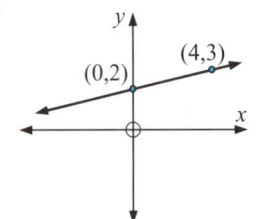

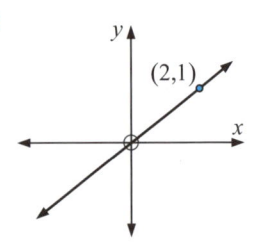

d graph through (0,2) and (2,0)

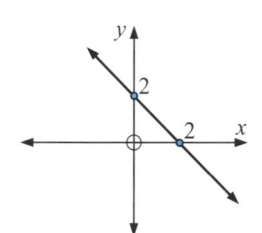

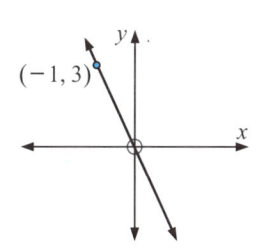

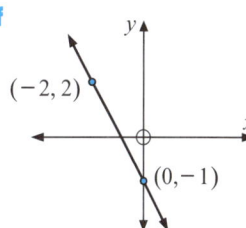

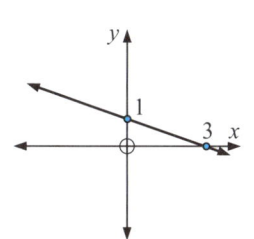

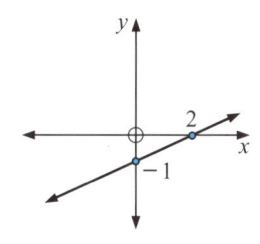

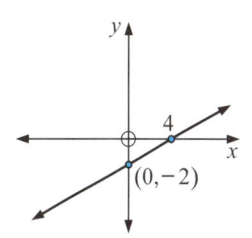

e graph through (−1, 3) and origin

f graph through (−2, 2) and (0, −1)

g graph through (0, 1) and (3, 0)

h graph through (0, 2) and (0, −1)... line through (0,−1) and (2,0)

i graph through (4, 0) and (0, −2)

2 Find the rule connecting the variables in:

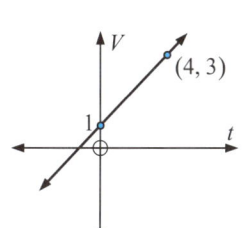

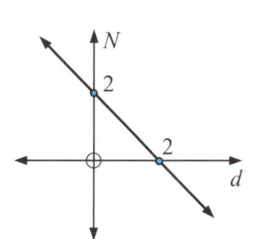

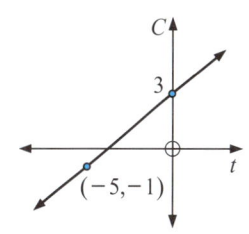

a line through (0, 1) and (4, 3), axes t and V

b line through (0, 2) and (2, 0), axes d and N

c line through (0, 3) and (−5, −1), axes t and C

I   POINTS ON LINES

Once we have found the equation of a line, we can easily check to see whether a given point lies on it.

We simply replace x by the x-coordinate of the point being tested and see if the equation produces the y-coordinate.

Example 16

Determine whether $(2, 11)$ and $(-3, -3)$ lie on the line with equation $y = 3x + 5$.

If $x = 2$, $y = 3 \times 2 + 5$
$= 6 + 5$
$= 11$

$\therefore$ $(2, 11)$ lies on the line.

If $x = -3$, $y = 3 \times (-3) + 5$
$= -9 + 5$
$= -4 \neq -3$

$\therefore$ $(-3, -3)$ does not lie on the line.

EXERCISE 13I

1 Determine whether the given point satisfies the given equation, or in other words whether the point lies on the graph of the line:

   a $(2, 5)$, $y = 4x - 3$ **b** $(3, -1)$, $y = 2x - 7$

   c $(-4, 2)$, $y = -x + 3$ **d** $(-1, 7)$, $y = -2x + 5$

   e $(4, -1)$, $y = -2x + 7$ **f** $(1, 6)$, $y = -3x + 5$

INVESTIGATION 4   THE GRAPH OF $y = \sqrt{x}$

This investigation is best attempted using a **graphing package** or **graphics calculator**.

What to do:

1
  a Draw the graph of $y = \sqrt{x}$ from a table of values.
  b Use technology to check your graph.
  c Explain why there is no graph to the left of the vertical axis.
  d Explain why no part of the graph is below the x-axis.

2
  a On the same set of axes, graph $y = \sqrt{x}$ and $y = -\sqrt{x}$.
  b What is the geometrical relationship between the two graphs?

3
  a Draw the graphs of $y = x^2$ and $y = \sqrt{x}$ on the same set of axes.
  b What is the geometrical relationship between the two graphs?

4
  a On the same set of axes graph $y = \sqrt{x}$, $y = \sqrt{x} + 3$ and $y = \sqrt{x} - 3$.
  b What is the geometrical relationship between the three graphs?
  c Do the graphs have the same basic shape?

5
  a On the same set of axes plot the graphs of $y = \sqrt{x}$, $y = \sqrt{x-3}$ and $y = \sqrt{x+3}$.
  b Do the graphs have the same basic shape?
  c What is the geometrical relationship between the three graphs?

HOW FAR IS IT FROM YOUR CHIN TO YOUR FINGERTIPS?

Areas of interaction:
Approaches to learning

REVIEW SET 13A

1. On a set of axes show all points with an x-coordinate equal to -2.

2. A lawyer charges a €75 consultation fee and then €120 per hour thereafter.
   a Identify the dependent and independent variables.
   b Make a table of values for the cost €C of an appointment with the lawyer for time t hours where $t = 0, 1, 2, 3, 4$.
   c Is the relationship between C and t linear?
   d If you graphed this relationship, is it sensible to join the points graphed with a straight line? Give a reason for your answer.
   e For every increase of 1 hour for t, what is the change in C?
   f For an appointment with the lawyer, what is:
      i the fixed cost   ii the variable cost?

3. For the equation $y = -2x + 3$:
   a Construct a table of values with $x = -3, -2, -1, 0, 1, 2, 3$.
   b Plot the graph.
   c Find: i the y-intercept   ii the x-intercept.

4. Find, by inspection, the equation of the straight line passing through the points:

x	0	1	2	3	4	5
y	3	2	1	0	-1	-2

5. State the gradients of the given lines:
   a   b

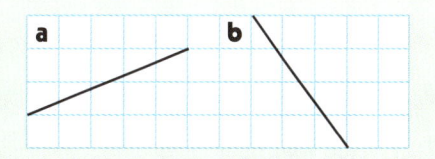

6. Use the gradient formula to find the gradient of the straight line through the points A$(-2, 3)$ and B$(1, -4)$.

7. Write down the equation of the line with gradient 5 and y-intercept -2.

8. For the line with equation $y = -\frac{1}{3}x + 2$:
   a find the gradient and the y-intercept, and hence
   b sketch the graph.

9. Use axes intercepts to draw the graph of $2x - 3y = 6$.

10. For the line alongside, find:
    a the gradient
    b the y-intercept
    c the equation of the line.

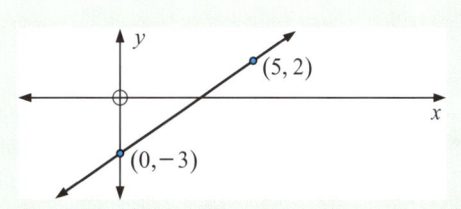

    $(5, 2)$
    $(0, -3)$

11. Determine whether the point $(-2, 5)$ lies on the line with equation $y = -2x + 1$.

REVIEW SET 13B

1. Illustrate on a set of axes the region where both x and y are negative.

2. A tank contains 400 litres of water. The tap is left on and 25 litres of water escape per minute. V is the volume of water remaining in the tank t minutes after the tap is switched on.

   a What are the dependent and independent variables?

   b Make a table of values for V and t.

   c Is the relationship between V and t linear?

   d If you graphed this relationship, is it sensible to join the points graphed with a straight line? Give a reason for your answer.

   e For every increase of 1 minute for t, what is the change in V?

3. For the equation $y = 3x - 2$:

   a Construct a table of values with $x = -2, -1, 0, 1, 2$.

   b Plot the graph.

   c Find: **i** the y-intercept **ii** the x-intercept.

4. Find, by inspection, the equation of the straight line passing through the points:

x	0	1	2	3	4
y	0	-3	-6	-9	-12

5. State the gradients of the given lines:

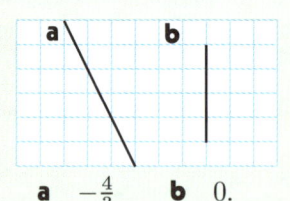

6. On grid paper, draw a line with a gradient of: **a** $-\frac{4}{3}$ **b** 0.

7. For the line with equation $y = \frac{3}{4}x + 2$:

   a find the gradient and the y-intercept, and hence

   b sketch the graph.

8. Find the gradient of the line with equation $5x - 2y = 12$.

9. For the line alongside, find:

   a the gradient

   b the y-intercept

   c the equation of the line.

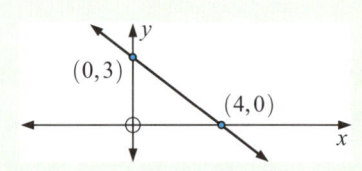

10. Find:

    a the gradient of the line shown

    b the equation connecting the variables.

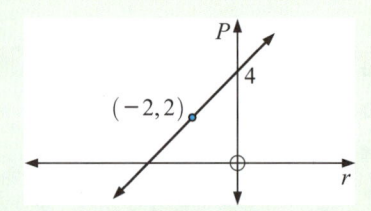

11. Determine whether the point $(1, 2)$ lies on the line with equation $y = 3x - 5$.

Chapter 14

Simultaneous equations

Contents:
- **A** Trial and error solution
- **B** Graphical solution
- **C** Solution by substitution
- **D** Solution by elimination
- **E** Problem solving with simultaneous equations

OPENING PROBLEM

The graph alongside shows the straight lines with equations $x + y = 4$ and $x - 2y = -2$. How can we find the point where the graphs meet?

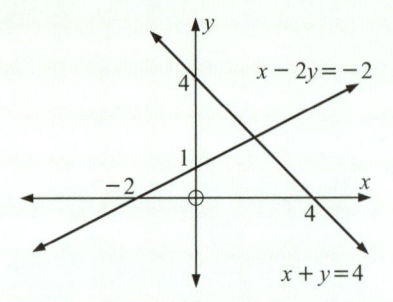

In the **Opening Problem** we have **two equations** involving the **two variables** x and y.

From the graph we can see the lines meet in exactly one point. This means there is exactly one solution for x and y which satisfies *both* equations.

In this chapter we discuss how to solve two equations **simultaneously**, which means at the same time.

For the **Opening Problem**, we say that $\begin{cases} x + y = 4 \\ x - 2y = -2 \end{cases}$ are simultaneous equations in the two unknowns x and y.

Sometimes this is referred to as a **2 × 2 system** of 2 equations in 2 unknowns.

We will examine four different methods of solution for simultaneous equations:

- **trial and error** solution
- **graphical** solution
- solution by **substitution**
- solution by **elimination**

A   TRIAL AND ERROR SOLUTION

Example 1

Solve the system of equations $\begin{cases} x + y = 4 \\ x - 2y = -2 \end{cases}$ simultaneously by trial and error.

Hence find where the graphs of these equations meet.

From the graph, we know the x-coordinate of the point of intersection must lie between 0 and 4. We also know that x and y obey the rule $x + y = 4$. We construct a table of values for $x = 0, 1, 2, 3$ or 4:

x	y	$x+y$	$x-2y$
0	4	4	-8
1	3	4	-5
2	2	4	-2
3	1	4	1
4	0	4	3

We see that when $x = 2$ and $y = 2$, $x + y = 4$ and $x - 2y = -2$.
So, the graphs meet at the point $(2, 2)$.

EXERCISE 14A

1 By completing a table, find integers x and y which simultaneously satisfy:

  a $x + y = 4$ **b** $x + y = 11$ **c** $y = x + 2$ **d** $y = 6 + x$
      $3x + 5y = 14$ $4x + 3y = 40$ $9x - 4y = 7$ $8x - 3y = -3$

2 You are given a possible solution for each pair of simultaneous equations. Check whether the solution is correct.

  a $x - y = 3$ $\{x = 5,\ y = 2\}$ **b** $x + y = 9$ $\{x = 5,\ y = 4\}$
      $2x + y = 11$ $2x - y = 6$

  c $a + b = 2$ $\{a = 5,\ b = -3\}$ **d** $2p + q = 7$ $\{p = 4,\ q = -1\}$
      $a - b = 8$ $3p + 2q = 10$

3 Find by *trial and error* the simultaneous solution of the following equation pairs, given that the solutions are integers.

  a $x + y = 4$ **b** $x + y = 6$ **c** $a - b = 1$ **d** $p - q = 3$
      $2x - y = 5$ $2x + y = 10$ $2a + 3b = 2$ $5p + 2q = 29$

B   GRAPHICAL SOLUTION

The graphs of any two straight lines which are not parallel will meet somewhere. The point where they meet is called the **point of intersection**.

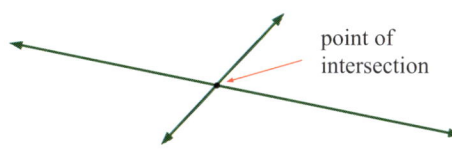

The point of intersection is the only point common to both lines.

The point of intersection corresponds to the **simultaneous solution** of **both equations**.

Example 2   ◀) Self Tutor

Find the point of intersection of the lines with equations $y = 2x + 5$ and $y = -x - 1$.

For $y = 2x + 5$:   when $x = 0$, $y = 5$
                    when $y = 0$, $2x + 5 = 0$
                                  $\therefore\ 2x = -5$
                                  $\therefore\ x = -\tfrac{5}{2}$
So, $(0, 5)$ and $(-\tfrac{5}{2}, 0)$ lie on it.

For $y = -x - 1$:   when $x = 0$, $y = -1$
                     when $y = 0$, $-x - 1 = 0$
                                   $\therefore\ -x = 1$
                                   $\therefore\ x = -1$
So, $(0, -1)$ and $(-1, 0)$ lie on it.

$\therefore$ the graphs meet at the point $(-2, 1)$.

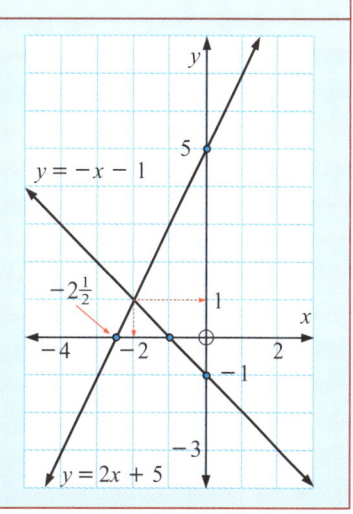

Not all line pairs meet at one point. Two other situations could occur, both resulting from the lines being parallel.

These are:

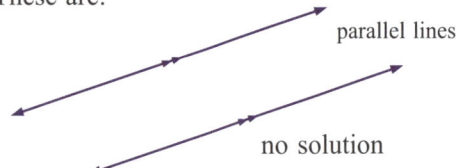

parallel lines

no solution

coincident lines

infinitely many solutions.

EXERCISE 14B

1 Find the point of intersection of the following pairs of lines by drawing the graphs of the two lines on the same set of axes:

a $y = x$
$y = 2 - x$

b $y = x + 3$
$y = -2x$

c $y = 3x + 2$
$y = x - 4$

d $y = -2x + 3$
$y = 5 - x$

e $y = 2 - 3x$
$y = x - 2$

f $y = 3x + 4$
$y = 2x + 1$

2 Find the simultaneous solution of the following pairs of equations using graphical methods:

a $y = x + 1$
$y = 2x - 3$

b $y = x + 4$
$y = -x + 2$

c $y = x + 2$
$y = -2x + 5$

d $y = 2x - 2$
$y = 1 - x$

e $y = 3x - 1$
$y = 2x - 2$

f $y = -2x + 3$
$y = x + 6$

3 Graph the following pairs of lines to find how many solutions these simultaneous equations have:

a $y = 2x + 3$
$y = 2x - 2$

b $x + y = 2$
$2x + 2y = 4$ Give reasons for your answers.

4 Explain when solving simultaneous equations by 'trial and error' and by 'graphing' would be inadequate.

C   SOLUTION BY SUBSTITUTION

Solution by **substitution** is an algebraic method used to solve simultaneous equations. This method is used when one of the variables is given in terms of the other.

For example, if one of the equations is $y = 2x - 1$, then y is given in terms of x and we say that y is the **subject** of the equation.

Example 3   ◀) Self Tutor

Find the simultaneous solution of the following pair of equations:
$y = 2x - 1$, $y = x + 3$

If $y = 2x - 1$ and $y = x + 3$, then

$2x - 1 = x + 3$ {equating ys}

$\therefore\ 2x - 1 - x = x + 3 - x$ {subtracting x from both sides}

$\therefore\ x - 1 = 3$ {simplifying}

$\therefore\ x = 4$ {adding 1 to both sides}

and so $y = 4 + 3$ {using $y = x + 3$}

$\therefore\ y = 7$

So, the simultaneous solution is $x = 4$ and $y = 7$.

(*Check:* In $y = 2x - 1$, $y = 2 \times 4 - 1 = 8 - 1 = 7$ ✓)

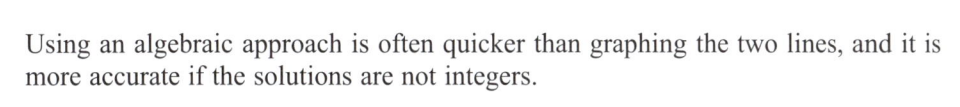

Always check your solution in both equations.

Using an algebraic approach is often quicker than graphing the two lines, and it is more accurate if the solutions are not integers.

EXERCISE 14C

1 Find the simultaneous solution of the following pairs of equations using an algebraic method:

a $y = x + 1$
$y = 2x - 3$

b $y = x + 4$
$y = -x + 2$

c $y = x + 2$
$y = -2x + 5$

d $y = -2x - 4$
$y = x - 4$

e $y = -x + 4$
$y = 2x - 8$

f $y = 2x + 3$
$y = 2x - 2$

g $y = 3x + 7$
$y = -x - 6$

h $y = -2x + 3$
$y = -2x + 6$

i $y = 5 - 3x$
$y = 10 - 6x$

Example 4 ◀) Self Tutor

Solve simultaneously by substitution: $y = 2x + 3$
$3x - 4y = 8$

$y = 2x + 3$ ...... (1)
$3x - 4y = 8$ ...... (2)

Substituting (1) into (2) gives $3x - 4(2x + 3) = 8$

$\therefore\ 3x - 8x - 12 = 8$

$\therefore\ -5x - 12 = 8$

$\therefore\ -5x = 20$

$\therefore\ x = -4$

Substituting $x = -4$ into (1) gives $y = 2(-4) + 3$

$\therefore\ y = -8 + 3$

$\therefore\ y = -5$

$\therefore\ $ the solution is $x = -4$, $y = -5$.

In equation (1) y is given in terms of x, so we substitute this into (2).

2 Use the method of substitution to solve:

- **a** $x = 1 + 2y$
  $2x + y = 17$
- **b** $y + 4x = 6$
  $y = 2x + 3$
- **c** $x = 2y - 6$
  $2x + y = 8$
- **d** $3x - 2y = 5$
  $y = 3 - 4x$
- **e** $x = 1 - 2y$
  $3x + y = 13$
- **f** $x = 3y + 12$
  $3x - 2y = 8$
- **g** $y = 3x - 2$
  $2x - 5y = 27$
- **h** $x = 4y - 1$
  $3x + 4y = -1$
- **i** $y = 5x + 7$
  $2x - 3y = 8$

Example 5   Self Tutor

Find the point of intersection of the two lines $y = 2x + 5$ and $y = -x - 1$.

The lines meet when

$2x + 5 = -x - 1$ {equating ys}
$\therefore \ 2x + 5 + x = -x - 1 + x$ {adding x to both sides}
$\therefore \ 3x + 5 = -1$
$\therefore \ 3x + 5 - 5 = -1 - 5$ {subtracting 5 from both sides}
$\therefore \ 3x = -6$ {collecting like terms}
$\therefore \ x = -2$ {divide both sides by 3}

Thus, $y = 2 \times (-2) + 5$ {using $y = 2x + 5$}
$\therefore \ y = -4 + 5$
$\therefore \ y = 1$ So, the lines meet at $(-2, 1)$.

3 Use substitution to find the point of intersection of the following lines:

- **a** $y = 2x + 3$
  $y = x + 5$
- **b** $y = x - 3$
  $y = 3x + 1$
- **c** $y = 2 - x$
  $2x + y = -1$
- **d** $y = 3x + 2$
  $3x + 7y = -10$
- **e** $y = 2x - 5$
  $3x + y = 7$
- **f** $4x + 7y = 10$
  $y = 5 - 3x$

D   SOLUTION BY ELIMINATION

Solution by **elimination** is used to solve simultaneous equations such as
$\begin{cases} 3x + 2y = -2 \\ 5x - y = 27 \end{cases}$ where neither variable is given as the subject of an equation.

However, if we make the coefficients of one of the variables equal in size but opposite in sign, we can add the equations to eliminate that variable. To do this we multiply both sides of one of the equations by an appropriate constant.

There is always a choice whether we wish to eliminate x or y. However, our choice is usually determined by the ease of eliminating one of the variables.

Example 6

Solve $\begin{array}{l} 3x + 2y = -2 \\ 5x - y = 27 \end{array}$ using the method of elimination.

$3x + 2y = -2$ ...... (1)
$5x - y = 27$ ...... (2)

Multiplying both sides of (2) by 2 gives $\quad 3x + 2y = -2$
$ 10x - 2y = 54$
$ \text{adding} \quad 13x = 52$
$ \therefore \quad x = 4$

Always check that your solutions are correct.

Substituting $x = 4$ into (1),
$\quad 3(4) + 2y = -2$
$\therefore \quad 12 + 2y = -2$
$\therefore \quad 2y = -14$
$\therefore \quad y = -7 \quad$ Hence $x = 4$, $y = -7$ is the solution.

Check: In (1), $3x + 2y = 3(4) + 2(-7)$
$ = 12 - 14$
$ = -2 \checkmark$

In (2), $\quad 5x - y = 5(4) - (-7)$
$ = 20 + 7$
$ = 27 \checkmark$

Sometimes it is easier to eliminate a variable if we multiply both of the equations by different constants.

Example 7

Solve simultaneously, by elimination: $\begin{array}{l} 5x + 3y = 12 \\ 7x + 2y = 19 \end{array}$

$5x + 3y = 12$ ...... (1)
$7x + 2y = 19$ ...... (2)

We multiply (1) by 2 and (2) by -3:
$ 10x + 6y = 24$
$ -21x - 6y = -57$
$ \text{adding} \quad -11x = -33$
$ \therefore \quad x = 3$

Substituting $x = 3$ into (1), $\quad 5(3) + 3y = 12$
$ \therefore \quad 15 + 3y = 12$
$ \therefore \quad 3y = -3$
$ \therefore \quad y = -1 \quad$ Hence $x = 3$, $y = -1$.

EXERCISE 14D

1 What equation results when:

- **a** $2x - 3y = 5$ is multiplied by 2
- **b** $x + 3y = 7$ is multiplied by -3
- **c** $2x + 5y = 1$ is multiplied by 4
- **d** $3x - 2y = 8$ is multiplied by -2
- **e** $5x - y = 2$ is multiplied by 5
- **f** $-2x + 5y = -1$ is multiplied by -1?

2 What equation results when the following are added vertically?

- **a** $3x + 2y = 6$
  $x - 2y = 10$
- **b** $3x - y = 8$
  $2x + y = 7$
- **c** $x + y = 5$
  $x - y = 7$
- **d** $3x - y = 4$
  $-3x + 4y = 2$
- **e** $5x - y = 6$
  $-5x + 3y = -8$
- **f** $-8x + 2y = 11$
  $8x - 3y = -7$

3 Solve the following simultaneously using the method of elimination:

- **a** $3x + y = 13$
  $x - y = 3$
- **b** $2x - y = 8$
  $3x + y = 7$
- **c** $x + 3y = 13$
  $-x + y = 7$
- **d** $5x + 2y = -19$
  $3x - 4y = -1$
- **e** $2x + 3y = 11$
  $7x - y = 50$
- **f** $2x + y = 1$
  $x + 3y = -12$
- **g** $4x + y = 19$
  $3x + 4y = -2$
- **h** $7x + 2y = -5$
  $3x - 5y = -49$
- **i** $6x + 5y = -2$
  $3x - y = 13$
- **j** $4x - 3y = 12$
  $-x + 5y = -3$
- **k** $3x + 2y = 7$
  $8x + 7y = 12$
- **l** $3x + 7y = 47$
  $7x + 3y = 43$
- **m** $2x + 7y = -51$
  $3x - 2y = 11$
- **n** $3x + y = 17$
  $2x - y = 23$
- **o** $2x - 3y = 14$
  $5x - 7y = 34$

INVESTIGATION — FINDING WHERE GRAPHS MEET

Click on the icon to run a graphing package.

Type in $y = 3x + 2$ and click on PLOT.

Now type in $y = 5 - x$ and click on PLOT.

GRAPHING PACKAGE

Now click on Intersect. Move the cursor near the point of intersection and click again.

Your answer should be $(\frac{3}{4}, 4\frac{1}{4})$. For a fresh start click on CLEAR ALL.

What to do:

1 Show that the point of intersection of $y = 2x + 1$ and $y = 7 - 5x$ is at about $(0.857, 2.714)$.

2 Type in $2x + 3y = 5$ and plot it. Then type in $3x - 4y = 10$ and plot it. Find the point of intersection of the two lines.

3 Use the graphing package to solve these simultaneously:

- **a** $2x + 3y = 10$
  $5x + 7y = -4$
- **b** $3x + 7y = 38$
  $4x + 11y = 56$
- **c** $3x - 8y = 49$
  $4x - 17y = 8$

E PROBLEM SOLVING WITH SIMULTANEOUS EQUATIONS

In this section we deal with problems given in sentences. We need to interpret the information and use it to write two equations in two unknowns. Once we have solved them we need to describe what the solution means in terms of the problem.

Example 8

Two numbers have a sum of 30 and a difference of 5. Find the numbers.

Let x and y be the unknown numbers, with $x > y$.

So, $x + y = 30$ ...... (1) {'sum' means add}
and $x - y = 5$ ...... (2) {'difference' means subtract}

adding $2x = 35$
$\therefore x = 17\frac{1}{2}$

Substituting into (1), $17\frac{1}{2} + y = 30$ Check: $17\frac{1}{2} + 12\frac{1}{2} = 30$ ✓
$\therefore y = 12\frac{1}{2}$ $17\frac{1}{2} - 12\frac{1}{2} = 5$ ✓

The numbers are $17\frac{1}{2}$ and $12\frac{1}{2}$.

EXERCISE 14E

1 Two numbers have a sum of 200 and a difference of 37. Find the numbers.

2 The difference between two numbers is 84 and their sum is 278. What are the numbers?

3 One number exceeds another by 11. The sum of the two numbers is 5. What are the numbers?

4 The larger of two numbers is four times the smaller and their sum is 85. Find the two numbers.

5 Find two integers such that three times the smaller is 33 more than twice the larger, and twice the smaller plus five times the larger equals 250.

Example 9

At a clearance sale all CDs are sold for one price and all DVDs are sold for another price.
Marisa bought 3 CDs and 2 DVDs for a total of $34.50, and Nico bought 2 CDs and 5 DVDs for a total of $56.

Find the cost of each item.

Let x cents be the cost of one CD and y cents be the cost of one DVD.

3 CDs and 2 DVDs cost $34.50, so $3x + 2y = 3450$ ...... (1)
2 CDs and 5 DVDs cost $56, so $2x + 5y = 5600$ ...... (2)

We will eliminate x by multiplying equation (1) by 2 and equation (2) by -3.

$$\therefore \quad 6x + 4y = 6900$$
$$-6x - 15y = -16\,800$$

adding $\quad -11y = -9900$

$$\therefore \quad y = 900$$

Substituting in equation (1) gives $\quad 3x + 2 \times 900 = 3450$

$$\therefore \quad 3x + 1800 = 3450$$
$$\therefore \quad 3x = 1650$$
$$\therefore \quad x = 550$$

So, the cost of one CD is $5.50 and the cost of one DVD is $9.

6 Two hammers and a screwdriver cost a total of $34. A hammer and 3 screwdrivers cost a total of $32. Find the price of each type of tool.

7 Four adults and three children go to a theatre for £74, whereas two adults and five children are charged £58. Find the price of an adult's ticket and a child's ticket.

8 Three blankets and a sheet cost me RM190. Two sheets and a blanket cost a total of RM100. Find the cost of one blanket and one sheet.

9 Seven peaches plus eight nashi cost me ¥273 altogether. However, three peaches and one nashi cost a total of ¥66. Find the cost of one piece of each fruit.

10 A purse contains $3.75 in 5 cent and 20 cent coins. If there are 33 coins altogether, how many of each type of coin are in the purse?

Example 10

A carpenter makes cabinets and desks. Each cabinet has 2 doors and 3 drawers, and each desk has 1 door and 5 drawers, the same as are used for the cabinets. The carpenter has 41 doors and 100 drawers available. How many of each item of furniture should he make to use his entire supply of doors and drawers?

Suppose the carpenter makes x cabinets and y desks.

$\therefore \quad 2x + y = 41$ ...... (1) {total number of doors}

$3x + 5y = 100$ ...... (2) {total number of drawers}

Item	Number	Doors	Drawers
Cabinet	x	$2x$	$3x$
Desk	y	y	$5y$
Total		41	100

Multiplying (1) by -5 gives $\quad -10x - 5y = -205$

$$3x + 5y = 100$$

adding $\quad -7x \quad = -105$

$$\therefore \quad x = 15 \quad \text{\{dividing both sides by } -7\text{\}}$$

Substitituting $x = 15$ into (1) gives $2 \times 15 + y = 41$
$$\therefore \quad 30 + y = 41$$
$$\therefore \quad y = 11$$
So, the carpenter should make 15 cabinets and 11 desks.

Example 11

◀)) **Self Tutor**

An equilateral triangle has sides of length $(3x - y)$ cm, $(x + 5)$ cm and $(y + 3)$ cm. Find the length of each side.

The sides of an equilateral triangle are equal.
$$\therefore \quad 3x - y = y + 3$$
$$\therefore \quad 3x - 2y = 3 \quad \ldots\ldots \text{ (1)} \quad \{\text{subtracting } y \text{ from both sides}\}$$
Also $\quad 3x - y = x + 5$
$$\therefore \quad 2x - y = 5 \quad \ldots\ldots \text{ (2)} \quad \{\text{subtracting } x \text{ from both sides}\}$$

$$\quad\quad\quad\quad\quad 3x - 2y = 3$$
Multiplying (2) by $-2 \quad -4x + 2y = -10$
adding $\quad\quad\quad -x \quad\quad = -7$
$$\therefore \quad x = 7$$

Substituting in (1) $\quad 3(7) - 2y = 3$
$$\therefore \quad 21 - 2y = 3$$
$$\therefore \quad -2y = -18$$
$$\therefore \quad y = 9$$

$3x - y = 21 - 9 = 12$, $\quad x + 5 = 7 + 5 = 12 \quad$ and $\quad y + 3 = 9 + 3 = 12$
$\therefore$ the sides are 12 cm long.

11 A yard contains rabbits and pheasants only. There are 35 heads and 98 feet in the yard. How many rabbits and pheasants does the yard contain?

12 Milk is sold in one litre and two litre cartons. A delicatessen owner orders 120 litres of milk and receives 97 cartons. How many of each type did she receive?

13 The figure alongside is a rectangle. Find x and y.

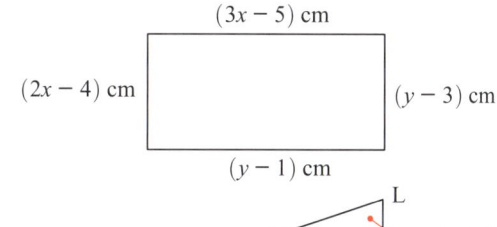

$(3x - 5)$ cm
$(2x - 4)$ cm
$(y - 3)$ cm
$(y - 1)$ cm

14 KLM is an isosceles triangle. Find x and y and hence find the measure of the angle at K.

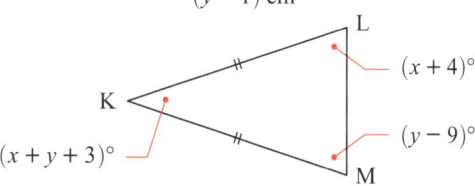

$(x + 4)°$
$(y - 9)°$
$(x + y + 3)°$

15 Twelve years ago Jane was five times as old as Anne. In three years' time Anne will be half Jane's age. How old is each girl at the moment?

16 Nine years ago a woman was three times as old as her son. In eight years from now the sum of their ages will be 78. How old are they today?

17 The weekly wages of Sam and Ben are in the ratio of $2:1$. Their living costs are in the ratio of $9:4$. If each saves $100 per week, find their weekly incomes.

REVIEW SET 14A

1 On the same set of axes draw accurate graphs of the lines with equations $y = 2x - 1$ and $y = x - 2$.
From your graphs, find the simultaneous solution of $\quad y = 2x - 1$
$\qquad\qquad\qquad\qquad\qquad\qquad\qquad\qquad\qquad\qquad\qquad\quad y = x - 2$

2 Solve by substitution: $\quad y = 2x - 3$
$\qquad\qquad\qquad\qquad\qquad 3x - 2y = 4$

3 Solve by elimination: $\quad 3x + 2y = 3$
$\qquad\qquad\qquad\qquad\qquad 5x + 3y = 4$

4 Solve the following problems:

a Two pencils and a ruler cost 49 cents in total. One pencil and two rulers cost 62 cents in total. Find the cost of each item.

b I have only 2 cent and 5 cent coins. The total number of coins is 25, and their total value is 92 cents. How many of each coin do I have?

REVIEW SET 14B

1 On the same set of axes draw accurate graphs of the lines with equations $y = 2x - 3$ and $y = 2 - 3x$.

a Use your graph to solve simultaneously: $\quad y = 2x - 3$
$\qquad\qquad\qquad\qquad\qquad\qquad\qquad\qquad\qquad y = 2 - 3x$

b Check your answer to **a** by substitution.

2 Find the simultaneous solution of $y + 3x = 16$ and $y = 2x - 4$ using the substitution method.

3 Use elimination to solve: $\quad y = 2x + 1$
$\qquad\qquad\qquad\qquad\qquad\quad y = -x - 5$

Do the lines with equations $y = 2x + 1$, $y = -x - 5$ and $y = -3x - 9$ meet at a common point of intersection?

4 Solve the following problems:

a John is two years older than Paula. Three times John's age plus four times Paula's age is 55 years. How old are John and Paula?

b A baker's basket contains bread rolls and sandwich loaves. The loaves weigh 750 g and the rolls 150 g. The total number of loaves and rolls is 16 and their total weight is 6 kg. How many rolls and how many loaves are in the basket?

Chapter 15

Estimating probabilities

Contents:
- **A** Probability by experiment
- **B** Probabilities from tabled data
- **C** Probabilities from two way tables
- **D** Chance investigations

OPENING PROBLEM

A triangular prism is made of plastic with the dimensions shown.

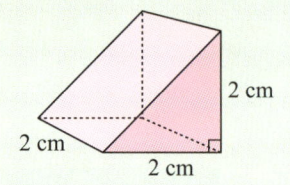

When it is thrown in the air it could come down and finish on:

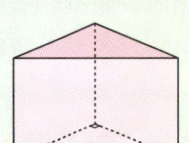

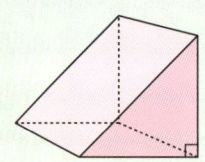

a **triangular face**   a **square face**   a **rectangular face**

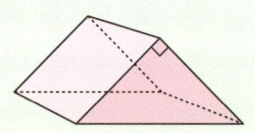

Things to think about:

- Which side do you think the prism is most likely to finish on?
- How can we estimate the probability of the prism ending up on a triangular face?
- How can the estimate be improved?

PROBABILITIES

The **probability** of an event happening is a measure of the likelihood or chance of it occurring.

Probabilities can be given as percentages from 0% to 100%, or as proper fractions or decimal numbers between 0 and 1.

An **impossible** event which has 0% chance of happening is assigned a probability of 0.
A **certain** event which has 100% chance of happening is assigned a probability of 1.
All other events are assigned a probability between 0 and 1.

The number line below shows how we could interpret different probabilities:

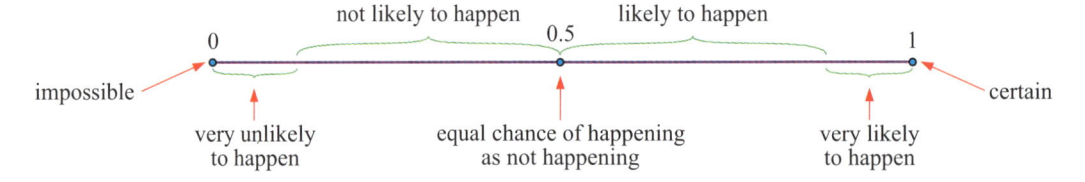

The assigning of probabilities is usually based on either:

- observing the results of an experiment (**experimental probability**),   or
- using arguments of symmetry (**theoretical probability**).

In general, the probability of an event occurring is

$$P(\text{event}) = \frac{\text{number of ways the event can happen}}{\text{total number of outcomes}}$$

HISTORICAL NOTE

A dispute between gamblers in the 17th Century led to the creation of a new branch of mathematics called **theoretical probability**.

Chevalier de Méré, a French aristocrat and a gambler, wanted to know the answer to this question:

"Should I bet even money on the occurrence of at least one 'double six' when rolling a pair of dice 24 times?"

De Méré's experience of playing this game convinced him that the answer was yes.

He asked two French mathematicians, **Blaise Pascal** and **Pierre de Fermat**, to prove that his theory was true.

Not only did they correctly argue the result, but they became interested in solving other questions of this kind.

A PROBABILITY BY EXPERIMENT

The probabilities for some events can only be found by experimentation.

Here are some words and phrases which we need to understand:

- The **number of trials** is the total number of times the experiment is repeated.
- The **outcomes** are the different results possible for one trial of the experiment.
- The **frequency** of a particular outcome is the number of times that this outcome is observed.
- The **relative frequency** of an outcome is the frequency of that outcome divided by the total number of trials.

The more times an experiment is repeated, the better the estimate of the probability of the event.

EXPERIMENTAL PROBABILITY

Consider the **Opening Problem** again. A prism was made in this exact shape and was thrown in the air 200 times.

The results were: Rectangular 77,   Square 85   and   Triangular 38

We say that:

- the number of trials was 200
- the possible outcomes were   Rectangular, Square or Triangular.
- the frequencies were 77 for Rectangular, 85 for Square and 38 for Triangular
- the relative frequencies were $\frac{77}{200}$ for Rectangular, $\frac{85}{200}$ for Square and $\frac{38}{200}$ for Triangular.

318   ESTIMATING PROBABILITIES   (Chapter 15)

We use the relative frequencies, usually written as decimals, to estimate the probabilities.

The **estimated experimental probability** is the relative frequency of the outcome.

We write: P(Rectangular) ≈ 0.385,   P(Square) ≈ 0.425   and   P(Triangular) ≈ 0.190

When the experiment was performed again the results for 250 repetitions were: Rectangular 90,   Square 112   and   Triangular 48.

This time   P(Rectangular) ≈ 0.360,   P(Square) ≈ 0.448,   P(Triangular) ≈ 0.192

DISCUSSION — EXPERIMENTAL RESULTS

Discuss:
- why the two repetitions of the experiment of the **Opening Problem** give different results and what this may be due to
- the ways these results may be combined.

Example 1

Find the experimental probability of:

a tossing a head with one toss of a coin if it falls tails 36 times in 80 tosses

b rolling a pair of sixes with a pair of dice given that when they were rolled 300 times a double six occurred 9 times.

a   P(a head)
   ≈ relative frequency of a head
   ≈ $\frac{36}{80}$
   ≈ 0.45

b   P(a double six)
   ≈ relative frequency of a double six
   ≈ $\frac{9}{300}$
   ≈ 0.03

EXERCISE 15A

1 Jacinta has been given an indoor golf hole to practice her putting. Out of her first 91 attempts to hit the ball into the hole, she succeeds 23 times. Find the experimental probability of Jacinta hitting the ball into the hole.

2 When John makes an error in his work he crushes the sheet of paper into a ball and throws it at the waste paper basket. At the end of the day he has scored 16 hits into the basket and 5 misses. Find the experimental probability that he scores a hit into the basket.

3 In the first round of a competition Sasha recorded 77 hits out of 80 shots at her target.

   a Use this result to estimate her chances of hitting the target.

   b On the next day in the final round of the competition she scored 105 hits out of 120 shots. Obtain the 'best' estimate of her hitting the target with any shot.

> Find the best estimate by adding the numbers of hits and dividing by the total number of shots.

4 Paulo catches a 7.45 am tram to school. During a period of 79 days he arrives at school on time on 53 occasions. Estimate the probability Paulo:

   a arrives on time   **b** arrives late.

5 A circular target has 8 sectors numbered 1 to 8. The sectors all have angle $45°$. The target rotates about its centre at high speed. When Max throws a dart into it 120 times, the dart hits the '8' sector 17 times. Find the experimental probability of hitting the '8' sector.

6 Don threw a tin can into the air 180 times. From these trials it landed on its side 137 times. Later that afternoon he threw the same tin can into the air 150 more times. It landed on its side 92 times.

   a Find the experimental probability of 'landing on the side' for both sets of trials.

   b List possible reasons for the differences in the results.

B   PROBABILITIES FROM TABLED DATA

When data is collected, it is often summarised and displayed in a frequency table. We can use such a table to help calculate probabilities.

Example 2

A marketing company surveys 50 randomly selected people to discover what brand of toothpaste they use. The results are in the table:

Brand	Frequency	Relative Frequency
Shine	10	0.20
Starbright	14	0.28
Brite	4	0.08
Clean	12	0.24
No Name	10	0.20

a Find the experimental probability that a community member uses:

   i Starbright   **ii** Clean.

b Would you classify the estimate of **a** to be very good, good, or poor? Why?

a   **i** Experimental P(Starbright) ≈ 0.28

    ii Experimental P(Clean) ≈ 0.24

b Poor, as the sample size is very small.

EXERCISE 15B

1 A street vendor is selling toffee apples. Some apples are red and others are green. On one day 247 toffee apples are sold.

Colour	Freq.	Rel. Freq.
Red	149	
Green		
Total		

   a Copy and complete the table.

   b Estimate the probability that the next customer buys:

     i a red toffee apple   **ii** a green toffee apple.

2 Three types of tickets are available for a concert. These are Adult, Pensioner and Child. All tickets were sold and a summary appears in the table.

Type	Freq.	Rel. Freq.
Adult	238	
Pensioner	143	
Child	119	
Total		

  a Copy and complete the table given.
  b How many seats does the theatre have?
  c If the seats are numbered and one number is chosen at random, find the probability that the person sitting at that seat is a child.
  d Is this an experimental probability?

3 A supermarket sells four fragrances of air freshener. During a period of a week it sells the numbers shown in the table opposite.

Fragrance	Freq.	Rel. Freq.
Rose	59	
Violet	72	
Lavender	81	
Woodland Breeze	104	
Total		

  a Copy and complete the table.
  b Estimate the probability that the next customer will buy:
  i Violet
  ii Rose or Woodland Breeze.

4 A small island country imports four models of cars which we will call A, B, C and D.

Model	Freq.	Rel. Freq.
A		0.25
B		0.35
C	40	
D		0.275
Total		

  a Copy and complete the given table.
  b Estimate the probability that the next car which passes the town hall is model:
  i C **ii** C or D.

C PROBABILITIES FROM TWO WAY TABLES

Sometimes data is categorised by not only one, but two variables, and the data is represented in a **two way table**. We can estimate probabilities from a two way table just as we do from a regular frequency table.

Example 3

60 students were randomly selected and asked whether they studied Physics and English.

		Physics		
		Yes	No	Total
English	Yes	15	12	
	No	13	20	
	Total			

  a Copy and complete the table by finding the total of each row and column.
  b What does the 13 in the table represent?
  c Estimate the probability that a randomly selected student who studies English also studies Physics.
  d Estimate the probability that a randomly selected student studies English but not Physics.

a

	Physics		
	Yes	No	Total
English Yes	15	12	27
English No	13	20	33
Total	28	32	60

b 13 of the selected students study Physics but do not study English.

c 27 students study English, 15 of whom also study Physics.

$\therefore$ P(randomly selected student who studies English also studies Physics) $\approx \frac{15}{27}$
≈ 0.556

d 12 out of the 60 students study English but not Physics.

$\therefore$ P(randomly selected student studies English but not Physics) $\approx \frac{12}{60} \approx 0.2$

Since the data only represents a sample of the population, the results are only **estimates** of the true probabilities. The larger the size of the sample, the more accurate the estimates will be.

EXERCISE 15C

1 Students at a high school were surveyed to determine whether they played a sport or a musical instrument.

a Copy and complete the table alongside.

b Estimate the probability that a randomly chosen student:

  i who plays sport does not play an instrument
  ii plays an instrument.

	Instrument		
	Yes	No	Total
Sport Yes	19	25	
Sport No	11	14	
Total			

2 A sample of adults were asked whether they had a driver's licence. The results were further categorised by gender as shown:

a Copy and complete the table alongside.

b Estimate the probability that a randomly chosen:

  i male has a driver's licence   **ii** female has a driver's licence.

c Which of the estimates in **b** is more likely to be accurate? Explain your answer.

	Gender		
	Male	Female	Total
Licence Yes	62	17	
Licence No	8	3	
Total			

3 At a supermarket, a taste-testing stall was set up to determine whether people could taste the difference between two brands of cola, A and B. 100 randomly selected shoppers were given either A or B, then asked to say what they were drinking.

a Copy and complete the table.

b Estimate the probability that a randomly selected shopper who is given:

  i A could correctly identify their drink.
  ii B could correctly identify their drink.

	Said		
	A	B	Total
Given A	38	12	
Given B	17	33	
Total			

4 100 randomly chosen members of an electorate are asked whether they will vote for the current mayor in the upcoming election. The results are categorised by age.

		Yes	Undecided	No	Total
Age	under 30	15	19	14	
	over 30	26	16	10	
	Total				

Vote

a Copy and complete the table.

b Estimate the probability that a randomly chosen person:
  i over 30 has decided to vote for the current mayor
  ii has decided not to vote for the current mayor
  iii is over 30 and is undecided
  iv under 30 has decided whether or not to vote for the current mayor.

D   CHANCE INVESTIGATIONS

When we perform experiments, the **relative frequency** of an outcome gives us an **estimate** for the **probability** of that outcome. The greater the number of trials, the more we can rely on our estimate of the probability.

The most commonly used equipment for experimental probability and games of chance are described below:

COINS

When a **coin** is tossed there are two possible sides that could show upwards: the *head* which is usually the head of a monarch, president, or leader, and the *tail* which is the other side of the coin. We expect a head (H) and a tail (T) to have equal chance of occurring, so we expect each to occur 50% of the time. So,

the probability of obtaining a head is $\frac{1}{2}$, and

the probability of obtaining a tail is $\frac{1}{2}$.

The table below shows actual experimental results obtained for tossing a coin:

Number of tosses	H	T	%H	%T
10	7	3	70.0	30.0
100	56	44	56.0	44.0
1000	491	509	49.1	50.9

each is nearly 50%

These experimental results support our expectations and suggest the general rule:

"The more times we repeat an experiment, the closer the results will be to the theoretical results we expect to obtain."

DICE

Dice is the plural of **die**.

The most commonly used dice are small cubes with the numbers 1, 2, 3, 4, 5 and 6 marked on them using dots. The numbers on the face of a cubic die are arranged such that the sum of each pair of opposite faces is seven.

SPINNERS

A simple **spinner** consists of a regular polygon or sometimes a circle with equal sectors. We place a toothpick or match through its centre.

Alongside is a square spinner. It shows a result of 1 since it has come to rest on the side marked 1.

A spinner such as that alongside may be used instead of a die, providing all angles are exactly $60°$.

The result shown is 2, since the pointer came to rest on the sector marked 2.

The **roulette wheel** is an example of a much more sophisticated spinner.

PLAYING CARDS

A standard deck of playing cards consists of 52 cards. There are 4 **suits**: hearts and diamonds (red), and spades and clubs (black).

Each suit contains 13 cards with face values Ace, 2, 3, 4, 5, 6, 7, 8, 9, 10, Jack, Queen, King.

Jacks, Queens and Kings are all called 'picture' cards.

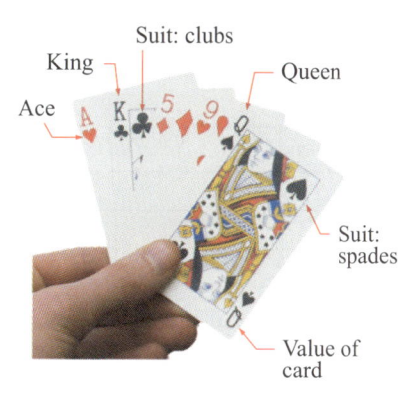

In the following investigations you use technology to run simulations of experiments. The use of technology enables us to gather vast numbers of results almost instantaneously, and in a form which is easy to recognise and interpret.

INVESTIGATION 1   ROLLING A PAIR OF DICE

You will need: 2 normal six-sided dice with numbers 1 to 6 on the faces.

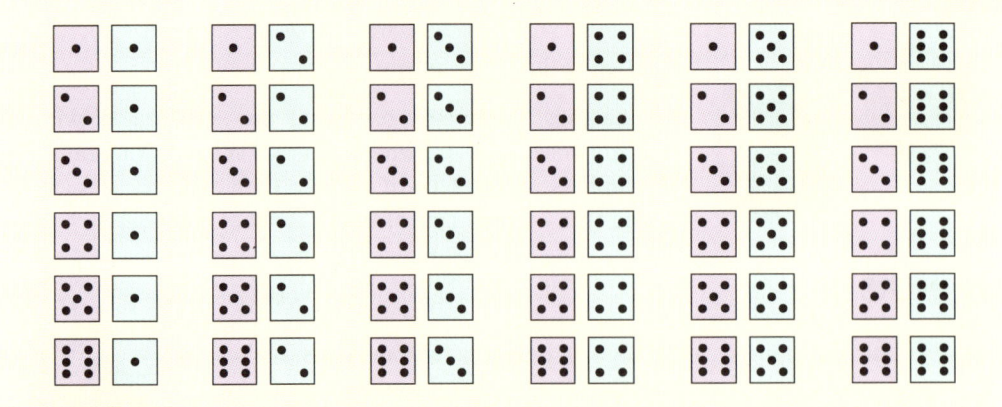

What to do:

1 The illustration shows that when two dice are rolled, there are 36 possible outcomes. Of these, {1, 3}, {2, 2} and {3, 1} give a sum of 4.

Copy and complete the table of expected or theoretical results:

Sum	2	3	4	5	...	12
Fraction of total			$\frac{3}{36}$			
Fraction as decimal			0.083			

2 If a pair of dice is rolled 360 times, how many of each result (2, 3, 4, ..., 12) would you expect to get? Extend your table by adding another row. Write your **expected frequencies** within it.

3 Toss the two dice 360 times. Record the *sum of the two numbers* for each toss using a table.

Sum	Tally	Frequency	Relative Frequency
2			
3			
4			
5			
⋮			
12			
Total		360	1

WORKSHEET

4 Pool as much data as you can with other students. Find the overall relative frequency of each *sum*.

5 Use the two dice simulation from the computer package on the CD to roll the pair of dice 10 000 times. Repeat this 10 times and on each occasion record your results in a table like that in **3**. Are your results consistent with your expectations?

SIMULATION

INVESTIGATION 2 — BLACKJACK

Blackjack is a game which uses playing cards. It is most commonly played in casinos.

In blackjack, each playing card is assigned a points value:

- cards 2 through to 10 are worth their face value, so 2s are worth 2 points, 3s are worth 3 points, and so on
- Jacks, Queens and Kings are worth 10 points
- Aces are worth 1 *or* 11 points, depending on which is better for the player.

Players are initially dealt two cards. They must then decide whether to accept additional cards in an attempt to obtain a total points value as close as possible to 21, without going over.

We will now find experimental probabilities for obtaining the various point scores possible from the initial 2 card deal.

What to do:

1 Shuffle a pack of cards, and draw the top two cards from the deck.

2 Calculate the sum of the points value of these two cards.
For example,
$\quad\quad = 5 + 8 = 13 \quad\quad = 10 + 4 = 14$

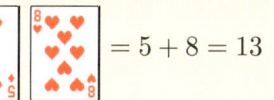

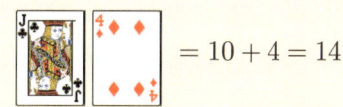

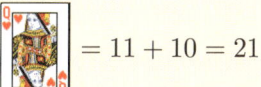

$\quad\quad = 11 + 10 = 21$

3 Return the cards to the pack.

4 Do this 200 times, recording your results in a table:

Sum	Tally	Frequency	Relative Frequency
4			
5			
6			
⋮			
21			
	Total	200	1

> Count aces as 11, except for 2 aces which is $11 + 1 = 12$ since $11 + 11 = 22$ and this is more than 21.

5 From your data, which point score occurs most frequently after the two card deal?

6 Use the simulation to repeat this process 10 000 times. Compare your results with those of the simulation.

INVESTIGATION 3 — CONCEALED NUMBER TICKETS

Many clubs have ticket machines which contain sets of consecutive numbers from 0001, 0002, 0003, ... up to 2000. These games are relatively inexpensive to play and are used as fund-raisers for the club.

Tickets are ejected from the machine at random at a cost of 50 cents each. A small cardboard cover is removed to reveal the concealed number.

Suppose a golf club can buy golf balls as prizes for $5.50 each and a set of 2000 tickets for the machine at $50. The club shows the following winners table:

Winning Numbers	Prize
777	4 golf balls
1000, 2000	2 golf balls
any multiple of 25	1 golf ball

What to do:

1 If all tickets are sold, how many balls are paid out as prizes?

2 Determine the total cost to the club for a complete round of 2000 tickets going through the machine.

3 What profit is made by the club?

4 If you purchase one ticket, what is your chance of winning at least one ball?

INVESTIGATION 4 — FURTHER SIMULATIONS

A INSTANT MONEY AND BINGO

Click on the icon to access this investigation.

WORKSHEET

B DICE GOLF

Over a long period of time, Joe noticed that on 'par 3' golf holes he scores a two, a three, a four or a five in the ratio 1 : 2 : 2 : 1.

Simulate Joe's golf scoring for par 3 holes using a die which has *two* on one face, *three* on two faces, *four* on two faces and *five* on one face.

What to do:

1 Roll the die 100 times to simulate Joe's next 100 par 3 hole scores.

2 Find Joe's average score per hole for the results in **1**.

3 **a** Find $\frac{1}{6} \times 2 + \frac{2}{6} \times 3 + \frac{2}{6} \times 4 + \frac{1}{6} \times 5$.

   b Explain the significance of this calculation.

   c How is this calculation related to **2**?

C MATHEMATICS COMPETITION

Click on the icon. This simulation tests your ability to select correct answers by guessing or by chance alone. Run the simulation several times.

SIMULATION

REVIEW SET 15A

1. A cube has 2 faces painted green and 4 faces painted red. When it is tossed 97 times, the uppermost face is green on 35 occasions. Find the experimental probability of the uppermost face being red.

2. In a large country hospital, 72 girls and 61 boys were born in a month.
   a. How many children were born in total?
   b. Estimate the probability that the next baby born at this hospital will be:
      i. a girl   ii. a boy.

3. A survey of three-child families was conducted and the following results obtained:
   a. How many families were surveyed?
   b. Copy and complete the table.
   c. Estimate the chance of a randomly selected 3-child family containing:
      i. 2 boys and 1 girl   ii. 3 girls.

Result	Frequency	Rel. Freq.
3 boys	21	
2 boys, 1 girl	62	
1 boy, 2 girls	55	
3 girls	18	
Total		

4. The year 8 students in a school were all given a maths test. After the test a sample of students were asked whether they studied for the test and whether they passed or failed.

	Test Pass	Test Fail	Total
Studied Yes	21	7	
Studied No	12	8	
Total			

   a. Copy and complete the table.
   b. If a year 8 student is chosen at random, estimate the probability that he or she:
      i. passed the test   ii. did not study and failed the test.
   c. If a student who studied for the test is selected at random, estimate the probability that he or she passed the test.

REVIEW SET 15B

1. A spinner is made using a regular pentagon, as shown. When the spinner was twirled 378 times it finished on red 72 times. Find the experimental probability of spinning a red.

2. Two coins are tossed many times and the number of heads recorded each time. The results are given in the table.
   a. Copy and complete the table.
   b. Use the data to estimate the probability that the result of the next toss will be:
      i. 2 heads   ii. at least 1 head.

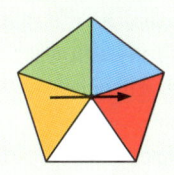

Result	Frequency	Rel. Freq.
2 heads	78	
1 head	149	
0 heads	73	
Total		

3 A marketing company was commissioned to investigate the types of cereal people preferred for breakfast. The results of the survey are shown below:

    a How many people were randomly selected in this survey?

    b Calculate the relative frequency of each brand of cereal.

    c Using the results of the survey, estimate the probability that a randomly selected person:

        i prefers Wheat Bites
        ii does not prefer Bran Snacks?

Brand	Freq.	Rel. Freq.
Wheat Bites	198	
Corn Crisps	115	
Rice Flakes	110	
Bran Snacks	77	
Total		

4 The table shows the number of students in a school with *fair hair* and *dark hair*.

    a Copy and complete the table.

    b How many students are there:

        i who are boys
        ii who have dark hair   **iii** in the school?

    c If a student is randomly chosen from this school, what is the probability that the student:

        i is a girl   **ii** has dark hair
        iii has fair hair, if we know that the student is a girl?

	Fair hair	Dark hair	Total
Boys	418	577	
Girls	327	638	
Total			

KARL FRIEDRICH GAUSS (1777-1855)

Karl Friedrich Gauss is one of the greatest mathematicians ever. As a young student he was interested in the study of languages and was in fact fluent in German, Latin, Greek, Sanskit, Russian and English. When he was only 3 years old he is believed to have corrected the wages of a team of bricklayers as calculated by his father.

It is written that Karl's mathematics teacher loved to set ridiculously long arithmetic sums as impositions for his students who misbehaved. On one occasion Karl and the other naughty boys were set the task of adding a long string of consecutive large whole numbers. Karl devised a simple method which enabled him to calculate such a sum within a few seconds.

His method for the sum $1 + 2 + 3 + 4 + 5 + 6 + \ldots + 98 + 99 + 100$, say, was to add the numbers in pairs. That is,

$$(1 + 99) + (2 + 98) + (3 + 97) + \ldots + (49 + 51) + 50 + 100$$
$$= 49 \times 100 + 100 + 50$$
$$= 5050$$

Needless to say, his teacher had to find other forms of punishment.

Chapter 16

Transformations, similarity and congruence

Contents:
- **A** Translations
- **B** Reflections and line symmetry
- **C** Rotations and rotational symmetry
- **D** Enlargements and reductions
- **E** Similar figures
- **F** Similar triangles
- **G** Areas and volumes of similar objects
- **H** Congruence of triangles

TRANSFORMATIONS, SIMILARITY AND CONGRUENCE (Chapter 16)

OPENING PROBLEM

Jacob makes conical tanks of different *sizes*, but all with the same *shape*. His smallest tank has a height of 2 m and a radius of 0.8 m. If he wants to manufacture another tank which is to have a base radius of 1 m, what will be the next tank's:

- height
- area of the top
- capacity?

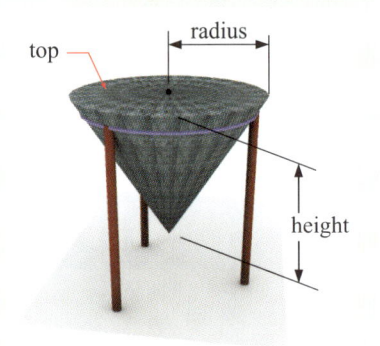

This chapter examines the geometrical ideas of transformations, similarity and congruence.

The transformations we consider are:
- translations
- reflections
- rotations
- enlargements and reductions

A   TRANSLATIONS

A **translation** of a figure occurs when every point on that figure is moved the same distance in the same direction.

For example,

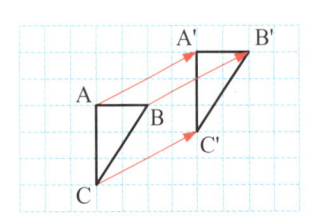

Triangle ABC is translated to a new position by sliding every point of ABC the same distance in the same direction. We call the new triangle A′B′C′.

We say, for example, that A is an **object point** and A′ is its **image**.

We can give details of a translation by using a **translation vector**. In the above example, each point has moved 4 units to the right and 2 units upwards.

The translation vector is therefore $\begin{pmatrix} 4 \\ 2 \end{pmatrix}$ ← horizontal step
← vertical step

Notice that A′B′C′ can be translated back to ABC using $\begin{pmatrix} -4 \\ -2 \end{pmatrix}$.

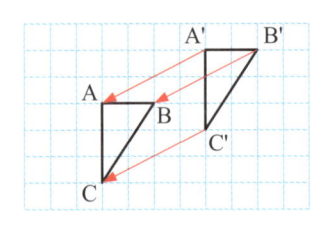

EXERCISE 16A

1 For the figures alongside, give the translation vector which maps:

- **a** A onto B
- **b** B onto A
- **c** B onto C
- **d** C onto B
- **e** D onto C
- **f** C onto D
- **g** B onto D
- **h** D onto B.

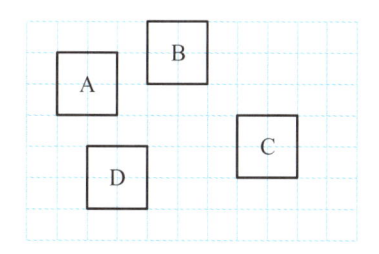

2 Copy these figures onto grid paper and translate using the given vector:

a $\begin{pmatrix} 4 \\ -2 \end{pmatrix}$ **b** $\begin{pmatrix} -3 \\ 2 \end{pmatrix}$ **c** $\begin{pmatrix} 0 \\ -3 \end{pmatrix}$

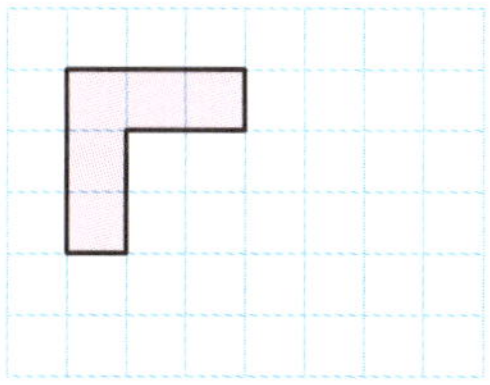

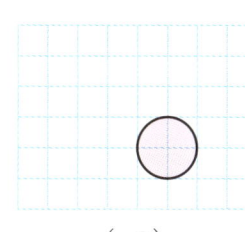

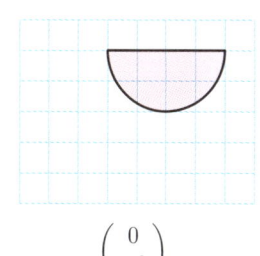

d $\begin{pmatrix} 4 \\ 0 \end{pmatrix}$ **e** $\begin{pmatrix} -2 \\ -4 \end{pmatrix}$ **f** $\begin{pmatrix} -3 \\ 3 \end{pmatrix}$

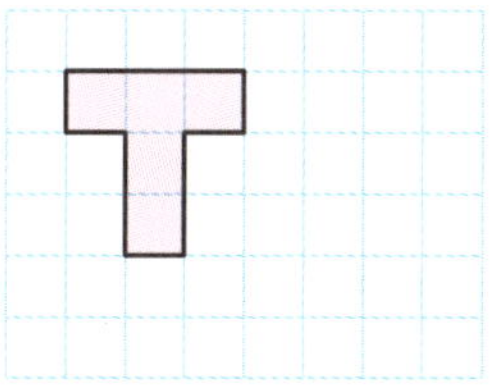

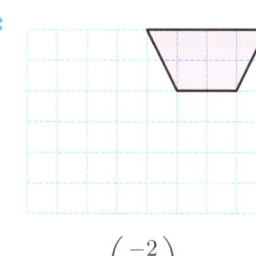

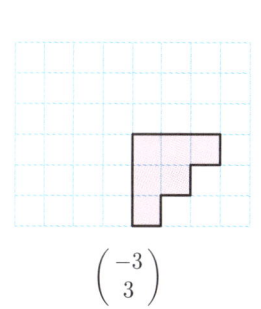

3 a What distances do the figures in question **2** move under their respective translations?

b What distance does a figure move under a translation of $\begin{pmatrix} a \\ b \end{pmatrix}$?

B REFLECTIONS AND LINE SYMMETRY

REFLECTIONS

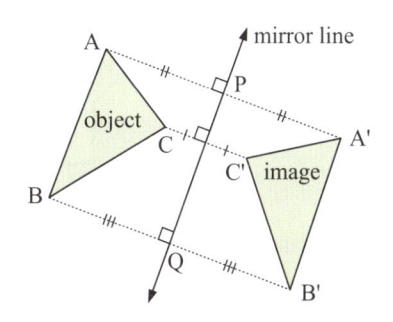

When a figure or **object** is reflected in a line to a new position, the resulting figure is called the **image**.
The image points are the same distance from the mirror line as the object points are from it.

AP = A'P',   BQ = B'Q',   and so on.

[AA'], [BB'], [CC'], and so on are always **perpendicular** to the mirror line.

332   TRANSFORMATIONS, SIMILARITY AND CONGRUENCE   (Chapter 16)

Example 1

Reflect this figure in the mirror line given.

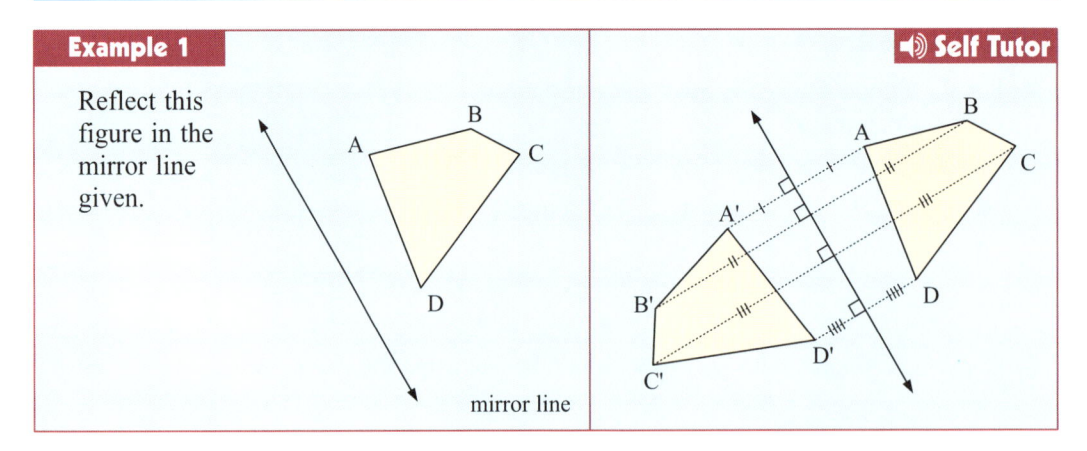

We can check our reflection drawings by placing a small mirror on the mirror line.

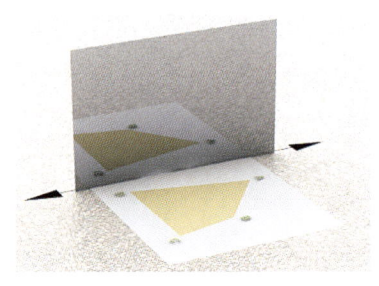

EXERCISE 16B.1

1   Draw the reflections of the following in the dashed mirror lines given:

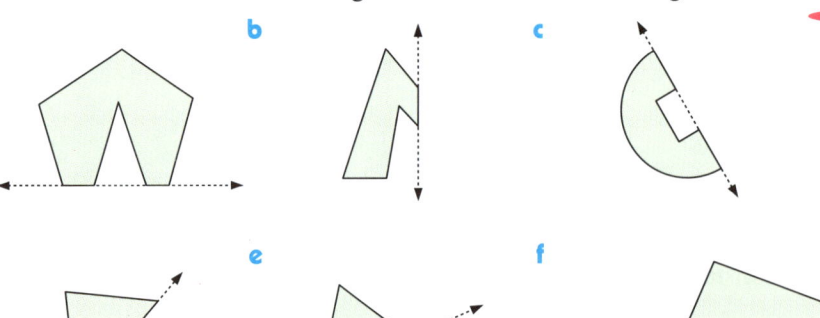

   a   b   c
   d   e   f

2   On grid paper, reflect these shapes in the given mirror lines:

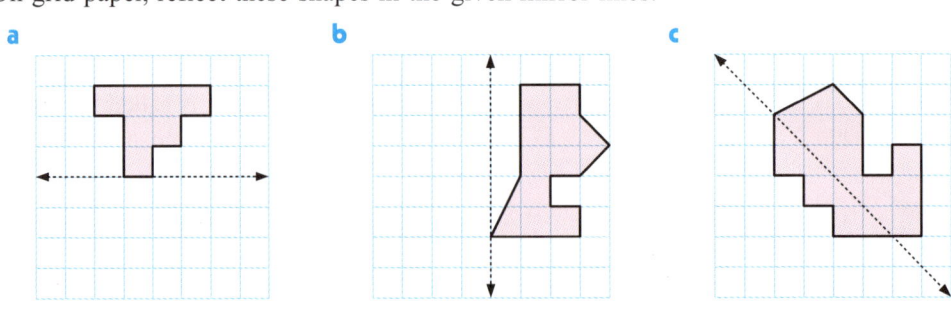

   a   b   c

LINE SYMMETRY

A shape has **line symmetry** if it can be folded on a line so that one half of the figure matches the other half exactly.

For example, a square has line symmetry.

In fact it has 4 lines of symmetry.

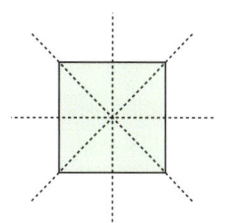

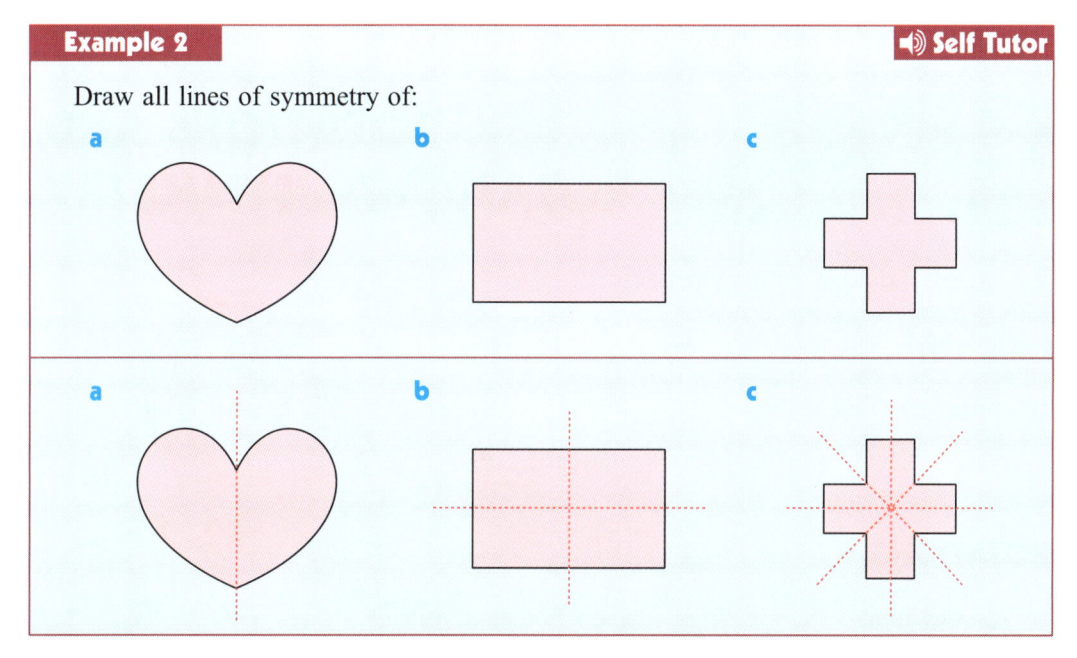

Example 2

Draw all lines of symmetry of:

a   b   c

a   b   c

EXERCISE 16B.2

1 Copy these figures and draw their lines of symmetry:

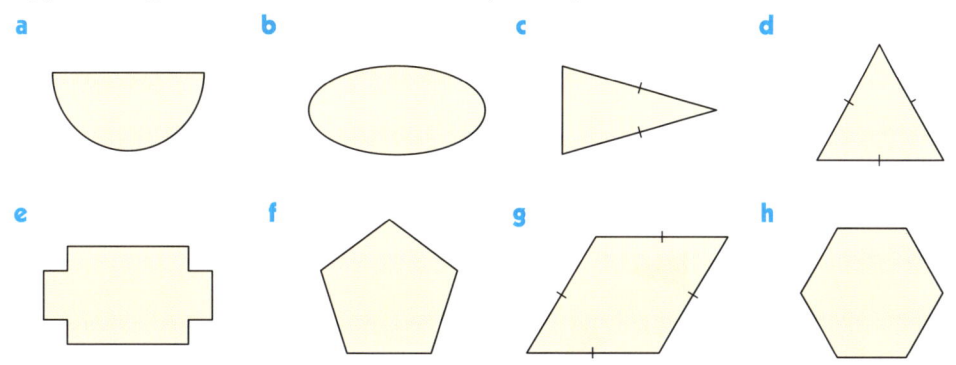

a   b   c   d

e   f   g   h

2 Draw and name a figure which has exactly 8 lines of symmetry.

3 Justin was convinced that the illustrated parallelogram has two lines of symmetry.
Draw the figure folded along [AC] to show Justin he is not correct.

4 **a** Can a parallelogram have:
  i 2 lines of symmetry **ii** 4 lines of symmetry?
  b Name a figure which has infinitely many lines of symmetry. Describe one of these lines.
  c How many lines of symmetry can a triangle have? Draw the different cases.
  d How many lines of symmetry can a quadrilateral have? Draw the different cases.

C ROTATIONS AND ROTATIONAL SYMMETRY

We are all familiar with objects which rotate, such as the hands of a clock, wheels, and propellers. We know that the earth rotates on its axis once every day.

ROTATIONS

A **rotation** turns a shape or figure about a point and through a given angle.
The point about which a figure rotates is called the **centre of rotation**. We often label this point O.

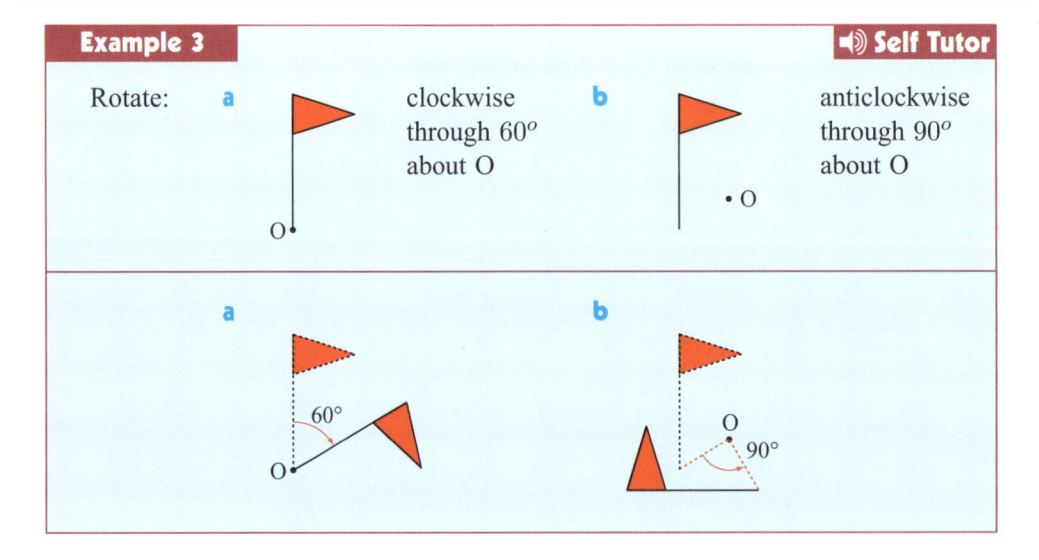

Example 3

Rotate: **a** clockwise through $60°$ about O **b** anticlockwise through $90°$ about O

EXERCISE 16C.1

1 Copy the figure and rotate it: 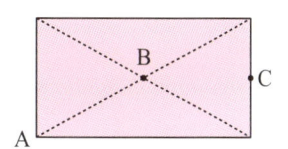
   a clockwise through 90° about A
   b clockwise through 90° about B
   c clockwise through 90° about C
   d anticlockwise through 180° about A
   e anticlockwise through 180° about B
   f anticlockwise through 180° about C.

2 Copy the figure and rotate it: 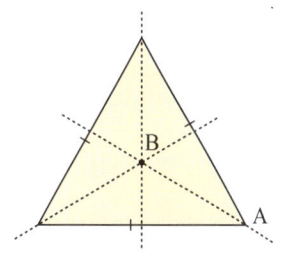
   a clockwise about A through 60°
   b anticlockwise about A through 120°
   c clockwise about B through 120°.

3 Copy each figure and rotate it clockwise about O through the given angle:

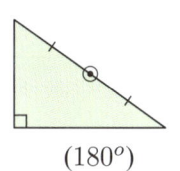

   a (90°)   b (180°)   c (180°)

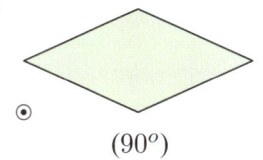

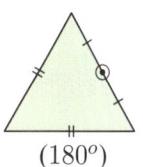

4 Rotate anticlockwise about O through 90°:

   a   b 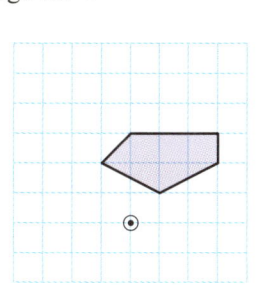   c

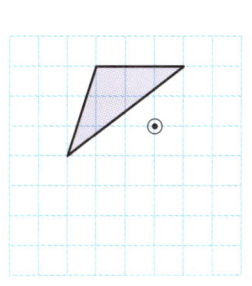

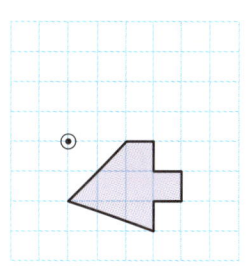

ROTATIONAL OR POINT SYMMETRY

A shape has **rotational symmetry** or **point symmetry** about a **point** if it can be rotated about that point through an angle **less than 360°** so that it maps onto itself.

For example, this propeller shape has rotational symmetry. If it is rotated about O through 180° then it will still look identical to how it did at the start.

Every shape will map onto itself under a 360° rotation, but this is not rotational symmetry.

The **order** of rotational symmetry is the number of times a shape maps onto itself during a complete $360°$ turn.

For example,

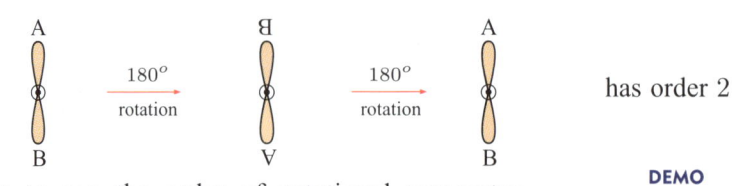

A ⟶ $180°$ rotation ⟶ B ⟶ $180°$ rotation ⟶ A   has order 2
B   V   B

Click on the icon to see the order of rotational symmetry demonstrated for an equilateral triangle.

DEMO

Example 4   ◀) Self Tutor

For each of these figures, find the centre of rotational symmetry O and the order of rotational symmetry.

a   (ellipse)   b   (4-pointed star)

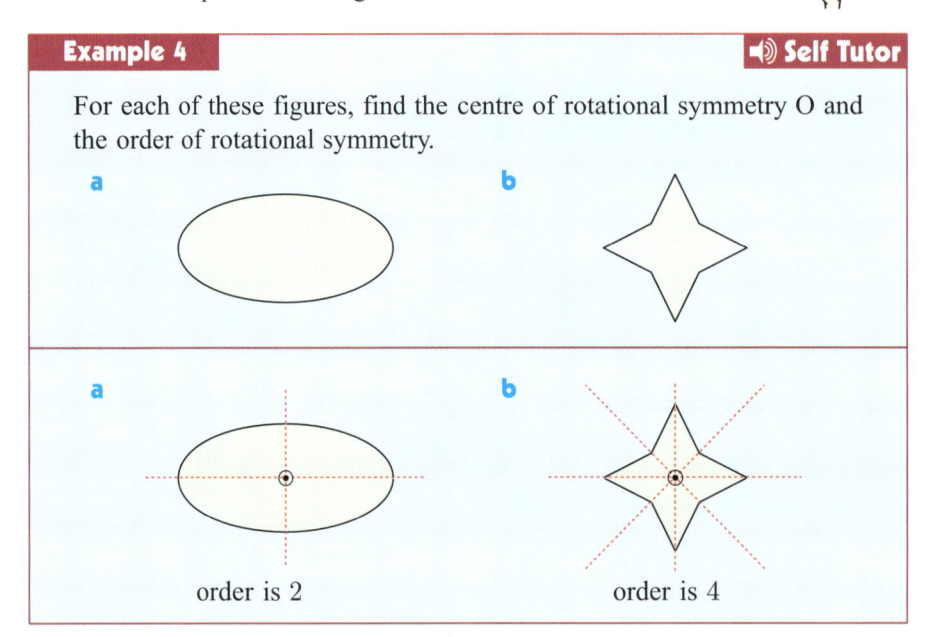

a   order is 2   b   order is 4

DISCUSSION

- Is there a connection between line symmetry and rotational symmetry?
- Does a figure need to have a line of symmetry in order to have rotational symmetry?
- If a figure has exactly one line of symmetry, can it have rotational symmetry?
- If a figure has more than one line of symmetry, will it have rotational symmetry? If so, what do the lines of symmetry tell us about the centre of rotation?

EXERCISE 16C.2

1 Find the centre of rotational symmetry in the following. Illustrate your answers.

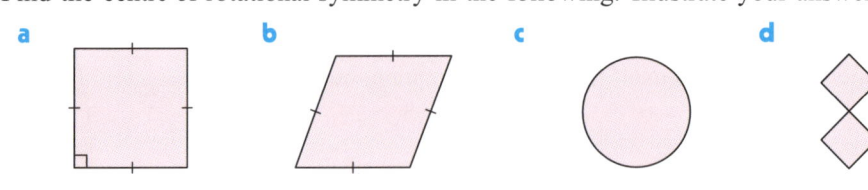

a (square)   b (parallelogram)   c (circle)   d (two diamonds)

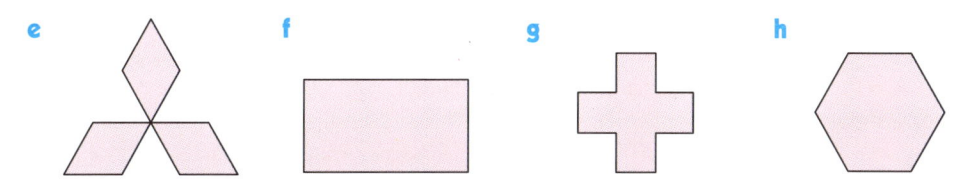

TRANSFORMATIONS, SIMILARITY AND CONGRUENCE (Chapter 16) 337

e **f** **g** **h**

2 Find the order of rotational symmetry for the figures in **1**.

3 Draw a figure which has order of rotational symmetry: **a** 5 **b** 8.

D ENLARGEMENTS AND REDUCTIONS

Consider the rectangles illustrated below. They are clearly not the same *size*, but they do have the same *shape*. Their side lengths are in the same proportions.

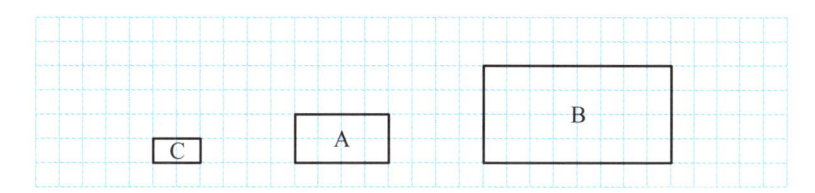

B is an **enlargement** of A and C is a **reduction** of A.

When A is enlarged to B, the lengths are *doubled*.
We say that the scale factor $k = 2$.

When A is reduced to C, the lengths are *halved*.
We say that the scale factor $k = \frac{1}{2}$.

If a scale factor is > 1, an **enlargement** occurs.
If a scale factor is < 1, a **reduction** occurs.

Example 5

Enlarge or reduce using a scale factor of:

a 2 **b** $\frac{1}{2}$.

a

b

EXERCISE 16D

1 If A is the object and B is the image, state whether each of the following is an enlargement or a reduction:

a   **b** 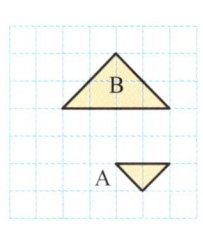   **c**

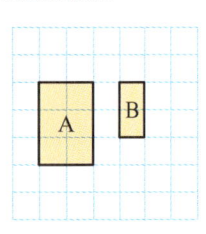

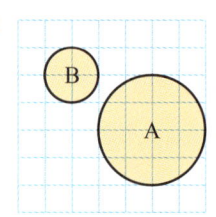

2 Find the scale factors for these enlargements and reductions:

a   **b** 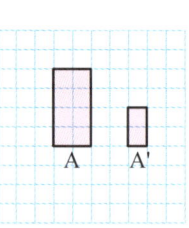   **c**

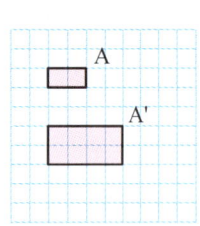

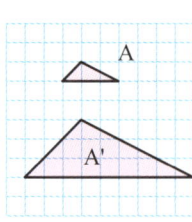

d 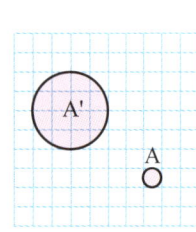   **e** 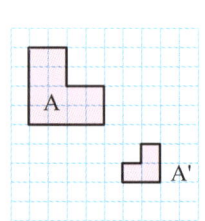   **f**

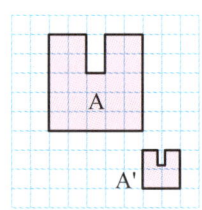

3 For each figure in **2**, what is the scale factor when A′ is mapped back to A?

E — SIMILAR FIGURES

Two figures are **similar** if one is an enlargement of the other.

Under an enlargement all distances between corresponding points are either increased or reduced by the scale factor k.

For example,

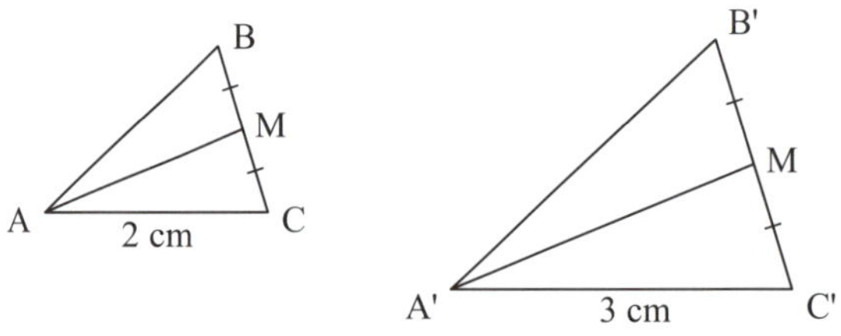

Since $k = \frac{3}{2}$,

$A'M' = \frac{3}{2}(AM)$.

Notice that $\dfrac{A'B'}{AB} = \dfrac{B'C'}{BC} = \dfrac{A'C'}{AC} = \dfrac{A'M'}{AM} = \dfrac{3}{2}$.

Similar figures are **equiangular** and have corresponding **sides in the same ratio** or **same proportion**.

Example 6

Find x given these figures are similar.

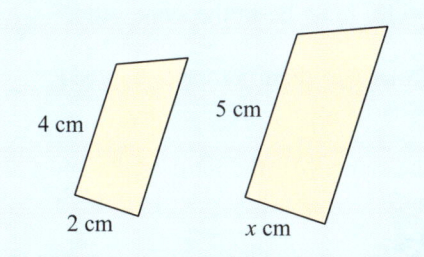

Since the figures are similar, corresponding sides are in the same ratio.

$$\therefore \quad \frac{x}{5} = \frac{2}{4}$$

$$\therefore \quad x = \frac{2}{4} \times 5$$

$$\therefore \quad x = 2\tfrac{1}{2}$$

EXERCISE 16E

1 Find x given that the figures are similar:

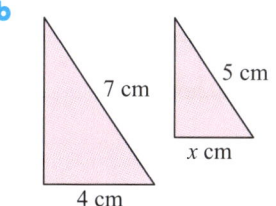

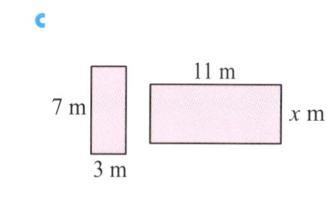

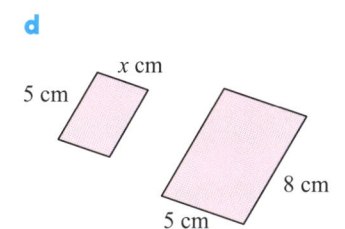

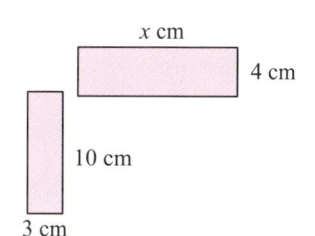

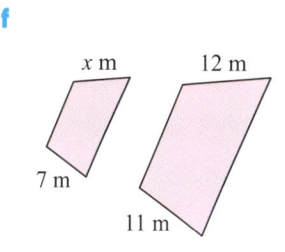

a 3 m, 5 m, 4 m, x m

b 7 cm, 5 cm, 4 cm, x cm

c 11 m, 7 m, 3 m, x m

d x cm, 5 cm, 8 cm, 5 cm

e x cm, 4 cm, 10 cm, 3 cm

f x m, 12 m, 7 m, 11 m

2 True or false? Give reasons for your answers.

  a All squares are similar.
  b All circles are similar.
  c All rectangles are similar.

3 A 20 cm wide picture frame surrounds a painting which is 100 cm by 60 cm.

Are the two rectangles shown here similar?

4 Sketch two quadrilaterals which:
  a are equiangular but not similar
  b have sides in proportion but are not similar.

F — SIMILAR TRIANGLES

We have seen in **Exercise 16E** question **4** that quadrilaterals that are equiangular are not necessarily similar, and quadrilaterals that have sides in proportion are not necessarily similar.

Triangles differ from quadrilaterals when it comes to similarity.

If triangles are equiangular then their corresponding sides must be in the same ratio.

> If two triangles are equiangular then they are similar and their corresponding sides are in the same ratio.

If we can show that two triangles have two angles the same then the third angles must also be equal and the triangles are similar.

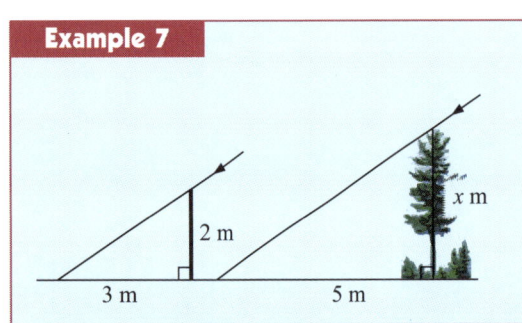

Example 7

At 4 pm one day the shadow of a pine tree was 5 m long. At the same time a 2 m long broom handle had a shadow which was 3 m long.

How high is the pine tree?

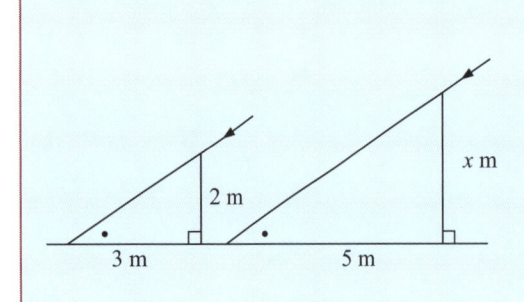

As the rays of light are parallel, we can mark the angles • {equal corresponding angles}.

Also each triangle is right angled.

∴ the triangles are similar.

So, $\dfrac{x}{5} = \dfrac{2}{3}$

∴ $x = \dfrac{2}{3} \times 5$

∴ $x = \dfrac{10}{3} \approx 3.33$

So, the pine tree is about 3.33 m high.

EXERCISE 16F

1 Give brief reasons why these figures possess similar triangles:

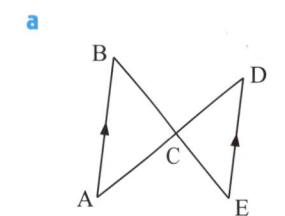

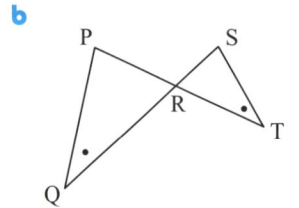

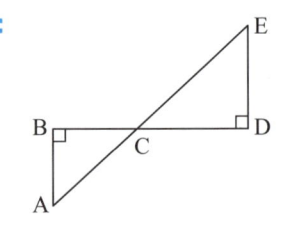

a, b, c

TRANSFORMATIONS, SIMILARITY AND CONGRUENCE (Chapter 16)

2 After establishing similarity, find the unknowns in:

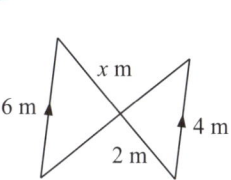

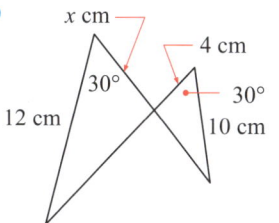

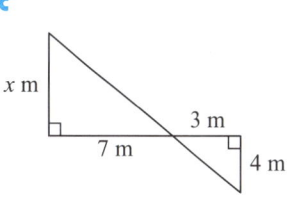

a [triangles with sides 6 m, x m, 4 m, 2 m]

b [x cm, 4 cm, 30°, 30°, 12 cm, 10 cm]

c [x m, 7 m, 3 m, 4 m]

3 A Canadian redwood casts a shadow which is 9.4 m long at the same time as a vertical metre rule casts a shadow which is 1.32 m long. How high is the tree?

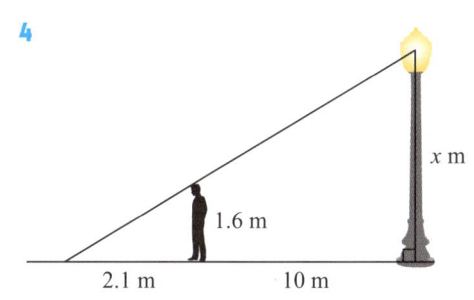

4 When a 1.6 m tall person stands 10 m from the base of an electric light pole the shadow of the person is 2.1 m long.

   a Establish similarity of triangles.
   b Find the height of the globe above ground level.

5 The diagram alongside has not been drawn to scale.

A building sits on horizontal ground and Yong uses two poles 6 m apart to help find the height of the building.

Pole A is 1 m high and pole B is 3 m high.

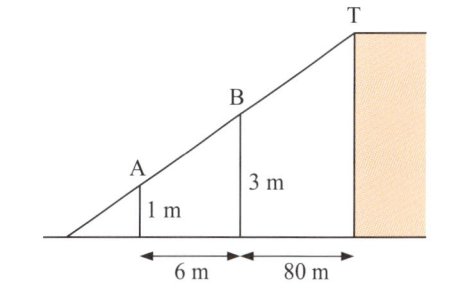

   a By drawing one horizontal line explain how the information given can be used to find the height of the building.
   b Find the height of the building to the nearest 10 cm.

G AREAS AND VOLUMES OF SIMILAR OBJECTS

AREAS

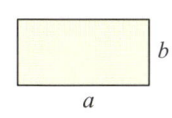

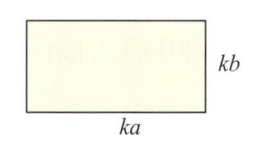

If the sides of a rectangle are multiplied by k, a similar rectangle is obtained.

The new area $= ka \times kb$
$\phantom{\text{The new area }} = k^2 ab$
$\phantom{\text{The new area }} = k^2 \times$ the old area

342 TRANSFORMATIONS, SIMILARITY AND CONGRUENCE (Chapter 16)

If the radius of a circle is multiplied by k, a similar circle is obtained.

The new area $= \pi \times (kr)^2$
$= \pi \times k^2 r^2$
$= k^2 \pi r^2$
$= k^2 \times$ the old area

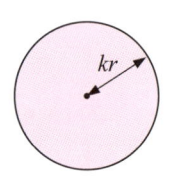

If an object or figure is enlarged by a scale factor of k, then the area of the image $= k^2 \times$ the area of the object.

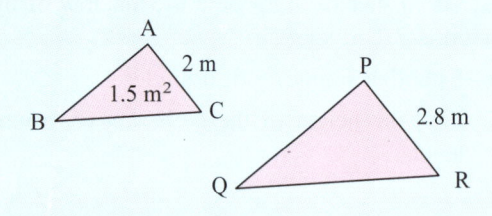

Example 8 ◀)) Self Tutor

Triangles ABC and PQR are similar and the area of triangle ABC is 1.5 m². What is the area of triangle PQR?

If we enlarge $\triangle ABC$ to make $\triangle PQR$, $k = \dfrac{2.8}{2} = 1.4$

Area $\triangle PQR = k^2 \times$ area $\triangle ABC$
$= 1.4^2 \times 1.5$
$= 2.94$ m²

Example 9 ◀)) Self Tutor

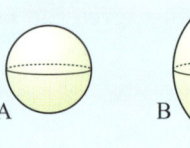

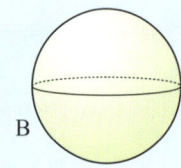

Two spheres have surface areas of 201 cm² and 452 cm² respectively.

Find the radius of the larger sphere.

radius 4 cm   radius r cm

If we enlarge A into B,   area of B $= k^2 \times$ area of A
$\therefore$ $452 = k^2 \times 201$
$\therefore$ $\dfrac{452}{201} = k^2$
$\therefore$ $k = \sqrt{\dfrac{452}{201}}$ $\{k > 0\}$
$\therefore$ $k \approx 1.50$

Now $r = k \times 4$
$\therefore$ $r \approx 6.00$

So, B has radius 6 cm.

TRANSFORMATIONS, SIMILARITY AND CONGRUENCE (Chapter 16)

EXERCISE 16G.1

1 Consider the following similar shapes. Find:
  i the scale factor **ii** the length or area marked by the unknown.

a 40 cm², 10 cm → 10 cm², x cm

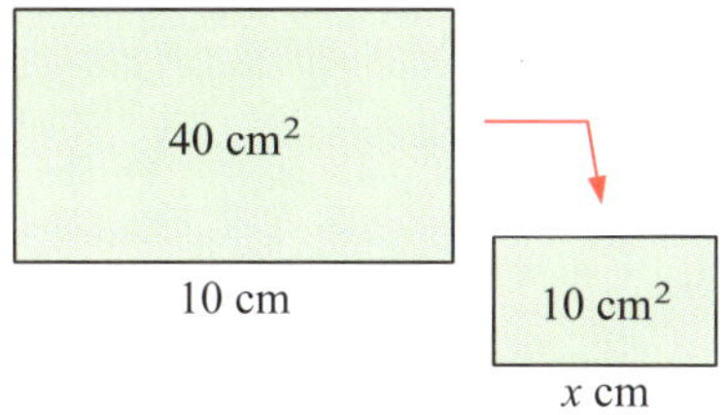

b 8 cm², 6 cm → x cm², 9 cm

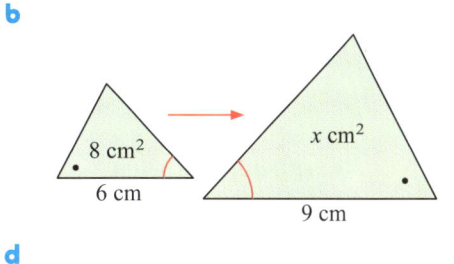

c 2 cm, x cm², 5 cm → 25 cm²

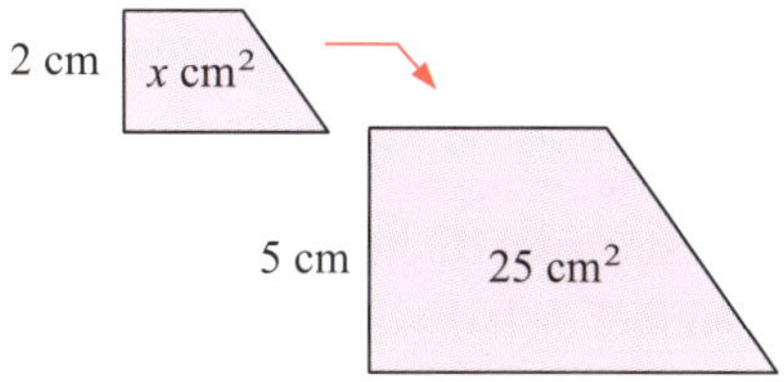

d 20 cm², 8 cm → 6 cm², x cm

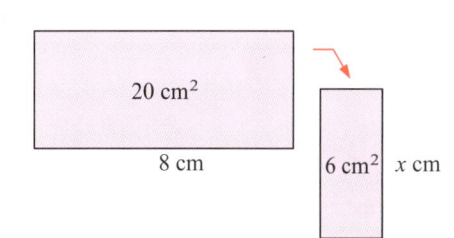

e 4.2 m, 55.4 m² → x m, 31.8 m²

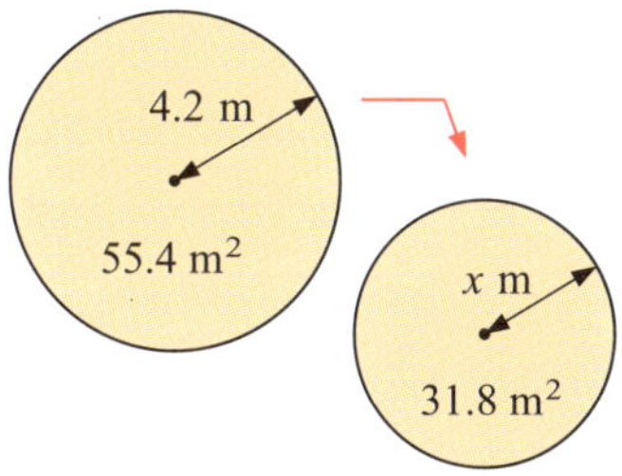

f 5 cm, x cm² → 70 cm², 7.25 cm

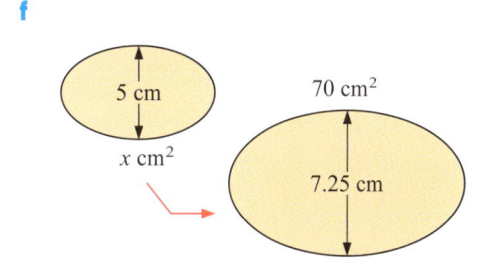

2 The sides of a triangular stained glass window pane are 5 m, 6 m and 7 m. Another pane is similar to it with longest side 21 m. Find:
  a the scale factor
  b the lengths of the other two sides
  c the ratio of the areas of the two panes.

3 Two rectangular photographs are similar and one has area double the other.
  a What is the scale factor?
  b If the larger one is 20 cm by 10 cm, what are the dimensions of the smaller one?

4 Two circles are such that one has area three times the other.
  a What is the scale factor?
  b If the smaller circle has a circumference of 35.8 m, what is the circumference of the larger one?

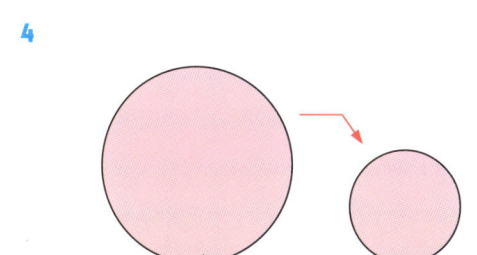

VOLUMES

If the sides of a rectangular prism are multiplied by k, a similar prism is obtained.

The new volume $= ka \times kb \times kc$
$= k^3 abc$
$= k^3 \times$ old volume

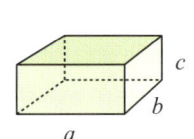

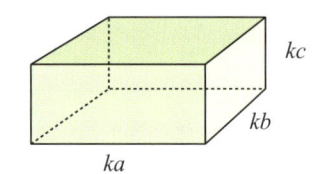

If a 3-dimensional object is enlarged by a scale factor of k, then the volume of the image $= k^3 \times$ the volume of the object.

Example 10   Self Tutor

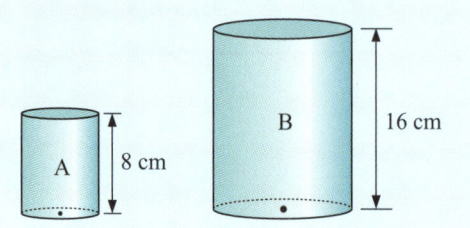

Two soup cans are similar and have heights of 8 cm and 16 cm respectively. Cylinder A has volume 225 cm^3.

Find: **a** the ratio of their radii
         b the volume of B.

a When A is enlarged to give B, $k = \frac{16}{8} = 2$

$\therefore$ the ratio of radii $= 1 : 2$

b Volume of B $= k^3 \times$ volume of A
$= 2^3 \times 225$ cm^3
$= 1800$ cm^3

Example 11   Self Tutor

Two rectangular prisms have volumes of 48 m^3 and 6 m^3 respectively. The larger one has length 5 m. Find:

  a the scale factor
  b the corresponding length of the smaller prism
  c the ratio of their surface areas.

a Volume of larger $= k^3 \times$ volume of smaller
$\therefore \; 48 = k^3 \times 6$
$\therefore \; k^3 = 8$
$\therefore \; k = 2$

b Length of larger $= k \times$ length of smaller
$\therefore \; 5 = 2 \times x$
$\therefore \; \frac{5}{2} = x$

So, the smaller one has length 2.5 m.

TRANSFORMATIONS, SIMILARITY AND CONGRUENCE (Chapter 16) 345

c Area of larger $= k^2 \times$ area of smaller

$\therefore \dfrac{\text{area of larger}}{\text{area of smaller}} = k^2 = 4$

$\therefore$ the ratio is $4:1$.

EXERCISE 16G.2

1 The following contain similar solids. Find the unknown length or volume:

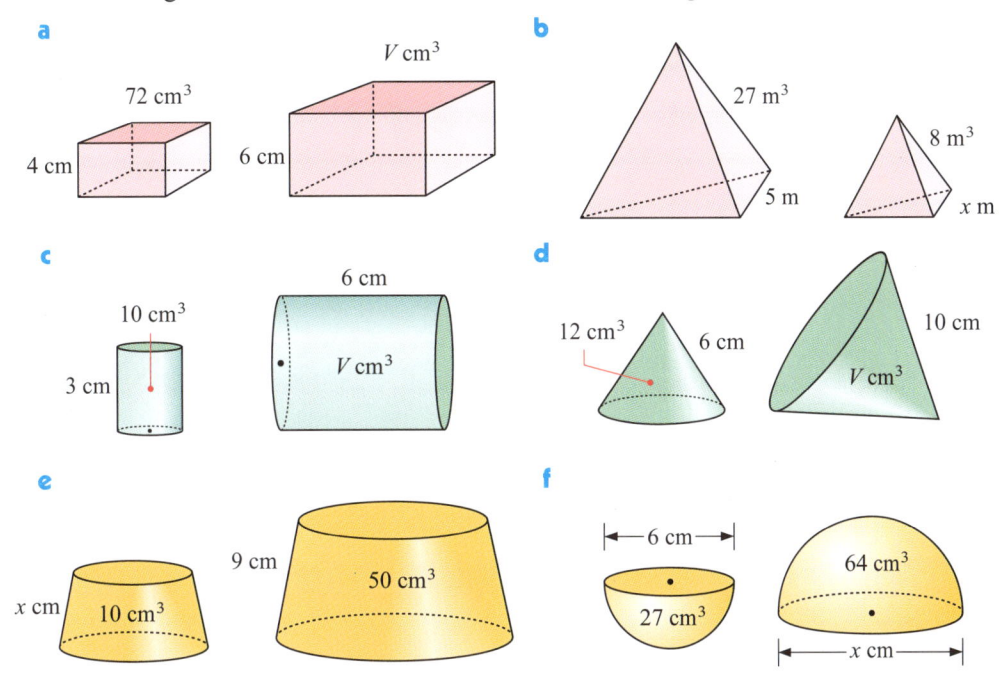

a 72 cm³, 4 cm; V cm³, 6 cm

b 27 m³, 5 m; 8 m³, x m

c 10 cm³, 3 cm; 6 cm, V cm³

d 12 cm³, 6 cm; 10 cm, V cm³

e x cm, 10 cm³; 9 cm, 50 cm³

f 6 cm, 27 cm³; 64 cm³, x cm

2 The surface areas of two similar cylinders are 6 cm² and 54 cm² respectively.
  a Find the scale factor for the enlargement.
  b If the larger cylinder has height 12 cm, how high is the smaller one?
  c What is the ratio of their volumes?

3 Two similar cones have volumes of 4 cm³ and 108 cm³ respectively.
   If the larger one has surface area 54 cm², find the surface area of the smaller one.

4 Two buckets are similar in shape. The smaller one is 30 cm tall and the larger one is 45 cm tall. Both have water in them to a depth equal to half of their heights. The volume of water in the smaller bucket is 4400 cm³.
  a What is the scale factor in comparing the bucket sizes?
  b What is the volume of water in the larger bucket?
  c The surface area of the water in the larger bucket is 630 cm².
     What is the surface area of the water in the smaller bucket?

H — CONGRUENCE OF TRIANGLES

Two triangles are **congruent** if they are identical in every respect apart from position.

If we are given the lengths of three sides of a triangle we can construct it in only one way.

For example, the triangle with sides of length 3 cm, 5 cm and 6 cm is shown opposite.

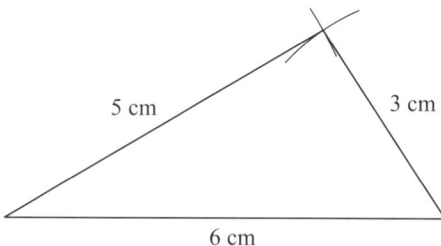

If we are given the measures of three angles of a triangle we can construct it in more than one way.

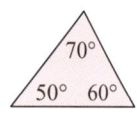

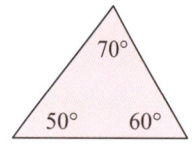

These are similar but not congruent.

What other information do we need to know that would allow us to construct a triangle in only one way?

INVESTIGATION — CONGRUENT TRIANGLES

You need to have: a ruler, a sharp pencil, protractor, and compass.

What to do:

1. Accurately construct triangle ABC with AB = 6 cm, $B\hat{A}C = 45°$ and AC = 4 cm. Is there one and only one possible triangle?

2. Draw a horizontal line with A at the left end.
   Use your protractor to measure an angle of 40° at A.
   Draw [AC] with length 6 cm.
   With compass point on C draw an arc of a circle with radius 5 cm to cut the base line at B. 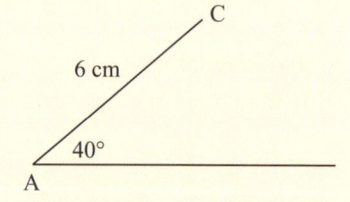
   - How many possible positions are there for B?
   - How many triangles ABC can be drawn given AC = 6 cm, $B\hat{A}C = 40°$ and BC = 5 cm?

3. Now draw a horizontal line with B at the right end. At B draw a right angle and on the perpendicular mark C where BC = 3 cm. With C as centre, draw an arc of radius 4 cm to cut the original base line at A.
   How many different triangles can be drawn from this information?

4 Accurately draw triangle ABC in which $A\hat{B}C = 40°$, $A\hat{C}B = 50°$ and BC = 4 cm. How many different triangles can be drawn from this information?

5 Accurately draw triangle ABC in which $A\hat{B}C = 40°$, $A\hat{C}B = 50°$ and a side other than [BC] has length 4 cm.
How many different triangles can be formed now?

6 Write a summary indicating when one and only one triangle can be drawn from given information involving 3 angles or sides.

If a given set of information allows us to construct a triangle in only one way, then this information is sufficient to state that two triangles are congruent. From the investigation above, therefore, we can state four acceptable tests for congruence:

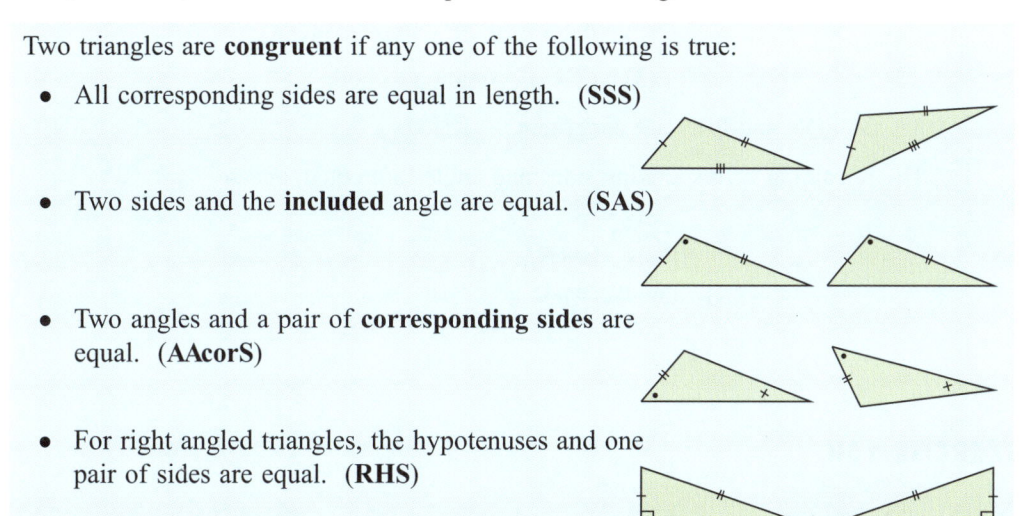

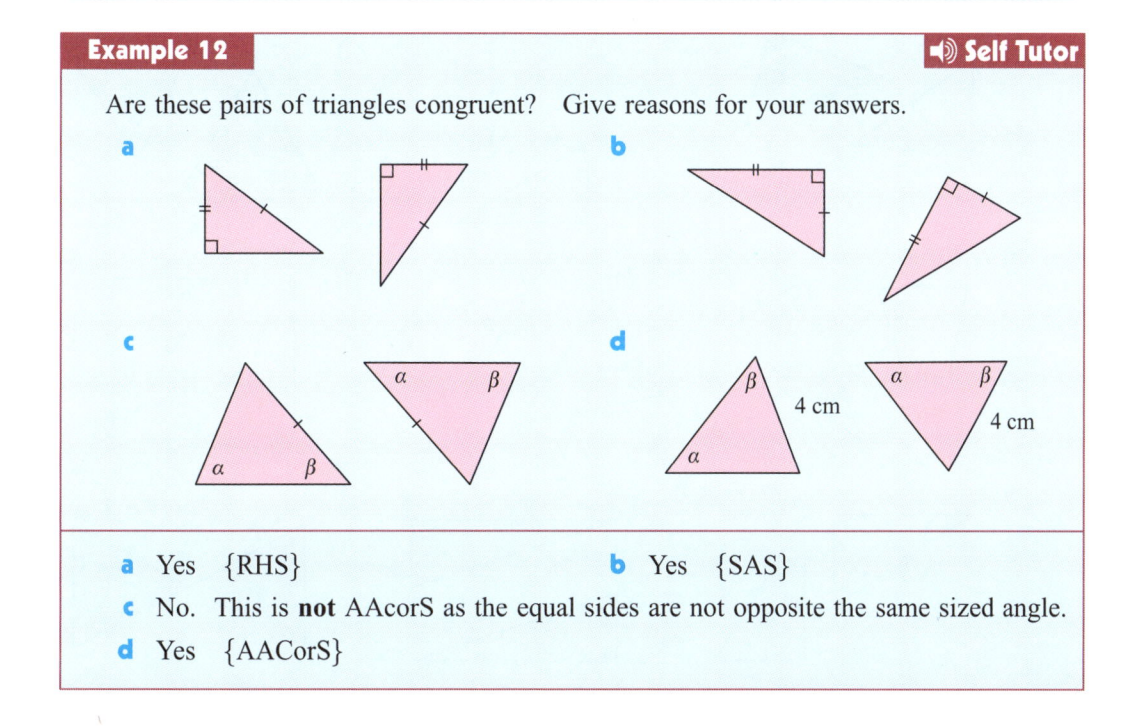

Two triangles are **congruent** if any one of the following is true:

- All corresponding sides are equal in length. (**SSS**)

- Two sides and the **included** angle are equal. (**SAS**)

- Two angles and a pair of **corresponding sides** are equal. (**AAcorS**)

- For right angled triangles, the hypotenuses and one pair of sides are equal. (**RHS**)

Example 12

Are these pairs of triangles congruent? Give reasons for your answers.

a

b

c

d

a Yes {RHS}
b Yes {SAS}
c No. This is **not** AAcorS as the equal sides are not opposite the same sized angle.
d Yes {AACorS}

Example 13

Are there congruent triangles in the given figure?

If so, what can be deduced?

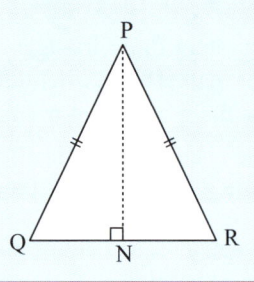

In $\triangle$s PQN and PRN: (1) PQ = PR {given}
(2) $P\hat{N}Q = P\hat{N}R = 90°$ {given}
(3) [PN] is common to both

$\therefore$ $\triangle$s PQN and PRN are congruent. {RHS}

The remaining corresponding sides and angles are equal, and so
$$QN = RN,$$
$$P\hat{Q}N = P\hat{R}N,$$
and $Q\hat{P}N = R\hat{P}N$

EXERCISE 16H

1 State whether these pairs of triangles are congruent, giving reasons for your answers:

a

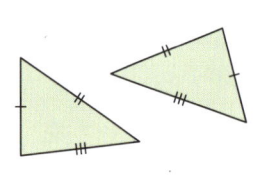

b

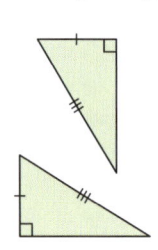

c

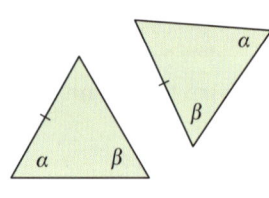

d

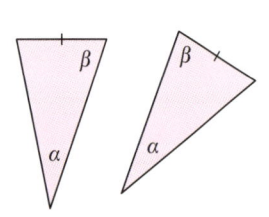

e

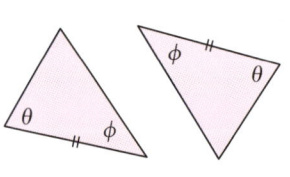

f

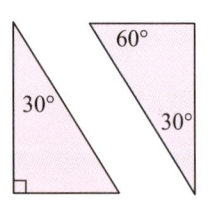

g

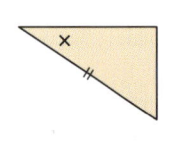

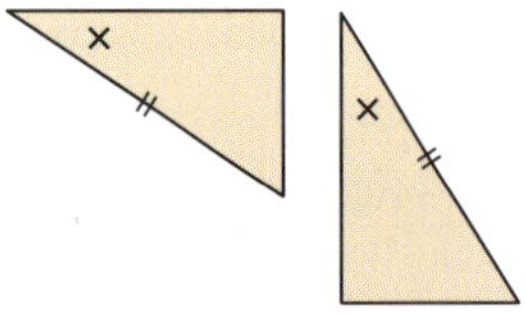

h

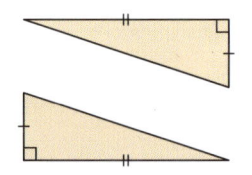

i

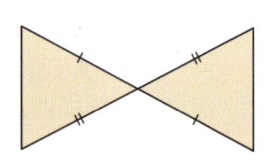

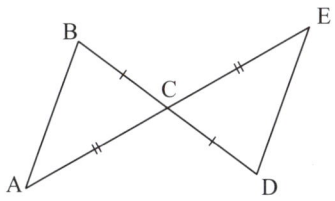

TRANSFORMATIONS, SIMILARITY AND CONGRUENCE (Chapter 16)

2 For the given figure, copy and complete:
In △s CAB and CED
1. CB = CD {........}
2. AC = ... {........}
3. .... = ... {..................}

∴ these triangles are congruent. {........}

Consequently AB̂C = ...

∴ [AB] ∥ .... {equal ....}

3
 a Show that △s CAN and CBN are congruent.
 b What are the consequences of this congruence?

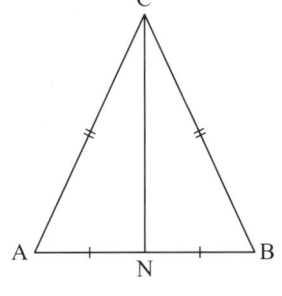

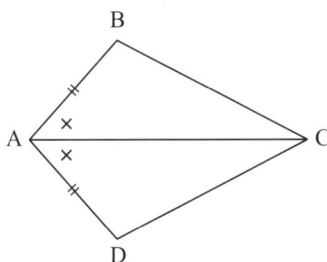

4
 a Show that △s ABC and ADC are congruent.
 b What are the consequences of this congruence?

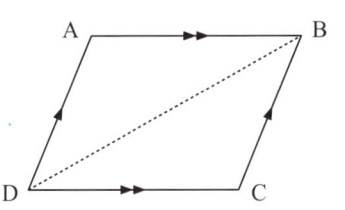

5
 a ABCD is a parallelogram and [DB] is one of its diagonals.
   Use properties of parallel lines to show that △s ABD and CDB are congruent.
 b What are the consequences of this congruence?

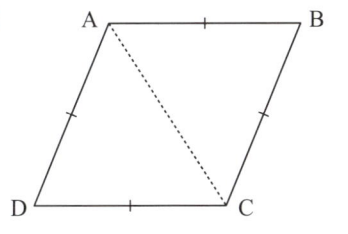

6
 a ABCD is a rhombus and [AC] is one of its diagonals.
   Without assuming parallel sides, explain why △s ABC and ADC are congruent.
 b Deduce from **a** that ABCD is a parallelogram.

THE MATHEMATICS OF AIR HOCKEY

LINKS
click here

Areas of interaction:
Approaches to learning

REVIEW SET 16A

1 a What translation vector moves Q to P?

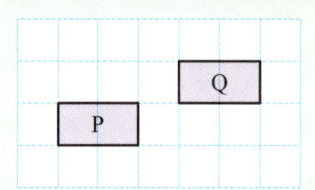

b On grid paper redraw the given figure and translate it $\begin{pmatrix} -4 \\ 1 \end{pmatrix}$.

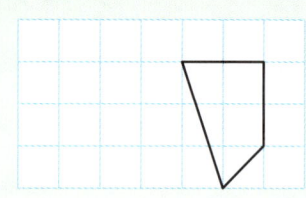

2 Copy and reflect the shape in the mirror line.

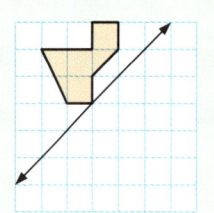

3 Draw lines of symmetry for:

  a   **b**

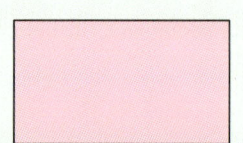

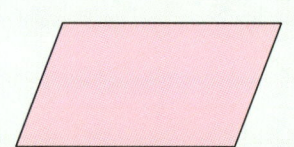

4 Copy and rotate the following figures about O clockwise through 90°:

  a   **b**

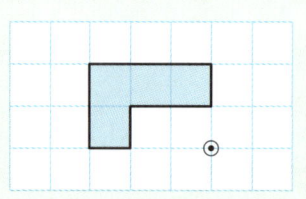

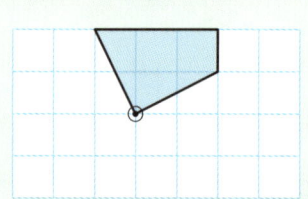

5 Find any points of rotational symmetry and state the order of rotational symmetry:

  a   **b**

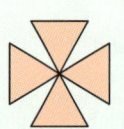

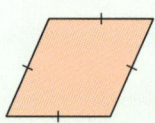

6 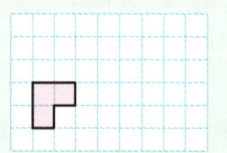 Copy and enlarge the shape with a scale factor $k = \frac{5}{2}$.

7 Figure A is reduced to figure B.

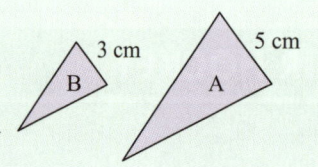

  a What is the scale factor?

  b If A has area 15 cm², find the area of B.

8 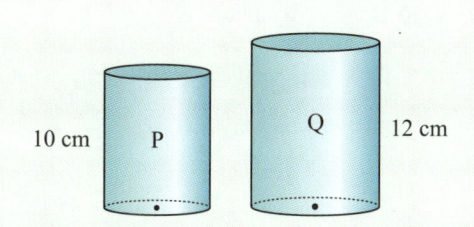 P and Q are similar solid cylindrical cans with heights as shown.

    a What is the scale factor?

    b If P has an end surface area of 50 cm^2, what is the end surface area of Q?

    c If Q has volume 2400 cm^3, find the volume of P.

9 State whether these pairs of triangles are congruent, giving reasons for your answer:

    a

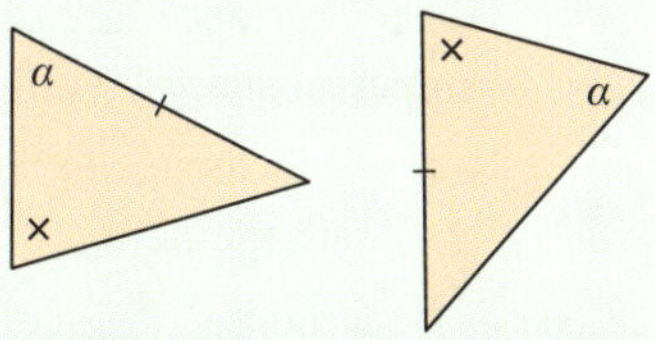

    b

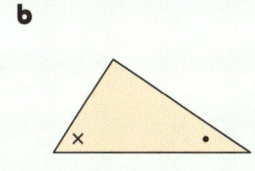

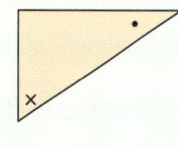

10 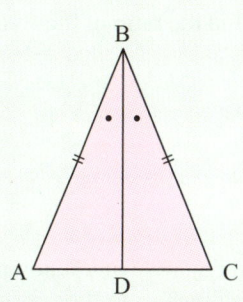 Triangle ABC is isosceles with BA = BC.

[BD] is the angle bisector of $\widehat{ABC}$.

    a Show that triangles DAB and DCB are congruent.

    b Show that a consequence of **a** is that [BD] is perpendicular to [AC].

REVIEW SET 16B

1 Copy and reflect the shape in the mirror line:

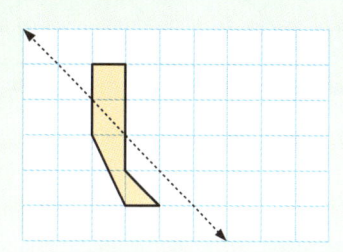

2

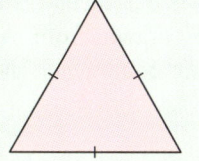

    a How many lines of symmetry does an equilateral triangle have?

    b Does it have a point of rotational symmetry?

    c Illustrate **a** and **b** on a sketch.

3 Copy and rotate this figure:

    a clockwise about A through 180°

    b anticlockwise about B through 90°.

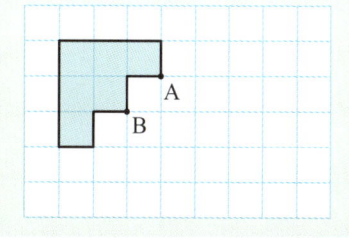

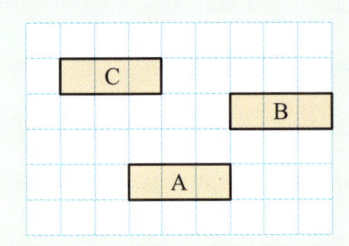

4 What translation vector would move:
  a C to B   **b** B to A?

5 Draw a figure which possesses rotational symmetry of order 6.

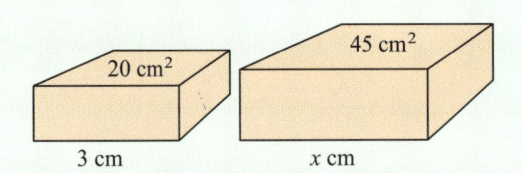

6 Two blocks of cheese are similar. The surface areas which are uppermost are 20 cm² and 45 cm².

  a Find the scale factor k for the enlargement.
  b Find x.
  c Find the ratio of their volumes.

7 Copy the given figure and reduce it by a factor of $k = \frac{2}{3}$.

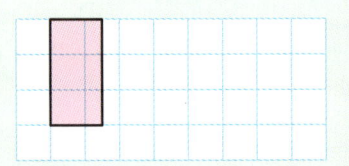

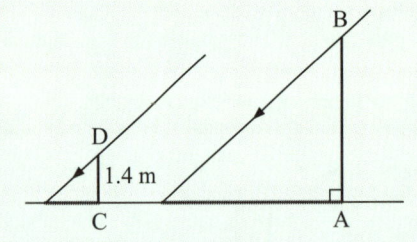

8 [AB] is a vertical flag pole of unknown height. [CD] is a vertical stick.
When the shadow of the flag pole is 12.3 m long, the shadow of the stick is 1.65 m long. Find, correct to 3 significant figures, the height of the flag pole.

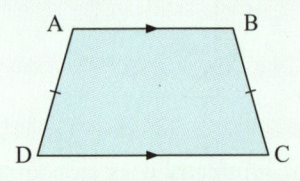

9 The figure alongside is called an *isosceles trapezium* as its non-parallel sides are equal in length.
Claudia is convinced that the angles at C and D are also equal. To prove her theory, she added two lines to the figure, drawn from A and B respectively. Explain using congruence the rest of Claudia's proof.

Chapter 17

Algebraic factorisation

Contents:
- **A** Common factors
- **B** Factorising with common factors
- **C** Difference of two squares factorising
- **D** Perfect square factorisation
- **E** Factorising quadratic trinomials
- **F** Miscellaneous factorisation

When an expression is written as a **product** of its **factors**, it is said to have been **factorised**.

For example, we can factorise the expression $3x + 15$ as $3 \times (x + 5)$ where the factors are 3 and $(x + 5)$.

Notice that $3(x + 5) = 3x + 15$ using the **distributive law** and so **factorisation** is really the **reverse** process of **expansion**.

Factorisation is an important process which we will use to solve **quadratic equations** such as $x^2 + 3x - 40 = 0$.

A   COMMON FACTORS

We have seen how numbers can be expressed as the product of **factors**.

We know that **prime numbers** have only two different factors, the number itself and 1.

Factors that are prime numbers are called **prime factors**. Prime factors of any number can be found by repeated division.

For example:

$$\begin{array}{r|r} 2 & 30 \\ \hline 3 & 15 \\ \hline 5 & 5 \\ \hline & 1 \end{array} \quad \therefore \; 30 = 2 \times 3 \times 5 \qquad \begin{array}{r|r} 3 & 45 \\ \hline 3 & 15 \\ \hline 5 & 5 \\ \hline & 1 \end{array} \quad \therefore \; 45 = 3 \times 3 \times 5$$

COMMON FACTORS AND HCF

Notice that 3 and 5 are factors of both 30 and 45. They are called **common factors**. 15 which is 3×5, must also be a common factor.

> **Common factors** are numbers that are factors of two or more numbers.
>
> The **highest common factor** or **HCF** of the numbers is the largest factor that is common to all of them.

To find the highest common factor of a group of numbers it is often best to express the numbers as products of prime factors. The common prime factors are identified and multiplied to give the HCF.

Example 1   ◀) Self Tutor

Find the highest common factor of 36 and 81.

$$\begin{array}{r|r} 2 & 36 \\ \hline 2 & 18 \\ \hline 3 & 9 \\ \hline 3 & 3 \\ \hline & 1 \end{array} \quad \therefore \; 36 = 2 \times 2 \times 3 \times 3 \qquad \begin{array}{r|r} 3 & 81 \\ \hline 3 & 27 \\ \hline 3 & 9 \\ \hline 3 & 3 \\ \hline & 1 \end{array} \quad \therefore \; 81 = 3 \times 3 \times 3 \times 3$$

$\therefore$ HCF $= 3 \times 3 = 9$

Algebraic products are also made up of factors. We can find the **highest common factor** of a group of algebraic products.

Example 2 ◀) Self Tutor

Find the highest common factor of:

a $8a$ and $12b$ **b** $4x^2$ and $6xy$

Write each term as a product of its factors!

a
$8a = 2 \times 2 \times 2 \times a$
$12b = 2 \times 2 \times 3 \times b$
$\therefore$ HCF $= 2 \times 2$
$= 4$

b
$4x^2 = 2 \times 2 \times x \times x$
$6xy = 2 \times 3 \times x \times y$
$\therefore$ HCF $= 2 \times x$
$= 2x$

EXERCISE 17A

1 Find the highest common factor of:
   a 18 and 27
   b 25 and 15
   c 32 and 36
   d 50 and 75
   e 98 and 42
   f 48 and 84

2 Find the missing factor:
   a $4 \times \square = 8x$
   b $5 \times \square = 15y$
   c $3 \times \square = 9a^2$
   d $3x^2 \times \square = 12x^2$
   e $\square \times 7y = 7y^2$
   f $\square \times 2a = -8a$
   g $p \times \square = -pq$
   h $\square \times 3a = 6a^3$
   i $8s \times \square = -24st$

3 Find the highest common factor of:
   a $4x$ and 8
   b $3a$ and a
   c $5b$ and 15
   d $7y$ and $5y$
   e $8c$ and $24c$
   f $6d$ and $15d$
   g $7x$ and 9
   h $18y$ and $27y$
   i $81x$ and $63x$

4 Find the HCF of:
   a $17st$ and $13ts$
   b xy and $2xy$
   c $16x$ and $24xy$
   d x and x^2
   e a^3 and $2a$
   f a^2 and a^3
   g $6b$ and $2b^3$
   h $5a^2$ and $25a$
   i $6b^2$ and $12b^3$
   j $14ab$ and $49ba$
   k $8ab$ and $16ab^2$
   l $9a^2b$ and $18ab^2$
   m $10f$, $15fg$ and $25g$
   n $6abc$, $8ab$ and $12bc$
   o $16x^2y$ and $36xy^2$

Example 3 ◀) Self Tutor

Find the HCF of $3(x+3)$ and $(x+3)(x+1)$.

$3(x+3) = 3 \times (x+3)$ $\quad (x+3)(x+1) = (x+3) \times (x+1)$
$\therefore$ HCF $= (x+3)$

5 Find the HCF of:

- **a** $5(a+7)$ and $(a+1)(a+7)$
- **b** $3(2+b)^2$ and $3(6+b)(2+b)$
- **c** $x^2(x-4)$ and $x(x-4)$
- **d** $15(x-2)^2$ and $5(x-2)(x+3)$
- **e** $6(x-1)^2$ and $16(x-7)(x-1)$
- **f** $9y(y+1)$ and $6y(y+1)^2$

ACTIVITY — WHICH EXPRESSION AM I?

1 I am an expression of the form $kx^\square y^\square$ where k is a single digit integer.
The HCF of myself and $2x^2y$ is $2xy$.
The HCF of myself and $3xy^2$ is $3xy$.
Which expression am I?

2 I am an expression of the form $ka^\square b^\square c^\square$ where k is a two digit integer.
The HCF of myself and $9ab^2c^4$ is $3ab^2c^3$.
The HCF of myself and $20a^3b^4c^3$ is $4a^2b^4c^3$.
The HCF of myself and $16a^2b^6c$ is $8a^2b^5c$.
Which expression am I?

B FACTORISING WITH COMMON FACTORS

Factorisation is the process of writing an expression as a **product** of its **factors**.

Factorisation is the reverse process of **expansion**.

When we expand an expression we remove its brackets.

When we factorise an expression we insert brackets.

Notice that $5(x-1)$ is the *product of the two factors*, 5 and $x-1$.

The brackets are essential since $5(x-1)$ multiplies 5 by the whole of $x-1$, whereas in $5x-1$ only the x is multiplied by 5.

in **expansion**

$$5(x-1) = 5x - 5$$

is **factorisation**

To factorise an algebraic expression involving a number of terms, we look for the HCF of the terms. We write it in front of a set of brackets. We then identify the contents of the brackets.

For example, $6a^2$ and $2ab$ have HCF of $2a$,

so $6a^2 + 2ab = 2a \times 3a + 2a \times b$
$= 2a(3a+b)$

FACTORISING FULLY

Consider the expression $8x + 4 = 2(4x + 2)$. This expression is not fully factorised since $(4x + 2)$ still has a common factor of 2 which could be removed. So, although 2 was a common factor, it was not the HCF. The HCF is 4 and so

$$8x + 4 = 4(2x + 1) \text{ is } \textbf{fully factorised}.$$

Example 4

Fully factorise: **a** $3a + 6$ **b** $ab - 2bc$

a $3a + 6$
$= 3 \times a + 3 \times 2$
$= 3(a + 2)$ {HCF is 3}

b $ab - 2bc$
$= a \times b - 2 \times b \times c$
$= b(a - 2c)$ {HCF is b}

With practice the middle line is not necessary.

EXERCISE 17B

1 Copy and complete:
- **a** $3x + 6 = 3(x + \ldots)$
- **b** $4a - 8 = 4(a - \ldots)$
- **c** $16 - 4b = 4(\ldots - b)$
- **d** $14x + 21 = 7(\ldots + 3)$
- **e** $6p^2 - p = p(6p - \ldots)$
- **f** $15x^2 + 10x = 5x(\ldots + 2)$

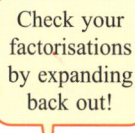

Check your factorisations by expanding back out!

2 Copy and complete:
- **a** $6a + 12 = 6(\ldots + \ldots)$
- **b** $3b - 3 = 3(\ldots - \ldots)$
- **c** $9 + 3c = 3(\ldots + \ldots)$
- **d** $16d - 12 = \ldots(4d - \ldots)$
- **e** $15xy + 20y = \ldots(3x + 4)$
- **f** $12y - 18y^2 = 6\ldots(2 - \ldots)$
- **g** $3xy - xy^2 = \ldots(3 - \ldots)$
- **h** $5xy - yz = y(\ldots - \ldots)$

3 Fully factorise:
- **a** $2x - 4$
- **b** $7d + 28$
- **c** $9x - 27$
- **d** $12 + 3x$
- **e** $11a + 11b$
- **f** $pr + qr$
- **g** $35 - 14x$
- **h** $xy + x$
- **i** $a + ab$
- **j** $x - xy$
- **k** $2c + cd$
- **l** $7x - xy$
- **m** $pq - 8qr$
- **n** $ab - bc$
- **o** $2xy - yz$
- **p** $12x - 18xy$

Example 5

Fully factorise: **a** $8x^2 + 12x$ **b** $3y^2 - 6xy$

a $8x^2 + 12x$
$= 2 \times 4 \times x \times x + 3 \times 4 \times x$
$= 4x(2x + 3)$ {HCF is $4x$}

b $3y^2 - 6xy$
$= 3 \times y \times y - 2 \times 3 \times x \times y$
$= 3y(y - 2x)$ {HCF is $3y$}

4 Fully factorise:

- **a** $x^2 + 5x$
- **b** $5x^2 + 15x$
- **c** $14x - 2x^2$
- **d** $4x - 16x^2$
- **e** $8x^2 + 12x$
- **f** $x^3 + 2x^2$
- **g** $x^3 + 3x$
- **h** $7x^3 - x^2$
- **i** $a^2b - ab^2$
- **j** $x + x^2 + x^3$
- **k** $5x^2 - 10x + 15$
- **l** $2x^2 - 8x - 4x^3$

Example 6 — Self Tutor

Fully factorise: $-2a + 6ab$

$-2a + 6ab$
$= 6ab - 2a$ {Rewrite with $6ab$ first.}
$= 2 \times 3 \times a \times b - 2 \times a$
$= 2a(3b - 1)$ {as $2a$ is the HCF}

---

5 Fully factorise:

- **a** $-2a + 4$
- **b** $-15 + 3b$
- **c** $-6c + 12d$
- **d** $-xy + 3y$
- **e** $-x + xy$
- **f** $-x^2 + x$
- **g** $-12y + 6y^2$
- **h** $-ab + 2b^2$
- **i** $-c^2 + c$

Example 7 — Self Tutor

Fully factorise: $-2x^2 - 4x$

$-2x^2 - 4x$
$= -2 \times x \times x + -2 \times 2 \times x$
$= -2x(x + 2)$ {as HCF is $-2x$}

---

6 Fully factorise:

- **a** $-8x - 32$
- **b** $-7 - 7x$
- **c** $-3x - 3y$
- **d** $-4c - 2d$
- **e** $-xy - x$
- **f** $-5a - 15a^2$
- **g** $-12b^2 - 6b$
- **h** $-8c^2 - 6cd$
- **i** $-22e^2 - 33e$

Example 8 — Self Tutor

Fully factorise:
a $2(x + 3) + x(x + 3)$
b $x(x + 4) - (x + 4)$

a $\quad 2(x + 3) + x(x + 3)$ {HCF $= (x + 3)$}
$= (x + 3)(2 + x)$

b $\quad x(x + 4) - (x + 4)$ {HCF $= (x + 4)$}
$= x(x + 4) - 1(x + 4)$
$= (x + 4)(x - 1)$

7 Fully factorise:

a $4(x+1) + x(x+1)$
b $5(x-3) + x(x-3)$
c $3(x+7) - x(x+7)$
d $x(x+4) + (x+4)$
e $a(c-1) - b(c-1)$
f $a(2+x) - b(2+x)$
g $x(y+z) - (y+z)$
h $x(x-2) + x - 2$

Example 9 — Self Tutor

Fully factorise $(x-1)(x+2) + 3(x-1)$

$(x-1)(x+2) + 3(x-1)$ {HCF = $(x-1)$}
$= (x-1)[(x+2) + 3]$
$= (x-1)(x+5)$

Notice the use of square brackets in the second line.

8 Fully factorise:

a $(x+1)(x+5) + 2(x+1)$
b $7(x+3) + (x+3)(x-2)$
c $(x-5)(x+2) - 7(x+2)$
d $(x-9)^2 + 3(x-9)$
e $(a+3)^2 + (a+7)(a+3)$
f $(a-b)(b-1) - 3(b-1)$
g $12(a+3)^2 - 8(a+3)$
h $(x-8)^2 - 2(x-8)(x+4)$
i $m(m-7) - 2(m-7)(m+1)$
j $2(n-3) - 7(n-3)^2$

C DIFFERENCE OF TWO SQUARES FACTORISING

INVESTIGATION   THE DIFFERENCE OF TWO SQUARES

In the diagram alongside, a b by b square has been cut from an a by a square.

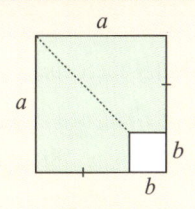

What to do:

1 Explain why the green shaded area is given by $a^2 - b^2$.

2 Copy the above diagram, or print the **worksheet** from the CD. Cut along the dotted line.

3 Rearrange the two trapezia to form a rectangle as shown.

4 Find, in terms of a and b, the lengths of [AB] and [BC].

5 Find, the area of the rectangle in the form (......)(......).

6 What can be deduced by comparing areas? How does your answer relate to question **1**?

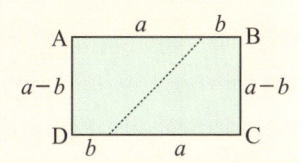

On expanding, $(a+b)(a-b) = a^2 - ab + ab - b^2 = a^2 - b^2$ {using FOIL}

So, the difference of two squares $a^2 - b^2 = (a+b)(a-b)$

Example 10

Fully factorise:

a $x^2 - 4$ **b** $1 - 25y^2$

a $\quad x^2 - 4$
$= x^2 - 2^2$
$= (x+2)(x-2)$

b $\quad 1 - 25y^2$
$= 1^2 - (5y)^2$
$= (1+5y)(1-5y)$

Write each term as a square.

EXERCISE 17C

1 Fully factorise:

    a $c^2 - d^2$ **b** $m^2 - n^2$ **c** $n^2 - m^2$ **d** $a^2 - b^2$

    e $x^2 - 16$ **f** $x^2 - 36$ **g** $a^2 - 25$ **h** $4x^2 - 1$

    i $4b^2 - 25$ **j** $9y^2 - 16$ **k** $49 - c^2$ **l** $9 - 4y^2$

Example 11

Fully factorise:

a $2x^2 - 18$ **b** $x^3 - xy^2$

a $\quad 2x^2 - 18$
$= 2(x^2 - 9)$
$= 2(x+3)(x-3)$

b $\quad x^3 - xy^2$
$= x(x^2 - y^2)$
$= x(x+y)(x-y)$

When factorising, always look for common factors first.

2 Fully factorise:

    a $3x^2 - 12$ **b** $8x^2 - 72$ **c** $2a^2 - 50$ **d** $4x^2 - 25$

    e $9b^2 - 900$ **f** $3b^2 - 48$ **g** $\pi R^2 - \pi r^2$ **h** $10 - 10x^2$

    i $p^3 - 4p$ **j** $x^3 - x$ **k** $x^4 - x^2$ **l** $x^3y - xy^3$

Example 12

Fully factorise: **a** $4a^2 - 9b^2$ **b** $x^2y^2 - 16$

a $\quad 4a^2 - 9b^2$
$= (2a)^2 - (3b)^2$
$= (2a+3b)(2a-3b)$

b $\quad x^2y^2 - 16$
$= (xy)^2 - 4^2$
$= (xy+4)(xy-4)$

3 Fully factorise:

    a $49a^2 - b^2$ **b** $y^2 - 36x^2$ **c** $9x^2 - 25y^2$ **d** $9a^2 - 16b^2$

    e $a^2 - 81b^2$ **f** $a^2b^2 - 4$ **g** $36x^2 - p^2q^2$ **h** $16a^2 - 25b^2c^2$

Example 13   ◀)) **Self Tutor**

Fully factorise: **a** $(x+2)^2 - 9$ **b** $25 - (x-2)^2$

Notice the use of the square brackets.

a $(x+2)^2 - 9$
$= (x+2)^2 - 3^2$
$= [(x+2) + 3][(x+2) - 3]$
$= [x + 2 + 3][x + 2 - 3]$
$= (x+5)(x-1)$

b $25 - (x-2)^2$
$= 5^2 - (x-2)^2$
$= [5 + (x-2)][5 - (x-2)]$
$= [5 + x - 2][5 - x + 2]$
$= (x+3)(7-x)$

4 Fully factorise:

    a $(x+3)^2 - 4$ **b** $(x-2)^2 - 25$ **c** $16 - (x+1)^2$

    d $36 - (x-3)^2$ **e** $(x+4)^2 - 1$ **f** $1 - (x-4)^2$

    g $4(x+1)^2 - 9$ **h** $81 - 16(x+1)^2$ **i** $(x+2)^2 - 9(x-1)^2$

    j $4(x-5)^2 - (x-1)^2$ **k** $9x^2 - (x+2)^2$ **l** $(x+5)^2 - 4x^2$

    m $(x+3)^2 - (x+1)^2$ **n** $(x-4)^2 - 16(x+2)^2$ **o** $4(x+1)^2 - (2-x)^2$

D   PERFECT SQUARE FACTORISATION

We have seen that $(a+b)^2$ and $(a-b)^2$
$= (a+b)(a+b)$ $= (a-b)(a-b)$
$= a^2 + ab + ab + b^2$ $= a^2 - ab - ab + b^2$
$= a^2 + 2ab + b^2$ $= a^2 - 2ab + b^2$

Expressions such as $a^2 + 2ab + b^2$ and $a^2 - 2ab + b^2$ are called **perfect squares** because they factorise into the product of two identical factors, or a factor squared.

$$a^2 + 2ab + b^2 = (a+b)^2 \quad \text{and} \quad a^2 - 2ab + b^2 = (a-b)^2 \ .$$

For example, $x^2 + 6x + 9$ and $x^2 - 6x + 9$ are perfect squares because they factorise into two identical factors:

$$x^2 + 6x + 9 = (x+3)^2 \quad \text{and} \quad x^2 - 6x + 9 = (x-3)^2$$

You can check this for yourself by expanding $(x+3)^2$ and $(x-3)^2$.

IDENTIFYING PERFECT SQUARES

Notice that $(a+b)^2 = a^2 + 2ab + b^2$ and $(a-b)^2 = a^2 - 2ab + b^2$.

The a^2 and b^2 terms are perfect squares.

So, a perfect square must be one of these two forms. It must contain **two squares and a middle term** of $\pm 2ab$.

For example,
$$x^2 + 10x + 25$$
$$= x^2 + 2 \times 5 \times x + 5^2$$
$$= (x+5)^2$$

and
$$x^2 - 10x + 25$$
$$= x^2 - 2 \times 5 \times x + 5^2$$
$$= (x-5)^2$$

We can see that $x^2 + 10x + 25$ is a perfect square because $x^2 + 10x + 25$ contains two squares x^2 and 5^2 and a middle term $2 \times 5 \times x$.

$x^2 + 10x + 26$ does not satisfy these conditions.

Example 14 ◀)) Self Tutor

Find all perfect squares of the form: **a** $x^2 + \square + 25$ **b** $4x^2 + \square + 9$

a $x^2 + \square + 25 = x^2 + \square + 5^2$
This is of the form $(a+b)^2 = a^2 + 2ab + b^2$ with $a = x$ and $b = \pm 5$.
$\therefore \quad 2ab = 2 \times x \times \pm 5 = \pm 10x$
$\therefore$ the perfect squares are $x^2 + 10x + 25$ and $x^2 - 10x + 25$.

b $4x^2 + \square + 9 = (2x)^2 + \square + 3^2$
This is of the form $(a+b)^2 = a^2 + 2ab + b^2$ with $a = 2x$ and $b = \pm 3$.
$\therefore \quad 2ab = 2 \times 2x \times \pm 3 = \pm 12x$
$\therefore$ the perfect squares are $4x^2 + 12x + 9$ and $4x^2 - 12x + 9$.

EXERCISE 17D

1   Find all perfect squares of the form:

   a $x^2 + \square + 1$ **b** $x^2 + \square + 4$ **c** $x^2 + \square + 16$
   d $4x^2 + \square + 1$ **e** $9x^2 + \square + 4$ **f** $16x^2 + \square + 81$
   g $4x^2 + \square + c^2$ **h** $x^2 + \square + 4d^2$ **i** $a^2c^2 + \square + 4$

Example 15 ◀)) Self Tutor

Factorise:
   a $x^2 + 20x + 100$ **b** $x^2 - 8x + 16$

a $x^2 + 20x + 100$
$= x^2 + 2 \times x \times 10 + 10^2$
$= (x+10)^2$

b $x^2 - 8x + 16$
$= x^2 - 2 \times x \times 4 + 4^2$
$= (x-4)^2$

2 Factorise:

    a $x^2 + 2x + 1$ **b** $x^2 - 4x + 4$ **c** $x^2 - 6x + 9$

    d $x^2 + 10x + 25$ **e** $x^2 - 16x + 64$ **f** $x^2 + 20x + 100$

    g $x^2 - 12x + 36$ **h** $x^2 + 14x + 49$ **i** $x^2 - 18x + 81$

Example 16   🔊 Self Tutor

Factorise:

    a $16x^2 + 24x + 9$ **b** $4x^2 - 20x + 25$

a $16x^2 + 24x + 9$
     $= (4x)^2 + 2 \times 4x \times 3 + 3^2$
     $= (4x + 3)^2$

b $4x^2 - 20x + 25$
     $= (2x)^2 - 2 \times 2x \times 5 + 5^2$
     $= (2x - 5)^2$

---

3 Factorise:

    a $4x^2 + 4x + 1$ **b** $16x^2 - 40x + 25$ **c** $4x^2 + 28x + 49$

    d $4x^2 - 12x + 9$ **e** $9x^2 + 6x + 1$ **f** $9x^2 - 30x + 25$

Example 17   🔊 Self Tutor

Fully factorise:

    a $3x^2 - 18x + 27$ **b** $-2x^2 + 8x - 8$

a $3x^2 - 18x + 27$
     $= 3(x^2 - 6x + 9)$
     $= 3(x^2 - 2 \times x \times 3 + 3^2)$
     $= 3(x - 3)^2$

b $-2x^2 + 8x - 8$
     $= -2(x^2 - 4x + 4)$
     $= -2(x^2 - 2 \times x \times 2 + 2^2)$
     $= -2(x - 2)^2$

---

4 Fully factorise:

    a $2x^2 + 4x + 2$ **b** $2x^2 - 12x + 18$ **c** $3x^2 + 30x + 75$

    d $-x^2 + 6x - 9$ **e** $-x^2 - 8x - 16$ **f** $-x^2 + 16x - 64$

    g $-2x^2 + 40x - 200$ **h** $-4b^2 + 28b - 49$ **i** $ax^2 - 10ax + 25a$

E   FACTORISING QUADRATIC TRINOMIALS

A **quadratic trinomial** is an algebraic expression of the form $ax^2 + bx + c$ where x is a variable and a, b, c are constants, $a \neq 0$.

Using FOIL, $(x+3)(x+6) = x^2 + \underbrace{6x + 3x}_{\text{the sum of the 'inners' and 'outers'}} + \underbrace{18}_{\text{the product of the 'lasts'}}$

So, $(x+3)(x+6) = x^2 + [6+3]x + [6 \times 3]$
$= x^2 + [\text{sum of 6 and 3}]x + [\text{product of 6 and 3}]$
$= x^2 + 9x + 18$

In order to factorise a quadratic trinomial such as $x^2 + 9x + 18$ into the form $(x + ...)(x + ...)$ we must find two numbers which have a *sum* of 9 and a *product* of 18.

In the general case, $x^2 + \underbrace{(a+b)x}_{\substack{\text{the coefficient} \\ \text{of } x \text{ is the sum} \\ \text{of } a \text{ and } b}} + \underbrace{ab}_{\substack{\text{the constant term} \\ \text{is the product} \\ \text{of } a \text{ and } b}} = (x+a)(x+b)$

Example 18 ◀)) Self Tutor

Factorise: $x^2 + 11x + 24$

We need to find two numbers with sum 11 and product 24.
Pairs of factors of 24:

Factor product	1 × 24	2 × 12	3 × 8	4 × 6
Factor sum	25	14	11	10

↑ this one

The numbers we want are 3 and 8.
So, $x^2 + 11x + 24$
$= (x+3)(x+8)$

Most of the time we can find these two numbers mentally. We then don't need to show all of the working.

EXERCISE 17E

1 Find two numbers which have:
  a product 8 and sum 6
  b product 14 and sum 9
  c product 21 and sum 10
  d product -6 and sum 5
  e product -7 and sum -6
  f product -22 and sum -9
  g product 16 and sum -10
  h product 24 and sum -11

2 Factorise:
  a $x^2 + 3x + 2$
  b $x^2 + 10x + 24$
  c $x^2 + 11x + 18$
  d $x^2 + 13x + 36$
  e $x^2 + 12x + 35$
  f $x^2 + 26x + 25$
  g $x^2 + 7x + 12$
  h $x^2 + 15x + 54$
  i $x^2 + 52x + 100$

Example 19

Factorise: $x^2 - 7x + 12$

sum $= -7$ and product $= 12$

∴ the numbers are -3 and -4

So, $x^2 - 7x + 12$
$= (x - 3)(x - 4)$

The sum is negative but the product is positive, so both numbers must be negative.

3 Factorise:

a $x^2 - 10x + 9$
b $x^2 - 6x + 8$
c $x^2 - 13x + 12$
d $x^2 - 11x + 18$
e $x^2 - 14x + 33$
f $x^2 - 10x + 24$
g $x^2 - 14x + 45$
h $x^2 - 24x + 80$
i $x^2 - 16x + 48$

Example 20

Factorise: a $x^2 - 2x - 15$ b $x^2 + x - 6$

a sum $= -2$ and product $= -15$
∴ the numbers are -5 and $+3$
So, $x^2 - 2x - 15$
$= (x - 5)(x + 3)$

b sum $= 1$ and product $= -6$
∴ the numbers are -2 and $+3$
So, $x^2 + x - 6$
$= (x - 2)(x + 3)$

Since the product is negative, the numbers are opposite in sign.

4 Factorise:

a $x^2 - x - 2$
b $x^2 - x - 6$
c $x^2 + x - 6$
d $x^2 + 3x - 28$
e $x^2 + 4x - 45$
f $x^2 - 2x - 15$
g $x^2 - 3x - 18$
h $x^2 + 6x - 27$
i $x^2 - x - 30$
j $x^2 + 13x - 30$
k $x^2 + 7x - 60$
l $x^2 - 21x - 100$

Example 21

Fully factorise by first removing a common factor: $3x^2 + 6x - 72$

$3x^2 + 6x - 72$ {look for a **common factor**}
$= 3(x^2 + 2x - 24)$ {sum $= 2$, product $= -24$
$= 3(x + 6)(x - 4)$ ∴ the numbers are 6 and -4}

5 Fully factorise by first removing a common factor:

a $2x^2 + 10x + 12$
b $2x^2 + 18x + 28$
c $3x^2 + 21x + 36$
d $5x^2 - 10x - 15$
e $4x^2 + 40x + 36$
f $5x^2 + 20x + 15$
g $6x^2 - 24x - 30$
h $10x^2 - 80x + 120$
i $5x^2 - 60x + 100$
j $7x^2 - 28x + 28$
k $6x^2 + 30x - 36$
l $9x^2 - 54x + 72$
m $x^3 + 14x^2 + 48x$
n $x^3 - 9x^2 - 36x$
o $x^3 + 6x^2 - 55x$

F MISCELLANEOUS FACTORISATION

The following flowchart may prove useful:

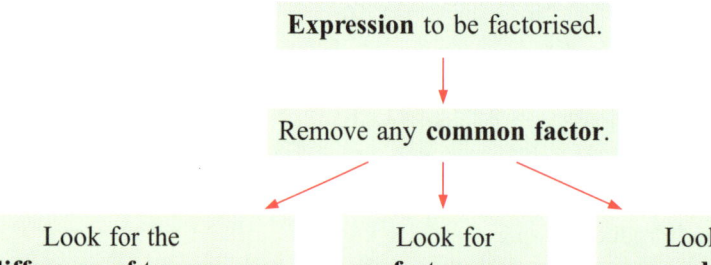

Expression to be factorised.

↓

Remove any **common factor**.

↓

Look for the **difference of two squares**.   Look for **perfect squares**.   Look for **sum and product type**.

EXERCISE 17F

1 Fully factorise:

a $5a^2 + 10a$
b $6b^2 + 12$
c $5x - 25y$
d $d^2 + 12d + 27$
e $x^2 - 11x + 24$
f $y^2 - 4y - 21$
g $-x^2 - 16x$
h $q^2 + q^3$
i $a^2b - 2ab$
j $-7x^2 - 28$
k $s^2 - s - 42$
l $16x - 2x^3$
m $2x - 28xy$
n $m^2 + 9mn$
o $y^2 - 8y + 15$
p $6x^2 - 6x - 36$
q $6x^2 - 36x + 54$
r $x^3 + 2x^2 + x$

2 Find the pattern in the following expressions and factorise:

a $x^2 - 8x + 16$
b $x^2 - 64$
c $9c^2 - 81$
d $9 - 9p^2$
e $3x^2 - 27$
f $5a^2 + 10a + 5$
g $25x^2 - 4y^2$
h $x^3 - 2x^2 + x$
i $2x^2 - 32x + 128$

3 Fully factorise:

a $xy - xz + x$
b $3x^3 - 3x^2$
c $x^2y^2 - 5xy$
d $9x - 4x^3$
e $(x+1)^2 - (x+1)$
f $x^2y - z^2y$
g $a(x+2) - b(x+2)$
h $3(x+y) - x(x+y)$
i $a(a+b) - b(a+b)$
j $x^3 - 16x$
k $3x^2 + 30x + 75$
l $4xy^2 - x^3$

REVIEW SET 17A

1 Find the HCF of:
   a $3a^2b$ and $6ab$
   b $3(x+1)$ and $6(x+1)^2$

2 Fully factorise:
   a $x^2 - 3x$
   b $3mn + 6n^2$
   c $ax^3 + 2ax^2 + 3ax$

3 Fully factorise:
   a $-2x^2 - 32x$
   b $d(t+2) - 4(t+2)$
   c $(x-1)^2 - (x-1)$
   d $2x(x+3) - 5(x+3)$
   e $3(g+1)^2 - 9(g+1)$
   f $b(b-c) - c(b-c)$

4 Fully factorise:
   a $9 - 16x^2$
   b $4x^2 + 20x + 25$
   c $9x^2 - 6x + 1$
   d $5x^2 - 20x + 20$
   e $9a^2 - 4b^2$
   f $6x^2 - 24$

5 Fully factorise:
   a $x^2 + 10x + 21$
   b $x^2 + 4x - 21$
   c $x^2 - 4x - 21$
   d $6 - 5x + x^2$
   e $4x^2 - 8x - 12$
   f $-x^2 - 13x - 36$
   g $20 + 9x + x^2$
   h $2x^2 - 2x - 60$
   i $3x^2 - 30x + 48$

REVIEW SET 17B

1 Find the HCF of:
   a $6y^2$ and $8y$
   b $4(x-2)$ and $2(x-2)(x+3)$

2 Fully factorise:
   a $2x^2 + 6x$
   b $-2xy - 4x$
   c $a^2x + ax^2 - 2ax$

3 Fully factorise:
   a $xy^3 - 16xy$
   b $3x^2 - 60x + 300$
   c $p(a+2) - q(a+2)$
   d $4cd^2 - 6c^2d$
   e $(k-3) + (k-3)^2$
   f $x(x-1) + 3x$

4 Fully factorise:
   a $2x^2 - 50$
   b $x^2 - 12x + 36$
   c $n^2 - 6n + 9$
   d $49 - 9z^2$
   e $2x^2 - 4x + 2$
   f $x^3 + 8x^2 + 16x$

5 Fully factorise:
   a $x^2 + 12x + 35$
   b $x^2 + 2x - 35$
   c $x^2 - 12x + 35$
   d $2x^2 - 4x - 70$
   e $30 - 11x + x^2$
   f $x^2 - 8x - 20$
   g $x^2 - 14x + 33$
   h $4x^2 - 36x - 88$
   i $x^3 + 5x^2 - 36x$

HISTORICAL NOTE — NORBERT WIENER 1894 - 1964

Norbert Wiener was born in Columbia, Missouri, USA in 1894. Norbert's father was determined that his son should succeed, and Norbert, who was obviously highly intelligent, was expected to study hard. At 18 years of age he achieved his doctorate in mathematics at Harvard University, and being too young for an academic position, he travelled overseas on scholarship, and studied in England and in Germany. His first paper 'Messenger in Mathematics' was published in 1913.

In 1919 Norbert accepted a position as mathematics instructor at the Massachusetts Institute of Technology (MIT). In time he was promoted to the chair of mathematics, and remained professor of mathematics until he retired in 1960.

He travelled extensively, investigating the latest research and findings by mathematicians. In 1933 he shared the Bocher Prize for mathematicians.

He wrote and published many important mathematical papers, especially 'Differential Space' (1923), 'Generalised Harmonic Analysis' (1930), and 'Tauberian Theorems' (1932).

During World War 2 Norbert's work on gunfire control and range finding led him to discover the theory on 'predicting stationary time series' which in turn led to his most famous work on the concept of 'cybernetics'. His famous book 'Cybernetics or Control and Communication in the Animal and the Machine' was first published in 1948.

In 1964 Norbert was awarded the National Medal of Science. His renown as a teacher helped to make MIT one of the finest centres for learning in the sciences in the world.

Chapter 18

Comparing categorical data

Contents:
- **A** Categorical data
- **B** Examining categorical data
- **C** Comparing and reporting categorical data
- **D** Data collection
- **E** Misleading graphs

HISTORICAL NOTE — FLORENCE NIGHTINGALE

Florence Nightingale (1820 - 1910) was born into an upper class English family. Her father believed that women should have an education, and she learnt Italian, Latin, Greek and history, and had an excellent early preparation in mathematics.

She served as a nurse during the Crimean War, and became known as 'the lady with the lamp'. During this time she collected data and kept systematic records.

After the war she came to believe that most of the soldiers in hospital were killed by insanitary living conditions rather than dying from their wounds.

She wrote detailed statistical reports and represented her statistical data graphically. She demonstrated that statistics provided an organised way of learning and this led to improvements in medical and surgical practices.

OPENING PROBLEM

A construction company is building a new high-rise apartment building in Tokyo. It will be 24 floors high with 8 apartments on each floor.

The company needs to know some information about the people who will be buying the apartments. They prepare a form which is published in all local papers and on-line:

HANAKO CONSTRUCTIONS – NEW APARTMENTS

¥70 to 400 million

Please respond only if you have *some interest* in owning your own residence in this prestigious new block.

Marital status:
☐ married ☐ single

Age group:
☐ 18 to 35 ☐ 36 to 59 ☐ 60+

Desired number of bedrooms:
☐ 1 ☐ 2 ☐ 3

Name: ....
Current address: ....
Phone number: ....

The statistical officer receives 272 responses and these are typed in coded form.

Marital Status	Married (M) Single (S)
Age group	18 to 35 (Y) 36 to 59 (I) 60+ (O)
Apartment size	1 2 3 bedrooms

The results are:

MY1	MI3	MI2	MO2	MY2	MO2	MO2	MY2	MO2	MI2
SY1	MO2	MY1	MI3	MO2	SO1	MI3	SO2	MO2	MO2
MI3	SO3	SO2	MI3	MI1	MO3	SI3	MO2	SO2	SO1
SO1	MI3	MO2	SO1	SY2	MO1	MY1	MI2	MO1	MO1
MO2	SO1	SO2	MI3	MO1	MI3	SI1	SI2	MO2	MO1
SO1	MO2	MI3	MI3	MO1	MI2	MO2	MO2	MO1	MO1
MO2	MI3	SY2	MO3	MO1	MI3	MI3	MI3	MO1	SO3
SO1	MO2	SI2	SO1	MO3	MI3	SI2	MO1	MI3	MO1
MO2	MO1	MI3	MY2	MY3	MI3	MI1	MY1	SY2	MI3
SO1	MY2	MI3	MO1	SI3	SI1	SY3	MO1	MO1	SO1
MY1	MI3	MI3	MI3	MY2	MO3	MO2	SO2	MI3	MO1
MO1	MI1	SI2	MO3	MI1	MI3	MI3	MY3	MO2	MO1
MO2	MY2	SO2	MY2	SO1	SI2	SO3	MO3	MI3	MI3
SO2	MI3	MI3	SO1	MY2	MI3	SY2	MO1	MI2	MI3
SO1	SO2	MI3	MO3	SO2	SY1	SO2	SI1	MY2	SI1
MI2	MI3	MI3	MY2	MY2	MI3	MO2	MO3	MO1	MI3
MO1	SO1	MO1	MO2	MO2	SO2	MI3	SO1	MI3	SI1
MI2	MY2	MI3	SI1	MI3	MO2	MI3	MI3	MO1	MO2
MI3	SI1	MI3	MI3	SY2	SO2	MO1	SI2	SO2	SO1
SO1	MI2	MO2	MO2	MO1	MI3	MI3	MI3	MO3	MO2
MI2	MI3	MO1	MI3	SO1	SO2	SI2	SO1	SI2	
SO1	MI3	MI3	MO3	MO2	MY1	MO2	MI3	MO3	
MI1	SY2	MO3	SO1	MY2	SI2	MI2	MI3	SI1	
MO1	MO2	MO3	MI3	MO1	SO1	MI2	MI3	MO2	
MI3	MI3	MI3	SO1	MI3	MI3	SY2	SI3	MO2	
MI1	SO1	MI3	MY2	SY3	MI3	MI2	SO2	MO2	
SO1	MI3	MI3	MY1	MI1	MO2	MY1	MI2	MO3	
MI1	MI3	MI3	SI1	MO3	MO1	SI1	SO1	SI1	

Things to think about:

- What problems are the construction company trying to solve?
- Is the company's investigation a census or a survey?
- What are the variables?
- Are the variables categorical or quantitative?
- What are the categories of the categorical variables?
- Can you explain why the construction company is interested in these categories?
- Is the data being collected in an unbiased way?
- Why were the names, addresses and phone numbers of respondents asked for?
- Can you make sense of the data in its present form?
- How could you reorganise the data so that it can be summarised and displayed?
- What methods of display are appropriate here?
- Can you make a conclusion regarding the data and write a report of your findings?

Statistics is the art of solving problems and answering questions by collecting and analysing data.

The facts or pieces of information we collect are called **data**.

One piece of information is known as one piece of *datum* (singular), whereas lots of pieces of information are known as *data* (plural).

A list of information is called a **data set**. If it is not in organised form it is called **raw data**.

A   CATEGORICAL DATA

VARIABLES

There are two types of variables that we commonly deal with:

- A **categorical variable** describes a particular quality or characteristic. The data is divided into **categories**, and the information collected is called **categorical data**.

    Examples of categorical variables are:

    Getting to school: the categories could be train, bus, car and walking.

    Colour of eyes: the categories could be blue, brown, hazel, green, grey.

- A **quantitative variable** has a numerical value and is often called a **numerical variable**. The information collected is called **numerical data**.

    Quantitative variables can be either discrete or continuous.

    A **quantitative discrete variable** takes exact number values and is often a result of **counting**.

    Examples of discrete quantitative variables are:

    The number of people in a household: the variable could take the values 1, 2, 3, ...

    The score out of 30 for a test: the variable could take the values 0, 1, 2, 3, ..., 30.

    A **quantitative continuous variable** takes numerical values within a certain continuous range. It is usually a result of **measuring**.

    Examples of quantitative continuous variables are:

    The weight of newborn babies: the variable could take any positive value on the number line but is likely to be in the range 0.5 kg to 8 kg.

    The heights of 14 year old students: the variable would be measured in centimetres. A student whose height is recorded as 145 cm could have exact height anywhere between 144.5 cm and 145.5 cm.

CENSUS OR SAMPLE

The two methods of data collection are by census or sample.

> A **census** involves collecting data about every individual in a *whole population*.

The individuals in a population may be people or objects. A census is detailed and accurate but is expensive, time consuming, and often impractical.

> A **sample** involves collecting data about a *part of the population* only.

A sample is cheaper and quicker than a census but is not as detailed or as accurate. Conclusions drawn from samples always involve some error.

A sample must truly reflect the characteristics of the whole population. To ensure this it must be **unbiased** and **large enough**.

Just how large a sample needs to be is discussed in future courses.

> In a **biased sample**, the data has been unfairly influenced by the collection process. It is not truly representative of the whole population.

STATISTICAL GRAPHS

Two variables under consideration are usually linked by one being *dependent* on the other.

For example: The *total cost of a dinner* depends on the *number of guests present*.
The *total cost of a dinner* is the dependent variable.
The *number of guests present* is the **independent variable**.

When drawing **graphs** involving two variables, the *independent variable* is usually placed on the **horizontal axis** and the *dependent variable* is placed on the **vertical axis**. An exception to this is when we draw a horizontal bar chart.

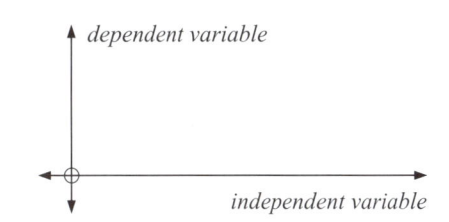

Acceptable graphs which display categorical data are:

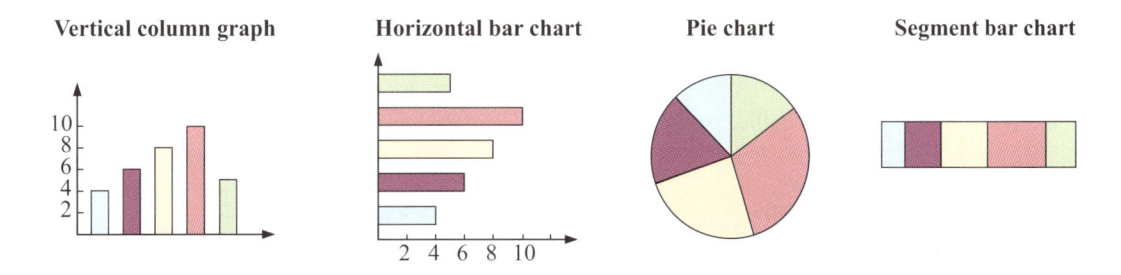

Vertical column graph   **Horizontal bar chart**   **Pie chart**   **Segment bar chart**

The **mode** of a set of categorical data is the category which occurs most frequently.

THE STATISTICAL METHOD

The process of **statistical enquiry** or **investigation** includes the following steps:

Step 1: Examine the problem which may be solved using data. Pose the correct questions.

Step 2: Collect unbiased data.

Step 3: Organise the data.

Step 4: Summarise and display the data.

Step 5: Analyse the data and make a conclusion in the form of a **conjecture**.

Step 6: Write a report.

GRAPHING USING A COMPUTER PACKAGE

Click on the icon to obtain a computer package which can be used to draw:

- graphs of a single set of categorical data using:
  - a vertical column graph
  - a horizontal bar chart
  - a pie chart
  - a segment bar chart
- comparative graphs of categorical data using:
  - a side-by-side column graph
  - a back-to-back bar chart.

EXERCISE 18A

1 Classify the following variables as either categorical or numerical:
  - **a** the number of text messages you send in a day
  - **b** the places where you access the internet
  - **c** the brands of breakfast cereal
  - **d** the heights of students in your class
  - **e** the daily maximum temperature for your city
  - **f** the number of road fatalities each day
  - **g** the breeds of horses
  - **h** the number of hours you sleep each night.

2 Write down possible categories for the following categorical variables:
  - **a** brands of cars
  - **b** methods of transport
  - **c** types of instruments in a band
  - **d** methods of advertising.

3 For each of the following possible investigations, classify the variable as categorical, quantitative discrete, or quantitative continuous:
  - **a** the types of flowers available from a florist

b the numbers on playing cards in a pack of cards

  c the heights of trees that were planted one year ago

  d the masses of oranges in a 5 kg bag

  e the times for runners in a 400 metre race

  f the number of oranges in the 5 kg bags at a supermarket

  g the varieties of peaches

  h the amount of rain each day for a month

  i the speeds of cars passing through an intersection

  j the types of fiction

  k the pulse rates of horses at the end of a race

  l the weekly cost of groceries for your family

  m the number of passengers for a taxi driver each day for a month

  n the number of students absent from school each day for a term.

4 State whether a census or a sample would be used for these investigations:

  a the country of origin of the parents of students in your class

  b the number of people in your country who are concerned about global warming

  c people's opinions about the public transport system in your capital city

  d the favourite desserts in your local restaurant

  e the most popular candidate for the next election in your state or county.

5 Comment on any possible bias in the following situations:

  a Members of a dog club are asked if dogs make the best pets.

  b School students are asked about the benefits of homework.

  c Commuters at peak hour are asked about crowding in buses.

6 Guests of a hotel in Paris were asked which country they lived in. The results are shown in the vertical column graph.

  a What are the variables in this investigation?

  b What is the dependent variable?

  c What is the sample size?

  d Find the mode of the data.

  e Construct a pie chart for the data. If possible, use a spreadsheet.

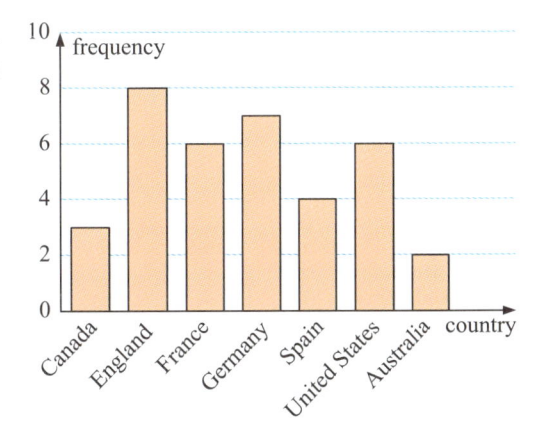

7 Fifty households of one street were asked which brand of television they owned. The data alongside was collected.

TV Brand	Frequency
A	9
B	4
C	12
D	8
E	7
F	10

  a What are the dependent and independent variables in this investigation?

  b If we are trying to determine the buying patterns of a whole city, is the sample unbiased? Explain your answer.

  c Find the mode of the data.

  d Construct a horizontal bar chart for the data.

8 Find the sector angle of a pie chart if the frequency of the category is:

  a 23 in a sample of 180
  b 128 in a sample of 720
  c 238 in a sample of 1250.

9 A sample of many people was taken, asking them their favourite fruit. On a pie chart a sector angle of 68° represented 277 people whose favourite fruit was an orange.
Find, to the nearest 10, the size of the sample used.

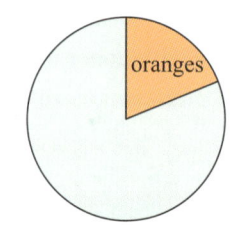

B EXAMINING CATEGORICAL DATA

For the **Opening Problem** data, the statistical officer first extracts the data for single people responding to the survey. Her findings are:

SY1	2	SI1	11	SO1	26	39
SY2	7	SI2	9	SO2	15	31
SY3	2	SI3	3	SO3	3	8
	11		23		44	78

In order to make a report to the construction company, she displays this data in the form of a **two way table**:

		Age of single respondent			Totals
		18 to 35	36 to 59	60+	
Number of bedrooms	1	2	11	26	39
	2	7	9	15	31
	3	2	3	3	8
	Totals	11	23	44	78

She then uses a spreadsheet to create a series of graphs. Here are two of them:

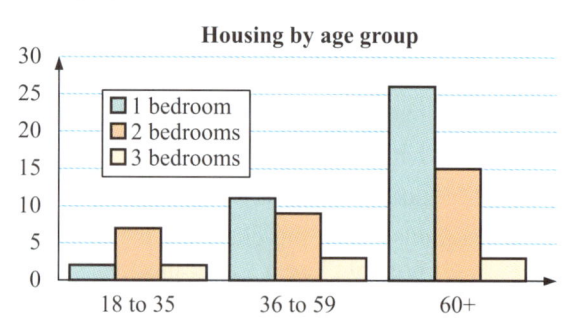

If we **transpose** the data by interchanging the rows and columns, we also get an interesting comparison.

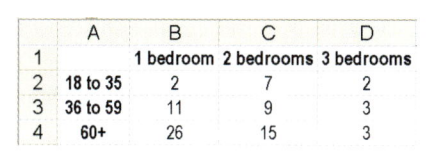

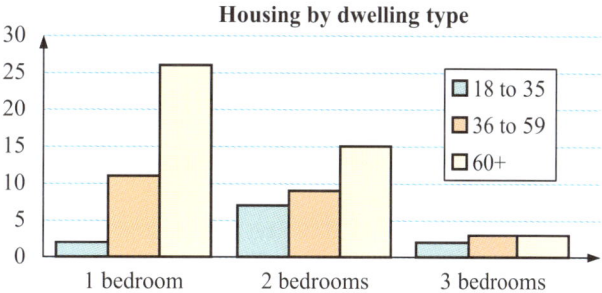

	A	B	C	D
1		1 bedroom	2 bedrooms	3 bedrooms
2	18 to 35	2	7	2
3	36 to 59	11	9	3
4	60+	26	15	3

Find out how to transpose your table without having to retype the data into new cells.

From the table of counts and from graphs, various questions can be answered. In many cases tables containing percentages may be more appropriate to use.

Example 1

A survey was conducted to determine willingness to be an organ donor. The results are shown alongside:

Marital status

		Single	Married	Totals
Organ donor	Yes	63	79	
	No	25	27	
	Totals			

a Complete the table to find the total of each row and column.

b How many people surveyed were married but not willing to be an organ donor?

c What percentage of single people surveyed were willing to be organ donors?

d What percentage of people surveyed were married?

a **Marital status**

		Single	Married	Totals
Organ donor	Yes	63	79	142
	No	25	27	52
	Totals	88	106	194

b From the table, 27 people were married but were not willing to be an organ donor.

c Percentage of single people who were willing to be organ donors
$= \frac{63}{88} \times 100\%$
$\approx 71.6\%$

d Percentage of people surveyed who were married $= \frac{106}{194} \times 100\% \approx 54.6\%$

EXERCISE 18B

1 Residents of a suburb were sent a survey in the mail. It asked them to indicate their gender and whether they would prefer a tennis court or a basketball court built in their suburb. The results are given alongside.

Gender

		Male	Female	Totals
Preference	Basketball	21	20	
	Tennis	9	35	
	Totals			

a Complete the table to find the total of each row and column.

b Did more males or females respond to the survey?

c What percentage of people responding to the survey preferred a basketball court?

d What percentage of people responding to the survey who preferred a tennis court were female?

2 To determine where the need for public transport is greatest, residents of a city were asked to indicate whether they lived to the north or south of the city centre, and the method of transport they used to go to work.

Position

Transport method		North	South	Totals
	Public	85	64	149
	Car	71	57	128
	Totals	156	121	277

a What percentage of people living north of the city centre take public transport to work?

b What percentage of people surveyed live south of the city centre and drive their car to work?

c Is the percentage of people using public transport greater to the north or the south of the city centre?

3 A survey was conducted in 1997, and another in 2007, to investigate how many people had a computer in their home. The results are given in the table alongside:

Year

Home computer		1997	2007	Totals
	Yes	113	281	
	No	159	23	
	Totals			

a Complete the table to find the total of each row and column.

b What percentage of people surveyed in 1997 had a computer in their home?

c What percentage of people surveyed in 2007 did not have a computer in their home?

d Find the increase in computer ownership percentage from 1997 to 2007, according to the survey.

4 A country town in England is organising a food festival. Residents interested in attending were asked to indicate their age group and whether they preferred Italian or Greek food.

Age group

Food preference		Under 30	Over 30	Totals
	Italian	29	38	67
	Greek	55	24	79
	Totals	84	62	146

a How many people responding to the survey expressed a preference for Greek food?

b What percentage of people who indicated they preferred Italian food were under 30?

c What percentage of people over 30 preferred Greek food?

d Which age group showed the most interest in the festival, and which type of food did that group prefer?

5 For the Singles' data from the **Opening Problem**:

a create your own tally on a spreadsheet and obtain the side-by-side column graph

b transpose the data on the spreadsheet and draw the new side-by-side column graph

c answer the following questions:

  i How many singles responded to the survey?

  ii What percentage of the total respondents were single?

  iii Which singles' age group showed the most interest in the new development and what form of housing interested them most?

  iv What percentage of the 36 to 59 singles age group were interested in 3 bedroom apartments?

  v What percentage of the single respondents were interested in buying a 2 bedroom apartment?

d True or false?

  i The 18 to 35 singles group has shown little interest in the new apartments.

  ii There is much interest amongst the single respondents in one bedroom apartments.

  iii The 60+ singles age group has shown most interest in the new apartments and the vast majority of them want them with 2 or 3 bedrooms.

INVESTIGATION   THE OPENING PROBLEM

Your task now is to organise the data from the married respondents for the **Opening Problem**. You could do this without using a spreadsheet and simply count from the raw data originally given. However, you could use the spreadsheet found on your CD. Click on the icon to find it.

It contains all 272 responses so the singles data should first be eliminated. **SPREADSHEET**

What to do:

1 Follow these steps to analyse the apartment size by age group:

 Step 1:   Open the spreadsheet by clicking on the icon.

 Step 2:   Enter the formula =COUNTIF($A:$A,"M"&D$3&$C4) into cell D4.

      the formula to count the number of times "MY1" appears in the data

      data in column A

      constructs "MY1" from the table row and column headings

	A	B	C	D	E	F	G
1	MY1						
2	SY1				Married people		
3	MI3			Y	I	O	Total
4	SO1		1	=COUNTIF($A:$A,"M"&D$3&$C4)			
5	MO2		2				
6	SO1		3				
7	MO2		Total				
8	SO1						
9	MO2						
10	SO1						

 Step 3:   Fill the formula in D4 down and across to cell F6.

 Step 4:   Highlight the cell range D4:G7 and click the sum button Σ on the toolbar.

 Step 5:   Highlight the cell range C3:F6 and click on the Chart Wizard button on the toolbar. Choose the first type of column graph and click the Finish button. A column graph of your tabulated data should appear.

2 The next task is to suitably graph the married respondents' data so that it can be compared:
- in categories
- with the singles' data to find similarities and differences.

Produce similar graphs for the singles' data.

3 Construct your own report for the construction company. It should include:
- tabulation of the data in summarised form
- graphical representation of the data
- discussion and conclusion.

4 What conclusions can you draw from the data?

C COMPARING AND REPORTING CATEGORICAL DATA

DISPLAY

To display **categorical data sets** for comparison we could use:

- a **side-by-side column graph** 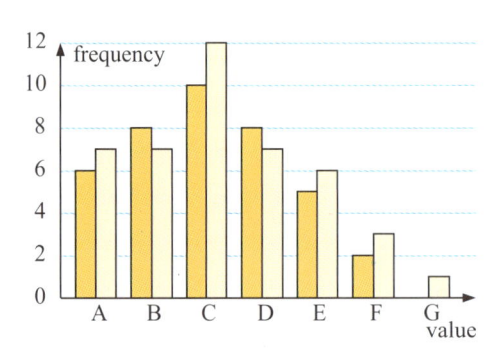
- a **back-to-back bar chart**.

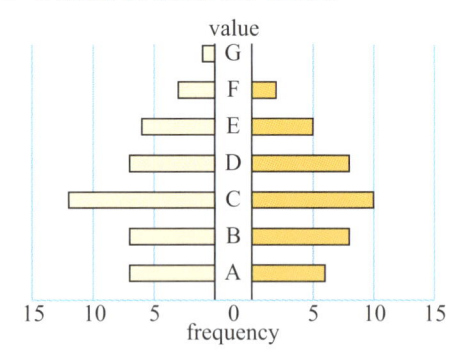

Example 2

In order to compare the popularity of car colours in London and Paris, a sample of 120 people from each city were asked their favourite car colour.

	Colour			
City	Red	Blue	Black	White
London	35	26	38	21
Paris	27	19	34	40

a Draw a side-by-side column graph comparing the data from London and Paris.

b Which colour is most popular in London?

c In which city are blue cars more popular?

d Which colour shows the largest difference in popularity between the two cities?

a

Car colours

(bar chart: no of votes vs colour; London and Paris bars for red, blue, black, white)

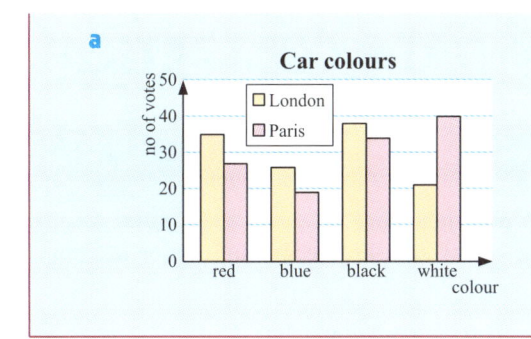

b Black is the most popular colour in London, with 38 people preferring black.

c From the graph, blue cars are more popular in London.

d The largest difference in popularity occurs in white cars, with 21 people in London compared to 40 people in Paris.

EXERCISE 18C

1 100 boys and girls were asked to indicate their favourite subjects. The results were:

	Maths	Science	Geography	Art
Boys	30	26	21	22
Girls	20	15	40	25

Subject / Gender

a Draw a back-to-back bar chart comparing the data for boys and girls.

b What is the most popular subject for girls?

c Do boys or girls show less variation in their subject preferences?

d In which subject were the boys' and girls' preferences closest?

2 People from two different age groups were surveyed about their favourite type of movie.

	Action	Comedy	Drama	Horror
Under 30	38	42	29	31
Over 30	17	21	25	7

Movie type / Age

a Draw a side-by-side column graph comparing movie preferences of the under 30s and over 30s.

b Is this a sensible way to compare the groups? Give a reason for your answer.

c Draw a side-by-side column graph again, this time using relative frequencies. Is this a more sensible way of comparing the groups?

d Which age group likes drama movies more?

e Which type of movie is preferred equally by each age group?

3 In the lead up to an election, 100 people from the electorates of Arton and Burnley were polled to see how they intended to vote on election day. The results are shown in the following table:

	Labor	Liberal	Independent	Undecided
Arton	37	28	14	21
Burnley	33	36	15	16

Party / Electorate

a Draw a back-to-back bar chart comparing the data from Arton and Burnley.

b Which party is the most popular in Arton?

c In which electorate is the Liberal Party performing the best?

d In which electorate is the intended voting closest?

D. DATA COLLECTION

DATA COLLECTION

There are a number of ways in which data can be misleading. It is always a good idea to check the source and method of collection of a set of data before making major decisions based on statistics.

Before data is collected the following **decisions** need to be made:

1. Should data for the investigation be collected from the whole **population** or a **sample** of the population?

   In most statistical investigations surveying the whole population is impractical; it is either too time consuming or too costly. In these cases a sample is chosen to represent the population. Conclusions for an investigation from a sample will not provide the same degree of accuracy as conclusions made from the population.

   In this context, **population** means all the people or things that the conclusions of a statistical investigation would apply to.

   For example, if you want to investigate a theory related only to your school then the population is all the students who attend your school. The population in this case would be accessible although the investigation could also be done with a carefully selected sample.

2. How should the **sample** be collected?

   If data is to be collected from a **sample** then a sample that represents the population must be chosen so that reliable conclusions about the population can be made.

   Samples must be chosen so that the results will not show **bias** towards a particular outcome. For example, if the purpose of a survey is to get an accurate indication of how the population of a city is going to vote at the next election then surveying a sample of voters from only one suburb would not provide information that represents all of the city. It would give a *biased* sample.

   One way of choosing an unbiased sample is to use **simple random sampling** where every member of the population has an equal chance of being chosen.

3. What should the **sample size** be?

   The **sample size** is an important feature to be considered if conclusions about the population are to be made from the sample.

   For example, measuring a group of three fifteen-year-olds would be insufficient to give a very reliable estimate of the height of fifteen-year-olds.

PROJECT

Decide on a worthwhile project of a statistical nature.
The data collected should be categorical in nature.

- Discuss the project with your teacher who will judge if it is appropriate.
- Make sure that your sample is **sufficiently large** to accurately reflect the population.
- Make sure that your sample is **not biased**.
- Write a detailed, factual report including your data and your conclusions.

EXERCISE 18D

1 A school has 820 students. An investigation concerning the school uniform is being conducted. 40 students from the school are randomly selected to complete the survey on their school uniform.

a What is the population size?

b What is the size of the sample?

c Explain why data collected in the following ways would not produce a sample representative of the population.

  i The surveyor's ten best friends are asked to complete the survey.

  ii All the students in one class are surveyed.

  iii Volunteers are asked to complete the survey.

2 A research company wants to know peoples' opinions on whether smoking should be banned in all public places.

They ask people standing outside buildings in the city during office hours. Explain why the data collected is likely to be biased.

3 A polling agency is employed to survey the voting intention of residents of a particular electorate in the coming election. From the data collected they are to predict the election result in that electorate.

Explain why each of the following situations would produce a biased sample:

a A random selection of people in the local large shopping complex is surveyed between 1 pm and 3 pm on a weekday.

b All the members of the local golf club are surveyed.

c A random sample of people on the local train station between 7 am and 9 am are surveyed.

d A doorknock is undertaken, surveying every voter in a particular street.

E | MISLEADING GRAPHS

Graphs can also be **misleading**. There are two ways this usually happens:

USING A 'CUT-OFF' SCALE ON THE VERTICAL AXIS

For example, consider the graph shown:

A close look at the graph reveals that the vertical scale does not start at zero and so has exaggerated the increase in profits.

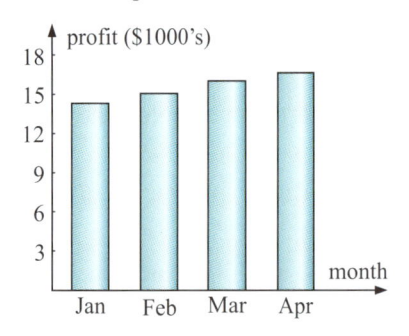

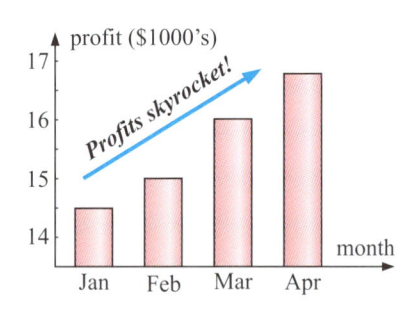

The graph should look like that on the left, which gives a better picture of the profit increases. It probably should be labelled *'A slow but steady increase in profits'*.

MISREPRESENTING THE 'BARS' ON A BAR CHART OR COLUMN GRAPH

Sometimes the 'bars' on a bar chart or column graph are shown with misleading area or volume.

For example, consider the graph below comparing sales of different flavours of drink.

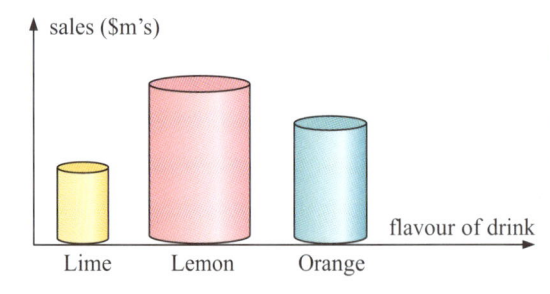

By giving the 'bars' the appearance of volume, the sales of lemon drinks look to be about eight times the sales of lime drinks.

However, on a bar chart the frequency is proportional to the height of the bar only, and so the graph should look like this:

The sales of lemon are just over twice the sales of lime.

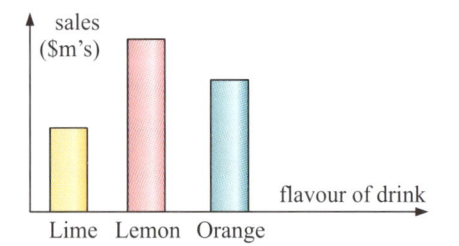

EXERCISE 18E

1 Describe the misleading or poor features of each of the following graphs:

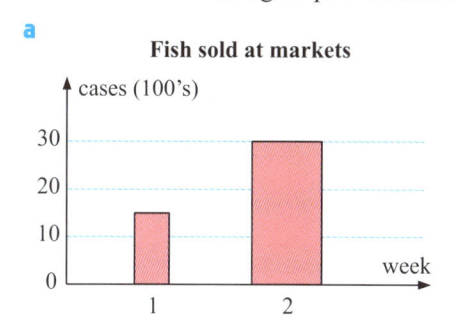

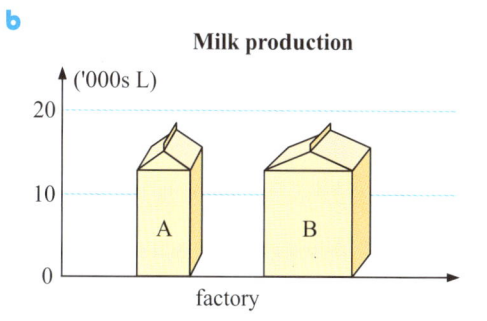

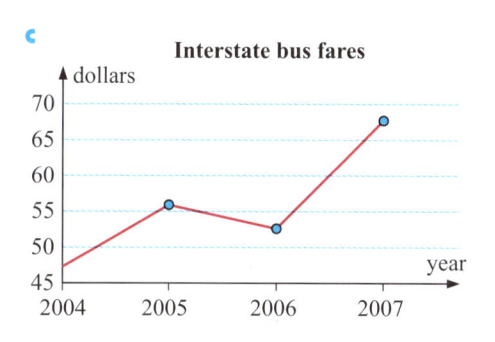

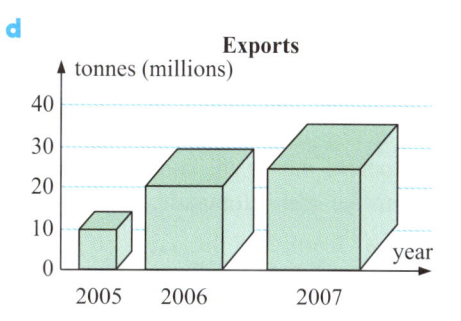

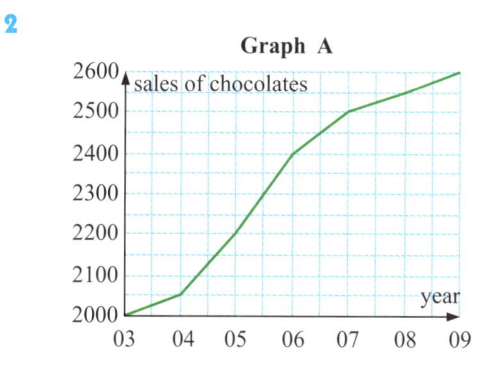

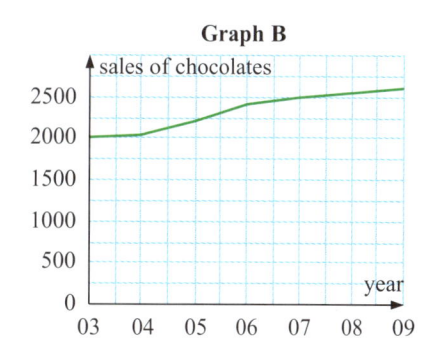

a Fish sold at markets

b Milk production

c Interstate bus fares

d Exports

2

Graph A — sales of chocolates

Graph B — sales of chocolates

a Which graph gives the impression of rapidly increasing sales?

b Have sales in fact rapidly increased over this 6 year period?

c According to graph A, the sales for 2006 appear to be double those of 2005. Is this true?

REVIEW SET 18A

1 For each of the following investigations, classify the variable as categorical, quantitative discrete, or quantitative continuous:

  a the favourite television programs watched by class members

  b the number of visitors to an art gallery each week.

2 To find out which foods at a school canteen the students eat most, 80 year 12 students were asked to nominate the item they purchased most often. The following data was collected:

Type of food	Frequency
Pie	20
Hot dog	16
Pasta	9
Sandwich	17
Apple	13
Chips	5

   a What are the variables in the investigation?

   b What are the dependent and independent variables?

   c In what way is the sample biased?

   d Construct a vertical column graph to illustrate the data.

3 A sample of people were asked whether they owned an analogue or a digital radio. The results were sorted by the age of the people surveyed, and are shown in the table alongside:

Radio type

Age		Analogue	Digital	Totals
	Under 30s	32	23	
	Over 30s	38	21	
	Totals			

   a Complete the table to find the total of each row and column.

   b How many people surveyed were over 30?

   c What percentage of under 30s surveyed own an analogue radio?

   d What percentage of people surveyed were over 30s who have a digital radio?

4 The ticket sales for a movie theatre over a two day period are given in the table alongside:

Ticket Group

	Adult	Concession	Children
Friday	121	71	63
Saturday	139	34	82

   a Draw a side-by-side column graph comparing the ticket sales from Friday and Saturday for each ticket group.

   b Which day is more popular with adults?

   c Which ticket group was least popular on Friday?

   d Which ticket group was most influenced by the day of the week?

5 To compare the sporting preferences of Hillsvale and Greensdale High Schools, 100 students from each school were asked to indicate their favourite sports:

Sport

	Gridiron	Ice Hockey	Basketball	Baseball	Football
Hillsvale	24	28	17	22	9
Greensdale	18	30	14	12	26

a Draw a back-to-back bar graph comparing the results for Hillsvale and Greensdale High Schools.

b Which is the most favoured sport at Hillsvale?

c Basketball is more popular in which school?

d Which sport is best described as "a mainly Greensdale School Sport"?

6 To investigate the public's opinion on whether money should be spent upgrading the local library, a questionnaire form is placed in the library for members of the public to fill out.
Explain why this sample is likely to be biased.

REVIEW SET 18B

1 For each of the following investigations, classify the variable as categorical, quantitative discrete, or quantitative continuous:
   a the area of each block of land on a street
   b the marital status of people in a particular suburb.

2 State whether a census or a sample would be used for these investigations:
   a finding the percentage of people who own a dog
   b finding the number of pets that students in a particular class own
   c finding the amount of rain a city receives each month.

3 To investigate whether being left or right handed has any effect on eyesight, a sample of people were asked whether they were left or right handed and whether they required glasses for driving. The results are given in the table alongside:

Require glasses

	Yes	No
Left handed	39	56
Right handed	229	311

   a How many people were surveyed?
   b What percentage of people surveyed were left handed?
   c What percentage of right handed people required glasses for driving?
   d Was there a significant difference between the percentages of right handed and left handed people who required glasses for driving?

4 A newspaper surveys 150 people aged under 30 and 150 people over 30 about an upcoming election. They want to find out which issues are most important to each age group.

Election Issues

	Unemployment	Inflation	Health	Education
Under 30	68	20	23	39
Over 30	52	27	50	21

a Draw a back-to-back bar graph comparing the results for the under 30s and the over 30s.

b Which issue is most important to the people aged under 30?

c Which issue is the least important to the people aged over 30?

d Which issue is mainly an "over 30s issue"?

5 A council is considering whether to occupy a block of land with a hotel, a shopping centre, or a park. To find the local residents' opinions, the council surveys 200 spectators at the local football match. The results are shown alongside:

Preference

	Hotel	Shopping	Park
Male	83	39	48
Female	4	16	10

a Which option was most preferred by the people surveyed?

b Would it be reasonable for the council to make a decision based on the answer given in **a**? Give a reason for your answer.

c Draw a side-by-side column graph comparing the preferences of males and females, using relative frequencies.

d Is the option of a park preferred more by males or females?

6 The Government releases the following graph showing the increase in employment in the tourism industry over recent years.

a Explain why the graph is misleading.

b Redraw the graph in a way that more accurately indicates the increase in employment.

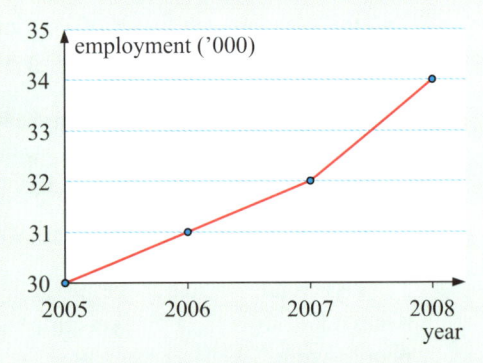

Chapter 19

Quadratic equations

Contents:
- **A** The Null Factor law
- **B** Equations of the form $ax^2 + bx = 0$
- **C** Solving equations using the 'difference of squares'
- **D** Solving equations of the form $x^2 + bx + c = 0$
- **E** Problem solving with quadratic equations
- **F** Simultaneous equations involving quadratic equations

Equations of the form $ax^2+bx+c=0$ where $a \neq 0$ are called **quadratic equations**.

For example, $2x^2 - 3x + 5 = 0$ and $x^2 + 3x = 0$ are quadratic equations whereas $x^2 + 5 + \dfrac{1}{x} = 0$ is not.

Consider the equation $x^2 = 4x$.

One might be tempted to divide both sides by x to get $x = 4$. However, in doing this the obvious solution $x = 0$ is lost.

We therefore need another method of solution to ensure that no solutions are lost.

A   THE NULL FACTOR LAW

The Null Factor law is an essential part of the process for solving quadratic equations.

THE NULL FACTOR LAW

When the product of two or more numbers is zero, then at least one of them must be zero.

So, if $ab = 0$ then $a = 0$ or $b = 0$.

For example:
- if $2xy = 0$ then $x = 0$ or $y = 0$
- if $x(x - 2) = 0$ then $x = 0$ or $x - 2 = 0$
- if $xyz = 0$ then $x = 0$, $y = 0$, or $z = 0$.

Example 1   ◀) Self Tutor

Solve for x: **a** $5x(x+2) = 0$ **b** $(x+4)(x-1) = 0$

a
$$5x(x+2) = 0$$
$\therefore\ 5x = 0$ or $x + 2 = 0$ {Null Factor law}
$\therefore\ x = 0$ or $x = -2$ {solving linear equations}
So, $x = 0$ or -2

b
$$(x+4)(x-1) = 0$$
$\therefore\ x + 4 = 0$ or $x - 1 = 0$ {Null Factor law}
$\therefore\ x = -4$ or $x = 1$ {solving linear equations}
So, $x = -4$ or 1

EXERCISE 19A

1 Explain what can be deduced from:

a $ac = 0$ **b** $bd = 0$ **c** $abc = 0$ **d** $3x = 0$

e $x(x-3) = 0$ **f** $x^2 = 0$ **g** $(x-5)y = 0$ **h** $x^2y = 0$

2 Solve for x:

   a $2x(x-1) = 0$ **b** $x(x+5) = 0$ **c** $3x(x+2) = 0$

   d $(x-1)^2 = 0$ **e** $-x(x-4) = 0$ **f** $-2x(x+3) = 0$

   g $x(2x+1) = 0$ **h** $3x(4x-3) = 0$

3 Solve for x:

   a $(x-1)(x-5) = 0$ **b** $(x+2)(x-4) = 0$ **c** $(x+3)(x+7) = 0$

   d $(x+7)(x-11) = 0$ **e** $2x(x-8) = 0$ **f** $(x+12)(x-5) = 0$

   g $-3x(x+7) = 0$ **h** $(2x+1)(x-3) = 0$ **i** $(x+6)(3x-1) = 0$

   j $(2x+1)(x+6) = 0$ **k** $x(3x+5) = 0$ **l** $(x-31)(x+11) = 0$

   m $(x+4)(4x-1) = 0$ **n** $-3x(x+3) = 0$ **o** $(2-x)(3x+4) = 0$

B   EQUATIONS OF THE FORM $ax^2 + bx = 0$

To solve quadratic equations of the form $ax^2 + bx = 0$ where $a \neq 0$ we first of all take out x as a common factor. We can then use the *Null Factor law*.

Example 2

Solve for x: $x^2 = 4x$

$$x^2 = 4x$$
$$\therefore\ x^2 - 4x = 0 \quad \{\text{subtracting } 4x \text{ from both sides to make RHS} = 0\}$$
$$\therefore\ x(x-4) = 0 \quad \{\text{factorising the LHS}\}$$
$$\therefore\ x = 0 \text{ or } x - 4 = 0 \quad \{\text{using the Null Factor law}\}$$
$$\therefore\ x = 0 \text{ or } x = 4$$

$\dfrac{x^2}{x} = \dfrac{4x}{x}$ gives $x = 4$ only. We need the Null Factor law to ensure the solution $x = 0$ is not lost.

EXERCISE 19B

1 Solve for x:

   a $x^2 - x = 0$ **b** $x^2 - 13x = 0$ **c** $x^2 + 8x = 0$

   d $x^2 + 3x = 0$ **e** $2x + x^2 = 0$ **f** $5x - x^2 = 0$

   g $12x - x^2 = 0$ **h** $x^2 + 7x = 0$ **i** $x^2 - 4x = 0$

   j $2x^2 - 7x = 0$ **k** $3x^2 - 15x = 0$ **l** $2x^2 + 8x = 0$

2 Solve for x:

    a $x^2 = 3x$ **b** $x^2 = 10x$ **c** $x^2 + x = 0$

    d $x^2 = -6x$ **e** $2x^2 + 7x = 0$ **f** $5x = x^2$

    g $8x = x^2$ **h** $3x^2 = 18x$ **i** $5x^2 = 6x$

    j $7x + x^2 = x$ **k** $x^2 - 4 = 2x - 4$ **l** $2x^2 + x = 3x$

C   SOLVING EQUATIONS USING THE 'DIFFERENCE OF SQUARES'

Equations like $x^2 - 9 = 0$ and $4x^2 - 1 = 0$ have the 'difference of squares' on the LHS of the equals sign.

We can use $a^2 - b^2 = (a + b)(a - b)$ to convert the difference into a product.

Example 3   ◀)) Self Tutor

Solve for x: **a** $x^2 - 4 = 0$ **b** $x^2 = 9$

a
$$x^2 - 4 = 0$$
$$\therefore (x+2)(x-2) = 0$$
$$\therefore x + 2 = 0 \quad \text{or} \quad x - 2 = 0$$
$$\therefore x = -2 \quad \text{or} \quad 2$$
So, $x = \pm 2$

b
$$x^2 = 9$$
$$\therefore x^2 - 9 = 0$$
$$\therefore (x+3)(x-3) = 0$$
$$\therefore x + 3 = 0 \quad \text{or} \quad x - 3 = 0$$
$$\therefore x = -3 \quad \text{or} \quad 3$$
So, $x = \pm 3$

EXERCISE 19C

1 Solve for x:

    a $x^2 - 16 = 0$ **b** $x^2 - 49 = 0$ **c** $x^2 - 1 = 0$

    d $x^2 = 25$ **e** $x^2 = 144$ **f** $x^2 = 81$

    g $2x^2 - 8 = 0$ **h** $3x^2 - 27 = 0$ **i** $5x^2 - 20 = 0$

    j $-3x^2 + 12 = 0$ **k** $-2x^2 + 8 = 0$ **l** $x^2 + 4 = 0$

2 Solve for x:

    a $2 - 8x^2 = 0$ **b** $1 - 9x^2 = 0$ **c** $4 - 25x^2 = 0$ **d** $4x^2 - 1 = 0$

    e $4x^2 - 9 = 0$ **f** $9x^2 - 4 = 0$ **g** $3x^2 + 12 = 0$ **h** $16x^2 - 25 = 0$

D SOLVING EQUATIONS OF THE FORM $x^2 + bx + c = 0$

To solve $x^2 - 5x + 6 = 0$ we must first factorise $x^2 - 5x + 6$.

To do this we have to find two numbers with a **sum** of -5 and a **product** of 6.

The numbers required are -2 and -3, so $x^2 - 5x + 6 = (x-2)(x-3)$.

Example 4 ◀) Self Tutor

Solve for x: **a** $x^2 - 3x + 2 = 0$ **b** $x^2 = x + 12$ **c** $x^2 + 4 = 4x$

a $x^2 - 3x + 2 = 0$ {We need two numbers with sum -3
$\therefore (x-1)(x-2) = 0$ and product 2. These are -1 and -2.}
$\therefore x - 1 = 0$ or $x - 2 = 0$
$\therefore x = 1$ or 2

b $x^2 = x + 12$ {Make RHS $= 0$ by subtracting $x + 12$ from both sides}
$\therefore x^2 - x - 12 = 0$ {We need two numbers with sum -1
$\therefore (x-4)(x+3) = 0$ and product -12. These are -4 and $+3$.}
$\therefore x - 4 = 0$ or $x + 3 = 0$
$\therefore x = 4$ or -3

c $x^2 + 4 = 4x$ {Make RHS $= 0$ by subtracting $4x$ from both sides}
$\therefore x^2 - 4x + 4 = 0$ {We need two numbers with sum -4 and product $+4$.
$\therefore (x-2)(x-2) = 0$ These are -2 and -2.}
$\therefore x = 2$

Sometimes each term in an equation contains a **constant common factor**. We can simplify these equations by dividing each term by the constant.

For example, consider $3x^2 + 21x + 30 = 0$.
If we divide each term by 3 then $x^2 + 7x + 10 = 0$.

EXERCISE 19D

1 Solve for x:

a $x^2 + 7x + 10 = 0$ **b** $x^2 + 6x + 8 = 0$ **c** $x^2 + 11x + 10 = 0$
d $x^2 - 8x + 12 = 0$ **e** $x^2 - 5x + 4 = 0$ **f** $x^2 - 11x + 24 = 0$
g $x^2 + 10x + 25 = 0$ **h** $x^2 - 3x - 18 = 0$ **i** $x^2 + 7x - 18 = 0$
j $x^2 - 22x + 121 = 0$ **k** $x^2 - 6x + 9 = 0$ **l** $x^2 - 5x - 6 = 0$
m $x^2 + 11x - 60 = 0$ **n** $x^2 + 18x - 63 = 0$ **o** $x^2 - 12x - 64 = 0$

2 Solve for x:

a $3x^2 + 21x + 30 = 0$ b $2x^2 + 4x - 30 = 0$ c $2x^2 - 24x + 72 = 0$

d $3x^2 - 21x + 36 = 0$ e $5x^2 - 5x - 210 = 0$ f $4x^2 + 32x + 48 = 0$

3 Solve for x:

a $x^2 - 14x = 15$ b $x^2 + 2 = 3x$ c $x^2 = 3x + 28$

d $x^2 = 20 + x$ e $8 = x^2 + 7x$ f $x^2 = 5x + 24$

g $2x^2 + 2x = 24$ h $x^2 = 4x + 45$ i $3x^2 = 30x - 48$

j $x^2 + 1 = 2x$ k $x^2 = 19x + 20$ l $5x^2 = 20(x + 8)$

4 Solve for x:

a $x(x + 2) = 15$ b $x(x - 2) = 5(x + 12)$ c $2x - 6 = x(x - 5)$

d $x^2 - 4 = x + 2$ e $2(x + 5) = x^2 + 11$ f $5 - x^2 = 2x - 3$

INVESTIGATION — SOLUTIONS OF A QUADRATIC EQUATION

How many solutions can a quadratic equation have?

This investigation should help to answer this question.

What to do:

1 Show that $(x - 1)^2 = 4$, $(x - 1)^2 = 0$ and $(x - 1)^2 = -4$ can all be put into quadratic form $ax^2 + bx + c = 0$.

2 a Show that $(x - 1)^2 = 4$ has two different solutions.

b Show that $(x - 1)^2 = 0$ has one solution.

c Explain why $(x - 1)^2 = -4$ has no solutions.

3 Use the graphing package to graph $y = (x - 1)^2$.

GRAPHING PACKAGE

a Now graph $y = 4$.
The graphs meet when $(x - 1)^2 = 4$.
Use this to solve the equation $(x - 1)^2 = 4$.

b Erase the graph of $y = 4$ and replace it with $y = 0$.
Use this to solve the equation $(x - 1)^2 = 0$.

c Erase the graph of $y = 0$ and replace it with $y = -4$.
Use this to solve the equation $(x - 1)^2 = -4$.

E   PROBLEM SOLVING WITH QUADRATIC EQUATIONS

Many problems when converted to algebraic form result in a **quadratic equation**.

We use **factorisation** and the **Null Factor law** to solve these equations.

PROBLEM SOLVING METHOD

- Carefully **read the question** until you **understand** it. A **rough sketch** may be useful.
- Decide on the **unknown** quantity. Label it with a variable such as x.
- Find an **equation** which connects x and the information you are given.
- **Solve** the equation using factorisation and the **Null Factor law**.
- **Check** that any solutions satisfy the original problem.
- Write your answer to the question in **sentence form**.

Example 5 — Self Tutor

The sum of a number and its square is 30. Find the number.

Let the number be x.

$$\begin{aligned} \text{So,} \quad x + x^2 &= 30 &&\{\text{the number plus its square is 30}\} \\ \therefore \quad x^2 + x &= 30 &&\{\text{rearranging}\} \\ \therefore \quad x^2 + x - 30 &= 0 &&\{\text{subtracting 30 from both sides}\} \\ \therefore \quad (x+6)(x-5) &= 0 &&\{\text{factorising}\} \\ \therefore \quad x = -6 \ \text{or} \ x &= 5 \end{aligned}$$

$\therefore$ the numbers are -6 and 5.

Check: If $x = -6$, we have $-6 + (-6)^2 = -6 + 36 = 30$ ✓
If $x = 5$, we have $5 + 5^2 = 5 + 25 = 30$ ✓

Example 6 — Self Tutor

Two numbers have a sum of 10 and the sum of their squares is 58. Find the numbers.

Let one of the numbers be x.

$\therefore$ the other number is $10 - x$. {their sum is 10}

$$\begin{aligned} \text{So,} \quad x^2 + (10-x)^2 &= 58 &&\{\text{insert brackets around } 10 - x\} \\ \therefore \quad x^2 + 100 - 20x + x^2 &= 58 &&\{\text{expand the brackets}\} \\ \therefore \quad 2x^2 - 20x + 100 - 58 &= 0 &&\{\text{subtract 58 from both sides}\} \\ \therefore \quad 2x^2 - 20x + 42 &= 0 &&\{\text{collect like terms}\} \\ \therefore \quad x^2 - 10x + 21 &= 0 &&\{\text{divide each term by the common factor 2}\} \\ \therefore \quad (x-3)(x-7) &= 0 &&\{\text{factorise}\} \\ \therefore \quad x = 3 \ \text{or} \ 7 \end{aligned}$$

If $x = 3$, $10 - x = 7$.
If $x = 7$, $10 - x = 3$.

$\therefore$ the numbers are 3 and 7.

EXERCISE 19E

1. The sum of a number and its square is 42. Find the number.

2. When a number is squared, the result is five times the original number. Find the number.

3. When a number is subtracted from its square, the result is 56. Find the number.

4. Find two consecutive integers such that the square of the smaller plus twice the larger is 50.

5. Two numbers have a sum of 9 and the sum of their squares is 153. Find the numbers.

6. The product of two consecutive integers is 156. Find the integers.

7. The sum of the squares of two consecutive odd numbers is 290. Find the numbers.

8. When the square of a number is added to the number trebled the result is 108. What is the number?

9. Two numbers differ by 4. The product of the two numbers is 221. What are the numbers?

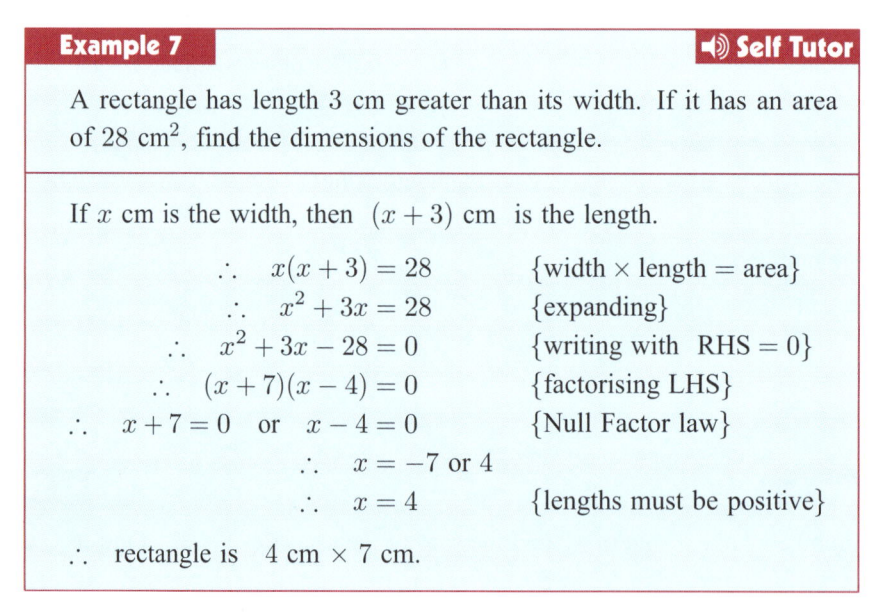

Example 7   ◀) Self Tutor

A rectangle has length 3 cm greater than its width. If it has an area of 28 cm², find the dimensions of the rectangle.

If x cm is the width, then $(x+3)$ cm is the length.

$\therefore \quad x(x+3) = 28$ {width × length = area}
$\therefore \quad x^2 + 3x = 28$ {expanding}
$\therefore \quad x^2 + 3x - 28 = 0$ {writing with RHS = 0}
$\therefore \quad (x+7)(x-4) = 0$ {factorising LHS}
$\therefore \quad x + 7 = 0$ or $x - 4 = 0$ {Null Factor law}
$\therefore \quad x = -7$ or 4
$\therefore \quad x = 4$ {lengths must be positive}

$\therefore$ rectangle is 4 cm × 7 cm.

10. The length of a rectangle is 4 cm more than the width. If the area is 96 cm², find the width of the rectangle.

11. 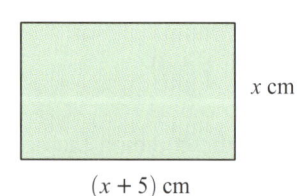
    a Write down an expression for the rectangle's:
       i area   ii perimeter.
    b If the perimeter is 21.6 cm, what is the rectangle's area?
    c If the area is 176 cm², what is the rectangle's perimeter?

    (rectangle with width x cm and length $(x+5)$ cm)

12. A triangle has altitude 4 cm less than its base. If the area is $38\frac{1}{2}$ cm², find the base of the triangle.

13. A rectangle has sides which differ in length by 3 cm. If the area is 154 cm², find the perimeter of the rectangle.

14 A rectangle has length 4 cm longer than its width. It has an area numerically equal to its perimeter.
    a Find the width of the rectangle.   **b** Check your answer to **a**.

15 A floor is 18 m by 16 m. A carpet is placed in its centre so that an equal width of uncovered floor remains all the way around the carpet. The area of the floor remaining is 120 m². Find the dimensions of the carpet.
Hint: Let the remaining strip of floor have width x m.

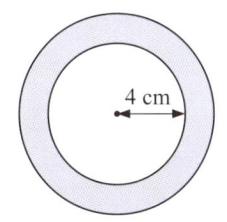

16 The shaded region has area 33π cm².
Find the radius of the outer circle.

17 **a** Kelly claims that the equation $x^2 + ax + b = 0$ has solutions $x = 2$ and $x = -5$ but has forgotten the values of a and b. Find a and b to help Kelly.
    b Fredrik knows that $x^2 + ax + b = 0$ has only one solution and this is $x = -1\frac{1}{2}$. What are the values of a and b?

18 The sum of the squares of three consecutive integers is 110.
    a Let the smallest integer be x and find a quadratic equation involving x.
    b Solve the quadratic equation and hence write down the three integers.
    c This time let the middle integer be x and find the quadratic equation involving x.
    d Solve the equation in **c** and hence write down the three integers.
    e Which method is better, starting with the smallest being x or the middle number being x? Why?

19 The sum of the squares of three consecutive odd numbers is 371. What are the numbers?

20 Three numbers are of the form $x - 1$, x and $x + 1$.
The square of the middle number is twice the product of the other two numbers.
What are the numbers given that each of them is positive?

21 The sum of the squares of five consecutive integers is 15. What are the integers?

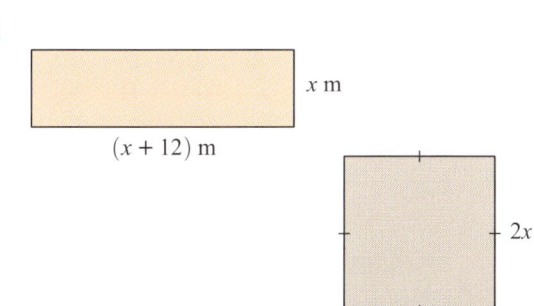

22 Alongside are the dimensions of two flower beds of equal area.
    a Find their dimensions.
    b What is the total length of border needed to enclose both of them?

F SIMULTANEOUS EQUATIONS INVOLVING QUADRATIC EQUATIONS

Often the solution of simultaneous equations involves a quadratic equation. To solve these problems we use **substitution** of one equation into the other.

Example 8

Solve simultaneously: $y = x^2$ and $y = 2x + 3$.

We substitute x^2 for y in the second equation.

So, $x^2 = 2x + 3$
$\therefore \ x^2 - 2x - 3 = 0$
$\therefore \ (x - 3)(x + 1) = 0$
$\therefore \ x - 3 = 0$ or $x + 1 = 0$
$\therefore \ x = 3$ or $x = -1$

When $x = 3$, $y = 3^2 = 9$.
When $x = -1$, $y = (-1)^2 = 1$.

Thus the solutions are $x = 3, y = 9$ or $x = -1, y = 1$.

Example 9

Solve simultaneously: $xy = -6$ and $y = x - 5$.

We substitute $(x - 5)$ for y in the first equation.

So, $x(x - 5) = -6$
$\therefore \ x^2 - 5x + 6 = 0$
$\therefore \ (x - 2)(x - 3) = 0$
$\therefore \ x - 2 = 0$ or $x - 3 = 0$
$\therefore \ x = 2$ or $x = 3$

When $x = 2$, $y = 2 - 5 = -3$.
When $x = 3$, $y = 3 - 5 = -2$.

Thus the solutions are $x = 2, y = -3$ or $x = 3, y = -2$.

EXERCISE 19F

1 Solve simultaneously:

a $y = x + 6$ and $y = x^2$
b $y = x + 12$ and $y = x^2$
c $y = x^2$ and $y = 2x - 1$
d $y = x^2$ and $x + y = 12$

    e $y = 8 - x$ and $xy = 7$ **f** $xy = -5$ and $y = x - 6$

    g $xy = 4$ and $y = 4 - x$ **h** $xy + 6 = 0$ and $x + y = 1$

2 Two numbers have a product of 24 and one of them is five more than the other. What are the numbers?

3 One number is the square of another number and is also 8 more than twice that number. What are the numbers?

HOW FAR WILL A CAR TRAVEL WHEN BRAKING?

LINKS   click here

Areas of interaction:
Community and service, Health and social education

REVIEW SET 19A

1 Solve for x:

   a $-5x = 0$ **b** $2(x+2)(x-8) = 0$ **c** $-2(2x-1)^2 = 0$

   d $4x^2 + 8x = 0$ **e** $x^2 - 5x - 24 = 0$ **f** $x^2 = 7x + 18$

2 Solve for x:

   a $x^2 - 9 = x + 3$ **b** $x(x+4) = 8x - 3$

3 Solve simultaneously:

   a $y = x^2$ and $y = x + 2$ **b** $x^2 + y^2 = 25$ and $y = x + 7$.

4 If a number is subtracted from its square, the result is 56. What is the number?

5 A rectangle has length 6 cm larger than its width and has area 72 cm². What is the width of the rectangle?

6 The height of a triangle is 4 cm more than its base. Find the length of its base given that its area is 58.5 cm².

7 A square has sides of length $3x$ cm. A rectangle is $2x$ cm by $(x+7)$ cm. The area of the square is twice that of the rectangle. Find the dimensions of each figure.

8 Two numbers have a product of -6 and one of them is 5 more than the other. Find the numbers.

REVIEW SET 19B

1 Solve for x:

   a $-4x = 0$ **b** $3x(2x-1) = 0$ **c** $x^2 = 14x - 33$

   d $(1-3x)^2 = 0$ **e** $5x - 10x^2 = 0$ **f** $x^2 + 7x + 12 = 0$

2 Solve for x:

   a $x(x-3) = 10$ **b** $(x+2)(x-3) = 2x(x-3) - 2$

3 Solve simultaneously:

   a $xy = -8$ and $y = 2 - x$ **b** $x^2 + y = 10$ and $y = 2x - 5$.

4 The square of a number is subtracted from the original number and the result is -110. Find the number.

5 A rectangular plot has length 5 m more than its width. If its area is 84 m^2, find the dimensions of the plot.

6 A rectangle has one side 4 m longer and the other side 2 m shorter than a square. The rectangle's area is 14 m^2 more than that of the square. What is the area of the rectangle?

7 The sum of the squares of three consecutive even numbers is 308. What are the integers?

8 The sum of the squares of two numbers is 5 and one of the numbers is 3 more than the other. Find the numbers.

ADA BYRON LOVELACE
(1815 - 1852)

Ada Byron Lovelace was born in England. She was the daughter of the famous poet, **Lord Byron**. However, most of her basic mathematical knowledge was taught to her by her mother who was very interested and capable in the subject.

When friends of her parents recognised her ability they suggested that she should go and see **Charles Babbage** who was one of the notable mathematicians of that era. At that time Babbage was using inventions of his own which were actually very basic mechanical computers. He called two of these machines the *Difference Engine* and the *Analytic Engine*.

At the age of 18, Lovelace had easily grasped the concepts involved in these machines and was greatly motivated to pursue a study of mathematics. Babbage was so impressed by her insight into the workings of his equipment that he readily agreed when she asked if she could work with him.

Later she published several essays explaining how and why the machines worked. Simultaneously, she developed a language for "communicating with machines". This language served the same purpose as does present day computer programming.

Like most people, Ada enjoyed mathematical games, and she was delighted when she discovered winning strategies. Soon after Ada purchased the game of "Solitaire" from a toy shop she was able to complete it successfully every time. Not satisfied with this achievement she asked Babbage if it were possible to find a formula for achieving a successful solution to this game.

Chapter 20
Quantitative statistics

Contents:
- **A** Quantitative data
- **B** Grouped discrete data
- **C** Measuring the centre
- **D** Comparing and reporting discrete data

OPENING PROBLEM

Jamima is investigating whether non-smokers are generally healthier people than those who smoke.

She selected 100 smokers and 100 non-smokers, each of whom were middle-aged males. She asked each of them how many sick days they had taken from work in the last 12 months. The results were:

Non-smokers

2 4 1 0 2 3 3 4 5 2 1 1 2 0 3 4 1 2 1 3 2 1 3 6 4
5 2 1 3 1 3 2 0 3 2 1 2 5 3 1 0 6 1 2 2 7 3 2 1 2
4 2 3 0 1 3 1 4 2 8 3 2 0 1 1 3 2 4 1 3 2 5 0 1 3
2 7 4 3 1 1 2 6 5 4 2 3 4 5 0 2 4 1 2 5 3 0 6 4 2

Smokers

3 2 4 5 2 1 4 5 5 3 6 4 8 7 3 1 2 5 6 4 0 1 4 7 4
5 9 1 2 4 3 6 7 4 6 5 3 1 2 5 3 0 7 1 5 3 6 2 4 5
2 4 6 5 4 3 7 4 3 5 9 4 2 3 7 4 6 13 3 6 4 2 1 5 0
5 8 3 6 7 2 4 5 1 6 3 4 2 7 3 0 5 4 1 8 2 3 6 3 4

Thing to think about:

- Can you clearly state the problem Jamima wants to solve?
- How has Jamima tried to make a fair comparison?
- What is the best way of organising this data?
- What are suitable methods of displaying the data?
- How can we best indicate the most typical response?
- Can a satisfactory conclusion be made?

A QUANTITATIVE DATA

A **quantitative variable** has a numerical value and is often called a **numerical variable**. The information collected is called **numerical data**.

There are two types of quantitative variables:

A **quantitative discrete variable** takes exact number values and is often a result of **counting**.

For example:

- *The number of telephone calls received each day:*   the variable could have values: 0, 1, 2, 3, 4, ...
- *Shoe size:*   the variable could take the values of 3, $3\frac{1}{2}$, 4, $4\frac{1}{2}$, 5, $5\frac{1}{2}$, ...

A **quantitative continuous variable** takes numerical values within a certain continuous range. It is usually a result of **measuring**.

For example:

- *The time taken to text a message:* the variable could take any value from about 10 seconds to 2 minutes.
- *The speed of cars on a stretch of highway:* the variable can take any value from 0 km per hour to the fastest speed that a car can travel but is most likely to be in the range 50 km per hour to 180 km per hour.

ORGANISATION AND DISPLAY OF DISCRETE DATA

In the **Opening Problem**, *the number of sick days* is a **discrete quantitative variable**.

To organise the data a **tally-frequency table** could be used. We count the data systematically and use | to indicate one data value, or ||||| to represent 5.

Below is the tally-frequency table for non-smokers:

Number of sick days	Tally	Frequency
0											9
1																							21
2																											25
3																					19
4														12
5									7
6						4
7				2
8			1

We could use a **dot plot** or a **column graph** to display the results.

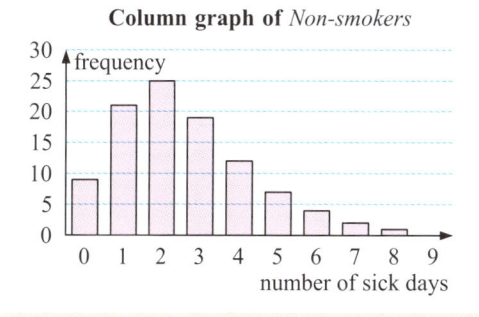

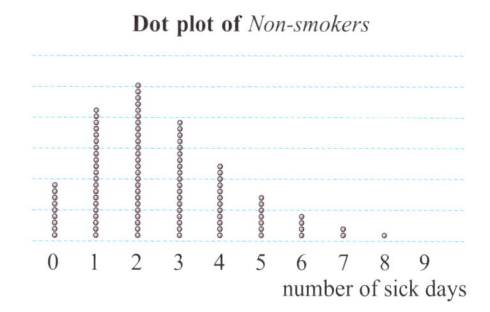

DISCUSSION

What are the advantages and disadvantages of using a dot plot as opposed to a column graph?

From both graphs we can make observations and calculations such as:

- 2 sick days is the **mode** of the *Non-smokers* data, since it is the most frequently occurring value
- 74% of non-smokers had fewer than 4 sick days.

DESCRIBING THE DISTRIBUTION OF THE DATA SET

Many data sets show **symmetry** or **partial symmetry** about the centre of the distribution. We can see this by drawing a curve of a column graph or dot plot. For example, if we place a curve over the column graph opposite, we see the curve is symmetric. We say we have a **symmetrical distribution** of data.

For the *Non-smokers* data we draw the curve alongside. This distribution is said to be **positively skewed** since it is 'stretched' on the right or positive side of the centre.

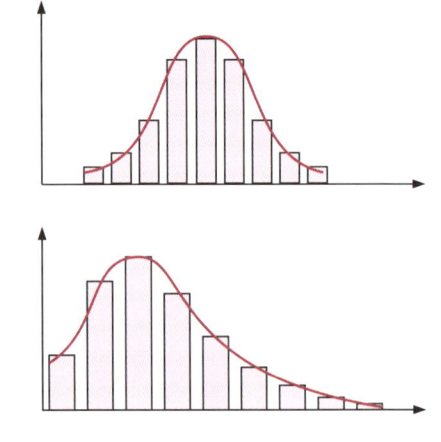

So we have:

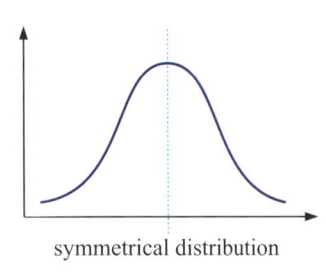

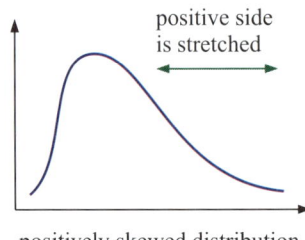

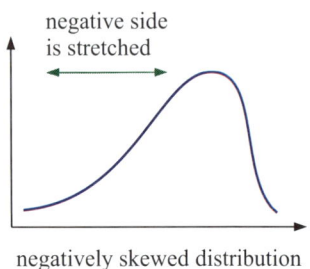

symmetrical distribution   positively skewed distribution   negatively skewed distribution

OUTLIERS

Outliers are data values that are either much larger or much smaller than the general body of data. Outliers appear separated from the body of data on a frequency graph.

For example, in the *Non-smokers* data from the **Opening Problem**, suppose one non-smoker had taken 12 sick days.

The data value 12 would be considered an outlier since it is much larger than the other data. On the column graph it would appear separated:

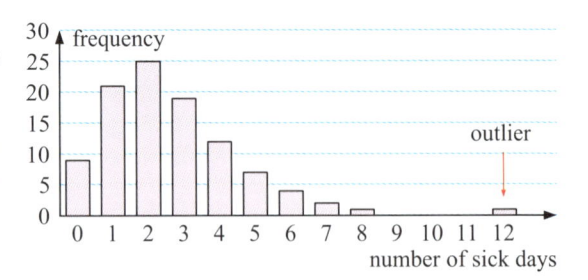

EXERCISE 20A

1 A randomly selected sample of teenagers were asked 'How many times per week do you eat red meat?' A column graph has been constructed from the results.

    a How many teenagers gave data in the survey?

    b How many of the teenagers ate red meat at least once per week?

    c What percentage of the teenagers ate red meat more than twice per week?

    d Describe the distribution of the data.

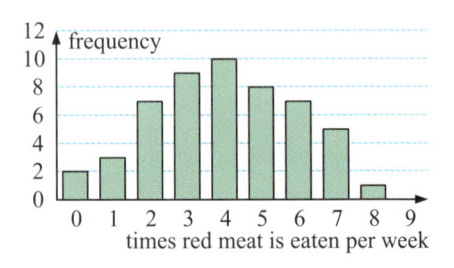

2 As part of a Health Survey, a class of 25 students was asked how many times they had been to the doctor in the past year.

The following dot plot was constructed from the data:

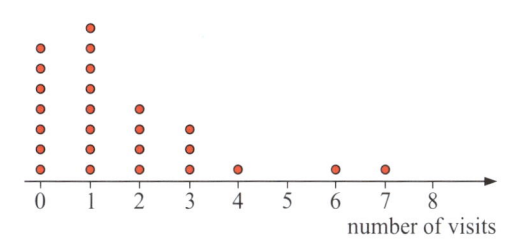

Visits to the doctor

number of visits

    a What is the variable in this investigation?

    b Explain why the data is discrete numerical data.

    c What percentage of the students did not go to the doctor in the past year?

    d What percentage of the students made more than one visit to the doctor in the past year?

    e Copy and complete: "The *mode* or most frequent number of visits made was ......"

    f Describe the distribution of the data.

    g How would you describe the data values 6 and 7?

3 Alfred has 15 hens. He records the number of eggs that are laid each day for 1 month.

    12 13 12 14 14 12 11 8 10 14 15 13 13 14 13
    14 15 14 12 13 14 13 13 11 12 14 13 15 13 13

    a What is the variable in this investigation?

    b Is the data continuous or discrete numerical data?

    c Construct a frequency table for this data.

    d Display the data using a bar chart.

    e Describe the distribution of the data.

    f On what percentage of days were 14 or more eggs laid?

    g List any outliers in this data.

4 25 customers in a newsagency were asked how many magazines they bought each week. The following data was collected:

    1 0 1 1 2 2 1 3 2 4 3 1 2 0 0 1 1 0 2 2 1 0 1 0 1

    a What is the variable in this investigation?

    b Is the data discrete or continuous? Why?

    c Construct a dot plot to display the data. Include a heading for the graph and a scale, and label the axes.

    d Describe the distribution of the data. Is it symmetrical, positively skewed or negatively skewed? Are there any outliers?

    e What percentage of the customers bought no magazines?

    f What percentage of the customers bought two or more magazines?

5 Consider the *Smokers* data in the **Opening Problem**.

    a Organise the data in a tally-frequency table.   **b** Draw a column graph of the data.

    c Are there any outliers?   **d** Is the data skewed?

    e What evidence is there that the smokers take more sick days than the non-smokers?

B GROUPED DISCRETE DATA

In situations where there are large numbers of different data values, it is not sensible to organise the data in a frequency table. It is also often inappropriate to display the data by dot plot or column graph.

For example, a local kindergarten was concerned about the number of vehicles passing by between 8.45 am and 9.00 am. Over 30 consecutive week days they recorded data.

The results were: 27, 30, 17, 13, 46, 23, 40, 28, 38, 24, 23, 22, 18, 29, 16, 35, 24, 18, 24, 44, 32, 52, 31, 39, 32, 9, 41, 38, 24, 32

In situations like this, it is appropriate to group the data into **class intervals**. In this case we use class intervals of length 10.

The tally-frequency table is:

Number of cars	Tally	Frequency
0 to 9			1
10 to 19	||||	5
20 to 29	|||| ||||	10
30 to 39	|||| ||||	9
40 to 49	||||	4
50 to 59			1
Total		30

STEM-AND-LEAF PLOTS

A **stem-and-leaf plot** or **stemplot** is a way of recording the data in groups. It is used for small data sets. It shows actual data values and gives a visual comparison of frequencies.

For numbers with two digits, the first digit forms part of the **stem** and the second digit forms a **leaf**. For example, for the data value 18, 1 is recorded on the stem and 8 is a leaf value.

Two different stem-and-leaf plots are shown for the traffic data.

The **ordered stem-and-leaf plot** arranges all data from smallest to largest.

The **stem-and-leaf plot** is:

Stem	Leaf
0	9
1	7 3 8 6 8
2	7 3 8 4 3 2 9 4 4 4
3	0 8 5 2 1 9 2 8 2
4	6 0 4 1
5	2 **Note:** 1	7 means 17

The **ordered stem-and-leaf plot** is:

Stem	Leaf
0	9
1	3 6 7 8 8
2	2 3 3 4 4 4 4 7 8 9
3	0 1 2 2 2 5 8 8 9
4	0 1 4 6
5	2

Notice the following features:

- all the actual data is shown
- the minimum or smallest data value is 9
- the maximum or largest data value is 52
- the 'twenties' interval (20 to 29) occurred most often.

Example 1 🔊 Self Tutor

The ages of guests at a 21st birthday party were:

22 20 18 27 35 21 48 19 21 47 17 26 49
16 21 48 19 22 31 20 18 21 19 45 22

a Draw a stem-and-leaf plot for the data.
b Redraw the stem-and-leaf plot so that it is ordered.
c How many guests attended the party?   **d** How old was the youngest guest?
e How many guests were at least 30 years old?
f What percentage of guests were in their twenties?

a The stem-and-leaf plot is:

Stem	Leaf
1	8 9 7 6 9 8 9
2	2 0 7 1 1 6 1 2 0 1 2
3	5 1
4	8 7 9 8 5

1 | 8   means 18

b The ordered stem-and-leaf plot is:

Stem	Leaf
1	6 7 8 8 9 9 9
2	0 0 1 1 1 1 2 2 2 6 7
3	1 5
4	5 7 8 8 9

c 25 guests attended the party.   **d** The youngest guest was 16 years old.
e 7 guests were at least 30 years old.
f 11 guests were in their twenties.

$\therefore$ percentage of guests who were in their twenties $= \frac{11}{25} \times 100\%$
$= 44\%$

EXERCISE 20B

1 Dave plays golf almost every day. The data set shown are his scores for his last 40 rounds of golf.

72 81 78 77 82 78 89 82
85 76 75 81 74 87 84 77
80 83 79 82 75 74 74 71
75 79 72 76 71 75 82 78
76 76 81 77 72 84 87 83

a Construct a tally and frequency table for this data using class intervals 70 - 74, 75 - 79, 80 - 84, 85 - 89.

b What percentage of Dave's scores were more than 84?

c What percentage of Dave's scores were less than 75?

d Copy and complete the following:
More scores were in the interval .... than in any other interval.

2 a Draw a stem-and-leaf plot for the following data using stems 1, 2, 3, 4, and 5:
27, 34, 19, 36, 52, 34, 42, 51, 18, 48, 29, 27, 33, 30, 46, 19, 35, 24, 21, 56

b Redraw the stem-and-leaf plot from **a** so that it is ordered.

3 For the ordered stem-and-leaf plot given, find:

Stem	Leaf
1	3 4 6 7 8 9 9
2	0 0 1 1 2 3 3 5 5 6 7 8 8
3	1 1 2 4 4 5 8 9
4	2 3 7
5	
6	2

2 | 0 means 20

a the minimum value
b the maximum value
c the number of data with values greater than 25
d the number of data with values of at least 40
e the percentage of the data with values less than 15.

4 The number of students absent from City Bay High School is recorded for 40 days during winter:

21 16 23 24 18 29 35 37 41 38 33 28 29 31 25 23 17 26 34 33
49 52 43 41 32 34 27 24 20 25 23 19 22 17 15 14 14 10 12 16

  a Construct a stem-and-leaf plot for this data using 1, 2, 3, 4, and 5 as the stems.
  b Redraw the stem-and-leaf plot so that it is ordered.
  c What advantage does a stem-and-leaf plot have over a frequency table?
  d What was the **i** highest **ii** lowest number of absences for the period?
  e On what percentage of the days were there 40 or more students absent?
  f Attendance is described as 'good' if there are less than 25 absences per day in winter. On what percentage of the days was the attendance 'good'?
  g Describe the distribution of the data.

5 Jason obtains statistics on the winners of an 80-player professional tennis tournament. The data which follows is *the number of points needed to win a first round match*. This variable is a discrete numerical variable that can take values of 48, 49, 50, 51, ...

74   136 134 111 109 114 132 120 83   119 62   150 90   91
96   140 78   86   167 129 145 68   98   103 93   110 125 119
105 134 106 121 104 84   117 102 86   142 90   108

  a Construct a stem-and-leaf plot for the data using the stems 06, 07, 08, 09, ..., 16.
  b Order the stem-and-leaf plot and find the:
      i maximum   **ii** minimum   points won.
  c Which class interval has the most number of points won?
  d How many matches were won in less than 80 points?
  e What percentage of the matches were won after 130 points or more?
  f Describe the distribution of the data.
  g Are there any outliers in this data set?

C MEASURING THE CENTRE

We can gain a better understanding of a data set by locating the **middle** or **centre** of the data and by measuring its **spread**. Knowing one of these without the other is often of little use.

There are *three statistics* that are used to measure the **centre** of a data set. These are the **mean**, the **median** and the **mode**.

THE MEAN

> The **mean** of a data set is the statistical name for the arithmetic average.
> $$\text{mean} = \frac{\text{sum of all data values}}{\text{the number of data values}}$$

The mean gives us a single number which indicates a centre of the data set. It is not necessarily a member of the data set.

For example, suppose the mean success rate of a basketball team from the free throw line is 78%, then several of the players scored less than 78% and several scored above it. It does not necessarily mean that a player scored 78%.

THE MEDIAN

> The **median** is the *middle value* of an ordered data set.

An ordered data set is obtained by listing the data, usually from smallest to largest.

The median splits the data in two halves. Half of the data are less than or equal to the median and half are greater than or equal to it.

For example, if the median success rate of a basketball team from the free throw line is 78%, then half of the team has scored less than or equal to 78% and half has scored greater than or equal to 78%.

> For an **odd number** of data, the median is one of the data.
>
> For an **even number** of data, the median is the average of the two middle values and may not be one of the original data.

Here is a **rule for finding the median**:

> If there are n data values, find the value of $\frac{n+1}{2}$.
>
> The median is the $\left(\frac{n+1}{2}\right)$th data value.

For example:

When $n = 9$, $\frac{9+1}{2} = 5$, so the median = 5th ordered data value.

When $n = 12$, $\frac{12+1}{2} = 6.5$, so the median = average of 6th and 7th ordered data values.

THE MODE

The **mode** is the most frequently occurring value in the data set.

Example 2

The number of games won by a football team over 9 seasons is   5 7 3 6 5 9 8 7 5.
For this data set, find:

a the mean   **b** the median   **c** the mode.

a   mean $= \dfrac{5+7+3+6+5+9+8+7+5}{9}$ ← sum of the data
              ← 9 data values

$= \dfrac{55}{9}$

≈ 6.11 wins

b The ordered data set is: 3̶ 5̶ 5̶ 5̶ 6 7̶ 7̶ 8̶ 9̶ $\{n = 9, \; \frac{n+1}{2} = 5\}$

∴ median $= 6$ wins

c 5 is the score which occurs the most often

∴ mode $= 5$ wins

How are the measures of the middle affected if the team in **Example 2** wins 7 games in the next season?

We expect the mean to increase because the new data value is greater than the old mean.

In fact,   new mean $= \dfrac{55+7}{10}$

$= \dfrac{62}{10}$

$= 6.2$ wins

The new ordered data set would be: 3̶ 5̶ 5̶ 5̶ 6 7 7̶ 7̶ 8̶ 9̶

  two middle scores

∴ median $= \dfrac{6+7}{2} = 6.5$ wins

This new data set has two modes. The modes are 5 and 7 wins.

Example 3

The weights of the fish caught on a one day fishing trip are displayed in the stem-and-leaf plot shown. Find the median weight.

Weight in kg
0 | 7 8
1 | 1 4 6 6 7 8 9
2 | 1 5 5 5 6
3 | 1 1 2 4 9
4 | 3   4 | 3 means 43

```
0 | 7̶ 8̶
1 | 1̶ 4̶ 6̶ 6̶ 7̶ 8̶ 9̶
2 | 1 5 5̶ 5̶ 6̶
3 | 1̶ 1̶ 2 4̶ 9̶
4 | 3̶
```
Crossing off in pairs from the top and bottom, 21 and 25 remain

∴ median = 23 kg

{the average of these two scores}

EXERCISE 20C.1

1 Find the **i** mean **ii** median **iii** mode for each of the following data sets:
  a 2, 3, 3, 3, 4, 4, 4, 5, 5, 5, 5, 6, 6, 6, 6, 6, 7, 7, 8, 8, 8, 9, 9
  b 10, 12, 12, 15, 15, 16, 16, 17, 18, 18, 18, 18, 19, 20, 21
  c 22.4, 24.6, 21.8, 26.4, 24.9, 25.0, 23.5, 26.1, 25.3, 29.5, 23.5
  d 127, 123, 115, 105, 145, 133, 142, 115, 135, 148, 129, 127, 103, 130, 146, 140, 125, 124, 119, 128, 141

2 The annual salaries of ten office workers are: €33 000, €56 000, €52 000, €48 000, €38 000, €45 000, €33 000, €48 000, €33 000, €42 000
  a Find the mean, median and modal salaries of this group.
  b Explain why the mode is an unsatisfactory measure of the middle in this case.

3 For each of the following stem-and-leaf plots, find the median and mode.

  a
  ```
  2 | 2 5
  3 | 0 1 3 7
  4 | 2 2 4 5 9
  5 | 0 4 8
  6 | 1      2 | 2 means 22
  ```
  b
  ```
  4 | 0 6
  5 | 1 2 3 3 3 9
  6 | 4 4 5 6 7 7 8
  7 | 1 2 5
          4 | 0 means 40
  ```
  c
  ```
  1 | 2 3 7
  2 | 0 0 2 1 6
  3 | 2 4 4 5 5 5 8
  4 | 0 1 7 7
  5 | 6        1 | 2 means 120
  ```

4 The ages of the employees of International Sports Coaching Clinics are given below:
  23, 18, 29, 31, 25, 24, 17, 33, 22, 20, 21, 25, 16, 34
  21, 23, 22, 27, 28, 30, 28, 19, 20, 22, 22, 21, 27, 26
  a Draw a stem-and-leaf plot for the data.
  b Find the: **i** median age **ii** mean age.

5 It started raining on Sunday October 1st and 11 mm of rain fell. On the next 5 days 24 mm, 28 mm, 22 mm, 16 mm and 13 mm of rain fell.
  a Find the mean rainfall from Sunday to Friday.
  b How much rain would need to fall on Saturday for the mean to remain the same?
  c If 10 mm of rain fell on Saturday, calculate the mean rainfall for the week.
  d If no more rain fell for the month, find the mean rainfall for October.

6 Huang does casual work at a petrol outlet. On average, he has earned $214.50 per week for the last 6 weeks. How much has he earned in total?

7 Magda calculates that she spends, on average, a total of 1 hour 40 minutes per day travelling to and from work. How long will she spend travelling if she works 5 days?

MEASURES OF THE CENTRE FROM OTHER SOURCES

When the same data appear several times we often summarise the data in table form.

Consider the data of the given table:

We can find the measures of the centre directly from the table.

Data value	Frequency	Product
3	1	$3 \times 1 = 3$
4	1	$4 \times 1 = 4$
5	3	$5 \times 3 = 15$
6	7	$6 \times 7 = 42$
7	15	$7 \times 15 = 105$
8	8	$8 \times 8 = 64$
9	5	$9 \times 5 = 45$
Total	40	278

THE MODE

There are 15 of data value 7 which is more than any other data value.
The mode is therefore 7.

THE MEAN

Adding a 'Product' column to the table helps to add all scores.

For example, there are 15 data of value 7 and these add to $15 \times 7 = 105$.

So, the mean $= \dfrac{278}{40} = 6.95$

THE MEDIAN

There are 40 data values, an even number, so there are *two middle* data values.

As the sample size $n = 40$, $\dfrac{n+1}{2} = \dfrac{41}{2} = 20.5$

$\therefore$ the median is the average of the 20th and 21st data values.

In the table, the blue numbers show us accumulated values.

Data value	Frequency	
3	1	1 — one number is 3
4	1	2 — two numbers are 4 or less
5	3	5 — five numbers are 5 or less
6	7	12 — 12 numbers are 6 or less
7	15	27 — 27 numbers are 7 or less
8	8	
9	5	
Total	40	

Remember that the median is the middle of the ordered data set.

We can see that the 20th and 21st data values (in order) are both 7s,

$\therefore$ median $= \dfrac{7+7}{2} = 7$

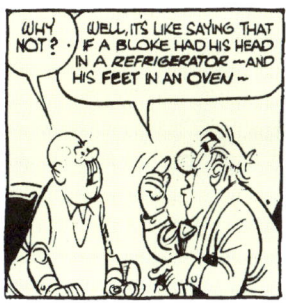

Example 4

A class of 20 students all take a spelling test. Their results out of 10 are shown in the table.

Calculate the:

a mean
b median
c mode

of the scores.

Score	Number of students
5	1
6	2
7	4
8	7
9	4
10	2
Total	20

a

Score	Number of students	sum of scores
5	1	$5 \times 1 = 5$
6	2	$6 \times 2 = 12$
7	4	$7 \times 4 = 28$
8	7	$8 \times 7 = 56$
9	4	$9 \times 4 = 36$
10	2	$10 \times 2 = 20$
Total	20	157

The mean score
$$= \frac{\text{total of scores}}{20}$$
$$= \frac{157}{20}$$
$$= 7.85$$

b There are 20 scores, and so the median is the average of the 10th and 11th.

Score	Number of students	
5	1	← 1st student
6	2	← 2nd and 3rd student
7	4	← 4th, 5th, 6th and 7th student
8	7	← 8th, 9th, **10th, 11th**, 12th, 13th, 14th student
9	4	
10	2	
Total	20	

The 10th and 11th students both scored 8 $\therefore$ median $= 8$.

c The highest frequency is 7 when the score is 8, so the mode $= 8$.

EXERCISE 20C.2

1 A class of 30 students were asked how many pets they owned. The following data was obtained:

Number of pets	Frequency
0	4
1	12
2	11
3	3
Total	30

Calculate the:

  a mode   **b** median   **c** mean.

2 Sarah recorded the number of occupants in each car that drove down her street one day. The results are shown in the frequency column graph.

  a Construct a frequency table from the graph.
  b How many cars did Sarah record data for?
  c Find the:
    i mode   **ii** median   **iii** mean.

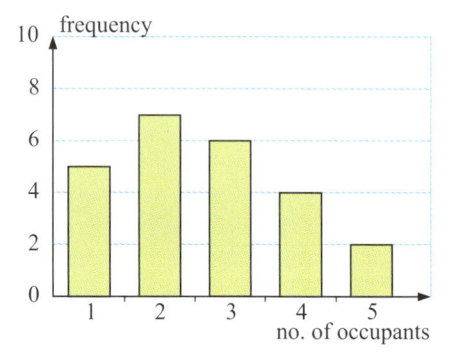

3 50 people were asked how many times they had moved house. The results are given in the frequency table:

No. of house moves	Frequency
0	5
1	9
2	13
3	8
4	6
5	3
6	3
7	2
8	1

  a For this data, find the:
    i mode   **ii** median   **iii** mean.
  b Construct a column graph for the data and show the position of the measures of centre on the horizontal axis.
  c Describe the distribution of the data.
  d Why is the mean larger than the median for this data?
  e Which measure of centre would be the most suitable for this data set?

4 Revisit the **Opening Problem**.

  a Use the frequency table for the *Non-smokers* data on page **403** to find the:
    i mode   **ii** median   **iii** mean   number of sick days.
  b Use the frequency table for the *Smokers* data from **Exercise 20A**, question **5** to find the:
    i mode   **ii** median   **iii** mean   number of sick days.
  c Which measure of the centre is appropriate to use in a report on this data?
  d Is there a significant difference in the number of sick days taken by the smokers and the non-smokers?

D COMPARING AND REPORTING DISCRETE DATA

Sometimes we may be asked to **compare** two sets of data.

To display **discrete ungrouped data sets** for comparison, we usually use a **back-to-back stem-and-leaf plot**.

For example,

Leaf	Stem	Leaf
	2	7
8	3	0 1 8
9 5 3 3 0	4	2 5 6 7 7 9
9 6 4 4 2 2 2 1 1	5	0 1 2 3 3 3 5 7 7 8
9 8 7 6 4 4 2 0	6	4 5 5 9
9 9 8 8 6 6 5	7	0 8
8 5 5 3	8	1

Data set A   Data set B

where 4 | 2 means 42

PREPARING A REPORT

If you are required to gather and interpret statistics, an acceptable way to report your observations and findings is to base your argument around these steps.

To properly compare two sets of data, you should:

Step 1: **Display** both sets of data.

Step 2: Look for any **outliers**. If you are sure they are data which have been recorded wrongly, you should discard them.

Step 3: Examine and describe the **shape of each distribution**. Is it symmetric, negatively skewed, positively skewed, or something else?

Step 4: Compare the **middle of each distribution** usually using the mean and median.

Step 5: Make a **conclusion**, but be careful not to exaggerate your case.

Example 5

Two football teams, Northfield and Southbeach, are due to play against each other in the grand final. To determine if either team has a height advantage, the following data was collected. It shows the heights of the players from each team in cm.

Northfield: 182   193   187   177   195   190   184   187   182   198
                    201   185   175   192   183   182   202   198   184   192

Southbeach: 184   187   172   194   188   168   189   201   180   178
                    190   182   182   175   167   187   196   188   177   186

a Construct a back-to-back stem-and-leaf plot for this data using 16, 17, 18, 19, and 20 as the stems.

b Describe the shape of each distribution.

c Compare the mean and median heights of the teams.

d Copy and complete: "In general, the players from Southbeach are ...... than the players from Northfield."

a

Northfield		Southbeach
	16	7 8
7 5	17	2 5 7 8
7 7 5 4 4 3 2 2 2	18	0 2 2 4 6 7 7 8 8 9
8 8 5 3 2 2 0	19	0 4 6
2 1	20	1

20 | 1 means 201 cm

b Both distributions are reasonably symmetrical.

c Northfield has a higher mean height than Southbeach (188.5 cm compared to 183.6 cm) and a higher median height (187 cm compared to 185 cm).

d "In general, the players from Southbeach are **shorter** than the players from Northfield."

EXERCISE 20D

1 Pedro operates a Mexican restaurant. He wants to see how effective his new advertising will be on the number of customers he has at his restaurant. He records his numbers of customers for thirty days before he starts advertising, and then for thirty days after he starts advertising. He collects the following data:

Before advertising: 74 82 63 77 89 91 74 71 57 62 83 79 75 62 59 84 93 78 68 94 73 77 84 66 72 61 56 76 88 64

After advertising: 93 98 108 84 89 76 92 69 93 85 101 78 47 99 90 88 70 93 104 108 95 80 103 79 92 98 84 106 98 101

   a Construct a back-to-back stem-and-leaf plot for this data.
   b Are there any outliers in the data?
   c Describe the shape of each distribution.
   d Compare the mean and median of each data set.
   e Copy and complete: "The number of customers coming to the restaurant appears to have .... as a result of the advertising."

2 Two professional tennis players, Andre and Andrew, want to find out who has the faster serve. To decide, each player serves 25 times. The speeds are recorded in km per hour, as shown below:

Andre: 192 201 199 212 182 191 203 194 187 195 206 215 197 217 208 187 222 195 208 192 204 218 206 188 213

Andrew: 209 213 198 219 223 197 205 217 216 203 188 224 211
          219 206 192 215 200 220 217 206 224 191 207 219

- **a** Construct a back-to-back stem-and-leafplot for this data.
- **b** Are there any outliers in the data?
- **c** Describe the shape of each distribution.
- **d** Compare the mean and median of each data set.
- **e** Copy and complete:
  "...... generally serves the ball faster than ......".

3 Mary drives her car to and from work each day. She wants to know if she takes longer getting to work in the mornings, or getting home in the evenings. Every work day for a month she records how long it takes her to get to and from work. The results, in minutes, are shown below:

Going to work: 16.7 18.9 17.3 17.7 16.5 15.8 17.2 18.2 17.3 17.8 16.6
                  15.7 16.9 17.8 16.7 15.7 17.1 18.5 17.1 16.6 17.4 16.3

Returning from   18.8 17.6 16.5 18.7 19.2 18.9 17.9 17.6 18.5 17.7 18.5
work: 17.2 18.2 19.7 18.9 17.9 16.8 17.6 22.3 18.8 17.4 16.6

- **a** Construct a back-to-back stem-and-leaf plot for this data using 15, 16, 17, ... and so on as the stems.
- **b** Are there any outliers in the data?
- **c** Describe the shape of each distribution.
- **d** Compare the mean and median value of each data set.
- **e** Copy and complete: "In general it takes Mary ...... time to get to work than it does to return home from work."

AT WHAT RATE SHOULD YOU BREATHE?

Areas of interaction:
Health and social education

REVIEW SET 20A

1 A class of 20 students was asked "*How many children are there in your household?*" The following data was collected:

   1 2 3 3 2 4 5 4 2 3 8 1 2 1 3 2 1 2 1 2

- **a** What is the variable in the investigation?
- **b** Is the data discrete or continuous? Why?
- **c** Construct a dot plot to display the data. Include a heading for the graph, a scale, and clearly labelled axes.
- **d** How would you describe the distribution of the data? Is it symmetrical, positively or negatively skewed? Are there any outliers?

2 Find the **a** mode **b** median **c** mean for the following data set:
34.4, 36.6, 33.8, 38.4, 36.9, 37.0, 35.5, 38.1, 37.3, 41.5, 35.5

3 For the following sample of weights (in kg) of year 8 students, find:
  a the minimum weight
  b the maximum weight
  c the median weight
  d the number of students with a weight of at least 70 kg
  e the percentage of students with a weight less than 48 kg.

Stem	Leaf
3	2 4 8
4	0 4 4 7 9 9 9
5	0 0 1 2 2 3 3 5 5 6 8 8
6	0 1 2 4 4 5 7 9
7	0 2 6
8	4
9	1

9 | 1 represents 91

4 Using the frequency column graph alongside:
  a construct a frequency table
  b determine the total number of assists
  c for the assists given, find the:
    i mode **ii** median **iii** mean.

Assists per game by a basketballer

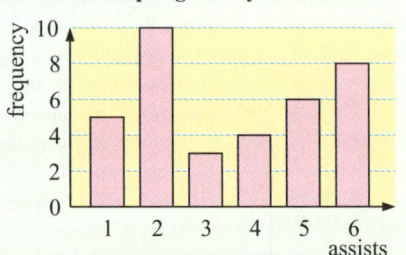

5 The test scores out of 40 marks were recorded for a group of 30 students:

25 18 35 32 34 28 24 39 29 33 22 34 39 31 36
35 36 33 35 40 26 25 20 18 9 40 32 23 28 27

  a Construct a stem-and-leaf plot for this data using 0, 1, 2, 3 and 4 as the stems.
  b Redraw the stem-and-leaf plot so that it is ordered.
  c What advantage does the stem-and-leaf plot have over a frequency table?
  d What is the **i** highest **ii** lowest mark scored for the test?
  e If an 'A' was awarded to students who scored 36 or more for the test, what percentage of students scored an 'A'?

6 A survey is carried out to determine the number of motor vehicles passing through two suburban intersections in a given time period during peak hour traffic.

Intersection A
49 37 47 42 51 54 46 59
59 48 64 53 57 46 62 65
54 45 47 51 62 59 43 55

Intersection B
48 25 29 48 47 40 53 58
62 66 51 64 37 43 51 47
41 64 46 55 37 52 57 37

  a Construct a back-to-back stem-and-leaf plot comparing the two data sets.
  b Find the median of each data set.
  c Find the mean of each data set.
  d Comment on the shape of each distribution.

REVIEW SET 20B

1 The numbers of goals scored by a hockey team in their games during a season were:

1 2 5 0 3 4 5 0 3 1 2 4 3 5 1 0 2 0
3 5 7 4 1 3 1 2 5 2 3 3 4 3 2 4 2 3

  a What is the variable in this data set?
  b Is the data discrete or continuous? Why?
  c Construct a frequency table for this data.
  d Display the data using a horizontal bar chart.
  e In what percentage of the games did the team score 4 or more goals?

2 The data set below is the scores out of 100 of 45 students in a Maths examination.

58 31 80 69 70 71 82 91 94 60 68 58 90 83 72
75 65 76 69 66 64 57 58 77 92 94 49 61 66 91
64 53 89 91 78 61 74 82 97 70 82 66 55 45 63

  a Construct a stem-and-leaf plot for this data using 3, 4, 5, 6, 7, 8 and 9 as the stems.
  b Redraw the stem-and-leaf plot so that it is ordered.
  c What is the **i** highest **ii** lowest mark scored for the examination?
  d If a distinction was awarded to students who scored 75 or more for the examination, what percentage of students scored a distinction?
  e Would you describe this distribution as:
    A symmetric   **B** skewed   **C** neither symmetric nor skewed?

3 Find the **a** mode **b** median **c** mean for the following data set:
69 72 75 82 65 85 75 81 79 83 65 65 80 63 61 80 68 85

4 The given table shows the distribution of scores in a fitness test for 13 year olds.

Score	Frequency
6	2
7	4
8	7
9	12
10	5
Total	30

  a Calculate the: **i** mode **ii** median **iii** mean.
  b The average score for all 13 year olds in China was 7.2. How does this class compare to the national average?
  c The data set is skewed. Is the skewness positive or negative?

5

Stem	Leaf
3	8 9
4	2 2 5
5	0 1 1 7 9
6	1 3 4
7	0

7 | 0 represents 70

For the data displayed in the stem-and-leaf plot, find the:

  a mode   **b** median   **c** mean.

6 In order to find out whether doctors or lawyers work longer hours, 20 doctors and 20 lawyers were each asked how many hours they worked in an average month. The following data was collected:

Doctors	212	203	228	215	200	194	216	222	210	232
	211	225	209	217	217	199	213	235	219	207
Lawyers	227	216	238	221	206	228	233	214	229	232
	220	210	197	238	224	226	219	171	225	236

a Draw a back-to-back stemplot comparing the two data sets.
b Are there any outliers in the data?
c Describe the shape of each distribution.
d Compare the mean and median of each data set.
e Copy and complete:
  "From the samples above, it appears that .... generally work longer hours than ...."

LEONHARD EULER
(1707 - 1783)

Leonhard Euler (pronounced 'oiler') was born in 1707 in Switzerland.

- Euler has been described as the most productive mathematician of the eighteenth century - if not of all time. His complete works would fill 16 000 pages.
- Euler was a brilliant calculator. He could mentally determine products of many digit numbers with great accuracy.
- He was awarded a Masters Degree at the age of 17 and won the Paris Academy prize 12 times.
- He was married twice and had 13 children.
- Euler was totally blind at age 59 but this did not interrupt his enormous productivity. Due to his incredible memory he continued to make great progress and he dictated his discoveries to a servant. At death he had published 560 books and papers on nearly every field of mathematics which exists in his day.

Chapter 21

Algebraic fractions

Contents:
- **A** Evaluating algebraic fractions
- **B** Simplifying algebraic fractions
- **C** Multiplying and dividing algebraic fractions
- **D** Adding and subtracting algebraic fractions
- **E** Simplifying more complicated fractions

Algebraic fractions are fractions which contain at least one variable or unknown.

The variable may be in the numerator, the denominator, or in both of these places.

For example, $\dfrac{a}{b}$, $\dfrac{-3}{x+2}$ and $\dfrac{x-y}{x+y}$ are all algebraic fractions.

Algebraic fractions are sometimes called **rational expressions**.

A EVALUATING ALGEBRAIC FRACTIONS

To **evaluate** an algebraic expression we replace the variables with their known values. We simplify the expression so we can give our answer in simplest form.

Example 1 — Self Tutor

If $x = 3$, $y = -2$ and $z = 4$ evaluate: **a** $\dfrac{y}{z}$ **b** $\dfrac{2x-z}{y}$ **c** $\dfrac{x-y-z}{z-x}$

a $\dfrac{y}{z}$
$= \dfrac{(-2)}{4}$
$= -\dfrac{2}{4}$
$= -\dfrac{1}{2}$

b $\dfrac{2x-z}{y}$
$= \dfrac{2(3)-4}{(-2)}$
$= \dfrac{6-4}{-2}$
$= \dfrac{2}{-2}$
$= -1$

c $\dfrac{x-y-z}{z-x}$
$= \dfrac{3-(-2)-4}{4-3}$
$= \dfrac{3+2-4}{4-3}$
$= \dfrac{1}{1}$
$= 1$

EXERCISE 21A

1 If $a = 2$, $b = 3$, $c = 5$, evaluate:

a $\dfrac{a}{2}$ **b** $\dfrac{b}{6}$ **c** $\dfrac{b+1}{a}$ **d** $\dfrac{a+2b}{c}$ **e** $\dfrac{c-b}{a}$

f $\dfrac{3c-a}{b}$ **g** $\dfrac{a^2}{b-1}$ **h** $\dfrac{ab}{-1-c}$ **i** $\dfrac{2a^2}{b+1}$ **j** $\dfrac{ac}{b^2+1}$

2 If $x = -1$, $y = 2$, $z = -3$, evaluate:

a $\dfrac{y}{x}$ **b** $\dfrac{z}{x}$ **c** $-\dfrac{z}{y+1}$ **d** $\dfrac{y^2}{-4}$ **e** $\dfrac{z-y}{x}$

f $\dfrac{x-y}{z}$ **g** $\dfrac{y}{x+z}$ **h** $\dfrac{x+y}{x-y}$ **i** $\dfrac{x+z}{y^2}$ **j** $\dfrac{x^2y}{z-1}$

k $\dfrac{x^2+y^2}{10}$ **l** $\dfrac{x^2+z^2}{y}$ **m** $\dfrac{x-z^2}{y}$ **n** $\dfrac{y^2-z^2}{-2y}$ **o** $\dfrac{3x-2y}{z^2}$

B SIMPLIFYING ALGEBRAIC FRACTIONS

Simplification of algebraic fractions is sometimes, but not always, possible.

We have observed that number fractions can be simplified by cancelling common factors.

For example, $\dfrac{16}{24} = \dfrac{2 \times \cancel{8}^{1}}{3 \times \cancel{8}_{1}} = \dfrac{2}{3}$ where we cancel the common factor of 8.

If the numerator and denominator of an algebraic fraction are both written in factored form and common factors are found, we can simplify by **cancelling the common factors**.

For example, $\dfrac{4x}{8xy} = \dfrac{\cancel{2}^{1} \times \cancel{2}^{1} \times \cancel{x}^{1}}{\cancel{2}_{1} \times \cancel{2}_{1} \times 2 \times \cancel{x}_{1} \times y}$ {fully factorised}

$= \dfrac{1}{2y}$ {after cancellation}

> Always check the numerator and denominator to see if they can be expressed as the product of factors, then look for common factors which can be cancelled.

Example 2   ◀) Self Tutor

Simplify if possible: **a** $\dfrac{a^2}{2a}$ **b** $\dfrac{6a^3}{3a^2}$

a $\dfrac{a^2}{2a}$

$= \dfrac{a \times \cancel{a}^{1}}{2 \times \cancel{a}_{1}}$

$= \dfrac{a}{2}$

b $\dfrac{6a^3}{3a^2}$

$= \dfrac{\cancel{6}^{2} \times a \times \cancel{a}^{1} \times a}{\cancel{3}_{1} \times \cancel{a}_{1} \times \cancel{a}_{1}}$

$= \dfrac{2 \times a}{1}$

$= 2a$

Example 3

Simplify: **a** $\dfrac{3a^4}{-a^2}$ **b** $\dfrac{-6t^2}{-2t^3}$

a $\dfrac{3a^4}{-a^2}$

$= \dfrac{3 \times a \times a \times \overset{1}{\cancel{a}} \times \overset{1}{\cancel{a}}}{-1 \times \underset{1}{\cancel{a}} \times \underset{1}{\cancel{a}}}$

$= -3a^2$

b $\dfrac{-6t^2}{-2t^3}$

$= \dfrac{\overset{3}{\cancel{-6}} \times \overset{1}{\cancel{t}} \times \overset{1}{\cancel{t}}}{\underset{1}{\cancel{-2}} \times t \times \underset{1}{\cancel{t}} \times \underset{1}{\cancel{t}}}$

$= \dfrac{3}{t}$

Example 4

Simplify if possible: **a** $\dfrac{(3x)^2}{x}$ **b** $\dfrac{(-4b)^2}{2b}$

a $\dfrac{(3x)^2}{x}$

$= \dfrac{3x \times 3x}{x}$

$= \dfrac{3 \times x \times 3 \times \overset{1}{\cancel{x}}}{\underset{1}{\cancel{x}}}$

$= 9x$

b $\dfrac{(-4b)^2}{2b}$

$= \dfrac{-4b \times -4b}{2 \times b}$

$= \dfrac{\overset{8}{\cancel{16}} \times b \times \overset{1}{\cancel{b}}}{\underset{1}{\cancel{2}} \times \underset{1}{\cancel{b}}}$

$= 8b$

EXERCISE 21B

1 Simplify:

a $\dfrac{7x}{14}$ **b** $\dfrac{15y}{5}$ **c** $\dfrac{9r}{r}$ **d** $\dfrac{8p}{16p}$

e $\dfrac{3a}{a^2}$ **f** $\dfrac{8b^3}{4b}$ **g** $\dfrac{13c^2}{c^3}$ **h** $\dfrac{7d^3}{d^2}$

2 Simplify:

a $\dfrac{a^2}{-2a}$ **b** $\dfrac{-a}{2a^2}$ **c** $\dfrac{-a^3}{-4a}$ **d** $\dfrac{4a^2}{-a^2}$

e $\dfrac{-6t}{-3t^2}$ **f** $\dfrac{4d^2}{-2d}$ **g** $\dfrac{-ab^2}{2ab}$ **h** $\dfrac{-4ab^2}{6a^2b}$

3 Simplify if possible:

a $\dfrac{(5a)^2}{a}$ **b** $\dfrac{(5a)^2}{5}$ **c** $\dfrac{5a}{(-a)^2}$ **d** $\dfrac{(2a)^2}{-a}$

e $\dfrac{(-3b)^2}{6}$ **f** $\dfrac{(-4c)^2}{8}$ **g** $\dfrac{(3d)^2}{d^2}$ **h** $\dfrac{(e^3)^2}{e^3}$

C. MULTIPLYING AND DIVIDING ALGEBRAIC FRACTIONS

The rules for multiplying and dividing algebraic fractions are identical to those for numerical fractions.

To **multiply** two or more fractions, we multiply the numerators to form the new numerator, and we multiply the denominators to form the new denominator.

Since $\frac{2}{5} \times \frac{3}{7} = \frac{2 \times 3}{5 \times 7}$,

$$\frac{a}{b} \times \frac{c}{d} = \frac{a \times c}{b \times d} = \frac{ac}{bd}$$

To **divide** by a fraction we multiply by its reciprocal.

Since $\frac{2}{5} \div \frac{3}{7} = \frac{2}{5} \times \frac{7}{3}$,

$$\frac{a}{b} \div \frac{c}{d} = \frac{a}{b} \times \frac{d}{c} = \frac{ad}{bc}$$

MULTIPLICATION

Step 1: Multiply numerators and multiply denominators.
Step 2: Separate the factors.
Step 3: Cancel any common factors.
Step 4: Write in simplest form.

For example,
$$\frac{x}{2} \times \frac{3}{x^2} = \frac{x \times 3}{2 \times x^2} \quad \{Step\ 1\}$$
$$= \frac{\cancel{x}^1 \times 3}{2 \times x \times \cancel{x}_1} \quad \{Step\ 2\ and\ 3\}$$
$$= \frac{3}{2x} \quad \{Step\ 4\}$$

Example 5   ◀)) Self Tutor

Simplify:

a $\dfrac{a}{4} \times \dfrac{2}{3a}$

b $n^2 \times \dfrac{3}{n}$

a $\dfrac{a}{4} \times \dfrac{2}{3a} = \dfrac{\cancel{a}^1 \times \cancel{2}^1}{\cancel{2}_1 \times 2 \times 3 \times \cancel{a}^1}$

$= \dfrac{1}{6}$

b $n^2 \times \dfrac{3}{n} = \dfrac{n^2 \times 3}{n}$

$= \dfrac{\cancel{n}^1 \times n \times 3}{\cancel{n}_1}$

$= \dfrac{3n}{1}$

$= 3n$

DIVISION

Step 1: To divide by a fraction, multiply by its reciprocal.
Step 2: Multiply numerators and multiply denominators.
Step 3: Cancel any common factors.
Step 4: Write in simplest form.

For example, $\dfrac{x}{3} \div \dfrac{2x}{9} = \dfrac{x}{3} \times \dfrac{9}{2x}$ {*Step 1*}

$= \dfrac{\cancel{x} \times \cancel{9}^{\,3} \times 3}{\cancel{3} \times 2 \times \cancel{x}}$ {*Step 2 and 3*}

$= \dfrac{3}{2}$ {*Step 4*}

Example 6 ◀) Self Tutor

Simplify:

a $\dfrac{3}{x^2} \div \dfrac{6}{x}$ **b** $\dfrac{4x}{3} \div 2x$

a $\dfrac{3}{x^2} \div \dfrac{6}{x}$

$= \dfrac{3}{x^2} \times \dfrac{x}{6}$

$= \dfrac{\cancel{3} \times \cancel{x}}{\cancel{x} \times x \times \cancel{6}}$

$= \dfrac{1}{x \times 2}$

$= \dfrac{1}{2x}$

b $\dfrac{4x}{3} \div 2x$

$= \dfrac{4x}{3} \times \dfrac{1}{2x}$

$= \dfrac{\cancel{4}^{\,2} \times \cancel{x} \times 1}{3 \times \cancel{2} \times \cancel{x}}$

$= \dfrac{2}{3}$

> The reciprocal of $\dfrac{a}{b}$ is $\dfrac{b}{a}$.

EXERCISE 21C

1 Multiply each of the following by $\dfrac{x}{2}$:

a $\dfrac{2}{3}$ **b** $\dfrac{2}{x}$ **c** $\dfrac{4}{3x}$ **d** $\dfrac{x}{3}$

2 Simplify:

a $\dfrac{a}{3} \times \dfrac{b}{5}$ **b** $\dfrac{a}{5} \times \dfrac{2}{a}$ **c** $\dfrac{b}{7} \times b$ **d** $\dfrac{b}{6} \times \dfrac{4}{3b}$

e $\dfrac{a}{5} \times \dfrac{1}{a^2}$ **f** $\dfrac{7}{b} \times b$ **g** $\dfrac{4}{c} \times c^2$ **h** $\left(\dfrac{3}{d}\right)^2$

i $\left(\dfrac{y}{3}\right)^3$ **j** $\left(\dfrac{3a}{b}\right)^2$ **k** $x \times \left(\dfrac{y}{x}\right)^2$ **l** $2a \times \left(\dfrac{a}{4}\right)^2$

3 Divide each of the following by $\frac{a}{2}$:

   a $\frac{3}{2}$ **b** $\frac{a}{2}$ **c** $\frac{3}{a}$ **d** $\frac{5a}{4}$

4 Simplify:

   a $\frac{x}{5} \div \frac{x}{3}$ **b** $\frac{2}{3} \div \frac{3}{x}$ **c** $\frac{5}{y} \div \frac{2}{y}$ **d** $\frac{y}{6} \div 3$

   e $\frac{x}{3} \div x$ **f** $x \div \frac{x}{7}$ **g** $2 \div \frac{x}{y}$ **h** $\frac{6}{x} \div \frac{4}{x^2}$

D   ADDING AND SUBTRACTING ALGEBRAIC FRACTIONS

Variables are used in algebraic fractions to represent unknown numbers. We can treat algebraic fractions in the same way that we treat numerical fractions since they are in fact *representing* numerical fractions.

The rules for addition and subtraction of algebraic fractions are identical to those used with numerical fractions.

To **add** two or more fractions we obtain the *lowest common denominator* then add the resulting numerators.

Since $\frac{1}{5} + \frac{3}{5} = \frac{1+3}{5}$,

$$\frac{a}{c} + \frac{b}{c} = \frac{a+b}{c}$$

To **subtract** two or more fractions we obtain the *lowest common denominator* and then subtract the resulting numerators.

Since $\frac{5}{7} - \frac{2}{7} = \frac{5-2}{7}$,

$$\frac{a}{c} - \frac{d}{c} = \frac{a-d}{c}$$

To find the lowest common denominator, we look for the **lowest common multiple of the denominators**.

For example,   when adding $\frac{1}{2} + \frac{1}{3}$,   the lowest common denominator is 6,

                 when adding $\frac{2}{3} + \frac{3}{4}$,   the lowest common denominator is 12,

                 when adding $\frac{1}{6} + \frac{5}{9}$,   the lowest common denominator is 18.

The same method is used when there are variables in the denominator.

For example,   when adding $\frac{2}{3} + \frac{1}{x}$,   the lowest common denominator is $3x$,

                 when adding $\frac{2}{a} + \frac{3}{2a}$,   the lowest common denominator is $2a$,

                 when adding $\frac{3}{4a} + \frac{5}{6b}$,   the lowest common denominator is $12ab$.

To find $\dfrac{2}{3a} + \dfrac{3}{2a}$, we find the LCD and then proceed in the same way as for ordinary fractions.

The LCM of $3a$ and $2a$ is $6a$, so the LCD is $6a$.

$$\therefore \quad \dfrac{2}{3a} + \dfrac{3}{2a} = \dfrac{2 \times 2}{3a \times 2} + \dfrac{3 \times 3}{2a \times 3}$$

$$= \dfrac{4}{6a} + \dfrac{9}{6a}$$

$$= \dfrac{13}{6a}$$

Example 7 — Self Tutor

Simplify:

a $\dfrac{2x}{3} + \dfrac{x}{2}$ **b** $\dfrac{a}{2} - \dfrac{3a}{7}$

a $\dfrac{2x}{3} + \dfrac{x}{2}$ $\quad \{\text{LCD} = 6\}$

$= \dfrac{2x \times 2}{3 \times 2} + \dfrac{x \times 3}{2 \times 3}$

$= \dfrac{4x}{6} + \dfrac{3x}{6}$

$= \dfrac{4x + 3x}{6}$

$= \dfrac{7x}{6}$

b $\dfrac{a}{2} - \dfrac{3a}{7}$ $\quad \{\text{LCD} = 14\}$

$= \dfrac{a \times 7}{2 \times 7} - \dfrac{3a \times 2}{7 \times 2}$

$= \dfrac{7a}{14} - \dfrac{6a}{14}$

$= \dfrac{7a - 6a}{14}$

$= \dfrac{a}{14}$

EXERCISE 21D

1 Add $\dfrac{x}{2}$ to each of the following:

  a $\dfrac{x}{3}$ **b** $\dfrac{x}{4}$ **c** $\dfrac{x}{5}$ **d** $\dfrac{x}{6}$

2 Subtract $\dfrac{a}{3}$ from each of the following:

  a $\dfrac{a}{2}$ **b** $\dfrac{2a}{3}$ **c** $\dfrac{3a}{4}$ **d** $\dfrac{5a}{6}$

3 Simplify by writing as a single fraction:

  a $\dfrac{x}{7} + \dfrac{x}{2}$ **b** $\dfrac{y}{2} - \dfrac{y}{3}$ **c** $\dfrac{2a}{5} + \dfrac{3a}{10}$ **d** $\dfrac{b}{3} - \dfrac{b}{5}$

  e $\dfrac{c}{7} + \dfrac{c}{2}$ **f** $\dfrac{d}{4} - \dfrac{3d}{8}$ **g** $\dfrac{e}{6} + \dfrac{2e}{3}$ **h** $\dfrac{3f}{7} - \dfrac{f}{14}$

  i $\dfrac{n}{5} + \dfrac{3n}{2}$ **j** $\dfrac{p}{7} - \dfrac{2p}{3}$ **k** $\dfrac{2k}{3} + \dfrac{3k}{4}$ **l** $\dfrac{3s}{8} - \dfrac{s}{2}$

Example 8

Simplify: a $\dfrac{3}{x} + \dfrac{2}{y}$ b $\dfrac{2}{3a} - \dfrac{1}{2a}$

a $\dfrac{3}{x} + \dfrac{2}{y}$ {LCD = xy}

$= \dfrac{3 \times y}{x \times y} + \dfrac{2 \times x}{y \times x}$

$= \dfrac{3y}{xy} + \dfrac{2x}{xy}$

$= \dfrac{3y + 2x}{xy}$

b $\dfrac{2}{3a} - \dfrac{1}{2a}$ {LCD = $6a$}

$= \dfrac{2 \times 2}{3a \times 2} - \dfrac{1 \times 3}{2a \times 3}$

$= \dfrac{4}{6a} - \dfrac{3}{6a}$

$= \dfrac{1}{6a}$

4 Simplify:

a $\dfrac{2}{x} + \dfrac{3}{x}$ b $\dfrac{1}{x} + \dfrac{3}{2x}$ c $\dfrac{1}{2} + \dfrac{1}{x}$ d $\dfrac{1}{x} - \dfrac{1}{2}$

5 Simplify:

a $\dfrac{5}{p} + \dfrac{3}{q}$ b $\dfrac{7}{r} + \dfrac{2}{s}$ c $\dfrac{4}{p} + \dfrac{3}{q}$ d $\dfrac{2t}{s} - \dfrac{t}{2s}$

e $\dfrac{a}{7} + \dfrac{2}{3}$ f $\dfrac{5}{b} - \dfrac{1}{2b}$ g $\dfrac{a}{b} + \dfrac{3}{5}$ h $\dfrac{a}{b} + \dfrac{c}{3b}$

6 Simplify:

a $\dfrac{a}{5} + 1$ b $\dfrac{b}{7} - 2$ c $c + \dfrac{c}{3}$ d $4 - \dfrac{d}{2}$

e $4 + \dfrac{p}{3}$ f $7 - \dfrac{q}{2}$ g $8 + \dfrac{1}{r}$ h $4 - \dfrac{3}{s}$

7 Simplify:

a $\dfrac{3x}{4} + \dfrac{x}{3}$ b $\dfrac{5y}{2} - \dfrac{2y}{3}$ c $\dfrac{5}{2p} + \dfrac{3}{2p}$ d $\dfrac{7}{2q} - \dfrac{4}{3q}$

e $\dfrac{2}{x} + \dfrac{5}{y}$ f $\dfrac{4}{3x} - \dfrac{2}{x}$ g $\dfrac{a}{6} + 3a$ h $3x - \dfrac{x}{2}$

8 Simplify:

a $\dfrac{3}{a} + \dfrac{2}{a^2}$ b $\dfrac{5}{b^2} + \dfrac{1}{b}$ c $\dfrac{6}{d} - \dfrac{1}{d^2}$ d $\dfrac{5}{x^2} - \dfrac{4}{x}$

e $1 + \dfrac{x^2}{2}$ f $1 + \dfrac{1}{x^2}$ g $x + \dfrac{2}{x}$ h $x + \dfrac{4}{x^2}$

i $5 - \dfrac{a^2}{4}$ j $6 - \dfrac{2}{b^2}$ k $x + \dfrac{x^2}{2}$ l $x - \dfrac{1}{x^2}$

m $4x + \dfrac{2}{x}$ n $6x - \dfrac{1}{x}$ o $\dfrac{3x}{4} - \dfrac{1}{x}$ p $\dfrac{1}{2x} + x$

E SIMPLIFYING MORE COMPLICATED FRACTIONS

In this section we try to simplify more complicated algebraic fractions. This is not always possible to do.

ILLEGAL CANCELLATION

Take care with fractions such as $\dfrac{x-6}{6}$.

The expression in the numerator, $x - 6$, cannot be written as the product of factors other than $1 \times (x - 6)$. x and -6 are terms of the expression, not factors.

A typical **error** in illegal cancellation is: $\dfrac{x - \cancel{6}^{1}}{{}_{1}\cancel{6}} = \dfrac{x-1}{1} = x-1.$

You can check that this cancellation of terms is incorrect by substituting a value for x.

For example, if $x = 12$, LHS $= \dfrac{x-6}{6} = \dfrac{12-6}{6} = \dfrac{6}{6} = 1$,

whereas RHS $= x - 1 = 12 - 1 = 11$.

Example 9

Simplify if possible:

a $\dfrac{10(2x+3)}{5}$

b $\dfrac{4(x+2)(x-1)}{2(x-1)}$

a $\dfrac{{}^{2}\cancel{10}(2x+3)}{\cancel{5}_{1}}$
$= 2(2x+3)$

b $\dfrac{{}^{2}\cancel{4}(x+2)\cancel{(x-1)}^{1}}{{}_{1}\cancel{2}\cancel{(x-1)}_{1}}$
$= \dfrac{2(x+2)}{1}$
$= 2(x+2)$

Example 10

Simplify if possible:

a $\dfrac{6(x+6)}{3}$

b $\dfrac{x+6}{3}$

a $\dfrac{{}^{2}\cancel{6}(x+6)}{{}_{1}\cancel{3}}$
$= 2(x+6)$

b $\dfrac{x+6}{3}$ cannot be simplified because the coefficient of x is not a multiple of 3, and so we cannot cancel the denominator.

EXERCISE 21E.1

1 Simplify if possible:

a $\dfrac{3(x-2)}{3}$ b $\dfrac{2(a+3)}{4}$

c $\dfrac{6(d+1)}{2}$ d $\dfrac{3(c-3)}{6}$

e $\dfrac{8}{2(z+3)}$ f $\dfrac{9}{6(1+x)}$

g $\dfrac{6(a+2)}{2(a+2)}$ h $\dfrac{5(x+2)}{10(x-2)}$

i $\dfrac{(x+y)(x-y)}{x(x+y)}$ j $\dfrac{(a+2)^2}{2(a+2)}$

k $\dfrac{3(b-4)}{6(b-4)^2}$ l $\dfrac{8(p+q)^2}{12(p+q)}$

Remember that $(x+y)^2 = (x+y)(x+y)$

2 Simplify if possible:

a $\dfrac{4(x+1)}{2}$ b $\dfrac{2(x-1)}{4}$ c $\dfrac{x+4}{2}$

d $\dfrac{x-9}{3}$ e $\dfrac{3(a+2)}{6(a-2)}$ f $\dfrac{2x+3}{9}$

g $\dfrac{2x-4}{2}$ h $\dfrac{2x-4}{4}$ i $\dfrac{2x-4}{x-2}$

j $\dfrac{2x-4}{x}$ k $\dfrac{9}{x+3}$ l $\dfrac{9}{3x+6}$

FACTORISATION THEN SIMPLIFICATION

Given an algebraic fraction, we factorise both the numerator and denominator. If they have a common factor then we can cancel it.

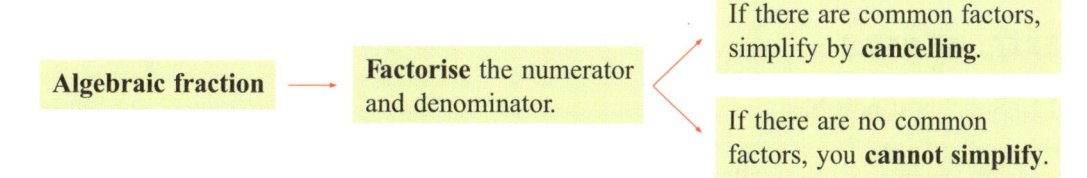

Algebraic fraction ⟶ **Factorise** the numerator and denominator.
- If there are common factors, simplify by **cancelling**.
- If there are no common factors, you **cannot simplify**.

For example, the fraction $\dfrac{3x+3y}{6x+6y}$ can be simplified by factorising the numerator and denominator **separately** using the distributive law, and **then** cancelling common factors:

$$\dfrac{3x+3y}{6x+6y} = \dfrac{\overset{1}{\cancel{3}}\cancel{(x+y)}^{1}}{\underset{2}{\cancel{6}}\cancel{(x+y)}_{1}} \quad \{\text{factorising separately}\}$$

$$= \tfrac{1}{2} \quad\quad\quad \{\text{simplifying by cancelling}\}$$

432	ALGEBRAIC FRACTIONS	(Chapter 21)

INVESTIGATION WHAT DOES $\dfrac{b-a}{a-b}$ SIMPLIFY TO?

Consider $\dfrac{x-5}{5-x}$. Can we simplify this expression?

What to do:

1 Copy and complete the table alongside:

2 What do you notice about the value for $\dfrac{b-a}{a-b}$ in every case?

3 Copy and complete:
   $b - a = ...(a - b)$ and $a - b = ...(b - a)$

a	b	$b-a$	$a-b$	$\dfrac{b-a}{a-b}$
5	2			
7	1			
12	5			
3	7			
2	6			

From the investigation above, you should have discovered the rule:

$$b - a = -1(a - b)$$

Example 11

Simplify: a $\dfrac{3a-9}{3}$ b $\dfrac{4x+6}{3}$

a $\dfrac{3a-9}{3}$
$= \dfrac{{}^1\cancel{3}(a-3)}{{}_1\cancel{3}}$
$= a - 3$

b $\dfrac{4x+6}{3}$
$= \dfrac{2(2x+3)}{3}$
which cannot be simplified as there are no common factors.

Factorise first and then see if you can cancel common factors.

EXERCISE 21E.2

1 Simplify if possible:

a $\dfrac{4x+6}{2}$ b $\dfrac{4x+6}{5}$ c $\dfrac{2x-6}{3}$ d $\dfrac{2x-6}{2}$

e $\dfrac{6a+2}{2}$ f $\dfrac{6a+2}{3}$ g $\dfrac{5b-10}{2}$ h $\dfrac{5b-10}{5}$

i $\dfrac{3x-15}{3}$ j $\dfrac{3x-15}{5}$ k $\dfrac{4y+12}{3}$ l $\dfrac{4y+12}{4}$

m $\dfrac{4x+16}{2}$ n $\dfrac{4x+16}{4}$ o $\dfrac{4x+16}{8}$ p $\dfrac{x^2+2x}{x}$

ALGEBRAIC FRACTIONS (Chapter 21) 433

Example 12 *Self Tutor*

Simplify by factorising: **a** $\dfrac{4x+8}{5x+10}$ **b** $\dfrac{ab-ac}{b-c}$

a $\dfrac{4x+8}{5x+10}$ ← HCF is 4
      ← HCF is 5

$= \dfrac{4(x+2)}{5(x+2)}$

$= \dfrac{4\cancel{(x+2)}^1}{5\cancel{(x+2)}^1}$ {cancelling}

$= \dfrac{4}{5}$

b $\dfrac{ab-ac}{b-c}$ ← HCF is a

$= \dfrac{a(b-c)}{1(b-c)}$

$= \dfrac{a\cancel{(b-c)}^1}{1\cancel{(b-c)}^1}$ {cancelling}

$= a$

2 Simplify by factorising:

a $\dfrac{2x+4}{3x+6}$ **b** $\dfrac{2x-10}{3x-15}$ **c** $\dfrac{4x+12}{2x+6}$ **d** $\dfrac{5x-20}{3x-12}$

e $\dfrac{7x-14}{x-2}$ **f** $\dfrac{x+4}{2x+8}$ **g** $\dfrac{xy+3x}{y+3}$ **h** $\dfrac{ax-ay}{x-y}$

i $\dfrac{12-3x}{4-x}$ **j** $\dfrac{ab+bc}{b}$ **k** $\dfrac{ab+bc}{a+c}$ **l** $\dfrac{ab+bc+b}{b}$

Example 13 *Self Tutor*

Simplify by factorising: **a** $\dfrac{x^2-3x}{x}$ **b** $\dfrac{2x^2+4x}{x^2+2x}$

a $\dfrac{x^2-3x}{x}$ ← HCF is x

$= \dfrac{x(x-3)}{x}$

$= \dfrac{^1\cancel{x}(x-3)}{_1\cancel{x}}$ {cancelling}

$= x-3$

b $\dfrac{2x^2+4x}{x^2+2x}$ ← HCF is $2x$
        ← HCF is x

$= \dfrac{2x(x+2)}{x(x+2)}$

$= \dfrac{2\cancel{x}^1\cancel{(x+2)}^1}{_1\cancel{x}\cancel{(x+2)}_1}$ {cancelling}

$= 2$

3 Simplify by factorising:

a $\dfrac{x^2+3x}{x}$ **b** $\dfrac{4x^2-8x}{4x}$ **c** $\dfrac{3x^2+9x}{x+3}$ **d** $\dfrac{5x^2-10x}{x-2}$

e $\dfrac{4x^2-12x}{x^2-3x}$ **f** $\dfrac{7x^2+14x}{2x^2+4x}$ **g** $\dfrac{4x^2-20x}{2x-10}$ **h** $\dfrac{x^2+2x}{x+2}$

i $\dfrac{x^3-x}{x}$ **j** $\dfrac{x^3-x}{x^2-1}$ **k** $\dfrac{ab^2-cb^2}{a-c}$ **l** $\dfrac{3xy+y^2}{6x+2y}$

Example 14

Simplify:

a $\dfrac{6a - 6b}{b - a}$

b $\dfrac{xy^2 - xy}{1 - y}$

Use the rule $b - a = -1(a - b)$.

a $\dfrac{6a - 6b}{b - a}$

$= \dfrac{6(a - b)}{-1(a - b)}$

$= -6$

b $\dfrac{xy^2 - xy}{1 - y}$

$= \dfrac{xy(y - 1)}{-1(y - 1)}$

$= -xy$

4 Simplify if possible:

a $\dfrac{m - n}{n - m}$

b $\dfrac{a + b}{b - a}$

c $\dfrac{2x - 2y}{y - x}$

d $\dfrac{4a - 4c}{3c - 3a}$

e $\dfrac{p - 2q}{6q - 3p}$

f $\dfrac{2a - 3b}{12b - 8a}$

g $\dfrac{1 - r}{r^2 - r}$

h $\dfrac{xy^2 - y}{2 - 2xy}$

HARDER SIMPLIFICATIONS (EXTENSION)

Look at the **expression** to be factorised → Remove any **common factors**

- Look for the **'difference of two squares'** $x^2 - a^2 = (x + a)(x - a)$
- Look for **'perfect squares'** $x^2 \pm 2ax + a^2 = (x \pm a)^2$
- Look for **'sum and product'** type $x^2 + [a + b]x + ab = (x + a)(x + b)$

Example 15

Simplify by factorising and cancelling common factors:

a $\dfrac{x^2 - 4}{x - 2}$

b $\dfrac{2a + 2b}{a^2 - b^2}$

Make sure that both the numerator and denominator are fully factorised before you attempt cancellation.

a $\dfrac{x^2 - 4}{x - 2}$

$= \dfrac{(x + 2)(x - 2)}{(x - 2)}$

$= x + 2$

b $\dfrac{2a + 2b}{a^2 - b^2}$

$= \dfrac{2(a + b)}{(a + b)(a - b)}$

$= \dfrac{2}{a - b}$

Example 16

Simplify by factorising and cancelling common factors: $\dfrac{x^2+x-6}{x+3}$

$\dfrac{x^2+x-6}{x+3}$

$= \dfrac{(x+3)(x-2)}{(x+3)}$

$= x - 2$

$x^2 + bx + c$ type where we need two numbers which multiply to give -6 and add to give $+1$.

These are $+3$ and -2.

$\therefore \ x^2 + x - 6 = (x+3)(x-2)$

EXERCISE 21E.3

1 Simplify:

a $\dfrac{x^2-1}{x-1}$ b $\dfrac{a^2-1}{a+1}$ c $\dfrac{2+m}{4-m^2}$ d $\dfrac{x^2-y^2}{x+y}$

e $\dfrac{x^2-1}{3x+3}$ f $\dfrac{x^2-16}{4-x}$ g $\dfrac{a^2-b^2}{ab-b^2}$ h $\dfrac{x^2-2xy}{2y^2-xy}$

2 Simplify by factorising and cancelling common factors:

a $\dfrac{(x+1)(x-2)}{x-2}$ b $\dfrac{(x-y)(x+y)}{y-x}$ c $\dfrac{(x-3)(2+x)}{(x+2)(3-x)}$

d $\dfrac{x^2-5x+6}{x-3}$ e $\dfrac{x+2}{x^2-3x-10}$ f $\dfrac{x^2+6x-7}{x-1}$

g $\dfrac{x^2+8x+12}{x^2+6x+8}$ h $\dfrac{x^2-x-6}{x^2-7x+12}$ i $\dfrac{x^2-6x+9}{x^2-3x}$

j $\dfrac{1-x^2}{x^2+4x+3}$ k $\dfrac{2x^2-18}{x^2+5x+6}$ l $\dfrac{x^2+7x+12}{x^2-x-12}$

m $\dfrac{x^2+3x-10}{x^2-10x+16}$ n $\dfrac{x^2-8x+16}{4x-x^2}$ o $\dfrac{x^2+10x+25}{25-x^2}$

REVIEW SET 21A

1 If $a = 3$ and $b = -2$, evaluate:

a $\dfrac{a}{2b}$ b $\dfrac{3b}{a}$ c $\dfrac{a-b}{a+b}$

2 Simplify:

a $\dfrac{3a^3}{6a}$ b $\dfrac{4x^3y}{8xy^2}$ c $\dfrac{-(2x^2)^2}{(-x)^2}$

3 Simplify:

   a $\dfrac{x}{3} + 2$ **b** $2 - \dfrac{x}{3}$ **c** $\dfrac{3a}{5} \times \dfrac{10}{a^2}$

   d $\dfrac{3a}{5} \div \dfrac{10}{a^2}$ **e** $\dfrac{5}{2x} - \dfrac{2}{x}$ **f** $\dfrac{5}{2x} \div \dfrac{2}{x}$

4 Simplify by factorising and then cancelling common factors:

   a $\dfrac{4x + 20}{4}$ **b** $\dfrac{3y + 12}{y + 4}$ **c** $\dfrac{x - 2}{2 - x}$

   d $\dfrac{5x^2 - 25x}{2x - 10}$ **e** $\dfrac{x^2 - 2x - 15}{x + 3}$ **f** $\dfrac{x^2 + 3x - 10}{2x^2 - 4x}$

   g $\dfrac{x^2 - 11x + 10}{3x - 3x^2}$ **h** $\dfrac{x^2 - 20x + 100}{100 - x^2}$ **i** $\dfrac{x^2 + x - 72}{x^2 - 20x + 96}$

REVIEW SET 21B

1 If $x = -4$ and $y = 2$, evaluate:

   a $\dfrac{x}{y}$ **b** $\dfrac{y^2}{x}$ **c** $\dfrac{xy}{y - x}$

2 Simplify:

   a $\dfrac{8x^4}{2x}$ **b** $\dfrac{x^2 y^3}{5xy^2}$ **c** $\dfrac{(-2x)^2}{x^3}$

3 Simplify:

   a $\dfrac{2a}{5} + \dfrac{a}{2}$ **b** $\dfrac{8}{x} \div \dfrac{2}{x^2}$ **c** $\dfrac{3}{2b} + \dfrac{4}{a}$

   d $\dfrac{3a}{5} - a$ **e** $\dfrac{8}{x} + \dfrac{2}{x^2}$ **f** $\dfrac{3}{2b} \times \dfrac{4}{a}$

4 Simplify by factorising and then cancelling common factors:

   a $\dfrac{12 - 3x}{3}$ **b** $\dfrac{7y - 21}{y - 3}$ **c** $\dfrac{4x + 12}{x^2 + 3x}$

   d $\dfrac{x^2 + 4x + 4}{x^2 - 4}$ **e** $\dfrac{x^2 - 5x + 4}{x^2 - x - 12}$ **f** $\dfrac{2x - 6}{x^2 - 6x + 9}$

   g $\dfrac{x^2 + 3x - 28}{x^2 - 10x + 24}$ **h** $\dfrac{36 - 4x^2}{x^2 - 6x + 9}$ **i** $\dfrac{x^2 - 14x + 45}{x^2 - 12x + 27}$

Chapter 22

Theoretical probability

Contents:
- **A** Sample space
- **B** Theoretical probability
- **C** Using grids to find probabilities
- **D** Multiplying probabilities
- **E** Using tree diagrams
- **F** Expectation
- **G** Odds

OPENING PROBLEM

Dieter has noticed that when he is driving, he is stopped by one in every two sets of traffic lights. We say the probability that Dieter has to stop at traffic lights at any given intersection is $\frac{1}{2}$.

Things to think about:

- If Dieter has to pass through two consecutive intersections with traffic lights, can you calculate the probability that he will have to stop?
- What do you think will be the probability that Dieter has to stop if he passes through four consecutive intersections with traffic lights?
- Do you think that this is realistic? What other factors should you consider?

A SAMPLE SPACE

The **outcomes** of an experiment are the different possible results we could obtain in one trial.

The **sample space** of an experiment is the set of its possible outcomes.

Suppose we have 10 cards with the numbers 1 to 10 written on them. If we take a card at random, it could have any of the numbers from 1 to 10 on it.

The outcomes are the numbers   1, 2, 3, 4, 5, 6, 7, 8, 9 or 10.

So, the sample space is   {1, 2, 3, 4, 5, 6, 7, 8, 9, 10}.

The number of elements in the sample space is 10.

An **event** is one or more of the outcomes of an experiment that have a particular characteristic.

In the example above, an event E could be 'getting a prime number'.

The outcomes in the event are 2, 3, 5 and 7. The number of outcomes in the event is 4.

EXERCISE 22A

1 List the sample space for:

    a taking a ticket at random from a box containing red and blue tickets

    b rolling a 6 sided die

    c taking a card at random from a pack of playing cards and looking at its suit

    d twirling a spinner with 6 segments marked A, B, C, D, E, and F.

    e choosing at random a day of the week

    f the results of a student sitting a test.

2 We have 12 cards which have the numbers from 1 to 12 written on them. A card is taken at random.

    a Find the number of elements in the sample space.

b Event A is 'getting an even number'.
   - **i** List the outcomes in the event.
   - **ii** Give the number of outcomes in the event.

   c Event B is 'getting a number less than 5'.
   - **i** List the outcomes in the event.
   - **ii** Give the number of outcomes in the event.

   d Event C is 'getting a multiple of 4'.
   - **i** List the outcomes in the event.
   - **ii** Give the number of outcomes in the event.

3 List the sample space for the genders of a litter of two puppies. Let MF represent 'the first is male and the second is female'.

B THEORETICAL PROBABILITY

Consider the **octagonal spinner** shown.

Since the spinner is symmetrical, when it is spun the arrowed marker could finish with **equal likelihood** on each of the sections marked 1 to 8.

We therefore say that the likelihood of obtaining a particular number, for example 4, is

$$1 \text{ chance in } 8, \quad \tfrac{1}{8}, \quad 12\tfrac{1}{2}\% \quad \text{or} \quad 0.125.$$

This is a **mathematical** or **theoretical** probability and is based on what we theoretically expect to occur.

> The **theoretical probability** of a particular event is the theoretical chance of that event occurring in any trial of the experiment.

Consider the event of getting '*6 or more*' from one spin of the octagonal spinner. There are three favourable outcomes (6, 7 or 8) out of the eight possible outcomes, and each of these is equally likely to occur.

So,   P(6 or more) $= \tfrac{3}{8}$

We read $\tfrac{3}{8}$ as '3 chances in 8'.

In general, for an event E containing **equally likely** possible results:

$$P(E) = \frac{\text{the number of outcomes in the event } E}{\text{the total number of possible outcomes}}.$$

Example 1

A ticket is *randomly selected* from a basket containing 3 green, 4 yellow and 5 blue tickets. Determine the probability of getting:

a a green ticket
b a green or yellow ticket
c an orange ticket
d a green, yellow or blue ticket

The sample space is $\{G_1, G_2, G_3, Y_1, Y_2, Y_3, Y_4, B_1, B_2, B_3, B_4, B_5\}$ which has $3 + 4 + 5 = 12$ outcomes.

a   P(green)
$= \frac{3}{12}$
$= \frac{1}{4}$

b   P(a green or a yellow)
$= \frac{3+4}{12}$
$= \frac{7}{12}$

c   P(orange)
$= \frac{0}{12}$
$= 0$

d   P(green, yellow or blue)
$= \frac{3+4+5}{12}$
$= \frac{12}{12}$
$= 1$

In **Example 1** notice that:

- in **c** an orange result cannot occur. The calculated probability is 0, which fits the fact that it has *no chance* of occurring.
- in **d** that a green, yellow or blue result is certain to occur. It is 100% likely or *certain* which is perfectly described using a 1.

For any event E, $0 \leqslant P(E) \leqslant 1$.

COMPLEMENTARY EVENTS

If E is an event, then E' is the **complementary event** of E, and
$$P(E) + P(E') = 1.$$

A useful rearrangement is: $P(E \text{ not occurring}) = 1 - P(E \text{ occurring})$

Example 2   ◀)) Self Tutor

An ordinary 6-sided die is rolled once. Determine the chance of:

a   getting a 6
b   not getting a 6
c   getting a 1 or 2
d   not getting a 1 or 2

The sample space of possible outcomes is $\{1, 2, 3, 4, 5, 6\}$.

a   P(6)
$= \frac{1}{6}$

b   P(not getting a 6)
$= P(1, 2, 3, 4 \text{ or } 5)$
$= \frac{5}{6}$

c   P(1 or 2)
$= \frac{2}{6}$

d   P(not getting a 1 or 2)
$= P(3, 4, 5 \text{ or } 6)$
$= \frac{4}{6}$

In **Example 2**, notice that $P(6) + P(\text{not getting a 6}) = 1$
and that $P(1 \text{ or } 2) + P(\text{not getting a 1 or 2}) = 1$.

This is no surprise as *getting a 6* and *not getting a 6* are **complementary events** where one of them **must occur**.

EXERCISE 22B

1 A marble is randomly selected from a box containing 5 green, 3 red and 7 blue marbles. Determine the probability that the marble is:

   a red   **b** green   **c** blue

   d not red   **e** neither green nor blue   **f** green or red.

2 A carton contains eight brown and four white eggs. Find the probability that an egg selected at random is:

   a brown   **b** white.

3 In a class of 32 students, eight have one first name, nineteen have two first names, and five have three first names. A student is selected at random. Determine the probability that the student has:

   a no first name   **b** one first name   **c** two first names   **d** three first names.

4 An ordinary six-sided die is rolled once. Determine the chance of getting:

   a a 5   **b** an odd number

   c a number greater than 1   **d** a multiple of 2.

5 In a club newsletter, 8 pages contain reports, 3 pages contain articles, and 5 pages contain advertising. The newsletter is opened to a page at random.

   a Determine the probability that it is:

      i a report   **ii** advertising

      iii not advertising   **iv** a report or articles.

   b Which of the events listed in **a** are complementary?

6 A disc is randomly selected from a box containing two discs marked 1, three discs marked 2, and five discs marked 3.

   a Determine the probability that the chosen disc will be marked:

      i 1   **ii** with an odd number.

   b State the event that is complementary to 'a disc with an odd number', and determine its probability.

7 A tennis club has 18 adult members, 13 teenage members and 19 junior members. The name of each member is written on a small card and placed in a box. One card is randomly chosen from the box. What is the probability that the member is:

   a a teenager   **b** an adult

   c a junior or a teenager   **d** a teenager and a junior?

C USING GRIDS TO FIND PROBABILITIES

When an experiment involves more than one operation we can still list the sample space.

If we have two operations we can use a **two-dimensional grid** to illustrate the sample space efficiently.

We can use the grid to count favourable outcomes and so calculate probabilities.

This grid shows the outcomes when two coins A and B are tossed.

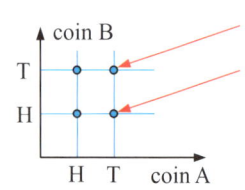

This point represents 'a tail from coin A' and 'a tail from coin B'.

This point represents 'a tail from coin A' and 'a head from coin B'.

There are four members of the sample space.

They are: HH, HT, TH, and TT.

Example 3

Use a two-dimensional grid to illustrate the sample space for tossing a coin and rolling a die simultaneously. From this grid determine the probability of:

a tossing a head
b rolling a 2
c getting a tail and a 5
d getting a tail or a 5.

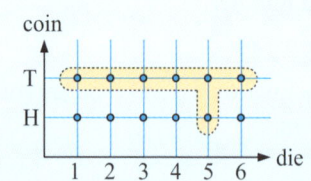

There are 12 members in the sample space.

a P(head) $= \frac{6}{12} = \frac{1}{2}$

b P(2) $= \frac{2}{12} = \frac{1}{6}$

c P(tail and a '5') $= \frac{1}{12}$

d P(tail or a '5') $= \frac{7}{12}$ {the enclosed points}

Example 4

Two square spinners, each with 1, 2, 3 and 4 on their edges, are twirled simultaneously. Draw a two-dimensional grid of the possible outcomes.
Use your grid to determine the probability of getting:

a a 3 with each spinner
b a 3 and a 1
c an even result with each spinner.

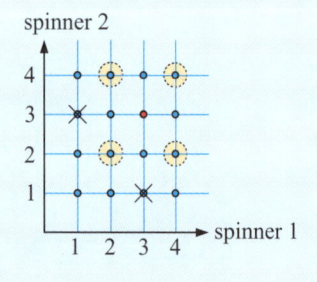

The sample space has 16 members.

a P(a 3 with each spinner) $= \frac{1}{16}$

b P(a 3 and a 1) $= \frac{2}{16}$ {crossed points}
   $= \frac{1}{8}$

c P(an even result for each spinner)
   $= \frac{4}{16} = \frac{1}{4}$ {circled points}

EXERCISE 22C

1 Draw the grid of the sample space when a $1 and a $2 coin are tossed simultaneously. Hence determine the probability of getting:

   a two heads   **b** two tails

   c exactly one head   **d** at least one head.

2 Bag A contains one red disc and one blue disc. Bag B contains one red, one blue, and one white disc. Draw a grid of the sample space when one disc is taken at random from each bag. Hence determine the probabilities of getting:

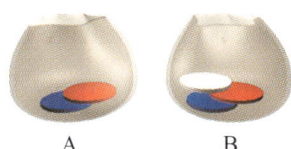

   a two red discs   **b** two discs the same colour

   c a white disc   **d** two discs that are different colours.

3 **a** Use a grid to illustrate the sample space when a coin is tossed and a spinner with 3 equal sectors A, B, and C is twirled.

   b **i** List the sample space.
        ii How many outcomes are possible?

   c Use your grid to determine the chance of getting:

      i an A and a head   **ii** a head and not an A
      iii an A   **iv** an A or a B and a tail.

4 **a** Draw a grid to represent the sample space when two spinners each with 3 equal sectors 1, 2, and 3 are twirled simultaneously.

   b List the sample space.

   c How many outcomes are possible?

   d Use your grid to determine the chance of getting:

      i two 2s   **ii** two odd numbers
      iii a 2 and a 3   **iv** two numbers with a sum of 3
      v two numbers the same   **vi** two numbers with a sum of 3 or 5.

5 A coin is tossed and a spinner with six equal sectors marked 1, 2, 3, 4, 5 and 6 is twirled.

   a Draw a grid of the sample space.

   b How many outcomes are possible?

   c Use your grid to determine the chance of getting:

      i a tail and a 3
      ii a head and an even number
     iii a tail and a number greater than 4
     iv a 6
      v no 6s
     vi any number except 5 and a head
     vii a head or a 6.

D MULTIPLYING PROBABILITIES

In the previous section we used two-dimensional grids to represent sample spaces and hence find answers to certain types of probability problems.

Consider tossing a coin and rolling a die simultaneously.

What is the probability of getting a head and a 5?

From the grid there are 12 possible outcomes but only one with the property that we want. So, the probability is $\frac{1}{12}$.

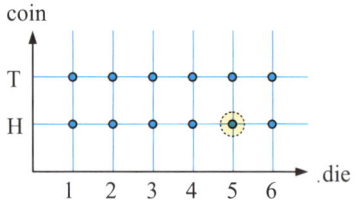

But P(a head) $= \frac{1}{2}$ and P(a '5') $= \frac{1}{6}$ and $\frac{1}{2} \times \frac{1}{6} = \frac{1}{12}$.

This suggests that P(a head **and** a '5') = P(a head) $\times$ P('5'), so we multiply the separate probabilities.

In general: If A and B are two events then P(A **and** B) = P(A) $\times$ P(B).

Example 5   ◀)) Self Tutor

Every Sunday morning Dagma and Karl go fishing. Karl says that he catches fish 9 mornings out of 10, and Dagma says she catches fish 4 mornings out of 5. If you can believe what they say, determine the probability that:

- **a** Dagma and Karl both caught fish last Sunday
- **b** only Dagma caught fish last Sunday
- **c** neither of them caught fish last Sunday.

P(Karl catches fish) $= \frac{9}{10}$
$\therefore$ P(Karl does not catch fish) $= 1 - \frac{9}{10} = \frac{1}{10}$
P(Dagma catches fish) $= \frac{4}{5}$
$\therefore$ P(Dagma does not catch fish) $= 1 - \frac{4}{5} = \frac{1}{5}$

- **a** P(both caught fish)
  = P(Dagma *and* Karl caught fish)
  = P(Dagma caught fish) $\times$ P(Karl caught fish)
  = $\frac{4}{5} \times \frac{9}{10} = \frac{18}{25}$
- **b** P(only Dagma caught fish)
  = P(Dagma caught fish *and* Karl did not catch fish)
  = P(Dagma caught fish) $\times$ P(Karl did not catch fish)
  = $\frac{4}{5} \times \frac{1}{10} = \frac{2}{25}$
- **c** P(neither caught fish)
  = P(Dagma did not catch fish *and* Karl did not catch fish)
  = P(Dagma did not catch fish) $\times$ P(Karl did not catch fish)
  = $\frac{1}{5} \times \frac{1}{10} = \frac{1}{50}$

EXERCISE 22D

1 Irena and Natasha are young ice skaters. They are learning to do a triple loop. Irena falls on average half the time when she attempts this jump, while Natasha falls on average once in every three times. If they each have one attempt at the triple loop, determine the probability that:

   a they are both successful   **b** they both fall   **c** Natasha succeeds but Irena falls.

2 Carlos does his shopping at the same time each Friday. He estimates that the probability that he has to queue at the supermarket checkout is $\frac{5}{6}$, and the probability that he has to queue at the post office is $\frac{1}{4}$. When he does his shopping next Friday, what is the probability that he will queue at: **a** both places   **b** neither place?

3 Helena has an 80% chance and Rodriquez has a 50% chance of obtaining 'A' grades in their History examination. Find the probability that:

   a both will obtain 'A' grades   **b** Rodriquez will get an 'A' and Helena will not

   c neither will obtain 'A' grades.

4 Nigel fires 500 arrows at a target and hits the target on 475 occasions. Use this information to estimate the probability that he will hit the target with every shot when he fires: **a** one arrow   **b** two arrows   **c** three arrows.

5 The probability of a woman giving birth to identical twins is approximately $\frac{1}{250}$.

Find the probability that a woman will have two sets of identical twins with her first two births.

E   USING TREE DIAGRAMS

Tree diagrams can be used to illustrate sample spaces provided that the alternatives are not too numerous.

Once the sample space is illustrated, the tree diagram can be used for determining probabilities.

Consider **Example 5** again. The tree diagram for this information is:

F = caught fish
N = did not catch fish

Karl's result   Dagma's result

$\frac{9}{10}$ → F $\frac{4}{5}$ → F $\frac{9}{10} \times \frac{4}{5} = \frac{36}{50}$

           $\frac{1}{5}$ → N $\frac{9}{10} \times \frac{1}{5} = \frac{9}{50}$

$\frac{1}{10}$ → N $\frac{4}{5}$ → F $\frac{1}{10} \times \frac{4}{5} = \frac{4}{50}$

           $\frac{1}{5}$ → N $\frac{1}{10} \times \frac{1}{5} = \frac{1}{50}$

Notice that:

- the probabilities for catching and not catching fish are marked on the branches
- there are *four* alternative paths and each path shows a particular outcome
- all outcomes are represented and the probabilities are obtained by **multiplying** the probabilities along each branch
- the probability of an event containing two or more outcomes is obtained by **adding** the probabilities of each of the outcomes.

Example 6

During the summer holidays, the probability that Hiroko plays tennis on any day is $\frac{5}{7}$, and the probability that she swims on any day is $\frac{3}{5}$.

a Draw a tree diagram to illustrate this situation.
b Use the tree diagram to determine the chance that on any day Hiroko:
  i plays tennis and swims
  ii swims but does not play tennis.

a Let T represent the event 'Hiroko plays tennis' and S represent the event 'Hiroko swims'.
$\therefore$ $P(T) = \frac{5}{7}$ and $P(T') = \frac{2}{7}$, also $P(S) = \frac{3}{5}$ and $P(S') = \frac{2}{5}$.

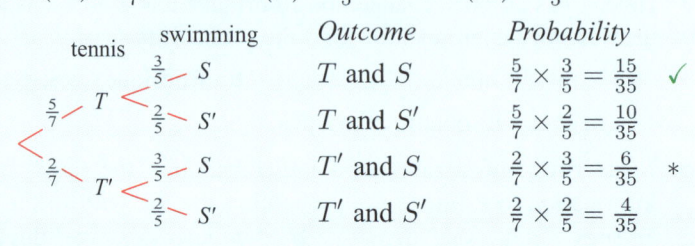

tennis	swimming	Outcome	Probability	
$\frac{5}{7}$ T	$\frac{3}{5}$ S	T and S	$\frac{5}{7} \times \frac{3}{5} = \frac{15}{35}$	✓
	$\frac{2}{5}$ S'	T and S'	$\frac{5}{7} \times \frac{2}{5} = \frac{10}{35}$	
$\frac{2}{7}$ T'	$\frac{3}{5}$ S	T' and S	$\frac{2}{7} \times \frac{3}{5} = \frac{6}{35}$	*
	$\frac{2}{5}$ S'	T' and S'	$\frac{2}{7} \times \frac{2}{5} = \frac{4}{35}$	

b i P(plays tennis and swims)
$= P(T \text{ and } S)$ ✓
$= \frac{5}{7} \times \frac{3}{5}$
$= \frac{3}{7}$

ii P(swims but does not play tennis)
$= P(S \text{ and } T')$ *
$= \frac{2}{7} \times \frac{3}{5}$
$= \frac{6}{35}$

Example 7

Bag A contains three red and two yellow tickets. Bag B contains one red and four yellow tickets. A bag is randomly selected by tossing a coin, and one ticket is removed from it. Determine the probability that it is yellow.

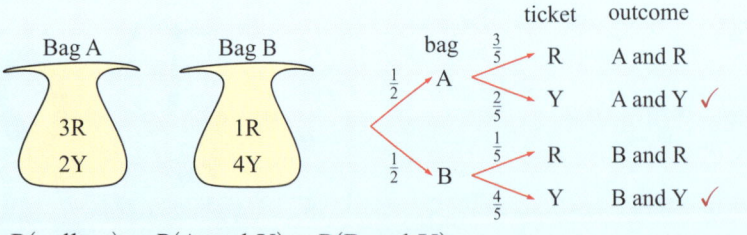

Bag A: 3R 2Y
Bag B: 1R 4Y

bag	ticket	outcome	
$\frac{1}{2}$ A	$\frac{3}{5}$ R	A and R	
	$\frac{2}{5}$ Y	A and Y	✓
$\frac{1}{2}$ B	$\frac{1}{5}$ R	B and R	
	$\frac{4}{5}$ Y	B and Y	✓

P(yellow) = P(A and Y) + P(B and Y)
$= \frac{1}{2} \times \frac{2}{5} + \frac{1}{2} \times \frac{4}{5}$ {branches marked with a ✓}
$= \frac{6}{10}$
$= \frac{3}{5}$

> To get a yellow we take either the first branch marked with a tick **or** the second one marked with a tick and **add** the probabilities.

EXERCISE 22E

1 Suppose this spinner is spun twice.

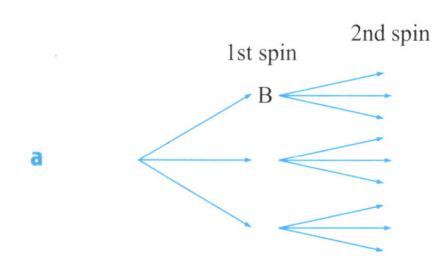

a Copy and complete the branches on the tree diagram shown.

b Find the probability that blue appears on both spins.
c Find the probability that white appears on both spins.
d Find the probability that different colours appear on the two spins.
e Find the probability that the same colour appears on the two spins.
f Find the probability that red appears on exactly one of the spins.

2 A die has four faces marked A and two faces marked B. A is the event 'the uppermost face is A', and B is the event 'the uppermost face is B'.

    a Determine: **i** $P(A)$ **ii** $P(B)$.
    b Copy and complete the tree diagram for two rolls of the die.
    c Using the tree diagram, determine the probability that:
        i both results are A
        ii both results are the same letter
        iii the first roll is B and the second roll is A
        iv the result is two different letters.

3 The weather forecast gives a 20% chance of rain tomorrow. If it is fine, the probability that Bernard will go sailing is 80%, but if it rains, the probability that he will go sailing is only 10%. Display the sample space of possible outcomes on a tree diagram.

Determine the probability that tomorrow:

    a is fine and Bernard goes sailing
    b is wet and Bernard does not go sailing
    c Bernard goes sailing.

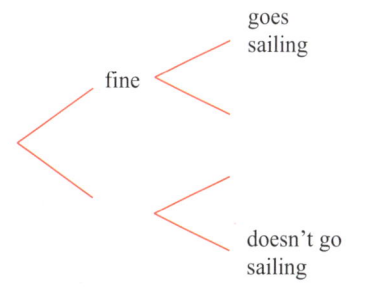

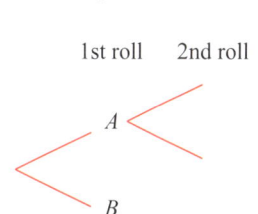

4 When Dieter passes through an intersection with traffic lights, the probability that he has to stop is $\frac{1}{2}$. If he has to pass through two consecutive intersections with traffic lights, draw a tree diagram to illustrate the possible outcomes.

Determine the probability that Dieter:
- **a** will not have to stop
- **b** will have to stop at both sets of lights
- **c** will have to stop at exactly one set of lights
- **d** will have to stop.

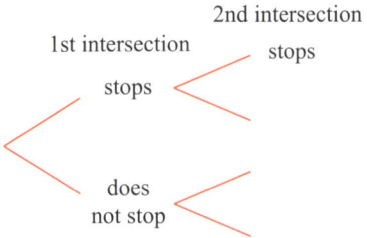

5 Luke and Gaston are chefs. Luke cooks 60% of the time and burns 4% of what he cooks. Gaston cooks the remainder of the time and burns 3% of his cooking.

Determine the probability that the next meal:
- **a** is cooked by Gaston and is burnt
- **b** is cooked by Luke and is good
- **c** is burnt.

6 Moira has two cartons each containing a dozen eggs. Carton A has three white and nine brown eggs, and carton B has eight white and four brown eggs. Moira chooses a carton at random and randomly selects an egg. Determine the probability that it is white.

7 Box X contains three green and two orange tickets. Box Y contains four green and six orange tickets. A box is chosen at random by flipping a coin and one ticket is taken from it. Determine the probability that the ticket is orange.

8 Three buckets A, B, and C, each contain some old and some new tennis balls. Bucket A has three new and three old balls, bucket B has four new and five old balls, and bucket C has two new and four old balls.

A bucket is selected using a triangular spinner with three equal sides marked A, B, and C. One tennis ball is selected at random from the bucket. Determine the probability that it is new.

F EXPECTATION

Suppose a die is rolled 120 times. On how many occasions would you *expect* the result to be a "six"?

The possible outcomes when rolling a die are 1, 2, 3, 4, 5 and 6, and each of these is equally likely to occur.

So, we would expect $\frac{1}{6}$ of them to be a "six".

Since $\frac{1}{6}$ of 120 is 20, we expect 20 of the 120 rolls of the die to yield a "six".

In general:

> If there are n trials of an experiment and the probability of an event occurring is p for each trial, then the **expectation** of the occurrence of that event is $n \times p$.

Example 8

Every box of Bran-Plus cereal has a 1 in 3 chance of containing a prize. In one month Stan buys 6 boxes of Bran-Plus. How many prizes would you expect him to win?

$p = $ P(box contains a prize) $= \frac{1}{3}$

For a sample of $n = 6$ boxes, the expected number of prizes is $\quad n \times p$
$= 6 \times \frac{1}{3}$
$= 2$

EXERCISE 22F

1 A pair of dice is rolled.
  a What is the probability of rolling a pair of ones?
  b If the dice are rolled 540 times, how many times would you expect a pair of ones to appear?

2 **a** If 3 coins are tossed, what is the chance that they all fall heads?
  b If the 3 coins are tossed 200 times, on how many occasions would you expect them all to fall heads?

3 A library found that the probability of a borrowed book being returned on time is 0.68. In one day the library lent 837 books. How many of those books can the library expect to be returned on time?

4 In a money wheel game, the wheel shown alongside is spun, and the player wins the amount in euros indicated by the marker.
  a What are your chances of spinning the wheel once and winning:
   i €9   **ii** €6   **iii** €3   **iv** €1?
  b Your expected return from spinning a 9 is $\frac{1}{12} \times$ €9. What is your expected return from spinning:
   i a 6   **ii** a 3   **iii** a 1?
  c Use **b** to find the total expected return from one spin of the wheel.
  d The game costs €4 to play. What is your expected profit or loss after one game?

G ODDS

In the horse and dog racing industries, the chances of *winning* (coming first) or *running a place* (coming first, second or third) are quoted as **odds**.

> **Odds** are usually given *against* a particular event occurring and are expressed as the ratio
> number of ways you can lose : number of ways you can win.

For example, if the odds of Rogue winning are $3:1$, then since $3+1=4$,
P(Rogue loses) $=\frac{3}{4}$ and P(Rogue wins) $=\frac{1}{4}$.

> In general, if the odds are $m:n$, then P(losing) $=\dfrac{m}{m+n}$, P(winning) $=\dfrac{n}{m+n}$.

Odds quoted as *evens* means $1:1$ and so P(losing) = P(winning) $=\frac{1}{2}$.

Betting also uses odds.

For example, if Rogue's odds are $3:1$ and Rogue wins, the bookmaker pays out $3 for every $1 bet.
So, if a punter bets $20 on Rogue to win and Rogue does win, the punter wins $60. The bookmaker makes a payment of $80 to the punter, the $20 original bet plus the $60 won.

Example 9

Rogue is at his peak in fitness and is quoted at odds of $3:5$.
a Determine the bookmaker's estimated probability that Rogue will:
  i lose **ii** win.
b If a punter bets $20 on Rogue to win, what is the punter's situation if Rogue:
  i loses **ii** wins?

a For odds of $3:5$, $3+5=8$
  i $\therefore$ P(loses) $=\frac{3}{8}$ **ii** P(wins) $=\frac{5}{8}$
b **i** If Rogue loses, the punter is *down* $20.
  ii If Rogue wins, for every $5 bet the punter wins $3.
  $\therefore$ the punter wins $3 \times 4 = \$12$.
  As the punter gets back the original bet, he or she is *up* $12.
  The *return* is $20 + \$12 = \$32$.

EXERCISE 22G

1 Determine the bookmaker's estimated probability of **i** winning **ii** losing when the odds are:

   a 2 : 1   **b** 5 : 1   **c** 50 : 1   **d** 1 : 1   **e** 2 : 3.

2 Calculate the amount won by a punter who places a bet of:

   a $10 on a horse at 4 : 1 and the horse wins

   b $80 on a horse at 2 : 3 and the horse wins.

3 A punter goes to a race meeting with $100. He has planned which horses to bet on in each race, and will keep betting until he runs out of money or there are no more races. There are 5 races at the meeting.

   a Copy and complete the following table, which is the punter's dream scenario:

Race	Odds *	Bet ($)	Result	Win/Lose ($)	Money remaining ($)
					100
1	2 : 1	20	W		
2	5 : 4	20	W		
3	10 : 1	5	W		
4	Evens	30	W		
5	1 : 4	60	W		

   * Odds for his chosen horse

   b At the end of the last race, what is the punter's "dream" situation?

   c In reality, the results of the punter's horses are: Lose, Win, Win, Lose, Lose.
At the end of the last race, what is the punter's "reality" situation?

   d Assuming the odds given accurately reflect the probability of each horse winning, work out the punter's *expectation* for the bet of $20 on one of the horses. Interpret the meaning of this answer.

   e Is it then reasonable to assume that the bookmaker also has zero expectation for the bet? If so, where does his profit come from?

REVIEW SET 22A

1 Draw a two-dimensional grid representing the sample space when an octahedral or 8-sided die is rolled and a coin is tossed simultaneously. Hence, determine the likelihood of:

   a a head *and* an 8   **b** an even number *and* a tail

   c an even number *or* a tail

2 A bag of mixed lollies contains 10 mints and 6 chocolate caramels. A second bag contains 8 mints and 8 chocolate caramels. A bag is randomly chosen by tossing a coin, and a lolly is then taken from it. Construct a tree diagram to show the sample space and hence determine the probability that:

   a a chocolate caramel will be selected   **b** a mint will be selected.

3 When Sam plays Joe at squash, Sam has a probability of $\frac{4}{7}$ of winning any set they play. If they play two sets, determine the likelihood that Sam wins:

   a the first set   **b** both sets   **c** neither set.

4 Display the possible 4-child families on a tree diagram. Determine the probability that a randomly selected 4-child family consists of two girls and two boys.

5 Sarah has developed a new gambling game in which you roll a die. The following payouts are made depending on the result:

     1 - $1,   2 - $2,   3 - $3,   4 - $5,   5 - $10,   6 - $25.

   a If you play one game, what is your expected return?

   b If you play 100 games paying $10 to play each game, how much would you expect to win or lose?

REVIEW SET 22B

1 **a** Illustrate on a 2-dimensional grid the sample space when a spinner with faces A, B, C and D is spun and a die is rolled.

   b Use this grid to determine the probability of getting:

     i an A *and* a six   **ii** an A *or* a six   **iii** a B *and* an even number.

2 Peter has a 3 in 4 chance of successfully hitting a target and Bill has a 4 in 5 chance of hitting the target. If they both fire simultaneously at the target, determine the probability that:

   a both hit   **b** both miss   **c** Peter hits *and* Bill misses.

3 Alec Smart and Joe Slow sit for an examination in Chemistry. Alec has a 95% chance of passing and Joe has a 25% chance of passing. Determine the probability that:

   a both pass   **b** both fail

   c Joe passes *and* Alec fails   **d** Alec passes *and* Joe fails

4 **a** Display the possible 3-child families on a tree diagram. Determine the probability that a randomly selected 3-child family consists of two boys and a girl.

   b In a survey of 200 randomly selected families with 3 children, how many would you expect to have two boys and a girl?

5 **a** A punter places a bet of £20 on a horse at 5 : 1 and the horse wins. How much does the punter win?

   b What is the estimated probability that the horse wins?

6 A die has 3 red, 2 blue and one white face. When the die is rolled, a red result wins €1, a blue result €2, and a white result €5. What is the "expected return" for one roll of this die?

Chapter 23

Trigonometry

Contents:
- **A** Using scale diagrams in geometry
- **B** Trigonometry
- **C** The trigonometric ratios
- **D** Problem solving with trigonometry

OPENING PROBLEM

Sometimes it is difficult or even impossible to measure angles, heights and distances directly. Consider trying to find the height of the mountain illustrated, where the angles of elevation to the top of the mountain are taken from two points A and B on the sea.

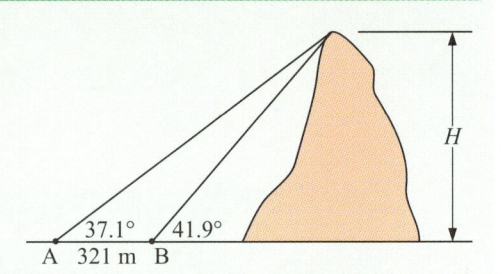

Things to think about:

- Heights of mountains are generally determined *'above sea level'*. Are the facts given sufficient to find the height of this mountain?
- How can we find a good estimate of the mountain's height?
- How accurate would you expect your final answer to be?
- Is there a mathematical method for determining an answer to greater accuracy?

A   USING SCALE DIAGRAMS IN GEOMETRY

Scale diagrams can be used to find the lengths of sides and angles of geometrical figures.

Example 1

From a drain, Jake measured the angle between the horizontal ground and the line of sight to the top of a building to be $50°$. The drain is 36.5 m from the base of the building. How high is the building?

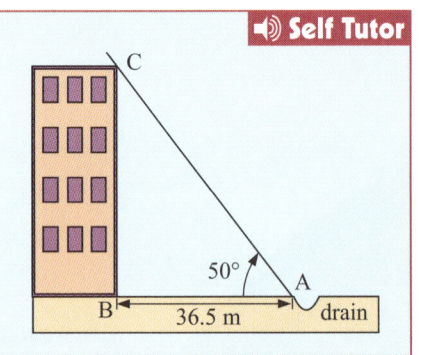

We choose a suitable *scale*, in this case
1 cm $\equiv$ 10 m   or   1 mm $\equiv$ 1 m.

We draw a horizontal line [BA] 36.5 mm long, and at the left end draw a vertical line using a set square.

We then use a protractor to draw a $50°$ angle at A. Where the two lines meet is C.

Measure [BC] in mm and use the scale to convert back to metres.

$\qquad$ BC $\approx$ 43.5 mm

$\therefore\;$ the building is approximately 43.5 metres high.

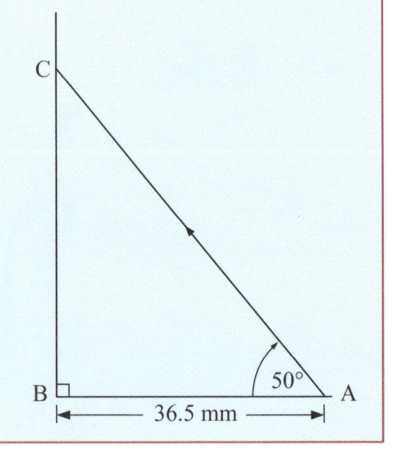

DISCUSSION

What factors could cause errors to be made in scale diagrams?
How accurate are the answers when using scale diagrams?

EXERCISE 23A

1 Convert this rough sketch into an accurate scale diagram using a scale of 1 mm ≡ 1 m.
  Use the scale diagram to find as accurately as you can the length of: **a** [BC]   **b** [AC]

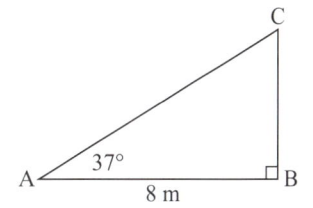

2 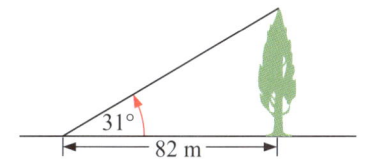 Use a scale diagram to find the height of the tree. Use a scale of 1 cm ≡ 10 m.

3 The triangular garden ABC has AB = 8 m, BC = 7.2 m and AC = 5.9 m.
  Use a compass and ruler to draw an accurate scale diagram of the garden with scale 1 cm ≡ 1 m. Hence find the measures of the garden's angles.

4 Use a scale diagram to estimate the height of the mountain in the **Opening Problem**.

B TRIGONOMETRY

Trigonometry is an important branch of mathematics which enables us to find lengths and angles to greater accuracy than is possible using scale diagrams. Loosely translated, *trigonometry* means *triangle measure*.

In this course we will consider only **right angled triangles**.

LABELLING RIGHT ANGLED TRIANGLES

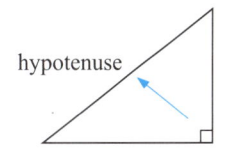

To label the angles of the triangle, we often use the Greek letters θ or 'theta' and ϕ or 'phi'.

The **hypotenuse** is the longest side of the triangle and is opposite the right angle.

For a given angle θ in a triangle, the **opposite** side is opposite the angle θ.

For example:

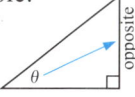

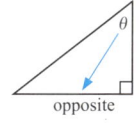

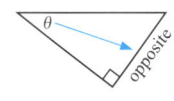

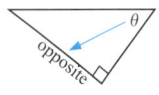

The third side is alongside the angle θ and so is called the **adjacent** side.

For example:

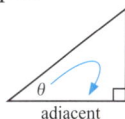

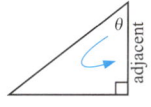

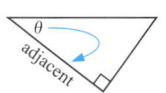

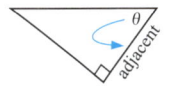

Example 2

In the diagram alongside, what is the:
- **a** hypotenuse
- **b** side opposite angle P
- **c** side adjacent to angle P
- **d** side opposite angle R
- **e** side adjacent to angle R?

- **a** The hypotenuse is [PR].
- **b** [QR] is the side opposite angle P.
- **c** [PQ] is the side adjacent to angle P.

- **d** [PQ] is the side opposite angle R.
- **e** [QR] is the side adjacent to angle R.

EXERCISE 23B.1

1 In the diagrams below, name the:
  - **i** hypotenuse
  - **ii** side opposite the angle marked θ
  - **iii** side adjacent to the angle marked θ.

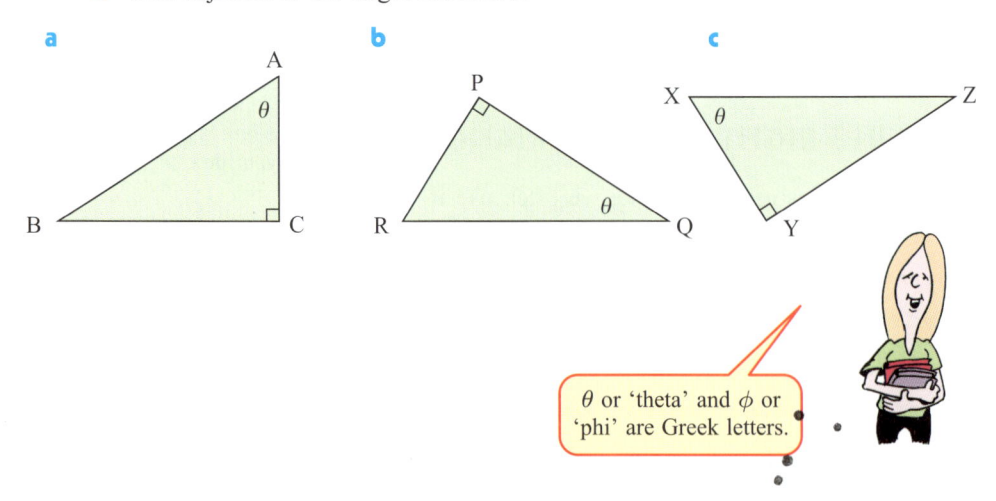

a **b** **c**

θ or 'theta' and ϕ or 'phi' are Greek letters.

2 The right angled triangle alongside has hypotenuse of length a units and other sides of length b units and c units. θ and ϕ are the two acute angles. Find the length of the side:
  - **a** opposite θ
  - **b** opposite ϕ
  - **c** adjacent to θ
  - **d** adjacent to ϕ.

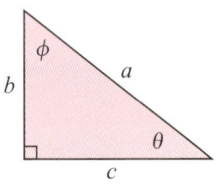

THE UNIT CIRCLE (SINE AND COSINE)

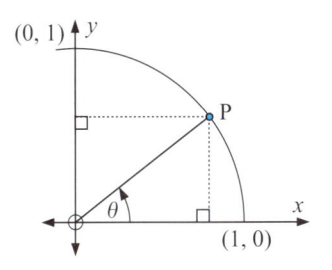

The circle of radius 1 unit with its centre at O is called the **unit circle**.

Suppose [OP] can rotate about O in the first quadrant and [OP] makes an angle θ with the x-axis as shown.

For any sized angle θ we could use an accurate scale diagram to find the coordinates of P.

We give the coordinates of P special names.

- The y-coordinate is called the **sine** of angle θ or **sin θ**.
- The x-coordinate is called the **cosine** of angle θ or **cos θ**.

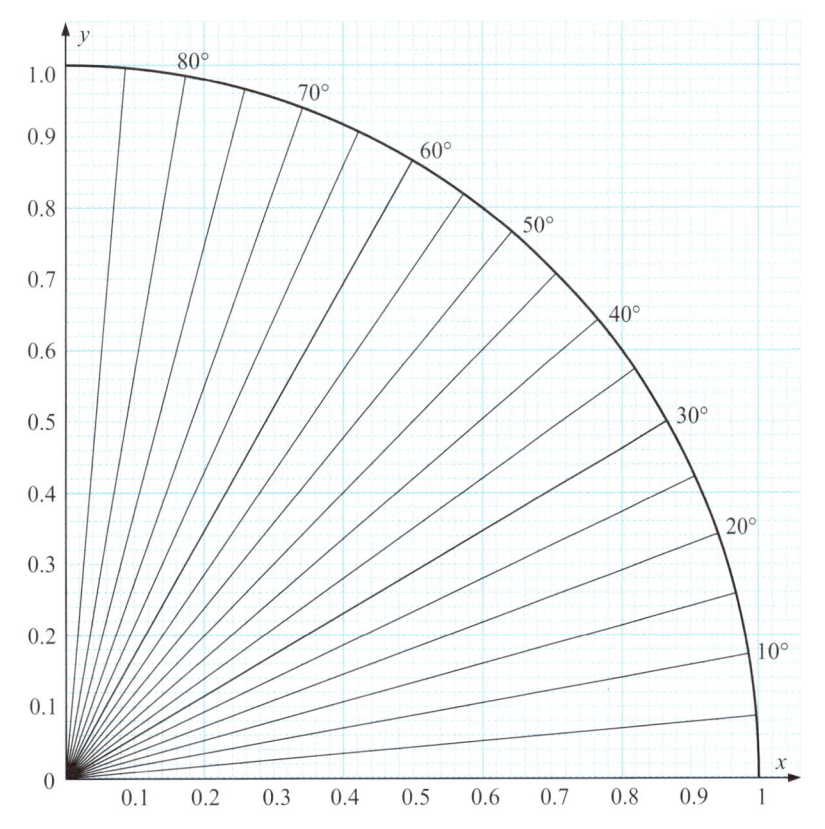

Example 3

Use the unit circle to find:

a $\sin 50°$ **b** $\cos 20°$ **c** the coordinates of P if $\theta = 40°$

a The y-coordinate at $50°$ is about 0.77, so $\sin 50° \approx 0.77$.
b The x-coordinate at $20°$ is about 0.94, so $\cos 20° \approx 0.94$.
c For $\theta = 40°$, P is $(\cos 40°, \sin 40°) \approx (0.77, 0.64)$.

EXERCISE 23B.2

1 Use the unit circle to find the value of:
- **a** $\sin 0°$
- **b** $\sin 10°$
- **c** $\sin 25°$
- **d** $\sin 30°$
- **e** $\sin 45°$
- **f** $\sin 60°$
- **g** $\sin 70°$
- **h** $\sin 90°$

2 To find $\sin 50°$ on a calculator, press [sin] 50 [)] [ENTER] or [sin] 50 [=].
The answer 0.766 044 443 can be rounded to whatever accuracy you require. Use your calculator to check your answers to question **1**.

3 Use the unit circle diagram to find the value of:
- **a** $\cos 0°$
- **b** $\cos 10°$
- **c** $\cos 25°$
- **d** $\cos 30°$
- **e** $\cos 45°$
- **f** $\cos 60°$
- **g** $\cos 70°$
- **h** $\cos 90°$

4 To find $\cos 20°$ on a calculator, press [cos] 20 [)] [ENTER] or [cos] 20 [=].
Use your calculator to check your answers to question **3**.

5 Use the unit circle diagram to find the coordinates of the point on the unit circle where [OP] makes an angle of $35°$ with the x-axis. Use your calculator to check this answer.

6 Use your results from **1** and **3** to complete the following table:

θ	$0°$	$30°$	$45°$	$60°$	$90°$
$\sin \theta$					
$\cos \theta$					

THE UNIT CIRCLE AND TANGENTS

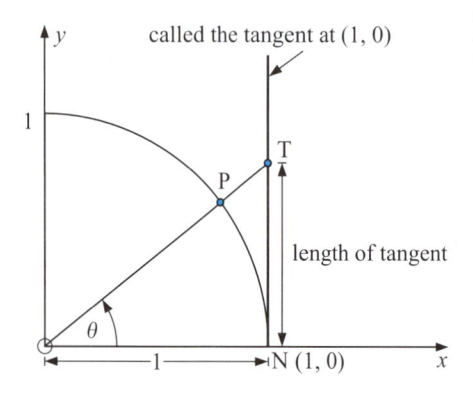

Consider extending [OP] to meet the tangent at N(1, 0). We call the point of intersection T.

The length of the tangent [NT] is called the **tangent** of angle θ or $\tan \theta$.

The diagram at the top of the next page shows how the tangent of an angle is found. Notice that $\tan 40° \approx 0.84$ and $\tan 55° \approx 1.43$.

EXERCISE 23B.3

1 Use the unit circle diagram to find the value of:
- **a** $\tan 0°$
- **b** $\tan 10°$
- **c** $\tan 15°$
- **d** $\tan 25°$
- **e** $\tan 35°$
- **f** $\tan 40°$
- **g** $\tan 45°$
- **h** $\tan 50°$

$\tan 55° \approx 1.43$

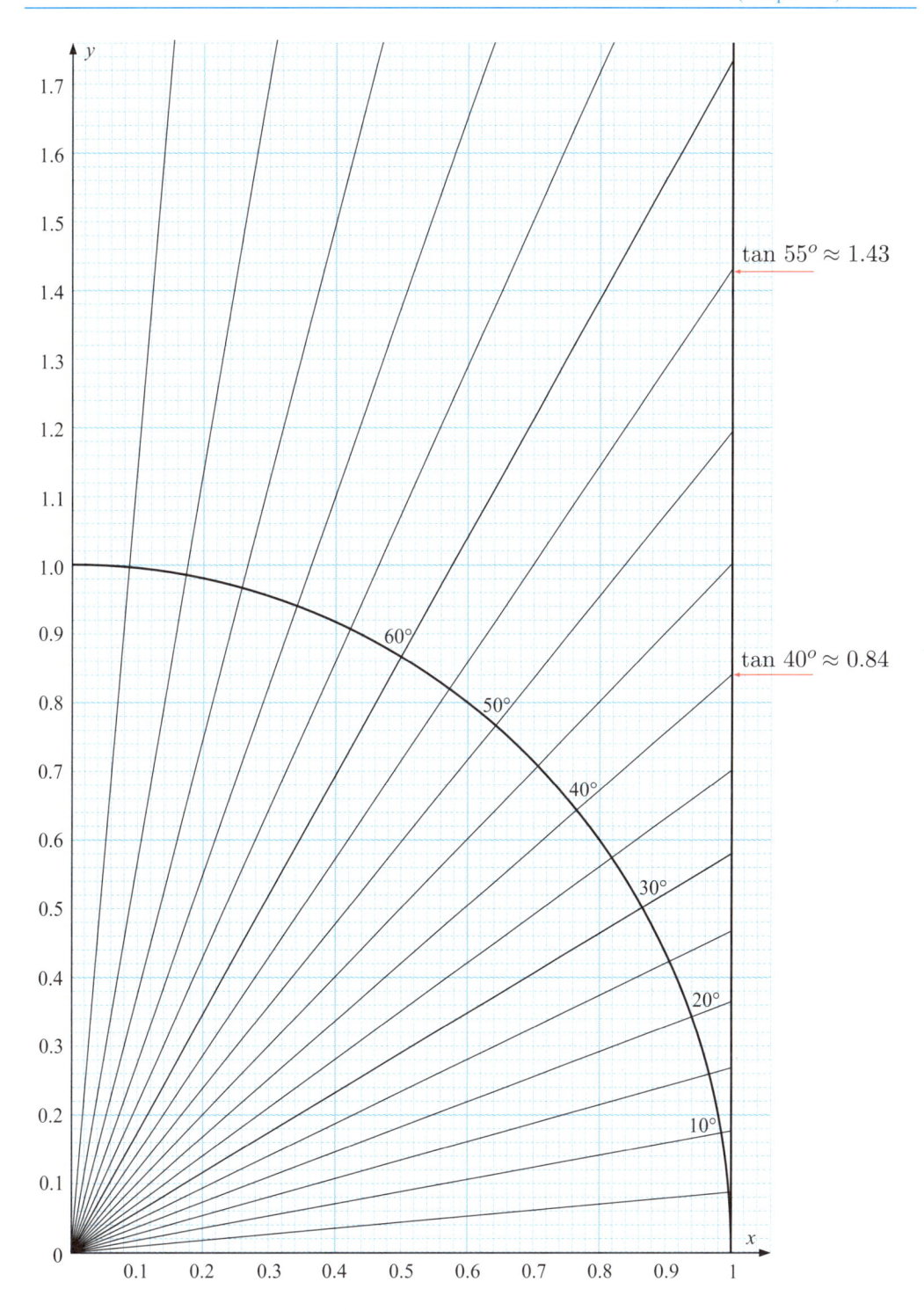

$\tan 40° \approx 0.84$

2 To find $\tan 25°$ on a calculator, press [tan] 25 [)] [ENTER] or [tan] 25 [=].
Use your calculator to check your answers to question **1**.

3 Why have you not been asked to find $\tan 90°$ using the unit circle diagram?
Find $\tan 90°$ using your calculator.

4 Explain why $\tan 45° = 1$ exactly.

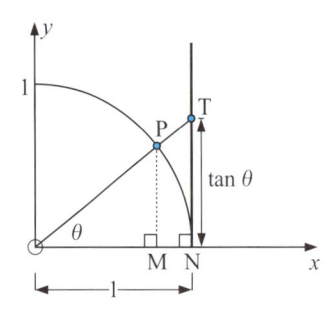

5
  a Find the coordinates of P in terms of θ.
  b Find the length of:
   i [OM]   **ii** [PM]   **iii** [TN].
  c Use similarity to show that:
  $$\tan \theta = \frac{\sin \theta}{\cos \theta}$$

C THE TRIGONOMETRIC RATIOS

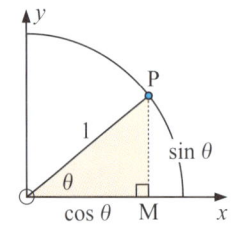

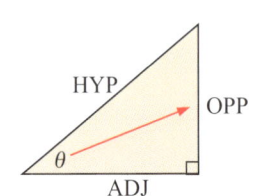

Consider a right angled triangle which is similar to $\triangle$OMP. We label its sides OPP for opposite, ADJ for adjacent, and HYP for hypotenuse.

Notice that $\quad \dfrac{\sin \theta}{1} = \dfrac{\text{OPP}}{\text{HYP}}, \quad \dfrac{\cos \theta}{1} = \dfrac{\text{ADJ}}{\text{HYP}}, \quad$ and $\quad \dfrac{\sin \theta}{\cos \theta} = \dfrac{\text{OPP}}{\text{ADJ}}.$

We saw in **Exercise 23B.3** question **5c** that $\tan \theta = \dfrac{\sin \theta}{\cos \theta}$.

So, $\quad \mathbf{\sin \theta = \dfrac{OPP}{HYP}}, \quad \mathbf{\cos \theta = \dfrac{ADJ}{HYP}}, \quad$ and $\quad \mathbf{\tan \theta = \dfrac{OPP}{ADJ}}.$

These three formulae are called the **trigonometric ratios**. They are the tools we use for finding sides and angles of right angled triangles.

FINDING SIDES

In a right angled triangle, if we are given another angle and a side, we can find:
- the third angle using the 'angle sum of a triangle is $180°$'
- the other sides using trigonometry.

Step 1: Redraw the figure and mark on it HYP, OPP, ADJ relative to the angle given.
Step 2: For the given angle, choose the correct trigonometric ratio which can be used to set up an equation.
Step 3: Set up the equation.
Step 4: Solve to find the unknown.

Example 4

Find the unknown length in the following correct to 2 decimal places:

a (triangle: 67° angle, hypotenuse 12.8 cm, opposite side x cm, right angle)

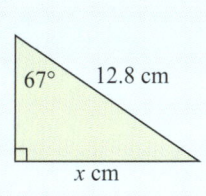

b (triangle: 39° angle, opposite 8.9 m, adjacent x m, right angle)

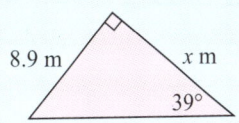

a

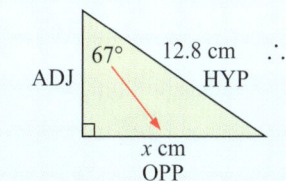

(labeled triangle: 67°, ADJ, HYP 12.8 cm, OPP x cm)

Now $\sin 67° = \dfrac{x}{12.8}$ $\{\sin\theta = \dfrac{\text{OPP}}{\text{HYP}}\}$

$\therefore\ \sin 67° \times 12.8 = x$ {multiplying both sides by 12.8}

$\therefore\ x = 11.78$ { [sin] 67 [)] [×] 12.8 [ENTER] }

b

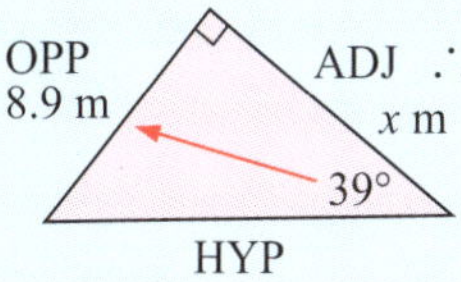

(labeled triangle: OPP 8.9 m, ADJ x m, 39°, HYP)

Now $\tan 39° = \dfrac{8.9}{x}$ $\{\tan\theta = \dfrac{\text{OPP}}{\text{ADJ}}\}$

$\therefore\ x \times \tan 39° = 8.9$ {multiplying both sides by x}

$\therefore\ x = \dfrac{8.9}{\tan 39°}$ {dividing both sides by $\tan 39°$}

$\therefore\ x = 10.99$ {8.9 [÷] [tan] 39 [)] [ENTER] }

EXERCISE 23C.1

1 Set up a trigonometric equation connecting the angle with the sides given:

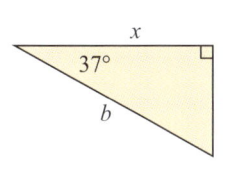

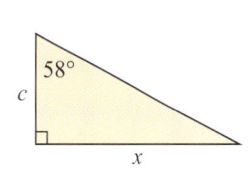

a (triangle: 68°, sides x and a)

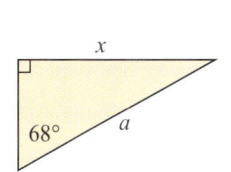

b (triangle: 37°, sides x and b)

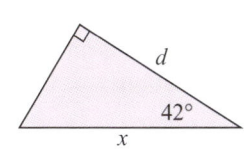

c (triangle: 58°, sides c and x)

d (triangle: 42°, sides d and x)

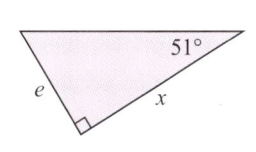

e (triangle: 51°, sides e and x)

f (triangle: 71°, sides f and x)

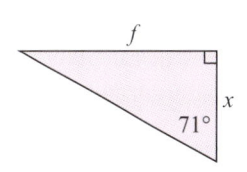

2 Find, to 2 decimal places, the unknown length in:

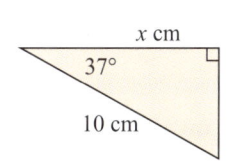

a (triangle: 68°, x cm, 9 cm)

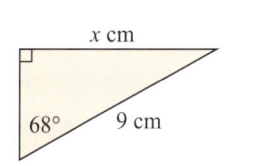

b (triangle: 37°, x cm, 10 cm)

c (triangle: 58°, 3.82 m, x m)

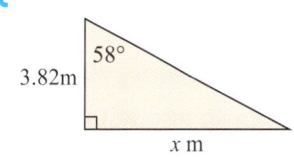

462 TRIGONOMETRY (Chapter 23)

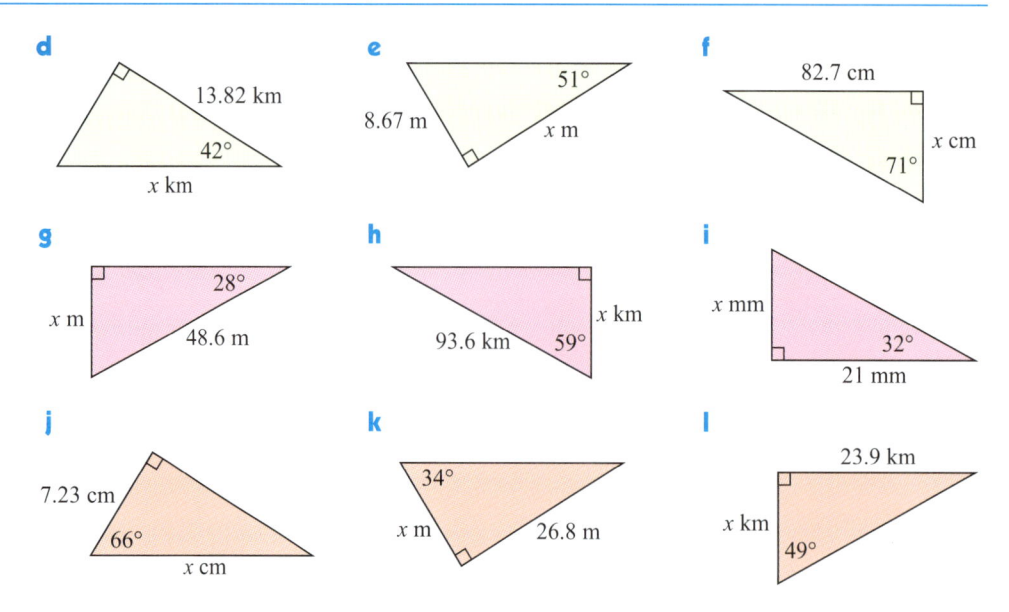

d 13.82 km, 42°, x km

e 8.67 m, 51°, x m

f 82.7 cm, 71°, x cm

g 28°, 48.6 m, x m

h 93.6 km, 59°, x km

i x mm, 32°, 21 mm

j 7.23 cm, 66°, x cm

k 34°, x m, 26.8 m

l 23.9 km, x km, 49°

3 Find, to one decimal place, *all* the unknown angles and sides of:

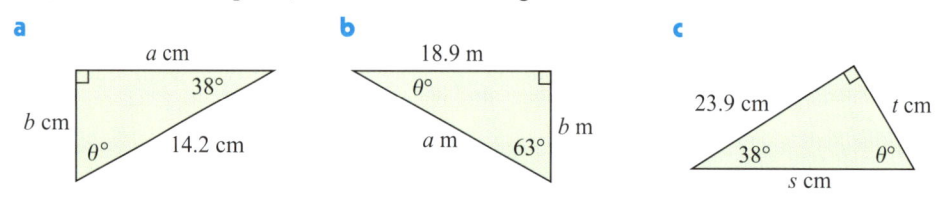

a a cm, 38°, b cm, $\theta°$, 14.2 cm

b 18.9 m, $\theta°$, a m, 63°, b m

c 23.9 cm, t cm, 38°, $\theta°$, s cm

FINDING ANGLES

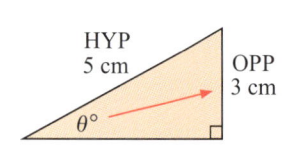

HYP 5 cm, OPP 3 cm, $\theta°$

In the right angled triangle, $\sin \theta = \frac{3}{5}$.

How do we find θ from this equation?

We need to find an angle θ with a sine of $\frac{3}{5}$.

If $\sin^{-1}(\ldots\ldots)$ reads "the angle with a sine of ......", we can write $\theta = \sin^{-1}\left(\frac{3}{5}\right)$.

We say that θ is the **inverse sine** of $\frac{3}{5}$.

We can calculate θ using our calculator. The keys you will need depend on the calculator you are using. You will probably need one of the following combinations:

$$\begin{cases} \boxed{\text{2nd F}} \ \boxed{\sin} \ \boxed{(} \ \boxed{3} \ \boxed{\div} \ \boxed{5} \ \boxed{)} \ \boxed{\text{ENTER}} \\ \boxed{\text{INV}} \ \boxed{\sin} \ \boxed{(} \ \boxed{3} \ \boxed{\div} \ \boxed{5} \ \boxed{)} \ \boxed{=} \\ \boxed{\text{SHIFT}} \ \boxed{\sin} \ \boxed{(} \ \boxed{3} \ \boxed{\div} \ \boxed{5} \ \boxed{)} \ \boxed{\text{EXE}} \end{cases}$$

The answer should be $\theta \approx 36.87°$.

We can find an **inverse cosine** or **inverse tangent** using a similar method.

Example 5

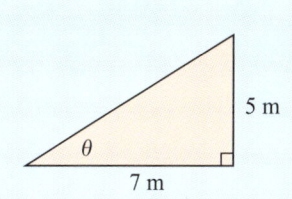

Find, to one decimal place, the measure of the angle marked θ in:

a (triangle with 5 m opposite, 7 m adjacent to θ)

b (right triangle with 5.92 km hypotenuse, 2.67 km adjacent to θ)

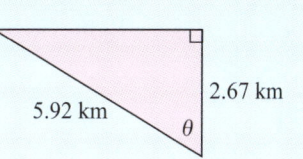

a $\tan\theta = \dfrac{\text{OPP}}{\text{ADJ}}$

$\therefore\ \tan\theta = \tfrac{5}{7}$

$\therefore\ \theta = \tan^{-1}\left(\tfrac{5}{7}\right)$

$\therefore\ \theta \approx 35.5$ 　　{ 2nd tan (5 ÷ 7) ENTER }

So, the angle measure is $35.5°$.

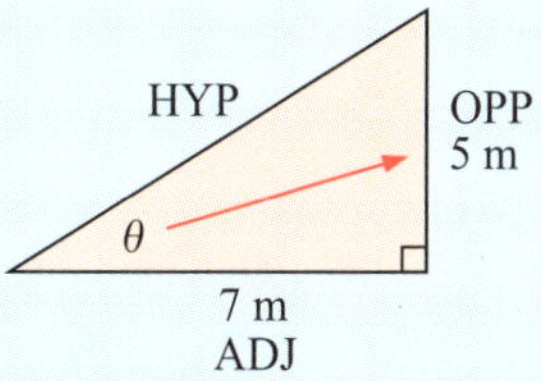

b $\cos\theta = \dfrac{\text{ADJ}}{\text{HYP}}$

$\therefore\ \cos\theta = \dfrac{2.67}{5.92}$

$\therefore\ \theta = \cos^{-1}\left(\dfrac{2.67}{5.92}\right)$

$\therefore\ \theta \approx 63.2$ 　　{ 2nd tan (2.67 ÷ 5.92) ENTER }

So, the angle measure is $63.2°$.

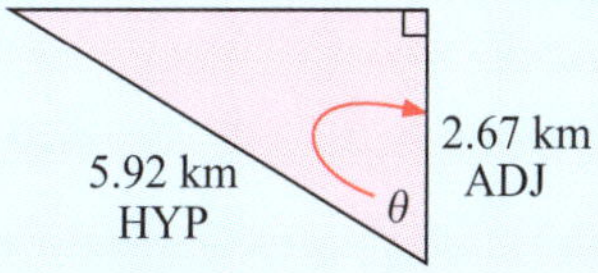

EXERCISE 23C.2

1 Find, to one decimal place, the measure of the angle marked θ in:

a (right triangle: 5 cm, 3 cm, θ)

b (right triangle: 6 cm, 3 cm, θ)

c (triangle: 3 m, 4 m, θ)

d (right triangle: 2.1 m, 4.1 m, θ)

e (triangle: 4.2 km, 3.2 km, θ)

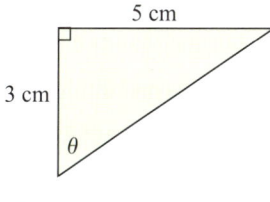

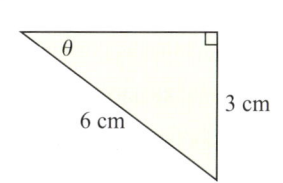

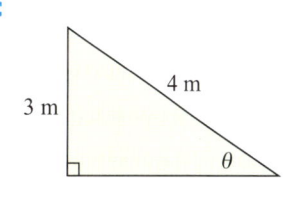

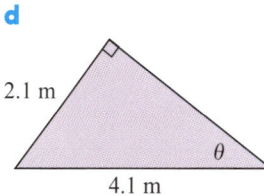

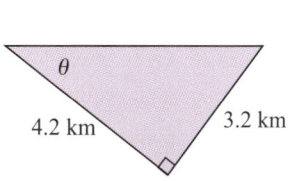

f (right triangle: 2.7 cm, 1.6 cm, θ)

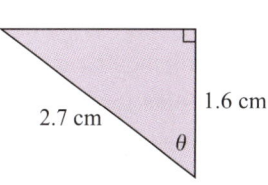

g 7.9 m, 11.2 m, θ

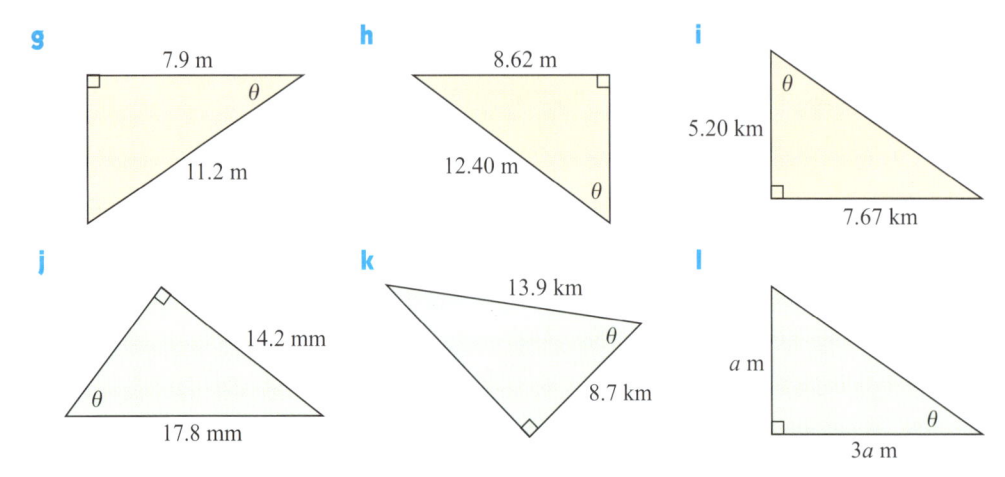

h 8.62 m, 12.40 m, θ

i θ, 5.20 km, 7.67 km

j 14.2 mm, 17.8 mm, θ

k 13.9 km, 8.7 km, θ

l a m, $3a$ m, θ

2 Find, to one decimal place, all the unknown sides and angles of the following:

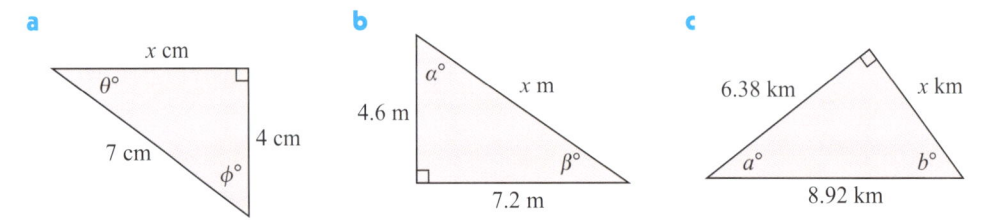

a x cm, 4 cm, 7 cm, θ°, φ°

b 4.6 m, x m, 7.2 m, α°, β°

c 6.38 km, x km, 8.92 km, α°, β°

3 Check your answer for x in each part of question **2** using Pythagoras' theorem.

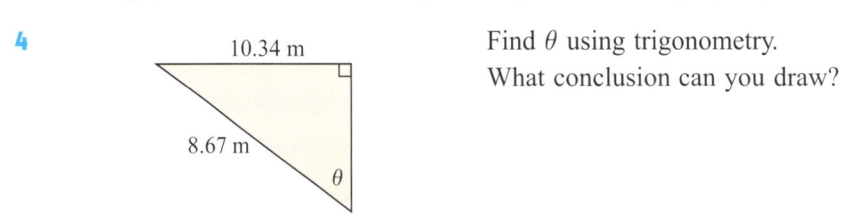

4 10.34 m, 8.67 m, θ

Find θ using trigonometry.
What conclusion can you draw?

D PROBLEM SOLVING WITH TRIGONOMETRY

When solving problems involving trigonometry, you should follow these steps:

- Draw a **diagram** to illustrate the situation.
- Mark on the diagram the **unknown** angle or side that needs to be calculated. We often use x for a length and θ for an angle.
- **Check** any assumptions about horizontal lines, vertical lines or right angles.
- Write a **relationship** between an angle and two sides of the triangle using one of the trigonometric ratios.
- **Solve** for the unknown.
- **Write** your answer in sentence form.

TRIGONOMETRY   (Chapter 23)   465

Example 6

A ladder leaning against a vertical wall reaches 3.5 m up the wall and makes an angle of 55° with the ground.
Find the length of the ladder.

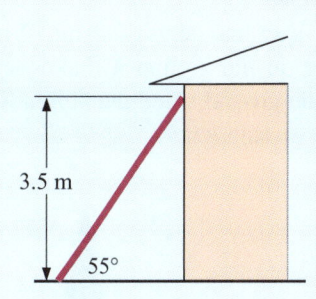

Let the ladder be x m long.

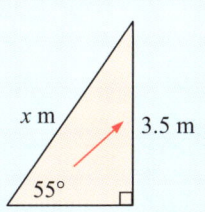

$$\sin \theta = \frac{\text{OPP}}{\text{HYP}}$$

$$\therefore \quad \sin 55° = \frac{3.5}{x}$$

$$\therefore \quad x \times \sin 55° = 3.5 \qquad \{\text{multiplying both sides by } x\}$$

$$\therefore \quad x = \frac{3.5}{\sin 55°} \qquad \{\text{dividing both sides by } \sin 55°\}$$

$$\therefore \quad x \approx 4.273$$

{Calculator: 3.5 ÷ sin 55) ENTER }

$\therefore$ the ladder is about 4.27 m long.

Example 7

Determine the length of the roofing beam required to support the roof shown alongside:

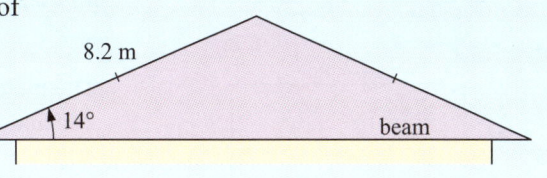

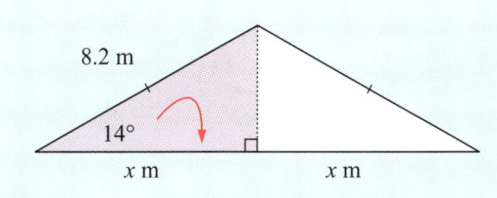

$$\cos \theta = \frac{\text{ADJ}}{\text{HYP}}$$

$$\therefore \quad \cos 14° = \frac{x}{8.2}$$

$$\therefore \quad x = 8.2 \times \cos 14°$$

$$\therefore \quad x \approx 7.956$$

{Calculator: 8.2 × cos 14) ENTER }

$\therefore$ the length of the beam $= 2 \times 7.956$ m
$\qquad \qquad \qquad \qquad \qquad \approx 15.9$ m

EXERCISE 23D

1 A see-saw has length 5.2 m. When one end is resting on the ground it makes an angle of 23° with the ground. Find the height of the other end above ground level.

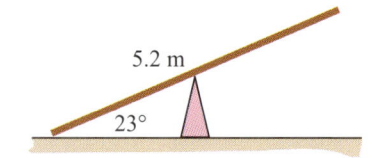

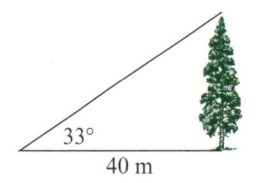

2 The shadow of a tree is 40 m in length. The angle from the end of the shadow to the top of the tree is 33°. Find the height of the tree to the nearest 10 cm.

3 At the point 25 metres from the base of a flagpole, the angle of elevation of the top of the pole is 35°. Find the height of the flagpole.

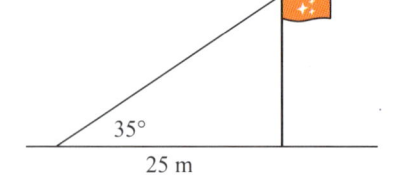

4 An isosceles triangle has sides 7 cm, 7 cm and 8 cm in length. Find the measure of the base angles correct to 4 significant figures.

5 Lucas starts at the base of a hill. He walks up a steep path at an angle of 22° to the ground for 100 metres. Find his height above ground level.

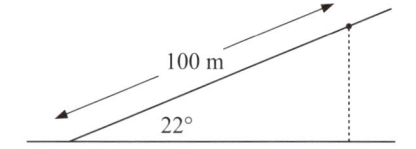

6 An aeroplane takes off at a constant angle of 20°. At the time it has flown 1000 m, what is its altitude? Give your answer correct to the nearest metre.

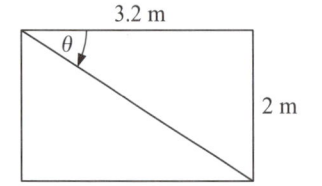

7 The metal frame of a rectangular gate has height 2 m and length 3.2 m. A diagonal strut is welded in place to support the frame. Find the measure of the angle θ between this diagonal strut and the top of the frame.

8 A driver travels 2 km up a long steady incline which is angled at 15° to the horizontal. How far has the driver moved horizontally?

9 A boat has an anchor rope of length 55 m. The boat drifts with the ocean current so that the rope makes an angle of 63° with the surface of the water. Find the depth of the water at the position where the anchor lies on the bottom.

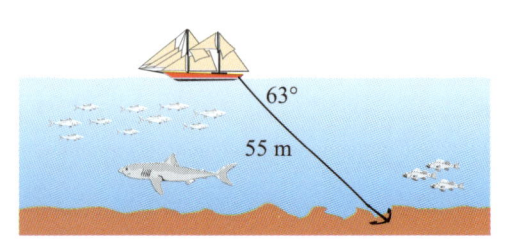

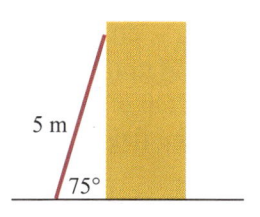

10 A ladder is 5 m long and makes an angle of 75° with the ground. How far from the wall is the base of the ladder? Give your answer correct to the nearest cm.

11 A beam of length 4.8 metres supports a garage roof. The pitch of the roof is 12°. Find the length of the sloping sides.

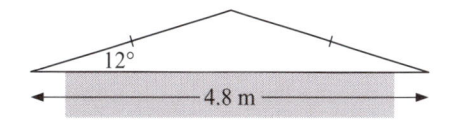

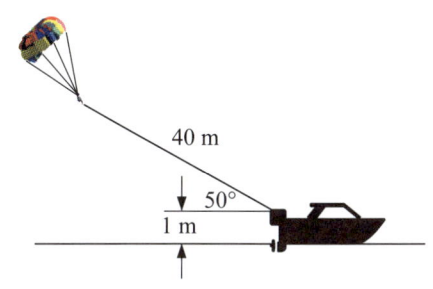

12 A parasailer is towed behind a boat. The towing cable is 40 metres long and makes an angle of 50° with the deck of the boat. How high is the parasailer above the water?

13 An isosceles triangle has equal sides of length 13 cm and base angles of 40°. Find the length of the base.

14 A flagpole is supported by four metal braces. Each brace makes an angle of 55° with the ground and meets the pole 6.2 m above ground level. Find the total length of the metal braces.

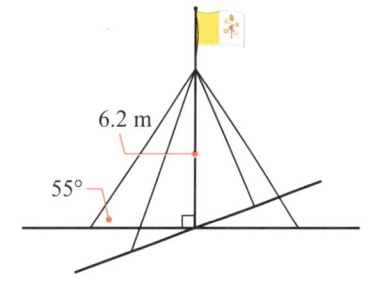

15 A rhombus has sides of length 15 cm and one diagonal of length 20 cm. Find the measure of the angles of the rhombus.

16 An aeroplane flying at an altitude of 10 000 m is directly overhead. 2 minutes later it is at an angle of 38° to the horizontal. How fast is the aeroplane flying in km per hour?

17 A 7 m long ladder leaning against a vertical wall makes an angle of 50° to the horizontal. If the foot of the ladder is pushed towards the wall until an angle of 65° is obtained, how much further up the wall will the ladder reach?

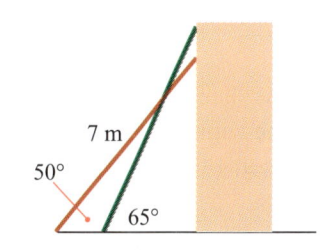

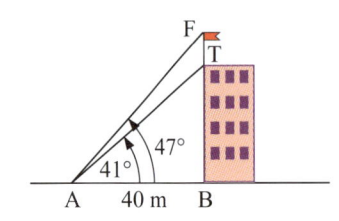

18 From a point A that is 40 m from the base of a building B, the angle to the top of the building T is 41°, and to the top of the flagpole F is 47°. Find the height of the flagpole [FT].

19 Use trigonometry to find the height of the mountain in the **Opening Problem** on page **454**.

20 A cube has sides of length 10 cm. Find the angle between the diagonal [AB] of the cube and [AC].

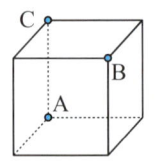

MEASURING INACCESSIBLE DISTANCES

LINKS
click here

Areas of interaction:
Human ingenuity, Approaches to learning

REVIEW SET 23A

1 For the triangle alongside, state the length of the side:
  a opposite θ
  b opposite ϕ
  c adjacent to θ
  d adjacent to ϕ.

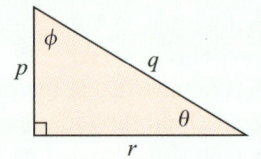

2 Find:
  a $\sin \theta$
  b $\cos \theta$
  c $\tan \theta$

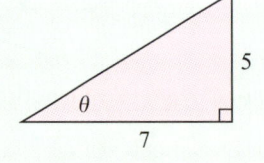

3 Find x in the following figures, giving answers correct to 1 decimal place:
  a
  b
  c

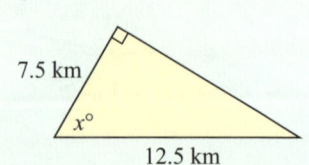

4 The shadow of a tree is 17.5 m in length. The angle from the end of the shadow to the tree top is 38°. Find the height of the tree.

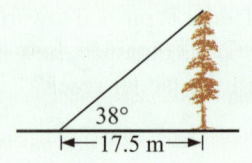

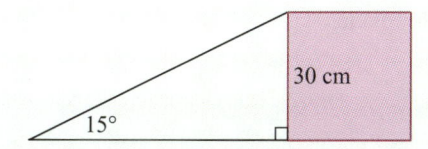

5 A ramp with an incline of 15° is needed to climb a step of height 30 cm. What is the length of the ramp?

6 A building is 100 m tall, and the angle from the top of the building to the foot of the building across the street is 9°. How far apart are the buildings?

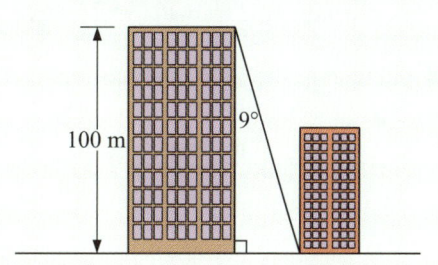

7 A cyclist travels for 5 km up a steady incline, and in that time she climbs a vertical distance of 800 m. What is the angle of the incline?

8 Two kayakers Greg and Tim, starting at point S, cross a river 400 m wide. Greg kayaks directly across the river to point A, while Tim travels at an angle of 32° to [SA] to get to point B. How much further does Tim travel than Greg?

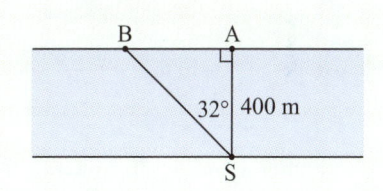

REVIEW SET 23B

1 Find the value of y, correct to 1 decimal place:

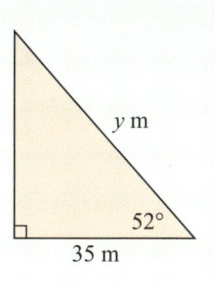

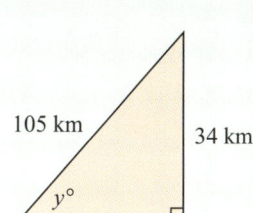

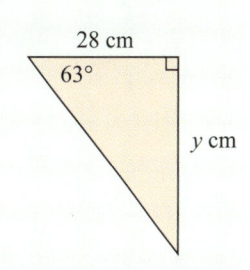

   a (triangle with y m, 52°, 35 m)

   b (triangle with 105 km, 34 km, $y°$)

   c (triangle with 28 cm, 63°, y cm)

2 Find the value of θ, correct to 1 decimal place:

   a $\sin \theta = 0.3642$ **b** $\cos \theta = 0.8157$ **c** $\tan \theta = 2.134$

3 Determine the height of a man who casts a 1.2 m shadow when the sun is 55° above the horizon.

4 A farmer is fencing an isosceles triangle shaped paddock which has equal angles of 55° and a base of length 240 m. Determine the total length of wire required if the fence has five strands of wire.

5 For the angle θ shown in the diagram alongside, name:
   a the adjacent side
   b the opposite side
   c find: **i** $\sin \theta$ **ii** $\cos \theta$ **iii** $\tan \theta$.

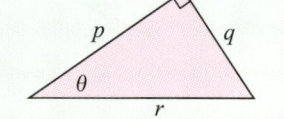

6 Find x in the following, correct to 1 decimal place:

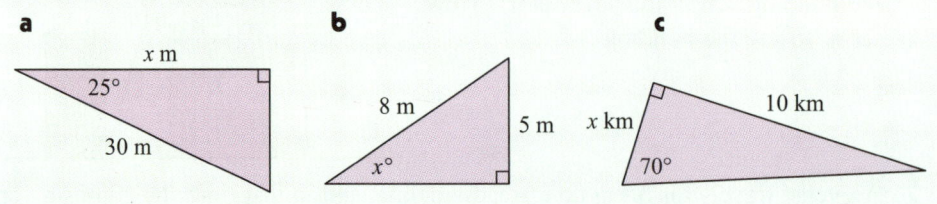

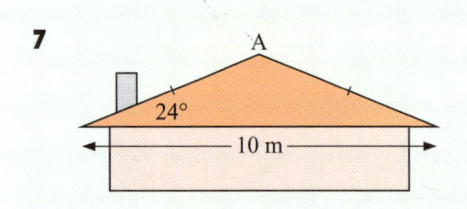

   a
   x m, 25°, 30 m

   b
   8 m, 5 m, $x°$

   c
   10 km, x km, 70°

7
A, 24°, 10 m

The pitch of the roof of a house is the angle between the ceiling and the roof. The pitch of the roof alongside is 24°. How high is the highest point A above the ceiling?

8 An archer standing 30 m away from a target fires an arrow at the bullseye, but misses to the right by 20 cm. By what angle was the archer off target?

Chapter 24

Introduction to networks

Contents:
- **A** Network diagrams
- **B** Constructing networks
- **C** Precedence networks
- **D** Counting pathways

472　INTRODUCTION TO NETWORKS　(Chapter 24)

Networks can be used to show the connections between objects. They have been used to solve problems of:

- mail delivery
- traffic flow on roads
- scheduling of trains
- bed occupancy in hospitals
- the management of projects

OPENING PROBLEM

If you can only move from left to right, how many different paths are possible starting at A and finishing at B? How many paths would there be if:
- the path must pass through point X
- the path must not pass through point X?

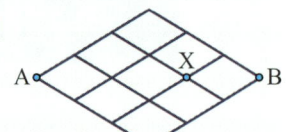

A   NETWORK DIAGRAMS

A **network diagram** or **finite graph** is a structure where things of interest are linked by physical connections or relationships.

TERMINOLOGY

- A **graph** or **network** is a set of points, some or all of which are connected by a set of lines.

- The points are known as **vertices** (singular vertex).

- In a graph, we can move from vertex to vertex along the lines. If we are allowed to move in either direction along the lines, the lines are called **edges** and the graph is **undirected**. Pairs of vertices that are directly connected by edges are said to be **adjacent**.

- If we are only allowed to move in one direction along the lines, the lines are called **arcs**.
  The graph is then known as a **digraph** or **directed graph**.

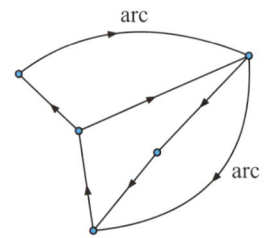

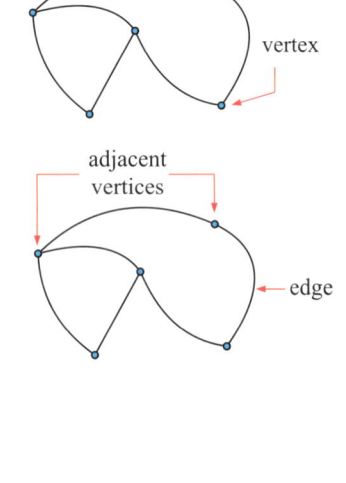

- An edge or arc may sometimes be assigned a number called its **weight**. This may represent the cost, time, or distance required to travel along that line.

  The lengths of the arcs and edges are not drawn to scale. They are not in proportion to their weight.

- A **path** is a connected sequence of edges or arcs showing a route that starts at one vertex and ends at another.
  For example: A - B - E - D

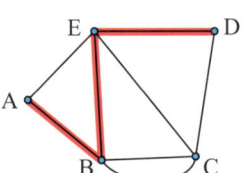

EXERCISE 24A

1 a For the network shown:
  i state the number of vertices
  ii list the edges
  iii state the number of edges.

  b Is the network directed or undirected?

  c What vertices are adjacent to:
  i A   **ii** F?

  d Name all paths which go from:
  i A to F without passing through C or D
  ii D to A without passing through E.

2 a For the given network:
  i state the vertices
  ii state the number of arcs.

  b Is the network directed or undirected?

  c What vertices are adjacent to:
  i B   **ii** E?

  d Name the paths which could be taken to get from:
  i B to C   **ii** A to C.

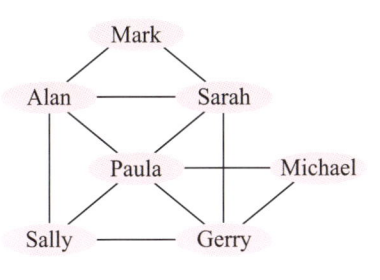

3 Consider the network showing which people are friends in a table tennis club.

  a What do the vertices of this graph represent?
  b What do the edges represent?
  c Who is Michael friendly with?
  d Who has the most friends?
  e How could we indicate that while Alan really likes Paula, Paula does not like Alan?

4 The best four tennis players at school played a round-robin set of matches. The graph is shown alongside.

  a What are the vertices of the graph?
  b What do the edges represent?
  c How many matches must be played?
  d How could you indicate who beat whom on the network diagram?

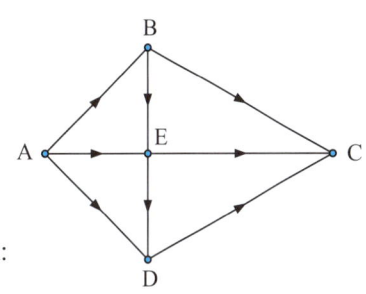

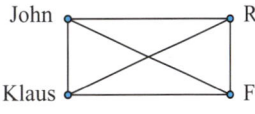

5 Jon constructed a network model of his morning activities from waking up to leaving for school.

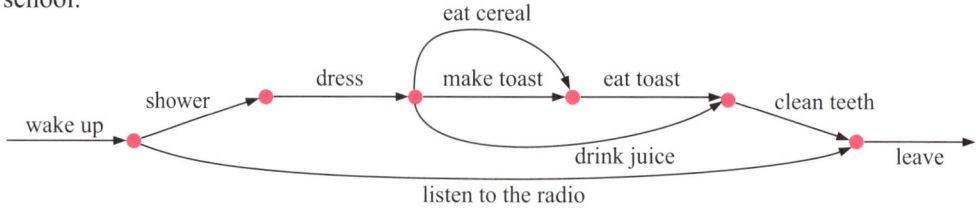

Write a brief account of Jon's morning activities indicating the order in which events occur.

6 The network alongside represents the possible ways for travelling to school from home. The weights on the arcs represent time in minutes.

Which route is the quickest to get from home to school?

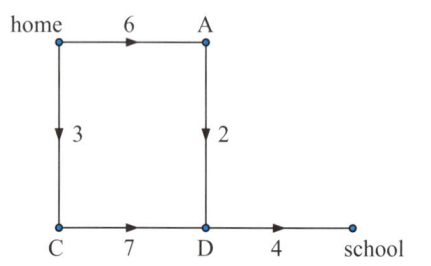

B   CONSTRUCTING NETWORKS

Often we are given data in the form of a table, a list of jobs, or a verbal description. We need to use this information to construct a network that accurately displays the situation.

Example 1   ◆) Self Tutor

Draw a network diagram to model a Local Area Network (LAN) of three computers connected through a server to a printer and scanner.

Example 2   ◆) Self Tutor

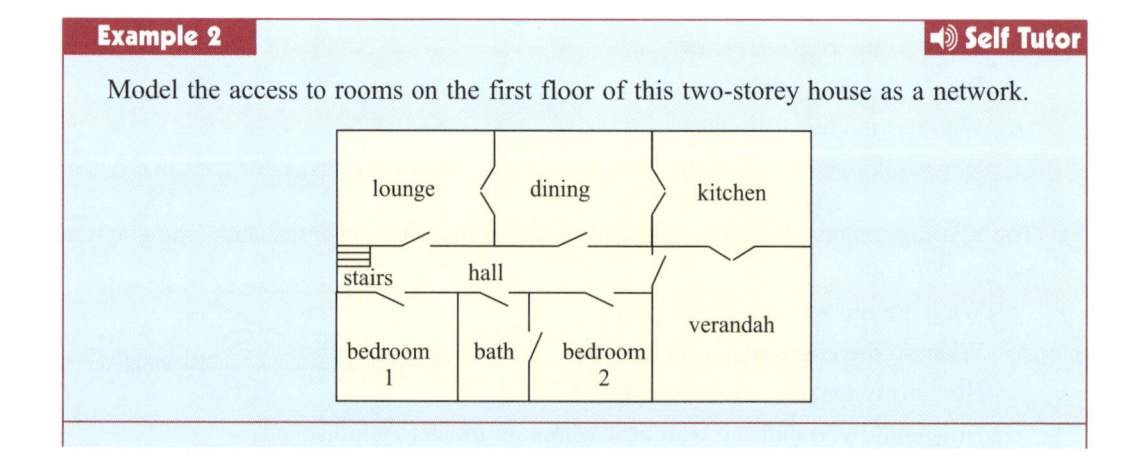

Model the access to rooms on the first floor of this two-storey house as a network.

INTRODUCTION TO NETWORKS (Chapter 24) 475

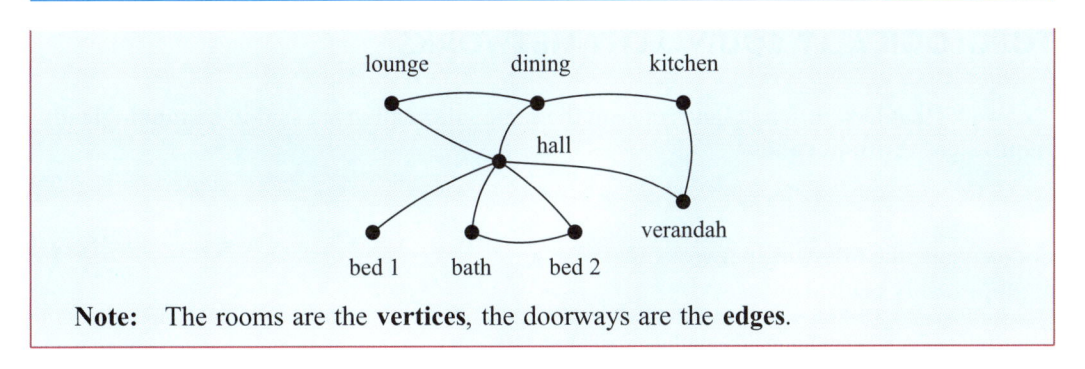

[Diagram showing rooms as vertices connected by edges: lounge, dining, kitchen, hall, bed 1, bath, bed 2, verandah]

Note: The rooms are the **vertices**, the doorways are the **edges**.

EXERCISE 24B.1

1 Draw a network diagram to represent the roads between towns P, Q, R, S and T if:
Town P is 23 km from town Q and 17 km from town T
Town Q is 20 km from town R and 38 km from town S
Town R is 31 km from town S.

2 Draw a network diagram of friendships if: A has friends B, D and F;
B has friends A, C and E;
C has friends D, E and F.

3 a Model the room access on the first floor of the house plan below as a network diagram.

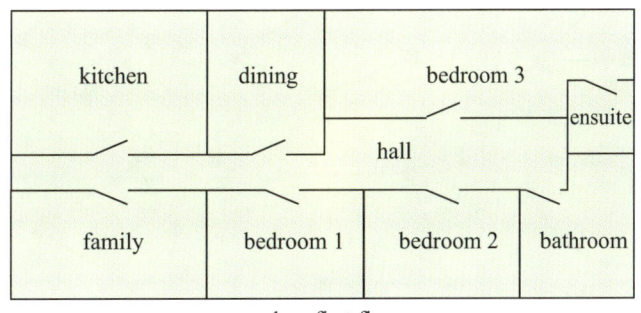

plan: first floor

b Model access to rooms and the outside for the ground floor of the house plan below as a network diagram. Consider outside as an external room represented by a single vertex.

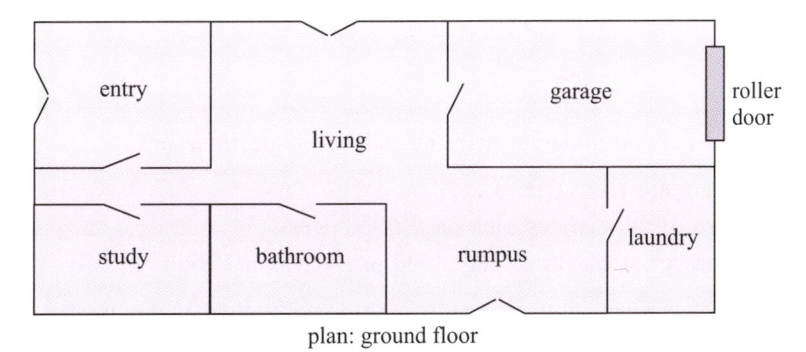

plan: ground floor

TOPOLOGICALLY EQUIVALENT NETWORKS

Networks that look different but represent the same information are said to be **topologically equivalent** or **isomorphic**.

For example, the following networks are topologically equivalent:

The number of vertices is the same in each network.

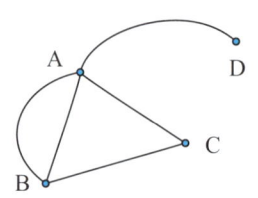

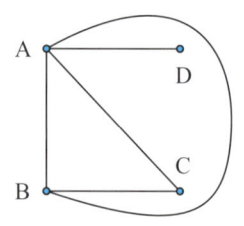

Check each vertex in turn to make sure it has the correct connections to the other vertices.

EXERCISE 24B.2

1 Which of the networks in the diagrams following are topologically equivalent?

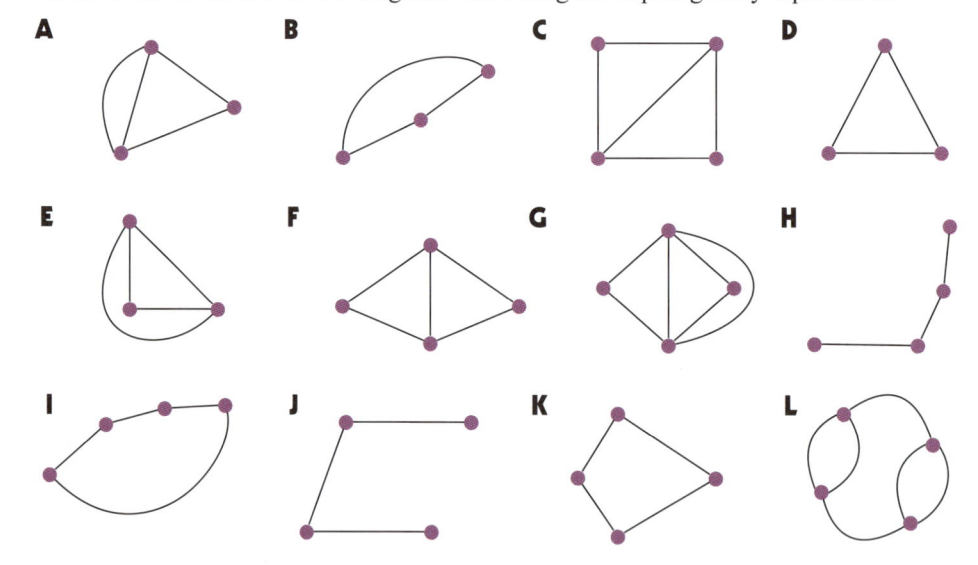

A   **B**   **C**   **D**

E   **F**   **G**   **H**

I   **J**   **K**   **L**

2 Label corresponding vertices of the following networks to show their topological equivalence:

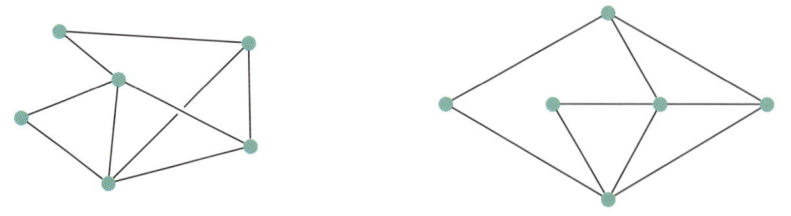

3 Draw a network diagram with the following specifications:
- there are five vertices
- two of the vertices each have two edges
- one vertex has three edges and one vertex has four.

Remember when comparing your solution with others that networks may appear different but be topologically equivalent.

C PRECEDENCE NETWORKS

Networks may be used to represent the steps involved in a project.

Building a house, constructing a newsletter, and cooking an evening meal, all require many separate tasks to be completed.

Some of the tasks may happen *concurrently* (at the same time) while others are dependent upon the completion of another task.

If task B cannot begin until task A is completed, then task A is a **prerequisite** for task B.

For example, putting water in the kettle is a *prerequisite* to boiling it.

If we are given a list of tasks necessary to complete a project, we need to

- write the tasks in the order in which they must be performed
- determine any prerequisite tasks
- construct a network to accurately represent the project.

Consider the tasks involved in making a cup of tea. They are listed below, along with their respective times (in seconds) for completion. A table like this is called a **precedence table** or an **activity table**.

A	Retrieve the cups.	15
B	Place tea bags into cups.	10
C	Fill the kettle with water.	20
D	Boil the water in the kettle.	100
E	Pour the boiling water into the cups.	10
F	Add the milk and sugar.	15
G	Stir the tea.	10

Example 3

The steps involved in preparing a home-made pizza are listed below.

A	Defrost the pizza base.
B	Prepare the toppings.
C	Place the sauce and toppings on the pizza.
D	Heat the oven.
E	Cook the pizza.

a Which tasks can be performed concurrently?
b Which tasks are prerequisite tasks?
c Draw a precedence table for the project.
d Draw a network diagram for the project.

a Tasks A, B and D may be performed *concurrently*, i.e., the pizza base could be defrosting and the oven could be heating up while the toppings are prepared.

b The toppings cannot be placed on the pizza until after the toppings have been prepared.
∴ task B is a prerequisite for task C.
The pizza cannot be cooked until everything else is done.
∴ tasks A, B, C and D are all prerequisites for task E.

c A precedence table shows the tasks and any prerequisite tasks.

Task	Prerequisite Tasks
A	
B	
C	B
D	
E	A, B, C, D

d The network diagram may now be drawn.

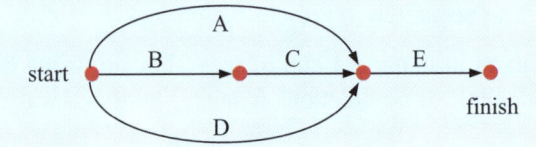

EXERCISE 24C

1 The tasks for the following projects are not in the correct order. For each project write the correct order in which the tasks should be completed.

a Preparing an evening meal:
1 find a recipe
2 clean up
3 prepare ingredients
4 cook casserole
5 set table
6 serve meals

b Planting a garden:
1 dig the holes
2 purchase the trees
3 water the trees
4 plant the trees
5 decide on the trees required

2 Which tasks in question **1** could be performed concurrently?

3 The activities involved in preparing, barbecuing and serving a meal of hamburgers are given in the table alongside. Draw a network diagram to represent this project.

Task		Prerequisite
A	Gather ingredients	-
B	Pre-heat barbecue	-
C	Mix and shape hamburgers	A
D	Cook hamburgers	B, C
E	Prepare salad and rolls	A
F	Assemble hamburgers and serve	D, E

4 Your friend's birthday is approaching and you decide to bake a cake. The individual tasks are listed below:

A	Mix the ingredients.
B	Heat the oven.
C	Place the cake mixture into the cake tin.
D	Bake the cake.
E	Cool the cake.
F	Mix the icing.
G	Ice the cake.

  a Draw a precedence table for the project.
  b Which tasks may be performed concurrently?
  c Draw a network diagram for the project.

5 The construction of a back yard shed includes the following steps:

A	Prepare the area for the shed.
B	Prepare the formwork for the concrete.
C	Lay the concrete.
D	Let concrete dry.
E	Purchase the timber and iron sheeting.
F	Build the timber frame.
G	Fix iron sheeting to frame.
H	Add window, door and flashing.

  a Draw a precedence table for the project.
  b Which tasks may be performed concurrently?
  c Draw a network diagram for the project.

6 The separate steps involved in hosting a party are listed below:

A	Decide on a date to hold the party.
B	Prepare invitations.
C	Post the invitations.
D	Wait for RSVPs.
E	Clean and tidy the house.
F	Organise food and drinks.
G	Organise entertainment.

Draw a network diagram to model the project, indicating which tasks may be performed concurrently and any prerequisites that exist.

D COUNTING PATHWAYS

One of the simplest examples of a network problem is in counting the number of pathways to get from one place to another. In these problems we assume that no backtracking is allowed.

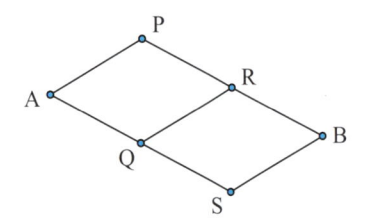

In the network alongside we want to get from A to B. Only movement to the right is allowed.

We could take any one of these three paths:

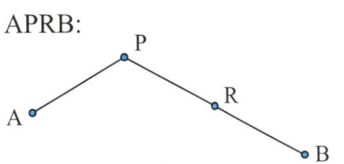

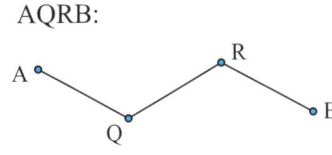

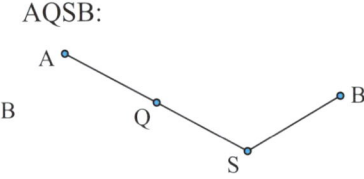

APRB: AQRB: AQSB:

However, drawing and counting possibilities is not desirable for more complicated networks.

Consider the diagram alongside:

There are 70 different pathways from A to B.

How can we find this number without listing them?

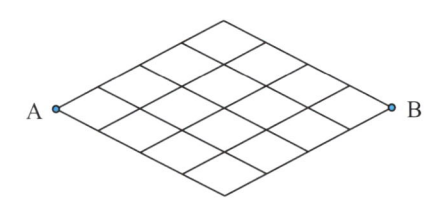

Example 4

How many pathways are there from A to B if the motion is only allowed from left to right?

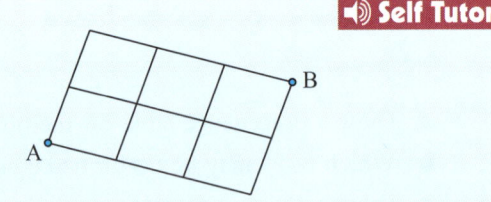

We label the other vertices as shown.

There is only 1 way to get from A to C and from A to F, so 1s are written at these vertices.

To get to J there is only 1 way as you must come from F.

To get to G you may come from F or from C, so there are 2 ways.

To get to D you must come from C, so there is 1 way.

To get to K you may come from J or G in $1 + 2 = 3$ ways.

We continue this process until the diagram is completed.

So, there are 10 different pathways.

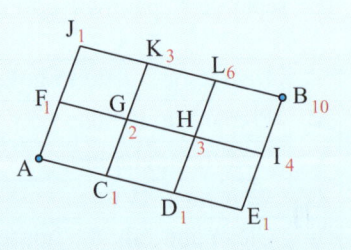

INTRODUCTION TO NETWORKS (Chapter 24) 481

In practice, we do not write out the wordy explanation. We simply write the numbers shown in red at appropriate vertices and **add** numbers from the preceding vertices:

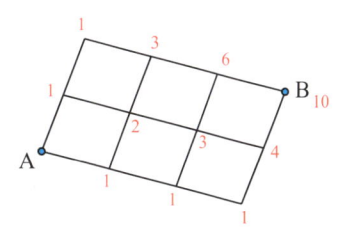

EXERCISE 24D

1 Find the number of different pathways from A to B in:

a

b

c

d

e

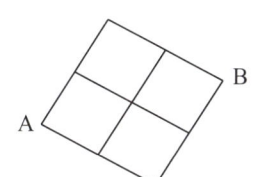

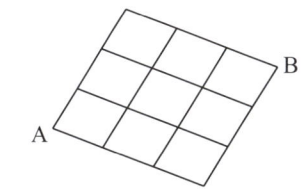

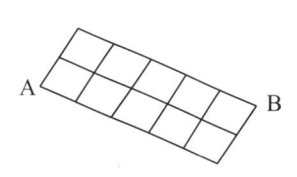

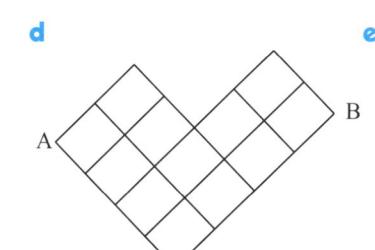

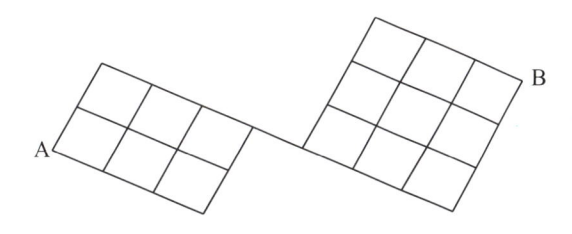

Example 5

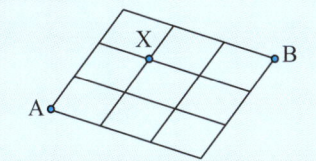

How many pathways go from A to B if:
a we must pass through X
b we must not pass through X?

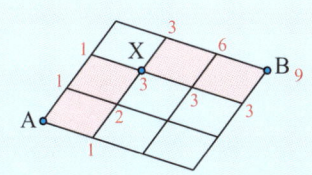

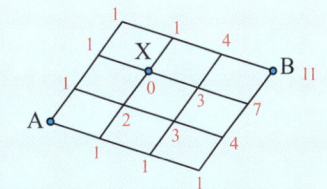

a Movement is restricted to the edges for the shaded portion.
∴ there are 9 different pathways.

b As we cannot go through X we put a 0 at this vertex.
We procede to count in the usual way.
∴ there are 11 different pathways.

2 For the following networks, find the number of different pathways from A to B which pass through X:

a

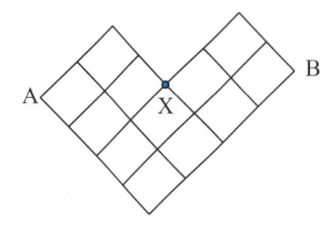

b

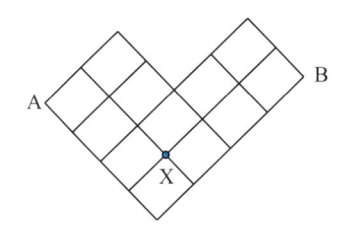

3 For the following networks, find the number of different pathways from A to B which do *not* pass through X:

a

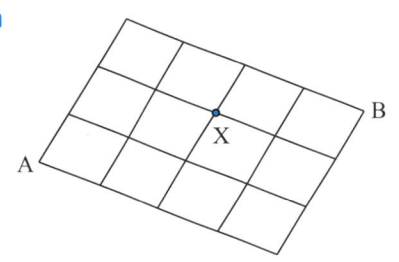

b

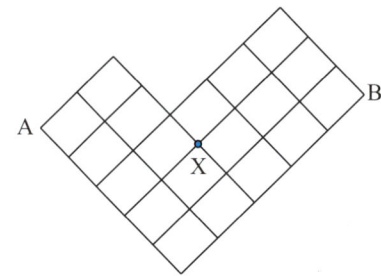

REVIEW SET 24A

1 a For the given network state the number of:
   i vertices   **ii** edges.
  b Is the network directed or undirected?
  c What vertices are adjacent to:
   i A   **ii** D?
  d Name all paths which go from:
   i A to D without passing through C
   ii B to E.

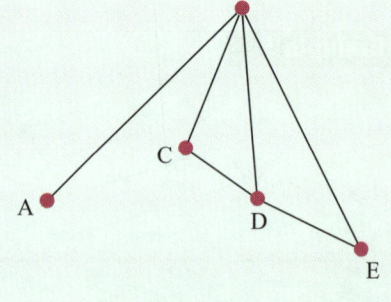

2 Is the network in **1** topologically equivalent to the network given? Give reasons for your answer.

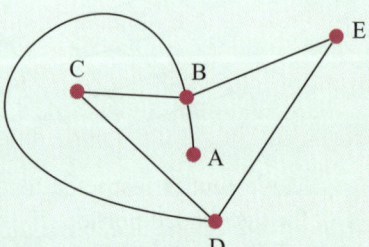

3 Draw a network diagram to represent this situation:
Angelina sends text messages to Malia and Sam. Sam texts Xi and Roman. Roman texts Malia three times and she replies twice. Xi texts Malia and Roman.

4 In a small business the Production Manager, the Sales Manager and the Accounts Manager report to the General Manager. The General Manager and the Sales Manager are organised by the same secretary. The Sales Manager has a team of three, one of whom also does work for the Accounts Manager. The Production Manager has a team of 5. Use a network to represent the lines of communication in this business.

5 Construct a network diagram for the project of renovating a room. Use the following tasks:

	Task	Prerequisite Tasks
A	Remove carpet	-
B	Sand timber floor	A
C	Plaster walls	-
D	Electrical work	-
E	Paint room	A, B, C, D
F	Seal floor	A, B, C, D, E

6 Movement to the right only is possible. 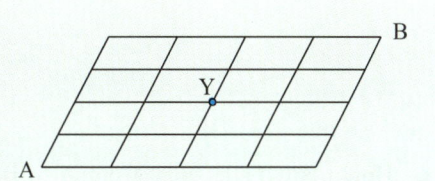
  a How many paths lead from A to B?
  b How many of these paths:
    i pass through Y
    ii do not pass through Y?

REVIEW SET 24B

1 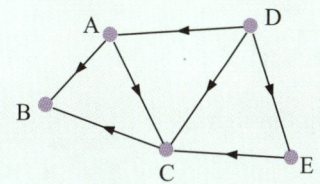
  a State the number of vertices in the given network.
  b Is the network directed?
  c Name all paths which could be taken to get from:
    i D to B   **ii** B to E

2 Consider the network showing roads connecting three towns A, B, and C. The weights on the edges represent distance in km. 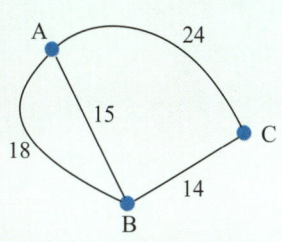
  a What do the vertices of this graph represent?
  b How are the roads represented on this diagram?
  c What is the shortest distance from A to C?
  d What is the shortest distance from A to C through B?
  e If the road from B to C was partly blocked by a fallen tree, how could we indicate that traffic could only travel in the direction B to C?

3 Construct a network that models the access to the rooms and outside for a house with the given floor plan.

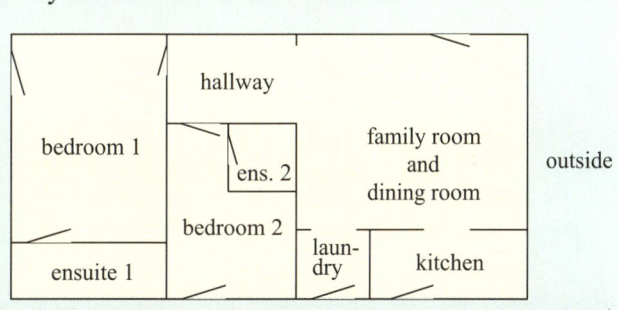

4 The results of a darts tournament were:
  Anya beat Brod,
  Brod beat Anya, Con and Dave
  Dave beat Brod, Con and Eva
  Eva beat Anya and Con.
Draw a network diagram which shows the results of the darts matches.

5 Uri wishes to make a cake from a packet. He makes a list of his tasks:

  a Draw a precedence table for the project.
  b Which tasks may be performed concurrently?
  c Draw a network diagram for the project.

A	Read the instructions
B	Preheat the oven
C	Tip the contents of the packet into a bowl
D	Add milk and eggs
E	Beat the mixture
F	Place in a cooking dish
G	Cook the cake
H	Ice the cake when cold

6 How many paths exist from A to B which pass through X?

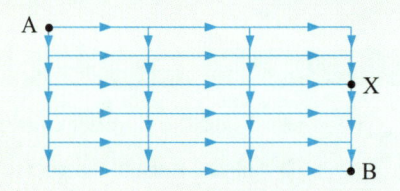

7 How many paths exist from P to R without passing through Q?

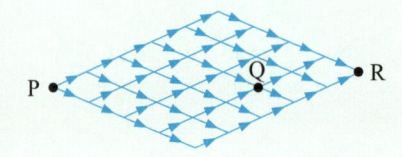

Chapter 25

Locus

Contents:
- **A** Everyday applications of loci
- **B** Experiments in locus
- **C** Locus in geometry

OPENING PROBLEM

A goat is tethered to a pole which is located 1 m from a shed as shown.

The rope is 3.8 m long, and so when the rope is taut the goat can eat grass 4 m from the pole.

Plan view (above)

pole   rope   goat

1 m

shed   1 m

2 m

Can you draw an accurate scale diagram of the region that the goat can eat?

A   EVERYDAY APPLICATIONS OF LOCI

The **locus** of a moving object is the path it takes. Loci is the plural of locus.

For example:

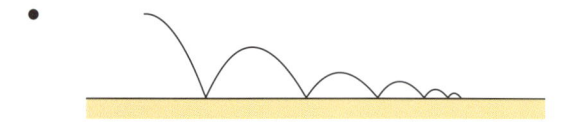

- could be the locus of a tennis ball hit over the net and left to bounce.

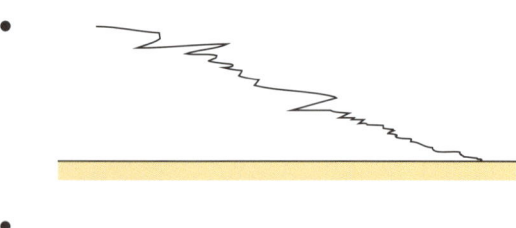

- could be the locus of an autumn leaf which has fallen from a tree.

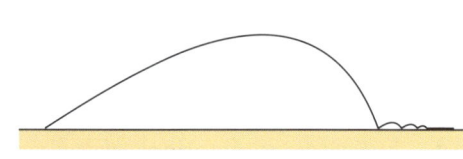

- could be the locus of a golf ball.

Loci can be used to describe special shapes such as a circle or an ellipse.

They can also be used to describe regions within special shapes.

Example 1   ◀)) Self Tutor

A sheep is tethered to a pole by a rope. When the rope is taut the sheep can eat grass 5 m from the pole. Illustrate and describe the region the sheep is able to eat.

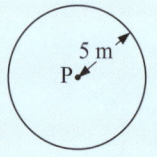

Let P represent the pole.

The sheep can eat all grass within a 5 m radius circle with centre P.

EXERCISE 25A

1 Draw the locus or path for:

   a a constant fine jet of water from a hose

   b the path of a basketball thrown from the free throw line, bouncing off the back board and going through the ring.

   c the path of an aeroplane moving along the runway and taking off

   d the path taken by a watermelon falling from the back of a moving truck.

2 The fences which border a roadway are parallel.
Draw the locus of all points which are equidistant from each fence.

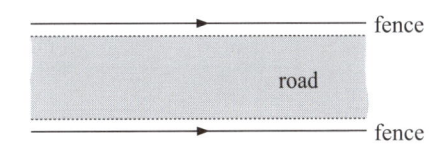

3 Two sprinklers are situated 10 m apart. Each sprinkler sprays water in all directions to a maximum distance of 7 m.
Illustrate the region that can be watered by the sprinklers.

4 Two small towns A and B each have their own post office. The post offices are 6 km apart.

   a Show on a sketch all points which are equidistant from both of the post offices.

   b All homes and businesses in the district are serviced by whichever post office is closer to them. Shade the region serviced by post office A.

5 Triangle ABC is equilateral with sides 6 m long. Stakes are placed at A, B and C, and a dog is tethered to each stake. Each dog has a 3 m lead. If I am standing inside the triangle so that no dog can reach me, illustrate the region where I could be.

6 Jeremy has a pet dog. He attaches a lead to the dog's collar and ties the other end to a 'running wire' between two points 30 m apart.

Shade the region the dog is able to wander in.

7 A, B, C and D are radar stations at different airports around the country. Each station covers a circular region of 250 km.

   a Draw an accurate diagram of the situation using the scale $1 \text{ mm} \equiv 10 \text{ km}$.

   b Shade the locus of points in the centre of the region which are *not* covered by radar.

   c Shade differently the region(s) covered by more than one radar.

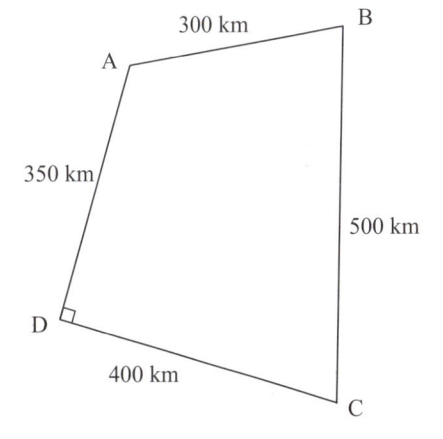

8 Draw scale diagrams of the region Sam the sheep can eat in the following situations. Use the scale 1 cm ≡ 1 m. In each case the rope is 4 m long.

a

5 m — pole — 5 m — fence

S

b

fence — pole — 1 m

S

fence

c

4 m, 4 m

2 m

pole

S

d

pole

S

2 m

3 m

B EXPERIMENTS IN LOCUS

ACTIVITY 1

What is the locus of all points P given that for two fixed points A and B, the sum of the lengths AP + BP is a constant?

What to do:

Obtain a strong piece of string about a metre long. One student should hold the ends of the string fixed to the whiteboard about 70 cm apart. A second student places a whiteboard marker inside the string loop and makes the string taut.

The second student then moves the marker to all possible positions keeping the string taut. Swapping to the other side of the string is necessary. What figure is traced out?

Experiment with the fixed points being further apart and closer together. Write a brief report of your findings.

ACTIVITY 2

You will need:

- two nails
- a sheet of particle board
- a sheet of cardboard.

What to do:

1. Hammer in the nails 10 cm apart so that each nail head is 10 mm above the board. Label the nails N_1 and N_2.

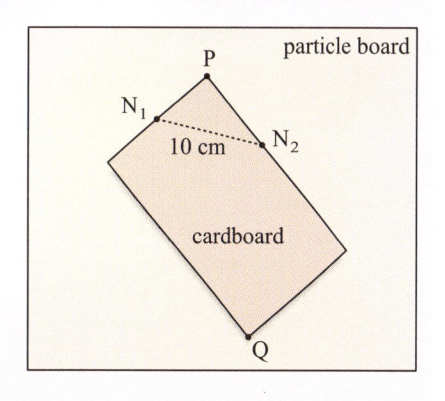

2. Place the cardboard as shown in the diagram so that its two adjacent sides are touching the nails. Use a pencil to mark the exact position of point P.

3. Move the cardboard to a new position so that it still touches the nails. Mark the new position of P. Repeat until you have marked at least 20 points.

4. What path is traced out by P as the cardboard moves through all possible positions with point Q remaining on the same side of the nails?

ACTIVITY 3

You will need:

- a piece of paper
- a strip of card exactly 10 cm long with midpoint M clearly marked.

What to do:

1. Draw a set of perpendicular axes in the middle of the piece of paper. Mark on the paper the four regions (1) to (4).

2. Place the strip so that corners A and B are on the perpendicular lines. Mark a dot on the bottom sheet to show where M is.

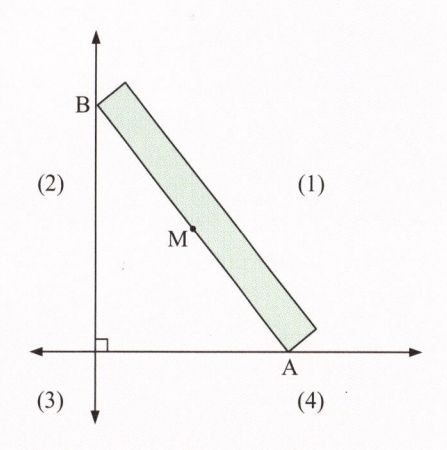

3. Move the strip to 20 more positions, each time marking where M is located.

4. Repeat this process for each of the 4 regions marked (1) to (4).

5. What path is traced out by M as the strip moves through all possible positions with A on the horizontal line and B on the vertical line?

ACTIVITY 4

You will need:
- a sheet of paper
- a small set square which could be made from cardboard

What to do:

1 Draw a set of perpendicular axes in the middle of the piece of paper. Mark on the paper the four regions (1) to (4).

2 Place the set square with the non-right angle vertices on the perpendicular lines as shown. Mark where R is located.

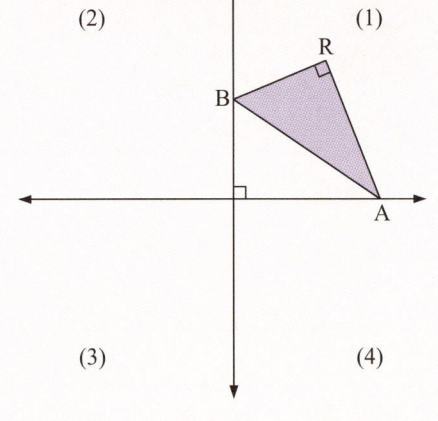

3 Move the set square to many more positions, keeping A on the horizontal line and B on the vertical line. Each time mark the position of R with a dot.

4 Repeat this process for each of the 4 regions marked (1) to (4).

5 What path is traced out by R as the set square moves through every possible position?

6 Repeat steps **1** to **5** using an equilateral triangle.

ACTIVITY 5

You will need:
- a sheet of paper
- a 10 cm long strip of card with A marked on one end and B marked at the other.
- a set square

What to do:

1 Draw a set of perpendicular lines on the sheet of paper.

2 Place the strip so that points A and B are on the perpendicular lines. Place the set square against the strip as shown. Move it so that the other side passes through the point O where the perpendicular lines meet. Mark the position of P with a dot.

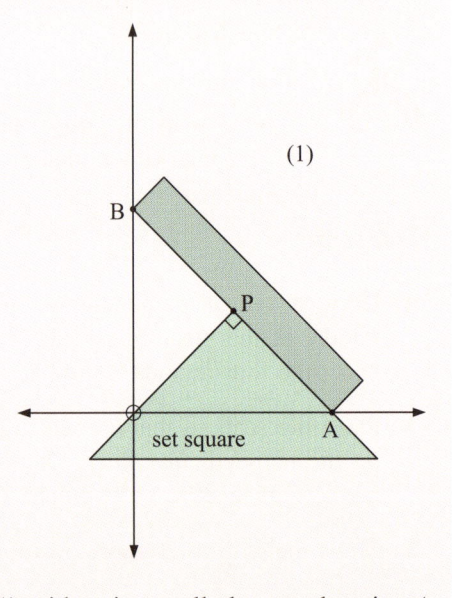

3 Move the strip to many positions in region (1) with quite small changes, keeping A on the horizontal line and B on the vertical line. Mark the new position of P for each point.

4 What shape is traced out in region (1)? If this experiment is carried out in the other three regions, what overall shape will be traced out?

C LOCUS IN GEOMETRY

Locus is used to describe mathematical lines, shapes and regions. In this section we will examine some of these.

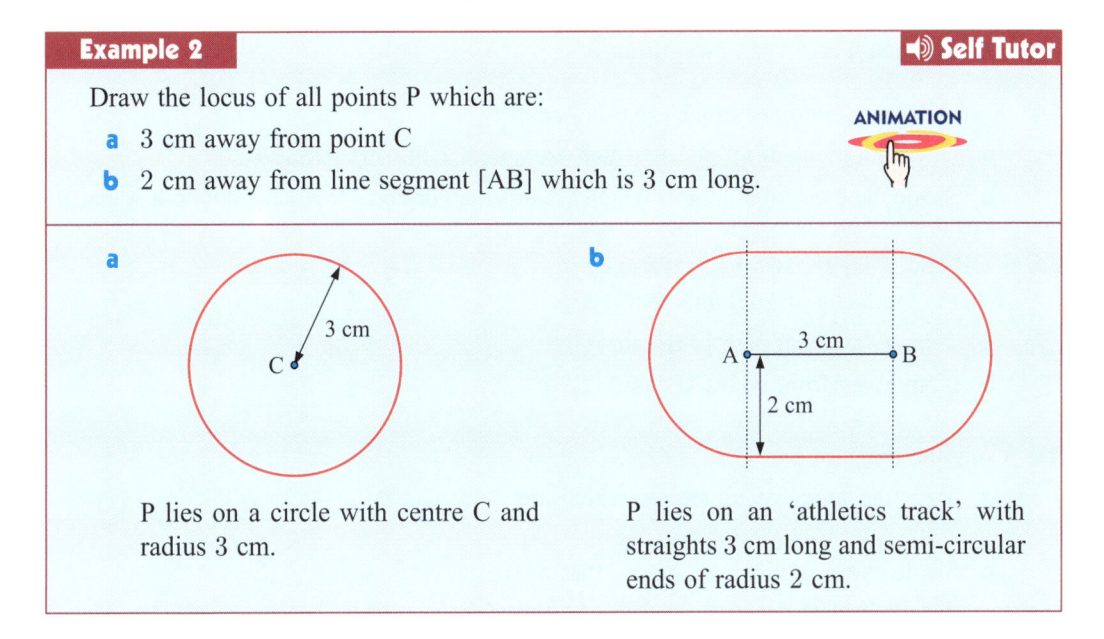

Example 2

Draw the locus of all points P which are:

a 3 cm away from point C

b 2 cm away from line segment [AB] which is 3 cm long.

a P lies on a circle with centre C and radius 3 cm.

b P lies on an 'athletics track' with straights 3 cm long and semi-circular ends of radius 2 cm.

EXERCISE 25C

1. Draw the locus of points P that are 4 cm away from a fixed point R.

2. Draw the locus of all points P that are 2 cm away from the infinitely long line passing through points D and E.

3. Draw the locus of all points P which are 1 cm away from segment [AB] which is 2 cm long.

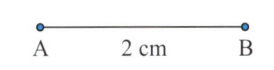

4. Draw the locus of all points P which are equidistant (the same distance away) from points B and C which are 4 cm apart.

5. A and B are two points which are 5 cm apart.
    a Accurately draw these two points.
    b Draw the locus of all points P that are 4 cm away from A.
    c Draw all points Q that are 3 cm away from B.
    d Shade the locus of all points which are within 4 cm of A and within 3 cm of B.

6. Consider a circle of radius 4 cm. Describe and illustrate the locus of all points which are 2 cm from the circle.

7. Consider a circle of radius 3 cm. Describe and illustrate the locus of all points which are 3 cm from the circle.

8 **a** Consider a square with 4 cm long sides. Illustrate the locus of points which are outside the square and 1 cm from it.

b Repeat **a** but this time replace the square with an equilateral triangle with sides 4 cm.

9 Draw the locus of all points that are:

a 3 cm from fixed point R

b greater than 3 cm from fixed point R

c between 3 and 4 cm away from R.

10 A and B are two points which are 6 cm apart.

a Draw the locus of all points which are equidistant from A and B.

b Shade the locus of all points which are less than or equal to 4 cm from both A and B.

11 [AB] and [CD] are two line segments.
What is the locus of all points that are:

a 1 cm away from both [AB] and [CD]

b 2 cm away from both [AB] and [CD]?

12 Copy the diagram and:

a draw the locus of all points which are 3 cm from C.

b Shade the region of all points that are less than or equal to 3 cm from C, but closer to [TU] than [RS].

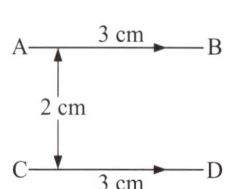

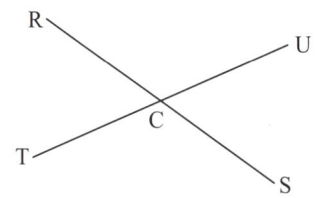

RESEARCH — VORONOI DIAGRAMS

Peter Dirichlet (1850) and later **Voronoi** (1908) considered the following problem:

"For a collection of points in the two-dimensional plane, how can we partition the plane so that the partition lines are equidistant to two or more points?"

As Voronoi published solutions to the problem, the diagrams were named after him.

Voronoi diagrams have applications in zoology, archaeology, communications, crystallography, and motion planning.

For example, Voronoi diagrams are useful in the solution to the problem of where to site mobile telephone towers. Given three towers, how can we ensure that any particular mobile call is carried by the closest tower?

Various methods or **algorithms** are used to construct Voronoi diagrams. However, Steve Fortune (1985) and his *plane-sweep* method greatly reduced the time needed to draw them.

Following is a Voronoi diagram for three distinct, non-collinear points A, B and C.

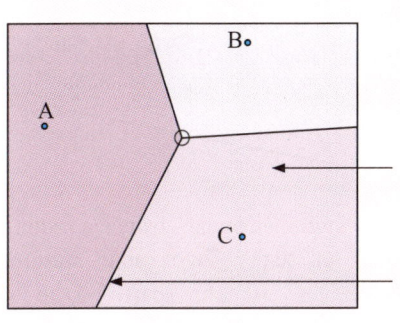

The plane alongside has been partitioned into three regions. Each partition line is equidistant from any two of the points.

Points A, B and C are called **sites**.

This region is called the **Voronoi region** for site C. Every point in this region is closer to C than to any other site.

This is a **Voronoi edge**, a boundary line between Voronoi regions. O is called a **Voronoi vertex**.

REVIEW SET 25

1 Sketch the locus of all points which are:

  a 1 cm from a fixed line segment which is 4 cm long

  b 1 cm from a fixed circle of radius 2 cm

  c equidistant from two 4 cm long parallel line segments

  d 2 cm from a fixed point P

  e more than 2 cm from a fixed point Q.

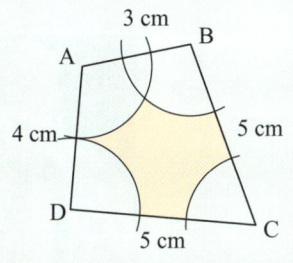

2 Four arcs of circles are drawn within quadrilateral ABCD as shown. Each arc has radius 2 cm. Describe the shaded region.

3
  a Draw an accurate scale scale diagram of the fence and shed given. The view is from above.

  b When the rope is fully extended, the sheep can eat grass 4 m away from the pole. Accurately draw the region that can be eaten by the sheep. Show all important lengths on the figure.

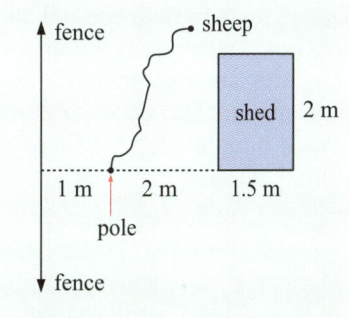

4 A and B are two farm houses 2 km apart. Draw the locus of all points which are:

  a equidistant from A and B

  b closer to A than they are from B

  c no more than 3 km away from both A and B.

5 [AB] is a fixed line segment 3 cm long. X is a point which can move but only such that $A\hat{X}B$ is fixed at $90°$.

Sketch the locus of X. Give reasons for your answer.

Hint: A set square could be used to help answer this question.

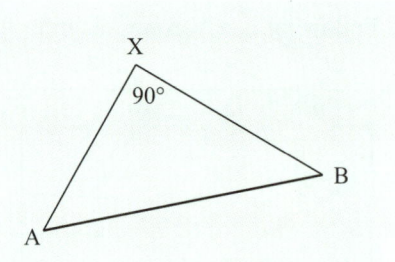

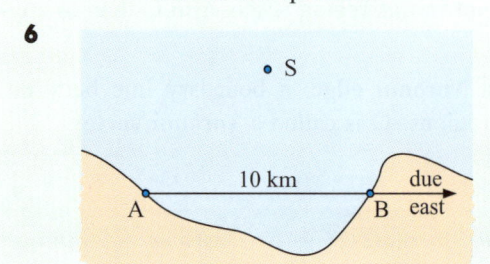

6 A distress signal comes from a small fishing boat at sea. Two radar stations are at A and B, 10 km apart. Due to poor weather conditions, the stations have difficulty locating the boat's position exactly. Station A reports that the boat is somewhere between $040°$ and $045°$. Station B reports the boat lies between $320°$ and $330°$.

a Draw an accurate scale diagram of the possible search region.

b Estimate the area of the search region.

PYTHAGORAS
(Approximately 580 BC to 500 BC)

Pythagoras was born around 580 BC in Samos, Greece. He was a famous mathematician and philosopher. He found the "Pythagorean brotherhood", a religious order, which had considerable influence on the development of mathematics and philosophy. As none of his original writings has survived, it is difficult to determine which work should be credited to him and which is a result of the work of some of his followers.

The Pythagorean school of thought was applied not only to areas of mathematics but also to astronomy, music theory and acoustics among other topics. In fact, it was recognised by Copernicus that some of Pythagoras's ideas on astronomy helped him develop his theories on the rotation of the planets around the sun.

The study of square numbers (1, 4, 9, 16, ...) and rectangular numbers (2, 6, 12, 20, ...) is credited to the Pythagorean school of study. However, the most well known of Pythagoras's mathematical ideas is his theory relating the lengths of the sides of a right-angled triangle, i.e., for a triangle as shown in the diagram.

$$a^2 + b^2 = c^2$$

Whether or not Pythagoras was himself directly responsible for some of the ideas credited to him is not particularly important. What is evident is that, as a result of his teaching and motivation, people were inspired to think creatively about mathematics, philosophy and associated areas such as music and astronomy.

Chapter 26

Activities

ACTIVITY 1 — TRIANGULAR NUMBERS

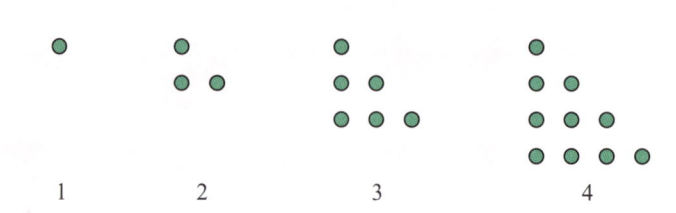

```
   •         •          •             •
            • •        • •           • •
                      • • •         • • •
                                   • • • •
   1         2          3             4
```

Let T_n be the number of dots in the nth triangular number. The first four triangular numbers are illustrated above.

What to do:

1. Draw the 5th, 6th and 7th triangular numbers. State the values of T_1, T_2, T_3, ..., T_7.

2. Find $T_2 - T_1$, $T_3 - T_2$, $T_4 - T_3$, and $T_5 - T_4$. Hence predict:
   a. $T_{40} - T_{39}$
   b. $T_n - T_{n-1}$

3. Find $T_1 + T_2$, $T_2 + T_3$, $T_3 + T_4$, and $T_4 + T_5$. Hence predict:
   a. $T_{31} + T_{32}$
   b. $T_n + T_{n+1}$

4. Find $2T_1 + 2$, $2T_2 + 3$, $2T_3 + 4$, and $2T_4 + 5$. Hence predict:
   a. $2T_{17} + 18$
   b. $2T_n + (n+1)$

5. The result in **3** can be illustrated geometrically by

   $T_1 + T_2 = $ [figure] $= 2^2$, $T_2 + T_3 = $ [figure] $= 3^2$,   and so on.

   Illustrate the result in **4** geometrically.

ACTIVITY 2 — WORD MAZE

The maze below contains the following words, not necessarily in the order given. You can move in any direction except diagonally.

TREE DIAGRAM	EXPERIMENT	SPINNER	PROBABILITY
EVENT	EXPECTATION	LIKELIHOOD	DICE
COINS	CHANCE	SAMPLE SPACE	OUTCOME

```
          N  T  E  X  P  E  R  E  S  ⟶ out
          E  N  E  M  I  R  E  X  N  I
          V  T  L  I  K  E  N  P  C  O
          E  E  C  H  I  L  N  E  N  O
   in ⟶  D  I  O  S  P  I  C  T  I
          E  L  D  O  M  A  R  G  A  T
          S  P  S  E  O  U  T  A  I  D
          P  M  A  C  H  C  C  O  M  E
          A  P  R  N  A  Y  T  I  E  E
          C  E  O  B  A  B  I  L  T  R
```

ACTIVITY 3 — COPS AND ROBBERS

Constable Ambrose (A) is walking down a city street towards an intersection.

At exactly 10:00 am he is 200 m from the intersection. He sees a man carrying a bag emerge from a bank at the corner of the intersection and run down the street at right angles to the street where he walks.

Constable Ambrose suspects that the man R is a bank robber, so he gives chase at his top speed of 28 km per hour.

The suspect has indeed robbed the Bank. He sees Constable Ambrose and runs down the street at 20 km per hour, to try to escape.

Fortunately for Constable Ambrose, there is a vacant lot on the corner of the intersection, so he runs across it directly towards the robber.

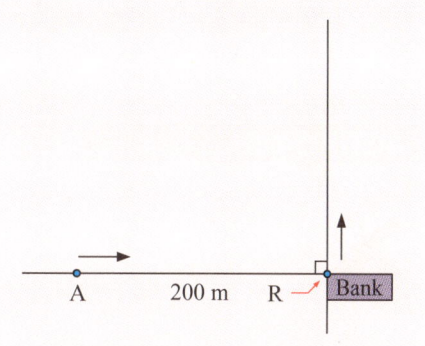

After a few seconds, Constable Ambrose, who was at A_0 when he saw the robber, is now at A_1, and the robber who started at R_0 is now at R_1. Constable Ambrose adjusts his direction so he can keep running directly at the robber.

What to do:

1. Convert the constable's speed and the bank robber's speed to metres per second.

2. Draw a scale diagram of the pursuit using 1 cm ≡ 50 m.
   As accurately as possible, plot the position of both men at 1 second intervals.
   Hence, find the approximate time of capture.

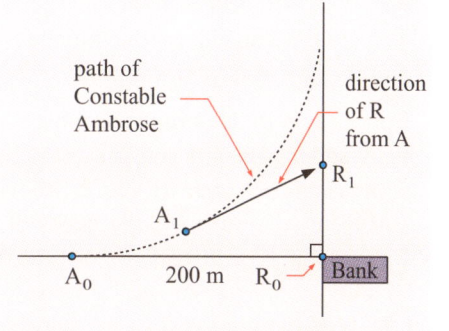

3. Would your answer's accuracy be improved if you plotted points at $\frac{1}{2}$ second intervals? Discuss the problems with plotting the paths which may occur when the time interval is reduced, and how you could overcome them.

4. Devise a 'curve of pursuit' problem of your own and ask a friend to solve it.

ACTIVITY 4 — TRANSLATIONS ON A CHESSBOARD

The knight in chess can be translated to another position on the board by moving in an L-shape as shown alongside.

498   ACTIVITIES   (Chapter 26)

What to do:

1 If a knight is placed near the middle of the chessboard, how many squares can it "protect"?

2 If a knight is placed in the corner of a chessboard, how many squares can it "protect"?

3 Can you place 12 knights on a chessboard so that every square is "protected"?

4 Can this be done with less than 12 knights?

ACTIVITY 5   SHORTEST DISCTANCE

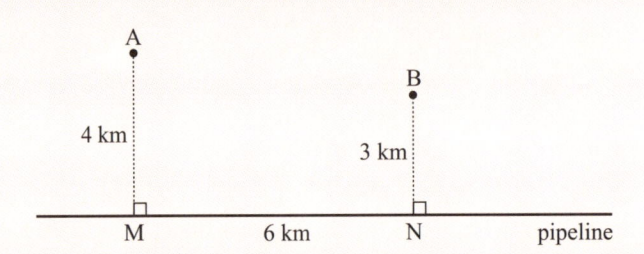

A and B are two homesteads which are 4 km and 3 km away from a water pipeline. M and N are the nearest points (on the pipeline) to A and B respectively, and MN = 6 km. The cost of running a spur pipeline across country from the pipe line is $3000 per km and the cost of a pump is $8000.

Your task is to determine the most economic way of pumping the water from the pipeline to A and B. Should you use two pumps located at M and N, or use one pump located somewhere between M and N knowing that one pump would be satisfactory to pump sufficient water to meet the needs of both homesteads?

What to do:

1 Find the total cost of the pumps and pipelines if two pumps are used, one at M and the other at N.

2 Suppose one pump is used and it is located at P, the midpoint of [MN].

   a Find AP and PB to the nearest metre.

   b Find the total cost of the pipeline and pump in this case.

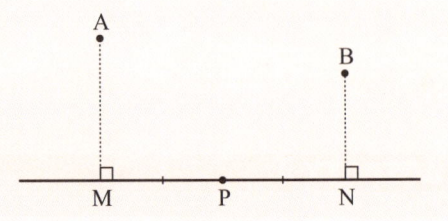

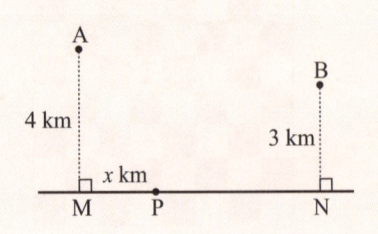

3 Suppose P is x km from M.

   a Show that AP + PB is given by $\sqrt{x^2 + 16} + \sqrt{x^2 - 12x + 45}$ km.

   b Use a **spreadsheet** to find AP + PB for $x = 0.1, 0.2, 0.3, ..., 5.9$.

4 Your spreadsheet could look like:

  a For what value of x is AP + PB least?

  b Use your spreadsheet to calculate the value of x that minimises AP + BP, correct to 3 decimal places.

	A	B	C
1		x-values	AP+PB
2		0.1	10.620
3		0.2	10.535
4		0.3	10.453

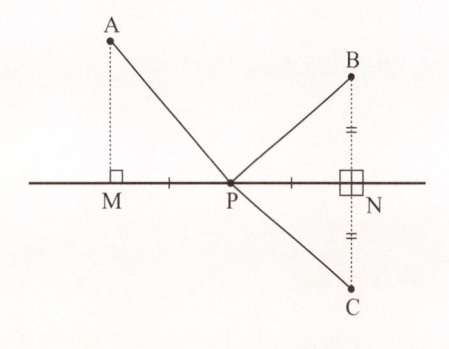

5 Now, consider the following geometrical argument:

Draw C on the opposite side of the pipeline, the same distance from the pipeline as B and directly opposite B.

  a Explain why AP + PB = AP + PC.

  b If P is anywhere on the pipeline between M and N, where should P be located so that AP + PC is as short as possible?

  c Find x.

  Hint: You could equate slopes of line segments.

  d Summarise what you have found from **a**, **b** and **c**.

ACTIVITY 6　　ENGAGED COUPLES

Two engaged couples, John and Mary, and Dominic and Maria, went shopping. Use the following clues to determine the number of the bus each person caught and what they bought:

- One couple caught odd numbered buses and the other couple caught even numbered buses.
- Maria, who did not catch bus 37, is engaged to the man who bought a video recorder.
- Dominic caught a bus numbered less than the person who bought the television.
- John, who bought the lounge suite, did not catch either bus 37 or 43.
- Mary did not catch bus 48.
- The person who caught bus 42 did not buy the bed.

Bus	Name	Purchase
37		
42		
43		
48		

ACTIVITY 7 — NUMBER CHAINS

In this activity we consider chains of numbers formed by repeating a procedure again and again.

Part 1:

Start with a two-digit number. → Add the tens digit to the treble of the units digit. → Stop if the result is the same as the previous number. Otherwise go back to the previous step.

If a single digit number results, such as 7, write it as 07.

For example: $43 \to 13 \to 10 \to 01 \to 03 \to 09 \to 27 \to \ldots$

What to do:

1. Continue the process started with 43 in the example above. Does the chain end? Why or why not?
2. Start with 68 and form the number chain.
3. Start with 87 and form the number chain.
4. What is special about 87?
5. Find **all** two digit numbers which behave in the same manner as 87.
6. Show that there are *two and only two* 2-digit numbers, one of which is 87, which 'stop'.
   Hint: Represent the 2-digit number 'ab' by $10a + b$.

Part 2:

Start with any number. → Find the sum of the squares of the digits. → Stop if the result is a single digit number. Otherwise go back to the previous step.

For example:

a $12 \to 1^2 + 2^2$
$= 1 + 4$
$= 5$

b $31 \to 3^2 + 1^2$
$= 9 + 1$
$= 10 \to 1^2 + 0^2$
$= 1^2$
$= 1$

What to do:

1. Find the first number after 10 whose chain ends with 1.
2. Write chains for the numbers between 10 and 50 inclusive. Which stops at the greatest number?
3. Try writing chains for 86, 129, and 912.
4. Write the chain for 537.

ACTIVITY 8   PAPER

In this activity we consider the size and weight of paper.

PAPER SIZE

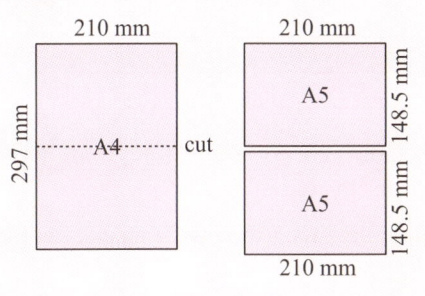

Nearly all paper used in schools has the size A4. Occasionally we use size A3 or A5.

A4 sheets are 297 mm × 210 mm.

A5 paper is made from A4 paper by cutting it in two equal halves, so A5 paper is 148.5 mm × 210 mm.

Two A4 sheets are cut from an A3 sheet, two A3 sheets are cut from an A2 sheet, two A2 sheets are cut from an A1 sheet, and two A1 sheets are cut from an original sheet of size A0.

PAPER WEIGHT

The weight of paper is determined by its area and its thickness. It is measured in **grams per square metre** or **gsm**.

What to do:

1 Ask your teacher to provide you with an unused pack of photocopying paper.

    a Explain how you can find the average thickness of one sheet.

    b Find the average thickness of one sheet using your method.

2 Find the area of one sheet of A4 paper in m^2. How many sheets are necessary to have a total surface area of $1\ m^2$? Copy and complete:

Sheet type	area (m^2)	number of sheets to make $1\ m^2$
A5		
A4		
A3		
A2		
A1		
A0		

3 **a** Find the approximate mass of one A4 sheet of 80 gsm paper?

    b Is 75 gsm paper thicker or thinner than 80 gsm paper? Explain your answer.

4 To find the ratio $\dfrac{\text{length}}{\text{width}}$ for each of the A-series sheet sizes, copy and complete the following table. Always record measurements with length > width.

Sheet type	length	width	$\dfrac{length}{width}$ (to 3 decimal places)
A5			
A4			
A3			
A2			
A1			
A0			

5 Use your calculator to find $\sqrt{2}$ to 3 decimal places.
Write a sentence which summarises what you discovered in **4**.

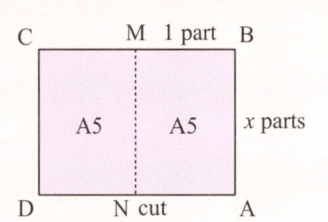

6 Consider the given sheet of A4 paper cut into two A5 sheets.
Let $AB : MB = x : 1$
Using similar figures, explain why $x = \sqrt{2}$.

7 You are given the task of creating a new paper size series. D0 should be 1.2 m², and the different sized D-series sheets must be similar with $\dfrac{length}{width} = \sqrt{2}$.
Find the sizes of D1, D2, D3, D4, D5 and D6 paper.

8 Research B-series paper sizes. You could consult a paper merchant, a printer, an encyclopedia, or use the internet.

ACTIVITY 9 — JOCKEYING FOR TRUTH

A horse race has just been completed and the jockeys on the first five horses all had differing views on the result. The photo showed that each jockey made one true and one false claim. Using the clues below, can you determine the order in which the jockeys finished?

	1st	2nd	3rd	4th	5th
Darren					
James					
Hugo					
Peter					
Warren					

Darren: Peter came second and I finished in third place.
James: I won and Hugo came second.
Hugo: I was third and James came last.
Peter: I finished second and Warren was fourth.
Warren: I came fourth and Darren won.

Hint: Assume Warren's fourth place is true and attempt to complete the table with ticks and crosses.

ANSWERS

EXERCISE 1A

1 **a** 1, 3, 9 **b** 1, 2, 3, 4, 6, 12 **c** 1, 19
   d 1, 2, 3, 4, 5, 6, 10, 12, 15, 20, 30, 60 **e** 1, 23
   f 1, 2, 3, 4, 6, 8, 12, 16, 24, 48 **g** 1, 7, 49
   h 1, 2, 3, 4, 6, 7, 12, 14, 21, 28, 42, 84

2 **a** 4, 8, 12, 16, 20 **b** 7, 14, 21, 28, 35
   c 9, 18, 27, 36, 45 **d** 15, 30, 45, 60, 75

3 **a** 2 **b** 6 **c** 6 **d** 24 **e** 3 **f** 4 **g** 3 **h** 24

4 **a** 994 **b** 1001 **c** 1989 **d** 10 005

5 **a** 40 **b** 12 **c** 40 **d** 90 **e** 12 **f** 60
   g 180 **h** 108

6 60 seconds

EXERCISE 1B

1 **a** i yes ii yes iii no iv no v yes
   b i no ii yes iii no iv yes v no
   c i yes ii no iii yes iv no v no
   d i yes ii yes iii no iv yes v yes
   e i no ii yes iii no iv no v no
   f i no ii yes iii no iv no v no
   g i no ii yes iii no iv no v no
   h i no ii yes iii no iv no v no

2 **a** 0, 2, 4, 6 or 8 **b** 0, 2, 4, 6 or 8 **c** any digit
   d no solutions

3 **a** 2, 5 or 8 **b** 1, 4 or 7 **c** 0, 3, 6 or 9 **d** 2, 5 or 8

4 **a** 0, 4 or 8 **b** 0, 2, 4, 6 or 8 **c** 0, 4, 8
   d 0, 2, 4, 6 or 8

5 **a** 0 or 5 **b** 0 or 5 **c** any digit **d** no solutions

6 **a** 0 or 6 **b** 2 or 8 **c** 1, 4 or 7 **d** 2, 5, 8

7 996 **8** 61 **9** 128

10 X = 1, Y = 7 or X = 2, Y = 3 or X = 4, Y = 7 or
    X = 5, Y = 3 or X = 7, Y = 7 or X = 8, Y = 3

11 6732

EXERCISE 1C

1 **a** 5 **b** 5 **c** 21 **d** −5 **e** −21 **f** −5
   g −5 **h** 21 **i** 41 **j** −9 **k** −9 **l** 41
   m 9 **n** −41 **o** 9 **p** 9

2 **a** 42 **b** −42 **c** −42 **d** 42 **e** 40 **f** −40
   g −40 **h** 40

3 **a** −25 **b** 25 **c** −1 **d** −1 **e** −30 **f** 30
   g −30 **h** 18 **i** −18 **j** −16 **k** 16 **l** 36

4 **a** 5 **b** −5 **c** −5 **d** 5 **e** 3 **f** −3
   g −3 **h** 3 **i** $\frac{1}{2}$ **j** $-\frac{1}{2}$ **k** $-\frac{1}{2}$ **l** $\frac{1}{2}$

EXERCISE 1D.1

1 **a** 10 **b** 0 **c** −6 **d** 4 **e** 4 **f** 25

2 **a** 25 **b** 22 **c** 7 **d** 0 **e** 21 **f** 15
   g 5 **h** 36 **i** 7 **j** 38 **k** 13 **l** −6
   m 24 **n** 11 **o** 2 **p** 7

3 **a** 15 **b** 15 **c** 0 **d** 4 **e** 82 **f** 12
   g 36 **h** 3 **i** 31 **j** 1 **k** 4 **l** −4
   m 96 **n** 16 **o** 1

4 **a** −3 **b** 8 **c** 2 **d** 39 **e** 25 **f** 18

5 **a** 3 **b** 3 **c** 2 **d** 4 **e** 8 **f** 5 **g** 57 **h** 1

6 **a** $9 - 3 + 2 = 8$ **b** $9 \times 3 - 2 = 25$ **c** $9 \div 3 + 2 = 5$

7 **a** $(8 - 6) \times 3 = 6$ **b** $120 \div (4 \times 2) = 15$
   c $120 \div 4 \times 2 = 60$ **d** $5 \times (7 - 3 - 1) = 15$
   e $5 \times 7 - (3 - 1) = 33$ **f** $5 \times (7 - 3) - 1 = 19$
   g $(3 + 2) \times 8 - 4 = 36$ **h** $3 + 2 \times (8 - 4) = 11$
   i $3 + 2 \times 8 - 4 = 15$

EXERCISE 1D.2

1 **a** 362 **b** 600 **c** 24 **d** 8 **e** −272 **f** 4
   g −4 **h** −33 **i** −5 **j** 4 **k** −6 **l** 2

EXERCISE 1E.1

1 **a** $\frac{9}{14}$ **b** $\frac{9}{16}$ **c** $1\frac{3}{8}$ **d** $\frac{17}{30}$ **e** $4\frac{2}{3}$ **f** $2\frac{1}{8}$
   g $3\frac{2}{3}$ **h** $6\frac{1}{12}$

2 **a** $\frac{5}{9}$ **b** $-\frac{1}{12}$ **c** $\frac{1}{14}$ **d** $\frac{3}{8}$ **e** $1\frac{7}{8}$ **f** $1\frac{7}{15}$
   g $-1\frac{2}{3}$ **h** $-1\frac{5}{12}$

EXERCISE 1E.2

1 **a** $\frac{5}{8}$ **b** $\frac{2}{7}$ **c** $1\frac{1}{2}$ **d** $2\frac{2}{3}$ **e** $\frac{15}{16}$ **f** $\frac{1}{2}$
   g $5\frac{4}{9}$ **h** $3\frac{3}{8}$

2 **a** $\frac{9}{10}$ **b** $1\frac{1}{8}$ **c** $\frac{7}{9}$ **d** $\frac{1}{6}$ **e** $2\frac{2}{3}$ **f** $2\frac{2}{5}$
   g $\frac{3}{10}$ **h** $\frac{28}{45}$

3 **a** $6\frac{31}{40}$ **b** $\frac{16}{81}$ **c** $3\frac{3}{4}$ **d** $\frac{9}{16}$ **e** 12 **f** $\frac{10}{11}$
   g $2\frac{3}{5}$ **h** $1\frac{3}{4}$

EXERCISE 1E.3

1 $\frac{7}{20}$ **2** $32 500 **3** pants £16, top £20

4 €180.15 **5** $\frac{2}{9}$ **6** $\frac{1}{5}$ **7** $\frac{2}{7}$ **8** 999 leaves

EXERCISE 1E.4

1 **a** $\frac{7}{12}$ **b** $1\frac{1}{21}$ **c** $\frac{5}{56}$ **d** $-\frac{1}{12}$ **e** $\frac{1}{3}$ **f** $\frac{10}{21}$
   g $\frac{6}{35}$ **h** $2\frac{7}{10}$ **i** $3\frac{1}{8}$ **j** $4\frac{2}{7}$ **k** 2

EXERCISE 1F.1

1 **a** $2 + \frac{5}{10}$ **b** $2 + \frac{5}{100}$ **c** $2 + \frac{5}{100} + \frac{1}{10\,000}$
   d $4 + \frac{5}{1000} + \frac{2}{10\,000}$ **e** $\frac{1}{100} + \frac{6}{10\,000}$

2 **a** 3.2 **b** 0.78 **c** 0.603 **d** 0.079 **e** 4.0001
   f 5.0302

3 **a** 600 **b** 60 **c** $\frac{6}{10}$ **d** $\frac{6}{1000}$ **e** $\frac{6}{100\,000}$

4 **a** 19.06 **b** 30.05 **c** 2.37 **d** 1.9
   e 4.746 **f** 4.335 **g** 0.4749 **h** −0.7
   i 0.106 **j** −0.579 **k** 2.742 **l** −6.31

5 **a** 1370 **b** 0.005 **c** 30 **d** 4 **e** 0.04
   f 1800 **g** 2.16 **h** 50 **i** 0.027 **j** 20
   k 0.004 **l** 0.031

6 **a** $\frac{1}{2}$ **b** $\frac{3}{5}$ **c** $3\frac{1}{4}$ **d** $\frac{5}{8}$ **e** $\frac{3}{80}$ **f** $\frac{21}{2500}$
   g $2\frac{3}{4}$ **h** $9\frac{1}{10}$ **i** $3\frac{1}{8}$ **j** $\frac{19}{250}$ **k** $\frac{7}{80}$ **l** $\frac{1}{2000}$

7 **a** 0.5 **b** 0.75 **c** 0.6 **d** 0.34 **e** $0.\overline{6}$
   f $0.\overline{2}$ **g** 0.225 **h** $0.8\overline{3}$ **i** 0.875 **j** 0.2125
   k 0.296 **l** $0.41\overline{6}$ **m** 0.15 **n** $0.\overline{36}$ **o** 0.44
   p $0.\overline{7}$ **q** $0.0\overline{7}$ **r** $0.\overline{07}$ **s** $0.\overline{007}$ **t** $0.\overline{0007}$

8 **a** £47.30 **b** €13.30 **c** $2.35
   d i $217 ii ≈ 26 cents **e** 14 000 cartons
   f 5000 bread rolls **g** 1000 dozen bottles
   h 8000 medallions

ANSWERS

EXERCISE 1F.2
1 a 3 b 6 c 20 d 201
2 a 3.1 b 10.4 c 4.9 d 4.0
3 a 9.43 b 13.13 c 9.31 d 0.19
4 a 499.32 b 228.84 c 9.11 d 31.75 e 0.88
   f 26.67 g 7.41 h 5.93 i 0.48
5 $34.77

EXERCISE 1G.1
1 a 10 : 7 b 2 : 5 c 80 : 50
   d 200 : 50 e 500 : 2000 f 800 : 1500
2 29 : 18   3 3700 : 800

EXERCISE 1G.2
1 a 1 : 2 b 3 : 1 c 5 : 2 d 3 : 4 e 5 : 3
   f 5 : 1 g 1 : 6 h 4 : 1
2 $\frac{5}{4}$, 5 : 4   3 a 2 : 3 b 15 : 8 c 39 : 8 d 50 : 39
4 a 5 : 3 b 1 : 4 c 2 : 5 d 5 : 7

EXERCISE 1G.3
1 a □ = 20 b □ = 9 c □ = 20 d □ = 9
   e □ = 12 f □ = 15
2 24 doctors   3 960 chickens   4 $1000

EXERCISE 1G.4
1 a $10, $40 b $15, $20   2 £560 000   3 64 girls
4 3 : 7   5 13 : 47

EXERCISE 1H
1 a 8 b 16 c 27 d 75 e 36
   f 1350 g 588 h 22 000
2 a 625 b 512 c 248 832 d −262 144
   e 2401 f −27 g 481.890 304 h 361
3 2, 3, 5, 7, 11, 13, 17, 19, 23, 29
4 a 2^3 b 3^3 c 2^6 d 5^4 e 7^3 f 3^5
   g 11^3 h 23^2
5 a $2^3 \times 7$ b $2^4 \times 3 \times 5$ c $2^3 \times 3^2 \times 7$ d $3 \times 5 \times 7^2$
   e $3^3 \times 11$ f 13×17 g $2^3 \times 3^2 \times 5$ h $2^3 \times 7 \times 17$
6 160
7 a 1575.296 b 561.968 c 162 538.705
   d 42.253 e 0.784 f 3.773
8 1   9 1   10 3, 33   11 $a = 4$

REVIEW SET 1A
1 a 15 b −6 c □ = 0, 2, 4, 6 or 8 d $\frac{4}{5}$
   e 1 : 5 f $2^2 \times 3 \times 11$ g 0.375 h 360
2 a HCF = 12, LCM = 72 b 986   3 $20.25
4 a 15.01 b 0.25 c 0.38
5 a $\frac{1}{6}$ b 1750 mL c 2500

REVIEW SET 1B
1 a 0.48 b $3\frac{2}{3}$ c −20 d $\frac{5}{6}$ e 0.28 f −5
   g 5 : 1 h $2^2 \times 3^3 \times 11$ i □ = 1, 4 or 7 j 2700
2 a HCF = 3, LCM = 135 b 2002   3 51 minutes
4 a $2\frac{31}{45}$ b 2.228
5 a 65 lengths, 40 cm b $34 000 c $\frac{5}{12}$

EXERCISE 2A
1 a $3m$ b $4k$ c $7n$ d $12b$ e $21a$ f $5dm$
   g $24m$ h $8mp$ i $7pq$ j $2pq$ k abc l dhp
2 a $ab + n$ b $3a + 2b$ c $ab + m$ d $ab - c$
   e $d - ac$ f $k - 4d$ g $ac + bd$ h $10 - 2ab$
   i $8(m + n)$ j $4(d - 2)$ k $3(b - d)$ l $ab(c + 1)$
3 a $2t$ b $3n$ c $2p + 3q + 3$ d $3d + e$
   e $x + 2y + 5$ f $4a + 2b$ g $3a + 5$ h $b - 2a$
   i b j $2s + 3t$ k $5 + 3d$ l $2a + 2b + 2$
4 a $3 - (a + a) = 3 - 2a$ whereas $3 - a + a = 3$
   b $m - (n + n + n) = m - 3n$ whereas
      $m - n + n + n = m + n$
5 a $a \times a \times a$ b $b \times b \times b \times b$ c $3 \times d \times d$ d $4 \times n \times n \times n$
   e $10 \times a \times a \times b$ f $4 \times a \times b \times b \times b$ g $2 \times a \times 2 \times a$
   h $2 \times a \times a$ i $a \times a + 2 \times b \times b$ j $a \times a \times a - 3 \times b \times b$
6 a $3a^2$ b $5b^3$ c $10a^2$ d $8a^2b$ e $5mn^3$
   f $12pq^2$ g p^3qr^2 h $20a^2$ i $6cd^2$ j $a + a^2$
   k $a^3 + a$ l $b^3 - a^2$ m $b^2 + 3b$ n $c^3 - 5c$
   o $3ab^2 - 5bc$ p $3a^2 + am$ q $4x + 2x^3$ r $4x(2x + 2)$

EXERCISE 2B
1 a 4 b −7 c 1 d −1 e 6 f −3 g −2 h 1
2 a 2 b −2 c 11 d −3 e −1 f −7 g 3
   h −13
3 a expression b 6 c i 5 ii −1 iii 6 iv −4
   d 6
4 a 3 b 4 c 5
5 a expression b expression c equation
   d equation e expression f equation

EXERCISE 2C
1 a $7 + 3$ b $y + 4$ c $t + 2p$ d $a + b + c$
2 a 7×3 b $4y$ c $2pt$ d abc
3 a $\frac{7}{3}$ b $\frac{4}{y}$ c $\frac{t}{2p}$ d $\frac{a+b}{c}$
4 a $\frac{7+3}{2}$ b $\frac{y+4}{2}$ c $\frac{t+2p}{2}$ d $\frac{a+b+c}{3}$
5 a $7 - 3$ b $y - 4$ c $4 - y$ d $c - (a + b)$
6 a $b + \frac{c}{3}$ b $\frac{b+c}{3}$ c $2 + x^2$ d $(2 + x)^2$
7 a $\frac{r+s}{3}$ b $3(b + c)$ c $m + n^3$ d $(m + n)^3$
8 a $b - 3x$ b ab^2 c $a + 5b$ d $t - 3$ e $a + 4$ f $9x^2$
   g $(cd)^2$ h $x^2 + y^2$ i $p^2 + q^2 + r^2$ j $\frac{c+d^2}{2}$
9 a the sum of a and 6 b the sum of b and 7
   c the sum of c and d d the sum of c and three times d
   e three times the sum of c and d f the product of b and c
   g the square of the sum of p and q
   h the sum of the squares of p and q
   i three times the square of x
   j the square of the product of three and x
   k the sum of a and one fifth of b
   l one fifth of the sum of a and b
   m the quotient of x and y
   n the square of the quotient of a and b

o the quotient of the squares of a and b
p the sum of a and b, all divided by c

EXERCISE 2D

1 a ¥1500 **b** ¥$(300a)$ **c** ¥(ac)

2 a €4 **b** €$\left(\dfrac{p}{2}\right)$ **c** €$\left(\dfrac{py}{100}\right)$

3 a \$67 **b** \$$(100-11x)$ **c** \$$(100-xy)$

4 $(14-x)$ years **5** $3t$ km

6 a $21x$ cm **b** $\left(35-\dfrac{21x}{100}\right)$ m **7** £$(45c+85t)$

8 a $(a+b)$ km **b** $\left(\dfrac{a+b}{5}\right)$ km per hour

9 a 400 km **b** st km

EXERCISE 2E

1 a 3 **b** 2 **c** -2 **d** 8 **e** -1 **f** 6
g 1 **h** 8 **i** 6 **j** 6 **k** 4 **l** 27

2 a 6 **b** 1 **c** -9 **d** 2 **e** 4 **f** 1
g 64 **h** -2 **i** 20 **j** -2 **k** 4 **l** 17

3 a 9 **b** -9 **c** 36 **d** 18 **e** 12 **f** 4
g -1 **h** 1 **i** 1 **j** 4 **k** 3 **l** 5

4 a 2 **b** 3 **c** -1 **d** -1 **e** 2 **f** 1
g -2 **h** -1 **i** -1 **j** $\frac{1}{2}$ **k** $\frac{5}{3}$ **l** $-\frac{5}{3}$

5 a -1 **b** -1 **c** $\frac{1}{2}$ **d** $\frac{2}{3}$ **e** -4 **f** $\frac{3}{2}$
g $\frac{2}{3}$ **h** $\frac{3}{4}$ **i** 4 **j** $\frac{1}{3}$ **k** $-\frac{2}{3}$ **l** $\frac{4}{3}$

EXERCISE 2F

1 a $x+8$ **b** $x+15$ **c** $p+10$ **d** $2a+12$ **e** $2b+3$
f $2b$ **g** $3x$ **h** $2a+10$ **i** $4x$ **j** x **k** $2x$ **l** $2a^2$
m $7x+3$ **n** $3x^2$ **o** $17x-7$ **p** $16x$ **q** $2b^2$ **r** $5ab$
s $3g$ **t** $2b-2$

2 a 0 **b** $10n$ **c** $11n-11$ **d** $4ab$ **e** $3xy$ **f** p^2
g $4a+6$ **h** $9a$ **i** $3b+7$ **j** $7xy$ **k** $5a+2b$
l $4a^2+3a$ **m** $4x$ **n** 0 **o** $3ab+2b^2$ **p** $10x-10$
q 0 **r** $9x$ **s** $2r^2+2r$ **t** x^2+x+2 **u** $8y+2$

3 a $11x$ **b** $-5x$ **c** $5x$ **d** $-11x$ **e** $6a$ **f** $4a$
g $-4a$ **h** $-6a$ **i** m^2+2m **j** $-8d$ **k** $2d$
l $-2d$ **m** $3b-3$ **n** $-4t$ **o** $-7g$ **p** $1-3m$
q $-2a+2$ **r** b **s** $2b$ **t** $4b$ **u** $3x$

4 a $-a-3$ **b** $4a-b$ **c** $-2ab-2$ **d** 0
e $-x$ **f** $3x^2-10$ **g** $-2n-5$ **h** $a-6b$
i $3-3bc$ **j** $2x^2-x$ **k** $-4x^2$ **l** $3x-2y$
m $-xy-2y$ **n** $-5x-10$

EXERCISE 2G.1

1 a xy **b** $3xy$ **c** x^2y **d** $2ab$ **e** x^2
f x^3 **g** $-2x^2$ **h** $-a^3$

2 a $3ab$ **b** $3ab^2$ **c** $6ab^2$ **d** $20a^2b^2$ **e** $16a^2$
f $9b^4$ **g** $8y^3$ **h** $10b^3$ **i** $5b^4$ **j** $12b^5$
k $-4x^2$ **l** $-3x^2$ **m** $-6x^2$ **n** $8x^2$ **o** $-2x^3$
p $-18x^3$ **q** $-5x^3$ **r** $-2x^4$ **s** $-4d^3$ **t** $8x^3$

3 a i x^4 **ii** x^5 **iii** x^7 **iv** x^9 **b** $x^m \times x^n = x^{m+n}$

EXERCISE 2G.2

1 a x^2 **b** x^3 **c** x^3 **d** x^2 **e** $3x^2$ **f** $5x^2$
g $5x^2$ **h** $2x^3$ **i** $2x^4$ **j** $2x^3$ **k** $2x^2$ **l** $\dfrac{x}{2}$
m $\dfrac{1}{2x}$ **n** $\dfrac{1}{2x^2}$ **o** $\dfrac{1}{2x}$ **p** $\dfrac{1}{3x^2}$

2 a i x^2 **ii** x^3 **iii** x^5 **iv** x^3 **b** $\dfrac{x^m}{x^n} = x^{m-n}$

REVIEW SET 2A

1 a $3mn^2$ **b** $18x^2$ **c** $3ab-2a^2$

2 a 6 **b** $7a$ and $-5a$, $-4ab$ and $3ab$ **c** 12
d -4 **e** $2a+12b-ab-4$

3 a $y+6$ **b** $q-p$ **c** \$$(r-pq)$

4 a -27 **b** -6 **c** 49 **5 a** $7p-7$ **b** $a+11b$

6 a $6m^3$ **b** $9m^4$ **c** $2a^2$ **d** $\dfrac{2}{3a}$

REVIEW SET 2B

1 a $12xy^2$ **b** $20x^3$ **c** $5a^3-5a$

2 a 5 **b** $7y$ and $-5y$ **c** -8 **d** 3 **e** $5x+2y-8xy+3$

3 a $x-4$ **b** p^2+q **c** €$\left(\dfrac{pq+rs}{100}\right)$

4 a 8 **b** -9 **c** -1 **5 a** $-2q+2$ **b** $3d-5c$

6 a $20x^3$ **b** $6x^3$ **c** $\dfrac{x^3}{2}$ **d** $\dfrac{2}{3x^2}$

EXERCISE 3A.1

1 a $\frac{70}{100}=70\%$ **b** $\frac{75}{100}=75\%$ **c** $\frac{14}{100}=14\%$
d $\frac{52}{100}=52\%$ **e** $\frac{100}{100}=100\%$ **f** $\frac{400}{100}=400\%$
g $\frac{55}{100}=55\%$ **h** $\frac{27.5}{100}=27\frac{1}{2}\%$

2 a 6% **b** 10% **c** 92% **d** 75% **e** 116%
f 527% **g** 6.4% **h** 102.4%

3 a 40% **b** 82% **c** 95% **d** 108.5%
e 516% **f** 101.2% **g** 325% **h** 85%
i $44\frac{4}{9}\%$ **j** 262.5% **k** $166\frac{2}{3}\%$ **l** $327\frac{3}{11}\%$

EXERCISE 3A.2

1 a $\frac{17}{20}$ **b** $\frac{21}{50}$ **c** $\frac{21}{20}$ **d** $\frac{3}{20}$ **e** $\frac{12}{25}$ **f** $\frac{3}{40}$
g $\frac{1}{16}$ **h** $\frac{33}{25}$ **i** $\frac{1}{6}$ **j** $\frac{1}{3}$ **k** $\frac{8}{5}$ **l** $\frac{1}{400}$

2 a 0.92 **b** 1.06 **c** 1.124 **d** 0.882
e 0.075 **f** 0.01 **g** 2.56 **h** 0.0005
i 11.5 **j** 0.000 037 **k** 3.428 **l** 0.637

3 a 80% **b** 60% **c** 12.5% **d** $33\frac{1}{3}\%$
e 13.79% **f** 5% **g** $16\frac{2}{3}\%$ **h** $8\frac{1}{3}\%$

4 Emma **5 a** $26\frac{2}{3}\%$ **b** $16\frac{2}{3}\%$ **c** $43\frac{1}{3}\%$ **d** $86\frac{2}{3}\%$

6 Science test

EXERCISE 3B

1 a \$1800 **b** 800 kg **c** 2.5 L **d** 3000 kg **e** \$1200
f 360 mL **g** 550 L **h** 720 kg **i** \$1244.68

2 a \$540 **b** 1152 kg **c** \$85 **d** 315 mL
e $870\frac{5}{6}$ kg **f** \$47.06

3 875 passengers **4** \$92 500 **5** 3200 people

6 a 700 students **b** 224 students

ANSWERS 507

EXERCISE 3C

1 **a** 27 kg   **b** €42.50   **c** 2 L   **d** 30 km
  e $35.10   **f** 4.75 m   **g** £665   **h** $804
2 **a** 36   **b** 108   **c** 2.7 L   **d** £6682.50
  e $40560   **f** €410
3 **a** ≈ 33.2 million   **b** ≈ 931 000 people

EXERCISE 3D.1

1 **a** **i** $240 profit   **ii** $540
  b **i** €292.50 loss   **ii** €357.50
  c **i** £20 550 profit   **ii** £157 550
  d **i** ¥565 400   **ii** ¥2 004 600
2 84.62%   3 **a** €125   **b** €625   4 £39, 18.06%
5 $1080, 18%   6 **a** £35 000   **b** 10.94%   7 $18, 6.57%

EXERCISE 3D.2

1 **a** discount €28, sale price €42
  b discount £37.50, sale price £112.50
  c discount $3, sale price $21
2 €11   3 €4224   4 ¥12 210   5 15%   6 35%   7 7.5%

EXERCISE 3E.1

1 **a** 1.4   **b** 1.06   **c** 0.8   **d** 0.85   **e** 0.58   **f** 1.12
2 **a** $138   **b** 540 kg   **c** £3648   **d** $662.40
  e 11 000 hectares   **f** 1408 tonnes
  g 12 317.5 m^2 **h** €125 835.37

EXERCISE 3E.2

1 **a** 20%   **b** 14.3%   **c** 17.2%   **d** 2.8%   **e** 16.7%
  f 5.1%   **g** 100%   **h** 17.7%
2 12.0%
3 **a** 12.5%   **b** 5.3%   **c** 33.3%   **d** 50%   **e** 9.7%
  f 75%
4 $990, i.e., less than the original value
5 $1.1^2 = 1.21$ i.e., 21% increase

EXERCISE 3E.3

1 €15 620   2 **a** $255   **b** 41.18%   3 €386 280
4 $11 560   5 $7.60   6 €308
7 **a** $136   **b** $115.60   **c** 44.5%   **d** $1497.60   **e** 15.6%
8 **a** $795.60   **b** 10.5%   9 €45 per week
10 **a** 44% increase   **b** 36% decrease   11 $64 800

EXERCISE 3F

1 **a** RM200   **b** $180   **c** £90
  d €45   **e** 184 pesos   **f** €12 000
2 $2430   3 €512   4 $295   5 $380

EXERCISE 3G

1 **a** $1600   **b** £495   **c** €525   **d** $9800
2 **a** $175   **b** €180   **c** ¥46 666.67   **d** £905.63
3 €1257.12   4 $248.75
5 **a** £2300   **b** £2160   **c** £2680
6 **a** $8910   **b** $148.50   7 €68

EXERCISE 3H.1

1 **a** €300   **b** €315.25   2 **a** £59 405   **b** £9405
3 **a** €665.60   **b** $2292.19   **c** £46.36

EXERCISE 3H.2

1 **a** $3993   **b** $993   2 €11 470.39
3 **a** £6000   **b** £6050   4 **a** $43 923   **b** $13 923
5 €23 602.32   6 **a** £7800   **b** £7935
7 **a** Option 1: €10 160 (better), Option 2: €10 077.70
  b yes
8 46.41%
9 **a** **i** $7012.76   **ii** $9835.76   **iii** $19 348.42
  b **i** 10 years 89 days   **ii** 20 years 179 days
    iii 30 years 268 days
  It takes the same length of time for the investment to increase from $10 000 to $20 000 as it does to increase from $20 000 to $40 000.

REVIEW SET 3A

1 **a** 1.08   **b** 0.93   2 $33\frac{1}{3}$% increase
3 **a** $131.20   **b** 132 kg   4 2000 kg   5 $320
6 £120 000   7 **a** $28\frac{1}{3}$%   **b** $119 000   8 $16.80
9 €2400   10 £8492.93   11 $8050

REVIEW SET 3B

1 **a** 0.975   **b** 1.073   2 $297.60   3 **a** $360   **b** $2640
4 18.75%   5 £3600   6 $200   7 95 kg
8 **a** 18.07%   **b** €115 710.84   9 **a** $2574   **b** $288.17
10 $4728.75   11 $396 000

EXERCISE 4A

1 **a** $2x + 14$ **b** $3x - 6$ **c** $4a + 12$ **d** $5a + 5c$
  e $6b - 18$ **f** $7m + 28$ **g** $2n - 2p$ **h** $4p - 4q$
  i $15 + 3x$ **j** $5y - 5x$ **k** $8t - 64$ **l** $28 + 4m$
  m $6d + 6e$ **n** $2x - 22$ **o** $21 + 3k$ **p** $5p - 5q$
  q $40 - 4j$ **r** $7y + 7n$ **s** $2n - 24$ **t** $88 - 8d$
2 **a** $18x + 9$ **b** $3 - 9x$ **c** $10a + 15$ **d** $11 - 22n$
  e $18x + 6y$ **f** $5x - 10y$ **g** $12b + 4c$ **h** $2a - 4b$
  i $7a - 35b$ **j** $24 + 36d$ **k** $24 - 32y$ **l** $30b + 18a$
  m $22x - 11y$ **n** $4p + 36q$ **o** $5a - 40b$ **p** $18 + 16x$
  q $27x + 3y$ **r** $7c - 63d$ **s** $6m + 42n$ **t** $64a - 8c$
3 **a** $x^2 + 2x$ **b** $5x - x^2$ **c** $2a^2 + 4a$ **d** $5b - 3b^2$
  e $ab + 2ac$ **f** $a^3 + a$ **g** $2a^2 - a^3$ **h** $6x - 8x^2$
  i $18x - 3x^2$ **j** $5x^2 - 20x$ **k** $4a - 4a^2$ **l** $7b^2 + 14b$
  m $2x^2 + 3x$ **n** $5x - 2x^2$ **o** $a^2b + ab^2$
  p $3a^2b - a^2b^2$ **q** $m^2n - mn^2$ **r** $ac^2 - 4a^2c$
  s $24p - 42p^2q$ **t** $3k^2 + 5kl^2$ **u** $7a^2b - 5b^2$
  v $x^2y + 9xy^2$ **w** $7xy - 4x^2y$ **x** $3t^2 - 5s^2t$
4 **a** $-2x - 4$ **b** $-3x - 12$ **c** $-4x + 8$ **d** $-25 + 5x$
  e $-a - 2$ **f** $-x + 3$ **g** $-5 + x$ **h** $-2x - 1$
  i $-12 + 3x$ **j** $-20x + 8$ **k** $-15 + 20c$ **l** $-x + 2$
5 **a** $-a^2 - a$ **b** $-b^2 - 4b$ **c** $-5c + c^2$
  d $-2x^2 - 4x$ **e** $-2x + 2x^2$ **f** $-3y^2 - 6y$
  g $-20a + 4a^2$ **h** $-18b + 12b^2$
6 **a** $5x + 12$ **b** $9x + 27$ **c** $9x - 28$ **d** $4x - 19$
  e $2m + 26$ **f** $3m - 17$ **g** $-x + 5$ **h** $-10x + 5$
  i $-5x + 20$ **j** $-13x + 10$ **k** $-11x + 35$ **l** $8y + 2$
  m 0   **n** $31t - 22$
7 **a** $x - 1$ **b** $-1 - 3x$ **c** $25 - 12x$ **d** $12x - 2$
  e $1 + 10x$ **f** $8 + 2x$ **g** $9 + 21x$ **h** $4x - 6$
  i $12x - 5$ **j** $6 + 2x$ **k** $9x - 5$ **l** $-47 + 15x$

8   **a** $3x^2 - 7x$ **b** $-2x^2 - x$ **c** $a + 7b$
    d $3x^3$ **e** $3x^3 - 7x$ **f** $9a - 3b - 30$

9   **a** $2y^2 + 4y + 6$ **b** $5a^2 - 20a - 10$
    c $6x^2 + 9x - 3$ **d** $-12b^2 - 8b + 12$
    e $3y^3 - 6y^2 + 21y$ **f** $8a^3 + 2a^2 - 2a$
    g $-10x^3 - 2x^2 + 8x$ **h** $-6b^3 - 12b^2 + 6b$
    i $-6y^3 + 2y^2 - 10y$

EXERCISE 4B

1   **a** $x^2 + 5x + 6$ **b** $a^2 + 9a + 20$
    c $b^2 - 3b - 10$ **d** $a^2 - 7a + 12$
    e $ax + bx + ay + by$ **f** $ap + aq + bp + bq$
    g $2x^2 + 5x + 3$ **h** $2x^2 + x - 3$
    i $3x^2 - 11x - 20$ **j** $3x^2 + 11x - 20$
    k $10x^2 - 19x + 7$ **l** $x^3 + x^2 + 4x + 4$

2   **a** $x^2 + 6x + 9$ **b** $x^2 - 6x + 9$ **c** $x^2 + 14x + 49$
    d $x^2 - 14x + 49$ **e** $4x^2 + 20x + 25$ **f** $4x^2 - 20x + 25$
    g $x^2 + 2xy + y^2$ **h** $x^2 - 2xy + y^2$ **i** $x^2 - 8x + 16$
    j $100 + 20x + x^2$ **k** $4 - 12x + 9x^2$ **l** $1 + 8x + 16x^2$

3   **a** $x^3 + 2x^2 + 4x + 3$ **b** $2x^3 + 5x^2 + 7x + 10$
    c $x^3 - 3x^2 - x + 6$ **d** $x^3 + 5x^2 + 5x + 4$
    e $2x^3 - 5x^2 + 7x - 6$ **f** $6x^3 + 17x^2 + 4x - 7$
    g $2x^3 + 5x^2 + 3x + 35$ **h** $x^3 + 7x^2 - 11x + 63$

EXERCISE 4C.1

1   **a** $pm + pn + qm + qn$ **b** $xr + xs + yr + ys$
    c $x^2 + 11x + 28$ **d** $x^2 + 4x + 3$ **e** $y^2 + 5y + 6$
    f $a^2 + 10a + 21$ **g** $x^2 - 4$ **h** $x^2 - 2x - 8$
    i $x^2 + 4x - 21$ **j** $x^2 - 7x - 18$ **k** $x^2 - x - 12$
    l $x^2 + 4x - 12$ **m** $x^2 - 7x + 12$ **n** $x^2 - 13x + 40$
    o $x^2 - 15x + 44$ **p** $2x^2 + x - 3$ **q** $3x^2 - 10x - 8$
    r $4x^2 - 2x - 12$

2   **a** $x^2 + 2x + 1$ **b** $x^2 + 8x + 16$ **c** $x^2 - 4x + 4$
    d $x^2 - 10x + 25$ **e** $9 + 6y + y^2$ **f** $9 - 6y + y^2$
    g $4x^2 + 4x + 1$ **h** $4x^2 - 4x + 1$ **i** $1 + 8a + 16a^2$
    j $1 - 8a + 16a^2$ **k** $a^2 + 2ab + b^2$ **l** $a^2 - 2ab + b^2$
    m $9x^2 + 12x + 4$ **n** $16x^2 - 24x + 9$
    o $81x^2 - 90x + 25$ **p** $49x^2 + 28x + 4$

3   **a** $x^2 - 4$ **b** $y^2 - 25$ **c** $a^2 - 49$ **d** $b^2 - 16$
    e $9 - x^2$ **f** $36 - y^2$ **g** $1 - a^2$ **h** $64 - b^2$
    i $4x^2 - 1$ **j** $9a^2 - 4$ **k** $9 - 25b^2$ **l** $25 - 16y^2$

4   With each of these, the inners and outers cancel. This suggests that $(a+b)(a-b) = (a-b)(a+b) = a^2 - b^2$.

EXERCISE 4C.2

1   **a** $c^2 + 2cd + d^2$ **b** $r^2 + 2rs + s^2$ **c** $m^2 + 2mn + n^2$
    d $a^2 + 6a + 9$ **e** $x^2 + 10x + 25$ **f** $x^2 + 22x + 121$
    g $4x^2 + 4x + 1$ **h** $9x^2 + 12x + 4$ **i** $16x^2 + 24x + 9$
    j $25 + 30x + 9x^2$ **k** $49x^2 + 14x + 1$ **l** $4x^2 + 4xy + y^2$
    m $36 + 12x + x^2$ **n** $9 + 30x + 25x^2$ **o** $x^4 + 2x^2 + 1$
    p $x^4 + 2x^3 + x^2$

2   **a** $x^2 - 2xy + y^2$ **b** $r^2 - 2rs + s^2$ **c** $d^2 - 2dc + c^2$
    d $d^2 - 6d + 9$ **e** $16 - 8a + a^2$ **f** $49 - 14x + x^2$
    g $9x^2 - 6x + 1$ **h** $25 - 10d + d^2$ **i** $4x^2 - 20x + 25$
    j $9 - 24a + 16a^2$ **k** $9a^2 - 12ab + 4b^2$ **l** $x^4 - 4x^2 + 4$
    m $36 - 12x + x^2$ **n** $9 - 30x + 25x^2$
    o $x^4 - 2x^3 + x^2$ **p** $x^2 - 4x^3 + 4x^4$

EXERCISE 4C.3

1   **a** $y^2 - 16$ **b** $b^2 - 1$ **c** $x^2 - 81$ **d** $a^2 - 64$
    e $25 - b^2$ **f** $4 - x^2$ **g** $100 - a^2$ **h** $49 - y^2$
    i $9x^2 - 4$ **j** $16x^2 - 9$ **k** $1 - 4y^2$ **l** $25 - 9a^2$

EXERCISE 4C.4

1   **a** $x^2 + 2x - 8$ **b** $x^2 - x - 6$ **c** $x^2 + 6x + 9$
    d $2 - 3x + x^2$ **e** $-x^2 + 6x - 8$ **f** $x^2 - 14x + 49$
    g $x^2 - 36$ **h** $x^2 + 20x + 100$ **i** $4x^2 - 49$
    j $2x^2 - 7x - 15$ **k** $4x^2 + 44x + 121$ **l** $x^2 - a^2$
    m $3x^2 - 13x - 10$ **n** $4x^2 - 36x + 81$ **o** $9x^2 - 25$
    p $-3x^2 + 2x + 8$ **q** $25 - 10x + x^2$ **r** $10x^2 + 13x - 3$

2   **b** $6\frac{1}{4}$ **c** **i** $12\frac{1}{4}$ **ii** $110\frac{1}{4}$ **iii** $420\frac{1}{4}$

EXERCISE 4C.5

1   **a** $2x^2 + 10x + 8$ **b** $3x^2 + 27x + 60$ **c** $4x^2 - 24x + 20$
    d $12 - 10x + 2x^2$ **e** $-5x^2 - 45x - 70$ **f** $-3x^2 + 3x + 18$
    g $-8 + 12x - 4x^2$ **h** $x^2 - x - 6$ **i** $x^2 - 3x - 10$
    j $63 - 7x^2$ **k** $2x^2 - 50$ **l** $-3x^2 + 24x - 48$

2   **a** $2x^2 + 12x + 18$ **b** $12 - 12x + 3x^2$
    c $5a^2 + 10ab + 5b^2$ **d** $-4x^2 - 8x - 4$
    e $-x^2 - 4x - 4$ **f** $8x^2 + 8x + 2$ **g** $2x^2 - 8x + 12$
    h $-3x^2 - 12x - 11$ **i** $-2x^2 + 16x - 24$

3   **a** $x^2 + 7x + 7$ **b** $x^2 + 14x - 7$ **c** $3x^2 + 2x + 3$
    d $3x^2 + 15x + 16$ **e** $2x - 5$ **f** $4x^2 - 4x + 4$
    g $5x^2 - 2x + 11$ **h** $-2x^2 - 22x + 7$
    i $-x^2 + 22x + 27$ **j** $2x^2 - 7x + 14$
    k $-18x^2 - 36x + 27$ **l** $x^2 + 14x - 5$

EXERCISE 4D

1   **a** 7   **b** 5   **c** 21   **d** 19   **e** 8   **f** 17   **g** 35   **h** 24

2   **a** 15   **b** 14   **c** 8   **d** 21   **e** 18   **f** 80
    g 12   **h** 50   **i** 30   **j** 30   **k** 24   **l** 4

3   **a** $9\sqrt{2}$ **b** $2\sqrt{3}$ **c** $13\sqrt{7}$ **d** $2\sqrt{3}$
    e $5\sqrt{2}$ **f** $2\sqrt{2} + 3$ **g** $-\sqrt{3}$ **h** $4\sqrt{2}$
    i $3\sqrt{2} + \sqrt{3}$ **j** $-\sqrt{3}$ **k** $4\sqrt{7}$ **l** $5\sqrt{5}$

4   **a** $3\sqrt{2} - 2$ **b** $3 + \sqrt{3}$ **c** $\sqrt{3} - 3$ **d** $7\sqrt{7} - 7$
    e $2\sqrt{5} - 5$ **f** $22 - \sqrt{11}$ **g** $\sqrt{6} - 12$ **h** $4\sqrt{2} + 4$
    i $6 - 3\sqrt{2}$ **j** $6\sqrt{2} - 4$ **k** $6\sqrt{5} - 10$ **l** $9 + 15\sqrt{3}$

5   **a** $2 - 3\sqrt{2}$ **b** $2 - 4\sqrt{2}$ **c** $-3 - \sqrt{3}$
    d $-2\sqrt{3} - 3$ **e** $-5 - 2\sqrt{5}$ **f** $-3 - \sqrt{2}$
    g $4\sqrt{5} - 5$ **h** $-3 + \sqrt{7}$ **i** $11 - 2\sqrt{11}$
    j $4 - 2\sqrt{2}$ **k** $9 - 15\sqrt{3}$ **l** $-21\sqrt{2} - 14$

6   **a** $4 + 3\sqrt{2}$ **b** $9 + 5\sqrt{3}$ **c** $1 + \sqrt{3}$ **d** $10 + \sqrt{2}$
    e -2 **f** $3 - 3\sqrt{7}$ **g** $-1 - \sqrt{5}$ **h** $9 + 4\sqrt{3}$
    i $14 - 7\sqrt{2}$ **j** $17 - 10\sqrt{3}$ **k** $-6 + 5\sqrt{2}$ **l** $23 + 16\sqrt{2}$

7   **a** $3 + 2\sqrt{2}$ **b** $7 - 4\sqrt{3}$ **c** $7 + 4\sqrt{3}$
    d $6 + 2\sqrt{5}$ **e** $27 - 10\sqrt{2}$ **f** $22 - 8\sqrt{6}$
    g $51 - 10\sqrt{2}$ **h** $17 - 12\sqrt{2}$ **i** $19 + 6\sqrt{2}$
    j $73 + 40\sqrt{3}$ **k** $16 - 6\sqrt{7}$ **l** $53 + 12\sqrt{11}$

8   **a** 13   **b** 23   **c** 31   **d** 2   **e** -2 **f** -1
    g 17   **h** 23   **i** -5

ANSWERS 509

REVIEW SET 4A
1 **a** $2x + 22$ **b** $14x - 4x^2$ **c** $8x - 12$
2 **a** $4x - 3$ **b** $17x - x^2$
3 **a** $x^3 + 8x^2 + 3x + 24$ **b** $x^2 - 8x + 16$ **c** $49 - 28x + 4x^2$
4 **a** $-x^3 - 2x^2 + 3x$ **b** $x^3 - x^2 - 5x + 2$
5 **a** $-2\sqrt{2}$ **b** $6 + \sqrt{6}$ **c** $-15 + 2\sqrt{5}$
6 **a** $7 - 4\sqrt{3}$ **b** $1 + \sqrt{2}$ **c** 7 **7** $2x^2 - 9x - 6$

REVIEW SET 4B
1 **a** $3x - 24$ **b** $6x - 12$ **c** $2x^4 - 2x^3 + 2x^2$
2 **a** $4x - x^2$ **b** $-x - 16$
3 **a** $x^2 + 12x + 36$ **b** $4x^2 - 20x + 25$ **c** $9x^2 - 49$
4 **a** $6x^3 + 15x^2 - 3x$ **b** $2x^3 - 5x^2 + 11x - 12$
5 **a** $7\sqrt{3}$ **b** $4\sqrt{5} - 20$ **c** $7 - 7\sqrt{7}$
6 **a** $12 + 6\sqrt{3}$ **b** $-4 + 5\sqrt{2}$ **c** 15 **7** $3x^2 - 8x - 3$

EXERCISE 5A
1 **a** concert **b** 1000 people **c** 29.7%
2 **a** Shows sales of Daily News figures from September 2004 to September 2007.
   b **i** 570 475 **ii** 581 384 **c** Sept 04 - Mar 05
   d **i** 28 188 **ii** 12 653 **e** 97.3%
3 **a** **i** £350 000 **ii** £269 000 **b** £42 000 **c** 91.4%
4 **a** **i** €4500 million **ii** 22.2% **b** 2004/2005, 2005/2006
   c 2005/2006, possible drought year
5 **a** New Zealand **b** **i** 23.7% **ii** 6.2%
   c **i** 1106 **ii** 5467
6 **a** driver **b** **i** 40 **ii** 22 **iii** 18
7 **a** **i** 35% **ii** 19% **b** **i** 29 **ii** 10
8 **a** 120 000 **b** 60% **c** 2003 **d** 33.3%
9 **a** 2007 **b** **i** $\approx$ \$13 **ii** $\approx$ \$20.50 **c** 26% **d** 20%
10 **a** Dairy, Edible oils, Meat/Fish/Eggs, Veg/Fruit
   b Decrease of 11.8% **c** **i** 14.2% **ii** 18.9%
   d 23.2% **e** In **c i** yes, in **c ii** no, in **d** no.
11 **a** **i** 131 km **ii** 2 hrs 20 mins
   b **i** 1 hr 50 mins **ii** 108 km
   c **i** 78 km **ii** Taupo and Rotorua
   d **i** Auckland (280 km from Taupo) and Palmerston North (263 km from Taupo)
      ii Auckland (131 km from Hamilton) and Taupo (149 km from Hamilton)
      iii Winding roads take longer to travel on than straight roads.

EXERCISE 5B
1 *(distance-time graph: rises from 0 to 15 km between 0 and 15 min, flat at 15 km from 15 to 45 min, descends to 0 at 60 min)*
2 **a** They travelled 50 km in the first hour and 70 km in the second. After stopping for 45 minutes, they continued at 10:45 am, and by 1 pm were at the 330 km mark. Here they stopped for an hour for lunch, and continued on at 2 pm. By 3:20 pm they had travelled a further 100 km, and after stopping for 20 minutes, they drove on again, arriving at Goa at 4:40 pm.

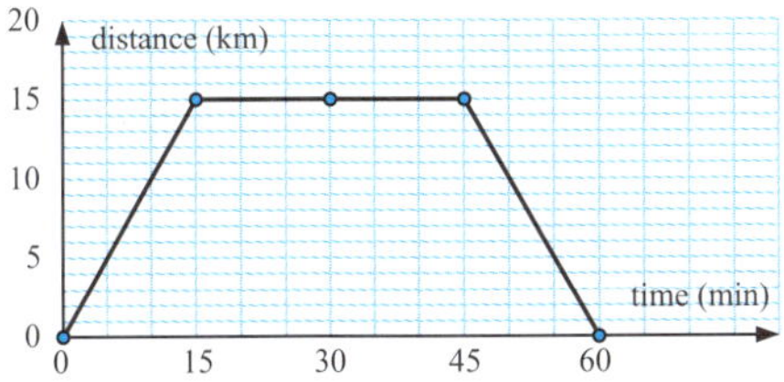

b **i** E **ii** between H and I **iii** I **iv** G
   v between A and B **vi** between D and E
3 **a** tortoise
   b *(graph: metres from starting line vs minutes, step-like curve reaching 800 m at 20 min, with dotted diagonal reference line)*
   c hare
   d *(graph: metres from starting line vs minutes, step-like curve reaching 800 m, with dotted diagonal reference line)*
4 **a** Route B **b** Route C **c** Route A
5 **a** 12 km **b** 26 minutes **c** **i** 4.5 km **ii** 8.5 km
   d **i** 14 mins **ii** 18.8 mins **e** 27.7 km per hour
6 **a** 40 mins **b** 390 km **c** $\approx$ 280 km
   d $X = 3$ hrs, Y : 4 hrs **e** 1 hour
   f X : 97.5 km per hour, Y : 78 km per hour

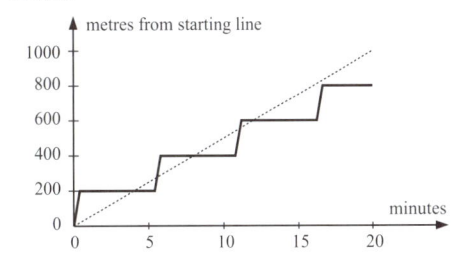

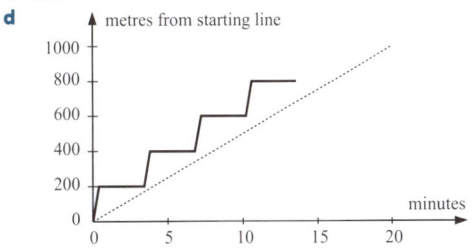

EXERCISE 5C
1 **a** A **b** C **c** B **2 a** C **b** B **c** A

EXERCISE 5D
1 **a**

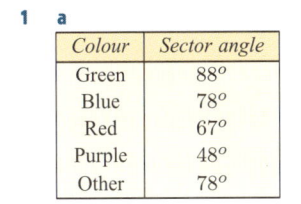

Colour	Sector angle
Green	$88°$
Blue	$78°$
Red	$67°$
Purple	$48°$
Other	$78°$

b *(pie chart with sectors: Green, Blue, Red, Purple, Other)*

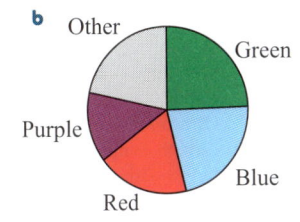

2 **a** 188 students **b** $9.5°$ **c** 1440 students
3 **a** *(bar chart: income after 5 years and after 10 years for Kaylene, Harry, Wei, Matthew)*
   b *(horizontal bar chart: after 5 years and after 10 years for Matthew, Wei, Harry, Kaylene)*

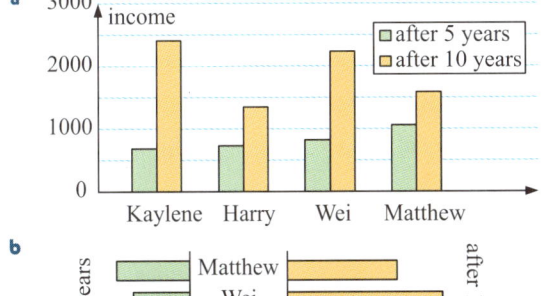

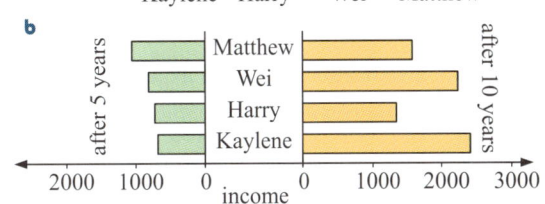

c

Graduate	% increase
Kaylene	252
Henry	84.8
Wei	173
Matthew	49.8

d Kaylene and Wei

REVIEW SET 5A

1 a i $21.6 million **ii** $15.84 million **b** $5.76 million **c i** 25% **ii** $4.14 million
2 a 745 **b** 26.6% **c** 82.6% **d** 55 - 64 **e** 20.1%
3 a i $\approx$ $80 000 **ii** $\approx$ $205 000 **b** $\approx$ 156%
 c March 2002 - March 2006
4 a The levels of ultraviolet radiation recorded from 8 am until 6 pm.
 b 12 noon **c** 6 **d** between 9:30 am and 3 pm
5 a 6000 km
 b The flight from B to A was completed 1 hour faster.
 c 3 hours
 d A to B: 857 km per hour, B to A: 1000 km per hour

REVIEW SET 5B

1 a production **b i** €500 000 **ii** €125 000
 c 20% decrease
2 a The total number of detections and revenue from speeding fines for the years 2004 - 2007.
 b 2005 **c** £35 163 339
 d A sharp decline in speeding fines in 2007.
3 a Shows the % cost breakdown in CD selling price.
 b retail margin **c** distribution **d** 23.8%
 e i $2.16 **ii** $3.20 **iii** $3.77
 f 99.9%, error due to rounding off
4 a December 2004 **b** $\approx$ 200 home sales **c** $\approx$ 650
 d $\approx$ 430 (April 2005)
 e Sale figures were higher in the June '04 to December '04 period than in the January '05 to June '05 period.
5 a 900 km **b** 1 hour
 c Gallelli family: 66.7 km per hour,
   Ortuso family: 100 km per hour
 d Gallelli family: 81.8 km per hour,
   Ortuso family: 75 km per hour

EXERCISE 6A

1 a $x = 7$ **b** $a = 4$ **c** $x = -4$ **d** $y = 1$
2 a A **b** A **c** D **d** A **e** B **f** C
 g D **h** A **i** B **j** C **k** E **l** A

EXERCISE 6B

1 a $x = 10$ **b** $x = 13$ **c** $2x = 14$ **d** $3x = 11$
2 a $x = 1$ **b** $x = -6$ **c** $2x = -5$ **d** $3x = -10$
3 a $3x = -9$ **b** $15x = 5$ **c** $x = 8$ **d** $x = -4$
 e $x = 6$ **f** $x = -40$
4 a $x = 4$ **b** $x = -6$ **c** $x + 4 = 0$
 d $x - 3 = 8$ **e** $x + 2 = -3$ **f** $x - 1 = 4$

EXERCISE 6C

1 a Start with x, multiply by 5, then add 2.
 b Start with x, multiply by -1, then add 7.
 c Start with x, add 6 and then multiply all of this by 5.
 d Start with x, subtract 3 and then multiply all of this by 8.
 e Start with x, add 2 and then divide all of this by 3.
 f Start with x, subtract 4 and then divide all of this by 5.
 g Start with x, divide by 7 and then add 2 to this fraction.
 h Start with x, divide by 3 and then subtract 4 from this fraction.
 i Start with x, multiply it by -2 and then add 1. Divide the whole of this by 3.
 j Start with x, multiply by 3 and then subtract 4. Divide the whole of this by 2.
 k Start with x, add 6 and then divide all of this by 3. Finally add 5 to this fraction.
 l Start with x, multiply by 2 and then subtract 1. Divide all of this by 4 and finally subtract 11 from this fraction.
2 a Subtract 5. **b** Add 7. **c** Divide by 2.
 d Multiply by 5. **e** Divide by 3. **f** Multiply by 4.
 g Add 6. **h** Subtract 11 and multiply or divide by -1.
 i Subtract 1, then divide by 2. **j** Add 2, then divide by 3.
 k Subtract 7, then divide by 5.
 l Subtract 1, then divide by -2.
 m Subtract 2, then divide by -4.
 n Subtract 17, then divide by -3.
 o Subtract 2, then multiply by 3.
 p Add 2, then multiply by 4.
 q Multiply by 2, then add 1 and then divide by 3.
 r Multiply by 3, then subtract 5 and then divide by 2.
 s Add 2, then multiply by 3 and then subtract 1.
 t Subtract 5, then multiply by 2 and then take 3.
 u Subtract 1, then multiply by $\frac{3}{2}$.
 v Subtract 6, then multiply by $-\frac{4}{3}$.
 w Multiply by 2, then add 5 and then divide by 6.
 x Multiply by 3, then subtract 1 and then divide by 4.

EXERCISE 6D

1 a $x = -3$ **b** $x = -3$ **c** $x = -2$ **d** $x = -\frac{2}{3}$
 e $x = 2$ **f** $x = 2\frac{1}{2}$ **g** $x = 2$ **h** $x = -4\frac{1}{3}$
 i $x = -1$ **j** $x = \frac{2}{3}$ **k** $x = 1$ **l** $x = -\frac{7}{2}$
2 a $x = 11$ **b** $x = -3\frac{3}{4}$ **c** $x = -2$ **d** $x = 3$
 e $x = \frac{5}{7}$ **f** $x = 9$ **g** $x = -4$ **h** $x = 8$
 i $x = -2\frac{1}{2}$ **j** $x = -1$ **k** $x = 3$ **l** $x = -5$
3 a $x = 10$ **b** $x = -6$ **c** $x = -16$ **d** $x = 9$
 e $x = 3$ **f** $x = -8$
4 a $x = -3\frac{1}{2}$ **b** $x = 1$ **c** $x = 5$ **d** $x = 3$
 e $x = 3$ **f** $x = -4\frac{1}{2}$

EXERCISE 6E

1 a $x = 3$ **b** $x = 3$ **c** $x = -2$ **d** $x = -6$
 e $x = -1$ **f** $x = 5\frac{1}{3}$
2 a $x = -2$ **b** $x = -5$ **c** $x = 5$ **d** $x = -2$
 e $x = 7$ **f** $x = 0$
3 a $x = 4$ **b** $x = -3\frac{1}{3}$ **c** $x = \frac{1}{4}$ **d** $x = 1$
 e $x = -3$ **f** $x = -6\frac{1}{2}$
4 a $x = -1$ **b** $x = 3$ **c** $x = 2\frac{1}{3}$ **d** $x = \frac{3}{5}$
 e $x = -2$ **f** $x = 1\frac{3}{4}$
5 a $x = 6$ **b** $x = \frac{1}{3}$ **c** $x = 2$ **d** $x = 2$
 e $x = -2$ **f** $x = 3$ **g** $x = 8$ **h** $x = 4$
 i $x = 2$ **j** $x = -1\frac{1}{3}$ **k** true for all x
 l no solution; impossible equation

EXERCISE 6F

1   **a** $x=10$ **b** $x=3\frac{1}{3}$ **c** $x=1$ **d** $x=\frac{3}{4}$
  e $x=2$ **f** $x=\frac{3}{25}$ **g** $x=1\frac{1}{5}$ **h** $x=\frac{5}{8}$

2   **a** $x=3$ **b** $x=8$ **c** $x=2\frac{1}{4}$ **d** $x=-5\frac{1}{2}$
  e $x=2$ **f** $x=-1\frac{3}{7}$ **g** $x=-1\frac{1}{4}$ **h** $x=1$
  i no solution; impossible equation

3   **a** $x=2\frac{6}{7}$ **b** $x=-5$ **c** $x=8$ **d** $x=-\frac{6}{17}$
  e $x=\frac{9}{56}$ **f** $x=-2\frac{18}{19}$

4   **a** $x=-\frac{1}{4}$ **b** $x=\frac{13}{18}$ **c** $x=-3\frac{7}{9}$ **d** $x=5\frac{1}{6}$
  e $x=-\frac{19}{68}$ **f** $x=4\frac{5}{14}$

5   **a** $x=35$ **b** $x=\frac{4}{3}$ **c** $x=-13\frac{1}{3}$
  d $x=3\frac{1}{2}$ **e** $x=0$ **f** $x=11$

EXERCISE 6G

1   **a** $x=10$ **b** $x=12$ **c** $x=3\frac{1}{2}$ **d** $x=1\frac{2}{3}$
  e $x=\frac{4}{9}$ **f** $x=\frac{2}{3}$ **g** $x=-\frac{7}{8}$ **h** $x=-\frac{3}{35}$

2   **a** $x=-\frac{1}{14}$ **b** $x=3$ **c** $x=-1\frac{3}{4}$ **d** $x=-2$
  e no solution; impossible equation   **f** $x=-2\frac{2}{7}$

REVIEW SET 6A

1   $x=7$ 2   B

3   Start with x, multiply it by 2 and then add 1. Divide the whole of this by 3.

4   Add 7 and then divide by 5.   5   Divide by 2 and then add 3.

6   **a** $x=-8$ **b** $x=22\frac{1}{2}$ **c** $x=-1$

7   **a** $x=3\frac{3}{4}$ **b** $x=-2$

8   **a** $x=\frac{1}{10}$ **b** $x=2$ **c** $x=11$

REVIEW SET 6B

1   $x=-3$ 2   A

3   Start with x, subtract 3 and then multiply all of this by 4.

4   Start with x, divide by 5 and then add 3 to this fraction.

5   Multiply by 4, subtract 3 and then divide by 2.

6   **a** $x=2$ **b** $x=-4\frac{1}{2}$ **c** $x=3$

7   **a** $x=2\frac{1}{2}$ **b** $x=1$

8   **a** $x=1\frac{5}{9}$ **b** $x=-6\frac{3}{4}$ **c** $x=-2\frac{3}{5}$

EXERCISE 7A

1   **a** true   **b** true   **c** false   **d** false   **e** false   **f** true

2   **a** $b=45$ **b** $a=113$ **c** $a=153$ **d** $b=180$
  e $b=91$ **f** $a=b=90$

3   **a** $54°$ **b** $19°$ **c** $(90-a)°$ **d** $x°$

4   **a** $101°$ **b** $67°$ **c** $(180-n)°$ **d** $m°$ **e** $(90-a)°$

5   **a** $x=108$ {vertically opposite angles}
  b $a=143$ {angles on a line}
  c $b=49$ {angles at a point}
  d $x=61$ {alternate angles}
  e $x=331$ {angles at a point}
  f $y=53$ {cointerior angles}
  g $a=51$ {complementary angles}
  h $z=110$ {cointerior angles}
  i $c=103$ {corresponding angles}
  j $m=226$ {angles at a point}
  k $g=123$ {cointerior angles}
  l $a=115$ {alternate angles}
  m $b=130$ {corresponding angles}
  n $x=39$, $y=39$ {vertically opposite, corresponding}
  o $a=60$, $b=60$ {angles on a line, corresponding}
  p $x=108$, $y=108$ {cointerior angles}
  q $n=140$ {angles at a point}
  r $a=90$ {angles on a line}
  s $a=55$, $b=55$ {angles on a line, corresponding}
  t $x=146$, $y=146$ {corresponding angles}
  u $a=120$, $b=120$, $c=60$, $d=60$
     {vertically opposite, corresponding, angles on a line}

6   **a** $d=130$ {angles at a point}
  b $g=54$ {angles at a point}
  c $e=120$ {angles at a point}
  d $h=60$ {angles on a line}
  e $n=36$ {angles on a line/equal corresponding angles}
  f $x=75$ {cointerior angles}
  g $x=45$ {angles on a line}
  h $x=5$ {complementary angles}
  i $x=42$ {angles at a point}

7   **a** parallel   {alternate angles are equal}
  b not parallel   {cointerior angles are not supplementary}
  c parallel   {corresponding angles are equal}

EXERCISE 7B

1   **a** $a=52$ {angles of a triangle}
  b $b=130$ {angles of a triangle}
  c $x=61$ {angles of a triangle}
  d $x=55$ {exterior angle of a triangle}
  e $y=120$ {exterior angle of a triangle}
  f $e=154$ {exterior angle of a triangle}

2   **a** [AC]   **b** [AB]   **c** [BC]   **d** [BC]   **e** [BC]
  f [BC]   **g** [BC]   **h** [AB]   **i** [BC]

3   **a** true   **b** false   **c** false   **d** false

4   **a** $m=60$ {angles of a triangle}
  b $b=36$ {angles of a triangle}
  c $x=80$, $y=60$
     {vertically opposite angles/angles of a triangle}
  d $a=80$, $b=50$
     {equal corresponding angles/angles of a triangle}
  e $a=50$, $b=120$
     {angles on a line/exterior angle of a triangle}
  f $a=80$, $b=60$, $c=140$, $d=40$
     {vertically opposite/angles on a line/exterior angle of a triangle}

5   $46°$, $52°$, $82°$

EXERCISE 7C

1   **a** $x=50$ {isosceles triangle/angles of a triangle}
  b $x=50$ {isosceles triangle/angles of a triangle}
  c $x=75$ {isosceles triangle/angles of a triangle}
  d $x=36$ {isosceles triangle/angles of a triangle}
  e $x=35$ {isosceles triangle/angles of a triangle}
  f $x=80$ {isosceles triangle/exterior angle of a triangle}

2   **a** $x=12$ {isosceles triangle}
  b $x=8$ {isosceles triangle}
  c $x=90$ {isosceles triangle/line to midpoint of base}

3 **a** equilateral **b** isosceles **c** equilateral **d** isosceles
  e isosceles **f** isosceles
4 **a** $x = 56$ **b** isosceles
5 **a** $x = 72$ **b** $y = 54$ **c** $108°$
6 **a** $x = 45$ **b** $y = 67\frac{1}{2}$ **c** $135°$

EXERCISE 7D.1

1 **a** two, $2 \times 180° = 360°$ **b** three, $3 \times 180° = 540°$
  c seven, $7 \times 180° = 1260°$
2 **a** $x = 87$ **b** $x = 43$ **c** $x = 36.5$ **d** $x = 90$
  e $x = 60$ **f** $x = 151$ **g** $x = 108$ **h** $x = 110$
  i $x = 120$
3 13 angles **4** No such polygon exists.
5

Regular polygon	No. of sides	No. of angles	Size of each angle
equilateral triangle	3	3	$60°$
square	4	4	$90°$
pentagon	5	5	$108°$
hexagon	6	6	$120°$
octagon	8	8	$135°$
decagon	10	10	$144°$

6 **a** $180(n-2)°$ **b** $\dfrac{180(n-2)°}{n}$ **7** 12 sides **8** No

EXERCISE 7D.2

1 **a** $x = 142$ **b** $x = 112$ **c** $x = 58$
2

Regular polygon	Sum of exterior angles	Size of each exterior angle	Size of each interior angle
square	$360°$	$90°$	$90°$
pentagon	$360°$	$72°$	$108°$
hexagon	$360°$	$60°$	$120°$
octagon	$360°$	$45°$	$135°$

EXERCISE 7E

1 **a** $x°$ **b** $x°$ **c** $x°$ [AE] bisects $\widehat{CAD}$
2 **b** $90°$ **c** $\widehat{APB}$ is $90°$
  e isosceles triangles, $AO = OP$ and $OB = OP$
  $\widehat{OPA} = x°$, $\widehat{OPB} = y°$, $\widehat{APB} = x° + y°$
  But $x + (x + y) + y = 180$
  $\therefore\ 2x + 2y = 180$ $\therefore\ x + y = 90$
  $\widehat{APB}$ is always a right angle.
3 **c** The angle at the centre is double the angle at the circumference.
  e We have created two isosceles triangles as $OA = OB = OC$.
  $\widehat{OCA} = a°$ and $\widehat{OCB} = b°$ $\therefore\ \widehat{ACB} = a° + b°$
  Now $\widehat{AOX} = 2a°$ Likewise $\widehat{BOX} = 2b°$
  $\therefore\ \widehat{AOB} = 2a° + 2b° = 2(a° + b°)$
  So, $\widehat{AOB}$ is always twice $\widehat{ACB}$.
4 **c** The opposite angles of a quadrilateral add to $180°$.
  e We have created four isosceles triangles as
  $OA = OB = OC = OD$.
  $\widehat{ODA} = a°$, $\widehat{OAB} = b°$, $\widehat{OBC} = c°$, $\widehat{OCD} = d°$
  Now $\widehat{DAB} + \widehat{DCB} = a° + b° + c° + d°$
  But the sum of the four original angles is
  $(a + b) + (b + c) + (c + d) + (d + a)$
  $= 2a + 2b + 2c + 2d$

$\therefore\ 2a + 2b + 2c + 2d = 360$
$\therefore\ a + b + c + d = 180$
So, opposite angles of a quadrilateral add to $180°$.

5 Hint: Find $\widehat{ABC}$, then $\widehat{DAX}$ and $\widehat{XDA}$.

EXERCISE 7F

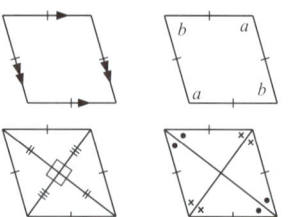

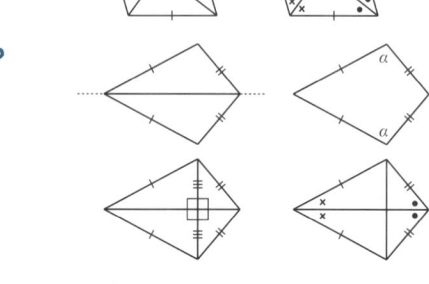

1 **a**

b

2 **a** $x = 40$ {opposite angles of a parallelogram}
  b $x = 6$, $y = 5$ {diagonals of a parallelogram}
  c $x = 90$, $y = 40$
    {diagonals of a rhombus/exterior angles of a triangle}
  d $a = 71$, $b = 124$ {cointerior angles are supplementary}
  e $x = 50$ {diagonals of a rhombus}
  f $x = 90$ {diagonals of a kite}
  g $y = 120$ {angles of a kite}
  h $x = 6$ {diagonals of a rhombus/Pythagoras}
  i $x = 2.5$ {Pythagoras/diagonals of a rectangle}
3 It is a rectangle. **4** It is a square.
5 a parallelogram, use Pythagoras' theorem, with a diagonal strut, congruent

REVIEW SET 7A

1 **a** $a = 110$ {angles on a line}
  b $b = 90$ {angles on a line}
  c $c = 130$ {vertically opposite angles}
  d $a = 70$, $b = 70$
    {vertically opposite angles/corresponding angles}
  e $a = 60$ {corresponding angles/angles of a triangle}
  f $a = 65$, $b = 75$, $c = 40$
    {alternate, corresponding angles/angles on a line}
2 **a** $x = 60$ {angles of a triangle}
  b $p = 75$ {exterior angle of a triangle}
  c $n = 114$ {exterior angle of an isosceles triangle}
  d $x = 70$ {base angles of an isosceles triangle}
  e $x = 102$ {angles of a pentagon}
  f $x = 60$ {exterior angles of a quadrilateral}
3 **a** true **b** true **c** false **d** false
4 **a** acute angled isosceles **b** obtuse angled scalene
  c right angled isosceles
5 **a** kite **b** parallelogram **c** trapezium

ANSWERS 513

REVIEW SET 7B

1
 a $b = 140$ {angles at a point}
 b $a = 54$ {angles at a point}
 c $x = 65$ {vertically opposite angles}
 d $x = 110$ {corresponding, cointerior angles}
 e $x = 120$, $y = 60$
   {opposite angles of rhombus/cointerior angles}
 f The parallelogram is a rectangle (as one angle is $90°$).
   The diagonals create 4 isosceles triangles.
   The bottom one has angles x, x and y.
   $\therefore\ 2x + y = 180°$ and $x = 40$ {alternate angles}
   $\therefore\ y = 100$.

2
 a $x = 25$ {exterior angle of a triangle}
 b $x = 65$, $y = 65$
   {angles of isosceles triangle/corresponding angles}
 c $x = 60$, $y = 45$ {cointerior angles}
 d $x = 65$ {alternate angles}
 e $a = 130$ {angles of a kite}
 f $x = 8$ {isosceles triangle/Pythagoras}

3
 a right angled scalene **b** equilateral triangle
 c obtuse angled isosceles

4
 a $x = 80$ {angles of an isosceles triangle}
 b $x = 130$ {exterior angle of a triangle}
 c $x = 115$ {exterior angle of an isosceles triangle}
 d $a = 60$ {angles of a quadrilateral}
 e $x = 70$ {angles of a quadrilateral}
 f $x = 8$ {isosceles triangles}

5
 a acute angled isosceles triangle {equal base angles}
 b regular pentagon {equal sides and equal angles}
 c parallelogram {pairs of opposite sides are parallel}

EXERCISE 8A

1 a a^2 **b** b^3 **c** c^4 **d** n^4 **e** m^3 **f** s^5
 g e^6 **h** k^5 **i** p^6 **j** p^3 **k** k^9 **l** m^4
 m k^7 **n** n^6 **o** e^8 **p** n^4

2 a a^4 **b** s^6 **c** g^6 **d** a^2c^2
 e m^8 **f** $9a^2b^2$ **g** $4a^4$ **h** $25b^4$
 i $9a^2b^4$ **j** $49m^4n^2$ **k** $64a^4c^2$ **l** $27x^6y^3$
 m a^2 **n** $4a^2$ **o** $-27b^3$ **p** $-50a^3$

3 a a **b** m^2 **c** 1 **d** y^2 **e** k^3 **f** p^2
 g $2n^4$ **h** $2r$ **i** $4g^3$ **j** $\dfrac{2d^5}{3}$ **k** $5e^5$ **l** $\dfrac{h^5}{3}$

EXERCISE 8B

1 a 2^6 **b** 3^4 **c** 5^7 **d** 7^5 **e** a^5 **f** n^5
 g x^{11} **h** b^7

2 a 2^3 **b** 3 **c** 5^2 **d** 10^3 **e** x^5 **f** y^6
 g a **h** b^5

3 a 2^6 **b** 10^8 **c** 3^{12} **d** 2^{15} **e** x^{12} **f** x^{10}
 g a^{20} **h** b^{21}

4 a a^5 **b** b^5 **c** c^7 **d** d^5 **e** a^{12} **f** b^3
 g b^{10} **h** a^{n+3} **i** b **j** m^9 **k** a^7 **l** g^{11}

5 a a^2 **b** $8b^5$ **c** $40h^5k^3$ **d** $7a^5$
 e $4ab^2$ **f** m^3n **g** m^5 **h** p^3

EXERCISE 8C

1 a a^4b^4 **b** x^3y^3 **c** a^4c^4 **d** $x^3y^3z^3$
 e $32x^5$ **f** $81a^4$ **g** $8m^3$ **h** $125a^3b^3$

2 a $\dfrac{x^2}{y^2}$ **b** $\dfrac{a^3}{b^3}$ **c** $\dfrac{p^4}{q^4}$ **d** $\dfrac{c^5}{d^5}$ **e** $\dfrac{9}{x^2}$
 f $\dfrac{y^3}{125}$ **g** $\dfrac{16}{a^4}$ **h** $\dfrac{b^5}{32}$

3 a $4a^6$ **b** $25n^4$ **c** $9x^4$ **d** $9a^6$
 e x^2y^4 **f** x^6y^3 **g** $12a^3$ **h** $9a^4b^2$
 i $27a^3b^6$ **j** $49a^6c^2$ **k** $16a^8b^4$ **l** $27a^3b^9$

4 a $\dfrac{a^2b^2}{4}$ **b** $\dfrac{9}{b^2c^2}$ **c** $\dfrac{8m^3}{n^3}$ **d** $\dfrac{m^4}{16}$ **e** $\dfrac{4a^4}{b^2}$
 f $\dfrac{c^6}{8d^3}$ **g** $\dfrac{16a^4}{9b^2}$ **h** $\dfrac{16a^4}{81b^{12}}$

EXERCISE 8D

1 a 1 **b** 1 **c** 1 **d** 1 **e** 1 if $y \neq 0$
 f 1 if $a \neq 0$ **g** 2 if $x \neq 0$ **h** 1 if $x \neq 0$
 i 1 if $x \neq 0$ **j** 1 if $b \neq 0$ **k** 4 **l** 4

2 a $\tfrac{1}{4}$ **b** $\tfrac{1}{2}$ **c** $\tfrac{1}{6}$ **d** $\tfrac{1}{8}$ **e** $\tfrac{1}{4}$ **f** $\tfrac{1}{9}$
 g $\tfrac{1}{49}$ **h** $\tfrac{1}{81}$ **i** $\tfrac{1}{27}$ **j** $\tfrac{1}{100\,000}$

3 a 2 **b** 4 **c** $\tfrac{5}{4}$ **d** $\tfrac{3}{5}$ **e** 9 **f** $\tfrac{3}{2}$
 g $\tfrac{9}{4}$ **h** $\tfrac{16}{49}$ **i** $\tfrac{64}{27}$ **j** $\tfrac{11}{3}$

4 a $\dfrac{2}{a}$ **b** $\dfrac{1}{2a}$ **c** $\dfrac{4}{b}$ **d** $\dfrac{1}{4b}$ **e** $\dfrac{3}{b^2}$ **f** $\dfrac{1}{9b^2}$
 g $\dfrac{1}{25c^2}$ **h** $\dfrac{5}{c^2}$ **i** $\dfrac{x}{y}$ **j** $\dfrac{1}{xy}$ **k** $\dfrac{x}{y^2}$
 l $\dfrac{1}{x^2y^2}$ **m** $\dfrac{2a}{b}$ **n** $\dfrac{1}{2ab}$ **o** $\dfrac{2}{ab}$ **p** $\dfrac{n^2}{3}$

5 a 10^3 **b** 10^6 **c** 10^{-3} **d** 10^{-8}

6 a 2^3 **b** 2^{-3} **c** 3^2 **d** 3^{-2} **e** 5^3 **f** 5^{-3}
 g 2^5 **h** 2^{-5} **i** 3^4 **j** 3^{-4} **k** 5^{-2} **l** 2^0, 3^0 or 5^0

EXERCISE 8E.1

1 a 10^2 **b** 10^3 **c** 10^1 **d** 10^5 **e** 10^{-1}
 f 10^{-2} **g** 10^{-4} **h** 10^8

2 a 2.59×10^2 **b** 2.59×10^5 **c** 2.59×10^0
 d 2.59×10^{-1} **e** 2.59×10^{-4} **f** 4.07×10^1
 g 4.07×10^3 **h** 4.07×10^{-2} **i** 4.07×10^5
 j 4.07×10^8 **k** 4.07×10^{-5}

3 a 1.495×10^{11} m **b** 3×10^{-4} mm **c** 1×10^{-3} mm
 d 1.4162×10^{-7} **e** 1.5×10^7 °C **f** 3×10^5

4 a 4000 **b** 500 **c** 2100 **d** $78\,000$ **e** $380\,000$
 f 86 **g** $43\,300\,000$ **h** $60\,000\,000$

5 a 0.004 **b** 0.05 **c** 0.0021 **d** $0.000\,78$
 e $0.000\,038$ **f** 0.86 **g** $0.000\,000\,433$ **h** $0.000\,000\,6$

6 a $0.000\,000\,9$ m **b** $6\,130\,000\,000$ people
 c $100\,000$ light years **d** $0.000\,01$ mm
 e $0.000\,000\,1$ kg

7 a 6×10^5 **b** 3.5×10^8 **c** 3×10^8 **d** 9×10^6
 e 2.5×10^9 **f** 6.4×10^{-3} **g** 2×10^2 **h** 4×10^2

514   ANSWERS

EXERCISE 8E.2

1 **a** 1.22^{06} **b** 4.64^{-05} **c** 1.26^{-04}
d 2.464^{10} **e** 2.14^{07} **f** 7.31^{-06}

2 **a** 3×10^{-8} **b** 1.36×10^{10} **c** 4.64×10^{10}
d 9.87×10^9 **e** 3.57×10^{-8} **f** 8.74×10^{-6}

3 **a** 1.64×10^{10} **b** 4.12×10^{-3} **c** 5.27×10^{-18}
d 1.36×10^2 **e** 2.63×10^{-6} **f** 1.73×10^9

4 **a** 1.30×10^5 km **b** 9.07×10^5 km **c** 9.47×10^7 km

5 **a** 1.8×10^{10} m **b** 2.59×10^{13} m **c** 9.47×10^{15} m

EXERCISE 8F

1 **a** 570 **b** 16 000 **c** 71 **d** 3.0 **e** 0.72
f 50 **g** 3.0 **h** 1800 **i** 0.041 **j** 46 000

2 **a** 43 600 **b** 10 100 **c** 0.667 **d** 0.0368 **e** 0.319
f 0.720 **g** 0.636 **h** 0.0637 **i** 19.0 **j** 257 000

3 **a** 28.04 **b** 0.005 362 **c** 23 680 **d** 42 370 000
e 0.038 79 **f** 0.006 378 **g** 0.000 900 0 **h** 43.08

4 3.06×10^{24} atoms

REVIEW SET 8A

1 **a** x^{11} **b** a^{12} **c** b^5 **2** **a** 3^6 **b** 3^4

3 **a** 3.762×10^3 **b** 1.043×10^{-4} **c** 8.62×10^0

4 **a** 43 **b** $\frac{7}{2}$ **c** $\frac{64}{25}$

5 **a** 6.4×10^{13} **b** 7×10^7 **c** 1.6×10^4

6 **a** $8x^{13}$ **b** $\frac{8a^6}{b^6}$ **7** **a** 2.66 **b** 0.000 620 **c** 3.14

8 **a** 3.47×10^8 **b** $\approx 1.69 \times 10^{14}$ km
c 6.9×10^{10} km per hour

REVIEW SET 8B

1 **a** a^9 **b** $32x^{15}$ **c** $42c^8$ **2** **a** 7^0 **b** 7^5

3 **a** 3.15×10^{-3} **b** 4.132×10^5 **c** 8.904×10^{-1}

4 **a** $\frac{4}{9}$ **b** $\frac{2}{3}$ **c** -1

5 **a** 6.4×10^{-5} **b** 5×10^5 **c** 3.6×10^5

6 **a** $20d^{31}$ **b** $\frac{16x^2}{y^6}$ **7** **a** 58.0 **b** 0.008 26 **c** 2.82

8 **a** 3.2×10^{-6} **b** $\approx €4.78 \times 10^{10}$
c 6.25×10^{10} cm per second

EXERCISE 9A

1 **a** 4 as $4^2 = 16$ **b** 6 as $6^2 = 36$ **c** 8 as $8^2 = 64$
d 12 as $12^2 = 144$ **e** 9 as $9^2 = 81$ **f** 11 as $11^2 = 121$
g 2 as $2^2 = 4$ **h** 1 as $1^2 = 1$ **i** 0 as $0^2 = 0$
j $\frac{1}{3}$ as $\left(\frac{1}{3}\right)^2 = \frac{1}{9}$ **k** $\frac{1}{7}$ as $\left(\frac{1}{7}\right)^2 = \frac{1}{49}$
l $\frac{5}{8}$ as $\left(\frac{5}{8}\right)^2 = \frac{25}{64}$

2 **a** 1 and 2 **b** 2 and 3 **c** 3 and 4 **d** 5 and 6
e 8 and 9 **f** 10 and 11 **g** 6 and 7 **h** 7 and 8

3 **a** 2.83 **b** 3.87 **c** 4.90 **d** 8.19
e 9.11 **f** 10.54 **g** 11.83 **h** 14.14
i 1.77 **j** 0.20 **k** 0.87 **l** 2.70

EXERCISE 9B

1 **a** 3 **b** 7 **c** 13 **d** 24 **e** $\sqrt{2}$ **f** 2
g 3 **h** $\sqrt{3}$ **i** 8 **j** 45 **k** 98 **l** 28

2 **a** $2\sqrt{2}$ **b** $2\sqrt{6}$ **c** $2\sqrt{7}$ **d** $2\sqrt{13}$ **e** $3\sqrt{2}$ **f** $4\sqrt{2}$
g $3\sqrt{3}$ **h** $4\sqrt{3}$ **i** $6\sqrt{2}$ **j** $5\sqrt{2}$ **k** $5\sqrt{5}$ **l** $3\sqrt{7}$
m $4\sqrt{5}$ **n** $10\sqrt{2}$ **o** $5\sqrt{3}$ **p** $4\sqrt{7}$

EXERCISE 9C

1 **a** $x = \pm 3$ **b** $x = \pm 6$ **c** $x = 0$
d $x = \pm 10$ **e** $x = \pm\sqrt{13}$ **f** $x = \pm\sqrt{29}$
g $x = \pm 4\sqrt{2}$ **h** $x = \pm 7$ **i** no solution
j no solution **k** $x = \pm 3\sqrt{2}$ **l** no solution

2 **a** $x = \pm 2$ **b** $x = \pm 4$ **c** $x = \pm 6$
d $x = \pm 5$ **e** $x = \pm 2$ **f** $x = \pm 2\sqrt{2}$
g $x = \pm 3\sqrt{2}$ **h** $x = \pm 2\sqrt{3}$ **i** $x = \pm 2\sqrt{10}$

3 **a** $x = \pm 3$ **b** $x = \pm 4$ **c** $x = \pm 5$
d $x = \pm 2\sqrt{6}$ **e** $x = \pm 5\sqrt{2}$ **f** $x = \pm 4\sqrt{2}$

EXERCISE 9D

1 **a** 5 cm **b** $\sqrt{65}$ m **c** $\sqrt{109}$ cm **d** 10 cm
e $\sqrt{34}$ cm **f** $2\sqrt{2}$ m

2 **a** 6 m **b** $2\sqrt{6}$ cm **c** $\sqrt{39}$ km **d** 3 km
e $\sqrt{21}$ cm **f** $4\sqrt{2}$ cm

3 **a** $y = 1$ **b** $y = 1$ **c** $y = 2$ **d** $y = 3\sqrt{2}$
e $y = 1$ **f** $y = 2$

4 **a** $x = \sqrt{5}$, $y = \sqrt{6}$ **b** $x = 3$, $y = \sqrt{34}$
c $x = 10$, $y = 2\sqrt{26}$ **d** $x = 6$, $y = \sqrt{13}$
e $x = \sqrt{2}$, $y = \sqrt{3}$, $z = 2$ **f** $x = 2\sqrt{51}$
g $x = \sqrt{10}$ **h** $x = 3\sqrt{3}$ **i** $x = 4\sqrt{2}$

EXERCISE 9E

1 **a** no **b** yes **c** no **d** no **e** no **f** yes

2 **a** right angled at $\widehat{ACB}$ **b** right angled at $\widehat{KLM}$
c right angled at $\widehat{QPR}$ **d** not right angled
e not right angled **f** right angled at $\widehat{XZY}$

EXERCISE 9F

1 **a** yes, $10^2 + 24^2 = 26^2$ **b** no, not integers
c no, $17^2 + 19^2 \neq 25^2$ **d** yes, $12^2 + 16^2 = 20^2$
e yes, $11^2 + 60^2 = 61^2$ **f** no, $23^2 + 36^2 \neq 45^2$

2 **a** $3^2 + 4^2 = 5^2$ **b** yes **c** $3 : 4 : 5$
d yes **e** $3 : 4 : 5$ **f** $x = 30$

4 **a** $x = 10$ **b** $x = 20$ **c** $x = 24$ **d** $x = 2.5$

5 **a** $x = 2\sqrt{2}$ **b** $x = 3\sqrt{2}$ **c** $x = 10\sqrt{2}$ **d** $x = 2$

6 **a** $k = 12$ **b** $k = 17$ **c** $k = 10$ **d** $k = 60$

EXERCISE 9G

1 **a** $\sqrt{117}$ cm **b** ≈ 10.8 cm

2 $\sqrt{35.28}$ (or $4.2\sqrt{2}$) cm ≈ 5.9 cm **3** $\sqrt{13}$ m ≈ 3.61 m

4 ≈ 14.4 cm **5** ≈ 2.74 km **6** 38.2 m **7** 3.46 m

8 **a** Yes, exactly to the bottom of the window.
b It reaches to be 21 m long $\therefore$ retract 3.81 m **c** 8 m

ANSWERS

9 12.8 km **10 a** 26.6 km **b** $\approx$ 2 hours 40 minutes
11 a B 32 km, C 36 km **b** 48.2 km **12** $\approx$ 361 m
13 $\approx$ 5.20 cm **14 a** 4 cm **b** 12 cm^2
15 a 15 cm **b** 1005 cm^3 **16** 33.9 cm
17 28.3 cm $\times$ 28.3 cm **18** 4.12 cm $\times$ 16.5 cm
19 11.5 cm **20** 43.3 cm^2 **21** $\sqrt{40} \approx 6.32$ m

EXERCISE 9H

1 $\sqrt{3} \approx 1.73$ cm **2** $\sqrt{34} \approx 5.83$ m **3** $\sqrt{35} \approx 5.92$ cm
4 $\sqrt{50} \approx 7.07$ cm

EXERCISE 9I

1 a 1 **b** -1 **c** -2 **d** 4 **e** -6 **f** 5
 g -5 **h** 10 **i** -10 **j** 7
2 a ≈ 1.59 **b** ≈ 2.71 **c** ≈ -4.64 **d** ≈ 6.30
 e ≈ -12.6
3 a $x = 2$ **b** $x = -5$ **c** $x = 4$ **d** $x = 0$
 e $x = -3$ **f** $x = -1$ **g** $x = 100$ **h** $x = -9$
4 a $x \approx 4.12$ **b** $x \approx 6.35$ **c** $x \approx -3.66$ **d** $x \approx 9.65$
5 ≈ 6.69 cm

REVIEW SET 9A

1 a no solutions **b** $x = \pm\sqrt{23}$ **c** $x = \pm 2\sqrt{2}$
2 a 11 **b** 12 **c** 5 **d** -3
3 a $3\sqrt{2}$ **b** $12\sqrt{2}$ **4** ≈ 22.5 cm **5** 10 cm
6 a $x = \sqrt{170}$ **b** $x = 4\sqrt{3}$ **c** $x = \sqrt{10}$
7 a no, $5^2 + 6^2 \neq 7^2$ **b** yes, since $(5x)^2 + (12x)^2 = (13x)^2$
8 3.32 m **9** $4\sqrt{5} \approx 8.9$ cm

REVIEW SET 9B

1 a $x = \pm 7$ **b** $x = \pm\sqrt{13}$ **c** $x = \pm 2\sqrt{3}$
2 a $\frac{1}{3}$ **b** 2 **c** 4 **3** $5\sqrt{2}$ **4** $x = -5$
5 a $x = \sqrt{69}$ **b** $x = \sqrt{65}$ **c** any value of $x > 0$
6 a yes, $18 : 24 : 30 = 3 : 4 : 5$ **b** no, $10^2 + 13^2 \neq 17^2$
7 $\sqrt{55} \approx 7.42$ cm **8** 20.6 km **9** 1.56 m **10** 89.4 cm

EXERCISE 10A.1

1 a kilometres **b** metres **c** metres
 d centimetres **e** centimetres **f** millimetres
2 a B **b** C **c** D
4 a 15 000 m **b** 24 cm **c** 3200 cm **d** 4500 mm
 e 4.32 km **f** 0.003 84 km
5 a 962.5 cm **b** 9.625 m **6 a** 6356 m **b** 6.356 km

EXERCISE 10A.2

1 a 15 cm **b** 22 cm **c** 30 cm **d** 26 cm
2 a 1500 m **b** 6000 m **c** \$744 **3** 77 m **4** 5 laps
5 a $P = 5x + 5$ cm **b** $P = 6x - 3$ cm **c** $P = 4x + 16$ cm
 d $P = 6x + 6$ cm **e** $P = 7x + 4$ cm **f** $P = 8x + 12$ cm
 g $P = a + b + c$ cm **h** $P = 9a$ cm **i** $P = 3a + 4$ cm

EXERCISE 10B

1 a 37.7 cm **b** 16.3 m **c** 19.5 cm
2 a 25.13 cm **b** 56.55 m **c** 45.24 km **3** ≈ 22.0 m
4 ≈ 15.7 m **5 a** 251.3 cm **b** 25.13 km **c** 3979 times
6 a 25.71 cm **b** 27.00 cm **c** 23.42 cm **d** 31.42 cm
 e 348.50 m **f** 33.13 cm **g** 37.70 cm **h** 57.13 cm
 i 56.55 cm
7 37.7 cm **8** Both distances are the same; 4π metres
9 15.9 cm **10 a** 1.885 m **b** $\approx 53\,100$ revolutions
11 a $\approx 45\,200$ km **b** $\approx 26\,400$ km per hour
12 a $P = 4\pi x$ **b** $P = 2x + \dfrac{\pi x}{2}$ **c** $P = \pi r + 2r$
 d $P = \pi x + 2x$ **e** $P = 2\pi x + 8x$ **f** $P = \dfrac{\pi\theta r}{180} + 2r$

EXERCISE 10C.1

1 a m^2 **b** cm^2 **c** mm^2 **d** ha **e** m^2 **f** km^2
2 a 2 350 000 cm^2 **b** 365 000 m^2 **c** 32.8 cm^2
 d 365.42 m^2 **e** 78.2 ha **f** 880 mm^2
 g 500 ha **h** 30 km^2 **i** 50 000 000 m^2

EXERCISE 10C.2

1 a 10.24 m^2 **b** 54 cm^2 **c** 42 m^2 **d** 85.5 cm^2
 e 10 cm^2 **f** 60 cm^2 **g** 120 m^2 **h** 35 cm^2
 i 72 cm^2
2 ≈ 3050 m^2 **3** 37.5% **4** 640 bricks
5 a $A = 18x^2$ cm^2 **b** $A = x^2 + 10x$ cm^2
 c $A = 3a^2 + 9a$ cm^2

EXERCISE 10D

1 a 153.94 cm^2 **b** 2463.01 cm^2 **c** 17 671.46 mm^2
 d 19.63 cm^2 **e** 37.70 m^2 **f** 40.11 cm^2
2 a 8.17 cm **b** 5.31 cm^2 **3** 36.3 m^2 **4** 91.6 m^2
5 a 55.0 cm^2 **b** 31.4 cm^2 **c** 20.0 m^2

EXERCISE 10E

1 a 78 m^2 **b** 46 m^2 **c** 30 cm^2 **d** 55 m^2
 e 54 cm^2 **f** 78 cm^2
2 a 17 853.98 m^2 **b** 42.06 cm^2 **c** 12.57 cm^2
 d 201.06 cm^2 **e** 16.86 cm^2 **f** 26.30 cm^2
3 225 tiles **4** 64.4 m^2 **5** ≈ 153 m^2 **6** 37.7 m^2
7 2.39 m^2 **8** decreased by 1.14 cm
9 a $A = 10x + 65$ cm^2 **b** $A = 2x^2 + 80x$ cm^2
 c $A = 3x^2 + 9x$ cm^2

EXERCISE 10F.1

1 a 150 mm^2 **b** 105.84 cm^2 **c** 433.5 cm^2
2 a 592 cm^2 **b** 8550 mm^2 **c** 168 m^2
3 a 108 cm^2 **b** 1056 cm^2 **c** 510 m^2
4 a 1264 cm^2 **b** 360 m^2 **c** ≈ 313 m^2
5 Surface area = 45.6 m^2 $\therefore$ 10 cans needed. So, €132.
6 ≈ 348 m^2 **7** $\approx$ £617

EXERCISE 10F.2

1 a ≈ 352 cm^2 **b** ≈ 341 cm^2 **c** ≈ 44.9 cm^2
 d ≈ 100 m^2 **e** ≈ 820 cm^2 **f** ≈ 292 m^2
2 a $\approx 11\,300$ cm^2 **b** ≈ 63.6 m^2 **c** ≈ 509 cm^2
3 a $A = 150x^2$ **b** $A = 14x^2$ **c** $A = 5x^2 + \sqrt{5}x^2$
 d $A = 10\pi x^2$ **e** $A = 9\pi x^2$ **f** $A = 64x^2 + 12\sqrt{5}x^2$

EXERCISE 10G

1 $\approx 21.5\%$ 2 a ≈ 1260 cm^2 b $\approx €8670$ 3 ≈ 27.4 m^2
4 1734 m   5 The rectangle has area 20 cm^2 extra.
6 ≈ 25.2 m   7 ≈ 11.3 cm   8 ≈ 11.9 cm   9 ≈ 35.6 litres
10 565 balls   11 The sphere is $16\pi \approx 50.3$ cm^2 extra.
12 $\approx 5.15 \times 10^8$ km^2

REVIEW SET 10A

1 a 9.5 cm   b 4800 m   c 31 500 m^2
   d 5.5 m^2 e 34 000 cm^2 f 1.85 ha
2 a 38 cm   b ≈ 24.3 m   c ≈ 514 m
3 a 50 cm^2 b ≈ 23.4 m^2 c ≈ 31.7 cm^2
4 a 76 cm^2 b ≈ 478 cm^2 c ≈ 1260 cm^2
5 a 352 m^2 b $2252.80   6 ≈ 13.7 cm^2
7 a i $P = 6x + 8$ cm   ii $A = 2x^2 + 5x + 3$ cm^2
   b i $P = x(\pi + 4)$ cm   ii $A = 2x^2 + \frac{1}{2}\pi x^2$ cm^2

REVIEW SET 10B

1 a 6.89 km   b 294 mm   c 0.88 ha
   d 76 000 m^2 e 8500 mm^2 f 3.4 cm^2
2 a ≈ 158 cm   b 48 m   c 25.1 cm
3 a 12.7 m^2 b 20.5 m^2 c 7.28 m^2
4 a 352 cm^2 b ≈ 129 cm^2 c 208 cm^2
5 $P = 10x + 2\pi x$ m, $A = 12x^2 + 2\pi x^2$ m^2
6 a $x = 3.75$ b 80 m   7 6.68 m   8 8.9 cm

EXERCISE 11A

1 a $x + 5$ b $x + 7$ c $a - 9$ d $x - 2$ e $d + 8$ f $\frac{x}{4}$
   g $2b$ h $2x + 11$ i $3s + 5$
2 a $x - 3$ b $2x$ c $x + 4$ d $\frac{x}{2}$ e $10 - x$ f $\frac{x}{3}$
   g $2x - 3$ h $3x + 7$
3 a $8 - x$ b $\frac{x}{3}$ c $5x$ d $30 - x$ e $x + 1$
   f $x + 1, x + 2$ g $x + 2$ h $x - 1, x - 2$
   i $x - 1, x + 1$ j $x + 7$
4 a $7 - a$ b $b + 1$ c $c - 1, c - 2$
   d $d + 2$ e $p - 2, p + 2$ f $n - t$
5 a $n + (n + 1)$ b $n(n + 2)$
   c $20x + 50(x - 2)$ pence   d $60x + 80(x + 5)$ watts

EXERCISE 11B

1 a $x + 5 = 7$ b $x - 3 = -1$ c $2(x + 5) = 33$
   d $2x + 3 = 7$ e $2x = x - 5$ f $4x = 35 - x$
2 a $x + (x + 1) = 21$ b $x + (x + 1) + (x + 2) = 162$
   c $x + (x + 2) = 78$ d $x + (x + 2) + (x + 4) = 123$
3 a $12(n + 3) + 23n = 281$ b $8h + 6(11 - h) = 80$
   c $2(f + 2) + 5f = 123$
4 a $3s + 11 = 2(s + 11)$ b $2x - 21 = 3(x - 21)$
   c $(x + 10) + 3 = 3(x + 3)$

EXERCISE 11C

1 63, 64   2 6   3 8   4 $2\frac{1}{2}$ 5 6   6 36
7 14 of them   8 12 onions   9 9 small and 5 large
10 $4\frac{1}{4}, 7\frac{3}{4}$ 11 $3\frac{2}{3}, 6\frac{2}{3}$ 12 8, 10, 12
13 8 years old   14 7 years old   15 17 years old

EXERCISE 11D

1 a 8 cm   b 2.5 m   2 a 10 m   b 10.5 cm
3 a 80 cm   b 12 planks
4 a 30 metres per second   b 2.5 seconds
5 a 2 cm   b 7 cm   6 a ≈ 6.37 cm   b ≈ 3.09 cm

EXERCISE 11E

1 a $S \leqslant 40$ km per hour   b $A \geqslant 18$ c $a > 3$ d $b \leqslant -3$
   e $d < 5$ f $-20 \geqslant x$ g $4 < y$ h $z \geqslant 0$
2 a $x > 2$ b $b < 5$ c $c \geqslant 2\frac{1}{2}$ d $d \leqslant -7$
   e $a < -19$ f $p > -3$
3 a [number line: open circle at 2, arrow right, x]
   b [number line: open circle at -3, arrow right, a]
   c [number line: closed circle at 2, arrow left, b]
   d [number line: closed circle at -1, arrow right, m]
   e [number line: open circle at 3, arrow right, x]
   f [number line: open circle at 2, arrow left, a]
   g [number line: closed circle at -2, arrow left, b]
   h [number line: closed circle at -2, arrow right, m]
4 a true   b false   c false   d false   e true   f false

EXERCISE 11F

1 a $a > 2$ [number line: open circle at 2, arrow right, a]
   b $b \leqslant -3$ [number line: closed circle at -3, arrow left, b]
   c $c < 6$ [number line: open circle at 6, arrow left, c]
   d $s < 6$ [number line: open circle at 6, arrow left, s]
   e $b < -4$ [number line: open circle at -4, arrow left, b]
   f $t > -5$ [number line: open circle at -5, arrow right, t]
   g $m \leqslant -60$ [number line: closed circle at -60, arrow left, m]
   h $x \geqslant -5$ [number line: closed circle at -5, arrow right, x]
   i $b \geqslant -\frac{2}{3}$ [number line: closed circle at $-\frac{2}{3}$, arrow right, b]
   j $a \geqslant 3\frac{1}{3}$ [number line: closed circle at $3\frac{1}{3}$, arrow right, a]
   k $a < -2$ [number line: open circle at -2, arrow left, a]
   l $b > 5$ [number line: open circle at 5, arrow right, b]
   m $s > -2$ [number line: open circle at -2, arrow right, s]
   n $a \leqslant 2$ [number line: closed circle at 2, arrow left, a]
   o $b < 3$ [number line: open circle at 3, arrow left, b]
   p $b \geqslant \frac{1}{3}$ [number line: closed circle at $\frac{1}{3}$, arrow right, b]
   q $n < -2$ [number line: open circle at -2, arrow left, n]

r $b \geq 1\frac{3}{4}$

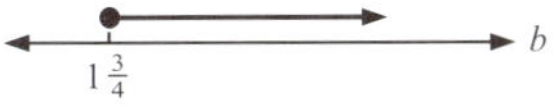

2 a $x > 9$

b $b \leq -5$

c $c \geq 16$

d $x < 9$

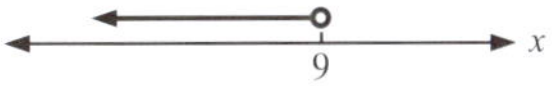

e $x \geq -4\frac{2}{3}$

f $x > -2$

g $x \leq 20$

h $x > 2\frac{1}{2}$

i $x < 9\frac{1}{3}$

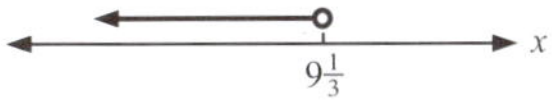

3 a $a < 15$

b $b \geq -1$

c $c \leq -2$

d $a < -6$

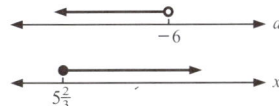

e $x \geq 5\frac{2}{3}$

f $x \leq 3$

4 a $c > 1\frac{2}{3}$ **b** $a \leq -\frac{3}{5}$ **c** $a \leq 1\frac{1}{3}$ **d** $a \leq -1$
e $a > \frac{1}{4}$ **f** $a > \frac{1}{8}$

5 a $x < 1$ **b** $c \geq -2$ **c** $b < -2$ **d** $a \geq 21$
e $d > 14$ **f** $p \leq 3\frac{2}{3}$

6 a $x > 2$

b $x \leq -3$

c $x < -1$

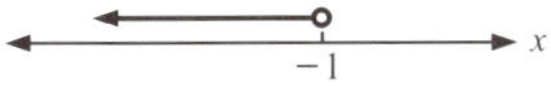

d $x < \frac{4}{5}$

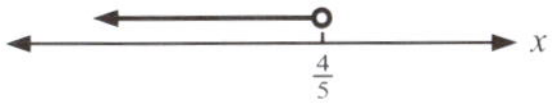

e $x \leq -3$

f $x \geq -2$

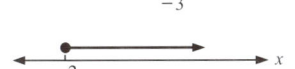

REVIEW SET 11A

1 a $x + 5$ **b** $x - 10$ **c** $2x + 1$
2 a $x + 7$ **b** $x^2 - 3$ **c** $x + 2$ **3** $50x + 10(x+2)$ cents
4 a $2(x-5) = 64$ **b** $x + (x+1) + (x+2) = 12$ **5** 6

6 13 5-pence coins **7 a** 28 metres per second **b** ≈ 128 m
8 a $x > 7$ **b** $-11 \leq x$ **9** $x \leq 3$
10 a

b

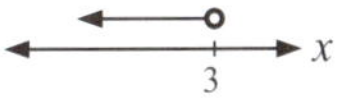

11 a $x \leq 3\frac{1}{2}$ **b** $x < -4\frac{1}{2}$ **c** $x \leq -\frac{4}{7}$

REVIEW SET 11B

1 a $x - 5$ **b** $x + 6$ **c** $\dfrac{x+1}{2}$
2 a $12 - x$ **b** $5x - 3$ **c** $25 - x$ **3** $10x + 20(2x)$ euros
4 a $3x = 48 - x$ **b** $x + (x+2) = 16$
5 16 **6** 4 10-cent coins **7 a** 320 000 units **b** 10 cm
8 a

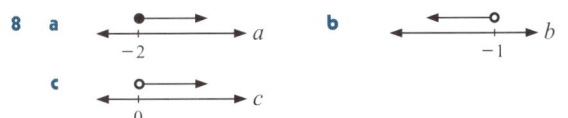

b

c

9 a $x \leq 1\frac{1}{2}$ **b** $x < 10$ **c** $x \geq 0$ **10** 45 years old

EXERCISE 12A

1 a cm³ or m³ **b** m³ **c** cm³ **d** km³ **e** mm³
f m³ **g** cm³ **h** m³ **i** mm³
2 a 2.4 cm³ **b** 6.8×10^6 cm³ **c** 0.083 cm³
d 7.48 m³ **e** 3.48×10^5 mm³ **f** 2 km³
g 7.2×10^9 m³ **h** 38.1 cm³ **i** 3.5×10^6 mm³

EXERCISE 12B

1 a 360 m³ **b** 125 cm³ **c** ≈ 368 cm³ **d** 2.6 m³
e 175 cm³ **f** $\approx 111\,000$ cm³ or 0.111 m³ **g** 819 cm³
h 576 cm³ **i** ≈ 0.0754 m³
2 a ≈ 66.7 cm³ **b** ≈ 236 cm³ **c** 60 cm³
d 60 cm³ **e** ≈ 3020 cm³ **f** ≈ 149 cm³
3 a ≈ 905 cm³ **b** ≈ 556 m³ **c** ≈ 56.5 m³
4 a $\frac{4}{3}\pi x^3$ m³ **b** $\frac{3}{4}\pi x^3$ m³ **c** $\frac{32}{3}x^3$ cm³
d $21\pi x^3$ cm³ **e** $12\pi x^3$ cm³ **f** $9x^3$ cm³
5 12 cm³ **6** ≈ 6810 cm³ **7** ≈ 4.45 cm³ **8** ≈ 6280 kg

EXERCISE 12C.1

1 a mL **b** L **c** mL **d** kL **e** ML **f** L
g L **h** kL
2 a 3.48 L **b** 4850 kL **c** 0.0725 kL **d** 8.6 ML
e 7800 L **f** 15 300 mL **g** 0.545 L **h** 0.048 kL
i 372.1 ML **j** 65 L **k** 820 L **l** 200 000 mL

EXERCISE 12C.2

1 a 250 cm³ **b** 9000 cm³ **c** 3900 m³ **d** 750 mL
e 4.1 L **f** 18.5 kL
2 ≈ 7.07 L **3** 20.9 kL **4** 7 jars
5 a $\approx 20\,900$ cm³ **b** ≈ 20.9 L **c** 698 boxes **6** 200 kL

EXERCISE 12D

1 a ≈ 1.47 m³ **b** ≈ 1410 kg **c** $\approx £1130$
2 21 676 bottles **3 a** 100 m² **b** $1650
4 1145 sinkers **5** 7.5 cm
6 3 : 5 in all cases, i.e., the same ratio
7 a ≈ 550 cm² **b** ≈ 0.110 m³ **c** $\approx \$14.85$
d ≈ 267 kg
8 $\approx 36\,200$ cm³ **9** ≈ 4.92 cm **10** ≈ 4.77 cm

11 a ≈ 1.56 m **b** ≈ 1.68 m   **12** $\frac{1}{3}$
13 $\sqrt[3]{\frac{4}{3}\pi} : 1 \approx 1.61 : 1$ **14** $h : r = 4 : 1$

REVIEW SET 12A

1 a 9.5 cm **b** 4800 m **c** 1.85 ha **d** 5.5 m²
  e 2.5×10^6 cm³ **f** 2.5 L
2 a ≈ 1570 cm³ **b** ≈ 1190 cm³ **c** ≈ 0.905 m³
3 44 door stops **4** 3 minutes 36 seconds **5** 69.1 cm
6 52.4% **7 a** ≈ 275 m² **b** ≈ $6.60 million
8 4 times larger

REVIEW SET 12B

1 a 6.89 km **b** 294 mm **c** 7.4 L
  d 76 000 m² **e** 8500 mm² **f** 3200 mm³
2 a ≈ 14.3 cm³ **b** ≈ 1130 cm³ **c** ≈ 75.4 m³
3 a ≈ 32.2 m² **b** ≈ 2.57 m³ **c** ≈ £193
4 ≈ 10.5 min **5** 40 cm **6** ≈ €1610
7 a 105 m² **b** 2100 kL
8 a ≈ 8.92 cm **b** ≈ 2970 cm³

EXERCISE 13A

1 P(3, −2), Q($-2\frac{1}{2}$, −1), R($1\frac{1}{2}$, 2), S(0, −1), T(−3, $2\frac{1}{2}$)

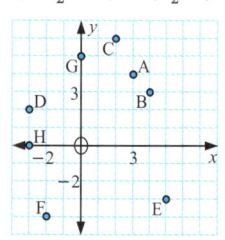

3 a 1st **b** 1st **c** 1st **d** 2nd **e** 4th **f** 3rd
  g None, it is on the positive y-axis.
  h None, it is on the negative x-axis.

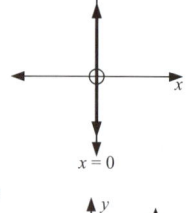

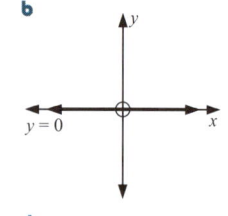

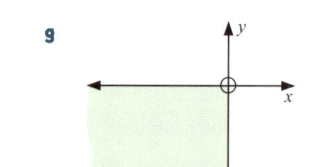

4 (graphs: a $x=0$; b $y=0$; c $x=3$; d $y=-2$; e, f shaded regions)

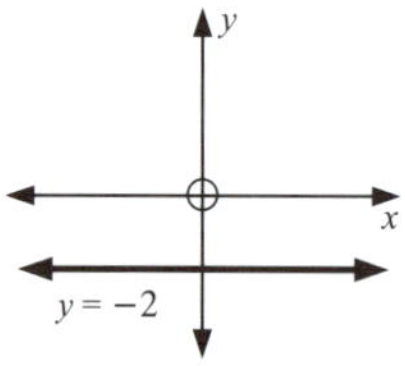

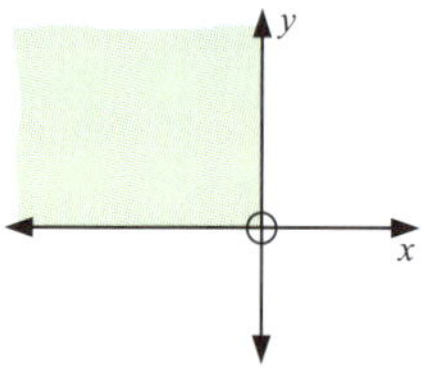

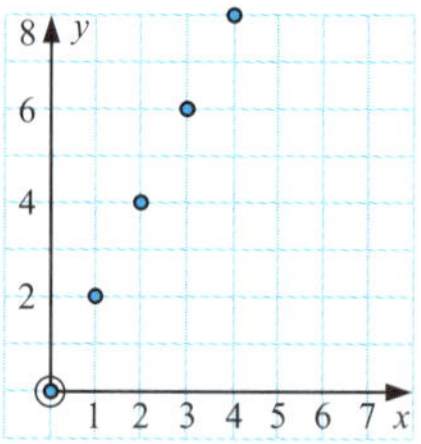

5 a (scatter plot) **i** yes **ii** E
  b (scatter plot) **i** yes **ii** C

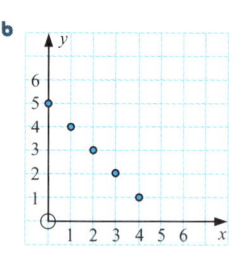

EXERCISE 13B

1 a Independent variable is number of tickets sold, dependent variable is amount agent is paid.

b

t	0	1	2	3	4	5
I	200	230	260	290	320	350

t	6	7	8	9	10
I	380	410	440	470	500

c yes **d** No, since we cannot sell part of a ticket.
e €30 **f i** €200 **ii** €30 per ticket sold

2 a

n	0	1	2	3	4	5
C	0	0.85	1.70	2.55	3.40	4.25

n	6	7	8
C	5.10	5.95	6.80

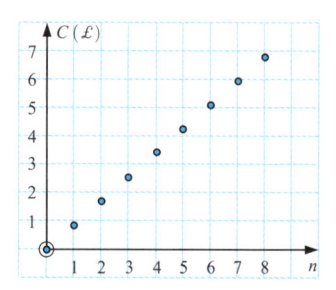

c Independent variable is the number of cartons bought, dependent variable is the cost in dollars.
d yes **e** No, since we cannot buy half a carton.
f £0.85 **g** £3.40 **h** 7 cartons

3 a

n	0	1	2	3	4	5
V	4	5.5	7	8.5	10	11.5

n	6	7	8
V	13	14.5	16

b Independent variable is the number of jugs emptied into the container, dependent variable is the volume of water in the container.

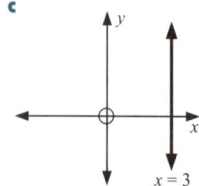

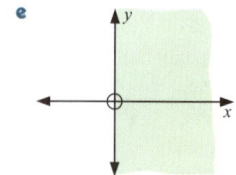

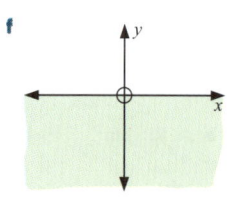

c

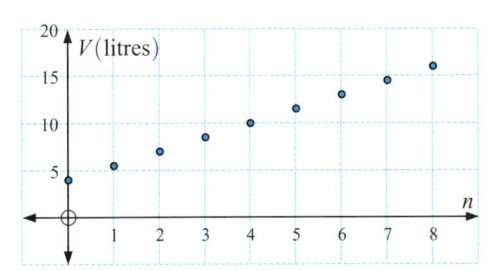

[Graph: V (litres) vs n, scatter plot showing points rising from about 4 at n=1 to about 16 at n=8]

d yes
e Yes, since Jason can empty part of a jug into the container.
f 1.5 L **g** 11.5 L **h** 7 jugs

4 b Independent variable is the temperature in degrees Celsius, dependent variable is the temperature in degrees Fahrenheit.

a/c

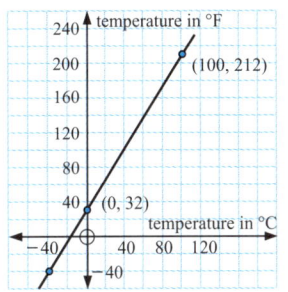

[Graph: temperature in °F vs temperature in °C, straight line through (0, 32) and (100, 212)]

d −40°C **e** **i** 7.8°C **ii** 2.2°C

f

°F	50	68	86	104	20	10	0
°C	10	20	30	40	−6.7	−12.2	−17.8

EXERCISE 13C

1 a i Independent variable is x, dependent variable is y.

ii

x	−3	−2	−1	0	1	2	3
y	−3	−2	−1	0	1	2	3

iii [Graph of $y = x$]

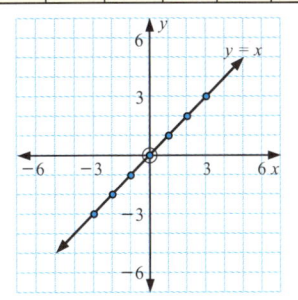

b i Independent variable is x, dependent variable is y.

ii

x	−3	−2	−1	0	1	2	3
y	−6	−4	−2	0	2	4	6

iii [Graph of $y = 2x$]

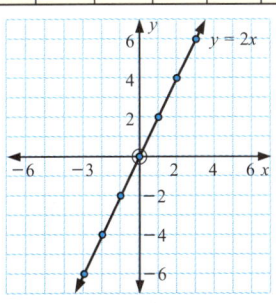

c i Independent variable is x, dependent variable is y.

ii

x	−3	−2	−1	0	1	2	3
y	$-\frac{3}{2}$	−1	$-\frac{1}{2}$	0	$\frac{1}{2}$	1	$\frac{3}{2}$

iii [Graph of $y = \frac{1}{2}x$]

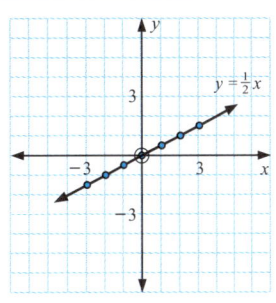

d i Independent variable is x, dependent variable is y.

ii

x	−3	−2	−1	0	1	2	3
y	6	4	2	0	−2	−4	−6

iii [Graph of $y = -2x$]

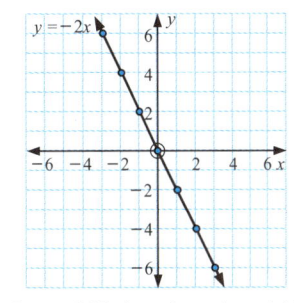

e i Independent variable is x, dependent variable is y.

ii

x	−3	−2	−1	0	1	2	3
y	−3	−1	1	3	5	7	9

iii [Graph of $y = 2x + 3$]

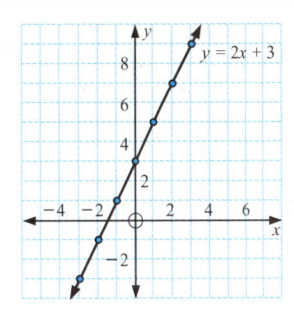

f i Independent variable is x, dependent variable is y.

ii

x	−3	−2	−1	0	1	2	3
y	9	7	5	3	1	−1	−3

iii [Graph of $y = -2x + 3$]

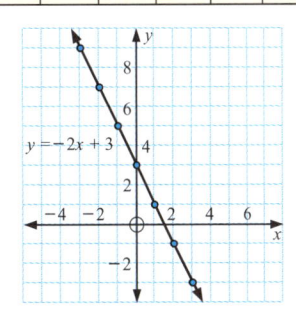

g i Independent variable is x, dependent variable is y.

ii

x	-3	-2	-1	0	1	2	3
y	$\frac{1}{4}$	$\frac{1}{2}$	$\frac{3}{4}$	1	$\frac{5}{4}$	$\frac{3}{2}$	$\frac{7}{4}$

iii (graph of $y = \frac{1}{4}x + 1$)

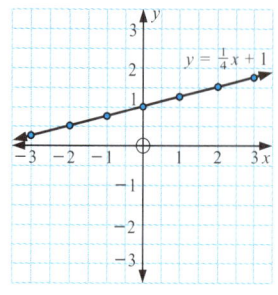

h **i** Independent variable is x, dependent variable is y.

ii

x	-3	-2	-1	0	1	2	3
y	$\frac{7}{4}$	$\frac{3}{2}$	$\frac{5}{4}$	1	$\frac{3}{4}$	$\frac{1}{2}$	$\frac{1}{4}$

iii (graph of $y = -\frac{1}{4}x + 1$)

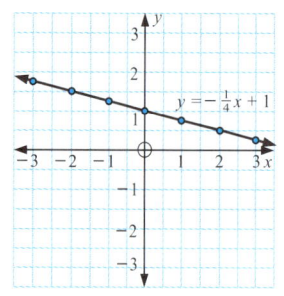

2 b, a, c; coefficient of x **3** sign of the coefficient of x
4 the constant term

EXERCISE 13D

1 a $y = x + 3$ gives the connection between the x and y-coordinates for every point on the line where the y-coordinate is the x-coordinate plus 3.
b $y = 5x$ gives the connection between the x and y-coordinates for every point on the line where the y-coordinate is five times the x-coordinate.
c $y = 2x - 6$ gives the connection between the x and y-coordinates for every point on the line where the y-coordinate is twice the x-coordinate, minus 6.
d $x + y = 5$ gives the connection between the x and y-coordinates for every point on the line where the sum of the x and y-coordinates is 5.

2 a $y = 4x$ **b** $y = x + 2$ **c** $y = -2x$
   d $y = 3 - x$ **e** $y = 2x + 1$ **f** $y = 2x - 1$

EXERCISE 13E.1

1 a $\frac{2}{3}$ **b** -1 **c** $\frac{1}{3}$ **d** $-\frac{4}{3}$ **e** $\frac{1}{6}$
   f undefined **g** -3 **h** $-\frac{1}{8}$ **i** 0

2 a, b, c, d, e, f, g, h (line segments on grid)

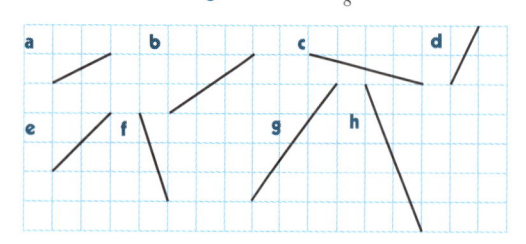

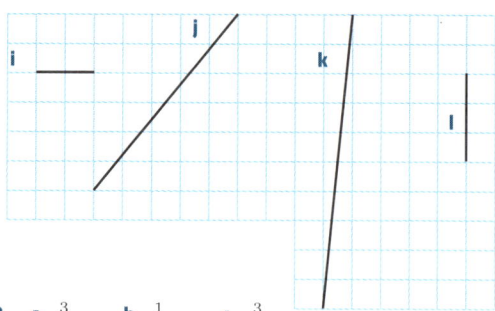

3 a $\frac{3}{4}$ **b** $\frac{1}{5}$ **c** $\frac{3}{20}$
4 a i 0 **ii** $\frac{1}{5}$ **iii** $\frac{3}{5}$ **iv** 1 **v** 2 **vi** 4
   vii undefined **viii** -4 **ix** $-\frac{1}{2}$
   b i 0 **ii** undefined **iii** increase in magnitude
5 a OP, PQ, RS, TU **b** QR, ST, UV **c** TU **d** ST
   e VW **f** PQ
6 a 3 **b** $-\frac{1}{2}$ **c** 3 **d** 1 **e** $-\frac{1}{2}$ **f** -1

EXERCISE 13E.2

1 a $\frac{4}{3}$ **b** $-\frac{5}{6}$ **c** $-\frac{4}{3}$ **d** 0
2 a 3 **b** $-\frac{1}{2}$ **c** -6 **d** -5 **e** undefined
   f 0 **g** 1 **h** 1 **i** $-\frac{1}{2}$ **j** -1
3 rule, grid needed is too large
4 a 0 **b** undefined
   c i 0 **ii** 1 **iii** undefined **iv** positive **v** negative

EXERCISE 13F.1

1 a $y = 2x + 11$ **b** $y = 4x - 6$ **c** $y = -3x + \frac{1}{2}$
   d $y = -x + 4$ **e** $y = 7$ **f** $y = \frac{2}{3}x + 6$
2 a i 4 **ii** 8 **b i** -3 **ii** 2 **c i** -1 **ii** 6
   d i -2 **ii** 3 **e i** 0 **ii** -2 **f i** -3 **ii** 11
   g i $\frac{1}{2}$ **ii** -5 **h i** $-\frac{3}{2}$ **ii** 3 **i i** $\frac{2}{5}$ **ii** $\frac{4}{5}$
   j i $\frac{1}{2}$ **ii** $\frac{1}{2}$ **k i** $\frac{2}{5}$ **ii** -2 **l i** $-\frac{3}{2}$ **ii** $\frac{11}{2}$

EXERCISE 13F.2

1 a i slope $= 1$, y-intercept $= 3$
   ii (graph of $y = x + 3$)
   b i slope $= -1$, y-intercept $= 4$
   ii (graph of $y = -x + 4$)
   c i slope $= 2$, y-intercept $= 2$
   ii (graph of $y = 2x + 2$)
   d i slope $= \frac{1}{2}$, y-intercept $= -1$
   ii (graph of $y = \frac{1}{2}x - 1$)

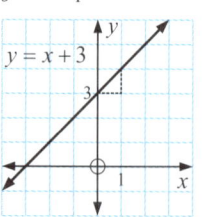

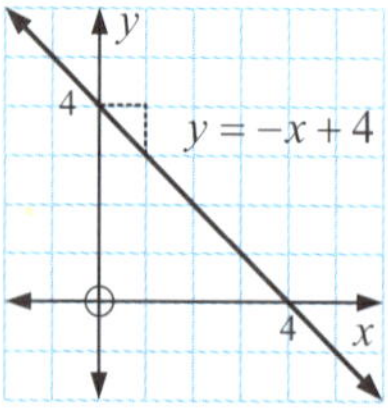

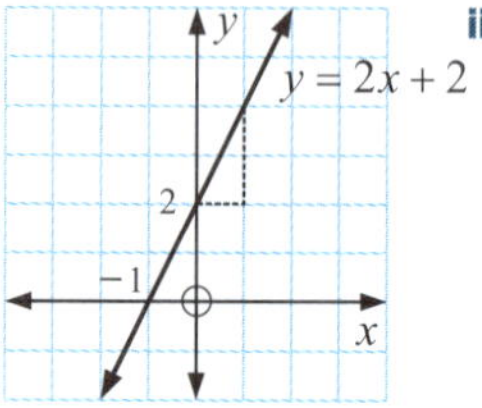

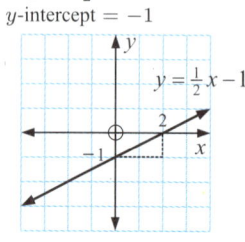

e **i** slope = 3, y-intercept = 0

ii [graph of $y = 3x$]

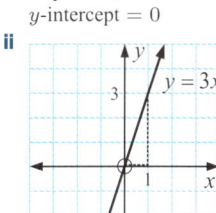

f **i** slope = $-\frac{1}{2}$, y-intercept = 0

ii [graph of $y = -\frac{1}{2}x$]

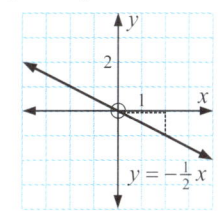

g **i** slope = -2, y-intercept = 1

ii [graph of $y = -2x + 1$]

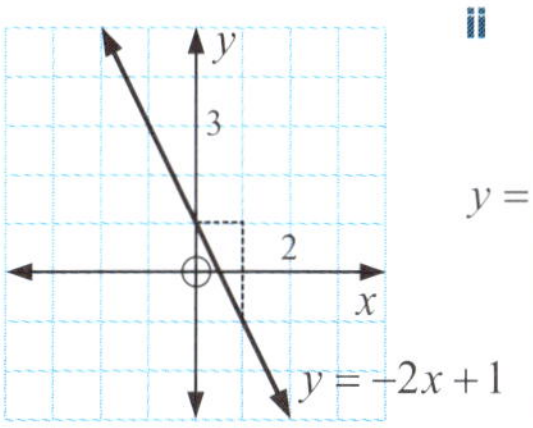

h **i** slope = $-\frac{1}{3}$, y-intercept = 3

ii [graph of $y = 3 - \frac{1}{3}x$]

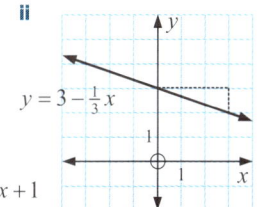

i **i** slope = 0, y-intercept = 3

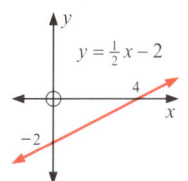

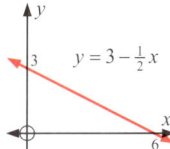

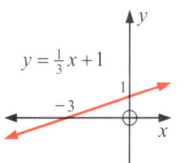

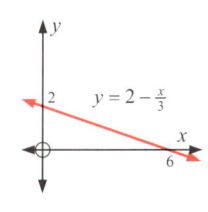

ii [graph of $y = 3$]

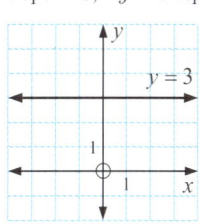

i [graph of $y = \frac{x+2}{3}$]

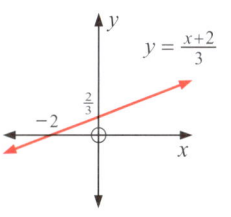

2 No, graph using the origin and one other point.

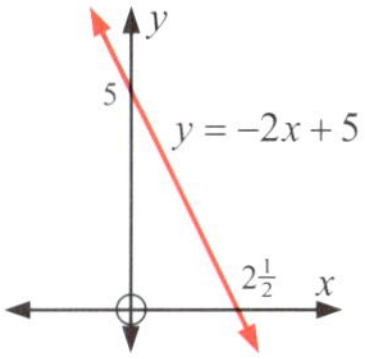

EXERCISE 13G.1

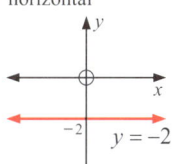

1 a horizontal [graph of $y = 3$]   **b** vertical [graph of $x = 4$]

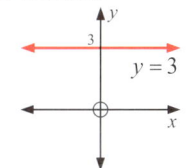

c horizontal [graph of $y = -2$]   **d** vertical [graph of $x = -6$]

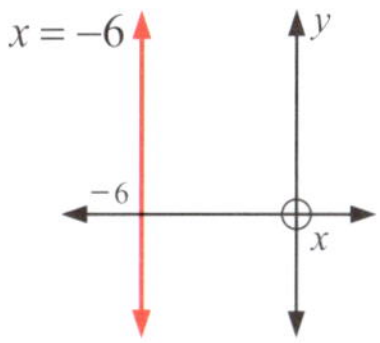

2 a horizontal   **b** vertical

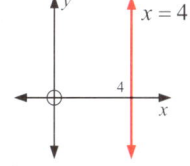

3 a $y = 0$ **b** $x = 0$ **c** $y = 2$ **d** $x = -3$

EXERCISE 13G.2

1 a 2   **b** -3 **c** $\frac{2}{3}$ **d** $\frac{3}{4}$ **e** -2 **f** -1

2 a $y = 5 - x$, -1 **b** $y = 4 - 2x$, -2
 c $y = 3x + 5$, 3   **d** $y = \frac{2}{3}x - 2$, $\frac{2}{3}$
 e $y = -\frac{1}{2}x + 3$, $-\frac{1}{2}$ **f** $y = \frac{5}{2}x + 3$, $\frac{5}{2}$
 g $y = -\frac{3}{7}x - 3$, $-\frac{3}{7}$ **h** $y = \frac{2}{5}x - 2$, $\frac{2}{5}$
 i $y = -\frac{5}{3}x + 10$, $-\frac{5}{3}$

3 a D   **b** H   **c** E   **d** B   **e** A   **f** C   **g** G   **h** F

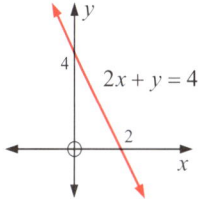

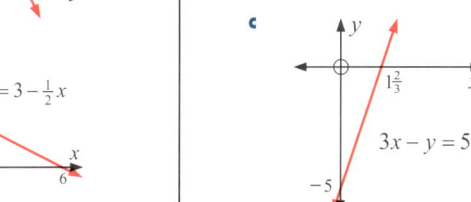

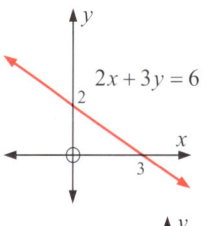

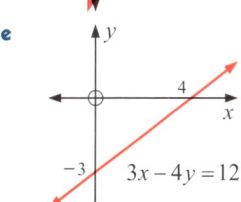

4 a [graph of $x + y = 6$]   **b** [graph of $2x + y = 4$]

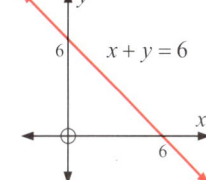

c [graph of $3x - y = 5$]   **d** [graph of $2x + 3y = 6$]

e [graph of $3x - 4y = 12$]   **f** [graph of $x + 3y = -6$]

EXERCISE 13F.3

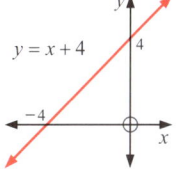

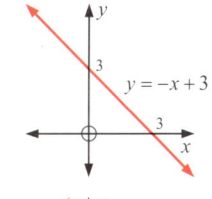

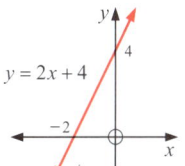

1 a [graph of $y = x + 4$]   **b** [graph of $y = -x + 3$]

c [graph of $y = 2x + 4$]   **d** [graph of $y = -2x + 5$]

e [graph of $y = \frac{1}{2}x - 2$]   **f** [graph of $y = 3 - \frac{1}{2}x$]

g [graph of $y = \frac{1}{3}x + 1$]   **h** [graph of $y = 2 - \frac{x}{3}$]

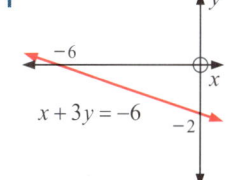

522 ANSWERS

g [graph: $2x - 5y = 10$, x-intercept 5, y-intercept -2]

h [graph: $2x + 7y = 14$, x-intercept 7, y-intercept 2]

i [graph: $3x - 4y = 8$, y-intercept -2, point $2\tfrac{2}{3}$ on x-axis]

c i 3   ii $\tfrac{3}{2}$

4 $y = -x + 3$ 5 a $\tfrac{2}{5}$ b $-\tfrac{4}{3}$ 6 $-\tfrac{7}{3}$ 7 $y = 5x - 2$

8 a slope $= -\tfrac{1}{3}$, y-intercept $= 2$

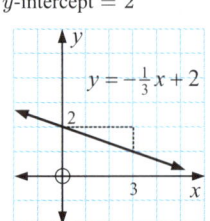

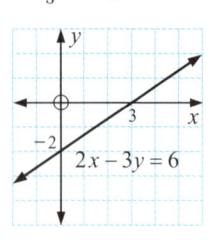

b [graph of $y = -\tfrac{1}{3}x + 2$]

9 [graph of $2x - 3y = 6$, x-intercept 3, y-intercept -2]

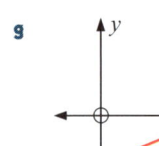

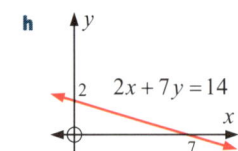

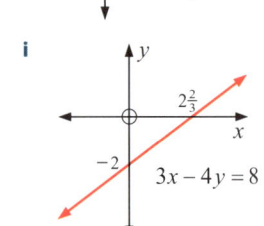

10 a 1   b -3 c $y = x - 3$ 11 yes

EXERCISE 13H

1 a i 1   ii 1   iii $y = x + 1$
   b i $\tfrac{1}{4}$ ii 2   iii $y = \tfrac{1}{4}x + 2$
   c i $\tfrac{1}{2}$ ii 0   iii $y = \tfrac{1}{2}x$
   d i -1 ii 2   iii $y = -x + 2$
   e i -3 ii 0   iii $y = -3x$
   f i $-\tfrac{3}{2}$ ii -1 iii $y = -\tfrac{3}{2}x - 1$
   g i $-\tfrac{1}{3}$ ii 1   iii $y = -\tfrac{1}{3}x + 1$
   h i $\tfrac{1}{2}$ ii -1 iii $y = \tfrac{1}{2}x - 1$
   i i $\tfrac{1}{2}$ ii -2 iii $y = \tfrac{1}{2}x - 2$

2 a $V = \tfrac{1}{2}t + 1$ b $N = 2 - d$ c $C = \tfrac{4}{5}t + 3$

EXERCISE 13I

1 a yes   b yes   c no   d yes   e yes   f no

REVIEW SET 13A

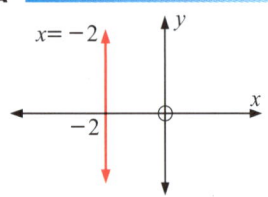

1 [graph of $x = -2$, vertical line through -2]

2 a Independent variable is the number of hours consultation, dependent variable is the consultation fee.

b
t	0	1	2	3	4
€	75	195	315	435	555

c yes

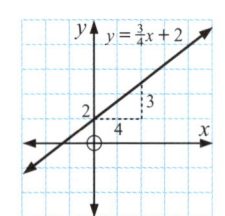

d Yes, since the lawyer may consult for part of an hour.
e an increase of €120   f i €75   ii €120 per hour

3 a
x	-3	-2	-1	0	1	2	3
y	9	7	5	3	1	-1	-3

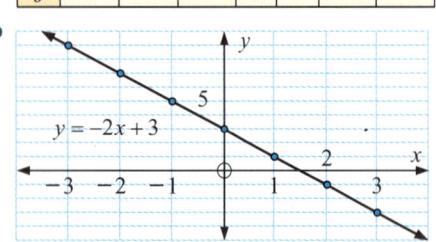

b [graph of $y = -2x + 3$]

REVIEW SET 13B

1 [graph: shaded region in third quadrant]

2 a Independent variable is t, dependent variable is V.

b
t	0	1	2	3	4	5	6	7
V	400	375	350	325	300	275	250	225

t	8	9	10	11	12	13	14	15	16
V	200	175	150	125	100	75	50	25	0

c yes   d Yes, since the water flows continuously.
e V decreases by 25 L

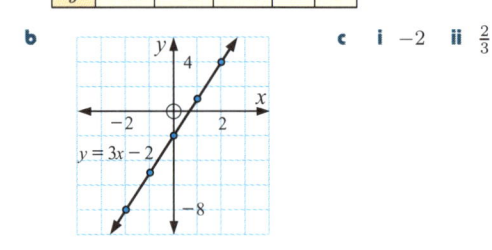

3 a
x	-2	-1	0	1	2
y	-8	-5	-2	1	4

b [graph of $y = 3x - 2$]   c i -2 ii $\tfrac{2}{3}$

4 $y = -3x$ 5 a -2 b undefined

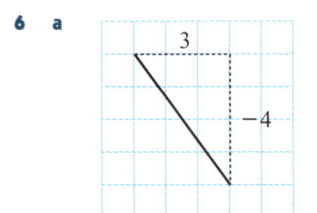

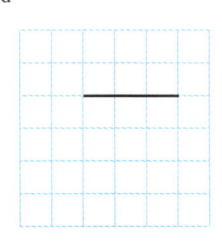

6 a [graph showing slope from 3 down to -4]   b [horizontal line graph]

7 a slope $= \tfrac{3}{4}$, y-intercept $= 2$

b [graph of $y = \tfrac{3}{4}x + 2$]

ANSWERS 523

8 $\frac{5}{2}$ **9 a** $-\frac{3}{4}$ **b** 3 **c** $y = -\frac{3}{4}x + 3$
10 a 1 **b** $P = r + 4$ **11** no

EXERCISE 14A
1 a $x = 3, \ y = 1$ **b** $x = 7, \ y = 4$ **c** $x = 3, \ y = 5$
   d $x = 3, \ y = 9$
2 a not correct **b** correct **c** correct **d** correct
3 a $x = 3, \ y = 1$ **b** $x = 4, \ y = 2$ **c** $a = 1, \ b = 0$
   d $p = 5, \ q = 2$

EXERCISE 14B
1 a $x = 1, \ y = 1$ **b** $x = -1, \ y = 2$
   c $x = -3, \ y = -7$ **d** $x = -2, \ y = 7$
   e $x = 1, \ y = -1$ **f** $x = -3, \ y = -5$
2 a $x = 4, \ y = 5$ **b** $x = -1, \ y = 3$ **c** $x = 1, \ y = 3$
   d $x = 1, \ y = 0$ **e** $x = -1, \ y = -4$ **f** $x = -1, \ y = 5$
3 a The lines are parallel $\therefore$ no solution exists.
   b Lines are coincident $\therefore$ infinitely many solutions exist
   e.g., $x = 1.24, \ y = 0.76$
4 Solving by 'trial and error' and by graphing is okay if the solutions are whole numbers, but not if they are fractions.

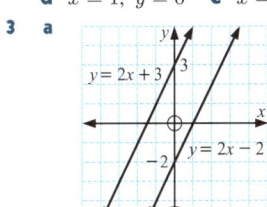

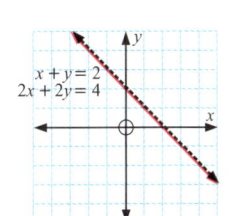

EXERCISE 14C
1 a $x = 4, \ y = 5$ **b** $x = -1, \ y = 3$ **c** $x = 1, \ y = 3$
   d $x = 0, \ y = -4$ **e** $x = 4, \ y = 0$ **f** no solution
   g $x = -\frac{13}{4}, \ y = -\frac{11}{4}$ **h** no solution **i** $x = \frac{5}{3}, \ y = 0$
2 a $x = 7, \ y = 3$ **b** $x = \frac{1}{2}, \ y = 4$ **c** $x = 2, \ y = 4$
   d $x = 1, \ y = -1$ **e** $x = 5, \ y = -2$
   f $x = 0, \ y = -4$ **g** $x = -\frac{17}{13}, \ y = -\frac{77}{13}$
   h $x = -\frac{1}{2}, \ y = \frac{1}{8}$ **i** $x = -\frac{29}{13}, \ y = -\frac{54}{13}$
3 a $(2, 7)$ **b** $(-2, -5)$ **c** $(-3, 5)$ **d** $(-1, -1)$
   e $(\frac{12}{5}, -\frac{1}{5})$ **f** $(\frac{25}{17}, \frac{10}{17})$

EXERCISE 14D
1 a $4x - 6y = 10$ **b** $-3x - 9y = -21$
   c $8x + 20y = 4$ **d** $-6x + 4y = -16$
   e $25x - 5y = 10$ **f** $2x - 5y = 1$
2 a $4x = 16$ **b** $5x = 15$ **c** $2x = 12$
   d $3y = 6$ **e** $2y = -2$ **f** $-y = 4$
3 a $x = 4, \ y = 1$ **b** $x = 3, \ y = -2$
   c $x = -2, \ y = 5$ **d** $x = -3, \ y = -2$
   e $x = 7, \ y = -1$ **f** $x = 3, \ y = -5$
   g $x = 6, \ y = -5$ **h** $x = -3, \ y = 8$
   i $x = 3, \ y = -4$ **j** $x = 3, \ y = 0$
   k $x = 5, \ y = -4$ **l** $x = 4, \ y = 5$
   m $x = -1, \ y = -7$ **n** $x = 8, \ y = -7$
   o $x = 4, \ y = -2$

EXERCISE 14E
1 $118\frac{1}{2}$ and $81\frac{1}{2}$ **2** 97 and 181 **3** -3 and 8
4 17 and 68 **5** 35 and 36 **6** hammer \$14, screwdriver \$6
7 adults £14, children £6 **8** blanket RM 56, sheet RM 22
9 peach ¥15, nashi ¥21
10 19 five cents and 14 twenty cents
11 14 rabbits, 21 pheasants **12** 74 one litre, 23 two litre
13 $x = 3, \ y = 5$ **14** $x = 39, \ y = 52$
15 Jane is 37, Anne is 17 **16** woman is 42, son is 20
17 Sam \$1000, Ben \$500

REVIEW SET 14A
1 $\therefore \ x = -1, \ y = -3$
2 $x = 2, \ y = 1$ **3** $x = -1, \ y = 3$
4 a pencil 12 cents, ruler 25 cents
   b 11 two cents, 14 five cents

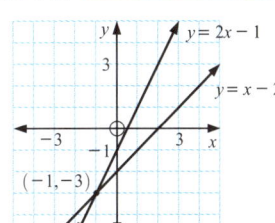

REVIEW SET 14B
1 $\therefore \ x = 1, \ y = -1$
2 $x = 4, \ y = 4$ **3** $x = -2, \ y = -3$; Yes
4 a John is 9, Paula is 7 **b** 6 loaves, 10 rolls

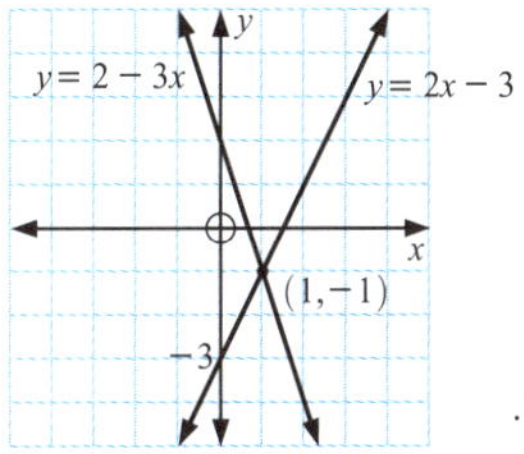

EXERCISE 15A
1 ≈ 0.253 **2** ≈ 0.762 **3 a** ≈ 0.963 **b** $\frac{182}{200} = 0.91$
4 a ≈ 0.671 **b** ≈ 0.329 **5** ≈ 0.142
6 a $\approx 0.761, \ \approx 0.613$
   b Assuming the can does not change shape, the difference is almost certainly due to chance alone.

EXERCISE 15B
1 a

Colour	Freq.	Rel. Freq.
Red	149	0.603
Green	98	0.397
Total	247	1.000

   b i ≈ 0.603 **ii** ≈ 0.397

2 a

Type	Freq.	Rel. Freq.
Adult	238	0.476
Pensioner	143	0.286
Child	119	0.238
Total	500	1.000

   b 500 seats **c** 0.238

   d No, as we know exactly how many of each category are at the concert.

3 a

Fragrance	Freq.	Rel. Freq.
Rose	59	0.187
Violet	72	0.228
Lavender	81	0.256
W/Breeze	104	0.329
Total	316	1.000

b i ≈ 0.228 **ii** ≈ 0.516

4 a

Model	Freq.	Rel. Freq.
A	80	0.25
B	112	0.35
C	40	0.125
D	88	0.275
Total	320	1.000

b i ≈ 0.125 **ii** ≈ 0.400

EXERCISE 15C

1 a

Sport	Instrument Yes	No	Total
Yes	19	25	44
No	11	14	25
Total	30	39	69

b i ≈ 0.568 **ii** ≈ 0.435

2 a

Licence	Gender Male	Female	Total
Yes	62	17	79
No	8	3	11
Total	70	20	90

b i ≈ 0.886 **ii** ≈ 0.850

c The Male estimate is likely to be more accurate as it is a much larger sample (70 compared with 20).

3 a

Given	Said A	B	Total
A	38	12	50
B	17	33	50
Total	55	45	100

b i ≈ 0.76 **ii** ≈ 0.66

4 a

Age	Vote Yes	Undecided	No	Total
under 30	15	19	14	48
over 30	26	16	10	52
Total	41	35	24	100

b i ≈ 0.500 **ii** ≈ 0.240 **iii** ≈ 0.160 **iv** ≈ 0.604

REVIEW SET 15A

1 ≈ 0.639 **2 a** 133   **b i** ≈ 0.541 **ii** ≈ 0.459

3 a 156 families   **b**

Result	Freq.	Rel. Freq.
3 boys	21	0.135
2 boys, 1 girl	62	0.397
1 boy, 2 girls	55	0.353
3 girls	18	0.115
Total	156	1.000

c i ≈ 0.397 **ii** ≈ 0.115

4 a

Studied	Test Pass	Fail	Total
Yes	21	7	28
No	12	8	20
Total	33	15	48

b i ≈ 0.688 **ii** ≈ 0.167 **c** ≈ 0.75

REVIEW SET 15B

1 ≈ 0.190

2 a

Result	Freq.	Rel. Freq.
2 heads	78	0.260
1 head	149	0.497
0 heads	73	0.243
Total	300	1.000

b i ≈ 0.260 **ii** ≈ 0.757

3 a 500   **b**

Brand	Freq.	Rel. Freq.
Wheat Bites	198	0.396
Corn Crisps	115	0.230
Rice Flakes	110	0.220
Bran Snacks	77	0.154
Total	500	1.000

c i ≈ 0.396 **ii** ≈ 0.846

4 a

	Fair hair	Dark hair	Total
Boys	418	577	995
Girls	327	638	965
Total	745	1215	1960

b i 995   **ii** 1215   **iii** 1960

c i ≈ 0.492 **ii** ≈ 0.620 **iii** ≈ 0.339

EXERCISE 16A

1 a $\binom{3}{1}$ **b** $\binom{-3}{-1}$ **c** $\binom{3}{-3}$ **d** $\binom{-3}{3}$ **e** $\binom{5}{1}$
f $\binom{-5}{-1}$ **g** $\binom{-2}{-4}$ **h** $\binom{2}{4}$

2 a b 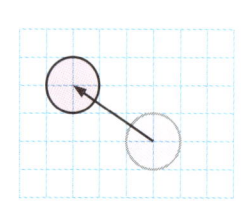 c 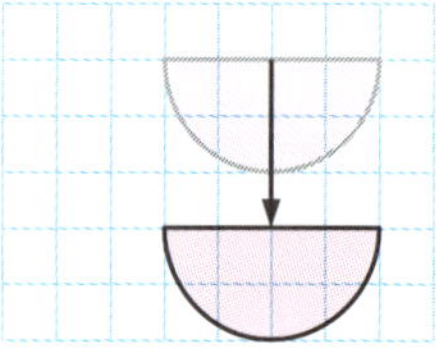 d 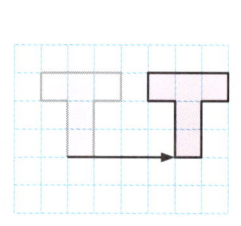 e 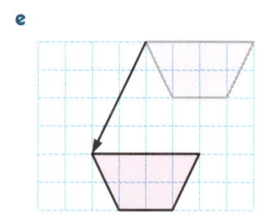 f

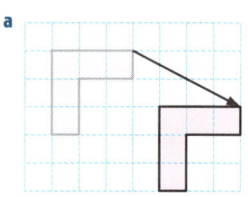

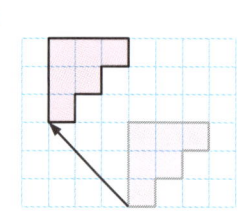

3 a a $2\sqrt{5}$ units   **b** $\sqrt{13}$ units   **c** 3 units
d 4 units   **e** $2\sqrt{5}$ units   **f** $3\sqrt{2}$ units
b $\sqrt{a^2 + b^2}$ units

EXERCISE 16B.1

1 a b

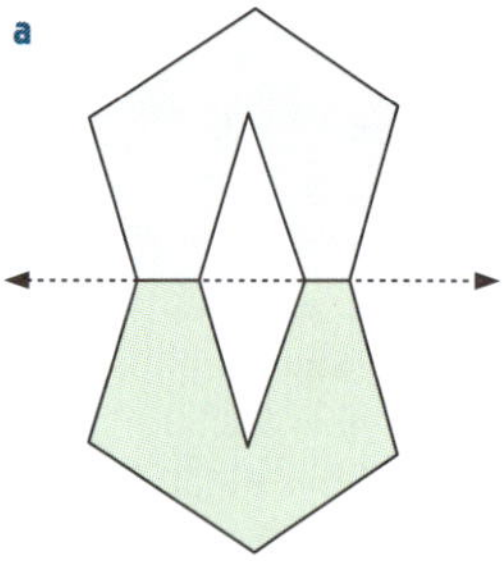

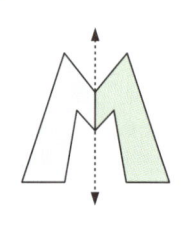

ANSWERS 525

c, d, e, f (figures)

2 a, b, c (figures)

EXERCISE 16B.2

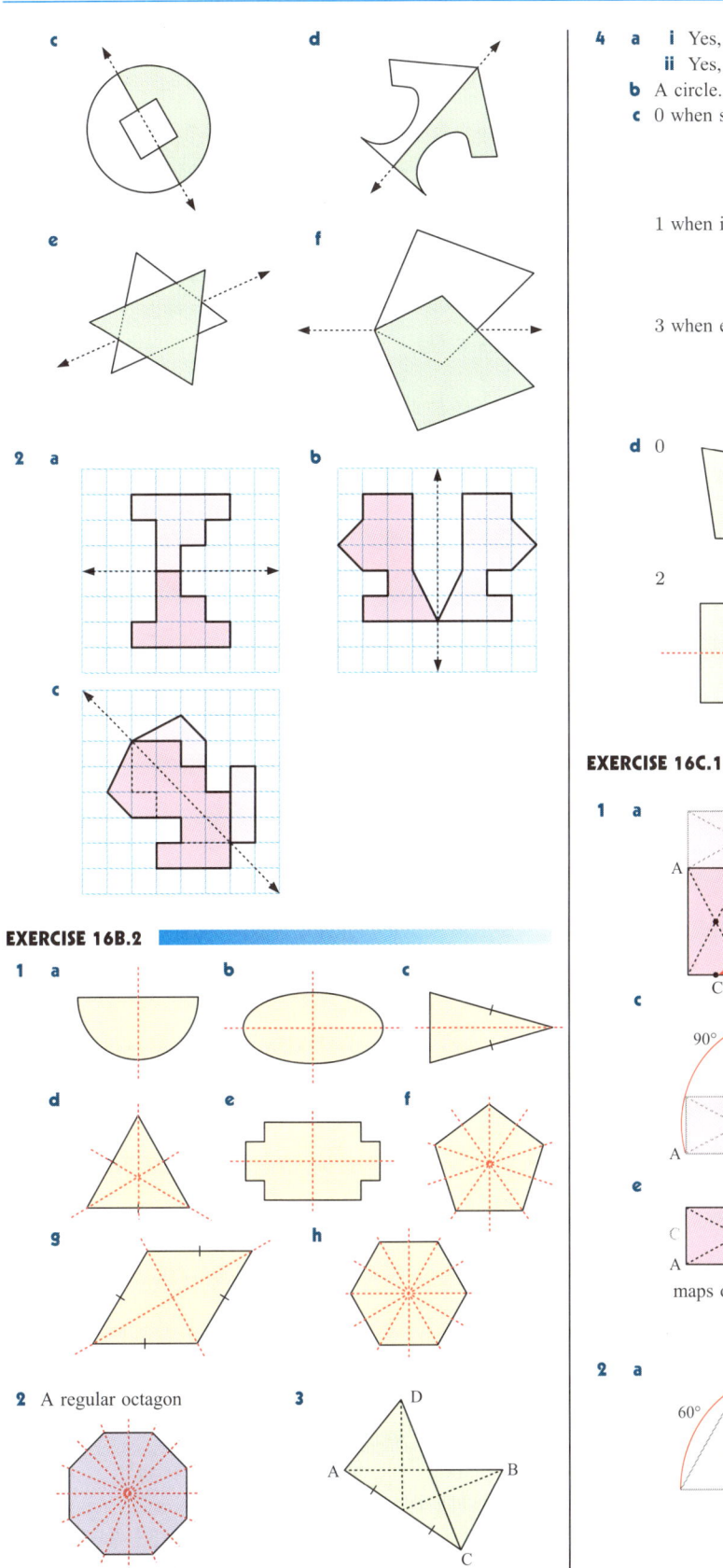

1 a, b, c, d, e, f, g, h (figures)

2 A regular octagon (figure)

3 (figure with points A, B, C, D)

4 a i Yes, when it is a rectangle.
 ii Yes, when it is a square.
 b A circle. Any diameter is an axis of symmetry.
 c 0 when scalene

 1 when isosceles

 3 when equilateral

 d 0   1

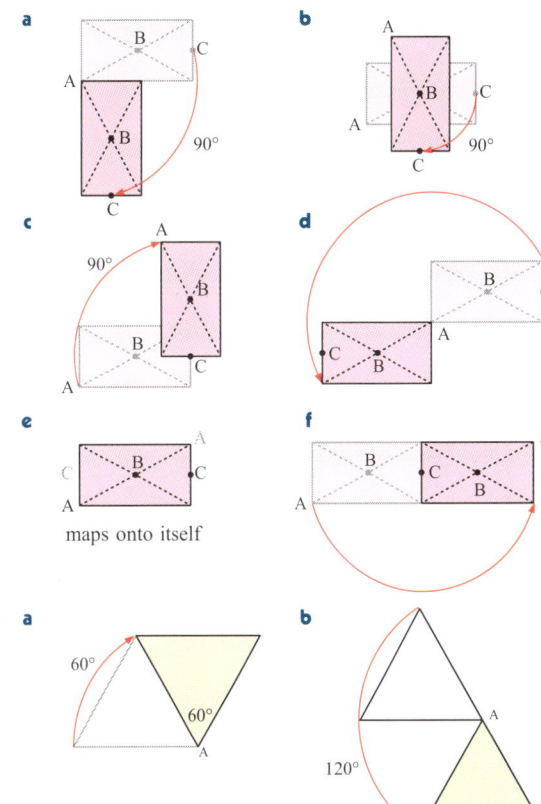

 2   4

EXERCISE 16C.1

1 a, b, c, d, e (maps onto itself), f (figures)

2 a (60°, 60°), b (120°) (figures)

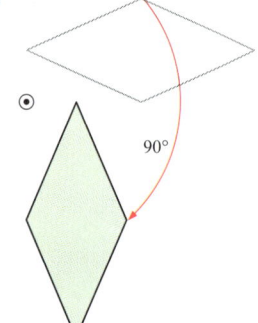

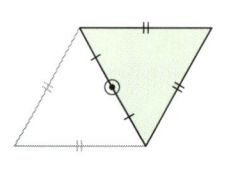

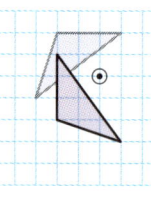

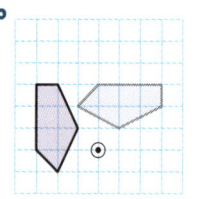

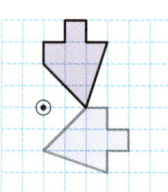

EXERCISE 16D

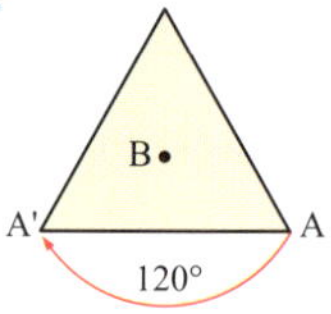

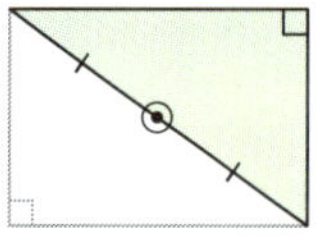

1 **a** neither; A has sides $3:2$, B $2:1$ **b** enlargement **c** reduction
2 **a** $k=2$ **b** $k=\frac{1}{2}$ **c** $k=3$ **d** $k=4$ **e** $k=\frac{1}{2}$ **f** $k=\frac{2}{5}$
3 **a** $k=\frac{1}{2}$ **b** $k=2$ **c** $k=\frac{1}{3}$ **d** $k=\frac{1}{4}$ **e** $k=2$ **f** $k=\frac{5}{2}$

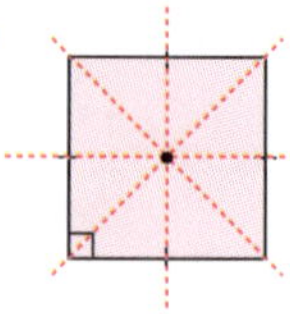

EXERCISE 16E

1 **a** $x=6\frac{2}{3}$ **b** $x=2\frac{6}{7}$ **c** $x=4\frac{5}{7}$ **d** $x=3\frac{1}{8}$ **e** $x=13\frac{1}{3}$ **f** $x=7\frac{7}{11}$
2 **a** true **b** true **c** false
3 Inside rectangle has sides in $5:3$. Outside rectangle has sides in $7:5$ and $5:3 \neq 7:5$ ∴ not similar.
4 **a** **b**

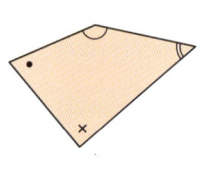

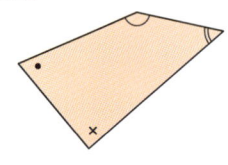

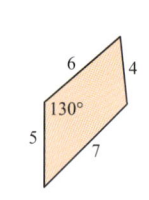

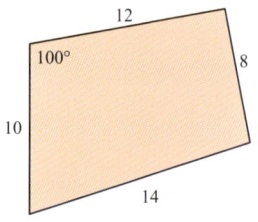

EXERCISE 16F

1 **a** $\widehat{ABE} = \widehat{DEB}$ {alternate}, $\widehat{ACB} = \widehat{DCE}$ {vert. opp.}
    So, triangles are equiangular and ∴ similar.
   b $\widehat{PQR} = \widehat{STR}$ {given}, $\widehat{PRQ} = \widehat{SRT}$ {vert. opp.}
    So, triangles are equiangular and ∴ similar.
   c Both triangles are right angled and $\widehat{BCA} = \widehat{DCE}$ {vert. opp.}
    So, triangles are equiangular and ∴ similar.
2 **a** $x=3$ **b** $x=4.8$ **c** $x=9\frac{1}{3}$
3 ≈ 7.12 m high 4 **b** ≈ 9.22 m 5 **b** ≈ 28.7 m

EXERCISE 16G.1

1 **a** **i** $k=\frac{1}{2}$ **ii** 5 cm **b** **i** $k=\frac{3}{2}$ **ii** 18 cm^2
   c **i** $k=\frac{5}{2}$ **ii** 4 cm^2
   d **i** $k \approx 0.548$ **ii** ≈ 4.38 cm
   e **i** $k \approx 0.758$ **ii** ≈ 3.18 m
   f **i** $k=1.45$ **ii** ≈ 33.3 cm^2
2 **a** $k=3$ **b** 15 m and 18 m **c** $1:9$
3 **a** $k=\sqrt{2}$ **b** ≈ 14.1 cm by 7.07 cm
4 **a** $k=\frac{1}{\sqrt{3}}$ **b** ≈ 62.0 m

EXERCISE 16G.2

1 **a** 243 cm^3 **b** $3\frac{1}{3}$ m **c** 80 cm^3
   d ≈ 55.6 cm^3 **e** ≈ 5.26 cm **f** 8 cm
2 **a** $k=3$ **b** 4 cm **c** $27:1$ or $1:27$ 3 6 cm^2
4 **a** $k=\frac{3}{2}$ **b** 14 850 cm^3 **c** 280 cm^2

---

c (triangle with B, A', A, 120°)

3 **a** (kite rotated 90°) **b** (right triangle) **c** (triangle)

4 **a** **b** **c**

EXERCISE 16C.2

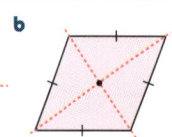

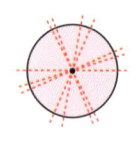

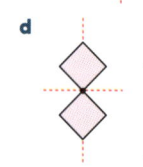

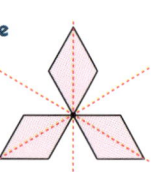

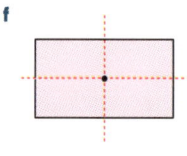

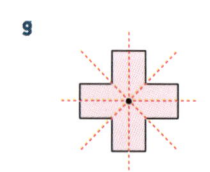

1 **a** square **b** rhombus **c** circle **d** **e** **f** rectangle **g** **h** hexagon

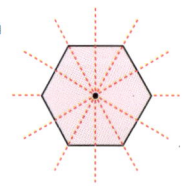

2 **a** 4 **b** 2 **c** infinite **d** 2 **e** 3 **f** 2 **g** 4 **h** 6
3 **a** Regular pentagon order 5 **b** Regular octagon order 8

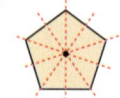

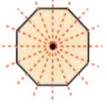

ANSWERS 527

EXERCISE 16H

1 **a** Yes (SSS) **b** Yes (RHS) **c** No
  d Yes (AAcorS) **e** Yes (AAcorS) **f** No **g** No
  h Yes (SAS) **i** Yes (SAS)

2 (1) CB = CD {given}
  (2) AC = EC {given}
  (3) $A\widehat{C}B = E\widehat{C}D$ {vertically opposite}
  ∴ these triangles are congruent {SAS}
  Consequently $A\widehat{B}C = E\widehat{D}C$
  ∴ [AB] ∥ [DE] {equal alternate angles}

3 **a** congruent (SSS) **b** • $A\widehat{C}N = B\widehat{C}N$
  • $C\widehat{A}N = C\widehat{B}N$
  • [CN] ⊥ [AB]

4 **a** congruent (SAS) **b** • BC = DC
  • $B\widehat{C}A = D\widehat{C}A$
  • $A\widehat{B}C = A\widehat{D}C$

5 **a** Hint: Show AAcorS
  b • Opposite sides are equal in length.
      • Opposite angles are equal.

6 **a** Hint: Show SSS
  b Consequence is $B\widehat{A}C = D\widehat{C}A$ and so [AB] ∥ [DC].
     Another consequence is $A\widehat{C}B = C\widehat{A}D$
     and so [AD] ∥ [BC].
     ∴ ABCD is a parallelogram.

REVIEW SET 16A

1 **a** $\begin{pmatrix} -3 \\ -1 \end{pmatrix}$ **b**

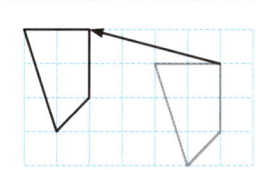

2

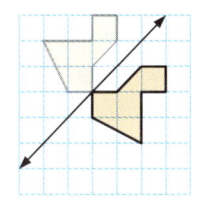

3 **a**
  b There are no lines of symmetry. 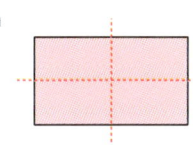

4 **a** **b**

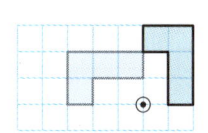

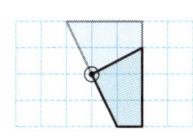

5 **a** order 4 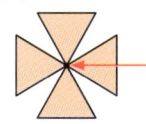 **b** order 2

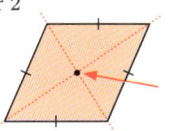

6

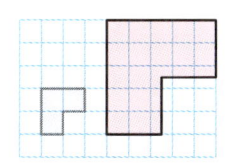

7 **a** $k = \frac{3}{5}$
  b 5.4 cm²

8 **a** $k = 1.2$ **b** 72 cm² **c** ≈ 1389 cm³
9 **a** not congruent **b** not congruent
10 **a** Hint: Show SAS

REVIEW SET 16B

1

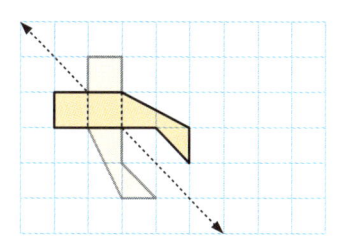

2 **a** 3 of them **b** Yes, where the 3 lines of symmetry meet.
  c

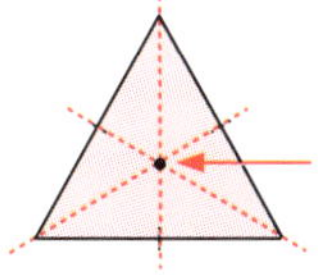

3

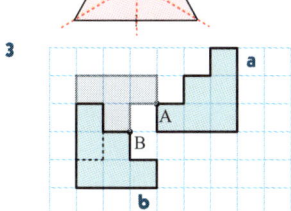

4 **a** $\begin{pmatrix} 5 \\ -1 \end{pmatrix}$
  b $\begin{pmatrix} -3 \\ -2 \end{pmatrix}$

5

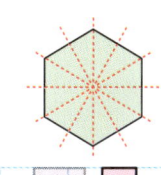

6 **a** $k = \frac{3}{2}$
  b $x = 4\frac{1}{2}$
  c 27 : 8

7

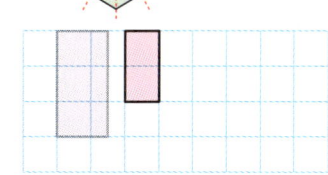

8 ≈ 10.4 m high
9 Hint:
  Explain why △s ADM, BCN are congruent, etc. 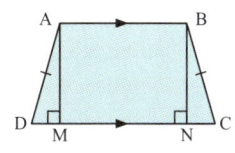

EXERCISE 17A

1 **a** 9 **b** 5 **c** 4 **d** 25 **e** 14 **f** 12
2 **a** 2x **b** 3y **c** 3a² **d** 4 **e** y **f** −4
  g −q **h** 2a² **i** −3t
3 **a** 4 **b** a **c** 5 **d** y **e** 8c **f** 3d
  g 1 **h** 9y **i** 9x
4 **a** st **b** xy **c** 8x **d** x **e** a **f** a²
  g 2b **h** 5a **i** 6b² **j** 7ab **k** 8ab **l** 9ab
  m 5 **n** 2b **o** 4xy
5 **a** (a + 7) **b** 3(2 + b) **c** x(x − 4) **d** 5(x − 2)
  e 2(x − 1) **f** 3y(y + 1)

EXERCISE 17B

1 **a** $3x+6 = 3(x+2)$ **b** $4a-8 = 4(a-2)$
  c $16-4b = 4(4-b)$ **d** $14x+21+7(2x+3)$
  e $6p^2-p = p(6p-1)$ **f** $15x^2+10x = 5x(3x+2)$

2 **a** $6a+12 = 6(a+2)$ **b** $3b-3 = 3(b-1)$
  c $9+3c = 3(3+c)$ **d** $16d-12 = 4(4d-3)$
  e $15xy+20y = 5y(3x+4)$ **f** $12y-18y^2 = 6y(2-3y)$
  g $3xy-xy^2 = xy(3-y)$ **h** $5xy-yz = y(5x-z)$

3 **a** $2(x-2)$ **b** $7(b+4)$ **c** $9(x-3)$ **d** $3(4+x)$
  e $11(a+b)$ **f** $r(p+q)$ **g** $7(5-2x)$ **h** $x(y+1)$
  i $a(1+b)$ **j** $x(1-y)$ **k** $c(2+d)$ **l** $x(7-y)$
  m $q(p-8r)$ **n** $b(a-c)$ **o** $y(2x-z)$ **p** $6x(2-3y)$

4 **a** $x(x+5)$ **b** $5x(x+3)$ **c** $2x(7-x)$
  d $4x(1-4x)$ **e** $4x(2x+3)$ **f** $x^2(x+2)$
  g $x(x^2+3)$ **h** $x^2(7x-1)$ **i** $ab(a-b)$
  j $x(1+x+x^2)$ **k** $5(x^2-2x+3)$ **l** $2x(x-4-2x^2)$

5 **a** $2(2-a)$ **b** $3(b-5)$ **c** $6(2d-c)$
  d $y(3-x)$ **e** $x(y-1)$ **f** $x(1-x)$
  g $6y(y-2)$ **h** $b(2b-a)$ **i** $c(1-c)$

6 **a** $-8(x+4)$ **b** $-7(1+x)$ **c** $-3(x+y)$
  d $-2(2c+d)$ **e** $-x(y+1)$ **f** $-5a(1+3a)$
  g $-6b(2b+1)$ **h** $-2c(4c+3d)$ **i** $-11e(2e+3)$

7 **a** $(x+1)(4+x)$ **b** $(x-3)(5+x)$ **c** $(x+7)(3-x)$
  d $(x+4)(x+1)$ **e** $(c-1)(a-b)$ **f** $(2+x)(a-b)$
  g $(y+z)(x-1)$ **h** $(x-2)(x+1)$

8 **a** $(x+1)(x+7)$ **b** $(x+3)(5+x)$
  c $(x+2)(x-12)$ **d** $(x-9)(x-6)$
  e $2(a+3)(a+5)$ **f** $(b-1)(a-b-3)$
  g $4(a+3)(3a+7)$ **h** $-(x-8)(x+16)$
  i $-(m-7)(m+2)$ **j** $(n-3)(23-7n)$

EXERCISE 17C

1 **a** $(c+d)(c-d)$ **b** $(m+n)(m-n)$
  c $(n+m)(n-m)$ **d** $(a+b)(a-b)$
  e $(x+4)(x-4)$ **f** $(x+6)(x-6)$
  g $(a+5)(a-5)$ **h** $(2x+1)(2x-1)$
  i $(4b+5)(4b-5)$ **j** $(3y+4)(3y-4)$
  k $(7+c)(7-c)$ **l** $(3+2y)(3-2y)$

2 **a** $3(x+2)(x-2)$ **b** $8(x+3)(x-3)$
  c $2(a+5)(a-5)$ **d** $(2x+5)(2x-5)$
  e $9(b+10)(b-10)$ **f** $3(b+4)(b-4)$
  g $\pi(R+r)(R-r)$ **h** $10(1+x)(1-x)$
  i $p(p+2)(p-2)$ **j** $x(x+1)(x-1)$
  k $x^2(x+1)(x-1)$ **l** $xy(x+y)(x-y)$

3 **a** $(7a+b)(7a-b)$ **b** $(y+6x)(y-6x)$
  c $(3x+5y)(3x-5y)$ **d** $(3a+4b)(3a-4b)$
  e $(a+9b)(a-9b)$ **f** $(ab+2)(ab-2)$
  g $(6x+pq)(6x-pq)$ **h** $(4a+5bc)(4a-5bc)$

4 **a** $(x+5)(x+1)$ **b** $(x+3)(x-7)$ **c** $(x+5)(3-x)$
  d $(x+3)(9-x)$ **e** $(x+5)(x+3)$ **f** $(5-x)(x-3)$
  g $(2x+5)(2x-1)$ **h** $(5-4x)(4x+13)$
  i $(4x-1)(5-2x)$ **j** $(3x-11)(x-9)$

k $4(2x+1)(x-1)$ **l** $(3x+5)(5-x)$
m $4(x+2)$ **n** $-3(x+4)(5x+4)$ **o** $3x(x+4)$

EXERCISE 17D

1 **a** x^2+2x+1 and x^2-2x+1
  b x^2+4x+4 and x^2-4x+4
  c $x^2+8x+16$ and $x^2-8x+16$
  d $4x^2+4x+1$ and $4x^2-4x+1$
  e $9x^2+12x+4$ and $9x^2-12x+4$
  f $16x^2+72x+81$ and $16x^2-72x+81$
  g $4x^2+4cx+c^2$ and $4x^2-4cx+c^2$
  h $x^2+4dx+4d^2$ and $x^2-4dx+4d^2$
  i $a^2c^2+4ac+4$ and $a^2c^2-4ac+4$

2 **a** $(x+1)^2$ **b** $(x-2)^2$ **c** $(x-3)^2$ **d** $(x+5)^2$
  e $(x-8)^2$ **f** $(x+10)^2$ **g** $(x-6)^2$ **h** $(x+7)^2$
  i $(x-9)^2$

3 **a** $(2x+1)^2$ **b** $(4x-5)^2$ **c** $(2x+7)^2$ **d** $(2x-3)^2$
  e $(3x+1)^2$ **f** $(3x-5)^2$

4 **a** $2(x+1)^2$ **b** $2(x-3)^2$ **c** $3(x+5)^2$
  d $-(x-3)^2$ **e** $-(x+4)^2$ **f** $-(x-8)^2$
  g $-2(x-10)^2$ **h** $-(2b-7)^2$ **i** $a(x-5)^2$

EXERCISE 17E

1 **a** 2 and 4 **b** 2 and 7 **c** 3 and 7 **d** 6 and -1
  e -7 and 1 **f** -11 and 2 **g** -2 and -8 **h** -8 and -3

2 **a** $(x+1)(x+2)$ **b** $(x+6)(x+4)$ **c** $(x+2)(x+9)$
  d $(x+4)(x+9)$ **e** $(x+5)(x+7)$ **f** $(x+25)(x+1)$
  g $(x+3)(x+4)$ **h** $(x+9)(x+6)$ **i** $(x+50)(x+2)$

3 **a** $(x-1)(x-9)$ **b** $(x-2)(x-4)$ **c** $(x-12)(x-1)$
  d $(x-2)(x-9)$ **e** $(x-11)(x-3)$ **f** $(x-6)(x-4)$
  g $(x-9)(x-5)$ **h** $(x-20)(x-4)$ **i** $(x-12)(x-4)$

4 **a** $(x-2)(x+1)$ **b** $(x-3)(x+2)$ **c** $(x+3)(x-2)$
  d $(x+7)(x-4)$ **e** $(x+9)(x-5)$ **f** $(x-5)(x+3)$
  g $(x-6)(x+3)$ **h** $(x+9)(x-3)$ **i** $(x-6)(x+5)$
  j $(x+15)(x-2)$ **k** $(x+12)(x-5)$ **l** $(x-25)(x+4)$

5 **a** $2(x+2)(x+3)$ **b** $2(x+2)(x+7)$
  c $3(x+3)(x+4)$ **d** $5(x-3)(x+1)$
  e $4(x+9)(x+1)$ **f** $5(x+1)(x+3)$
  g $6(x-5)(x+1)$ **h** $10(x-2)(x-6)$
  i $5(x-2)(x-10)$ **j** $7(x-2)^2$
  k $6(x+6)(x-1)$ **l** $9(x-2)(x-4)$
  m $x(x+6)(x+8)$ **n** $x(x-12)(x+3)$
  o $x(x+11)(x-5)$

EXERCISE 17F

1 **a** $5a(a+2)$ **b** $6(b^2+2)$ **c** $5(x-5y)$
  d $(d+3)(d+9)$ **e** $(x-3)(x-8)$ **f** $(y-7)(y+3)$
  g $-x(x+16)$ **h** $q^2(1+q)$ **i** $ab(a-2)$
  j $-7(x^2+4)$ **k** $(s-7)(s+6)$ **l** $2x(8-x^2)$
  m $2x(1-14y)$ **n** $m(m+9n)$ **o** $(y-3)(y-5)$
  p $6(x-3)(x+2)$ **q** $6(x-3)^2$ **r** $x(x+1)^2$

2 **a** $(x-4)^2$ **b** $(x+8)(x-8)$ **c** $9(c+3)(c-3)$
  d $9(1+p)(1-p)$ **e** $3(x+3)(x-3)$ **f** $5(a+1)^2$
  g $(5x+2y)(5x-2y)$ **h** $x(x-1)^2$ **i** $2(x-8)^2$

3 a $x(y-z+1)$ b $3x^2(x-1)$ c $xy(xy-5)$
  d $x(3+2x)(3-2x)$ e $x(x+1)$ f $y(x+z)(x-z)$
  g $(x+2)(a-b)$ h $(x+y)(3-x)$ i $(a+b)(a-b)$
  j $x(x+4)(x-4)$ k $3(x+5)^2$ l $x(2y+x)(2y-x)$

REVIEW SET 17A

1 a $3ab$ b $3(x+1)$
2 a $x(x-3)$ b $3n(m+2n)$ c $ax(x^2+2x+3)$
3 a $-2x(x+16)$ b $(t+2)(d-4)$ c $(x-1)(x-2)$
  d $(x+3)(2x-5)$ e $3(g+1)(g-2)$ f $(b-c)^2$
4 a $(3+4x)(3-4x)$ b $(2x+5)^2$ c $(3x-1)^2$
  d $5(x-2)^2$ e $(3a+2b)(3a-2b)$ f $6(x+2)(x-2)$
5 a $(x+7)(x+3)$ b $(x+7)(x-3)$ c $(x-7)(x+3)$
  d $(x-2)(x-3)$ e $4(x-3)(x+1)$ f $-(x+9)(x+4)$
  g $(x+5)(x+4)$ h $2(x-6)(x+5)$ i $3(x-2)(x-8)$

REVIEW SET 17B

1 a $2y$ b $2(x-2)$
2 a $2x(x+3)$ b $-2x(y+2)$ c $ax(a+x-2)$
3 a $xy(y+4)(y-4)$ b $3(x-10)^2$ c $(a+2)(p-q)$
  d $2cd(2d-3c)$ e $(k-3)(k-2)$ f $x(x+2)$
4 a $2(x+5)(x-5)$ b $(x-6)^2$ c $(n-3)^2$
  d $(7+3z)(7-3z)$ e $2(x-1)^2$ f $x(x+4)^2$
5 a $(x+5)(x+7)$ b $(x+7)(x-5)$ c $(x-5)(x-7)$
  d $2(x-7)(x+5)$ e $(x-6)(x-5)$
  f $(x-10)(x+2)$ g $(x-11)(x-3)$
  h $4(x-11)(x+2)$ i $x(x+9)(x-4)$

EXERCISE 18A

1 a numerical b categorical c categorical
  d numerical e numerical f numerical
  g categorical h numerical
2 a Ford, Mercedes, Fiat, Renault, ...
  b car, bus, train, bicycle, walk, ...
  c strings, woodwind, brass, percussion, ...
  d TV, newspaper, radio, internet, magazine, ...
3 a categorical b quantitative discrete
  c quantitative continuous d quantitative continuous
  e quantitative continuous f quantitative discrete
  g categorical h quantitative continuous
  i quantitative continuous j categorical
  k quantitative discrete l quantitative discrete
  m quantitative discrete n quantitative discrete
4 a census b sample c sample d census e sample
5 a Likely to be biased as members of a dog club generally like dogs.
  b Likely to be biased as most students probably don't realise the benefit of homework.
  c Commuters at peak hour are more likely to be unhappy about crowding in buses.
6 a country of origin and frequency
  b frequency
  c 36 people
  d England

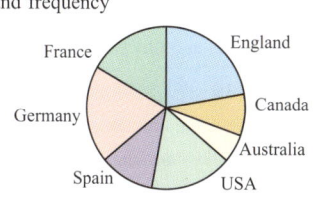

7 a Dependent *Frequency*; Independent *TV Brand*
  b Probably biased as only one street was used. A random sample of streets and people within them is essential.
  c C d

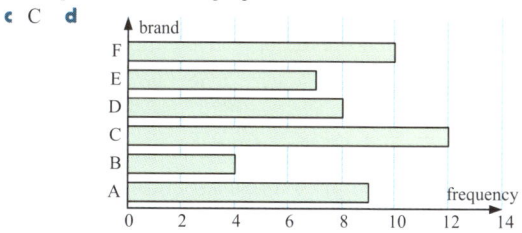

8 a $46°$ b $64°$ c $\approx 68.5°$ **9** 1470 people

EXERCISE 18B

1 a
Preference	Male	Female	Totals
Basketball	21	20	41
Tennis	9	35	44
Totals	30	55	85

  b females c 48.2% d 79.5%
2 a 54.5% b 20.6% c north
3 a
Home computer	1997	2007	Totals
Yes	113	281	394
No	159	23	182
Totals	272	304	576

  b $\approx 41.5\%$ c $\approx 7.57\%$ d $\approx 50.9\%$
4 a 79 b 43.3% c 38.7% d under 30, Greek food
5 a
Single People				
	18 to 35	36 to 59	60+	Total
1 bedroom	2	11	26	39
2 bedrooms	7	9	15	31
3 bedrooms	2	3	3	8
Totals	11	23	44	78

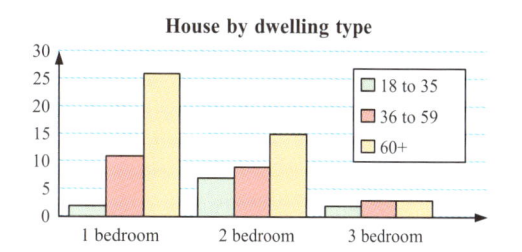

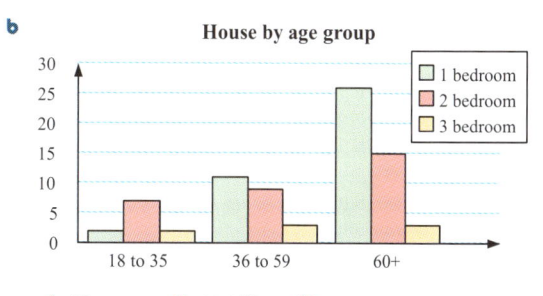

  c i 78 ii 28.7% iii 60+, 1 bedroom
  iv 18.0% v 39.7%
  d i true ii true iii false

ANSWERS

EXERCISE 18C

1 a

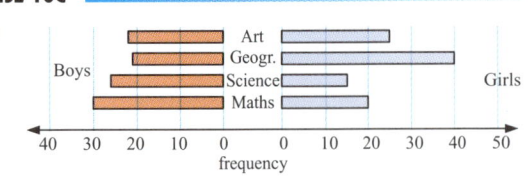

Boys / Girls bar chart: Art, Geogr., Science, Maths; frequency axis from 40 to 50.

b Geography **c** boys **d** Art

2 a Favourite movie types (under 30 / over 30):
- Action: ~38, ~17
- Comedy: ~41, ~20
- Drama: ~29, ~25
- Horror: ~31, ~7

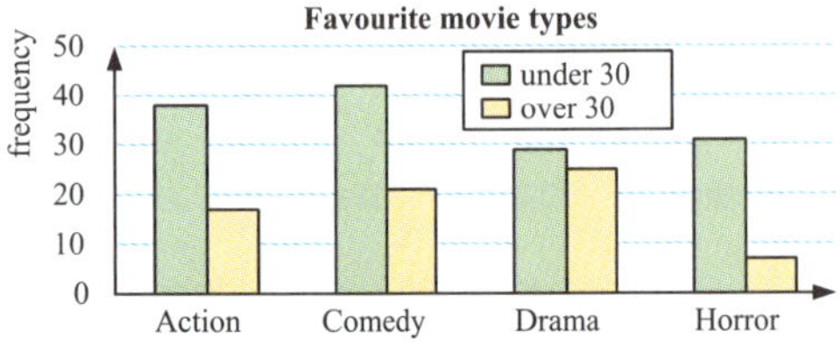

b No, the sample sizes were different because more people surveyed were under 30 than over 30.

c Favourite movie types (relative frequency):
- Action: 0.27, 0.24
- Comedy: 0.30, 0.30
- Drama: 0.21, 0.35
- Horror: 0.22, 0.10

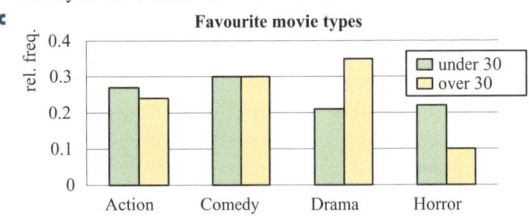

This is a more sensible way of comparing the groups.

d over 30s **e** Comedy

3 a Arton / Burnley side-by-side bar chart: Undecided, Independent, Liberal, Labor; frequency scale 0 to 40 each side.

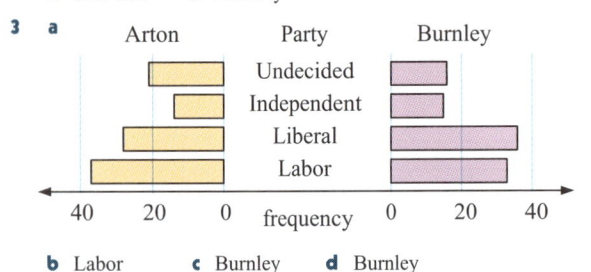

b Labor **c** Burnley **d** Burnley

EXERCISE 18D

1 a 820 **b** 40
  c
   i The best friends of the surveyor would probably have opinions like his.
   ii The students in one class will not represent students of all ages within the school.
   iii People who would volunteer to fill in the survey would be likely to have strong opinions and so not represent the population.

2 Those standing outside the office building are more likely to be smokers since smoking is banned in the workplace.

3 a Only people who do not work between 1 pm and 3 pm would be selected.
  b People who play golf are not likely to be representative of the whole population.
  c These people are likely to be students or the employed, not the unemployed, senior citizens, etc.
  d Only those people home at the time will be surveyed, and the people in that street may not have opinions indicative of the general population (street in a poor area, rich area, etc.).

EXERCISE 18E

1 a The fish sold at Market 2 looks to be 4 times as much as at Market 1 whereas it is actually only double.
  b A and B produce the same quantity of milk, but B looks more because a bigger carton is shown.
  c Because the y-axis does not begin at zero, it looks as though the increases are far greater than they really are.
  d The width of the boxes is increased, not just the height, so the increase in exports looks greater than it really is.

2 a A **b** no, only about 30% **c** no

REVIEW SET 18A

1 a categorical **b** quantitative discrete

2 a type of food and frequency
  b Type of food is the independent variable, frequency is the dependent variable.
  c Only year 12 students were asked, so the sample is not representative of all students.
  d frequency bar chart:
   - pie: 20
   - hot dog: 16
   - pasta: 9
   - sandwich: 17
   - apple: 13
   - chips: 5

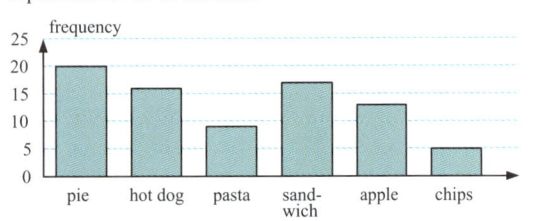

3 a

Age	Analogue	Digital	Totals
Under 30s	32	23	55
Over 30s	38	21	59
Totals	70	44	114

b 59 **c** 58.2% **d** 18.4%

4 a Friday / Saturday side-by-side bar chart:
- adult: 120, 140
- concession: 70, 35
- children: 65, 85

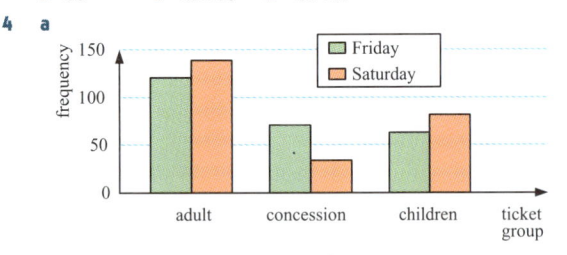

b Saturday **c** children **d** concession

5 a Hillsvale / Greensdale population pyramid – Sport: football, baseball, basketball, ice hockey, gridiron; frequency 0 to 40 each side.

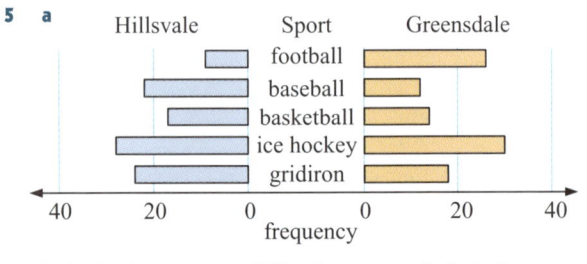

b ice hockey **c** Hillsvale **d** football

6 Only people who visit the library will be able to fill out the questionnaire, and this will not be representative of the public.

REVIEW SET 18B

1 a quantitative continuous **b** categorical

2 a sample **b** census **c** sample

3 a 635 **b** 15.0% **c** 42.4% **d** no

ANSWERS 531

4 a

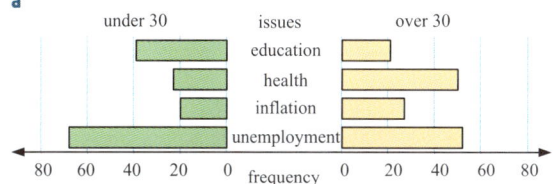

under 30 / over 30
issues: education, health, inflation, unemployment
frequency axis: 80 60 40 20 0 | 0 20 40 60 80

b unemployment **c** education **d** health

5 a hotel
b No, many more males were surveyed than females, so the sample is biased.
c (bar chart: rel freq. vs preference — hotel, shopping, park; male and female)
d females

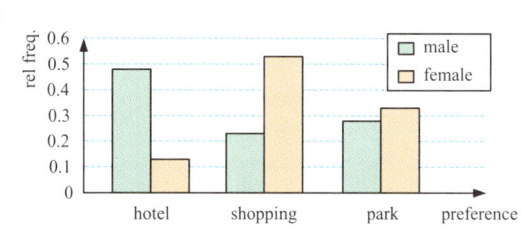

6 a Because the y-axis does not begin at zero, it looks as though the increase is greater than it really is.
b (line graph: employment ('000) vs year 2005–2008)

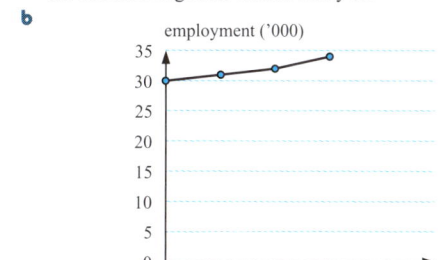

EXERCISE 19A

1 a $a = 0$ or $c = 0$ **b** $b = 0$ or $d = 0$
  c $a = 0$, $b = 0$ or $c = 0$ **d** $x = 0$ **e** $x = 0$ or 3
  f $x = 0$ **g** $x = 5$ or $y = 0$ **h** $x = 0$ or $y = 0$

2 a $x = 0$ or 1 **b** $x = 0$ or -5 **c** $x = 0$ or -2
  d $x = 1$ **e** $x = 0$ or 4 **f** $x = 0$ or -3
  g $x = 0$ or $-\frac{1}{2}$ **h** $x = 0$ or $\frac{3}{4}$

3 a $x = 1$ or 5 **b** $x = -2$ or 4 **c** $x = -3$ or -7
  d $x = -7$ or 11 **e** $x = 0$ or 8 **f** $x = -12$ or 5
  g $x = 0$ or -7 **h** $x = -\frac{1}{2}$ or 3 **i** $x = -6$ or $\frac{1}{3}$
  j $x = -\frac{1}{2}$ or -6 **k** $x = 0$ or $-\frac{5}{3}$ **l** $x = 31$ or -11
  m $x = -4$ or $\frac{1}{4}$ **n** $x = 0$ or -3 **o** $x = 2$ or $-\frac{4}{3}$

EXERCISE 19B

1 a $x = 0$ or 1 **b** $x = 0$ or 13 **c** $x = 0$ or -8
  d $x = 0$ or -3 **e** $x = 0$ or -2 **f** $x = 0$ or 5
  g $x = 0$ or 12 **h** $x = 0$ or -7 **i** $x = 0$ or 4
  j $x = 0$ or $\frac{7}{2}$ **k** $x = 0$ or 5 **l** $x = 0$ or -4

2 a $x = 0$ or 3 **b** $x = 0$ or 10 **c** $x = 0$ or -1
  d $x = 0$ or -6 **e** $x = 0$ or $-\frac{7}{2}$ **f** $x = 0$ or 5
  g $x = 0$ or 8 **h** $x = 0$ or 6 **i** $x = 0$ or $\frac{6}{5}$
  j $x = 0$ or -6 **k** $x = 0$ or 2 **l** $x = 0$ or 1

EXERCISE 19C

1 a $x = \pm 4$ **b** $x = \pm 7$ **c** $x = \pm 1$ **d** $x = \pm 5$
  e $x = \pm 12$ **f** $x = \pm 9$ **g** $x = \pm 2$ **h** $x = \pm 3$
  i $x = \pm 2$ **j** $x = \pm 2$ **k** $x = \pm 2$ **l** no solutions exist

2 a $x = \pm \frac{1}{2}$ **b** $x = \pm \frac{1}{3}$ **c** $x = \pm \frac{2}{5}$ **d** $x = \pm \frac{1}{2}$
  e $x = \pm \frac{3}{2}$ **f** $x = \pm \frac{2}{3}$ **g** no solutions exist **h** $x = \pm \frac{5}{4}$

EXERCISE 19D

1 a $x = -2$ or -5 **b** $x = -2$ or -4 **c** $x = -1$ or -10
  d $x = 2$ or 6 **e** $x = 1$ or 4 **f** $x = 3$ or 8
  g $x = -5$ **h** $x = 6$ or -3 **i** $x = -9$ or 2
  j $x = 11$ **k** $x = 3$ **l** $x = -1$ or 6
  m $x = 4$ or -15 **n** $x = 3$ or -21 **o** $x = -4$ or 16

2 a $x = -2$ or -5 **b** $x = 3$ or -5 **c** $x = 6$
  d $x = 3$ or 4 **e** $x = 7$ or -6 **f** $x = -2$ or -6

3 a $x = -1$ or 15 **b** $x = 1$ or 2 **c** $x = 7$ or -4
  d $x = 5$ or -4 **e** $x = -8$ or 1 **f** $x = -3$ or 8
  g $x = -4$ or 3 **h** $x = -5$ or 9 **i** $x = 2$ or 8
  j $x = 1$ **k** $x = -1$ or 20 **l** $x = -4$ or 8

4 a $x = -5$ or 3 **b** $x = -5$ or 12 **c** $x = 1$ or 6
  d $x = 3$ or -2 **e** $x = 1$ **f** $x = -4$ or 2

EXERCISE 19E

1 6 or -7 **2** 0 or 5 **3** 8 or -7
4 6 and 7 or -8 and -7 **5** 12 or -3
6 12 and 13 or -13 and -12
7 11 and 13 or -11 and -13 **8** -12 or 9
9 13 and 17 or -13 and -17 **10** 8 cm
11 a i $x(x+5)$ cm^2 **ii** $4x + 10$ cm **b** 22.91 cm^2
   c 54 cm
12 11 cm **13** 50 cm
14 a width $= 4\sqrt{2}$ cm **b** area = perimeter $= 8 + 8\sqrt{2}$
15 14 m by 12 m **16** 7 cm
17 a $a = 3$, $b = -10$ **b** $a = 3$, $b = 2\frac{1}{4}$
18 a $x^2 + 2x - 35 = 0$ **b** $-7, -6, -5$ or $5, 6, 7$
   c $x^2 = 36$ **d** $-7, -6, -5$ or $5, 6, 7$
   e Starting with the middle term being x.
19 9, 11 and 13 or $-9, -11$ and -13
20 $\sqrt{2} - 1$, $\sqrt{2}$ and $\sqrt{2} + 1$
21 $-1, 0, 1, 2, 3$ or $-3, -2, -1, 0, 1$
22 a square: 8 m by 8 m, rectangle: 4 m by 16 m **b** 72 m

EXERCISE 19F

1 a $x = 3, y = 9$ or $x = -2, y = 4$
  b $x = 4, y = 16$ or $x = -3, y = 9$ **c** $x = y = 1$
  d $x = -4, y = 16$ or $x = 3, y = 9$
  e $x = 1, y = 7$ or $x = 7, y = 1$
  f $x = 1, y = -5$ or $x = 5, y = -1$
  g $x = y = 2$ **h** $x = 3, y = -2$ or $x = -2, y = 3$

2 3 and 8 or -3 and -8 **3** 4 and 16 or -2 and 4

REVIEW SET 19A

1 a $x = 0$ **b** $x = -2$ or 8 **c** $x = \frac{1}{2}$
  d $x = 0$ or -2 **e** $x = 8$ or -3 **f** $x = 9$ or -2

2 a $x = -3$ or 4 **b** $x = 1$ or 3

3 a $x = 2, y = 4$ or $x = -1, y = 1$

532 ANSWERS

b $x = -3$, $y = 4$ or $x = -4$, $y = 3$
4 8 or -7 **5** 6 cm   **6** 9 cm
7 square: 16.8 cm by 16.8 cm
 rectangle: 12.6 cm by 11.2 cm
8 2 and -3 or -2 and 3

REVIEW SET 19B

1 a $x = 0$ **b** $x = 0$ or $\frac{1}{2}$ **c** $x = 3$ or 11
 d $x = \frac{1}{3}$ **e** $x = 0$ or $\frac{1}{2}$ **f** $x = -3$ or -4
2 a $x = 5$ or -2 **b** $x = 1$ or 4
3 a $x = 4$, $y = -2$ or $x = -2$, $y = 4$
 b $x = -5$, $y = -15$ or $x = 3$, $y = 1$
4 11 or -10 **5** 12 cm by 7 cm   **6** 135 m²
7 8, 10 and 12 or -12, -10, -8 **8** -1 and 2 or -2 and 1

EXERCISE 20A

1 a 52   **b** 50   **c** 76.9%   **d** approximately symmetrical
2 a number of visits
 b The number of visits to the doctor must be a whole number.
 c 28%   **d** 40%   **e** '.... 1'   **f** positively skewed
 g 6 and 7 are outliers
3 a number of eggs laid   **d** Number of eggs laid each day
 b discrete numerical
 c

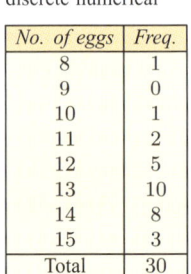

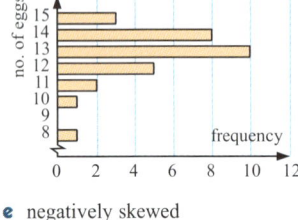

No. of eggs	Freq.
8	1
9	0
10	1
11	2
12	5
13	10
14	8
15	3
Total	30

 e negatively skewed
 f 36.7%
 g 8 is an outlier
4 a number of magazines bought each week
 b discrete, magazines can only be bought in whole number amounts
 c Magazines bought each week
 d positively skewed with no outliers   **e** 24%   **f** 36%
5 a

Number of sick days	Tally	Frequency
0	||||	4
1										9
2												12
3															16
4																		19
5														15
6											11
7									8
8					3
9				2
10		0
11		0
12		0
13			1
Total		100

b Number of sick days each year for smokers

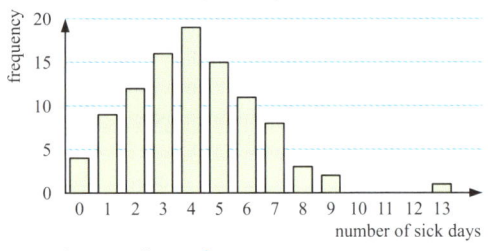

c yes, 13 is an outlier   **d** no
e The mode is higher for the *smokers* data (4 compared with 2 for the *non-smokers* data).

EXERCISE 20B

1 a

Score	Tally	Frequency
70 - 74	|||| |||	8
75 - 79	|||| |||| ||||		16
80 - 84	|||| |||| ||	12
85 - 89	||||	4
Total		40

 b 10%   **c** 20%   **d** '... 75 - 79 ...'

2 a
```
Stem | Leaf           Stem | Leaf
  1  | 9 8 9            1  | 8 9 9
  2  | 7 9 7 4 1        2  | 1 4 7 7 9
  3  | 4 6 4 3 0 5      3  | 0 3 4 4 5 6
  4  | 2 8 6            4  | 2 6 8
  5  | 2 1 6            5  | 1 2 6
```
1 | 9 means 19

3 a 13   **b** 62   **c** 16   **d** 4   **e** 6.25%

4 a
```
Stem | Leaf
  1  | 6 8 7 9 7 5 4 4 0 2 6
  2  | 1 3 4 9 8 9 5 3 6 7 4 0 5 3 2
  3  | 5 7 8 3 1 4 3 2 4
  4  | 1 9 3 1
  5  | 2
```
1 | 6 means 16

b
```
Stem | Leaf
  1  | 0 2 4 4 5 6 6 7 7 8 9
  2  | 0 1 2 3 3 3 4 4 5 5 6 7 8 9 9
  3  | 1 2 3 3 4 4 5 7 8
  4  | 1 1 3 9
  5  | 2
```
1 | 6 means 16

c All of the actual data values are shown.
d i 52   **ii** 10   **e** 12.5%   **f** 47.5%
g slightly positively skewed, no outliers

5 a
```
Stem | Leaf          Stem | Leaf
 06  | 2 8            06  | 2 8
 07  | 4 8            07  | 4 8
 08  | 3 6 4 6        08  | 3 4 6 6
 09  | 0 1 6 8 3 0    09  | 0 0 1 3 6 8
 10  | 9 3 5 6 4 2 8  10  | 2 3 4 5 6 8 9
 11  | 1 4 9 0 9 7    11  | 0 1 4 7 9 9
 12  | 0 9 5 1        12  | 0 1 5 9
 13  | 6 4 2 4        13  | 2 4 4 6
 14  | 0 5 2          14  | 0 2 5
 15  | 0              15  | 0
 16  | 7              16  | 7
```
06 | 2 means 62

 i 167   **ii** 62

c 100 - 109   **d** 4   **e** 22.5%   **f** symmetrical   **g** no

ANSWERS

EXERCISE 20C.1

1 a **i** 5.61 **ii** 6 **iii** 6 **b** **i** 16.3 **ii** 17 **iii** 18
  c **i** 24.8 **ii** 24.9 **iii** 23.5
  d **i** 128.6 **ii** 128 **iii** 115 and 127

2 a mean: €42 800; median: €43 500; mode: €33 000
  b The mode is the lowest value.

3 a median = 42, mode = 42 **b** median = 64, mode = 53
  c median = 340, mode = 350

4 a

Stem	Leaf
1	6 7 8 9
2	0 0 1 1 1 2 2 2 2 3 3 4 5 5 6 7 7 8 8 9
3	0 1 3 4 1 | 6 means 16

  b **i** 23 **ii** 24.1

5 a 19 mm **b** 19 mm **c** 17.7 mm **d** 4 mm

6 $1287 **7** 8 hours 20 minutes

EXERCISE 20C.2

1 a 1 **b** 1 **c** 1.43

2 a

No. of occupants	Frequency
1	5
2	7
3	6
4	4
5	2

  b 24 cars
  c **i** 2 **ii** 2.5 **iii** 2.63

3 a **i** 2 **ii** 2 **iii** 2.76
  b Number of times moving house (histogram, frequencies: 5, 9, 13, 8, 6, 3, 3, 2, 1; mode, median at 2; mean = 2.76)
  c positively skewed, no outliers
  d The mean is more affected by the higher values. **e** mean

4 a **i** 2 **ii** 2 **iii** 2.57 **b** **i** 4 **ii** 4 **iii** 4.09
  c mean
  d Yes, the mean is significantly higher for the *smokers* data.

EXERCISE 20D

1 a

```
        Before advertising          After advertising
                              4 | 7
                      9 7 6 | 5 |
                8 6 4 3 2 2 1 | 6 | 9
          9 8 7 7 6 5 4 4 3 2 1 | 7 | 0 6 8 9
                    9 8 4 4 3 2 | 8 | 0 4 4 5 8 9
                          4 3 1 | 9 | 0 2 2 3 3 3 5 8 8 8 9
                                | 10| 1 1 3 4 6 8 8
                                        4 | 7 means 47
```

  b yes, 47 is an outlier
  c *Before advertising*: symmetrical,
      After advertising: negatively skewed
  d The *After advertising* data has a higher mean (90.0 compared to 74.4) and median (92.5 compared to 74.5) than the *Before advertising* data.
  e increased

2 a

```
          Andre              Andrew
          8 7 7 2 | 18 | 8
    9 7 5 5 4 2 2 1 | 19 | 1 2 7 8
        8 8 6 6 4 3 1 | 20 | 0 3 5 6 6 7 9
              8 7 5 3 2 | 21 | 1 3 5 6 7 7 9 9 9
                      2 | 22 | 0 3 4 4    18 | 8 means 188
```

  b no
  c The data for Andre is positively skewed, while the data for Andrew is negatively skewed.
  d The data for Andrew has a higher mean (209.6 compared to 201.3) and median (211 compared to 201) than Andre.
  e Andrew generally serves the ball faster than Andre.

3 a

```
        Going to work           Returning from work
              8 7 7 | 15 |
        9 7 7 6 6 5 3 | 16 | 5 6 8
    8 8 7 4 3 3 2 1 1 | 17 | 2 4 6 6 6 7 9 9
                9 5 2 | 18 | 2 5 5 7 8 8 9 9
                      | 19 | 2 7
                      | 20 |
                      | 21 |
                      | 22 | 3        16 | 5 means 16.5
```

  b yes, 22.3 is an outlier
  c Both distributions are approximately symmetrical.
  d The *Returning from work* data has a higher mean (18.2 compared to 17.1) and median (18.1 compared to 17.1) than the *Going to work* data.
  e less

REVIEW SET 20A

1 a number of children in a household
  b discrete, only whole numbers are possible
  c Number of children in a household (dot plot, x-axis: no. of children 1–8)
  d positively skewed, 8 is an outlier

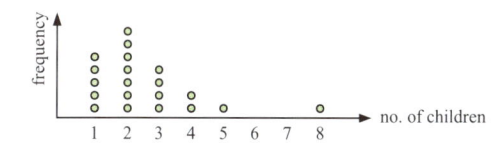

2 a 35.5 **b** 36.9 **c** 36.8

3 a 32 kg **b** 91 kg **c** 55 kg **d** 5 **e** 20%

4 a

Assists	Frequency
1	5
2	10
3	3
4	4
5	6
6	8
total	36

  b 128
  c **i** 2 **ii** 3.5 **iii** 3.56

5 a

Stem	Leaf
0	9
1	8 8
2	5 8 4 9 2 6 5 0 3 8 7
3	5 2 4 9 3 4 9 1 6 5 6 3 5 2
4	0 0 1 | 8 means 18

  b

Stem	Leaf
0	9
1	8 8
2	0 2 3 4 5 5 6 7 8 8 9
3	1 2 2 3 3 4 4 5 5 5 6 6 9 9
4	0 0 1 | 8 means 18

534 ANSWERS

c All the actual data values are shown.
d **i** 40 **ii** 9   **e** 20%

6 a
```
     Intersection A  |   | Intersection B
                   2 | 2 | 5 9
                   7 | 3 | 7 7 7
       9 8 7 7 6 6 5 3 2 | 4 | 0 1 3 6 7 7 8 8
       9 9 9 7 5 4 4 3 1 1 | 5 | 1 1 2 3 5 7 8
                 5 4 2 2 | 6 | 2 4 4 6        3 | 7 means 37
```
b Intersection A: 52; Intersection B: 48
c Intersection A: 52.3; Intersection B: 48.3
d Both distributions are approximately symmetrical.

REVIEW SET 20B

1 a number of goals scored
b discrete, only whole numbers are possible

c
Number of goals	Tally	Frequency
0	||||	4
1						5
2	|||| ||	7
3	|||| ||||	9
4						5
5						5
6		0
7	|	1
	Total	36

d Number of goals scored by hockey team (horizontal bar chart)

e 30.6%

2 a
```
Stem | Leaf
  3  | 1
  4  | 9 5
  5  | 8 8 7 8 3 5
  6  | 9 0 8 5 9 6 4 1 6 4 1 6 3
  7  | 0 1 2 5 6 7 8 4 0
  8  | 0 2 3 9 2 2
  9  | 1 4 0 2 4 1 1 7        3 | 1 means 31
```

b
```
Stem | Leaf
  3  | 1
  4  | 5 9
  5  | 3 5 7 8 8 8
  6  | 0 1 1 3 4 4 4 5 6 6 6 8 9 9
  7  | 0 0 1 2 4 5 6 7 8
  8  | 0 2 2 2 3 9
  9  | 0 1 1 1 2 4 4 7        3 | 1 means 31
```

c **i** 97 **ii** 31   **d** 40% **e** C

3 a 65 **b** 75   **c** 74.1
4 a **i** 9 **ii** 9 **iii** 8.47
b higher than the national average   **c** negative
5 a 42 and 51 **b** 51   **c** 52.3

6 a
```
     Doctors  |   | Lawyers
              | 17 | 1
              | 18 |
         9 4 | 19 | 7
       9 7 3 0 | 20 | 6
     9 7 7 6 5 3 2 1 0 | 21 | 0 4 6 9
         8 5 2 | 22 | 0 1 4 5 6 7 8 9
           5 2 | 23 | 2 3 6 8 8
                         20 | 6 means 206
```
b yes, 171 is an outlier
c Doctors: symmetrical; Lawyers: negatively skewed
d The Lawyers data has a higher mean (220.5 compared to 214.2) and median (224.5 compared to 214) than the Doctors data.
e From the samples above, it appears that lawyers generally work longer hours than doctors.

EXERCISE 21A

1 a 1 **b** $\frac{1}{2}$ **c** 2 **d** $1\frac{3}{5}$ **e** 1 **f** $4\frac{1}{3}$
  g 2 **h** -1 **i** 2 **j** 1
2 a -2 **b** 3 **c** 1 **d** -1 **e** 5 **f** 1
  g $-\frac{1}{2}$ **h** $-\frac{1}{3}$ **i** -1 **j** $-\frac{1}{2}$ **k** $\frac{1}{2}$ **l** 5
  m -5 **n** $1\frac{1}{4}$ **o** $-\frac{7}{9}$

EXERCISE 21B

1 a $\frac{x}{2}$ **b** $3y$ **c** 9 **d** $\frac{1}{2}$ **e** $\frac{3}{a}$ **f** $2b^2$
  g $\frac{13}{c}$ **h** $7d$
2 a $-\frac{a}{2}$ **b** $-\frac{1}{2a}$ **c** $\frac{a^2}{4}$ **d** -4 **e** $\frac{2}{t}$ **f** $-2d$
  g $-\frac{b}{2}$ **h** $-\frac{2b}{3a}$
3 a $25a$ **b** $5a^2$ **c** $\frac{5}{a}$ **d** $-4a$ **e** $\frac{3b^2}{2}$ **f** $2c^2$
  g 9 **h** e^3

EXERCISE 21C

1 a $\frac{x}{3}$ **b** 1 **c** $\frac{2}{3}$ **d** $\frac{x^2}{6}$
2 a $\frac{ab}{15}$ **b** $\frac{2}{5}$ **c** $\frac{b^2}{7}$ **d** $\frac{2}{9}$ **e** $\frac{1}{5a}$ **f** 7
  g $4c$ **h** $\frac{9}{d^2}$ **i** $\frac{y^3}{27}$ **j** $\frac{9a^2}{b^2}$ **k** $\frac{y^2}{x}$ **l** $\frac{a^3}{8}$
3 a $\frac{3}{a}$ **b** 1 **c** $\frac{6}{a^2}$ **d** $2\frac{1}{2}$
4 a $\frac{3}{5}$ **b** $\frac{2x}{9}$ **c** $2\frac{1}{2}$ **d** $\frac{y}{18}$ **e** $\frac{1}{3}$ **f** 7
  g $\frac{2y}{x}$ **h** $\frac{3x}{2}$

EXERCISE 21D

1 a $\frac{5x}{6}$ **b** $\frac{3x}{4}$ **c** $\frac{7x}{10}$ **d** $\frac{2x}{3}$
2 a $\frac{a}{6}$ **b** $\frac{a}{3}$ **c** $\frac{5a}{12}$ **d** $\frac{a}{2}$
3 a $\frac{9x}{14}$ **b** $\frac{y}{6}$ **c** $\frac{7a}{10}$ **d** $\frac{2b}{15}$ **e** $\frac{9c}{14}$ **f** $-\frac{d}{8}$
  g $\frac{5e}{6}$ **h** $\frac{5f}{14}$ **i** $\frac{17n}{10}$ **j** $-\frac{11p}{21}$ **k** $\frac{17k}{12}$ **l** $-\frac{s}{8}$

4 **a** $\dfrac{5}{x}$ **b** $\dfrac{5}{2x}$ **c** $\dfrac{x+2}{2x}$ **d** $\dfrac{2-x}{2x}$

5 **a** $\dfrac{5q+3p}{pq}$ **b** $\dfrac{7s+2r}{rs}$ **c** $\dfrac{4q+3p}{pq}$ **d** $\dfrac{3t}{2s}$
e $\dfrac{3a+14}{21}$ **f** $\dfrac{9}{2b}$ **g** $\dfrac{5a+3b}{5b}$ **h** $\dfrac{3a+c}{3b}$

6 **a** $\dfrac{a+5}{5}$ **b** $\dfrac{b-14}{7}$ **c** $\dfrac{4c}{3}$ **d** $\dfrac{8-d}{2}$
e $\dfrac{12+p}{3}$ **f** $\dfrac{14-q}{2}$ **g** $\dfrac{8r+1}{r}$ **h** $\dfrac{4s-3}{s}$

7 **a** $\dfrac{13x}{12}$ **b** $\dfrac{11y}{6}$ **c** $\dfrac{4}{p}$ **d** $\dfrac{13}{6q}$
e $\dfrac{2y+5x}{xy}$ **f** $-\dfrac{2}{3x}$ **g** $\dfrac{19a}{6}$ **h** $\dfrac{5x}{2}$

8 **a** $\dfrac{3a+2}{a^2}$ **b** $\dfrac{5+b}{b^2}$ **c** $\dfrac{6d-1}{d^2}$ **d** $\dfrac{5-4x}{x^2}$
e $\dfrac{2+x^2}{2}$ **f** $\dfrac{x^2+1}{x^2}$ **g** $\dfrac{x^2+2}{x}$ **h** $\dfrac{x^3+4}{x^2}$
i $\dfrac{20-a^2}{4}$ **j** $\dfrac{6b^2-2}{b^2}$ **k** $\dfrac{2x+x^2}{2}$ **l** $\dfrac{x^3-1}{x^2}$
m $\dfrac{4x^2+2}{x}$ **n** $\dfrac{6x^2-1}{x}$ **o** $\dfrac{3x^2-4}{4x}$ **p** $\dfrac{1+2x^2}{2x}$

EXERCISE 21E.1

1 **a** $x-2$ **b** $\dfrac{a+3}{2}$ **c** $3(d+1)$ **d** $\dfrac{c-3}{2}$
e $\dfrac{4}{z+3}$ **f** $\dfrac{3}{2(1+x)}$ **g** 3 **h** $\dfrac{x+2}{2(x-2)}$
i $\dfrac{x-y}{x}$ **j** $\dfrac{a+2}{2}$ **k** $\dfrac{1}{2(b-4)}$ **l** $\dfrac{2(p+q)}{3}$

2 **a** $2(x+1)$ **b** $\dfrac{x-1}{2}$ **c** cannot be simplified **d** cannot be simplified
e $\dfrac{a+2}{2(a-2)}$ **f** cannot be simplified **g** $x-2$ **h** $\dfrac{x-2}{2}$
i 2 **j** cannot be simplified **k** cannot be simplified **l** $\dfrac{3}{x+2}$

EXERCISE 21E.2

1 **a** $2x+3$ **b** cannot be simplified **c** cannot be simplified **d** $x-3$
e $3a+1$ **f** cannot be simplified **g** cannot be simplified **h** $b-2$
i $x-5$ **j** cannot be simplified **k** cannot be simplified **l** $y+3$
m $2x+8$ **n** $x+4$ **o** $\dfrac{x+4}{2}$ **p** $x+2$

2 **a** $\dfrac{2}{3}$ **b** $\dfrac{2}{3}$ **c** 2 **d** $1\dfrac{2}{3}$ **e** 7 **f** $\dfrac{1}{2}$ **g** x
h a **i** 3 **j** $a+c$ **k** b **l** $a+c+1$

3 **a** $x+3$ **b** $x-2$ **c** $3x$ **d** $5x$ **e** 4 **f** $3\dfrac{1}{2}$
g $2x$ **h** x **i** x^2-1 **j** x **k** b^2 **l** $\dfrac{y}{2}$

4 **a** -1 **b** cannot be simplified **c** -2 **d** $-1\dfrac{1}{3}$
e $-\dfrac{1}{3}$ **f** $-\dfrac{1}{4}$ **g** $-\dfrac{1}{r}$ **h** $-\dfrac{y}{2}$

EXERCISE 21E.3

1 **a** $x+1$ **b** $a-1$ **c** $\dfrac{1}{2-m}$ **d** $x-y$
e $\dfrac{x-1}{3}$ **f** $-(x+4)$ **g** $\dfrac{a+b}{b}$ **h** $-\dfrac{x}{y}$

2 **a** $x+1$ **b** $-(x+y)$ **c** -1 **d** $x-2$
e $\dfrac{1}{x-5}$ **f** $x+7$ **g** $\dfrac{x+6}{x+4}$ **h** $\dfrac{x+2}{x-4}$
i $\dfrac{x-3}{x}$ **j** $\dfrac{1-x}{x+3}$ **k** $\dfrac{2(x-3)}{x+2}$ **l** $\dfrac{x+4}{x-4}$
m $\dfrac{x+5}{x-8}$ **n** $\dfrac{4-x}{x}$ **o** $\dfrac{x+5}{5-x}$

REVIEW SET 21A

1 **a** $-\dfrac{3}{4}$ **b** -2 **c** 5 **2** **a** $\dfrac{a^2}{2}$ **b** $\dfrac{x^2}{2y}$ **c** $-4x^2$

3 **a** $\dfrac{x+6}{3}$ **b** $\dfrac{6-x}{3}$ **c** $\dfrac{6}{a}$ **d** $\dfrac{3a^3}{50}$ **e** $\dfrac{1}{2x}$ **f** $1\dfrac{1}{4}$

4 **a** $x+5$ **b** 3 **c** -1 **d** $\dfrac{5x}{2}$ **e** $x-5$
f $\dfrac{x+5}{2x}$ **g** $\dfrac{10-x}{3x}$ **h** $\dfrac{10-x}{x+10}$ **i** $\dfrac{x+9}{x-12}$

REVIEW SET 21B

1 **a** -2 **b** -1 **c** $-1\dfrac{1}{3}$ **2** **a** $4x^3$ **b** $\dfrac{xy}{5}$ **c** $\dfrac{4}{x}$

3 **a** $\dfrac{9a}{10}$ **b** $4x$ **c** $\dfrac{3a+8b}{2ab}$ **d** $-\dfrac{2a}{5}$ **e** $\dfrac{8x+2}{x^2}$ **f** $\dfrac{6}{ab}$

4 **a** $4-x$ **b** 7 **c** $\dfrac{4}{x}$ **d** $\dfrac{x+2}{x-2}$ **e** $\dfrac{x-1}{x+3}$
f $\dfrac{2}{x-3}$ **g** $\dfrac{x+7}{x-6}$ **h** $\dfrac{4(x+3)}{3-x}$ **i** $\dfrac{x-5}{x-3}$

EXERCISE 22A

1 **a** {red, blue} **b** {1, 2, 3, 4, 5, 6}
c {hearts, diamonds, clubs, spades} **d** {A, B, C, D, E, F}
e {Monday, Tuesday, Wednesday, Thursday, Friday, Saturday, Sunday}
f {A, B, C, D, Fail}

2 **a** 12 **b** **i** {2, 4, 6, 8, 10, 12} **ii** 6
c **i** {1, 2, 3, 4} **ii** 4 **d** **i** {4, 8, 12} **ii** 3

3 {MM, MF, FM, FF}

EXERCISE 22B

1 **a** $\dfrac{1}{5}$ **b** $\dfrac{1}{3}$ **c** $\dfrac{7}{15}$ **d** $\dfrac{4}{5}$ **e** $\dfrac{1}{5}$ **f** $\dfrac{8}{15}$

2 **a** $\dfrac{2}{3}$ **b** $\dfrac{1}{3}$ **3** **a** 0 **b** $\dfrac{1}{4}$ **c** $\dfrac{19}{32}$ **d** $\dfrac{5}{32}$

4 **a** $\dfrac{1}{6}$ **b** $\dfrac{1}{2}$ **c** $\dfrac{5}{6}$ **d** $\dfrac{1}{2}$

5 **a** **i** $\dfrac{1}{2}$ **ii** $\dfrac{5}{16}$ **iii** $\dfrac{11}{16}$ **iv** $\dfrac{11}{16}$
b **ii** and **iii**, or **ii** and **iv**

6 **a** **i** $\dfrac{1}{5}$ **ii** $\dfrac{7}{10}$ **b** a disc with an even number, $\dfrac{3}{10}$

7 **a** $\dfrac{13}{50}$ **b** $\dfrac{9}{25}$ **c** $\dfrac{16}{25}$ **d** 0

EXERCISE 22C

1 [grid diagram: $2 coin (T, H) vs $1 coin (H, T)]
  a $\frac{1}{4}$ **b** $\frac{1}{4}$ **c** $\frac{1}{2}$ **d** $\frac{3}{4}$

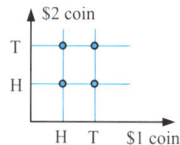

2 [grid diagram: bag B (W, R, B) vs bag A (R, B)]
  a $\frac{1}{6}$ **b** $\frac{1}{3}$ **c** $\frac{1}{3}$ **d** $\frac{2}{3}$

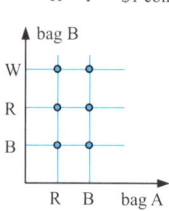

3 a [grid diagram: spinner (C, B, A) vs coin (H, T)]
  b i {HA, HB, HC, TA, TB, TC} **ii** 6
  c i $\frac{1}{6}$ **ii** $\frac{1}{3}$ **iii** $\frac{1}{3}$ **iv** $\frac{1}{3}$

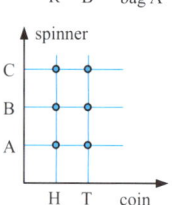

4 a [grid diagram: spinner 2 (1,2,3) vs spinner 1 (1,2,3)]
  b {11, 12, 13, 21, 22, 23, 31, 32, 33} **c** 9
  d i $\frac{1}{9}$ **ii** $\frac{4}{9}$ **iii** $\frac{2}{9}$ **iv** $\frac{2}{9}$ **v** $\frac{1}{3}$ **vi** $\frac{4}{9}$

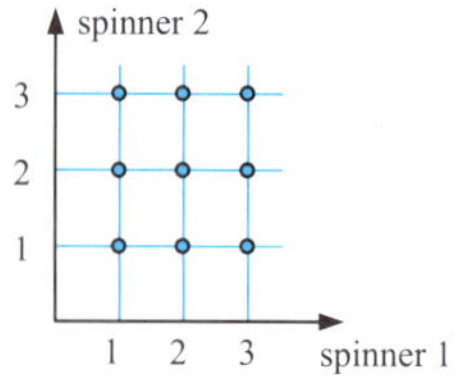

5 a [grid diagram: coin (T, H) vs spinner (1..6)] **b** 12
  c i $\frac{1}{12}$ **ii** $\frac{1}{4}$ **iii** $\frac{1}{6}$ **iv** $\frac{1}{6}$ **v** $\frac{5}{6}$ **vi** $\frac{5}{12}$ **vii** $\frac{7}{12}$

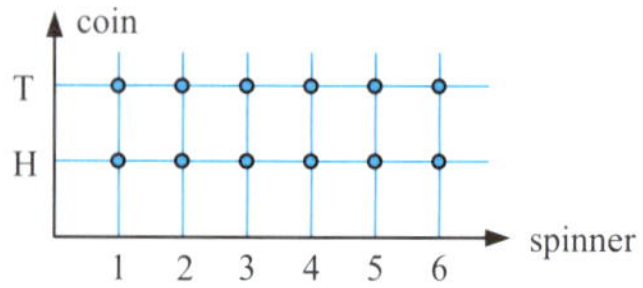

EXERCISE 22D

1 a $\frac{1}{3}$ **b** $\frac{1}{6}$ **c** $\frac{1}{3}$ **2 a** $\frac{5}{24}$ **b** $\frac{1}{8}$
3 a 0.4 **b** 0.1 **c** 0.1 **4 a** $\frac{19}{20}$ **b** $\frac{361}{400}$ **c** $\frac{6859}{8000}$
5 $\frac{1}{62\,500}$

EXERCISE 22E

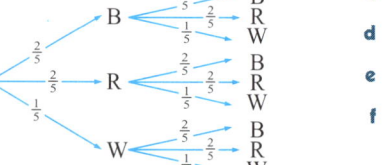

1 a [tree diagram: 1st spin B($\frac{2}{5}$), R($\frac{2}{5}$), W($\frac{1}{5}$); 2nd spin B($\frac{2}{5}$), R($\frac{2}{5}$), W($\frac{1}{5}$)]
  b $\frac{4}{25}$ **c** $\frac{1}{25}$ **d** $\frac{16}{25}$ **e** $\frac{9}{25}$ **f** $\frac{12}{25}$

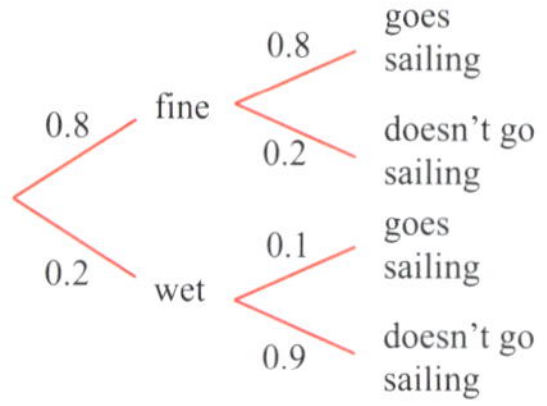

2 a i $\frac{2}{3}$ **ii** $\frac{1}{3}$ **b** [tree diagram: 1st roll A($\frac{2}{3}$), B($\frac{1}{3}$); 2nd roll A($\frac{2}{3}$), B($\frac{1}{3}$)]
  c i $\frac{4}{9}$ **ii** $\frac{5}{9}$ **iii** $\frac{2}{9}$ **iv** $\frac{4}{9}$

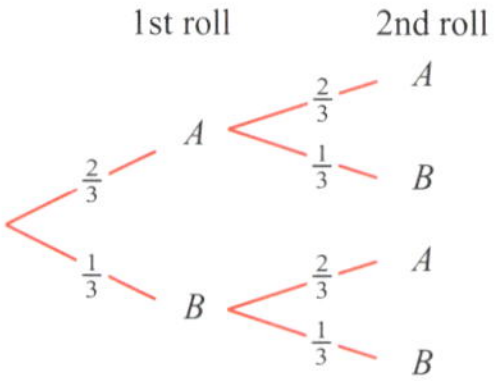

3 [tree diagram: fine (0.8) → goes sailing (0.8), doesn't go sailing (0.2); wet (0.2) → goes sailing (0.1), doesn't go sailing (0.9)]
  a 0.64 **b** 0.18 **c** 0.66

4 [tree diagram: 1st intersection stops ($\frac{1}{2}$) / does not stop ($\frac{1}{2}$); 2nd intersection stops ($\frac{1}{2}$) / does not stop ($\frac{1}{2}$)]
  a $\frac{1}{4}$ **b** $\frac{1}{4}$ **c** $\frac{1}{2}$ **d** $\frac{3}{4}$

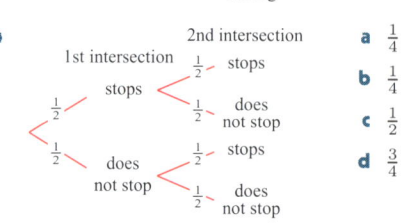

5 a 0.012 **b** 0.576 **c** 0.036 **6** $\frac{11}{24}$ **7** $\frac{1}{2}$ **8** $\frac{23}{54}$

EXERCISE 22F

1 a $\frac{1}{36}$ **b** 15 times **2 a** $\frac{1}{8}$ **b** 25 times **3** 569 times
4 a i $\frac{1}{12}$ **ii** $\frac{1}{6}$ **iii** $\frac{1}{4}$ **iv** $\frac{1}{2}$
  b i €1 **ii** €0.75 **iii** €0.50
  c €3 **d** expect to lose €1

EXERCISE 22G

1 a i $\frac{1}{3}$ **ii** $\frac{2}{3}$ **b i** $\frac{1}{6}$ **ii** $\frac{5}{6}$ **c i** $\frac{1}{51}$ **ii** $\frac{50}{51}$
  d i $\frac{1}{2}$ **ii** $\frac{1}{2}$ **e i** $\frac{3}{5}$ **ii** $\frac{2}{5}$
2 a $40 **b** $53.33

3 a

Race	Odds	($) Bet	Result	Win/Lose	Money ($) Remaining
					100
1	2 : 1	20	W	40	140
2	5 : 4	20	W	25	165
3	10 : 1	5	W	50	215
4	evens	30	W	30	245
5	1 : 4	60	W	15	260

  b he has won $160 **c** he has lost $35
  d $0. Assuming the odds given accurately reflect the probability of each horse winning, the punter can expect to break even.
  e The bookmaker would also have zero expectation in this case. In reality, the probability given by the odds are slightly higher than the horse's true probability of winning. This allows the bookmaker to make a profit.

REVIEW SET 22A

1 [grid diagram: coin (T, H) vs die (1..8)]
  a $\frac{1}{16}$ **b** $\frac{1}{4}$ **c** $\frac{3}{4}$

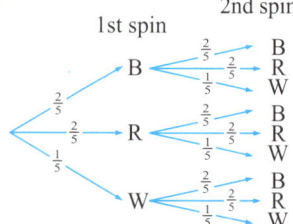

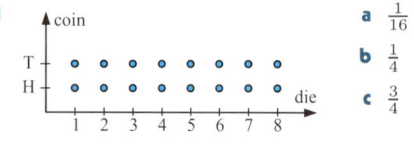

2 [tree diagram: Bag A ($\frac{1}{2}$) → M ($\frac{10}{16}$), C ($\frac{6}{16}$); Bag B ($\frac{1}{2}$) → M ($\frac{8}{16}$), C ($\frac{8}{16}$)]
  a $\frac{7}{16}$ **b** $\frac{9}{16}$

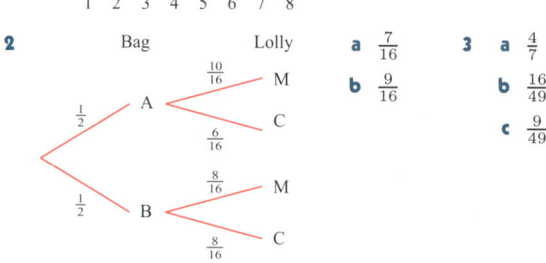

3 a $\frac{4}{7}$ **b** $\frac{16}{49}$ **c** $\frac{9}{49}$

ANSWERS 537

4

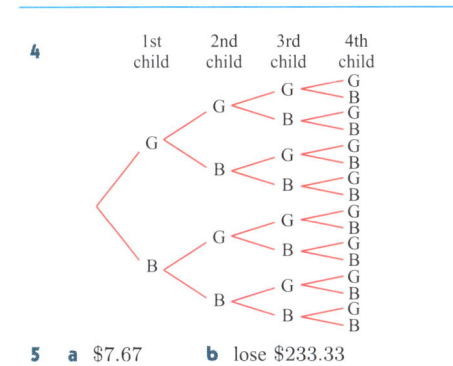

1st child	2nd child	3rd child	4th child

(tree diagram with G/B branches) $\frac{3}{8}$

5 a $7.67   **b** lose $233.33

REVIEW SET 22B

1 a (spinner diagram, die 1–6, rows A,B,C,D)   **b i** $\frac{1}{24}$ **ii** $\frac{3}{8}$ **iii** $\frac{1}{8}$

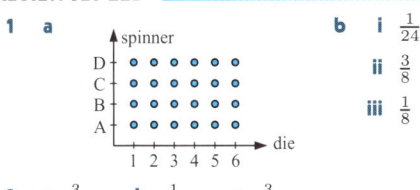

2 a $\frac{3}{5}$ **b** $\frac{1}{20}$ **c** $\frac{3}{20}$

3 a 0.2375   **b** 0.0375   **c** 0.0125   **d** 0.7125

4 a (1st, 2nd, 3rd child tree diagram) $\frac{3}{8}$ **b** 75

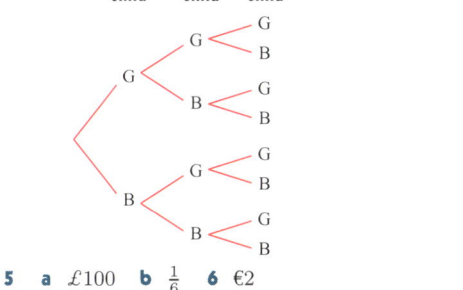

5 a £100   **b** $\frac{1}{6}$ **6** €2

EXERCISE 23A

1 a ≈ 6 m   **b** ≈ 10 m   **2** ≈ 49 m high
3 $\widehat{A} \approx 60°$, $\widehat{B} \approx 45°$, $\widehat{C} \approx 75°$ **4** ≈ 1550 m

EXERCISE 23B.1

1 a i [AB]   **ii** [BC]   **iii** [AC]
b i [RQ]   **ii** [PR]   **iii** [PQ]
c i [XZ]   **ii** [YZ]   **iii** [XY]

2 a b **b** c **c** c **d** b

EXERCISE 23B.2

1 a ≈ 0 **b** ≈ 0.17 **c** ≈ 0.42 **d** ≈ 0.50
e ≈ 0.71 **f** ≈ 0.87 **g** ≈ 0.94 **h** ≈ 1.00
3 a ≈ 1.00 **b** ≈ 0.98 **c** ≈ 0.91 **d** ≈ 0.87
e ≈ 0.71 **f** ≈ 0.50 **g** ≈ 0.34 **h** ≈ 0
5 $\approx (0.82, 0.57)$ **6**

θ	0°	30°	45°	60°	90°
$\sin\theta$	0	0.50	0.71	0.87	1
$\cos\theta$	1	0.87	0.71	0.50	0

EXERCISE 23B.3

1 a ≈ 0 **b** ≈ 0.18 **c** ≈ 0.27 **d** ≈ 0.47
e ≈ 0.70 **f** ≈ 0.84 **g** ≈ 1.00 **h** ≈ 1.19
3 This would be impossible as the tangent would be infinitely long.

4 $\triangle OAB$ is right angled isosceles.
$\therefore$ AB = OA = 1
i.e., tangent has length 1.
So, $\tan 45° = 1$.

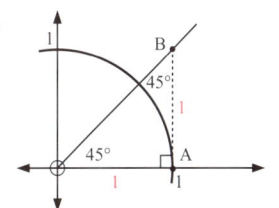

5 a $(\cos\theta, \sin\theta)$ **b i** $\cos\theta$ **ii** $\sin\theta$ **iii** $\tan\theta$
c $\dfrac{\tan\theta}{\text{ON}} = \dfrac{\text{PM}}{\text{OM}}$, etc.

EXERCISE 23C.1

1 a $\sin 68° = \dfrac{x}{a}$ **b** $\cos 37° = \dfrac{x}{b}$ **c** $\tan 58° = \dfrac{x}{c}$
d $\cos 42° = \dfrac{d}{x}$ **e** $\tan 51° = \dfrac{e}{x}$ **f** $\tan 71° = \dfrac{f}{x}$

2 a 8.34 cm   **b** 7.99 cm   **c** 6.11 m   **d** 18.60 km
e 7.02 m   **f** 28.48 cm   **g** 22.82 m   **h** 48.21 km
i 13.12 mm   **j** 17.78 cm   **k** 39.73 m   **l** 20.78 km

3 a $\theta = 52$, $a \approx 11.2$, $b \approx 8.7$
b $\theta = 27$, $a \approx 21.2$, $b \approx 9.6$
c $\theta = 52$, $s \approx 30.3$, $t \approx 18.7$

EXERCISE 23C.2

1 a 59.0°   **b** 30°   **c** 48.6°   **d** 30.8°   **e** 37.3°
f 53.7°   **g** 45.1°   **h** 44.0°   **i** 55.9°   **j** 52.9°
k 51.3°   **l** 18.4°

2 a $\theta \approx 34.8$, $\phi \approx 55.2$, $x \approx 5.7$
b $\alpha \approx 57.4$, $\beta \approx 32.6$, $x \approx 8.5$
c $a \approx 44.3$, $b \approx 45.7$, $x \approx 6.2$

3 a $5.7^2 + 4^2 = 48.49 \approx 7^2$ ✓
b $4.6^2 + 7.2^2 = 73 \approx 8.5^2$ ✓
c $8.92^2 - 6.38^2 \approx 38.86 \approx 6.2^2$ ✓

4 Impossible triangle, the hypotenuse must be the longest side.

EXERCISE 23D

1 ≈ 2.03 m   **2** ≈ 26.0 m   **3** ≈ 17.5 m   **4** $\approx 55.2°$
5 ≈ 37.5 m   **6** ≈ 342 m   **7** $\approx 32.0°$ **8** ≈ 1.93 km
9 ≈ 49.0 m   **10** ≈ 1.29 m   **11** ≈ 2.45 m   **12** ≈ 31.6 m
13 ≈ 19.9 cm   **14** ≈ 30.3 m   **15** 83.6° and 96.4°
16 ≈ 384 km per hour   **17** ≈ 98.2 cm   **18** ≈ 8.12 m
19 ≈ 1545 m   **20** $\approx 54.7°$

REVIEW SET 23A

1 a p **b** r **c** r **d** p **2 a** $\dfrac{5}{\sqrt{74}}$ **b** $\dfrac{7}{\sqrt{74}}$ **c** $\dfrac{5}{7}$
3 a $x \approx 64.3$ **b** $x \approx 38.7$ **c** $x \approx 53.1$ **4** ≈ 13.7 m
5 ≈ 116 cm   **6** ≈ 15.8 m   **7** $\approx 9.21°$ **8** ≈ 71.7 m

REVIEW SET 23B

1 a $y \approx 56.8$ **b** $y \approx 18.9$ **c** $y \approx 55.0$
2 a $\theta \approx 21.4$ **b** $\theta \approx 35.3$ **c** $\theta \approx 64.9$ **3** ≈ 1.71 m
4 3292 m   **5 a** p **b** q **c i** $\dfrac{q}{r}$ **ii** $\dfrac{p}{r}$ **iii** $\dfrac{q}{p}$
6 a $x \approx 27.2$ **b** $x \approx 38.7$ **c** $x \approx 3.6$
7 2.23 m   **8** $\approx 0.38°$

EXERCISE 24A

1 a **i** 6 **ii** AB, AE, BF, BC, CD, CF, DE, EF **iii** 8
  b undirected **c** **i** B and E **ii** B, C, and E
  d **i** A-B-F and A-E-F **ii** D-C-B-A and D-C-F-B-A

2 a **i** A, B, C, D, and E **ii** 8 **b** directed
  c **i** A, C, and E **ii** A, B, C, and D
  d **i** B-C, B-E-C, B-E-D-C
    ii A-B-C, A-D-C, A-E-C, A-B-E-C, A-E-D-C

3 a the people **b** friendships between the people
  c Paula and Gerry **d** Paula
  e adding a direction to the edge to make it an arc
    Alan → Paula

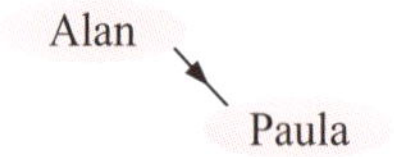

4 a the tennis players **b** the matches between players **c** 6
  d add a direction to the edge
    John → Rupesh could indicate that John beat Rupesh.

5 Jon wakes up and has a shower and dresses. He eats his cereal while he makes his toast. He drinks his juice while he makes and eats his toast. He then cleans his teeth and leaves for school. He listens to the radio from the time he wakes up until he leaves for school.

6 Home → A → D → school takes 12 minutes, which is quicker than home → C → D → school which takes 14 minutes.

EXERCISE 24B.1

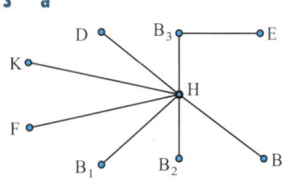

1 (graph with T-P-Q-R-S, weights 17, 23, 20, 31, 38)

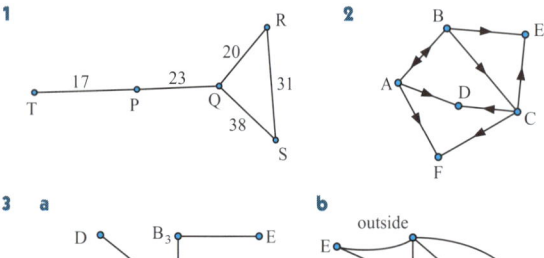

2 (directed graph with vertices A, B, C, D, E, F)

3 a (graph with vertices D, B₃, E, K, H, F, B₁, B₂, B)
  b (graph with outside, E, living, G, S, B, R, laundry)

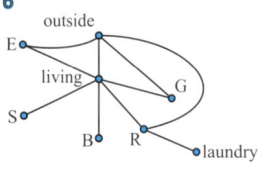

EXERCISE 24B.2

1 A and E, B and D, C and F, H and J, I and K

2 (two equivalent graphs shown)

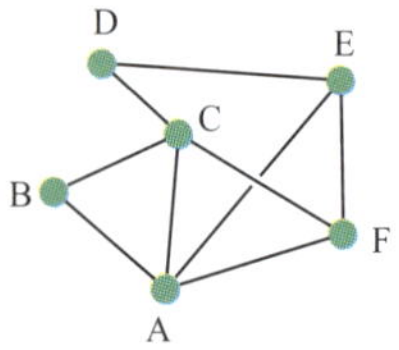

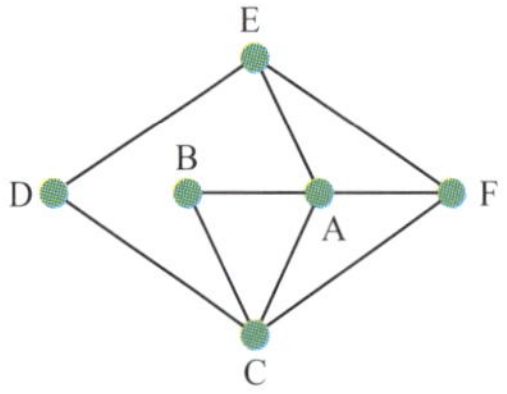

3 (graph shown) many other topologically equivalent solutions possible

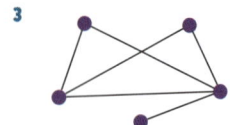

EXERCISE 24C

1 a Find a recipe, prepare ingredients, cook casserole, set table, serve meal, clean up.
  b Decide on trees required, dig the holes, purchase the trees, plant the trees, water the trees.

2 Cook casserole and set table.

3 (graph with vertices A, E, C, B, D, F)

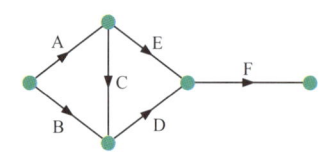

4 a

Task	Prerequisite task(s)
A	-
B	-
C	A
D	B, C
E	D
F	-
G	E, F

  b B can be performed concurrently with A and C.

  c (activity network diagram with A, B, C, D, E, F, G)

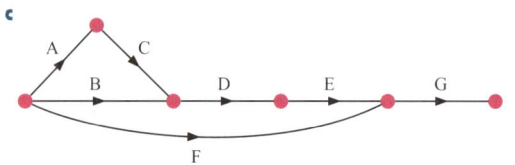

5 a

Task	Prerequisite task(s)
A	-
B	A
C	B
D	C
E	-
F	D, E
G	F
H	G

  b Task E can be performed concurrently with any of the tasks A, B, C or D. If the project is completed by a single person, then task E may be performed with task D only.

  c (activity network diagram with A, B, C, D, E, F, G, H)

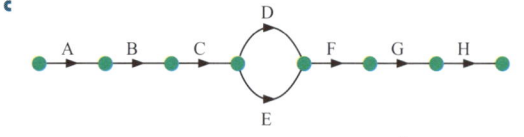

6 a

Task	Prerequisite task(s)
A	-
B	A
C	A, B
D	A, B, C
E	A
F	A, D
G	A, D

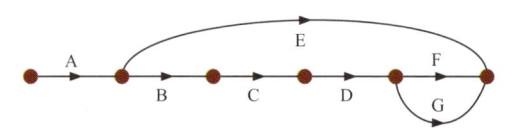

(activity network diagram with A, B, C, D, E, F, G)

EXERCISE 24D

1 a 6 **b** 20 **c** 21 **d** 53 **e** 200
2 a 36 **b** 16 **3 a** 17 **b** 86

REVIEW SET 24A

1 a **i** 5 **ii** 6 **b** undirected **c** **i** B **ii** B, C, and E
  d **i** A-B-D and A-B-E-D **ii** B-E, B-D-E and B-C-D-E

ANSWERS 539

2 It is topologically equivalent. It has the same number of vertices and corresponding vertices have the same connections on both diagrams.

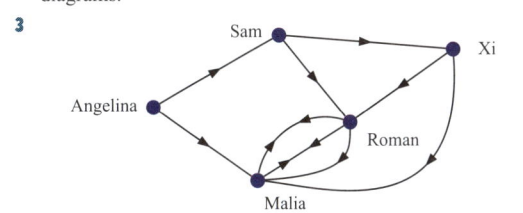

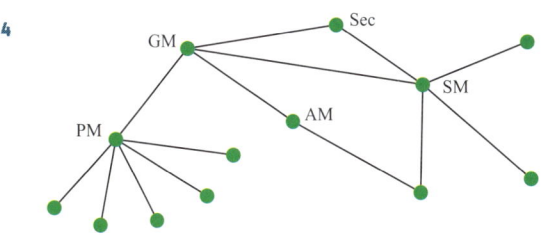

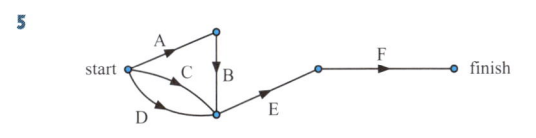

3

4

5

6 a 70 **b i** 36 **ii** 34

REVIEW SET 24B

1 a 5 **b** is directed
  c i D-A-B, D-C-B, D-A-C-B and D-E-C-B
   ii no path exists

2 a the towns **b** by edges **c** 24 km **d** 29 km
  e add a direction to the edge to make it an arc

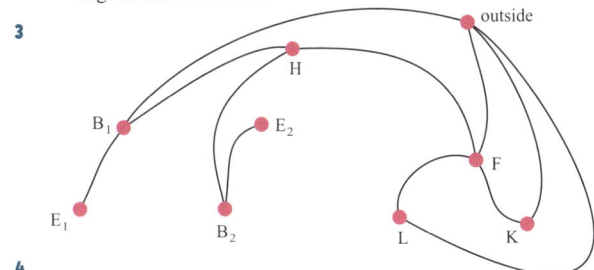

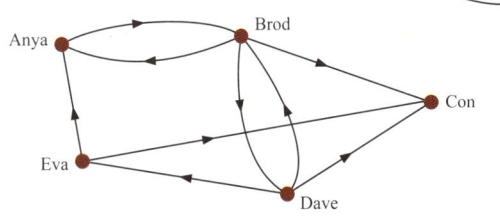

3

4

5 a

Task	Prerequisite task(s)
A Read instructions	-
B Preheat oven	-
C Contents into bowl	A
D Add milk and eggs	C
E Beat the mixture	D
F Place in cooking dish	E
G Cook cake	B, F
H Ice cake when cool	G

b Heating the oven can be done at the same time as A, C, D, E, and F.

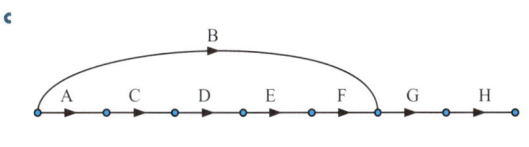

c

6 10   **7** 66

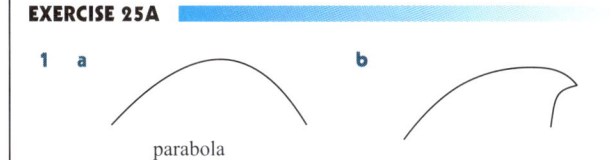

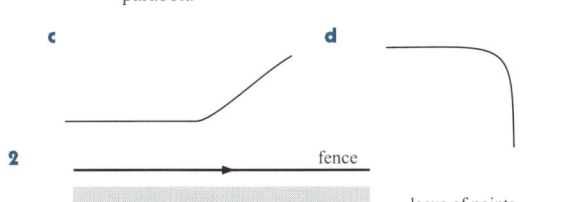

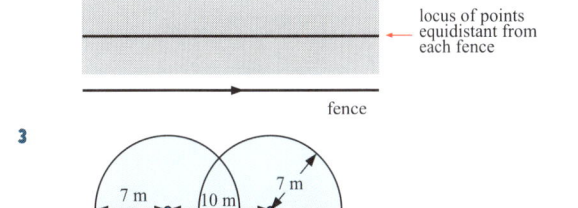

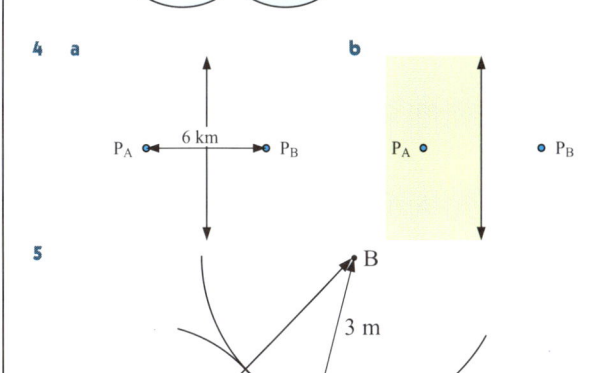

EXERCISE 25A

1 a   **b**

  parabola

  c   **d**

2 locus of points equidistant from each fence

3 7 m   10 m   7 m

4 a 6 km   **b**

5 Standing in this region.

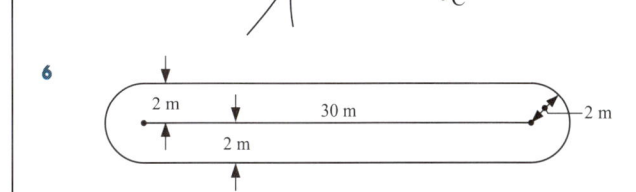

6 2 m   30 m   2 m
       2 m

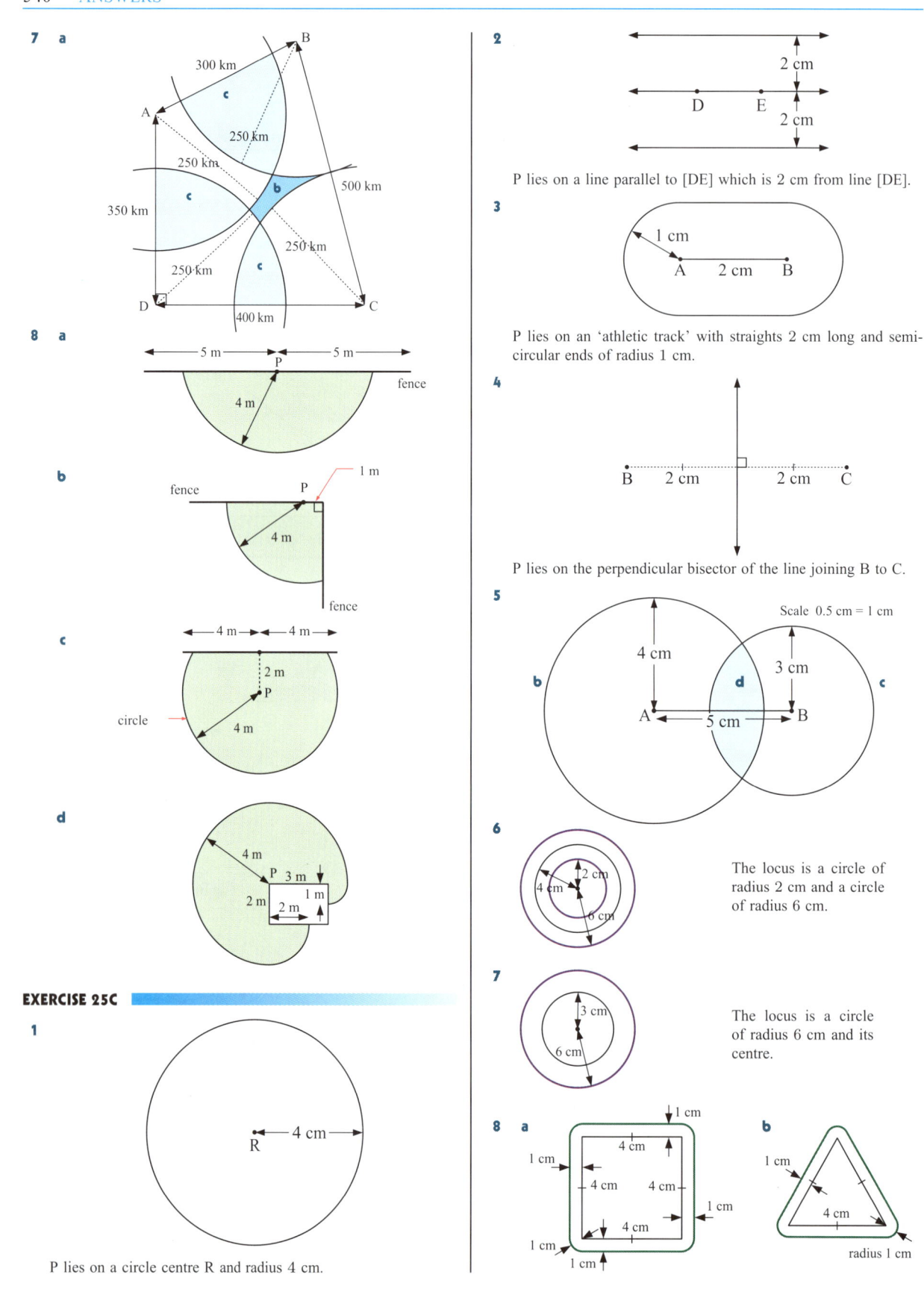

7 a [figure showing loci with arcs labelled 300 km, 250 km, 250 km, 350 km, 250 km, 250 km, 500 km, 400 km; points A, B, C, D; shaded region b]

8 a [figure: 5 m, 5 m, P, fence, 4 m semicircle]

b [figure: fence, P, 1 m, 4 m quarter circle, fence]

c [figure: 4 m, 4 m, 2 m, P, 4 m, circle]

d [figure: 4 m, P, 3 m, 2 m, 1 m, 2 m]

EXERCISE 25C

1 [circle centre R, radius 4 cm]

P lies on a circle centre R and radius 4 cm.

2 [figure showing parallel lines with D, E, 2 cm, 2 cm]

P lies on a line parallel to [DE] which is 2 cm from line [DE].

3 [athletic track figure: 1 cm, A, 2 cm, B]

P lies on an 'athletic track' with straights 2 cm long and semi-circular ends of radius 1 cm.

4 [figure: B, 2 cm, 2 cm, C with perpendicular bisector]

P lies on the perpendicular bisector of the line joining B to C.

5 [two overlapping circles: 4 cm, 3 cm, A, 5 cm, B, regions b, c, d] Scale 0.5 cm = 1 cm

6 [concentric circles: 2 cm, 4 cm, 6 cm]

The locus is a circle of radius 2 cm and a circle of radius 6 cm.

7 [circle with 3 cm, 6 cm]

The locus is a circle of radius 6 cm and its centre.

8 a [rounded square figure: 1 cm, 4 cm, 1 cm, 4 cm, 4 cm, 1 cm, 4 cm, 1 cm]

b [rounded triangle figure: 1 cm, 4 cm, radius 1 cm]

ANSWERS 541

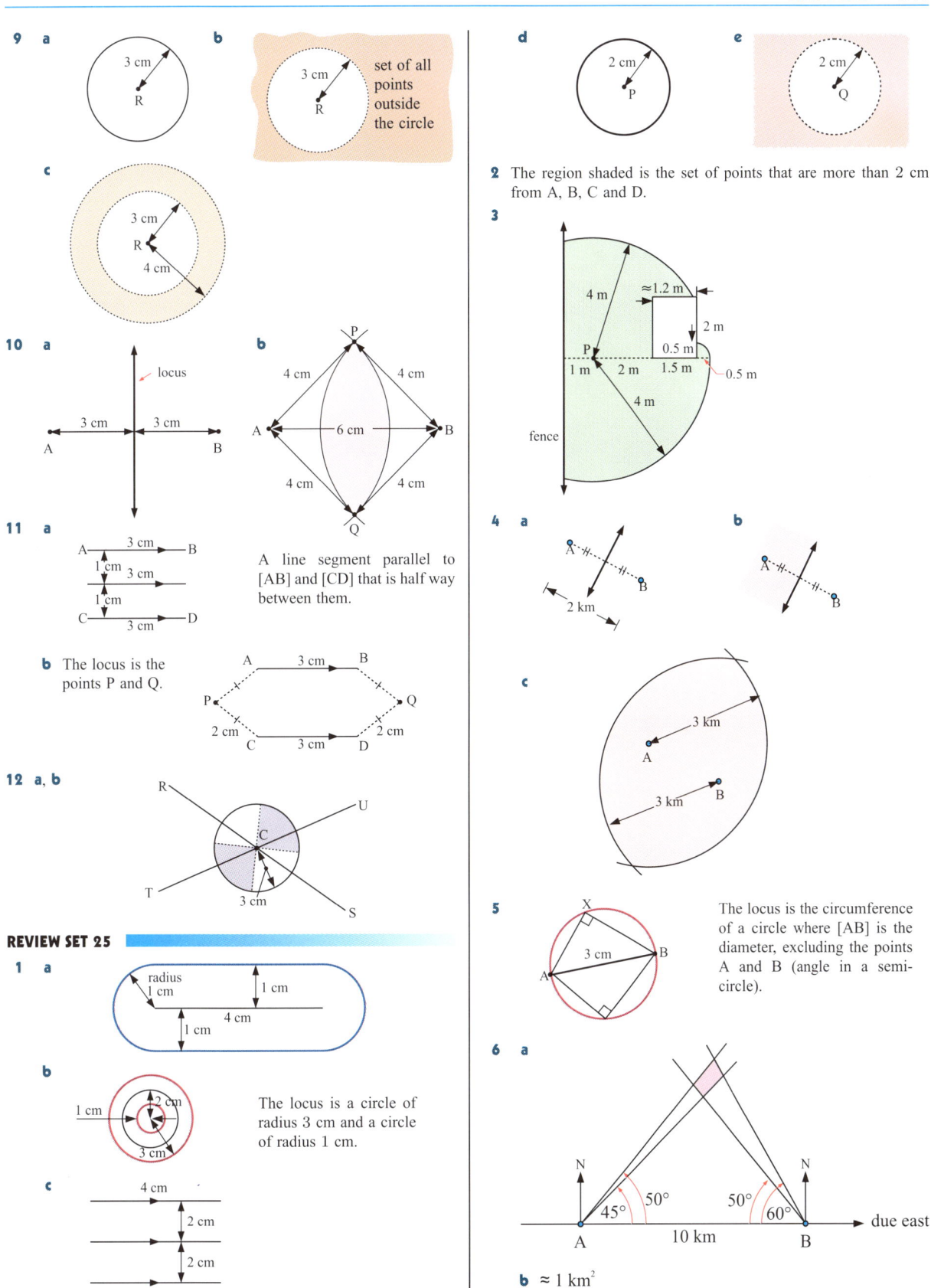

9 a [circle, radius 3 cm, centre R]
b set of all points outside the circle [dashed circle radius 3 cm, centre R]
c [annulus between 3 cm and 4 cm radii, centre R]
d [circle radius 2 cm, centre P]
e set of points outside dashed circle radius 2 cm, centre Q

2 The region shaded is the set of points that are more than 2 cm from A, B, C and D.

3 [diagram of semicircular region with fence, dimensions 4 m, ≈1.2 m, 2 m, 0.5 m, 1 m, 2 m, 1.5 m, 0.5 m, 4 m]

10 a [perpendicular bisector of AB, with 3 cm each side, labelled "locus"]
b [lens-shaped locus between A and B, 6 cm apart, with 4 cm arcs meeting at P and Q]

4 a [perpendicular bisector of AB, 2 km apart]
b [perpendicular bisector of AB]
c [circle through A and B with 3 km arcs]

11 a [parallel lines AB and CD, 3 cm each, with locus line halfway between, 1 cm from each] A line segment parallel to [AB] and [CD] that is half way between them.

b The locus is the points P and Q. [hexagonal arrangement with A, B, C, D and P, Q at ends; 3 cm and 2 cm distances]

5 [circle with diameter AB = 3 cm, point X on circumference] The locus is the circumference of a circle where [AB] is the diameter, excluding the points A and B (angle in a semi-circle).

12 a, b [circle centre C radius 3 cm with lines R, U, T, S through C, shaded sectors]

REVIEW SET 25

1 a [stadium shape: rectangle 4 cm × 2 cm with semicircular ends radius 1 cm]

b [two concentric circles, radii 3 cm and 1 cm, with 2 cm shown] The locus is a circle of radius 3 cm and a circle of radius 1 cm.

c [three parallel lines, 2 cm apart, middle is 4 cm line]

6 a [triangle with A and B 10 km apart on east line, bearings 045° and 050° from A, 050° and 060° from B]

b ≈ 1 km²

INDEX

acute angle	*151*
adjacent angles	*151*
algebraic equation	*134*
algebraic fraction	*70*
algebraic product	*57*
alternate angles	*153*
apex	*159*
area	*223*
average	*61*
back-to-back bar chart	*380*
biased sample	*373*
capacity	*268*
Cartesian plane	*278*
categorical variable	*372*
census	*373*
centre of rotation	*334*
circumference	*218*
co-interior angles	*153*
coefficient	*59*
coincident lines	*306*
collinear points	*152*
complementary angles	*151*
complementary event	*440*
composite figure	*230*
composite number	*50*
compound interest	*93*
concurrent lines	*152*
cone	*265*
congruent triangles	*346*
constant term	*59*
continuous	*372*
corresponding angles	*153*
cross-section	*264*
cube root	*209*
cubic units	*262*
cylinder	*236*
data set	*372*
decimal number	*41*
denominator	*37*
dependent variable	*281*
diameter	*218*
difference	*61*
directed graph	*472*
discrete	*372*
distance-time graph	*124*
distributive law	*100*
divisible	*30*
dot plot	*403*
ellipse	*229*
enlargement	*337*
equation	*59*
equation of line	*286*
equilateral triangle	*151*
equivalent fractions	*38*
expanded fractional form	*41*
expansion	*100*
expectation	*449*
expression	*59*
factor	*28*
factorisation	*356*
formula	*251*
fraction	*37*
frequency	*317*
general form	*296*
gradient	*287*
highest common factor	*29*
horizontal bar chart	*373*
horizontal line	*288, 295*
hypotenuse	*196*
image	*330*
improper fraction	*38*
included angle	*347*
independent variable	*281*
index laws	*176*
index notation	*50*
inequation	*253*
integer	*32*
inverse operation	*137*
irrational number	*191*
isosceles triangle	*151*
kite	*168*
like terms	*59*
line graph	*122*
line segment	*152*
line symmetry	*333*
linear equation	*134*
locus	*486*
loss	*81*
lowest common denominator	*143*
lowest common multiple	*29*
mean	*409*
median	*409*

INDEX

mixed number	38
mode	373, 410
multiple	29
multiplier	85
natural number	28
negatively skewed	404
network diagram	472
Null Factor law	390
number line	253
numerator	37
odds	450
ordered pair	278
origin	278
outlier	406
parallel lines	152
parallelogram	167
percentage change	121
perfect squares	108
perimeter	216
perpendicular lines	152
pie chart	120
point of intersection	305
polygon	162
positively skewed	404
precedence table	477
prime factored form	51
prime number	50
principal	91
probability	316
product	61
profit	81
pronumeral	56
proper fraction	38
pyramid	265
Pythagoras' theorem	197
Pythagorean triple	203
quadrant	279
quadratic equation	390
quadrilateral	162
quantitative variable	372, 402
quotient	61
radical	112
radius	219
ratio	46
rational number	37
raw data	372
reciprocal	37
rectangle	168
reduction	337
reflex angle	151
regular polygon	162
relative frequency	317
revolution	151
rhombus	168
right angle	151
right angled triangle	196
rotation	334
rotational symmetry	335
sample	373
sample space	438
scale factor	337
scalene triangle	151
scientific notation	183
segment bar chart	373
selling price	87
side-by-side column graph	380
significant figures	186
similar figures	338
similar triangles	340
simple interest	90
simultaneous solution	305
sphere	237
square	168
square root	112
stem-and-leaf plot	406
straight angle	151
sum	61
supplementary angles	151
surd	191
surface area	233
symmetrical distribution	404
tally-frequency table	403
terms	59
theoretical probability	439
translation	330
transversal	152
trapezium	168
tree diagram	445
trigonometric ratios	460
unit circle	457
variable	59
vertex	472
vertical column graph	373
vertical line	288, 295
vertically opposite angles	151
volume	262
Voronoi diagram	492